THE PUBLIC COMPANY TRANSFORMED

The Public Company Transformed

Brian R. Cheffins

OXFORD
UNIVERSITY PRESS

OXFORD
UNIVERSITY PRESS

Oxford University Press is a department of the University of Oxford. It furthers the University's objective of excellence in research, scholarship, and education by publishing worldwide. Oxford is a registered trademark of Oxford University Press in the UK and certain other countries.

Published in the United States of America by Oxford University Press
198 Madison Avenue, New York, NY 10016, United States of America.

Library of Congress Cataloging-in-Publication Data

Names: Cheffins, Brian R.
Title: The public company transformed / Brian R. Cheffins.
Description: New York, NY : Oxford University Press, 2019. | Includes bibliographical references and index.
Identifiers: LCCN 2018018657 | ISBN 9780190640323 ((hardback) : alk. paper)
Subjects: LCSH: Corporation law—United States—History. | Corporations—United States—History.
Classification: LCC KF1414 .C475 2018 | DDC 346.73/066—dc23
LC record available at https://lccn.loc.gov/2018018657

9 8 7 6 5 4 3 2 1

Printed by Sheridan Books, Inc., United States of America

Contents

List of Figures and Table

FIGURES

TABLE

Preface

THE PUBLIC COMPANY TRANSFORMED is a book about the history of the American public company, focusing on the period running from the mid-twentieth century through to the present day. Though the book is historical in orientation, the origins of this project were not. The departure point was a 2009 article in which I investigated the functioning of corporate governance during the 2008 financial crisis through case studies of the 37 companies removed from the S&P 500 stock market index in 2008.[1]

In my S&P 500 article I introduced readers to the key corporate governance mechanisms in public companies, describing in so doing the roles these mechanisms would ideally play. I drew upon history to do this, as past developments illustrate effectively the corporate governance challenges public companies pose and reveal the logic underlying the "fixes" that have evolved. This facet of my S&P 500 project set me on the path that culminated in this book. As I looked backward when researching the core governance features of public companies, I quickly discovered that in the voluminous literature on American corporate governance, historical analysis was thin. Nevertheless, I persevered with my plan to use history to introduce readers to corporate governance challenges and fixes.

Having become aware through my S&P 500 project that the history of corporate governance was under-researched, I continued to explore the topic. Various publications ensued.[2] As my research progressed I formulated a plan to write a book on the history of corporate

---

[1] Brian R. Cheffins, *Did Corporate Governance "Fail" during the 2008 Stock Market Meltdown? The Case of the S&P 500*, 65 BUS. LAW. 1 (2009).

[2] THE HISTORY OF MODERN US CORPORATE GOVERNANCE (Brian R. Cheffins ed., 2011); Brian R. Cheffins, *The History of Corporate Governance, in* THE OXFORD HANDBOOK OF CORPORATE GOVERNANCE 46 (Mike Wright, Donald Siegel, Kevin Keasey & Igor Filatotchev eds., 2013); Brian R. Cheffins, *Delaware and the*

governance. My idea was to focus on the United States because this was where, in the 1970s, managerial accountability issues were first considered by reference to the now ubiquitous "corporate governance" nomenclature.

A theme I emphasized in my writing on the history of corporate governance was that changes affecting public companies did much to account for corporate governance's rise to prominence in the 1970s and to explain how corporate governance evolved in subsequent decades. As I developed this insight, it became evident there was a paucity of historically contextualized research on changes US public companies underwent from the middle of the twentieth century through to the present day. This struck me as a curious gap in the literature, given the crucial economic role the US public company has played both in America and worldwide. I correspondingly decided to shift the emphasis of my research from corporate governance exclusively to the transformation of the public company more generally.

I switched my focus from corporate governance to the transformation of the public company with some trepidation. The shift was not merely incremental. The new project, I knew, would be considerably more ambitious in its scope and breadth. The change of direction was also exciting, however. I was aware from the research I had already conducted that the subject matter was fascinating. I also anticipated the book I was now intending to write would appeal to a wider audience. A book on the history of corporate governance may well have only caught the eye of those with a strong prior interest in governance. I felt that by examining changes affecting the public company in a general way I could write a book that would appeal not only to the corporate governance "crowd" but also to students of business history and those interested in a general way in the functioning and regulation of business enterprises.

While *The Public Company Transformed* is a considerably more ambitious book than what I first envisaged, the corporate governance origins with this project remain evident. Corporate governance can be defined as the checks and balances affecting those who run companies.[3] Boards of directors and shareholders are thought of as the primary corporate governance mechanisms in publicly traded firms. Boards and shareholders form an important part of the story which is told here. However, a historical account of publicly traded companies cannot begin and end with boards and shareholders. Events occurring in the mid-twentieth century illustrate this clearly.

During the 1950s and 1960s—the heyday of "managerial capitalism"—management was clearly in charge of large public companies. Boards and shareholders, which can be thought of as "internal" constraints on executives, were largely inert, absent a crisis. Nevertheless, managerial wrongdoing was rare and executives refrained from taking a freewheeling approach with the discretion seemingly available to them. What kept managerial capitalism era executives in check? Various "external" constraints were relevant. These included unions, substantial regulation at industry level, antitrust laws enforced in a way that discouraged horizontal mergers, and concerns among senior executives that criticism of big business could result in

Transformation of Corporate Governance, 40 Del. J. Corp. L. 1 (2015); Brian R. Cheffins, *The Rise of Corporate Governance in the UK: When and Why*, (2015) Current Legal Probs. 1.

[3] Robert E. Wright, Corporation Nation 152 (2014).

additional unwelcome state intervention. The fact that commercial and investment banks were conservative allocators of capital was also a potential obstacle for ambitious executives.

The identities of the internal and external constraints that impose checks on public company executives remain much the same as they did during the heyday of managerial capitalism. Their nature has changed considerably, however. *The Public Company Transformed* describes the history of the public company since the mid-twentieth century largely in terms of the development of these constraints. The result is a book that extends well beyond a history of corporate governance. Nevertheless, the orientation around checks on public company executives betrays the corporate governance origins of this project.

The book has, as the table of contents readily reveals, a strong chronological focus. Chapter 2 deals primarily with the 1950s and 1960s and Chapters 3 to 7 are organized on a decade-by-decade basis, beginning with the 1970s and concluding with an analysis of present-day circumstances combined with predictions regarding the future of the public company. This organizational format proved to be a convenient one for expository purposes and should aid a reader who wants to focus on a particular time period. Addressing satisfactorily the pertinent developments for each decade has made it necessary, however, to cover a substantial range of material in each chapter. The chapters correspondingly are each lengthy, averaging nearly 30,000 words. This has its drawbacks aesthetically. Dividing the chapters to shorten them would have resulted, however, in an undesirably fractionalized end product.

With respect to aesthetics, another feature of the book merits acknowledgment, namely the large number of footnotes. Various factors contributed. I am a legal academic, and law review articles tend to be heavily footnoted. Habits are hard to break, and there is an element of that involved here. It is also relevant that I use quotes liberally, usually from contemporary sources. Substantial footnoting was needed to provide relevant cites. Finally, many of the sources I have drawn upon are ones that have not been referenced in previous studies of the American public company. These sources merit signposting for those who might choose to research in more detail facets of the public company considered here, and the footnotes perform this function.

The history of the American public company indeed is a topic that merits further analysis. The public company has been a dominant force in the US economy for decades, so understanding how it has changed over time reveals a great deal about broader economic trends. The topic also is a lively one, involving various engaging personalities, firms scaling the heights of business success (think Microsoft), and firms that crashed spectacularly (think Enron). This book, moreover, does not provide the last word by any means on the historical development of the American public company. The focus here is primarily on the past 70 years; no attempt has been made to trace the story back to the earliest American public companies. Even with the decades the book focuses on most closely, with respect to particular companies, individuals, and institutions it has usually not been possible to do more than scratch the surface of their often fascinating histories. Finally, the transformation described here is only part of a larger historical story still being written. Contrary to various gloomy predictions offered as far back as the 1970s, the public company has a bright future. It is hoped this book, by providing the first detailed analysis of changes affecting the American public company since the mid-twentieth century, will provide a suitable departure point for further exploration of the public company's development over time.

Acknowledgments

I HAVE ACCUMULATED various debts of gratitude while working on *The Public Company Transformed*. The Leverhulme Trust is at the top of the list. The Trust, which provides grants and scholarships for research and education, awarded me a two year Major Research Fellowship to work on "The Transformation of the Public Company," tenable from September 2016 to September 2018. Funding from my fellowship was channelled primarily toward a buyout of my teaching and administrative duties at the Law Faculty at the University of Cambridge. Provision was also made for research expenditures, primarily for travel to draw upon library resources otherwise unavailable to me and to interview people with direct knowledge of events relevant to my research.

The Major Research Fellowship proved to be invaluable with this project. Having been given the opportunity to dedicate myself fully to my research, I was able to gather momentum that put me in a position to finish this book months, if not years, earlier than would have been feasible under normal circumstances. Research trips to the United States afforded me access to numerous sources I have drawn upon when writing this book. Conversations I had while traveling provided me with valuable context.

I am grateful to the Cambridge Law Faculty for extending its full support with my Leverhulme application. Faculty Research Grants Administrator Rosie Snajdr provided considerable assistance in this regard. She also handled the key administrative details with the Major Research Fellowship after it was awarded.

With my Major Research Fellowship funding I was able to carry out five research trips. The first was a two-week visit to Harvard Law School in October 2016. Jesse Fried went above and beyond the call in sorting out logistical issues on my behalf. The Dean RC Clark Corporate Governance Fund covered my accommodation expenses for this trip. I would like thank Robert Clark for arranging this.

The second trip was a two-week stint on the North American West Coast in January 2017. I spent one week at Stanford Law School, based in the law library, and a second week at the Peter A. Allard School of Law at the University of British Columbia. Michael Klausner was a wonderful host for my week at Stanford. I was a guest of the Centre for Business Law at Allard, courtesy of Director Cristie Ford and Executive Director Chiara Woods.

The third trip was to Georgetown Law School, where I spent one week in late February and early March 2017. Robert Thompson played the pivotal role in making this visit happen. Joshua Teitlebaum offered valuable assistance with logistics.

The fourth trip was to UCLA Law School, where I spent one week in late March and early April 2017. I was a guest of the Lowell Milken Institute for Business Law and Policy. Steve Bank, who was Faculty Director of the Institute at the time, did a great job setting things up for me.

The fifth and final trip was back to the University of British Columbia for one week in January 2018. This time I was a guest of the Political Science Department. Barbara Arneil, chair of the department, made the arrangements.

Before I began my Major Research Fellowship, I carried out two visits that contributed substantially to the research that culminated in this book. The first was to Harvard Business School, where I held the Thomas McCraw Fellowship in US Business History from September to November 2014. Geoffrey Jones and Walter Friedman, chair and director of the HBS Business History Initiative respectively, were excellent hosts.

The second valuable pre-Major Research Fellowship visit was to Columbia Law School. I was a visiting professor there for two weeks in March and April 2016. Jack Coffee played the crucial role in making this visit happen.

A substantial number of people with direct knowledge of the events this book canvasses have generously taken time to discuss facets of my research, usually face to face. I would like to thank in this regard James Barrall, David Benoit, Robert Clark, Joel Feuer, Ron Gilson, Daniel Goelzer, Jay Goldin, Jeff Gordon, Joe Grundfest, Jeff Gramm, Kenneth Guernsey, Ben Heineman, Roberta Karmel, Steve Kaufman, Donald Langevoort, Jay Lorsch, Jon Lukomnik, John Olson, Robert Pozen, Gerald Rosenfeld, Russell Stevenson, Richard Sylla, Tim Wu, and Andy Zelleke.

I received valuable feedback when giving presentations on facets of the book. As the project was getting underway, I provided overviews at a Blue Sky Lunch seminar at Columbia Law School, at a Centre for Business Law workshop at UBC's Allard School of Law, and to Professor Lucian Bebchuk's Corporate and Capital Markets Law and Policy class at Harvard Law School. I subsequently discussed the concluding chapter of the book at a seminar at the Allard School of Law co-organized by the Centre for Business Law and the Peter P. Dhillon Centre for Business Ethics and at a conference at Cardiff University hosted by the Cardiff Corporate Governance Research Group.

I would like to thank Joanna Cheffins and Brad Daisley for reading and commenting on facets of the book. I would also like to thank Joanna and my daughters Hannah and Lucy for their patience as I commandeered a considerable amount of what otherwise would have been family time as I was writing this book.

1 Introduction

NEARLY 9 OUT of 10 of America's largest corporations have shares publicly traded on the stock market.[1] Most Americans will encounter frequently each day products or services a US public company offers, such as social media (Facebook, for example), consumer goods (Procter & Gamble), telecommunications (AT&T), internet searching (Google, a subsidiary of Alphabet), transportation (General Motors), computer software (Microsoft), financial services (Bank of America) and shopping (Amazon or Walmart). Public company dominance of America's corporate economy has existed for decades. As of the early 1930s, only 11 of America's 200 largest non-financial corporations lacked an important public interest.[2]

Though the publicly traded company has been dominant for many decades, during this period of dominance the public company itself has been transformed. Large public firms of the 1950s and 1960s could count on substantial customer loyalty due to having few serious rivals. In today's digital age, warnings are issued regularly even to the biggest companies that there is no room to relax because competition is just a click away. During the middle

---

[1] As of 2017, 172 of America's 200 largest companies, ranked by annual revenue, were publicly traded. See *Largest US Corporations*, FORTUNE, June 15, 2017, F1; Andrea Murphy, *America's Largest Private Companies 2017*, available at https://www.forbes.com/largest-private-companies/list/ (accessed May 21, 2018). On what these sources reveal, see Chapter 7, notes 39–41, 106; Brian R. Cheffins, *The Future of the American Public Company*, unpublished working paper (2018).

[2] ADOLF A. BERLE & GARDINER C. MEANS, THE MODERN CORPORATION & PRIVATE PROPERTY 86 (1932). They list 12 such companies but one had over 12,000 shareholders and thus was clearly publicly traded. Their study is considered in more detail in Chapter 2—see notes 74–76 and related discussion. On public company dominance as of the mid-1990s, see MARK J. ROE, STRONG MANAGERS, WEAK OWNERS: THE POLITICAL ROOTS OF AMERICAN CORPORATE FINANCE 3 (1994).

decades of the twentieth century, unions were a meaningful source of countervailing power in the corporate context but are now mostly an afterthought. Senior executives of large mid-twentieth-century firms often thought of themselves as stewards of the enterprises they ran, seeking to balance if possible the interests of key corporate constituencies. Today's public company executives might envy such discretion but know they have to focus closely on shareholder returns because mediocre financial results can quickly put them in the firing line.

The transformation the public company has undergone since the mid-twentieth century is a fascinating one. There have been scandals, political controversy, wide swings in investor and public sentiment, mismanagement, entrepreneurial verve, noisy corporate "raiders," and various other larger-than-life personalities. Ascertaining how and why the public company has been transformed, however, is currently a challenging task.

Amidst the voluminous literature on corporations and big business there are innumerable valuable historical nuggets. One searches in vain, however, for a detailed analytical synthesis of changes affecting the public company since the end of World War II. This book correspondingly examines how the public company has been transformed from the mid-twentieth century through to the present day, using as the primary reference point senior corporate executives and the constraints affecting the choices available to them.

This introductory chapter provides necessary context. The basic chronology with the public company will be summarized first.[3] Next, the book's contribution to the vast literature on corporations will be spelled out. Case studies that will move the analysis from the abstract to the specific follow. The focus will be on two iconic American business enterprises, American Telephone and Telegraph Company (AT&T) and General Electric (GE). With both being prominent throughout the period the book covers, the case studies illustrate in a concrete fashion key market and regulatory trends examined in the chapters that follow. The chapter concludes with an overview of the remainder of the book.

The Public Company Transformed—A Brief Chronology

This book picks up the public company's story in earnest during the middle of the twentieth century. An extended treatment of earlier developments would be largely superfluous. This is primarily because of detailed research distinguished business historian Alfred Chandler, "the indispensable authority on the history of the company,"[4] carried out on the leading industrial enterprises of the late nineteenth and early twentieth centuries. He canvassed in considerable detail a shift in emphasis away from firms personally run by their owners toward firms where share ownership tended to be dispersed, and where operating decisions were increasingly concentrated in managers' hands.[5] His work on this new form

[3] Detailed citation of relevant sources will be provided in subsequent chapters rather than here.

[4] John Micklethwait & Adrian Wooldridge, The Company: A Short History of a Revolutionary Idea 184 (2003). See also Douglas Martin, *Alfred D. Chandler Jr., a Business Historian, Dies at 88*, NY Times, May 12, 2007, B7.

[5] See, for example, Alfred D. Chandler, Strategy and Structure: Chapters in the History of Industrial Enterprise (1962); Alfred D. Chandler, The Visible Hand: The Managerial Revolution in American Business (1977).

of capitalism—"managerial capitalism"—largely culminated with his 1990 book *Scale and Scope: The Dynamics of Industrial Capitalism*.[6] In *Scale and Scope* Chandler contrasted the development of the modern industrial enterprise in the United States between the 1880s and the 1940s with parallel trends in Germany and Britain. Chandler thus ended his detailed analysis just prior to the heyday of managerial capitalism, which occurred in the 1950s and 1960s.[7] This era provides the chronological and analytical departure point for this book.

For executives running larger American public companies immediately following World War II, "internal" constraints on their discretion—scrutiny by the board of directors and the shareholders—were more theoretical than actual. Boards operated on a largely collegial basis, at least absent a crisis. Most shares were owned by individual ("retail") investors with tiny shareholdings and little appetite for scrutinizing companies. There was correspondingly a real risk that senior executives would take advantage of what Adolf Berle and Gardiner Means famously described in 1932 as a separation of ownership and control to exercise their managerial authority in a manner that was contrary to the interests of stockholders and others closely affiliated with companies.[8]

Managerial wrongdoing was in fact rare during the middle decades of the twentieth century, with executives refraining for the most part from taking a freewheeling approach with the discretion available to them. Various "external" factors helped to keep managerial capitalism era executives in check. In numerous key industries organized labor was a powerful force, and in those industries collective bargaining functioned as a significant constraint for management. The mid-twentieth-century heyday of managerial capitalism was also an era of "regulated capitalism,"[9] as governmental action, or the threat thereof, impinged upon executive discretion in various significant ways. In many industrial sectors, including telecommunications, transport, and utilities, regulators exercised control over prices and imposed service provision standards. Moreover, robust antitrust enforcement essentially precluded horizontal mergers involving firms with a sizeable combined market share. Memories that the business community was deeply unpopular during the Depression were fresh. Fears that latent public antipathy toward corporations could translate into new and unwelcome regulation correspondingly provided incentives for executives running large companies to avoid taking steps that might spark an adverse public reaction.

Restricted access to capital could also be an obstacle for ambitious managerial capitalism era executives. Firms already in a dominant position in a market sector could rely on profits generated but not distributed to shareholders ("retained earnings") to finance plans executives might have. For enterprises without this luxury, progress could be difficult to achieve.

---

[6] Alfred D. Chandler, Scale and Scope: The Dynamics of Industrial Capitalism (1990).

[7] Chandler did discuss the post World War II era in Alfred D. Chandler, *The Competitive Performance of US Industrial Enterprises since the Second World War*, 63 Bus. Hist. Rev. 1 (1994). On the 1950s and 1960s being the heyday of managerial capitalism, see George P. Baker & George David Smith, The New Financial Capitalists: Kohlberg Kravis Roberts and the Creation of Corporate Value 10 (1998); Ronald Dore, William Lazonick & Mary O'Sullivan, *Varieties of Capitalism in the Twentieth Century*, 15(4) Oxford Rev. Econ. Pol'y 102, 109 (1999); Alexander Styhre, The Making of Shareholder Welfare Society: A Study in Corporate Governance 57 (2018).

[8] Berle & Means, *supra* note 2.

[9] David M. Kotz, The Rise and Fall of Neoliberal Capitalism 6, 50–53 (2015).

Commercial and investment banks were conservative allocators of capital, and the venture capital industry was a mere fledgling.

With mid-twentieth-century public company executives operating in a context of meaningful external constraints, the prevailing assumption was that the nature of managerial leadership had only a modest impact on corporate success, or lack thereof. In the mid-1950s chief executives "like(d) to remark jocularly that they (were) the most expendable men in their organizations."[10] Matters did not change markedly during the 1960s. A 1969 study of corporate "oligarchs" reported that senior management "gets the job done ... by mastering the 'science of muddling through.'"[11] "The relative indifference of the stock market" to the death or replacement of chief executives at that point in time was explained on the basis that shrewd investors deduced "changes at the top have little if any effect on the prospective earnings and growth of the company."[12] A groundbreaking 1972 empirical study of 167 major public companies lent credence to such logic.[13] Executive "leadership" was found to explain only a small proportion of corporate performance once the strength of the economy, the industry in which a corporation was operating, and a series of company-specific features were taken into account.[14]

By the market friendly 1980s, various external constraints affecting public company executives that were important during the managerial capitalism era were fading in importance. Unions were in decline, a deregulation trend was prompting the dismantling of controls in a wide range of industries, and antitrust enforcement was being relaxed. Growing competition in the banking sector accompanied by a wave of financial innovation eased restrictions on access to capital. The shift in market conditions was a particular boon for companies seeking to challenge market-dominating incumbents, which meant that concerns about losing out to rivals became a more potent external constraint on public company executives than had previously been the case.

With the downgrading of various key checks on managerial discretion executives began to spread their wings. A 1985 *New York Times* article on those serving as chief executive officer (CEO) of public companies, entitled "A New Breed of CEO," said that while "until fairly recently the most obvious trait of the CEO was his relentless dullness," various prominent chief executives were eschewing "the old ways of managing and have brought new excitement to rusty companies."[15] Jack Welch and Robert Goizueta, iconic chief executives of GE and Coca-Cola respectively, agreed in the mid-1990s that their jobs were "three times as fast" as when they were appointed in the early 1980s.[16]

---

[10] Herrymon Maurer, Great Enterprise: Growth and Behavior of the Big Corporation 81 (1955).

[11] David Finn, The Corporate Oligarch 18 (1969).

[12] *Id.* at 14–15.

[13] Stanley Lieberson & James F. O'Connor, *Leadership and Organizational Performance: A Study of Large Corporations*, 37 Amer. Soc. Rev. 117 (1972). On the characterization of the study, see Harris Collingwood, *Do CEOs Matter?*, The Atlantic, June 2009, available at https://www.theatlantic.com/magazine/archive/2009/06/do-ceos-matter/307437/ (accessed Dec. 12, 2017).

[14] Lieberson & O'Connor, *supra* note 13, 122–24, 127–29.

[15] N.R. Kleinfield, *A New Breed of CEO Enters the Public Eye*, NY Times, Dec. 1, 1985, Sunday Magazine, 76.

[16] John Micklethwait & Adrian Wooldridge, The Witch Doctors: What the Management Gurus Are Saying, Why It Matters and How to Make Sense of It 189 (1997).

Empirical evidence measuring the extent to which managerial capabilities dictated corporate success over time is scant.[17] The data available, however, tends to confirm that top management mattered more to the companies they ran as the twentieth century drew to a close compared with the 1950s and 1960s. A 2015 study that followed in the footsteps of the "ground breaking" 1972 study of the "CEO effect" found that the impact of CEOs on corporate performance was just under 10 percent in the 1950s and 1960s, hovered between 10 percent and 12 percent from 1970 until the mid-1980s and then grew to between 15 percent and 17 percent in the late 1990s.[18] Evidence indicating stock market reactions to unexpected chief executive deaths increased over time corroborates an intensifying CEO effect, as investors apparently attached greater weight to managerial contributions to corporate success.[19]

While various significant managerial capitalism era constraints were receding as the twentieth century concluded, in the 1980s an additional external constraint, a "market for corporate control" exemplified by unsolicited takeover bids ostensibly targeting underperforming companies, was helping to keep management on its toes. Such "hostile" takeover activity was prevalent amidst frenetic merger and acquisition (M&A) activity. "The Deal Decade," however, came to an abrupt end as the 1990s got underway. Executives thus were largely liberated from the anxiety associated with fending off a hostile bid. The 1990s would in its turn become an era of charismatic CEOs. Nevertheless, the muting of the market for corporate control did not afford executives untrammeled discretion. Under the mantle of better "corporate governance," a term rarely used before the mid-1970s, "internal" constraints had been strengthened since the heyday of managerial capitalism. Boards of directors, for instance, had been reconfigured to bolster the role of "outside" directors as monitors of management.

The Deal Decade and increased emphasis on governance-related internal constraints coincided with a reorientation of managerial priorities in favor of shareholder interests. During the managerial capitalism era, those running public companies, mindful of intense criticism of business in the Depression, took pains to emphasize the good citizenship of the firms they ran. The "traditional" model of the corporation catering to shareholders reputedly persisted "more in theory than in practice."[20] The Deal Decade helped to prompt a switch back in a shareholder-friendly direction. The surge in the number of hostile bids meant that the fate of publicly traded companies hinged on shareholder perceptions of the capabilities of the incumbent management team to an unprecedented extent.

When hostile takeovers subsided in the 1990s many thought increased shareholder activism would counteract the marginalization of the market for corporate control as a disciplinary mechanism. It was well known as far back as the 1950s that due to superior resources and larger ownership stakes "mainstream" institutional shareholders such as pension funds and mutual funds were better positioned to exercise influence over public company executives

---

[17] Timothy J. Quigley, Craig Crossland & Robert J. Campbell, *Shareholder Perceptions of the Changing Impact of CEOs: Market Reactions to Unexpected CEO Deaths, 1950–2009*, 38 STRAT. MGMT. J. 939, 940 (2017).

[18] Timothy J. Quigley & Donald C. Hambrick, *Has the "CEO Effect" Increased in Recent Decades? A New Explanation for the Great Rise in America's Attention to Corporate Leaders*, 36 STRAT. MGMT. J. 821 (2015).

[19] Quigley, Crossland & Campbell, *supra* note 17, at 944–45, 947.

[20] Covington Hardee, *Book Review: The Meaning of Modern Business*, 74 HARV. L. REV. 200, 201 (1960).

than were individual stockholders. By the 1990s, with institutional investors collectively owning as many shares as retail investors, and more in larger companies, there was optimism that asset managers would forsake a traditional bias in favor of passivity. In fact, high hopes for a meaningful governance contribution by institutional shareholders went largely unfulfilled. With isolated exceptions, pension funds and mutual funds refrained from intervening in the affairs of public companies as the twentieth century drew to a close.

While institutional investors generally stood back, shareholder value nevertheless emerged as the top priority for executives. During the 1990s, managerial compensation became primarily equity-based, largely in the form of stock options. Executives correspondingly focused intently on the expectations of investors who could send share prices tumbling in the event of an unwelcome earnings surprise. As of 2000, there was a general consensus "that . . . managers of the corporation should be charged with the obligation to manage the corporation in the interests of its shareholders."[21]

At the same time that internal constraints on executives were becoming more robust, competitive pressure from rival firms was growing in importance as an external constraint. As the twentieth century concluded, many industries experienced an influx of new entrants, the most effective of which became known as "disrupters." Access to finance continued to improve for these rivals to dominant firms. The challengers could also rely increasingly on technological innovation, such as the rise of the internet, to gain ready access to specialized resources that had previously provided dominant incumbents with a decisive and enduring competitive advantage.

While more robust corporate governance and increased competition from rivals counteracted to some degree the expansion of managerial discretion implied by deregulation, declining union power, and improved access to capital, public company executives retained considerable freedom of action. Abuse of the discretion available resulted in a series of major corporate scandals in the early 2000s. Corporate governance-related constraints were duly tightened, with regulatory reform playing a prominent role. "Activist" hedge funds specializing in buying up sizeable stakes in target companies and agitating for change also emerged as a significant disciplinary mechanism. Bank executives nevertheless retained considerable scope to engage in freewheeling practices that contributed to the onset of the 2008 financial crisis. Tougher regulation duly followed. By 2010, top executives arguably even qualified as "embattled."[22] The retreat has since ended, however, with CEO pay and CEO tenure both increasing since 2010.

There have been suggestions that the concentration of share ownership in the hands of leading institutional investors has reached the point where the separation of ownership and control Berle and Means identified is merely of historical interest. In fact, Berle and Means's characterization of public company governance remains apt. "Mainstream" institutional investors continue to be reluctant to intervene in the running of public companies. This seems unlikely to change for the foreseeable future, particularly given the rapid growth recently of investment funds that track well-known stock market indices rather than trying

---

[21] Henry Hansmann & Reinier Kraakman, *The End of History for Corporate Law*, 89 GEO. L.J. 439, 440–41 (2001).

[22] Marcel Kahan & Edward Rock, *Embattled CEOs*, 88 TEX. L. REV. 989 (2010).

to outperform the market. The cost-conscious investment model these "passive" funds follow greatly suppresses their incentive to become involved in the affairs of companies in which they own shares.

While the public company has been transformed since the managerial capitalism era, the basic legal foundation of such firms has remained unchanged. *The Structure of the Corporation*, a widely cited 1976 monograph by corporate law scholar Melvin Eisenberg, illustrates the point.[23] He sought in his book "to develop new and more highly articulated models of corporate structure."[24] As a departure point he described the "well known" outlines of "the received legal model of the corporation," saying "(u)nder this model, the board of directors manages the corporation's business and makes policy; the officers act as agents of the board and execute its decisions; and the shareholders elect the board. . . ."[25]

Eisenberg stressed that "the received legal model" did not accurately describe at the time how corporations functioned in practice.[26] Managerial power, he said, was vested as a practical matter in the hands of "officers" (i.e., full-time executives), and shareholder election of directors typically was an empty formality because existing management controlled the solicitation of proxies, the written documentation most shareholders would use to cast their votes.[27] Nevertheless, the model has proved to be durable. In a 2008 law review article William Bratton and Michael Wachter simultaneously cited examples of trends affecting public companies to show that "the corporate landscape changed dramatically" since 1976, while remarking upon the continuity of "the received legal model" Eisenberg had summarized.[28] The situation in Delaware, where a majority of US public companies are incorporated,[29] illustrates the continuity. Amidst incremental modifications in the years since the last major revision of the Delaware General Corporation Law in 1967, the provisions that vest the board with the authority to manage the company, authorize the appointment of corporate officers, and give shareholders the power to elect directors have not been altered materially.[30]

This Book's Contribution

For those familiar with developments affecting public companies over the past half century it will not be news that the public company of today differs considerably from its managerial capitalism era counterpart. Bratton and Wachter are hardly alone in acknowledging the corporate landscape has changed dramatically. Adrian Wooldridge, in a 2011 survey of

[23] MELVIN ARON EISENBERG, THE STRUCTURE OF THE CORPORATION: A LEGAL ANALYSIS (1976). On the book's prominence, see David A. Skeel, *Corporate Anatomy Lessons*, 113 YALE L.J. 1519, 1519 (2004).

[24] EISENBERG, *supra* note 23, at 6.

[25] *Id.* at 1.

[26] *Id.* at 3–5.

[27] *Id.* at 97–104, 139–41.

[28] William Bratton & Michael Wachter, *Shareholder Primacy's Corporatist Origins: Adolf Berle and the Modern Corporation*, 34 J. CORP. L. 99, 145 (2008).

[29] John Armour, Bernard Black & Brian Cheffins, *Delaware's Balancing Act*, 87 IND. L.J. 1345, 1348, 1382 (2012).

[30] DEL. CODE ANN., tit. 8, §§ 141(a), 142(a), (b), 211(b) (2018); Brian R. Cheffins, *Delaware and the Transformation of Corporate Governance*, 40 DEL. J. CORP. L. 1, 17 (2015).

developments in management theory, observed that companies "are remarkably fluid organizations. Over the past couple of decades they have been forced to rethink almost every tenet of managerial wisdom."[31] Rick Wartzman, an academic and journalist, observed in 2014 "there is no question that the ethos of corporate America had changed dramatically over the past 40 years."[32] Peter Clapman and Richard Koppes, venerable experts in the art of shareholder activism, noted in 2016 "(c)ompared with today, the corporate governance of the 1980s is nearly unrecognizable."[33] Likewise, according to a 2016 book review in the *Wall Street Journal*

> In *The New Industrial State*, published in 1967, John Kenneth Galbraith argued that big American companies were self-perpetuating automatons. They were responsible to no one, least of all indifferent stockholders. A half-century later, it's a rare day when some hedge fund titan fails to deliver an ultimatum to an under-achieving CEO to repurchase stock, or pay out a dividend, or else.[34]

While there is awareness of a significant break with the past with US public companies, historical analysis is patchy. There is, for instance, an extensive literature on corporate governance but the research is largely ahistorical.[35] From the 1980s through to the present day, dozens of articles and books have drawn attention to intensifying competitive pressure affecting companies and executives, but meaningful historical perspective has generally been lacking.[36]

Some may think the events involved are too recent to merit a historically oriented investigation. In fact, substantial water has now gone under the bridge. In 2015, Nitin Nohria planned to refer to Lee Iacocca, headline-grabbing chief executive of automaker Chrysler from 1978 to 1992, in Nohria's commencement address as dean of Harvard Business School. He changed his mind when staff told him that many of the students would not know who Iacocca was.[37]

A brief précis of the ground covered by a series of books that capably address significant facets of the transformation the US public company has undergone from the managerial capitalism era to the present day illustrates that important analytical gaps remain. Rakesh Khurana's *Searching for a Corporate Savior* (2002) has a chapter entitled "The Rise of the

---

31 Adrian Wooldridge, Masters of Management 146 (2011).

32 Quoted in Eduardo Porter, *Motivating Corporations to do Good*, NY Times, July 15, 2014, B1.

33 Peter Clapman & Richard Koppes, *Time to Rethink "One Share, One Vote,"* Wall St. J., June 24, 2016, A9. Clapman was chief investment counsel of TIAA, a retirement provider for academics and government employees, from 1972 to 2005, and Koppes was general counsel of the California Public Employees Retirement System from 1986 to 1996. On Koppes, see also Chapter 5, note 249 and related discussion.

34 James Grant, *Boardroom Brawlers*, Wall St. J., Mar. 1, 2016, A9.

35 James D. Cox, *How Delaware Law Can Support Better Corporate Governance, in* Perspectives on Corporate Governance 335, 335 (F. Scott Kieff & Troy A. Paredes eds., 2010). Roy Smith and Ingo Walter's Governing the Modern Corporation (2006) offers valuable historical background but does so primarily to provide context for an analysis of present-day corporate governance.

36 For a partial exception, see Amanda Bennett, The Death of the Organization Man (1990).

37 Nitin Nohria, *Getting the Steve Jobs Treatment*, NY Times, Oct. 25, 2015, B7.

Charismatic CEO" that provides various intriguing historical insights but the bulk of the book focuses on the position of the chief executive at the time of writing.[38] David Skeel's *Icarus in the Boardroom* (2005) offers a perceptive analysis of changes over time affecting public companies that set the scene for the corporate scandals occurring in the early 2000s but canvasses only cursorily other facets of publicly traded firms, and only touches briefly on the managerial capitalism era.[39]

The rapid financial sector growth that management professor Gerald Davis canvasses in *Managed by Markets: How Finance Reshaped America* (2009) had a significant impact on US public companies, but this was only one of a series of factors that transformed such firms.[40] In *The Vanishing American Corporation* (2016) Davis draws on history to explain why the public corporation's days may be numbered but deals primarily with the consequences of the purported corporate collapse and with what is likely to come next.[41] Mark Mizruchi's *The Fracturing of the American Corporate Elite* (2013) offers a perceptive take on changes affecting the public company in the decades following World War II but focuses primarily on politics as he argues that the decline of a pragmatic managerial elite from the early 1970s onward had unfortunate consequences for democracy.[42] David Kotz's *The Rise and Fall of Neoliberal Capitalism* (2015) covers much the same time period as this book and discusses big business with some regularity but concentrates on changes affecting capitalism generally rather than public companies specifically.[43] Finally, Rick Wartzman's *The End of Loyalty* (2017) offers rich historical detail on four iconic US corporations—Coca-Cola, GE, General Motors, and Kodak—but focuses pretty much exclusively on labor relations in those firms.[44]

This book will offer the purpose-built historical analysis of the transformation the public company has undergone since the mid-twentieth century that has thus far been lacking. With the rise of managerial capitalism providing the chronological departure point, the book focuses closely on circumstances affecting public company executives. The changes the public company has undergone will be described primarily by reference to constraints, both internal and external, on managerial discretion.

Canvassing the public company's transformation through the prism of constraints on public company executives is a helpful way of identifying relevant trends. As boards and shareholders are regarded as being theoretically pivotal "internal" checks on managerial discretion, developments concerning both will be analyzed in detail. Since unions were a potent "external" constraint during the managerial capitalism era before receding in importance, due account is taken of labor relations. Regulation, as another potentially significant external limitation on executive discretion, will be discussed in some detail. Likewise, because pressure

---

[38] Rakesh Khurana, Searching for a Corporate Savior: The Irrational Quest for Charismatic CEOs 71 (2002).

[39] David Skeel, Icarus in the Boardroom: The Fundamental Flaws in Corporate America and Where They Came From (2005).

[40] Gerald F. Davis, Managed by the Markets: How Finance Re-shaped America (2009).

[41] Gerald F. Davis, The Vanishing American Corporation: Navigating the Hazards of a New Economy 93 (2016).

[42] Mark S. Mizruchi, The Fracturing of the American Corporate Elite (2013).

[43] Kotz, *supra* note 9.

[44] Rick Wartzman, The End of Loyalty: The Rise and Fall of Good Jobs in America 95 (2017).

from rivals can do much to determine how public company managers conduct themselves, considerable attention will be paid to the intensity with which competitive forces operated.

Despite the emphasis placed on internal and external constraints, due regard will be had for key decade-specific developments impacting upon public companies and their executives. These include the market for corporate control in the 1980s, a "dot.com" stock market frenzy in the late 1990s, the corporate scandals of the early 2000s, and the financial crisis of 2008. The end result will be a history that draws together and places in chronological and theoretical context the inter-related trends that have transformed the American public company in myriad ways since the mid-twentieth century.

Given the insights the book offers, it should find an audience among US readers interested in business history and students of the public company's current configuration. For readers elsewhere, a caveat is in order, namely that in the corporate realm considerable care should be used when generalizing from the American experience. Corporate governance arrangements differ across borders depending on various factors.[45] Ownership patterns are particularly crucial.[46] Since the middle of the twentieth century, a separation of ownership and control has been a hallmark of US capitalism,[47] meaning that executives lacking a substantial equity stake have been the key corporate decision-makers in most of America's largest firms. This book, and the insights it provides, reflects this. In most other countries, in contrast, shareholders with ownership stakes large enough to exercise substantial control over management are the norm in major business enterprises.[48] The influence dominant shareholders exercise means that in most countries any account of changes affecting large companies must address their role in a way that is unnecessary in the American context.

While generalizing from the US experience must be done with care, the insights offered here regarding the public company should still resonate on a cross-border basis. American public companies were playing an outsized role in the global economy during the middle of the twentieth century and remain crucial players. As of 2017, ranked by annual revenue, 38 of the world's largest 100 companies were American, as were half of the top 10.[49] With publicly

---

[45] Business Sector Advisory Group on Corporate Governance, Corporate Governance: Improving Competitiveness and Access to Capital in Global Markets 9 (1998).

[46] Brian R. Cheffins, *The Rise of Corporate Governance in the UK: When and Why*, [2015] Current Legal Probs. 1, 42–43.

[47] Brian Cheffins & Steven Bank, *Is Berle and Means Really a Myth?*, 83 Bus. Hist. Rev. 443, 455–58, 463–66 (2009).

[48] Brian R. Cheffins, Corporate Ownership and Control: British Business Transformed 5–6 (2008) (indicating that an "insider/control-oriented" system of ownership and control is much more prevalent than the "outsider/arm's-length" regime existing in Britain and the United States); Gur Aminadav & Elias Papaioannou, *Corporate Control Around the World*, NBER Working Paper 23010 19 (2016) (reporting that with publicly traded companies from 85 countries as of 2012, the ownership stake of the largest shareholder averaged 31.5 percent); María Gutiérrez & Maribel Sáez Lacave, *Strong Shareholders, Weak Outside Investors*, 18 J. Corp. L. Stud. 1, 4 (2018) (table based on 2016 data from the Osiris database of Bureau Van Dijk, indicating that among 16 continental European countries in only 3 did a majority of large publicly traded firms lack a shareholder owning 25 percent or more of the shares).

[49] Forbes, *The World's Biggest Companies—2017 Ranking*, available at https://www.forbes.com/global2000/list/#tab:overall (accessed May 8, 2018).

traded companies, ranked by market capitalization, 55 of the 100 largest were American.[50] Moreover, even though due allowance must be made for differences between the corporate economy in the United States and in other countries, American developments have been a key reference point for what has occurred with business enterprises elsewhere. As a *Financial Times* columnist observed in 2015, "(a)s with much to do with capitalism, the debate centres on the US."[51] Insights this book offers correspondingly should be relevant in key respects for readers in countries where big business is organized differently than it is in the United States.

With respect to the book's contribution, there are two additional points the reader should bear in mind. The first relates to nomenclature. A reader might be expecting the deployment of a handy catchphrase to describe the form of capitalism that superseded managerial capitalism. No single label, however, captures properly the nuance involved.

While Chandler's *Scale and Scope* focused on the period between 1880 and 1940, he offered an afterword tracing developments from the 1950s onward.[52] He said the 1990 version of the modern industrial enterprise was undergoing changes that could be leading to a "new era of managerial capitalism" that "the historian is not yet in a position to analyze or evaluate."[53] We have moved on nearly three decades in the meantime and now know that what was occurring as Chandler wrote was not merely a new era of managerial capitalism but a new era entirely for the public company.

Various observers have sought to christen the post-managerial capitalism era, seeking primarily to capture the growing importance of shareholders and more particularly financial intermediaries such as mutual funds and pension funds. Contenders have included "fiduciary capitalism,"[54] "investor capitalism,"[55] and "shareholder capitalism."[56] These terms, however, fail to capture an important part of the story.

This book will describe in some detail how shareholders have grown in importance as an internal constraint on public company executives. An incorrect inference one might draw, however, from labels such as "fiduciary," "investor," or "shareholder" capitalism is that stockholders marginalized other potentially key players in the public company. In particular, with managerial capitalism displaced, one might assume that the power and influence of executives receded markedly, presumably with little room to maneuver as shareholder power grew. This did not happen.

---

[50] See Chapter 7, note 106 and related discussion.

[51] John Authers, *Vote of No-Confidence in Shareholder Capitalism*, FIN. TIMES, Oct. 24, 2015, 24. See also Mel Van Elteren, *Neoliberalization and Transnational Capitalism in the American Mold*, 43 J. AMER. STUD. 177, 178 (2009) ("US corporate values and practices continue to exert a domineering influence in the world of transnational corporations").

[52] CHANDLER, *supra* note 6, at 605–28.

[53] *Id.* at 621.

[54] JAMES P. HAWLEY & ANDREW T. WILLIAMS, THE RISE OF FIDUCIARY CAPITALISM: HOW INSTITUTIONAL INVESTORS CAN MAKE CORPORATE AMERICA MORE DEMOCRATIC (2000).

[55] MICHAEL USEEM, INVESTOR CAPITALISM: HOW MONEY MANAGERS ARE CHANGING THE FACE OF CORPORATE AMERICA (1996).

[56] DAVIS, *supra* note 40, at 63.

While shareholders moved up the priority list for public company executives as the twentieth century drew to a close, in various ways the discretion available to senior management was greater than it was when managerial capitalism prevailed. This resulted in "the advent of (a) new breed of corporate leader" at the expense of "the professional Organization Man who toiled in anonymity," culminating in the rise of "the charismatic CEO" as the twentieth century ended.[57] CEOs took a hit in the 2000s, but they remain a dominant force in public companies. As venerable corporate governance expert Bob Tricker said in a 2015 text on the topic "(m)anagement runs the business."[58] An appropriately pitched catchphrase for the post-managerial capitalism era must reflect the continuing importance of corporate executives, and for now we await a suitable moniker.

The second point for the reader to bear in mind is a normative stance not taken. The move away from mid-twentieth-century managerial capitalism could be a cause for regret. Donald Trump campaigned for president in 2016 using the slogan "Make America Great Again."[59] In so doing he was seeking to tap into nostalgia for a 1950s-style American Dream oriented around national prosperity, home ownership, secure gainful employment, and upward mobility.[60] The nostalgia could readily extend to the public company because it was a crucial element of mid-twentieth-century economic prosperity. There has indeed been some speculation that managerial capitalism might return, and that this could be a good thing.[61] This book refrains from offering an explicit value judgment on the merits of managerial capitalism as compared with what replaced it. This is because taking a normative stance on its passing is likely to be a moot exercise.

If there was a realistic possibility that managerial capitalism was likely to return, the analysis this book provides of its operation and demise would offer a solid evidentiary platform for deciding whether its restoration would be a "good" or "bad" thing. As the concluding chapter argues, however, it is highly unlikely that managerial capitalism or a regime closely resembling it will return. This verdict is akin to that offered by Wartzman in relation to a mid-twentieth-century labor-related "Golden Age" where "the American corporation used to act as a shock absorber" as part of a social contract between large corporate employers and their staff.[62] Wartzman admires the era and the social contract he says was in place. He concedes, however, that the corporate social contract cannot be reconstructed because "(t)he Golden Age was sui generis, and too much has changed since then."[63] The situation is, in all likelihood, the same with public companies and managerial capitalism.

---

[57] KHURANA, *supra* note 38, at 71.

[58] BOB TRICKER, CORPORATE GOVERNANCE: PRINCIPLES, POLICIES, AND PRACTICES 45 (3d ed. 2015).

[59] Karen Tumulty, *How Donald Trump Came Up with "Make America Great Again,"* WASHINGTON POST.COM, Jan.18, 2017, available at https://www.washingtonpost.com/politics/how-donald-trump-came-up-with-make-america-great-again/2017/01/17/fb6acf5e-dbf7-11e6-ad42-f3375f271c9c_story.html?utm_term=.1000e083de62 (accessed Feb. 1, 2018).

[60] Noam Cohen, *How Trump Disrupted Silicon Valley*, NY TIMES, Nov. 18, 2016, A31; Bryan Burrough, *In Good Company*, WALL ST. J., July 13, 2017, A13.

[61] Chapter 7, notes 476, 480–87 and accompanying text.

[62] WARTZMAN, *supra* note 44, at 5, 19, 81.

[63] *Id.* at 361.

The fact that the book does not stake out an explicit position on whether the passing of managerial capitalism was a "good" or "bad" thing does not mean this volume is an exercise in studied neutrality. For instance, while the hostile takeovers of the 1980s have been widely criticized, attention will be drawn to the fact they provided management with a potent incentive to focus on the bottom line in an era when neither boards nor shareholders were monitoring executives vigilantly and public company executives were being criticized for being counterproductively complacent. Likewise, though various observers have argued that academic theorizing did much to push shareholder value to the forefront in public companies as the twentieth century concluded, we will see that intellectual analysis played merely a subsidiary role. Moreover, while the dot.com stock market of the late 1990s is often characterized as a bubble, the point will be made that, with tech companies currently dominating the list of the world's largest companies, the internet-obsessed investors of that era were not engaging entirely in a flight of fancy.

Iconic Public Companies Transformed

The reader will now be aware in a general way how the public company has been transformed since the managerial capitalism era. Before we examine the key trends in detail in the chapters that follow, it is instructive to use case studies to illustrate the trends the book canvasses. The remainder of the book is organized chronologically rather than thematically. Cross-referencing is used to connect key themes across time, but the chronological orientation means the overall structure and shape of the story the book addresses may nevertheless be obscured to some degree. The case studies draw out in a concrete fashion the full narrative arc of the book.

We will consider the trajectory of two iconic American companies, namely the American Telephone and Telegraph Company and General Electric. Their prolonged prominence makes them atypical. AT&T and GE were the only two firms operating under their own names that *Forbes* included in rankings of the 50 largest companies in the United States as of 1917 and 2017.[64] Despite this abnormal continuity, both firms underwent great change, and did so in ways that were representative of trends affecting large public companies generally.

AT&T

The American Telephone and Telegraph Company was incorporated in 1885 and initially was a wholly owned subsidiary of the Bell Telephone Company that telephone pioneer Alexander Graham Bell cofounded in 1877.[65] In 1899 AT&T acquired the assets of the parent company and became the apex of the Bell system ("Ma Bell"), which encompassed licensees operating telephone networks throughout the United States.[66] AT&T would go on to become the largest company in the world and an iconic managerial enterprise before experiencing tumultuous changes from the 1980s onward. AT&T was distinctive in that for

---

[64] *America's Top Companies*, FORBES, Sept. 28, 2017, 38.

[65] Thunderbird School of Global Management, *AT&T: Twenty Years of Change*, Nov. 27, 2001, 1.

[66] JOHN BROOKS, TELEPHONE: THE FIRST HUNDRED YEARS 107 (1975).

decades it had federally sanctioned monopoly power that meant it "could be run like a family" to a greater extent than other large companies.[67] Nevertheless, *Time* referred to AT&T in 1995 as long having "been almost synonymous with Big Business."[68] Among America's elite corporations AT&T was for decades "the bluest blue chip," and its experience illustrates in various ways how "the corporate ethic . . . changed everywhere."[69]

Fully diffuse share ownership would become the norm in large US business enterprises during the middle decades of the twentieth century.[70] AT&T moved in this direction considerably earlier. Key AT&T patents relating to telephones expired in the 1890s and the corporation found responding to competition from new entrants to be a major financial drain.[71] This forced a group of Boston financiers who had exercised substantial control over the Bell system since 1880 to loosen their grip.[72] The number of AT&T shareholders was simultaneously growing rapidly, from 7,515 in 1900 to 40,381 in 1910.[73] When Clarence Mackay, a telegraph magnate, used the stock market in 1907 to buy up enough equity to become by far the largest single stockholder he only owned 5 percent of the shares.[74]

Elite Wall Street investment bank J.P. Morgan & Co. would supplant the Boston financiers as the locus of effective control for AT&T in 1906 due to extensive capital raising on the corporation's behalf.[75] The House of Morgan orchestrated behind the scenes the 1907 appointment of Theodore Vail, a former senior AT&T executive, to the top managerial post of president.[76] The bank's influence over AT&T waned after J.P. Morgan died in 1913.[77] Correspondingly, Vail, identified by the editor of *Forbes* in 1919 as one of America's six greatest business leaders,[78] had substantial discretion to run the company in the manner he thought best. That year he turned the presidency of the company over to Harry B. Thayer, a friend of Vail's who had worked as part of the Bell system since 1879.[79] Ownership of AT&T

---

[67] Stephanie Mehta, *Say Goodbye to AT&T*, FORTUNE, Oct. 1, 2001, 134 (quoting Bob Lucky, an employee for 31 years at AT&T's Bell Labs subsidiary).

[68] George J. Church & Tom Curry, *Just Three Easy Pieces*, TIME, Oct. 2, 1995, 38.

[69] Mehta, *supra* note 67.

[70] Chapter 2, notes 81–95 and related discussion.

[71] BROOKS, *supra* note 66, at 102–10, 120–22; Harry M. Trebing & Maurice Estabrooks, *AT&T's Grand Design for Dominance in the Global Information Age*, *in* MARKET DOMINANCE: HOW FIRMS GAIN, HOLD, OR LOSE IT AND THE IMPACT ON ECONOMIC PERFORMANCE 195, 197 (David I. Rosenbaum ed., 1998).

[72] BROOKS, *supra* note 66, at 122.

[73] Marco Becht & Bradford DeLong, *Why Has There Been So Little Blockholding in America?*, *in* A HISTORY OF CORPORATE GOVERNANCE AROUND THE WORLD: FAMILY BUSINESS GROUPS TO PROFESSIONAL MANAGERS 613, 641 (Randall K. Morck ed., 2005).

[74] BROOKS, *supra* note 66, at 123–24; Kenneth Lipartito & Yumiko Morii, *Rethinking the Separation of Ownership from Management in American History*, 33 SEATTLE UNIV. L. REV. 1025, 1025 (2010).

[75] BROOKS, *supra* note 66, at 122–23; Paul J. Miranti, *Innovation's Golden Triangle: Finance, Regulation, and Science at the Bell System*, 1877–1940, 90 BUS. HIST. REV. 277, 282–86 (2016).

[76] BROOKS, *supra* note 66, at 123; TIM WU, THE MASTER SWITCH: THE RISE AND FALL OF INFORMATION EMPIRES 50–51 (2010). Vail denied at the time of the appointment that Morgan had exercised any influence: *Vail Is Fish Successor*, BOS. GLOBE, May 1, 1907, 16.

[77] BROOKS, *supra* note 66, at 135.

[78] B.C. Forbes, *Theodore Vail: Business Statesman*, FORBES, Sept. 6, 1919, 1302.

[79] BROOKS, *supra* note 66, at 153, 160.

shares had dispersed still further in the meantime, with the company having 281,149 shareholders by 1923, more than any other US public company.[80]

A government investigator in the 1930s identified the periods of control for AT&T as being "banker" from 1907 to 1918, "government" from 1918 to 1919 due to a brief war-driven federal takeover of the telephone system, and "management" thereafter.[81] Berle and Means concurred with the post-1919 assessment in their 1932 classic *The Modern Corporation and Private Property*, part of which comprised a study of ownership and control of the 200 largest US industrial companies.[82] They listed AT&T as one of 21 firms that was under management control because there was affirmative evidence that the firms lacked a single shareholder group owning 20 percent or more of the shares.[83] Berle and Means, citing a 1930 press report, identified Sun Life Assurance Co. as AT&T's largest shareholder with 0.6 percent of the shares, and suggested AT&T, with its assets of nearly $5 billion and 568,000 shareholders, offered "perhaps the most advanced development of the corporate system."[84]

AT&T became in additional ways an early twentieth century exemplar of the sort of managerial capitalism that would flourish in corporate America during the middle decades of the century. AT&T had in place by 1910 a sophisticated central administration system that would change little until the 1970s.[85] As Alfred Chandler said, building, operating, and coordinating a long-distance telephone network "brought, indeed demanded, the creation of (a) modern managerially operated business (enterprise)."[86] Also, in a manner that would be familiar in the managerial capitalism era, AT&T eschewed the ruthless, hard-charging approach often associated with businesses that were dominant in the late nineteenth and early twentieth centuries.[87] Doing so would help to ensure that AT&T would retain quasi-monopolistic market power for decades to come.

Complaints by Mackay and a group of independent telephone companies that AT&T was violating antitrust laws ultimately resulted in AT&T agreeing in 1913 to a consent decree known as the "Kingsbury Commitment," named after Nathan Kingsbury, then AT&T's vice president.[88] AT&T provided an undertaking to the federal attorney general to divest itself of a dominant stake in Western Union, the telegraph company, thereby foreclosing any possibility of total AT&T control of wire communications. Independent telephone companies were also permitted access to AT&T's long-distance network at government-set rates that were "just and fair." Crucially for AT&T, though, it was given a license to acquire

[80] Becht & DeLong, *supra* note 73, at 641. AT&T had passed Pennsylvania Railroad as the corporation with the most shareholders by 1918—Berle & Means, *supra* note 2, at 52.

[81] N.S.B. Gras, Business and Capitalism: An Introduction to Business History 277 (1939).

[82] For a succinct overview of Berle and Means's empirical findings see Chapter 2, notes 74–76 and related discussion.

[83] Berle & Means, *supra* note 2, at 99, 107; Cheffins & Bank, *supra* note 47, at 453.

[84] Berle & Means, *supra* note 2, at 4–5, 99.

[85] Chandler, Visible, *supra* note 5, 202.

[86] *Id.* at 189.

[87] On the prevailing stance, see Maury Klein, The Genesis of Industrial America, 1870–1920, at 132–33 (2007).

[88] Brooks, *supra* note 66, at 136; Wu, *supra* note 76, at 55, 172.

rivals and integrate a nationwide telephone network unmolested, a pivotal competitive advantage locked in by statute in 1921 when Congress passed the Willis-Graham Act.[89]

The Kingsbury Commitment, by "sanction(ing) the most lucrative monopoly in history,"[90] set the stage for AT&T to become one of the world's most prominent corporations through much of the remainder of the twentieth century. At the same time, the deal could be characterized, as President Woodrow Wilson did, as an act of business statesmanship.[91] A 1975 history of the telephone industry in the United States explained why, saying that as of 1913 for AT&T and Vail, "(t)wo courses were now open—to push on toward monopoly at the expense of public hatred and a probable huge government antitrust suit to dismantle the company, or to compromise. Vail, in what is regarded, with justice, as one of his most statesmanlike acts, chose the latter course."[92] Timothy Wu, in a 2010 study of information empires, described Vail's efforts similarly:

> Proportionately, he probably delivered less profit for shareholders than Wall Street might expect today. Vail was acutely aware of how important the telephone network would be to the nation, and there is no evidence that he ever put AT&T's profitability ahead of the obligation to serve.[93]

The trading off of shareholder welfare against other interests that underpinned the Kingsbury Commitment reputedly was undertaken with some regularity by public company executives in the managerial capitalism era.[94] Certainly the ethos would be sustained at AT&T. Walter Gifford, who began working in the Bell System in 1904, succeeded Thayer as president in 1925 and would remain in charge for nearly a quarter of a century thereafter,[95] said in 1928 "a greater sense of responsibility is assumed by those who serve as managers for these great enterprises. Our job is to balance the relationships among the public, the stockholders and the employees so all three groups will be satisfied."[96]

A byproduct of "balance" was that AT&T delivered mediocre returns to shareholders. According to *Forbes*, few matched Gifford's "phenomenal record" in running what was the world's largest business enterprise.[97] The company's shareholders might have begged to differ. With regulation pushing down rates AT&T could charge, its share price in the late 1940s was much the same as it had been in 1901, implying a decline of roughly two-thirds in real terms.[98] Nevertheless, with AT&T paying generous dividends and with the wide dispersion

---

[89] 42 Stat. 27 (1921); Brooks, *supra* note 66, at 160; Wu, *supra* note 76, at 56, 59; Richard H.K. Vietor, Contrived Competition: Regulation and Deregulation in America 172–73 (1994).

[90] Wu, *supra* note 76, at 59.

[91] Brooks, *supra* note 66, at 136.

[92] *Id.* at 135–36.

[93] Wu, *supra* note 76, at 60. See also James Flanigan, *Executives Get Greedy despite Huge Paychecks*, LA Times, Dec. 4, 1988, D1 (indicating that under Vail the stock price did not go up but the dividends got paid).

[94] Chapter 2, notes 9, 238–50 and accompanying text.

[95] Brooks, *supra* note 66, at 168–69.

[96] John F. Sinclair, *American Bell Leader Limited*, LA Times, Apr. 8, 1928, B8. See also Brooks, *supra* note 66, at 172–73.

[97] Laurence Bell, *Men of Achievement: Walter S. Gifford*, Forbes, May 15, 1948, 18.

[98] Brooks, *supra* note 66, at 226–27.

of shares guaranteeing the president substantial autonomy, Gifford securely held one of the most powerful positions in American business as "a kind of king."[99]

In keeping with an established AT&T pattern, in 1948 Gifford took the lead in finding his successor and ultimately chose Leroy Wilson, who had been part of the Bell System since 1922, from among four internal candidates.[100] Consistent with a strong managerial capitalism norm in favor of elevating a current executive to the CEO post,[101] the tradition of chief executives coming "up the telephone pole"[102] would endure. In 1971 Haakon Romnes, then AT&T's chief executive, responded to a suggestion from a securities analyst that the company might need "fresh blood" by praising the company's management development system in the course of defending its promote-from-within policy.[103] Romnes's successors John deButts and Charles Brown both spent their entire business careers with AT&T.[104]

Vail and Gifford's public service ethos also endured at AT&T. Following World War II AT&T was an organization of "almost conspicuously average . . . likeable. . . . 'Bell-shaped men.' "[105] Supposedly "even those high in the executive ranks were exemplified by the repairmen who traditionally took their sweet time installing telephones and making sure they worked, even though many of these accounts were not profitable for AT&T."[106] Brown said in 1981 "(t)he people in this company understand—not only me, but others—that we operate a business that's essential to the public interest. These jobs carry with them a responsibility that is really like a public trust."[107]

With AT&T retaining its public service ethos, a corollary was that shareholder welfare remained a secondary consideration. In 1958 Fredrick Kappel, who became AT&T's president in 1956,[108] wrote in the *Christian Science Monitor* that he put service before profits.[109] This thinking permeated the managerial ranks. Reputedly, "AT&T's managers saw profit as a way to support and extend the monopoly, not an end in itself. Cost control was an issue less for corporate efficiency than for ensuring that outlays didn't upset the company's regulatory overseers."[110] The *New Yorker* observed in 1982 that while AT&T's stock performance was not particularly good despite being "the all-time champion favorite of widows and orphans or their trustees . . . the stockholder's loss had been the public's gain."[111]

---

[99] *Id.* at 226, 228.

[100] *Id.* at 228–29.

[101] Chapter 2, note 204 and related discussion; B.C. Forbes, *Today's 50 Foremost Business Leaders*, FORBES, Nov. 15, 1947, 37; Steven A. Bank, Brian R. Cheffins & Harwell Wells, *Executive Pay: What Worked?*, 42 J. CORP. L. 59, 97 (2016).

[102] *From the Bottom Up*, FORBES, Nov. 15, 1957, 35.

[103] *Old Bosses Bequeath New Problems*, BUS. WK., Jan. 1, 1972, 50.

[104] *Id.*; ROBERT L. SHOOK, THE CHIEF EXECUTIVE OFFICERS: MEN WHO RUN BIG BUSINESS IN AMERICA 33 (1981).

[105] Terrence E. Deal & Allan A. Kennedy, *The Corporate Right Stuff*, DIRECTORS & BOARDS, Winter 1983, 19, 21.

[106] *Id.*

[107] SHOOK, *supra* note 104, at 52.

[108] BROOKS, *supra* note 66, at 258.

[109] Fredrick R. Kappel, *Amount of Profit Keyed to Low Cost for Public*, CHRISTIAN SCI. MONITOR, Jan. 23, 1958, 12.

[110] Cynthia Crossen & Deborah Solomon, *Once a Corporate Icon, AT&T Finally Yields to a Humbler Role*, WALL ST. J., Oct. 26, 2000, A1.

[111] *The Talk of the Town: Notes and Comment*, NEW YORKER, Jan. 15, 1982, 25.

AT&T's "Bell-shaped men" toted up some impressive accomplishments. Relying on technology developed by its Bell Telephone Laboratories subsidiary, AT&T improved dramatically capabilities for long-distance telephone calls and more or less achieved universal telephone service in the United States with penetration increasing from 50 percent in 1945 to 90 percent in 1969.[112] Arno Penzias, a Nobel Prize-winning physicist who was a senior manager at Bell Labs from 1979 to 1998 said, "(t)he Bell System infused a million people with a common goal: We were taking care of the world."[113]

Despite the progress AT&T had made, by the 1970s its monopoly position was being eroded by technological innovations such as data transmission via microwave towers and the proliferation of equipment manufactured by AT&T competitors that could connect to AT&T's telephone network using phone jacks.[114] These changes coincided with an antitrust lawsuit the US government filed in 1974 arguing that AT&T's quasi-monopoly was no longer appropriate or necessary for long-distance telephone service.[115] AT&T, which had previously retaliated with sharp tactics when government regulators took tentative steps to foster competition in the parts of the telecommunications sector in which the company operated, realized that the 1974 lawsuit could jeopardize its future, and settled in 1982.[116]

Under the 1982 settlement AT&T committed to divesting itself of the wholly owned Bell operating companies that were providing local telephone service, which in turn would come to be known as "Baby Bells."[117] The government, for its part, agreed to the dismantling of a 1956 antitrust settlement under which AT&T had agreed to restrict its activities to the regulated business of the national telephone system and government projects.[118] In January 1984, pursuant to the 1982 settlement, "America's largest private employer was split into eight separate pieces."[119] Under the Telecommunications Act of 1996 the Baby Bells were explicitly authorized for the first time to compete in long distance services, though AT&T's share of the long distance market had already fallen to 50 percent from 90 percent 12 years earlier.[120]

After the 1984 divestment of the "Baby Bells," "AT&T suddenly found itself trying to operate in a world utterly foreign to its experience."[121] The switch from a regulated monopoly to a competitive environment necessitated a reinvention of its corporate culture to function

---

[112] Thunderbird School of Global Management, *supra* note 65, at 2; Trebing & Estabrooks, *supra* note 71, at 199.

[113] Mehta, *supra* note 67; Curriculum Vitae (Arno Penzias), available at http://www.nobelprize.org/nobel_prizes/physics/laureates/1978/penzias-cv.html (accessed May 13, 2018).

[114] Wu, *supra* note 76, at 189–90; Vietor, *supra* note 89, at 190–93, 196–201; Jacqueline Thompson, Future Rich: The People, Companies and Industries Creating America's Next Fortunes 161–70 (1985); Daniel Yergin & Joseph Stanislaw, The Commanding Heights: The Battle between Government and the Marketplace That Is Remaking the Modern World 347 (1998).

[115] Wu, *supra* note 76, at 192.

[116] *Id.* at 188–94; David Pauly, *Ma Bell's Big Breakup*, Newsweek, Jan. 18, 1982, 58.

[117] Wu, *supra* note 76, at 194.

[118] John Pinheiro, *AT&T Divestiture & the Telecommunications Market*, 2 High Tech. L.J. 303, 303, 305, 314, 316 (1987).

[119] Bruce Wasserstein, Big Deal: 2000 and Beyond 347 (2000).

[120] Thunderbird School of Global Management, *supra* note 65, at 3.

[121] Crossen & Solomon, *supra* note 110.

as a market participant with meaningful rivals.[122] This was a company for which genuine consumer choice was largely foreign, as exemplified by Lily Tomlin's Ernestine the Operator character on the late 1960s comedy sketch TV show *Laugh In*: "We don't care. We don't have to. We're the phone company."[123] Indeed, in 1982, "(t)o prepare itself for the free market," AT&T set up an academy "to teach its executives how to do what they haven't had to do much of: sell."[124] A byproduct of AT&T's introduction to market forces was that it would experience many of the trends transforming public companies generally in the United States in the late twentieth century, albeit often on a larger scale. After all, AT&T was, in the decades immediately following World War II, the largest public company in the world.[125]

Labor relations constituted one facet of AT&T's reinvention due to exposure to market forces. In the 1980s, unions were generally on the back foot,[126] and the trend was pronounced at AT&T. Traditionally at AT&T lifetime employment was a fact of life for the rank and file, with job security being akin to that afforded by the government.[127] Moreover, with AT&T's quasi-monopoly status leaving it well positioned to pass rising labor costs along to customers, its Communications Workers of America (CWA) membership grew as the phone company did.[128] In 1947, there were 650,000 AT&T employees, a new peak, most of who were union members.[129] This figure had increased to 1,009,000 by 1984.[130]

Things would soon change substantially. AT&T retained 373,000 employees after the 1984 divestiture.[131] AT&T announced later that year plans to eliminate 11,000 jobs.[132] The downsizing trend, which was pervasive among large American corporations during the 1980s, continued despite a nationwide strike in 1986 by the CWA against AT&T.[133] AT&T felt it must drive down costs to stay competitive with ambitious long distance rivals such as MCI Communications and Northern Telecom.[134] For AT&T staff the tradition of lifetime employment ended abruptly, leaving "people walking around . . . in a daze."[135] AT&T staffing figures fell to 273,000 by 1989, and by 1995 it was a clear downsizing leader, having eliminated 140,000 jobs since the 1984 breakup.[136]

---

[122] Thunderbird School of Global Management, *supra* note 65, at 3; *Corporate Culture*, BUS. WK., Oct. 27, 1980, 148.

[123] Mehta, *supra* note 67; Adam Cohen & William Dowell, *Ma Bell Calls It Splits*, TIME, Nov. 6, 2000, 96.

[124] *Ma Bell's New School of Selling*, NEWSWEEK, Oct. 25, 1982, 111.

[125] *To Eat or Sleep Well*, FORBES, Jan. 1, 1958, 35, 37; *Thinking Unaccustomed Thoughts*, FORBES, May 15, 1971, 54.

[126] Chapter 4, notes 405–06, 415–16 and related discussion.

[127] Bruce Keppel, *Olson Seeking to Take His Best Shot as Head of AT&T*, LA TIMES, Nov. 19, 1986, B1.

[128] *After the Bell Breakup: A New Ballgame for Unions*, BUS. WK., May 13, 1985, 50.

[129] Oliver J. Gingold, *AT&T Misses $9 Mark, But Sees Upturn*, BARRON'S, Dec. 8, 1947, 27.

[130] Thunderbird School of Global Management, *supra* note 65, at 2.

[131] *Id.*

[132] Bruce Keppell, *AT&T Plans to Cut 11,000 Jobs in Technology*, LA TIMES, Aug. 28, 1984, E2.

[133] Chapter 4, notes 313–16 and accompanying text; *AT&T, Union Yet to Feel Crunch of Strike*, HARTFORD COURANT, June 9, 1986, AC7; David Pauly, *The Wrong Battlefield*, NEWSWEEK, June 16, 1986, 52.

[134] *Robert Allen*, BUS. WK., Apr. 14, 1989, 109.

[135] *Can Jim Olson's Grand Design Get AT&T Going?*, BUS. WK., Dec. 22, 1986, 48.

[136] Church & Curry, *supra* note 68; Trebing & Estabrooks, *supra* note 71, at 203; *AT&T Freezes Hiring, Plans Shifts in Jobs*, LA TIMES, July 22, 1988, F2.

Hectic acquisition activity was another 1980s corporate trend with which AT&T fell into line. The 1980s were the Deal Decade and AT&T, aiming to diversify with its telephone monopoly gone,[137] joined the party, if slightly belatedly. Bob Allen, a long-time AT&T executive who became CEO in 1988,[138] had within a year of taking office "made millions of dollars' worth of acquisitions" and had plans to make more.[139] AT&T persevered despite takeover activity dropping sharply as the 1980s ended.[140] It even resorted in 1991 to a hostile takeover offer to acquire control of computer-maker NCR Corp. for $7.4 billion.[141] The NCR deal was the biggest takeover in the history of the computer business to that time but AT&T went one better in 1993, paying $12.6 billion in stock in a friendly deal to acquire McCaw Cellular Telecommunications Inc.[142]

AT&T's acquisition spree quickly went sour. In particular, the NCR acquisition proved to be "a disastrous marriage," resulting in losses of nearly $6 billion for AT&T.[143] This was a catalyst for a 1995 breakup of AT&T into three companies, a computer company (NCR), a systems and equipment business that would become Lucent Technologies, and a communications services company that remained AT&T.[144]

AT&T's unbundling was just one example of many during the 1980s and 1990s, as dozens of US public companies were restructured by way of split-ups and spin-offs.[145] Unlocking value for stockholders was an oft-cited rationale for such moves in an era when improving shareholder returns was increasingly identified as the top priority for public companies.[146] With its 1995 breakup, AT&T fell into line amidst complaints that AT&T was worth less than the sum of its parts.[147] Allen said that while "investors couldn't understand the strategy of the combined company," with the split they would "clearly understand it now."[148] So it seemed, at least initially, with the price of AT&T's shares rising 10 percent when Allen announced in September 1995 "AT&T is reinventing itself once again."[149]

---

[137] Trebing & Estabrooks, *supra* note 71, at 203, 205.

[138] Calvin Sims, *Robert Allen Is on the Line*, NY TIMES, Apr. 24, 1988, F5.

[139] *Robert Allen*, *supra* note 134.

[140] Chapter 4, notes 147, 152–54 and related discussion.

[141] Randall Smith, *The Corporate Raider of the '90s: Big Business*, WALL ST. J., Dec. 4, 1990, C1; *NCR's "Nancy Reagan Defense" May Not Work Much Longer*, BUS. WK., Apr. 1, 1991, 25; Annetta Miller & Bruce Shenitz, *Does This Deal Compute?*, NEWSWEEK, May 29, 1991, 147.

[142] *AT&T's Bold Bet*, BUS. WK., Aug. 30, 1993, 26.

[143] Sara Rimer, *A Hometown Feels Less Like Home*, NY TIMES, Mar. 6, 1996, A1; see also Crossen & Solomon, *supra* note 110.

[144] Thunderbird School of Global Management, *supra* note 65, at 4; Trebing & Estabrooks, *supra* note 71, at 215.

[145] Chapter 4, notes 100, 104 and accompanying text; Church & Curry, *supra* note 68; WESLEY B. TRUITT, THE CORPORATION 61–63 (2006).

[146] See, for example, Edward H. Bowman & Harbir Singh, *Overview of Corporate Restructuring Trends and Consequences*, *in* CORPORATE RESTRUCTURING: A GUIDE TO CREATING THE PREMIUM-VALUED COMPANY 8, 10–11 (Milton L. Rock & Robert H. Rock eds., 1990). On the emphasis placed on shareholder returns in the 1980s and 1990s, see Chapter 4, notes 293–305 and related discussion and Chapter 5, notes 192–95, 199 and accompanying text.

[147] USEEM, *supra* note 55, at 3–4; Steve Lohr, *To Divide Or Combine?*, NY TIMES, Sept. 25, 1995, D1; Greg Ip, *Dow Industrials Top 10000*, WALL ST. J., Mar. 30, 1999, A1.

[148] USEEM, *supra* note 55, at 4.

[149] William J. Cook & Kevin Whitelaw, *Dialing for Dollars*, US NEWS & WORLD REPORT, Oct. 2, 1995, 59.

The 1995 AT&T breakup would send the company further down the downsizing path, with AT&T announcing in January 1996 that 40,000 additional jobs would be cut as a result of its corporate shake-up.[150] Downsizing was at that moment very much in the media spotlight, and AT&T found itself to be a potent symbol of the phenomenon.[151] Allen was labeled a "corporate killer."[152] Allen protested, saying he hated firing people.[153] At the same time he acknowledged that there "used to be a lifelong commitment on the employee's part and our part. But our people now realize that the contract does not exist anymore."[154] The optics for AT&T also proved to be terrible. Investors responded to the January 1996 announcement of mass layoffs by adding $6 billion to AT&T's stock market valuation, prompting a *Newsweek* columnist to suggest it would have been timely for top AT&T executives to donate some of their executive compensation to a fund for the fired employees.[155]

The January 1996 downsizing would also embroil AT&T and Allen in a contretemps over executive pay, a highly controversial topic as the 1990s began and an issue in the 1992 election campaign that resulted in Bill Clinton becoming president.[156] The *Financial Times* observed in April 1996 that "(t)he increasingly vexed topic of US executive pay is in the news again" and attributed this primarily to a "roasting" over CEO compensation Allen had been subjected to at AT&T's annual stockholder meeting.[157] The controversy arose primarily because AT&T "disclosed a pay package for Allen that would have made Croesus blush, right on the heels of (the) massive layoff announcement" AT&T had made in January.[158] Allen was to be awarded stock options with a projected value of nearly $10 million, bringing his overall pay to $16 million.[159]

If the 1995 AT&T breakup had been a strategic success, this may have helped to cancel out the downsizing and executive pay criticism. *Fortune* indeed hailed the AT&T split as a move that would "go down as one of the classic organizational restructurings of American business."[160] Things quickly went awry, however, setting the stage for AT&T to conform to yet another trend affecting public companies as the twentieth century drew to a close, the hiring of an external candidate as CEO.[161]

Between 1995 and mid-1997, ATT suffered a "stock market debacle" as its share price fell by one-quarter during a bull market so potent that the next-weakest performance among the biggest 50 American public companies was telecommunications and electronics firm

---

[150] Allan Sloan, *The Hit Men*, NEWSWEEK, Feb. 26, 1996, 44.

[151] *Id.*; *The Year Downsizing Grew Up*, ECONOMIST, Dec. 21, 1996, 115 ("special shock"); Chapter 5, notes 45–46, 60–62 and accompanying text.

[152] Andrew Kupfer & Sheree Curry, *AT&T's Ready to Run, Nowhere to Hide*, FORTUNE, Apr. 29, 1996, 116.

[153] Allan Sloan, *For Whom Bell Tolls*, NEWSWEEK, Jan. 15, 1996, 44.

[154] Henry Allen, *Thanks, Folks. See Ya*, WASH. POST, Feb. 15, 1996, C1.

[155] Sloan, *supra* note 153.

[156] Chapter 5, notes 509–13 and accompanying text.

[157] Tony Jackson, *US Boardrooms Feel the Heat of Big Pay Increases*, FIN. TIMES, Apr. 19, 1996, 19.

[158] Andrew Kupfer, *AT&T Gets Lucky*, FORTUNE, Nov. 9, 1998, 108. See also Ira Millstein, *The Responsible Board*, 52 BUS. LAW. 407, 414 (1997).

[159] Jackson, *supra* note 157.

[160] David Kirkpatrick & Jane Furth, *AT&T Has the Plan. Is Mandl the Man?*, FORTUNE, Oct. 16, 1995, 54.

[161] Chapter 5, notes 489–90 and related discussion.

Motorola with a 23 percent increase.[162] *Business Week* said "(e)nough. It's time for the board of AT&T to find real leadership" and indicated that the company needed "a dynamic leader."[163] Allen himself concluded that the time had come to break with the AT&T tradition of chief executives being appointed from within the company.[164] He left it to the board to appoint his successor, which decided after a protracted search to choose Michael Armstrong, chief executive of Hughes Electronics.[165] A securities analyst enthused "AT&T appears to have gotten the superstar CEO it needs."[166]

Armstrong quickly sought to transform AT&T's "calcified corporate structure."[167] The most tangible manifestation was a new flurry of acquisitions that included a hostile takeover of cable giant MediaOne for which AT&T ended up paying $44 billion.[168] Initially, Armstrong enjoyed success, eliciting praise in the *Harvard Business Review* for "galvanizing AT&T" and for being "a real leader if there ever was one."[169] His "acquisition binge . . . ha(d) even his harshest critics marveling,"[170] and AT&T's stock rebounded strongly.[171] The share price rally, however, was likely underpinned indirectly by yet another trend impacting public companies in the early 2000s, namely a corporate-related scandal.

In late 1999, Armstrong indicated he was delighted to have persuaded Jack Grubman, a highly influential telecommunications securities analyst at the Salomon Smith Barney unit of Citigroup, to abandon a bearish outlook on AT&T stock of four years' standing.[172] Grubman explained at the time there had been some suspicion on Wall Street "that AT&T has been playing with the numbers to get the stock price up," but indicated that he felt Armstrong did not want to this to be part of his legacy and said "(i)f the numbers are real, the stock is huge."[173] Grubman's re-examination of AT&T was precipitated by Sandy Weill, Citigroup's chairman and an AT&T director, who had asked Grubman to take a "fresh look" at the stock.[174] Weill contemporaneously donated $1 million to a highly selective Manhattan preschool that in turn admitted Grubman's twin two-year-olds.[175] The result was a scandal

---

[162] Allan Sloan, *The Howling Wolves*, NEWSWEEK, Oct. 7, 1996, 59; Nelson D. Schwartz et al., *Time to Cash In Your Blue Chips*, FORTUNE, July 21, 1997, 120.

[163] Peter Elstrom, *AT&T: John Walter Isn't the Only One Who Should Go*, BUS. WK., July 28, 1997, 33.

[164] Ram Charan, *Why CEOs Fail*, FORTUNE, June 21, 1999, 68.

[165] Mehta, *supra* note 67.

[166] KHURANA, *supra* note 38, at 78.

[167] Jared Sandberg, *She's Baaack*, NEWSWEEK, Feb. 15, 1999, 44.

[168] Johnnie L. Roberts, *Cable-Hungry Ma Bell Turns Hostile*, NEWSWEEK, May 3, 1999, 56; Mark Ricciuti, *AT&T, MediaOne Merger a Done Deal*, CNET, Jan. 2, 2002, https://www.cnet.com/news/at-t-mediaone-merger-a-done-deal/ (accessed Dec. 12, 2017).

[169] Michael Maccoby, *Narcissistic Leaders: The Incredible Pros, the Inevitable Cons*, HARV. BUS. REV., Jan./Feb. 2000, 69, 72; Warren Bennis & James O'Toole, *Don't Hire the Wrong CEO*, HARV. BUS. REV., May/June 2000, 171, 173.

[170] Fred Vogelstein, *Michael Armstrong Finds His Calling*, US NEWS & WORLD REPORT, May 17, 1999, 58.

[171] Mehta, *supra* note 67.

[172] Janet Guyon, *AT&T's Big Bet Keeps Getting Dicier*, FORTUNE, Jan. 10, 2000, 126.

[173] *Id.*

[174] MONICA LANGLEY, TEARING DOWN THE WALLS 396 (2003).

[175] *Id.* at 415–18; ROGER LOWENSTEIN, ORIGINS OF THE CRASH: THE GREAT BUBBLE AND ITS UNDOING 212–13 (2004).

dubbed "nursery-schoolgate."[176] In 2003, in a settlement the federal Securities and Exchange Commission and other regulators reached with Grubman where he was banned for life from the financial services industry and had to pay a $15 million fine, his upgrading of AT&T was specifically cited as a factor relevant to the proceedings.[177]

Ultimately, Armstrong's flurry of M&A activity would work out no better than Allen's mid-1990s acquisition spree. AT&T's share price fell from $57 to $22 between the end of 1999 and late 2000.[178] Aware investors were disgruntled, Armstrong announced in October 2000 a plan to break the company up again into pieces.[179] In 2001, AT&T spun off AT&T Wireless and followed soon after with the sale of its cable business, leaving AT&T to operate in a long distance market buffeted by intense price competition.[180] *Fortune* remarked ruefully "(w)e really are witnessing the death of an American icon."[181] Armstrong jumped ship in 2002 to become chairman of the board of cable operator Comcast.[182] Harvard Business School's Rakesh Khurana cited Armstrong as an example of a chief executive hired on the often erroneous assumption that a managerial "savior" could solve a troubled company's problems.[183]

In 2005, SBC, known as Southwest Bell when it was one of the Baby Bells spun off in 1984, bought its former parent for $15 billion in stock.[184] SBC said at the time it would eliminate the historic AT&T brand.[185] SBC quickly changed its mind and decided to scrap its own name and style itself AT&T, reasoning that no one outside its service area knew what SBC meant.[186]

In terms of corporate lineage the legacy of the SBC/AT&T acquisition is somewhat ambiguous. A senior SBC executive said at the time of the name switch that it might be the same name as the old AT&T "but it's not the same company."[187] On the other hand, Tim Wu argued in his 2010 study of information empires that AT&T, "that perennial phoenix," "was back."[188] Regardless, for present purposes the key point is that AT&T, formerly a paradigmatic managerial capitalism company, was transformed from the 1980s onward in ways that illustrate numerous trends changing public companies over the same period.

---

[176] LANGLEY, *supra* note 174, at 416.

[177] Securities and Exchange Commission, *The Securities and Exchange Commission, New York Attorney General's Office, NASD and the New York Stock Exchange Permanently Bar Jack Grubman and Require $15 Million Payment*, Apr. 28, 2003, available at http://www.sec.gov/news/press/2003-55.htm (accessed May 21, 2018).

[178] Guyon, *supra* note 172; Fred Vogelstein, Paul Sloan & William J. Holstein, *Corporate Dowagers Go for a Makeover*, US NEWS & WORLD REPORT, Nov. 6, 2000, 40.

[179] Vogelstein, Sloan & Holstein, *supra* note 178.

[180] Mehta, *supra* note 67; Janet Guyon, *AT&T's Golden Boy Looks Back*, FORTUNE, July 25, 2005, 45.

[181] Mehta, *supra* note 67.

[182] Steve Rosenbush, *New Honcho, New AT&T*, BUS. WK., May 20, 2002, 130.

[183] *Are CEOs Worth Their Salaries?*, WASH. POST, Oct. 2, 2002, E1.

[184] Stephanie N. Mehta, *SBC Can't Resist a Blast from Its Past*, FORTUNE, Feb. 21, 2005, 30.

[185] Allan Sloan, *AT&T Hits Redial for an Old Strategy*, NEWSWEEK, Mar. 20, 2006, 14.

[186] *Id.*; *For AT&T, Back to the Future*, NY TIMES, Mar. 22, 2011, B7 (chart).

[187] Sloan, *supra* note 185.

[188] WU, *supra* note, 76, at 249, 252.

GENERAL ELECTRIC

Though AT&T illustrates effectively key trends that have affected US public companies historically it was, as a state-sanctioned monopolist for much of the twentieth century, a highly atypical corporation. One result was that regulatory developments such as its 1982 antitrust settlement dictated the pace of change to a greater extent than would have been the case for most publicly traded companies. General Electric's operations lacked the same sort of regulatory underpinning as AT&T. Market forces correspondingly did more to shape the myriad changes GE experienced since it began operations in the late nineteenth century, making it perhaps a more apt representative of corporate change than AT&T. GE indeed was itself often a trend-setting organizational and management model for other companies, typically respected and frequently admired by corporate peers.[189]

GE was the product of an 1892 merger of the two largest manufacturers in the electrical-equipment industry, Thompson-Houston and Edison General Electric.[190] Charles Coffin, Thomson-Houston's president, became GE's first president with the backing of J.P. Morgan & Co., which arranged the financing for the merger.[191] Anticipating by decades the heyday of managerial capitalism GE had from the outset a strong managerial orientation. As Alfred Chandler noted, "(f)rom almost its very beginning the key policy makers at General Electric were . . . its full-time salaried managers, Charles Coffin and his departmental vice presidents."[192] The board, dominated by outside financiers, continued to have a significant veto power. Otherwise, Chandler wrote in 1977, "the structure built at General Electric became and still remains today a standard way of organizing a modern integrated industrial enterprise."[193]

Coffin was GE's "dominating genius for a generation."[194] His managerial style, however, was far removed from the charismatic CEOs who would move to the forefront as the twentieth century concluded, including at GE. Coffin shrank from the limelight, believing "a company's job is to supply goods and sell them. The less said about personalities the better."[195] By the time Coffin stepped down as chairman of the board in 1922 "a hundred men" at GE had "received vastly more publicity than he."[196] At that point, Gerald Swope, an MIT engineer and GE lifer, took over as president, and Owen D. Young, GE's general counsel since 1912, became chairman of the board.[197] They would run GE jointly for 17 years until 1939, with each stepping down due to an age 65 retirement policy both had advocated.[198]

---

[189] David Warsh, *GE's Welch Proved That Candor Outshines Cosmetics*, CHI. TRIB., Feb. 7, 1993, G3; ALLAN A. KENNEDY, THE END OF SHAREHOLDER VALUE: CORPORATIONS AT THE CROSSROADS 63–64 (2000); CHRISTOPHER BYRON, TESTOSTERONE INC.: TALES OF CEOS GONE WILD 49 (2004).

[190] CHANDLER, *supra* note 6, at 213.

[191] CHANDLER, VISIBLE, *supra* note 5, at 429.

[192] *Id.* at 431.

[193] *Id.* at 433.

[194] B.C. Forbes, *New-Type Executive, Wizard of Plants and Markets*, FORBES, Feb. 3, 1923, 457.

[195] *Big Electric*, FORBES, Oct. 1, 1952, 45.

[196] Charles W. Wood, *New Revolution Predicted from Electricity's Amazing Advance*, BOS. GLOBE, Aug. 6, 1922, E4.

[197] Forbes, *supra* note 194; *OD Young's Career*, HARTFORD COURANT, Aug. 14, 1927, D2; WILLIAM E. ROTHSCHILD, THE SECRET TO GE'S SUCCESS 42 (2007).

[198] Paul D. Gesner, *Should a Successful Man Ever Retire?*, HARTFORD COURANT, Jan. 21, 1940, Sunday Magazine, 3; JOHN WINTHROP HAMMOND, MEN AND VOLTS: THE STORY OF GENERAL ELECTRIC 394 (1941).

They returned, however, to run the firm again from 1942 to 1944 when their successors were seconded to Washington, DC as senior administrators of the federal government's war production effort.[199]

Under Swope and Young, GE became a fully-fledged managerial enterprise. Outside financiers were replaced in the boardroom by a combination of top GE managerial personnel and senior executives from other large industrial enterprises.[200] GE's stockholder base expanded considerably, growing from 36,008 in 1923 to 49,481 in 1927, 194,753 in 1934, and 241,838 in 1945.[201] In 1928 Swope denied rumors that an eastern banking concern controlled GE, saying that no single shareholder owned more than 1 percent of the stock.[202] GE, as with AT&T, was one of the 21 companies in Berle and Means's 1932 study of ownership and control of the 200 largest US industrial companies to be deemed to be under management control because of affirmative evidence indicating the lack of a single shareholder group owning 20 percent or more of the shares. Berle and Means identified an employee investment company that was a GE subsidiary as GE's largest stockholder, with about 1.5 percent of the shares.[203]

Under Swope and Young GE anticipated an expansive approach to corporate constituencies that would become prevalent generally in large American corporations after World War II. For the most part, executives in the 1920s and 1930s considered themselves, in Swope's words, to be "paid attorneys of capital."[204] A 1941 history of GE commissioned by the company described how Swope and Young's approach encompassed a broader sense of corporate responsibility:

> They were almost the first to recognize a new conception of management's responsibilities—a conception of management, not as an agent of the owners, but as a trustee of all groups vitally interested in industry—owners, employees, and the general public, including customers. It was their determination to guard the interests of all three groups.[205]

GE's putting into production numerous new electrical appliances in the late 1920s was an example of a policy that ticked all of Swope and Young's corporate responsibility boxes. The company's revenues increased both from the sale of the appliances and additional use of electricity, new employment was provided for thousands, and domestic life was made easier for customers eager to buy GE products.[206]

---

199 *Two Who Are Not So Young Return to Duty*, BALT. SUN, Sept. 20, 1942, 10; *Wilson Made President of General Electric; Swope, Young Retire*, WALL ST. J., Sept. 9, 1944, 2.

200 CHANDLER, VISIBLE, *supra* note 5, at 451–52.

201 Becht & DeLong, *supra* note 73, at 641; *Real Wizards Bring Success to the General Electric Co.*, CHI. TRIB., Dec. 10, 1928, 33; *General Electric Co.'s Stockholders Increase*, CHRISTIAN SCI. MONITOR, Oct. 11, 1934, 11; *Number of Gen'l Electric Stockholders Increasing*, CHRISTIAN SCI. MONITOR, Jan. 10, 1946, 14.

202 *Real Wizards*, *supra* note 201.

203 BERLE & MEANS, *supra* note 2, at 100, 107. On Berle and Means's analysis of AT&T, see *supra* note 83 and related discussion.

204 WARTZMAN, *supra* note 44, at 31. See also HAMMOND, *supra* note 198, at 387.

205 HAMMOND, *supra* note 198, at 387. See also Forbes, *supra* note 194; Owen D. Young, *A Leader's Duties*, FORBES, Mar. 1, 1929, 60.

206 *Big Electric*, *supra* note 195; HAMMOND, *supra* note 198, at 389.

GE demonstrated in other ways an expansive approach to corporate responsibility under Swope and Young. GE improved employee benefits introduced during the Coffin era, such as a pension plan and a life insurance plan, and added new ones such as hospital coverage and housing assistance.[207] When the Depression hit, GE provided loans and other relief to staff it could no longer employ.[208] In the late 1930s, many companies fought bitterly against unionization campaigns legally bolstered by Depression-era federal labor law reforms. In contrast, Swope and Young embraced the national union movement, and GE acceded readily as the United Electrical and Radio Workers of America successfully unionized the workforce.[209]

In 1950 Ralph Cordiner, having spent most of his career at GE, succeeded Charles Wilson as president and became chairman of the board as well in 1958.[210] Cordiner's philosophy of corporate responsibility was similar to Swope and Young's, as might have been expected with that philosophy growing in popularity among post–World War II executives. Cordiner said just before becoming president "(m)anagement is a public trust.... And the public is our customer. If we do right by them—give them the best we can—they will buy the products that give labor employment and stockholders dividends."[211] In 1963, the year Cordiner stepped down,[212] a study of America's "managed economy" said GE "makes a greater public display than any other of its freedom from stockholder domination and its sense of social responsibility."[213] Nevertheless, Cordiner did not ignore stockholders. In a pioneering step for public corporations he set up in the early 1950s an investor relations department responsible for fostering realistic expectations about GE among the investment community and for communicating investor sentiment internally so executives understood what results were anticipated.[214]

Cordiner was "a model executive for his time, an Organization Man's Organization Man,"[215] refraining from maximizing personal fame and fortune and seeking to foster managerial autonomy. Though Cordiner spent most of his career at GE he was chief executive of Schick, an electric razor company, in the late 1930s and early 1940s and said "I learned from that experience that one should never work exclusively for financial reward."[216] He was eager for GE to have a large number of stockholders so no one individual or investment group could control the company.[217] As of 1961 the company had 405,000 shareholders and was one of the most widely held of all US public companies.[218] When Cordiner stepped down in

---

[207] WARTZMAN, *supra* note 44, at 30; ROTHSCHILD, *supra* note 197, at 47–49.

[208] ROTHSCHILD, *supra* note 197, at 48.

[209] WARTZMAN, *supra* note 44, at 32–34.

[210] *Id.* at 131–32; *Cordiner to Succeed Wilson as Head of General Electric*, BALT. SUN, Dec. 17, 1950, 4; *GE's Chairman Is Now the Boss*, BUS. WK., Apr. 26, 1958, 34.

[211] *Stepping Stone*, FORBES, June 15, 1949, 15.

[212] Vincent Butler, *Ralph Cordiner Closes Reign at General Electric*, CHI. TRIB., Dec. 21, 1963, B7.

[213] MICHAEL D. REAGAN, THE MANAGED ECONOMY 142 (1963).

[214] ROTHSCHILD, *supra* note 197, at 172; IRA M. MILLSTEIN, THE ACTIVIST DIRECTOR: LESSONS FROM THE BOARDROOM AND THE FUTURE OF THE CORPORATION 7 (2017).

[215] WARTZMAN, *supra* note 44, at 130.

[216] *Id.* at 132.

[217] ROTHSCHILD, *supra* note 197, at 89.

[218] Heinz H. Biel, *Concerning GE*, FORBES, Mar. 1, 1961, 40.

1963, he said of those occupying a chief executive post that "(n)o man is indispensable to the company and particularly yourself."[219]

GE's product lines, generally oriented around its electrical equipment base, expanded in number from 30 in 1910 to 281 in 1940 into the thousands by the early 1960s.[220] Cordiner overhauled an organizational structure that, despite GE's increasingly sprawling operations, had remained largely unchanged since the early twentieth century.[221] The primary emphasis was on decentralization, a 1950s management fad where Cordiner's moves were widely imitated.[222] Cordiner had a strong preference for delegation, saying "(a) man must have responsibility in his work."[223] To help to prepare GE's fast-growing crop of ostensibly self-sufficient managers, Cordiner had GE open in 1956 America's first corporate university, a 15-acre campus on the Hudson River north of New York City.[224] GE was also spending around $40 million annually on management education, nearly 10 percent of GE's pretax profit.[225]

Though GE in many ways exemplified managerial capitalism under Cordiner, it was not entirely a managerialist idyll. Profits, among the various result areas GE emphasized for its managers, were usually treated as the top priority.[226] Nevertheless, in the final few years Cordiner ran GE shareholders did not benefit particularly, as the company's profitability and share price lagged behind many other large corporations.[227] Labor relations were also not as harmonious as GE's managerialist rhetoric implied they would be. A corporate bargaining philosophy of "do right voluntarily" translated into inflexibility once a "fair but firm" offer was on the table, resulting in a ruling that the company's bargaining tactics amounted to an unfair labor practice with a 1960 strike that GE was thought to have won.[228]

Under Cordiner's leadership GE was also besmirched by a corporate scandal that "put a crack" in GE's "image of corporate citizenship based on regard for the welfare of the community."[229] In 1960 GE was fined after pleading guilty to collusion with other electrical systems and products companies to fix prices on government contracts.[230] GE fired numerous second-tier executives directly implicated in the price-fixing, including three who were jailed.[231] Perhaps benefitting indirectly from the company's decentralization policy, Cordiner

---

219 David R. Francis, *Cordiner Rejects "Indispensability,"* Bos. Globe, Dec. 23, 1963, 7.

220 Chandler, *supra* note 6, at 221; *How to Pioneer and Still Profit*, Forbes, Mar. 1, 1962, 18.

221 Chandler, *supra* note 6, at 220; Thomas F. O'Boyle, At Any Cost: Jack Welch, General Electric, and the Pursuit of Profit 50 (1998).

222 Philip D. Reed, *GE Keys Its Vast Operations to Decentralization of Authority*, Christian Sci. Monitor, Aug. 23, 1956, 12; Franklin G. Moore, Management: Organization and Practice 337 (1964); *GE's Fall from Grace*, Fin. Times, Sept. 30, 1970, 17.

223 *Chairman of General Electric Started Career in Bridgeport*, Hartford Courant, May 1, 1960, 25F.

224 Wartzman, *supra* note 44, at 133; Rothschild, *supra* note 197, at 103–04.

225 Wartzman, *supra* note 44, at 133.

226 *Id.* at 136.

227 *Tough Assignment*, Forbes, Sept. 15, 1964, 15.

228 Rothschild, *supra* note 197, at 117–19; Reagan, *supra* note 213, at 127–28; Harry Bernstein, *General Electric Girds for Long Labor Fight*, LA Times, Apr. 21, 1963, B1.

229 *Crisis of the Corporation (II)*, NY Times, Apr. 30, 1961, E10.

230 Wartzman, *supra* note 44, at 136; Rothschild, *supra* note 197, at 123.

231 Wartzman, *supra* note 44, 136–37; *General Electric Picks an Accountant, Too*, Bus. Wk., Aug. 5, 1961, 34.

and the rest of the top brass escaped direct blame because of lack of knowledge of the clandestine scheme even if they were criticized for inadequate supervision.[232]

Fred Borch, a GE lifer who succeeded Cordiner in 1963, continued his predecessor's decentralization strategy even as "profitless growth" prompted critics to characterize GE as "a beleaguered colossus."[233] Despite the grumbling, Borch anticipated later corporate governance trends by reorganizing GE's board to set up a number of committees, including an audit committee and compensation committee, primarily motivated by a desire to improve the review function of the board. *Business Week* said of the reforms "(i)f the idea spreads to other companies, some directors may miss their noonday naps, but shareholders may sleep better at night."[234] GE already had form with regard to boardroom innovation. Under Cordiner the board was structured so that outside directors substantially outnumbered executives, a format that was beginning to find favor in the 1950s.[235]

Despite the price-fixing scandal, Cordiner was generally thought of as "a real giant of American business."[236] Reginald Jones was the next GE chief executive in that category. Jones, who replaced Borch in 1972, quickly became widely regarded as one of the country's ablest CEOs and under his tutelage GE was thought of as perhaps the best-managed large US company.[237] By the time he left office in 1981, the reserved, scholarly Jones would be one of the most admired businessmen in the country and a corporate statesman exemplar, marked by service as an adviser to President Jimmy Carter on taxes, trade, and worker training.[238]

Jones's primary organizational innovation at GE was to step back from decentralization and implement a centrally coordinated strategic planning system that assumed resources were limited and should be allocated to GE business units that had the highest potential.[239] Jones and his management team treated GE's vast array of businesses as an investment portfolio, underpinned by the intention that top management would back the winners and prune the losers.[240] Divestiture was a realistic possibility, and indeed somewhat fashionable, because just before becoming CEO Jones had led on GE's behalf the sale of its failing computer business.[241] By 1979, 45 percent of companies in the *Fortune* 500, a list of America's largest 500

[232] Reagan, *supra* note 213, at 144–45; Inez Robb, *He Did It or He Isn't Running His Job Right*, Austin Am.-Statesman, Mar. 9, 1961, A6; *Cordiner Reaffirms His Stand*, Bus. Wk., June 10, 1961, 31.

[233] *GE: The Empire That Subdivided*, Bus. Wk., Oct. 7, 1970, 116; Noel M. Tichy & Stratford Sherman, Control Your Destiny or Someone Else Will: How Jack Welch Is Making General Electric the World's Most Competitive Corporation 39 (1993). See also *GE's Fall*, *supra* note 222; Robert Heller, The Naked Manager for the Nineties 39 (1994).

[234] *Waking Up the Directors*, Bus. Wk., July 15, 1972, 96. On the extent to which companies introduced audit and compensation committees during the 1970s, see Chapter 3, notes 278–79 and accompanying text.

[235] Rothschild, *supra* note 197, at 89; Chapter 2, notes 279–81 and related discussion.

[236] *GE's Fall*, *supra* note 222.

[237] Jeff Madrick, Taking America: How We Got from the First Hostile Takeover to Megamergers, Corporate Raiding and Scandal 90 (1987).

[238] Wartzman, *supra* note 44, at 228; *Chairman of GE Calls Activism Good Business*, Balt. Sun, Dec. 15, 1978, A19; Ken Gepfert, *GE Wants Others to Catch Up—by Using Its Products*, LA Times, Mar. 29, 1981, G1; Leo Hindrey, It Takes A CEO: It's Time to Lead with Integrity 164–65 (2005).

[239] Rothschild, *supra* note 197, at 154–55, 180; *Chairman of GE*, *supra* note 238.

[240] *GE's Jones Restructures His Top Team*, Bus. Wk., June 30, 1973, 38.

[241] *GE's New Strategy for Faster Growth*, Bus. Wk., July 8, 1972, 52; Nitin Nohria, Davis Dyer & Frederick Dalzell, Changing Fortunes: Remaking the Industrial Corporation 16 (2002).

companies ranked by annual revenues, were using business portfolio planning schemes akin to GE's.[242]

Under Jones GE's revenues doubled, the corporation averaged 15 percent annual earnings growth, and there was $2.2 billion in cash and marketable securities on hand when he left the company.[243] All was not well, however. GE's share price fell during Jones's tenure, modestly underperforming in difficult economic conditions the iconic Dow Jones Industrial Average stock market index, which encompasses 30 of America's largest public companies.[244] Jones, moreover, feared that bureaucracy was strangling GE, and believed the company had to be shaken to its roots.[245] He identified Jack Welch, who had quickly established a reputation at GE as a brash overachiever with a disdain for protocol, as the man to execute the needed changes.[246] The GE board appointed Welch CEO in 1981 after an exacting succession process involving the assessment of numerous internal executive contenders.[247]

Welch's appointment was recognized as a change of course for GE. Contemporaries said with the intense 45-year-old Welch GE had replaced "a legend with a live wire" and had picked "a new breed of executive."[248] Welch indeed would be in the executive vanguard in a couple of important ways by the time he left his post two decades later. The first related to treating shareholders as the top corporate priority. Emphasizing shareholder value was a practice with which Welch was closely associated,[249] in stark contrast to Swope, Young, and Cordiner's expansive corporate responsibility stance. The second involved the elevation of the late 1990s chief executive to iconic status. Welch would become emblematic of the CEO as charismatic leader,[250] somewhat ironically given that Cordiner was the quintessential "organization man" and given Jones's reserved air.

While Welch was destined to become a CEO exemplar by the time he stepped down, neither a shareholder value orientation nor executive charisma featured prominently during his first decade in office. When Welch was being considered for the CEO post he did acknowledge the need to appeal to stock market investors.[251] He was also eager by the late 1980s for GE's market capitalization to increase by a sufficiently large amount to pass IBM

---

242 MICKLETHWAIT & WOOLDRIDGE, *supra* note 16, 162. In 1995 the *Fortune* 500 was revamped to include service firms as well as industrial corporations—Martha Groves, *Service Now Counts with Fortune 500*, LA TIMES, Aug. 26, 1995, available at http://articles.latimes.com/1995-04-26/business/fi-59111_1_fortune-services-companies (accessed Mar. 25, 2018).

243 ROTHSCHILD, *supra* note 197, at 190; Gepfert, *supra* note 238; THOMAS O'BOYLE, JACK WELCH, GENERAL ELECTRIC, AND THE PURSUIT OF PROFIT 49 (1998).

244 TICHY & SHERMAN, *supra* note 233, at 30. On the selection philosophy involved with the Dow in recent decades, see Neil A. Martin, *Is the Dow a Dog?*, BARRON'S, Dec. 30, 2002, 15.

245 BYRON, *supra* note 189, at 101, 110, 112; TICHY & SHERMAN, *supra* note 233, at 32–33, 41; O'BOYLE, *supra* note 243, at 49–50.

246 WARTZMAN, *supra* note 44, at 233–34; O'BOYLE, *supra* note 243, at 58–63.

247 TICHY & SHERMAN, *supra* note 233, at 42–45; O'BOYLE, *supra* note 243, at 63–66.

248 John R. Emshwiller, *Reginald Jones Plans April 1 Retirement from GE; John Welch Will Succeed Him*, WALL ST. J., Dec. 22, 1980, 4; Thomas C. Hayes, *Changing the Guard at GE*, NY TIMES, Dec. 28, 1980, F1.

249 See, for example, KENNEDY, *supra* note 189, at 50-66.

250 KHURANA, *supra* note 38, at 69, 153.

251 JEFF MADRICK, AGE OF GREED: THE TRIUMPH OF FINANCE AND DECLINE OF AMERICA, 1970 TO THE PRESENT 192 (2011).

and leave GE as the stock market's largest company.[252] A 1981 speech Welch gave on steps that corporations should take to prosper in a slow growth economy has been cited as the birth of the shareholder value movement that influenced public companies as the 20th century ended.[253] Still, while he told his audience of the need to cut costs to increase profits he never mentioned the term "shareholder value."[254] The term was not even used in a GE annual report to shareholders until 1994.[255]

The manner in which a securities analyst characterized a $10 billion GE share buy-back in 1989 indicates that neither GE nor Welch yet had a distinctive reputation for prioritizing shareholder returns. The buy-back was the largest share repurchase ever by a US corporation up to that point.[256] Nevertheless, the analyst did not see GE as any sort of shareholder value pioneer, saying "(e)very chief executive considers the stock price a sort of report card and this should help Jack Welch's."[257]

As for CEO celebrity, the *Financial Times* did refer to Welch in 1989 as "charismatic," as articles and books on his management style began to appear with some regularity.[258] However, up to that point in time "the world at large barely noticed Jack Welch," and he ended up well down a list of 50 members of the corporate elite compiled by *Business Week* in 1985.[259] During the mid-1980s, Welch even referred to himself as nothing more than a corporate "grunt."[260] *Business Week* said of Welch in 1987 that he "seems to care little about being Corporate America's model manager."[261] Even in 1992, *Newsweek* suggested Welch was "notoriously press-shy."[262]

Welch was hardly idle during his first decade in office. His primary objective in the opening half of the 1980s was to improve GE's bottom line by cutting costs.[263] The general rule with GE divisions became "fix it, close it, or sell it," with the usual benchmark for survival as a GE unit being ranked first or second in the market in which it operated.[264] By 1985 more than $5.6 billion worth of businesses had been sold off.[265] GE's management style was also

---

[252] O'BOYLE, *supra* note 243, at 129–31; Geoffrey Colvin, *The Ultimate Manager*, FORTUNE, Nov. 22, 1999, 185.

[253] Betsy Morris, *The New Rules*, FORTUNE, July 24, 2006, 70; John Kay, *The Concept of the Corporation*, March 16, 2017, available at https://www.johnkay.com/2017/03/16/the-concept-of-the-corporation/ (accessed May 24, 2018).

[254] Francesco Guerrera, *Welch Slams the Obsession with Shareholder Value as a "Dumb Idea,"* FIN. TIMES, Mar. 13, 2009, 1.

[255] Blake Edward Taylor, *Reconsidering the Rise of "Shareholder Value" in the United States*, London School of Economics Economic History Working Paper No. 214/2015, 7.

[256] O'BOYLE, *supra* note 243, at 128.

[257] Paul Richter, *GE Will Spend Up to $10 Billion to Repurchase Its Own Stock*, LA TIMES, Nov. 18, 1989, D1.

[258] ROTHSCHILD, *supra* note 197, at 192; Christopher Lorenz & Geoffrey Owen, *Charismatic Takeover Specialist Looking for a Leading Role*, FIN. TIMES, Jan. 11, 1989, 26; Sherman P. Stratford & Cynthia Hutton, *Inside the Mind of Jack Welch*, FORTUNE, Mar. 27, 1989, 38.

[259] BYRON, *supra* note 189, at 157–58.

[260] Chapter 4, note 580 and related discussion.

[261] Russell Mitchell, *Jack Welch: How Good a Manager?*, BUS. WK., Dec. 14, 1987, 92.

[262] *He Brought GE to Life*, NEWSWEEK, Nov. 30, 1992, 62.

[263] WASSERSTEIN, *supra* note 119, at 285.

[264] WARTZMAN, *supra* note 44, at 234.

[265] WASSERSTEIN, *supra* note 119, at 287.

overhauled, with its heretofore renowned strategic planning system greatly streamlined and a complex managerial hierarchy flattened considerably.[266]

Though Welch was not yet a celebrity CEO during his first decade in office, he did achieve notoriety for GE employee layoffs,[267] of which there were 120,000 in the 1980s.[268] In 1982 *Newsweek* identified GE as a prime example of a large company cutting its payroll and nicknamed Welch "Neutron Jack," implying he emptied still-standing buildings of people, like a neutron bomb.[269] Welch objected strongly to what would become a popular moniker, believing that GE had no choice but to become more agile and arguing that GE had slimmed down responsibly by providing exit packages to those told to leave and by avoiding mass layoffs due to spreading out the process over a number of years.[270] Nevertheless, in what was a major change in approach for a company where there had been a paternalistic orientation that meant that only employees who messed up badly would be fired, Welch stressed GE could not and should not be offering assurances of lifetime employment because that would encourage underperformance and mediocrity.[271] GE was subsequently cited as a role model that made it easier for US corporations to dismiss workers at the earliest hint of trouble.[272]

The 1980s were renowned for M&A activity and GE participated fully, particularly in the second half of the decade with Welch looking to expand revenues as his confidence in the state of GE's existing businesses grew.[273] In 1986, GE acquired Kidder Peabody, a major investment bank, and, in the largest ever non-oil corporate acquisition to that point, paid $6.5 billion for RCA, a diversified electronics company that owned a national television network via the National Broadcasting Corporation.[274] While almost half of GE's earnings came from "core manufacturing" in 1980, after the Kidder Peabody and RCA deals nearly 80 percent came from services and high technology.[275] A host of other deals followed, including the acquisition of a major credit card business and the swapping of GE's consumer electronics unit for a sizeable medical equipment business.[276]

For US companies, the hectic dealmaking that characterized the 1980s ceased abruptly as the decade ended.[277] GE similarly stepped down its acquisition activity, as Welch was

---

[266] Thomas J. Lueck, *Why Jack Welch Is Changing GE*, NY TIMES, May 5, 1985, F1; Christopher Lorenz, *Why Strategy Has Been Put in the Hands of Line Managers*, FIN. TIMES, May 18, 1988, 20; *In "Flattening" Management Rolls, GE Chief Hopes to Shape Agile Giant*, LA TIMES, June 1, 1988, A16.

[267] BYRON, *supra* note 189, at 157; Nicholas Varchaver, *Glamour! Fame! Org Charts!*, FORTUNE, Nov. 15, 2004, 136.

[268] ANTHONY J. MAYO & NITIN NOHRIA, IN THEIR TIME: THE GREATEST BUSINESS LEADERS OF THE TWENTIETH CENTURY 307 (2005).

[269] Susan Dentzer, *White Collar: The "New Unemployed,"* NEWSWEEK, July 26, 1982, 63.

[270] WARTZMAN, *supra* note 44, at 241–42; Eric Gelman & Penelope Wang, *Jack Welch: GE's Live Wire*, NEWSWEEK, Dec. 23, 1985, 48.

[271] WARTZMAN, *supra* note 44, at 135, 242; BYRON, *supra* note 189, at 164; O'BOYLE, *supra* note 243, at 73–75, 238–45.

[272] Peter Grier, *Apostle of Change Institutes a Last One, by Retiring*, CHRISTIAN SCI. MONITOR, Sept. 7, 2001, 1.

[273] WASSERSTEIN, *supra* note 119, at 287.

[274] BYRON, *supra* note 189, at 129–31, 157; NOHRIA, DYER & DALZELL, *supra* note 241, at 19.

[275] Marilyn A. Harris & Judith Dobrzynski, *Not Just Another Takeover—Or Is It?*, BUS. WK., Dec. 30, 1985, 48.

[276] NOHRIA, DYER & DALZELL, *supra* note 241, at 19–20; Jeff B. Copeland, *And Then There Was One*, NEWSWEEK, Aug. 3, 1987, 36.

[277] *Supra* note 140 and accompanying text.

generally satisfied with the company's mix of businesses and sought to shift the emphasis to improving productivity.[278] GE continued, however, to carry out financial services acquisitions.[279] GE Capital, the group's financial services arm, became accustomed to growing larger under Welch, and it was increasingly the engine driving its parent's profits.[280] Financial services accounted for 6 percent of GE's net earnings just before Welch took the helm.[281] This figure then increased steadily from 13 percent in 1983 to 24 percent in 1990, 32 percent in 1992, and 42 percent as 2000 began.[282] GE exemplified in this way a "financialization" trend in the economy, with the proportion of total profits in the US economy accounted for by the financial sector rising from between 10 to 15 percent in the 1950s and 1960s to over 20 percent in the early 1990s before exceeding 40 percent in 2001.[283]

GE's financial services arm would ultimately contribute substantially to a remarkable run of success for GE under Welch. From 1983 through the late 1980s, GE underperformed the Dow Jones.[284] Welch said of the trend "I cannot understand it for the world," and portfolio managers were beginning to mutter "that's a bad stock."[285] *Barron's* noted in 1999 "(h)e certainly wasn't the world-class performer in the 'Eighties that he since has become."[286]

GE Capital would help to change its parent's luck. In sluggish economic conditions in the early 1990s GE Capital was "a veritable money machine."[287] In 1991 GE was rewarded as it achieved Welch's goal of becoming the largest company by market capitalization.[288] In a 1993 cover story *Business Week* contrasted GE Capital's approach "to the plodding, risk-averse attitude that pervades most banks," saying of GE's finance arm what is "most important is a culture that successfully blends an entrepreneurial spirit with the hard-driving and intensely competitive focus of its parent."[289]

GE's stock market performance went into overdrive for the remainder of the 1990s. During Welch's two decades as CEO, GE's share price increased approximately fortyfold, far outpacing the S&P 500, a prominent stock market index comprised of 500 of America's largest companies ranked by market capitalization.[290] With GE's earnings increasing eight times

---

278 NOHRIA, DYER & DALZELL, *supra* note 241, at 20–21.

279 KENNEDY, *supra* note 189, at 51–53 (setting out a list of major GE acquisitions and disposals from 1981 until the late 1990s); Tim Smart, *GE's Money Machine*, BUS. WK., Mar. 8, 1993, 63.

280 Smart, *supra* note 279; John Plender, *GE's Hidden Flaw*, FIN. TIMES, Aug. 1, 2000, 18.

281 Robert Barker, *Commanding General*, BARRON'S, Oct. 15, 1984, 8.

282 Smart, *supra* note 279; Plender, *supra* note 280; Barker, *supra* note 281; David W. Tice, *Cruisin' for a Bruisin'?*, BARRON'S, Oct. 22, 1990, 10.

283 KOTZ, *supra* note 9, at 35 (figure 2.8); GRETA R. KRIPPNER, CAPITALIZING ON CRISIS: THE POLITICAL ORIGINS OF THE RISE OF FINANCE 3, 28 (2011).

284 Janet Guyon, *GE Chairman Welch, Though Much Praised, Starts to Draw Critics*, WALL ST. J., Aug. 4, 1988, 1.

285 *Id.*; O'BOYLE, *supra* note 243, at 131–32; Janet Guyon, *GE Shares Lag Market Badly, Despite Plethora of Positives from Perplexed Welch's Efforts*, WALL ST. J., May 16, 1988, 45.

286 Jonathan R. Laing, *Riding Into the Sunset*, BARRON'S, Feb. 15, 1999, 23.

287 Smart, *supra* note 279.

288 O'BOYLE, *supra* note 243, at 132.

289 Smart, *supra* note 279.

290 LOWENSTEIN, *supra* note 175, at 56 ("(o)ver Welch's entire two decades as CEO, adjusting for later splits, GE's shares rose from $1.20 to roughly $50"); Jerry Useem, *Tyrants, Statesmen, and Destroyers (A Brief History of the CEO)*, FORTUNE, Nov. 18, 2002, 82 (5021 percent). On GE and the S&P 500 under Welch, see Jeffrey A. Krames, *The Price of Heroes*, BARRON'S, Oct. 30, 2000, 66; Andy Serwer, *A Rare Skeptic Takes On the Cult*

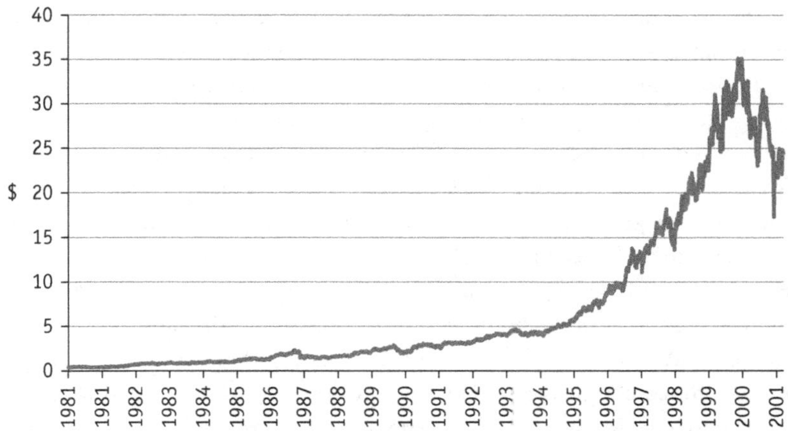

FIGURE 1.1 General Electric Share Price, 1981–2001, Adjusted for Splits and Dividends, $.
Source: Derived from data available via Macrotrends, *General Electric (GE)—55 Year Stock Price History*, available at http://www.macrotrends.net/stocks/charts/GE/prices/genl-electric-stock-price-history (accessed November 24, 2017).

during Welch's tenure, by the time he stepped down investors were paying roughly five times more for a dollar of GE's earnings than they were when he took over.[291] The rerating occurred primarily in the 1990s, when GE's stock price rose stratospherically (Figure 1.1).

As with GE Capital, one of the great bull markets in US stock market history, running from 1982 to the end of the 1990s largely without interruption,[292] contributed to GE's stellar stock market performance as the twentieth centuryconcluded. GE also benefitted from an unparalleled run of continuous earnings increases. In the 1990s, investors prepared to drive down the share price of companies announcing results that failed to meet market expectations would also reward handsomely companies that featured regular, consistent earnings growth.[293] GE was stellar in the latter regard. By February 2001, GE's earnings from continuing operations had increased 101 consecutive quarters, generally understood to be a record.[294] Investors came to believe GE was immune to twists of fate that would sideswipe lesser public companies, and correspondingly priced GE's shares much more generously.[295]

---

of GE, FORTUNE, Feb. 19, 2001, 237 (a 3098 percent increase for GE versus 896 percent for the S&P 500); Geoffrey Colvin, *Breaking Up Is Hard to Do*, FORTUNE, Sept. 1, 2015, 114 (chart comparing GE's cumulative stock return with that of the S&P 500 under different GE CEOs since 1945). On the composition of the S&P 500 see Brian R. Cheffins, *Did Corporate Governance "Fail" during the 2008 Stock Market Meltdown? The Case of the S&P 500*, 65 BUS. LAW. 1, 19–20 (2009).

[291] LOWENSTEIN, *supra* note 175, at 56. See also Pamela L. Moore, *The Man Who Would Be Welch*, BUS. WK., Dec. 11, 2000, 94 (indicating GE's price/earnings ratio was 9 in 1981 and 40 in 2000).

[292] Moore, *supra* note 291; ALEX BERENSON, THE NUMBER: HOW THE DRIVE FOR QUARTERLY EARNINGS CORRUPTED WALL STREET AND CORPORATE AMERICA 69–75 (2003); MAGGIE MAHAR, BULL! A HISTORY OF THE BOOM, 1982–1999 at 4–5, 48–49 (2003).

[293] Chapter 5, notes 279, 285 and related discussion.

[294] Serwer, *supra* note 290; Jon Birger, *GE's Glowing Numbers*, MONEY, Nov. 2000, 112.

[295] LOWENSTEIN, *supra* note 175, at 56–57; Birger, *supra* note 294; David Millon, *Why Is Corporate Management Obsessed with Quarterly Earnings and What Should Be Done about It?*, 70 GEO. WASH. L. REV. 890, 899 (2002).

Welch maintained when asked about GE's stellar track record "(c)onsistency comes from managing businesses, not earnings."[296] Skeptics, however, said GE used accounting gimmicks adeptly (if legally) to do what was required to hit financial targets and keep earnings rising steadily upwards.[297] GE Capital was identified as a particularly promising venue for squirreling away profits during good quarters and releasing them in tougher times.[298]

As Welch reached retirement as GE's CEO in 2001, enthusiastic acclaim drowned out a skunk or two at the garden party carping about the uncanny consistency of GE's smoothly rising earnings curve.[299] A securities analyst who followed GE said in 1998 "(t)his guy's legacy will be to create more shareholder value on the face of the planet than ever—forever."[300] *Business Week* said of Welch's ability to run so successfully "the most far-flung, complex organization in all of American business" that "(h)e does it through sheer force of personality, coupled with an unbridled passion for winning the game of business and a keen attention to details many chieftains would simply overlook."[301] A *Barron's* book reviewer suggested in 1999 that Welch was as close to an anointed saint as the business world came.[302] The same year *Fortune* named Welch "manager of the century."[303] A 2001 study of Welch hailed him as "(b)eyond a CEO," saying "he is seen as a management role model, an oracle, an icon for those people who hope to ascend the mountaintop of management."[304]

For US public companies buoyed in the 1990s by the bull market in stocks, the 2000s was akin to "the decade from hell" as share prices fell sharply to open the decade, corporate scandals hit the headlines in the early 2000s, and the financial crisis of 2008 created havoc.[305] The pattern was similar for GE, as the company was "under siege" as the 2000s concluded.[306] In 2009, the company announced its first dividend cut since 1938 and had its debt rating set below the top ranking of triple A for the first time since the 1960s.[307] GE, the world's most respected company in 2005 according to *Barron's*, fell to 11th in the rankings by 2008 and 43rd in 2009.[308]

Problems struck GE as the 2000s got underway, largely coinciding with Jeffrey Immelt taking over as CEO from Jack Welch in September 2001.[309] In early 2003, *Barron's* said

---

[296] Birger, *supra* note 294.

[297] *Id.*; Alan Abelson, *Next Time Around*, BARRON'S, Oct. 11, 1999, 5; Jeremy Kahn, *Accounting in Wonderland*, FORTUNE, Mar. 19, 2001, 134.

[298] Serwer, *supra* note 290; Birger, *supra* note 294.

[299] JANET LOWE, WELCH: AN AMERICAN ICON 46 (2001); Harris Collingwood, *The Earnings Cult*, NY TIMES, June 9, 2002, Sunday Magazine, 68.

[300] John A. Byrne, *Jack*, BUS. WK., June 8, 1998, 90.

[301] *Id.*

[302] Neil Lipschutz, *Selling the Sizzle, Often with No Steak*, BARRON'S, Jan. 4, 1999, 79.

[303] Colvin, *supra* note 252.

[304] LOWE, *supra* note 299, 41.

[305] Chapter 6, notes 6, 10 and related discussion.

[306] Geoff Colvin, *GE under Siege*, FORTUNE, Oct. 27, 2008, 84.

[307] Justin Baer & Francesco Guerrera, *GE's Dividend Cut for First Time since 1938*, FIN. TIMES, Feb. 28, 2009, 16; Francesco Guerrera, *GE's Pristine Rating Cut Back after 42 Years*, FIN. TIMES, Mar. 24, 2009, 21.

[308] Michael Santoli, *Kudos to You*, BARRON'S, Feb. 16, 2009, 25.

[309] Marc Gunther, *Money and Morals at GE*, FORTUNE, Nov. 15, 2004, 176. GE's share price did fall 33 percent in Welch's final year as CEO—BYRON, *supra* note 189, at 353.

GE, "long envied and emulated as the class act in American business, is looking more and more like a weary foot soldier these days."[310] "The house that Jack built," *Barron's* noted, had "proved no more immune than anyone else's to the ravages of a weak economy and a wicked bear market" as GE's shares had fallen 62 percent from the market high in August 2000.[311]

Accounting shenanigans were an integral element in the corporate scandals of the early 2000s.[312] GE responded by launching a major publicity campaign to assuage any doubts regarding its accounting practices and to distinguish itself from the scandalized companies, emphasizing the veracity of GE's numbers and providing additional details on the performance of GE Capital's key units.[313] Despite these reassurances, in 2009 GE agreed to pay $50 million to the Securities and Exchange Commission to settle charges of accounting fraud occurring in the early 2000s without admitting or denying what was alleged.[314]

Even Jack Welch could not escape scandal-like controversy in the early 2000s. Divorce proceedings put the spotlight on generous retirement benefits GE was paying Welch under a 1996 employment agreement, including sizeable consulting fees, the use of a luxury Manhattan corporate apartment, and access to company aircraft.[315] Citing the fact that corporate scandals had recently eroded public trust and confidence Welch announced he would forgo his consulting fees and pay personally for any facilities and services GE provided to him.[316]

During the mid-2000s GE trod water with Immelt garnering some praise despite GE underperforming a rallying stock market.[317] The financial turmoil that concluded the 2000s was then a major jolt. With GE Capital accounting for 46 percent of GE's earnings in 2007, when a "credit crunch" that year was followed by the full-blown financial crisis in the autumn of 2008 GE was highly exposed.[318] GE's market capitalization dropped by over $200 billion as the company's share price fell by more than half between October 2007 and October 2008.[319] In early October 2008, "in one of the more dramatic days in GE's 130-year history" the company sought to shore up confidence in its position by raising $15 billion as a "rainy day fund" by issuing securities to investors, including a $3 billion capital injection by Berkshire Hathaway and its legendary investor impresario Warren Buffett.[320] The *Wall Street Journal*

---

310 Jacqueline Doherty, *Turning on the Lights*, BARRON'S, Feb. 24, 2003, 19.

311 *Id.*

312 Chapter 6, note 31 and related discussion; Table 6.1.

313 Gretchen Morgenson, *Wait a Second: What Devils Lurk in the Details?*, NY TIMES, Apr. 14, 2002, B1; Steve Liesman, *Enron Triggers a Slew of Proposed Fixes, But What Will Stick?*, WALL ST. J., Mar. 7, 2002, A1; *A Helluva Problem*, ECONOMIST, Sept. 21, 2002, 81.

314 Securities and Exchange Commission, *SEC Charges General Electric with Accounting Fraud*, Aug. 4, 2009, available at https://www.sec.gov/news/press/2009/2009-178.htm (accessed June 26, 2018).

315 Matt Murray, Joann Lublin & Emma Silverman, *GE Pact with Welch Raises Eyebrows*, WALL ST. J., Sept. 9, 2002, B4.

316 Jack Welch, *My Dilemma—And How I Resolved It*, WALL ST. J., Sept. 16, 2002, A14.

317 Jerry Useem, *Another Boss, Another Revolution*, FORTUNE, Apr. 5, 2004, 112 ("Rushmorean"); Geoffrey Colvin, *The Bionic Manager*, FORTUNE, Sept. 19, 2005, 88; Francesco Guerrera, *Anxious GE Aims to Convince Sceptical Market*, FIN. TIMES, Feb. 26, 2007, 26; Vito J. Racanelli, *GE's Moment*, BARRON'S, June 4, 2007, 25 (chart with GE versus S&P 500, 2005–2007).

318 Geoff Colvin, Katie Benner & Doris Burke, *GE under Siege*, FORTUNE, Oct. 27, 2008, 84.

319 *Id.*

320 *Id.*; Paul Glader & Liz Rappaport, *GE Turns to Buffett for Infusion of $3 Billion*, WALL ST. J., Oct. 2, 2008, B1.

said at the time GE's strategy "dramatizes how the credit storm is prompting even the most stalwart companies to seek shelter."[321]

GE's crisis-induced 2008 capital injection and the economy stepping back from the brink in 2009 did not save GE's triple A credit rating or leave GE's long-standing dividend policy sacrosanct.[322] GE did survive the financial turmoil intact, however. Its share price even rose modestly in the early 2010s as it lowered the risk profile of and slimmed down GE Capital, which became subject to considerably tougher regulation after the financial crisis due to federal regulators deeming the unit to be a systematically important financial institution.[323] When GE announced in 2015 that it would sell off most of GE Capital, GE's shares went up 11 percent.[324] The same year Trian Fund Management, an activist hedge fund run by veteran corporate agitator Nelson Peltz, acquired a 1 percent stake in General Electric but, in a departure from usual hedge fund protocol, bought in as a supporter rather than a detractor of GE's strategic direction.[325] Still, GE's troubles were not over.

GE's share price and financial results were languishing as 2017 got underway, and Trian, unconvinced by reassurances Immelt was offering, pressed for change as speculation grew that the 61-year-old CEO would retire.[326] As investor concerns mounted, GE announced John Flannery, a three-decade GE veteran, would succeed Immelt.[327] Within a few months, GE had invited a Trian representative on the board, executed a fresh dividend cut, and announced plans to winnow down its portfolio of businesses to create a simpler and more efficient GE.[328]

A securities analyst quoted by the *New York Times* when GE announced Flannery's appointment advocated more forceful change than Flannery had suggested might be on the agenda, saying "GE needs an 'AT&T style' breakup."[329] Flannery himself subsequently acknowledged that a radical shakeup could be in the offing.[330] A breakup would be an ironic twist of fate for General Electric. The conglomerate, a corporation that owns companies operating in a number of largely separate market sectors and lacking a well-defined

---

[321] Glader & Rappaport, *supra* note 320.

[322] *Supra* note 307 and related discussion.

[323] Lawrence C. Strauss, *GE's Man on the Job*, BARRON'S, June 4, 2012, 38; Ted Mann & Joann S. Lublin, *Penned In, Finance Arm Lost Its Role at GE*, WALL ST. J., Oct. 14, 2015, A1.

[324] Colvin, *supra* note 290; James B. Stewart, *Do It All Era Ending as GE Returns to Core*, NY TIMES, Apr. 11, 2015, A1; Avi Salzman, *Time to Sell General Electric*, BARRON'S, Apr. 13, 2015, 19.

[325] Charley Grant, *Time to Up Voltage of GE Stock*, WALL ST. J., Oct. 6, 2015, C10; Thomas Gryta, David Benoit & Joann S. Lublin, *GE Adds Activist to Board as Stock Slumps*, WALL ST. J., Oct. 10, 2017, A1. On the business model of activist hedge funds, see Chapter 6, notes 301–05 and related discussion.

[326] Ted Mann & Joann S. Lublin, *Investors Ponder Succession at GE*, WALL ST. J., Feb. 21, 2017, B1; David Benoit, *Change May Ease Tensions with Trian*, WALL ST. J., June 13, 2017, A2; Thomas Gryta, David Benoit & Joann S. Lublin, *"Success Theater" Masked Rot at GE*, WALL ST. J., Feb. 22, 2018, A1.

[327] Ed Crooks & Adam Samson, *General Electric Replaces Immelt amid Growing Unrest among Shareholders*, FIN. TIMES, June 13, 2017, 1.

[328] Gryta, Benoit & Lublin, *supra* note 326; Thomas Gryta, *GE Takes Knife to Dividend*, WALL ST. J., Nov. 14, 2017, A1, Steve Lohr, *GE Tries a New Strategy: Less Is More*, NY TIMES, Oct. 21, 2017, B1.

[329] Steve Lohr, *The GE Puzzle, With the Diverse Pieces a New Chief Executive Must Make Fit His Plan*, NY TIMES, June 14, 2017, B3. See also *Judging Jeff*, ECONOMIST, June 17, 2017, 68 (acknowledging the possibility but saying it would be a bad idea).

[330] Thomas Gryta, *GE Puts a Breakup on the Table*, WALL ST. J., Jan. 17, 2018, A1.

connection between the products and services it offers,[331] rose to prominence in the 1960s, was discredited in the 1970s, and continues to prompt wariness among investors today.[332] Even having divested much of its financial operation GE remains today a conglomerate-like entity, with units specializing in power, healthcare, aviation, engines and generators, oil-field gear, and digital products.[333] Given the long-standing antipathy toward conglomerates, if an "AT&T style breakup" is in prospect for the next (final?) chapter in General Electric's history a corporation that has so often been a corporate trendsetter would become a much-belated follower of fashion.

Overview of the Book

This book's basic toolkit has now been revealed. All that remains as a matter of introduction is to provide a synopsis of what is to come. Chapter 2 sets the scene by focusing on the managerial capitalism era that prevailed prior to the myriad changes the public company would experience in the late twentieth and early twenty-first centuries. The chapter will describe how managerial capitalism began to take shape in the opening decades of the twentieth century and reached its zenith in the decades immediately following World War II. It will also discuss how managerial capitalism worked in practice during its heyday. In the 1950s and 1960s neither boards nor shareholders acted as a robust check on potentially wayward executives. Corporate scandals, however, were rare, with the prototypical executive being a bureaucratically inclined "organization man" who subordinated personal aspirations to foster the pursuit of corporate goals. The prevalence of industry-level regulation, robust antitrust enforcement, fears of additional heavy-handed governmental intrusions, powerful unions, and a banking sector reluctant to back risky corporate ventures all served to keep managerial ambition in check.

Chapter 3 focuses on the 1970s. Managerial capitalism continued to prevail but its moorings were now shaky. This was part of a broader trend, with many features of post–World War II America being called into question, including the efficacy of governmental institutions. Confidence in the public company and the managers who were running them suffered particularly due to the collapse in 1970 of Penn Central, then the seventh largest company in the United States, and revelations of illicit corporate payments, both domestically and abroad. These crises helped to set in motion a corporate governance "movement" oriented around reforming corporate decision-making processes that continues to this day.

Chapter 4 will consider the market-friendly 1980s, when the demise of managerial capitalism meant the transformation of the public company documented here moved into full

---

[331] Peter O. Steiner, Mergers: Motives, Effects, Policies 18 (1975); Harvey H. Segal, *The Urge to Merge: The Time of the Conglomerates*, NY Times, Oct. 27, 1968, 33.

[332] Chapter 2, note 210 and accompanying text; Chapter 3, notes 101–05, 111–16 and related discussion; Steve Lohr, *GE, Pressured by Its Investors, Changes Leader*, NY Times, June 13, 2017, A1.

[333] Lohr, *supra* note 329; Gryta, *supra* note 330. In 2017 GE sold off its utilities equipment business (Dana Mattioli & Thomas Gryta, *GE Jettisons Unit Edison Started*, Wall St. J., Sept. 26, 2017, B1) and in 2018 it merged its locomotive business with Wabtec Corp. (Thomas Gryta, *GE to Give Up Rail Unit in $11 Billion Deal*, Wall St. J., May 22, 2018, B1) and announced additional spin-off plans (Andrew Hill, *Back to Basics*, Fin. Times, June 30, 2018, 9).

swing. During "the Deal Decade" takeover bids, most conspicuously ones flamboyant corporate "raiders" made, constituted a potent "external" governance mechanism that provided executives with incentives to bolster shareholder returns to forestall an unwelcome approach. "Junk bonds" deployed widely during the takeover wave were a hallmark of a liberalization of corporate finance that would expand the options public company executives had in running their firms. Deregulation similarly enhanced managerial discretion in sectors formerly subject to industry-specific oversight but also intensified competitive pressure for incumbents previously insulated by regulatory barriers to entry.

Chapter 5 discusses the 1990s. During this generally prosperous decade, fluctuating market conditions dramatically affected perceptions of public companies and the executives in charge. There was considerable pessimism as the 1990s got underway, growing confidence during the middle of the decade, and borderline euphoria by the time the decade was drawing to a close. As the 1990s ended chief executives and the public companies they were running were riding high in a manner that was unmatched in the post–World War II era.

Chapter 6 analyzes the 2000s. In contrast with the euphoria that characterized the end of the 1990s, this was "the decade from hell" for American public companies and the executives who ran them. Stock prices fell, the number of public companies declined substantially, and scandals in the early 2000s and the financial crisis of 2008 eroded confidence in big business. The "imperial CEO" who was ruling the public company as the 1990s drew to a close was dethroned amidst a reversal of the deregulatory trend associated with the 1980s that continued in the 1990s.

Chapter 7 concludes. This chapter extrapolates from trends the previous chapters have identified to speculate on the future trajectory of the public company. The exercise is not one of pure historical deduction. Instead, salient developments from the 2010s are taken into account, with particular emphasis on those implying a path different from what would be anticipated given developments occurring from the mid-twentieth century through to the opening decade of the twenty-first century.

One forecast Chapter 7 makes bears mention now to put into proper context the transformation of the public company this book chronicles. Gerald Davis is by no means alone in suggesting the days of public company dominance are numbered.[334] Predictions of the death of the public company have been proffered with some regularity since the late 1970s and continue to be made today. If in fact the public company is on the verge of extinction then this book could serve as an epitaph, chronicling how the public company changed as it began its relegation from crucial economic instrument to business afterthought. Chapter 7, however, frames matters differently. Despite speculation to the contrary, the public company should remain a key element of the American economy for the foreseeable future. Hence, the transformation described here should end up being part of a larger story of the public company yet to be written.

---

[334] *Supra* note 41 and related discussion.

2 Managerial Capitalism

AS CHAPTER 1 INDICATED, the public company has been transformed since the middle decades of the twentieth century. Key trends include an "organization man" stereotype attributed to public company executives now being thoroughly outmoded and shareholders, boards, and competitors becoming increasingly important (though by no means infallible) checks on executive behavior. In addition, unions have declined in importance as a constraint and there has been a mixed pattern with regulation.

For public companies and their executives change did not begin in the 1950s and 1960s. Public company arrangements also evolved considerably during the opening half of the twentieth century. For instance, a divorce between share ownership and managerial control that would be a post–World War II hallmark of the large American corporation was underway. Indeed, the editors of *Fortune*, amongst others, were hailing in the 1950s "the transformation of American capitalism."[1]

As the editors of *Fortune* noted with respect to the transformed version of capitalism mid-twentieth century America had, a key feature was that "the big modern enterprise is . . . run by hired management."[2] Or as a 1955 study of 50 leading US corporations suggested "(t)his is not the age of would-be tycoons or enterprising manipulators. It is the

---

[1] EDITORS (FORTUNE), USA: THE PERMANENT REVOLUTION 65, 67 (1951). See also FREDRICK LEWIS ALLEN, THE BIG CHANGE: AMERICA TRANSFORMS ITSELF 1900–1950, at 241 (1952) ("the very nature of corporate business has been undergoing a change"); Robert Eagly, *American Capitalism: A Transformation?*, 33 BUS. HIST. REV. 549, 567 (1959).

[2] EDITORS (FORTUNE), *supra* note 1, at 78; see also Eagly, *supra* note 1, at 566.

age of management."[3] Harvard's Edward Mason said in 1958 because "(c)ontrol has passed from ownership hands into the hands of management" it was appropriate "to characterize this supposed transformation of American capitalism by the term 'managerial.' "[4] The term "managerial capitalism" has been widely used since to characterize arrangements in place in the middle decades of the twentieth century.[5] This managerial capitalism era provides the departure point for the public company transformation this book analyzes.

This chapter focuses on managerial capitalism and addresses the topic in three stages. First, to orient the reader, the key features will be outlined.[6] Second, managerial capitalism's rise to prominence will be considered. Third, the nature of managerial capitalism during its zenith in the 1950s and 1960s will be canvassed, with particular emphasis on constraints applicable to public company executives.

Key Features

Business historian Alfred Chandler has said of large American business enterprises "(b)y the 1950s, full-time salaried managers, with little equity in the enterprises they operated, were making nearly all operating and strategic decisions."[7] Direction and scrutiny from stockholders and boards was largely absent. Large public companies typically lacked dominant shareholders who were capable of and motivated to impose meaningful checks on top executives. Stock ownership instead was widely dispersed and the retail investors who owned the bulk of the shares lacked the expertise, information, and incentives to provide meaningful oversight. Stockholders who were dissatisfied with how a corporation was being run would sell their shares on the stock market. Public company boards, while formally vested with managerial authority, were also ill-suited to the task of holding management to account. Full-time managers held a substantial proportion of board seats, and chief executives would influence choices for the remaining directorships by shaping boardroom discussion about the directorial nominees to be put before the shareholders.

Corporate "first movers" from the late nineteenth and early twentieth centuries dominated numerous key sectors of the US economy in the middle decades of the twentieth century. As

---

[3] HERRYMON MAURER, GREAT ENTERPRISE: GROWTH AND BEHAVIOR OF THE BIG CORPORATION 292 (1955).

[4] Edward S. Mason, *The Apologetics of "Managerialism,"* 31 J. BUS. 1, 1 (1958).

[5] See, for example, Hyman P. Minsky, *Schumpeter: Finance and Evolution, in* EVOLVING TECHNOLOGY AND MARKET STRUCTURE: STUDIES IN SCHUMPETERIAN ECONOMICS 51, 68 (Arnold Heertje & Mark Perlman eds., 1990); Mark Mizruchi & Howard Kimeldorf, *The Historic Context of Shareholder Value Capitalism* 17 POL. POWER & SOC. THEORY 213, 214 (2005); GERALD F. DAVIS, MANAGED BY THE MARKETS: HOW FINANCE RE-SHAPED AMERICA 63 (2009); Michael Lind, *American Capitalism 6.0: The Search for a New Model,* SALON.COM, May 18, 2010, available at https://www.salon.com/2010/05/18/next_american_capitalism_model/ (accessed July 1, 2018).

[6] For sources describing managerial capitalism and drawing attention to the features discussed here see, for example, Mizruchi & Kimeldorf, *supra* note 5, at 214–16; Alfred D. Chandler, *The Competitive Performance of US Industrial Enterprises since the Second World War,* 63 BUS. HIST. REV. 1, 13–16 (1994); ROBERT REICH, SUPERCAPITALISM: THE BATTLE FOR DEMOCRACY IN AN AGE OF BIG BUSINESS 27–35, 45–49 (2007); Harwell Wells, *"Corporation Law Is Dead": Heroic Managerialism, Legal Change, and the Puzzle of Corporation Law at the Height of the American Century,* 15 U. PA. J. BUS. L. 305, 316–31 (2013).

[7] Chandler, *supra* note 6, at 14.

these firms moved to the forefront they invested heavily in production facilities, distribution networks, and marketing capabilities. They simultaneously developed sophisticated managerial hierarchies. Firms taking these steps were well-positioned to lock in the competitive advantages they had secured and create barriers to entry for potential challengers. During the prosperous decades following World War II market power translated into substantial earnings. With diffuse ownership forestalling pressure from shareholders to distribute profits, corporations were under little compunction to liberalize their dividend policies. Retained earnings duly accumulated. Managers of large corporate enterprises found in turn there was little need to access capital markets to execute plans they might have.

With shareholders and boards being largely disengaged, with barriers to entry helping to keep competitors at bay, and with retained earnings curtailing dependence on outside capital, executives of large corporations had in various key respects substantial discretion available to them. Nevertheless, the vast majority of executives refrained from taking improper personal advantage of their positions and the predominant managerial style was modest and unassuming. There were a few "pirates" and "buccaneers" plundering smaller public companies.[8] However, during the 1950s and 1960s heyday of managerial capitalism major scandals implicating large corporations were rare.

An evolving conception of the role executives were expected to play in managing their firms likely helped to temper corporate wrongdoing. In contrast with the rough and ready industrialists of the late nineteenth and early twentieth centuries, executives running large firms in the managerial capitalism era were not seeking ruthlessly to capture market share and maximize profits. Instead, business leaders were more akin to stewards for the enterprises they ran, fostering corporate growth while having due regard for constituencies such as labor, consumers, and the public at large (the now ubiquitous term "stakeholders" was not used in this context until the 1980s).[9]

To the extent that managerial capitalism era executives were conducting themselves as stewards rather than ruthless capitalists, there were external forces nudging them in this direction, characterized by noted economist John Kenneth Galbraith as sources of "countervailing power."[10] Organized labor, for instance, was a force to be reckoned with in many industries. Post–World War II unions had been fortified by growing membership, legal reform, and substantial public acceptance. Executives, fearful of debilitating strikes, would go to substantial lengths to keep unions onside.

---

[8] HILLEL BLACK, THE WATCHDOGS OF WALL STREET 19 (1962).

[9] Based on a search of academic journals available on the JSTOR database using the terms "shareholder" and "stakeholder," the first article to use the term "stakeholder" to refer generally to constituencies other than shareholders was George A. Luffman, Stephen F. Witt & Steven Lister, *A Quantitative Approach to Stakeholder Interests*, 3 MANAGERIAL & DECISIONS ECON. 70 (1982). On managerial capitalism era executives as stewards, see William K. Black & June Carbone, *Economic Ideology and the Rise of the Firm as a Criminal Enterprise*, 49 AKRON L. REV. 371, 384, 387 (2016); Lynne L. Dallas, *Is There Hope for Change? The Evolution of Conceptions of Good Corporate Governance*, 54 SAN DIEGO L. REV. 491, 506 (2017).

[10] JOHN KENNETH GALBRAITH, AMERICAN CAPITALISM: THE CONCEPT OF COUNTERVAILING POWER (rev. ed. 1956). For additional background on sources of countervailing power functioning as constraints on managerial discretion, see Brian R. Cheffins, *Corporate Governance and Countervailing Power*, BUS. LAW., forthcoming.

Government constituted another important source of countervailing power. The federal government's role in the economy expanded in the 1930s due to the New Deal Franklin Roosevelt launched in response to the Depression, and remained significant during World War II. Correspondingly, as the managerial capitalism era began there was substantial state regulation of business. Most strikingly, in key sectors such as telecommunications, transport, and utilities there was a system of "managed competition" with regulators enforcing standards and influencing pricing.[11] Barriers to entry that resulted reinforced market power that "first movers" were already enjoying due to their own efforts to bolster their production, distribution, marketing, and managerial capabilities.

The Rise of Managerial Capitalism

Alfred Chandler has observed "(m)ost histories have to begin before the beginning."[12] That is the case here. This book focuses on how the public company changed from the managerial capitalism era onward. To set the scene for the depiction of managerial capitalism this chapter offers, a summary of the rise and fall of "financial capitalism" that managerial capitalism superseded is provided now. An analysis of when and why the separation of ownership and control closely associated with managerial capitalism occurred supplies additional necessary context.

FINANCIAL CAPITALISM EMERGES

The *Saturday Evening Post* noted in 1937 that "(f)ifty years ago the corporate form was scarcely used, except by railroads, canals, banks and insurance enterprises. Individuals who incorporated were looked upon with suspicion."[13] Founders, or their families, usually controlled even the largest industrial firms, which lacked widely dispersed shareholdings and well-developed managerial hierarchies.[14] Substantial changes began during an era of "financial capitalism" when Wall Street banks such as J.P. Morgan & Co. exercised substantial control over corporate America.[15]

---

[11] RAKESH KHURANA, FROM HIGHER AIMS TO HIRED HANDS: THE SOCIAL TRANSFORMATION OF AMERICAN BUSINESS SCHOOLS AND THE UNFULFILLED PROMISE OF MANAGEMENT AS A PROFESSION 206 (2007).

[12] ALFRED D. CHANDLER, THE VISIBLE HAND: THE MANAGERIAL REVOLUTION IN AMERICAN BUSINESS 13 (1977).

[13] Samuel Crowther, *Five Men Cheat at Cards: What Is Right and Wrong about Corporations*, SATURDAY EVENING POST, Mar. 27, 1937, 27. Data on the activities and ownership structure of 19th century American corporations is typically fragmentary. See Eric Hilt, *When did Ownership Separate from Control? Corporate Governance in the Early Nineteenth Century*, 68 J. ECON. HIST. 645, 646 (2008).

[14] Thomas R. Navin & Marian V. Sears, *The Rise of a Market for Industrial Securities, 1887–1902*, 29 BUS. HIST. REV. 105, 106–12 (1955); Walter Werner, *Corporation Law in Search of Its Future*, 81 COLUM. L. REV. 1611, 1636–40 (1981); LOUIS GALAMBOS & JOSEPH PRATT, THE RISE OF THE CORPORATE COMMONWEALTH: UNITED STATES BUSINESS AND PUBLIC POLICY IN THE 20TH CENTURY 18–21, 25–27 (1988).

[15] George D. Smith & Richard Sylla, *The Transformation of Financial Capitalism: An Essay on the History of American Capital Markets*, 2(2) FIN. MARKETS, INSTITUTIONS & INSTRUMENTS 1, 17–18 (1993); J. Bradford DeLong, *Did J.P. Morgan's Men Add Value? An Economist's Perspective on Financial Capitalism, in* INSIDE THE

Before 1890 few business enterprises other than railways operated on a scale that required substantial long-term financing from outside sources.[16] The story was considerably different in the 1890s and the first decade of the twentieth century. Moves toward mass production and mass distribution associated with servicing increasingly national markets left forward-looking industrial firms capital hungry.[17] These pioneering business enterprises turned with some regularity to J.P. Morgan & Co. and its Wall Street peers, anticipating savvy, well-networked investment bankers could raise capital on a scale well beyond the capacity of a single lender or investor.[18] For instance, when in 1906 AT&T needed funds to improve efficiency and expand services in response to key patents expiring, J.P. Morgan & Co. took the lead in orchestrating a bond offering of $150 million.[19] The House of Morgan's pivotal intermediary role provided it with sufficient clout to orchestrate the appointment of a chief executive—Theodore Vail—the Morgan group was confident could execute AT&T's expansion successfully.[20]

Merger activity also placed Wall Street bankers front and center. The United States experienced a massive flurry of consolidation activity between 1897 and 1903, with a hallmark being the simultaneous amalgamation of numerous competitors in a single industry rather than merely the acquisition of a single enterprise.[21] J.P Morgan & Co. and leading investment banking rivals such as Kuhn Loeb and Kidder Peabody focused on the biggest deals.[22] Their primary role was to underwrite securities issued to finance the acquisition of the companies to be amalgamated, with the intention being to place the securities with a clientele of wealthy private investors and institutional buyers such as insurers and trust companies.[23]

Financial capitalism oriented around Wall Street banks prospered at the turn of the twentieth century partly because those running leading industrial firms were willing to accept outside leadership.[24] The president of a railroad involved in a reorganization conducted by

---

Business Enterprise: Historical Perspectives on the Use of Information 205, 205 (Peter Temin ed., 1991); J. Bradford DeLong, *What Morgan Wrought*, Wilson Q, Autumn 1992, at 16, 18.

[16] On investment banks and railway finance in the late nineteenth century, see, for example, Thomas J. Misa, A Nation of Steel: The Making of Modern America, 1865–1925, at 138–44 (1995); David A. Skeel, Debt's Dominion: A History of Bankruptcy Law in America 49–53, 66 (2001).

[17] Chandler, *supra* note 12, 285, 330; George W. Edwards, The Evolution of Finance Capitalism 201 (1938); Charles W. Calomiris & Carlos D. Ramirez, *Financing the American Corporation: The Changing Menu of Financial Relationships, in* The American Corporation Today 128, 148 (Carl Kaysen ed., 1996). Capital requirements of industrial firms usually remained modest, however, in comparison with railroad enterprises. See Mary O'Sullivan, Dividends of Development: Securities Markets in the History of US Capitalism, 1866–1922, at 67 (2016).

[18] Calomiris & Ramirez, *supra* note 17, at 148–49.

[19] Carlos D. Ramirez, *Did J.P. Morgan's Men Add Liquidity? Corporate Investment, Cash Flow, and Financial Structure at the Turn of the Twentieth Century*, 50 J. Fin. 661, 665–66 (1995).

[20] Chapter 1, note 76 and related discussion; DeLong, *What, supra* note 15, at 26.

[21] Brian R. Cheffins, *Mergers and Corporate Ownership Structure: The United States and Germany at the Turn of the 20th Century*, 51 Am. J Comp. L. 473, 477 (2003).

[22] Charles R. Morris, The Tycoons: How Andrew Carnegie, John D. Rockefeller, Jay Gould, and J.P. Morgan Invented the American Supereconomy 252 (2005).

[23] Cheffins, *supra* note 21, at 480.

[24] Robert H. Wiebe, The Search for Order: 1877–1920, at 25 (1967).

J.P. Morgan & Co. even said "I wear the Morgan collar and I am proud of it."[25] There was an element of necessity involved because a well-connected Wall Street bank could provide an entrée into otherwise inaccessible networks of well-heeled investors.[26] In addition, elite bankers could, due to reputations for neutrality and trustworthiness, serve as honest brokers to arbitrate disputes.[27] Amalgamations involving multiple competitors were a classic case because the parties were often distrustful of each other.[28]

Those running major industrial enterprises were also willing to accept outside leadership because banker involvement could foster confidence that the companies would be honestly managed in the interests of shareholders and bondholders.[29] Checks a Wall Street bank could and would impose if executives began pursuing ill-advised policies helped to put investors at ease in a laissez-faire environment where information about business enterprises was scant.[30] These banks would not meddle in day-to-day operations of the companies they oversaw.[31] They would, however, monitor developments closely, often relying on board representation to keep abreast of what executives were doing and to orchestrate managerial turnover should this be required.[32] Investors could with some justification place their faith in top Wall Street banks as governance intermediaries because the bankers had valuable business reputations to safeguard which wayward corporate clients could sully.[33] The fact that these elite firms were run by a handful of men who knew each other socially as well as professionally reinforced the pattern, albeit in circumstances where outside scrutiny was minimal.[34]

---

[25] Marco Becht & Bradford DeLong, *Why Has There Been So Little Blockholding in America?*, *in* A History of Corporate Governance around the World: Family Business Groups to Professional Managers 613, 631 (Randall K. Morck ed., 2005).

[26] Alan D. Morrison & William J. Wilhelm, Investment Banking: Institutions, Politics, and Law 175 (2007).

[27] Ron Chernow, The House of Morgan 82 (1990).

[28] *Id.* at 81–82.

[29] Calomiris & Ramirez, *supra* note 17, at 149; Morrison & Wilhelm, *supra* note 26, at 175; Thomas C. Cochran, American Business in the Twentieth Century 51 (1972).

[30] DeLong, *Did*, *supra* note 15, 209; N.S.B. Gras, Business and Capitalism: An Introduction to Business History 316 (1939); John C. Coffee, *The Rise of Dispersed Ownership: The Roles of Law and the State in the Separation of Ownership and Control*, 111 Yale L.J. 1, 30–31 (2001) (emphasizing the protection investment bankers could provide to minority shareholders in the event of an unanticipated takeover bid).

[31] Naomi Lamoreaux, *Entrepreneurship, Business Organization, and Economic Concentration*, *in* The Cambridge Economic History of the United States, Volume II: The Long Nineteenth Century 403, 428 (Stanley L. Engerman & Robert E. Gallman eds., 2000).

[32] DeLong, *Did*, *supra* note 15, at 216; Mark S. Mizruchi, The American Corporate Network 1904–1974, at 98 (1982); Ralph Gomory & Richard Sylla, *The American Corporation*, Daedalus, Spring 2013, at 102, 104–05.

[33] DeLong, *Did*, *supra* note 15, at 209–10, 214; Morrison & Wilhelm, *supra* note 26, at 175; George D. Smith & Richard Sylla, *Capital Markets*, *in* 3 Encyclopedia of the United States in the Twentieth Century 1209, 1217, 1233 (Stanley I. Kutler ed. 1996).

[34] Alfred D. Chandler & Richard S. Tedlow, The Coming of Managerial Capitalism: A Casebook on the History of American Economic Institutions 284 (1985); Steve Fraser, Every Man a Speculator: A History of Wall Street in American Life 170 (2005).

FINANCIAL CAPITALISM IN RETREAT

Financial capitalism reached its high-water mark in the years immediately prior to the 1914 outbreak of World War I in Europe.[35] At the same time, though, it was beginning to be a victim of its own success.[36] In 1907 J.P. Morgan personally led a rescue of a financial system panicked by the collapse of the Knickerbocker Trust Co.[37] The intervention was a personal triumph for Morgan.[38] Nevertheless, the 1907 rescue indicated there may be an undesirable level of economic dependence on a small coterie of Wall Street bankers.[39] Concerns also arose that Morgan and his investment bank were at the center of a competition-suppressing "money trust" featuring First National Bank, National City Bank, Kidder Peabody, Kuhn Loeb, and Lee, Higginson & Co.[40] The clamor led to the striking in 1912 of an investigatory subcommittee of the House Banking and Currency Committee chaired by Arsène Pujo, which reported in 1913.[41]

Congress largely ignored the Pujo Committee's recommendations.[42] The findings, however, were publicized effectively by a series of articles in *Harper's Weekly* by Louis Brandeis, then a corporation lawyer and adviser to President Woodrow Wilson.[43] Both the Pujo Committee's report and Brandeis emphasized the importance of directorships as a symbol of bank power, with the Pujo Committee indicating that J.P. Morgan & Co., First National Bank, and National City Bank collectively held 341 directorships in 112 corporations with an aggregate value of over $22 billion.[44]

During the financial capitalism era the presence of a banker director on a company's board usually meant little in practical terms day-to-day.[45] Nevertheless, to deflect criticism partners at J.P. Morgan & Co. and other members of Morgan's "inner group" gave up in 1914 a substantial number of the board seats they held.[46] The forsaking of directorships by bankers continued thereafter, resulting in a marked decline in the number of individuals holding a

---

[35] DeLong, *What, supra* note 15, at 26; MORRISON & WILHELM, *supra* note 26, at 185.

[36] Miguel Cantillo Simon, *The Rise and Fall of Bank Control in the United States: 1890–1939*, 88 AMER. ECON. REV. 1077, 1091 (1998).

[37] GALAMBOS & PRATT, *supra* note 14, at 65–66; ROBERT F. BRUNER & SEAN D. CARR, THE PANIC OF 1907: LESSONS LEARNED FROM THE MARKET'S PERFECT STORM 97–133 (2007).

[38] MORRISON & WILHELM, *supra* note 26, at 185.

[39] GALAMBOS & PRATT, *supra* note 14, at 66.

[40] MORRISON & WILHELM, *supra* note 26, at 199.

[41] REPORT OF THE COMMITTEE APPOINTED PURSUANT TO HOUSE RESOLUTIONS 429 AND 504 TO INVESTIGATE THE CONCENTRATION OF CONTROL OF MONEY AND CREDIT (1913) [hereinafter PUJO REPORT].

[42] JERRY W. MARKHAM, A FINANCIAL HISTORY OF THE UNITED STATES: FROM J.P. MORGAN TO THE INSTITUTIONAL INVESTOR (1900–1970) 53 (2002).

[43] MORRISON & WILHELM, *supra* note 26, at 201; FRASER, *supra* note 34, at 295–96; CEDRIC B. COWING, POPULISTS, PLUNGERS, AND PROGRESSIVES: A SOCIAL HISTORY OF STOCK AND COMMODITY SPECULATION, 1890–1936, at 50–52 (1965).

[44] PUJO REPORT, *supra* note 41, at 89–90.

[45] O'SULLIVAN, *supra* note 17, at 300–01; FREDRICK LEWIS ALLEN, THE LORDS OF CREATION 178–79 (1935).

[46] MORRISON & WILHELM, *supra* note 26, at 200–01; MARKHAM, *supra* note 42, at 55; *A Start, Untermeyer Says*, NY TIMES, Jan. 3, 1914, 2.

substantial number of directorships in large companies.[47] According to economic historian Naomi Lamoreaux, "(b)y the 1920s . . . the influence of bankers on the boards of major corporations had waned, and managers were left to run their companies largely unchecked."[48]

Changes to securities markets further compromised financial capitalism. Investment bankers enjoyed unparalleled prosperity in the 1920s as, amidst rapidly rising share prices, they exercised sway over larger aggregations of capital than they ever had before.[49] Still, "Wall Streeters realized that the Age of the Titans had passed."[50] Most relevant for public companies, J.P. Morgan & Co. and its ilk were no longer investment gatekeepers in the way they were at the turn of the twentieth century.

During the 1920s general economic optimism, revelations of new products and technologies, increasingly plentiful credit, and an element of speculative excess meant there was robust demand for shares without the imprimatur of J.P. Morgan & Co., Kuhn Loeb, and other elite Wall Street banks.[51] New financiers rose to prominence with the market for shares expanding.[52] As competition intensified, the sense of responsibility for investment quality among financial intermediaries diminished as old codes of conduct were disregarded and unsound sales practices proliferated.[53] The changes simultaneously democratized investment—according to one estimate the number of individuals owning stock in publicly traded companies increased from half a million in 1900 to 2 million in 1920 and 10 million in 1930[54]—while eroding the leverage J.P. Morgan Co. and its elite Wall Street peers had over both investors and public company executives.[55]

A revamp of the financing patterns of public companies also undermined financial capitalism. In the 1920s, leading enterprises in capital intensive industries such as electrical equipment retained substantial continuing ties to top Wall Street banks.[56] On the other hand, numerous successful companies that had formerly worked closely with Wall Street were striking out on their own, opting to finance their operations primarily through retained earnings.[57] There also were various sectors of the economy flourishing in the 1920s where Wall

---

[47] MIZRUCHI, *supra* note 32, at 100, 184–85; Smith & Sylla, *supra* note 33, at 1221; David Bunting & Mark S. Mizruchi, *Transfer of Control in Large Corporations*, 16 J. ECON. ISSUES 985, 995–96 (1982).

[48] Lamoreaux, *supra* note 31, at 428.

[49] GRAS, *supra* note 30, at 299; Paul M. Sweezy, *The Decline of the Investment Banker*, 1 ANTIOCH REV. 63, 63 (1941).

[50] ROBERT SOBEL, THE BIG BOARD: A HISTORY OF THE NEW YORK STOCK MARKET 237 (1965).

[51] DeLong, *What, supra* note 15, at 26–27 (investor demand and investment banks); STEVE FRASER, WALL STREET: A CULTURAL HISTORY 340–47 (2005) (summarizing factors contributing to investor demand).

[52] Smith & Sylla, *supra* note 33, at 1223; Mary O'Sullivan, *The Expansion of the U.S. Stock Market, 1885–1930: Historical Facts and Theoretical Fashions*, 8 ENTERPRISE & SOC'Y. 489, 531 (2007).

[53] Smith & Sylla, *supra* note 33, at 1223; ALLEN, *supra* note 45, at 341; O'Sullivan, *supra* note 52, at 531; THOMAS C. COCHRAN, 200 YEARS OF AMERICAN BUSINESS 150–51 (1977).

[54] JONATHAN BARRON BASKIN & PAUL J. MIRANTI, A HISTORY OF CORPORATE FINANCE 190 (1997).

[55] Smith & Sylla, *supra* note 15, at 28–29; COCHRAN, *supra* note 29, at 54.

[56] A.A. Berle, *High Finance: Master or Servant*, 23 YALE REV. 20, 25 (1933); ALFRED D. CHANDLER, SCALE AND SCOPE: THE DYNAMICS OF INDUSTRIAL CAPITALISM 82 (1990).

[57] EDITORS (FORTUNE), *supra* note 1, at 74; Smith & Sylla, *supra* note 33, at 1221-22; CHANDLER, *supra* note 56, at 81.

Street had never exercised substantial influence because of lack of involvement with early frontrunners.[58] Automobiles and motion pictures were prime examples.[59]

While investment bankers were prosperous in the 1920s even if financial capitalism was beginning to wane, the legacy of the 1930s was unambiguous—there was a "rout of the financiers."[60] A 1941 article entitled "The Decline of the Investment Banker" said "that in the short space of a single decade he has suffered a dramatic eclipse, and that such power as he still retains is largely rooted in a past that is gone forever."[61] Congressional hearings on the operation of securities markets held in the wake of the 1929 stock market crash where lead counsel Ferdinand Pecora played a starring role left a strong negative impression on public opinion.[62] Revelations of dubious ethics indicated that the sense of public duty that motivated J.P. Morgan's 1907 rescue of the financial markets had been lost by a generation of bankers prepared to exploit the financial system so as to advantage Wall Street "insiders."[63]

Legislative change closed the door further on financial capitalism. Provisions in 1933 banking legislation that came to be known as the Glass Steagall Act fragmented the financial sector by severing commercial banking, oriented around the taking of deposits and the making of loans, from investment banking, which relates primarily to the issuance, distribution, and trading of securities.[64] Commercial banks correspondingly divested themselves of securities affiliates and most private investment houses opted for investment banking.[65] Crucially for mid-twentieth-century public company executives, the combination of market trends and regulatory change meant the leverage bankers formerly had to circumscribe managerial discretion had largely dissipated.[66] As economic historian Bradford DeLong has said,

> (A)fter the Great Depression and World War II, American finance looked very different from how it had looked even in 1929 (footnote omitted).... (I)nvestment bankers ... no longer exercised substantial power over individual companies. No executive of any major corporation in the 1950s, '60s or '70s would have said under any circumstances that he wore the Morgan ... collar...."[67]

---

[58] FRASER, *supra* note 51, at 305; CHANDLER, *supra* note 56, at 82.

[59] SOBEL, *supra* note 50, at 185 (discussing the House of Morgan); JONATHAN A. KNEE, THE ACCIDENTIAL INVESTMENT BANKER: INSIDE THE DECADE THAT TRANSFORMED WALL STREET 46 (2007) (automobiles snubbed by "the Yankee houses").

[60] Smith & Sylla, *supra* note 33, at 1225.

[61] Sweezy, *supra* note 49, at 63.

[62] GALAMBOS & PRATT, *supra* note 14, at 102; YOUSSEF CASSIS, CAPITALS OF CAPITAL: THE RISE AND FALL OF INTERNATIONAL FINANCIAL CENTRES 1780–2009, at 188 (2006).

[63] GALAMBOS & PRATT, *supra* note 14, at 102; see also CASSIS, *supra* note 62, at 188.

[64] Banking Act of 1933, Pub. L. No. 73–66, 48 Stat. 162., s. 21; Smith & Sylla, *supra* note 15, at 38; CASSIS, *supra* note 62, at 188; Eugene White, *Banking and Finance in the Twentieth Century, in* THE CAMBRIDGE ECONOMIC HISTORY OF THE UNITED STATES, VOLUME III: THE TWENTIETH CENTURY 743, 766 (Stanley L. Engerman & Robert E. Gallman eds., 2000).

[65] MORRISON & WILHELM, *supra* note 26, at 209–10; Smith & Sylla, *supra* note 33, at 1125–26; CASSIS, note 62, at 188–89.

[66] Lind, *supra* note 5; DANIEL BELL, THE END OF IDEOLOGY: ON THE EXHAUSTION OF POLITICAL IDEAS IN THE FIFTIES 43 (1960).

[67] DeLong, *What, supra* note 15, at 27.

The "rout of the financiers" thus helped to foster the managerial dominance of public companies that characterized the middle decades of the twentieth century.

WHEN DID OWNERSHIP SEPARATE FROM CONTROL IN LARGE PUBLIC COMPANIES?

While the demise of financial capitalism helped to clear the way for managerial capitalism, also pivotal was a dispersion of share ownership that provided executives with substantial autonomy from stockholders. In public companies where one party (such as the founder) or a closely allied set of investors owns a dominant stake, the exercise of shareholder influence is likely to be a potent check on managerial discretion.[68] Dominant shareholders should have a financial stake that is large enough to motivate them to keep a careful watch on what is going on. The voting power "core" investors have at their disposal should also give them sufficient leverage to operate as a meaningful negative force capable of orchestrating corrective action if problems arise.[69] As law professor Mark Roe has said, "a shareholder with 25 percent of the company's stock could veto empire-building acquisitions, question managerial performance, and in extreme instances, replace the managers."[70]

While dominant shareholders can compromise managerial autonomy substantially, they were becoming the exception to the rule in large public companies as finance capitalism retreated. Adolf Berle and Gardiner Means maintained in 1932 in *The Modern Corporation and Private Property* that "in the largest American corporations, a new condition has developed.... (T)here are no dominant owners, and control is maintained in large measure apart from ownership."[71] This claim would have an enduring legacy. James Hawley and Andrew Williams suggested in 2000 "(t)he phenomenon Berle and Means identified in 1932—the divorce of ownership and control—would come to dominate most thinking about issues of corporate governance for the rest of the twentieth century."[72] The separation of ownership and control in public companies indeed became sufficiently closely associated with Berle and Means for a public company lacking a dominant shareholder to be referred to subsequently as a "Berle-Means corporation" or "Berle and Means corporation."[73] One might infer from

---

[68] Brian R. Cheffins, *Corporate Law and Ownership Structure: A Darwinian Link*, 25 U. NEW SOUTH WALES L.J. 346, 360.

[69] ROBERT A. GORDON, BUSINESS LEADERSHIP IN THE LARGE CORPORATION 173 (1945). *Cf.* Adolf A. Berle, *Economic Power and the Free Society, in* BUSINESS AND GOVERNMENT: THE PROBLEM OF POWER 2, 7–8 (Howard D. Marshall ed., 1970) (pointing out that the influence of a dominant minority shareholder would be compromised considerably if there was no support from otherwise neutral stockholders).

[70] Mark J. Roe, *A Political Theory of American Corporate Finance*, 91 COLUM. L. REV. 10, 12–13 (1991).

[71] ADOLF A. BERLE & GARDINER C. MEANS, THE MODERN CORPORATION & PRIVATE PROPERTY 110–11 (1932).

[72] JAMES P. HAWLEY & ANDREW T. WILLIAMS, THE RISE OF FIDUCIARY CAPITALISM: HOW INSTITUTIONAL INVESTORS CAN MAKE CORPORATE AMERICA MORE DEMOCRATIC 42 (2000).

[73] See, for example, Stephen M. Bainbridge, *The Politics of Corporate Governance*, 18 HARV. J.L. & PUB. POLICY 671, 674 (1995); Rafael La Porta, Florencio López-de-Silanes, Andrei Shleifer & Robert Vishny, *Corporate Ownership around the World*, 54 J. FIN. 471, 474 (1999); Sofie Cools, *The Real Difference in Corporate Law between the United States and Continental Europe: Distribution of Powers*, 30 DEL. J. CORP. L. 697, 698 (2005). Mark Roe originally coined the term: Roe, *supra* note 70, at 11.

all of this that dominant shareholders were already passé in large companies by 1932. In fact, the diffusion of share ownership that would help to underpin managerial capitalism still had some distance to go.

Berle and Means relied on empirical analysis to substantiate their claim that a separation of ownership and control characterized large US companies. Drawing on industrial manuals, press reports, and "street knowledge" they reported on control arrangements in the 42 railroads, 52 public utilities, and 106 industrials that comprised America's largest 200 non-financial corporations, ranked by assets.[74] Berle and Means categorized companies as being under (1) "private ownership" (an individual or compact group owning most or all of the shares), (2) "majority control" (ownership of a majority of stock by a single individual or small group), (3) "control through legal device" (use of corporate "pyramids," nonvoting shares, and voting trusts to secure the legal power to vote a majority of the voting shares), (4) "minority control" (an individual or small group holding a sufficiently large minority stake to hold sway due to share ownership), (5) "management control" (no individual or small group having a minority interest large enough—defined as 20 percent—to dominate the affairs of the company), and (6) in receivership.

Berle and Means's data did not match up fully with their rhetoric concerning the demise of dominant owners. Only a minority (88) of their 200 companies qualified as management controlled and only 21 of these 88 were categorized as management controlled on the basis on the basis of direct evidence of a lack of a shareholder having an ownership stake of 20 percent or more.[75] The other "management controlled" companies were ones where the locus of control was doubtful but was presumed to be held by management and where the dominant shareholders were themselves corporations that were management controlled.[76]

While Berle and Means spoke of a "new condition" in large business enterprises they did acknowledge "the separation of ownership and control has not yet become complete."[77] A 1940 study by the Temporary National Economic Committee (TNEC), which had been established jointly by Congress and President Roosevelt to investigate the concentration of economic power in the United States, underscored that large shareholders remained prominent in large companies in the 1930s.[78] The TNEC sought to identify as of 1939 centers of ownership control in America's 200 largest non-financial corporations. Statutory powers authorizing data gathering were relied upon to ascertain the percentage of shares owned by the 20 largest stockholders in each firm, and the TNEC's efforts were praised for both accuracy and reliability.[79]

---

[74] Berle & Means, *supra* note 71, at 19–27, 67–109.

[75] *Id.* at 98–101, 106. Berle and Means actually classified 88½ companies as being under management control. The half was awarded due to a "special situation," namely the utility Chicago Railways. Co. being in receivership (at 101).

[76] *Id.* at 90–97.

[77] *Id.* at 302.

[78] Raymond Goldsmith et al., The Distribution of Ownership in the 200 Largest Non-financial Corporations, TNEC Investigation of Concentration of Economic Power, Monograph No. 29 (1940).

[79] Don Villarejo, *Stock Ownership and the Control of Corporations (Parts I, II)*, New Univ. Thought, Autumn 1961, at 33, 50–51, 56; Philip H. Burch, The Managerial Revolution Reassessed: Family Control

The 1940 TNEC report distinguished between companies under ownership control, either by a family or another corporation, and those with no center of ownership control, the category akin to Berle and Means's management-controlled grouping. The TNEC assumed a center of ownership control existed where there was a sizeable concentration of equity in the hands of an identifiable dominant group or where the largest shareholders had managerial representation and remaining shareholdings were highly dispersed. Among the top 200 non-financial corporations, the TNEC found that only in 61 was there no center of ownership control. Of the remaining 139 companies, the TNEC classified 77 as being under family control, 56 as being controlled by other corporations, and 6 as being under joint control of family and corporate interest groups. The TNEC concluded control through ownership (albeit usually minority control) was the typical situation in large business enterprises.[80]

While Berle and Means's 1932 declaration that ownership and control were apart "in large measure" was an overstatement, matters were evolving in the direction they had suggested. The *New York Times* said in 1943 that "wealthy individuals (and) estates are disposing of important stockholdings piecemeal. . . . (T)his liquidation is being absorbed by an army of relatively small investors. . . . The current period will go down in financial history as one in which important changes were made in the ownership of corporations."[81] The same paper said in 1955 of public companies and their executives:

> A generation or so ago, most corporations were held by small groups of investors. Often as not, members of the founding family held the majority of shares. Then came in succession the Great Depression, high taxes on incomes and estates, and the need for new capital in a rapidly growing economy. Result: today, the stock of many companies is widely distributed among thousands or even hundreds of thousands of shareholders. Management, in effect, has become a high-priced employe(e).[82]

A 1955 study of the background of chief executives and board chairmen of large companies covering 1900, 1925, and 1950 confirmed "the general trend is toward increasing management control" unaffiliated with substantial share ownership, evidenced by the fact that as of 1950 at least three-quarters of the chief executives and chairmen owned less than 1 percent of their company's voting stock.[83] Berle concurred. In 1959 he acknowledged that as of 1929 large enterprises were usually under the "working control" of shareholders, but maintained that "management control . . . meaning . . . that no large concentrated stockholding exists that maintains a close working relationship with management" was "the norm" with "the bulk of American industry now."[84]

IN AMERICA'S LARGE CORPORATIONS 128 (1972); Dennis Leech, *Ownership Concentration and Control in Large US Corporations in the 1930s: An Analysis of the TNEC Sample*, 35 J. INDUST. ECON. 333, 333 (1987).

80 GORDON, *supra* note 69, at 42.

81 Edward J. Condlon, *Scattering of Big Security Blocks Speeded by Taxes, Post-War Views*, NY TIMES, Oct. 24, 1943, S7.

82 Richard Rutter, *Proxy Wards Shed No Gore, Much Ink*, NY TIMES, May 24, 1955, 44.

83 MABEL NEWCOMER, THE BIG BUSINESS EXECUTIVE: THE FACTORS THAT MADE HIM 5–6 (1955).

84 ADOLF A. BERLE, POWER WITHOUT PROPERTY: A NEW DEVELOPMENT IN AMERICAN POLITICAL ECONOMY 73–74 (1959).

Berle's 1959 assessment reflected the general consensus. *Forbes* indicated in 1957 "today's manager works for no single imperious owner. Instead he serves thousands, even hundreds of thousands of stockholder owners."[85] Carl Kaysen, a Harvard economist, said the same year of "the modern corporation" that dominated the US economy "(s)tockholding is widely dispersed; no single group of persons, in or out of management, has significant control over corporate action resting on stock ownership."[86] His colleague Edward Mason observed in 1959 "(a)lmost everyone now agrees that in the large corporation, the owner is, in general, a passive recipient; that typically control is in the hands of management; and that management normally selects its own replacements."[87] Princeton sociologist Wilbert Moore observed in 1962 that "the Berle-Means doctrine" had "achieved wide acceptance" and that managers had "acquired a large degree of independence from stockholders."[88]

While by the end of the 1950s it was widely accepted that in large public companies diffuse share ownership was the norm and dominant shareholders were a rarity, empirical data was "all too often scanty or badly out of date."[89] The TNEC's 1939 study remained the best source.[90] Matters changed in the 1960s and 1970s, with a number of studies of ownership and control being conducted. Economist Robert Larner, for instance, sought to replicate Berle and Means's methodology using data from 1963. He reported that 75 percent of the 500 largest companies in the United States were under management control and said his results showed the "managerial revolution" was "close to complete."[91] *Business Week* agreed, saying Larner's data established that "(m)anagement . . . holds sway in all but a minor share of America's corporate giants."[92]

Additional research typically confirmed Larner's finding that dispersed ownership was the norm in large business enterprises in the 1960s and 1970s.[93] There were studies indicating that only a minority of large companies had fully diffuse share ownership but most of these used a low threshold of share ownership of 5 percent or more to find "control."[94] Noted political theorist Robert Dahl said in 1970 that "(e)very literate person now rightly takes for granted what Berle and Means established four decades ago in their famous study."[95] There was by that point in time a solid empirical foundation for the received wisdom.

---

[85] *Not to Pioneer, But to Mesh . . .*, FORBES, Nov. 15, 1957, 27.

[86] Carl S. Kaysen, *The Social Significance of the Modern Corporation*, 47 AMER. ECON. REV. 311, 312 (1957).

[87] Edward S. Mason, *Introduction, in* THE CORPORATION IN MODERN SOCIETY 1, 4 (Edward S. Mason ed., 1959).

[88] WILBERT E. MOORE, THE CONDUCT OF THE CORPORATION 6–7 (1962).

[89] Villarejo, *supra* note 79, at 49.

[90] *Id.* at 51. See also ROBERT J. LARNER, MANAGEMENT CONTROL AND THE LARGE CORPORATION 7 (1970).

[91] LARNER, *supra* note 90, at 17; Robert J. Larner, *Ownership and Control in the 200 Largest Nonfinancial Corporations, 1929 and 1963*, 56 AMER. ECON. REV. 777, 787 (1966).

[92] *Managers Tighten Their Grip*, BUS. WK., Nov. 5, 1966, 63.

[93] For a summary, see Brian Cheffins & Steve Bank, *Is Berle and Means Really a Myth?*, 83 BUS. HIST. REV. 443, 468–69 (2009) (see Appendix 2).

[94] *Id.* at 458, 470–71 (Appendix 3).

[95] ROBERT A. DAHL, AFTER THE REVOLUTION 104 (1970).

WHY DID OWNERSHIP SEPARATE FROM CONTROL?

Having documented the diffusion of share ownership associated with the rise of managerial capitalism, we will consider now why the separation of ownership and control that accentuated managerial discretion became the norm in large public companies. Accounting for patterns of ownership and control in the corporate context is not a straightforward exercise. Economists Randall Morck and Lloyd Steier have said of theories advanced to explain cross-country differences on this point, "(i)t would be wonderful for economists if we could conclude that one is correct and discard the others, but economics is rarely so simple."[96] The United States is no different in this regard. Marco Becht and Bradford DeLong conceded in a 2005 paper seeking to account for the dearth of controlling shareholders in US public companies "the story we have to tell turns out not to be a neat one."[97] Nevertheless, as to why a divorce of ownership and control occurred in the United States, plausible conjectures can be offered.[98] A helpful way to start is to consider the extent to which basic business logic accounts for what occurred.

Business Logic

With a consensus having been reached during the mid-twentieth century that a separation of ownership and control was a hallmark of large American corporations, intense debate ensued as to whether stockholder passivity associated with diffuse share ownership begat counterproductively unconstrained executive power that necessitated a substantial regulatory response.[99] Underpinning the debate was widespread, if often implicit, agreement that, as a matter of business logic, most large corporations would feature diffuse share ownership and managerial control. Financial imperatives were part of that logic. Companies needing to raise large amounts of capital seemingly could proceed most readily if their equity was carved up into small units that could be distributed publicly to thousands of investors.[100] Dispersed share ownership should typically follow in turn. As Berle observed in 1954, a separation of ownership and control "was inevitable, granting that modern organizations of production and distribution must be so large as to be incapable of being owned by any individual or small group of individuals."[101]

Practical challenges associated with running large business enterprises were also thought to have fostered management's move to the forefront. As firms grew bigger, their operations were likely to become more complex and physically decentralized. Continued success under

---

[96] Randall K. Morck & Lloyd Steier, *The Global History of Corporate Governance: An Introduction*, *in* HISTORY OF CORPORATE GOVERNANCE, *supra* note 25, at 1, 29.

[97] Becht & DeLong, *supra* note 25, at 651.

[98] For a more expansive exposition of conjectures on point, see Brian R. Cheffins, *The Rise and Fall (?) of the Berle-Means Corporation*, forthcoming SEATTLE U. L. REV.

[99] Gregory A. Mark, *Realms of Choice: Finance Capitalism and Corporate Governance*, 95 COLUM. L. REV. 969, 973, 975–76 (1995); Brian R. Cheffins, *The Trajectory of (Corporate Law) Scholarship*, 63 CAMBRIDGE L.J. 456, 480–83 (2004).

[100] MARGARET BLAIR, OWNERSHIP AND CONTROL: RETHINKING CORPORATE GOVERNANCE FOR THE TWENTY-FIRST CENTURY 96 (1993); ROBIN MARRIS, MANAGERIAL CAPITALISM IN RETROSPECT 6–7 (1998).

[101] ADOLF A. BERLE, THE 20TH CENTURY CAPITALIST REVOLUTION 30 (1954). See also MAURER, *supra* note 3, at 186.

such circumstances, the thinking went, was contingent upon developing robust managerial capabilities underpinned by the hiring of career-oriented, professionally trained executives.[102] The available talent pool was expanded greatly due to neither wealth nor substantial stock ownership being necessary qualifications for top managerial posts. A split between ownership and control logically ensued.[103]

Alfred Chandler, with his work on the emergence of large, managerially-dominated firms in the late nineteenth and early twentieth centuries, was a leading exponent of the close association between the bolstering of managerial capabilities and the growth and success of business enterprises. According to Chandler, a new transportation and communication infrastructure oriented around railways, telegraph networks, and subsequently telephone service meant that for the first time successful firms were focusing on genuinely national markets for goods and services.[104] At the same time, technological innovations such as mass generation of electric power were fostering previously unimaginable economies of scale and thereby encouraging the centralization of production in large plants.[105] These changes set the scene for the emergence of what Chandler called "the modern business enterprise," with the existence of sophisticated managerial hierarchies being the defining characteristic.[106] Companies that invested in managerial capabilities, Chandler argued, could prosper—and dominate—because they would be coordinating production, distribution, and marketing more effectively than would be possible with heavy reliance on arm's-length transactions between independent businesses.[107] Hence, corporate success was associated with the growth of what Chandler termed "the visible hand" of management at the expense of the "invisible hand" market forces constituted.[108]

Chandler maintained the "visible hand" contributed to industrial success because large plants set up to exploit economies of scale had to feature effective capacity utilization, which in turn demanded "the constant attention of a managerial team or hierarchy."[109] The national scale on which leading corporations had begun to operate also favored investment in managerial capabilities. Expansion into new regions combined with the rolling out of wider ranges of products created risks that those overseeing increasingly sprawling enterprises would be overwhelmed by the volume and complexity of assigned tasks and that policy and planning would be handled inefficiently by negotiations between far-flung corporate fiefdoms.[110] The most effective response seemed to be a robust managerial hierarchy where divisional managers were assigned responsibility for running key business units day-to-day and senior head

---

102 Gordon, *supra* note 69, at 160; Oswald Knauth, Managerial Enterprise: Its Growth and Methods of Operation 43 (1948); Franklin G. Moore, Management: Organization and Practice 19 (1964).

103 Thomas C. Cochran, The American Business System: A Historical Perspective—1900–1955, at 11 (1957).

104 Chandler, *supra* note 12, at 8.

105 *Id.* at 207; Chandler, *supra* note 56, at 62.

106 Chandler, *supra* note 12, at 7.

107 *Id.* at 6–7.

108 *Id.* at 1.

109 Chandler and Tedlow, *supra* note 34, at 405. See also Chandler, *supra* note 12, at 7.

110 Oliver Williamson, *The Modern Corporation: Origins, Evolution, Attributes*, 19 J. Econ. Lit. 1537, 1555–56 (1981).

office executives dictated the general direction of the company supported by sophisticated financial control systems and cost management techniques.[111]

Chandler's research on the business logic underpinning the growth of managerial hierarchies dovetailed neatly with Berle and Means's characterization of the modern corporation as one where managers were in charge due to a separation of ownership and control.[112] Economist Richard Langlois said in 2013 "(w)e learned early on from Berle and Means (1932) that, by the early twentieth century, the owner-managed firm had given way in the United States to a corporate form in which ownership was diffuse and inactive and in which control had effectively passed to managers. Then we learned from Chandler (1977) that this managerial revolution was both inevitable and desirable."[113] Berle was indeed well aware of the connection between his work on the separation of ownership and control and Chandler's research. In a 1967 book entitled *Power* he cited research by Chandler from the early 1960s when describing how "corporation bureaucracy" emerged in the opening decades of the twentieth century because "enterprises became too big for personal dictatorship."[114]

Chandler only occasionally specifically referenced Berle and Means in his work on the emergence of managerial capitalism.[115] Nevertheless, he cited Larner's 1960s empirical research on ownership and control when saying in his 1977 book *The Visible Hand,* "by the 1950s the managerial firm had become the standard form of modern business enterprise in major sectors of the American economy," meaning "managerial capitalism had gained ascendancy over family and financial capitalism."[116] Chandler also acknowledged in his 1990 monograph *Scale and Scope* that Berle and Means had launched debate about the implications of ownership separating from management in large corporations.[117]

Ultimately, facets of Chandler's research became combined with Berle and Means's separation of ownership and control thesis to generate "a dominant theoretical narrative" that accounted for "our understanding of the evolution of corporate structure in the modern era."[118] Mark Roe described in 1994 a "dominant paradigm explaining the emergence and success of the large corporation in the United States" that saw "economies of scale and technology as producing a fragmentation of shareholding and a shift in power from shareholders to senior managers with specialized skills."[119] The *Economist* said similarly

> For many years, it has been argued that the present shape of the American corporation, in which a vast and dispersed group of shareholders exercises little or no control

---

[111] Chandler, *supra* note 6, at 11; CHANDLER, *supra* note 12, at 463.

[112] Kenneth Lipartito & Yumiko Morii, *Rethinking the Separation of Ownership from Management in American History*, 33 SEATTLE UNIV. L. REV. 1025, 1036 (2010).

[113] Richard N. Langlois, *Business Groups and the Natural State*, 88 J. ECON. BEH. & ORG. 14, 14 (2013).

[114] ADOLF A. BERLE, POWER 191 (1967), citing ALFRED D. CHANDLER, STRATEGY AND STRUCTURE: CHAPTERS IN THE HISTORY OF INDUSTRIAL ENTERPRISE (1962).

[115] Lipartito & Morii *supra* note 112, at 1036.

[116] CHANDLER, *supra* note 12, at 491, 493.

[117] CHANDLER, *supra* note 56, at 631. For other Berle and Means cites see Chandler, *supra* note 6, at 14; Alfred D. Chandler, *The Role of Business in the United States: A Historical Survey*, DAEDALUS, Winter 1969, at 23, 34.

[118] Langlois, *supra* note 113, at 14.

[119] MARK J. ROE, STRONG MANAGERS, WEAK OWNERS: THE POLITICAL ROOTS OF AMERICAN CORPORATE FINANCE xiii (1994). Roe did not cite Chandler's work explicitly in support of this proposition but did cite Chandler on a number of occasions when he elaborated on the point—see at 3–5.

over the firm's managers, is in some way preordained. Organising firms like this, runs the argument, is simply the most efficient way of adapting to the demands of modern capitalism.[120]

The received wisdom, in sum, became that business logic dictated that professional executives owning only a small percentage of widely held shares would dominate the typical modern large corporation.

Other Variables

Inconveniently for those who believed it was preordained for a successful large company to be widely held and run by career-oriented executives lacking a substantial equity stake, from a global perspective the norm for major business enterprises was (and is) to have dominant shareholders.[121] Still, managerially-oriented American companies were the powerhouses of the global corporate economy during the middle decades of the twentieth century.[122] Countries with different institutional characteristics thus could be safely ignored. After all, "neither laggards nor Neanderthals (compel) significant academic attention."[123]

The underlying economic context changed in the 1980s and early 1990s. Germany and Japan, countries where share ownership in large companies was considerably more concentrated than was the case in the United States, seemed to be enjoying greater economic success.[124] This implied, contrary to the business logic presumed to underpin the Berle-Means corporation's dominance in the United States, that a different ownership and control framework was fully capable of delivering similar or even superior results.[125] The possibility that there might be various ways to organize successful large firms raised, in turn, a question: Why was the American system of corporate governance oriented around diffuse share ownership?[126]

It is beyond the scope of this book to offer a definitive explanation why the Berle-Means corporation came to dominate in the United States and remained preeminent.[127] Relevant factors can be identified, however, by focusing on three core questions one needs to address to explain why ownership will separate from control in corporations.[128] These are: (1) Why

---

[120] *Owners versus Managers*, ECONOMIST, Oct. 8, 1994, 20.

[121] Chapter 1, note 48 and related discussion; La Porta, López-de-Silanes, Shleifer & Vishny, *supra* note 73, 491–98.

[122] *Infra* note 378 and related discussion.

[123] Ronald J. Gilson, *Corporate Governance and Economic Efficiency: When Do Institutions Matter?*, 74 WASH. U. L.Q. 327, 331 (1996).

[124] Roe, *supra* note 70, at 15; Chapter 5, note 41 and related discussion.

[125] Gilson, *supra* note 123, at 331–32.

[126] Mark J. Roe, *Some Differences in Corporate Structure in Germany, Japan, and the United States*, 102 YALE L.J. 1927, 1934 (1993).

[127] A monograph might be required to do the topic justice. See BRIAN R. CHEFFINS, CORPORATE OWNERSHIP AND CONTROL: BRITISH BUSINESS TRANSFORMED (2008) (seeking to account, primarily from a historical perspective, why a separation of ownership and control became the norm in UK public companies).

[128] The analysis here is borrowed from CHEFFINS, *supra* note 127, at 8.

might those owning large blocks of shares want to exit or accept dilution of their stake?, (2) Will there be demand for shares available for sale?, and (3) Will the new investors be inclined to exercise control themselves?

The answer to each question is by no means obvious. With question (1), blockholders, due to the influence over corporate affairs associated with their voting power, can benefit from their status in ways unavailable to other shareholders by securing "private benefits of control."[129] Given the advantages associated with being a blockholder, why stand down?[130] As a 1926 article in the *Los Angeles Times* indicated, "(n)aturally, the owners of an established business are not anxious to bargain for capital on terms that involves the possible loss of control. . . ."[131]

Sometimes a blockholder will exit a public company because there is a window of opportunity where the firm's shares are advantageously priced.[132] Other times a blockholder will sell shares because of a need for cash to pursue personal goals. For instance, to finance an expensive space rocket project Jeff Bezos, founder of e-tailing powerhouse Amazon, sold $2 billion worth of stock in 2017, reducing his stake in the company to 16 percent.[133] The 1955 quote above from the *New York Times* discussing public companies and their executives offers clues likely more relevant to that era as to why dominant shareholders might exit.[134] Sustained erosion of profits and income can leave a dominant shareholder exposed and welcoming the opportunity to sell out despite the theoretical potential for extracting private benefits of control.[135] The combination of tough economic times in the 1930s and the economic uncertainties and high taxes associated with World War II—from 1942 to 1947 employment and investment income above $200,000 was taxed at a rate of at least 86.5 percent[136]—likely meant numerous blockholders were in precisely this position.[137] The fact that capital gains arising from the sale of shares were taxed at a much lower rate than income, with the rate further reduced for assets held for a substantial period of time, provided a further tax-related incentive for blockholders to exit.[138]

---

[129] Ronald J. Gilson, *Controlling Shareholders and Corporate Governance: Complicating the Comparative Taxonomy*, 119 HARV. L. REV. 1641, 1651 (2006).

[130] MARRIS, *supra* note 100, at 9.

[131] Earle E. Crowe, *Public Buys Companies*, L.A. TIMES, Jan. 21, 1926, 13.

[132] CHEFFINS, *supra* note 127, at 73.

[133] *Control Freaks*, ECONOMIST, Nov. 25, 2017, 72.

[134] *Supra* note 82 and related discussion.

[135] CHEFFINS, *supra* note 127, at 67.

[136] Tax Policy Center, *Historical Individual Income Tax Parameters*, available at http://www.taxpolicycenter.org/taxfacts/displayafact.cfm?Docid=543 (accessed Dec. 15, 2017).

[137] For empirical evidence indicating that high tax rates prompt wealthy investors to sell shares over time, likely in favor of tax-advantaged investments, see Mihir A. Desai, Dhammika Dharmapala & Winnie Fung, *Taxation and the Evolution of Aggregate Corporate Ownership Concentration, in* TAXING CORPORATE INCOME IN THE 21ST CENTURY 345 (Alan Auerbach, James R. Hines Jr. & Joel Slemrod eds., 2007).

[138] CHARLES R. GEISST, VISIONARY CAPITALISM: FINANCIAL MARKETS AND THE AMERICAN DREAM IN THE TWENTIETH CENTURY 33 (1990); *US Federal Capital Gains Tax Rates: Historical Data from 1916*, available at http://forbestadvice.com/Money/Taxes/Federal-Tax-Rates/Historical_Federal_Capital_Gains_Tax_Rates_History.html (accessed July 15, 2018).

As for question (2), even if blockholders are prepared (indeed eager) to exit it is not self-evident why there will be sufficient demand for shares to permit the unwinding of dominant stakes. If those with capital available to invest buy shares in a company that continues to have a dominant shareholder, they can fall victim to extraction of private benefits of control. The circumstances may be no better in a company characterized by a separation of ownership and control because executives owning only a small percentage of the shares will have incentives to put their own interests ahead of those of the stockholders.[139]

Matters are also somewhat complicated with question (3). Assume there is sufficient demand for shares to facilitate exit by incumbent blockholders. There may well be among the new shareholders one investor (or a close alliance of investors) that will want to obtain a dominant stake, whether because of private benefits of control, concerns about keeping the executives in check, or a desire to set the company's strategic direction. One powerful blockholder may thus simply be substituted for another. If this occurs regularly, how does ownership separate from control?

In the early 1990s Mark Roe kicked off a lively debate about the determinants of ownership and control in large firms by advancing a theory that largely took for granted the first two of these questions, implicitly assuming blockholders had good reasons to exit and that it was sensible for investors to buy shares in public companies. What he sought to explain was why powerful financial intermediaries such as banks, insurance companies, mutual funds, and pension funds that had the wherewithal to buy enough shares in public companies to exercise dominance failed to follow through.[140] He suggested that at several points in the twentieth century, such intermediaries were poised to take substantial block positions in American business firms but politicians, mindful of a deeply ingrained popular mistrust of concentrated financial power, derailed the process.[141] Roe identified a variety of legislative provisions enacted in the twentieth century that discouraged the accumulation of large ownership stakes, indicating in so doing that the Pujo Committee and Pecora hearings that helped to bring financial capitalism to an end did much to set the antagonistic political tone.[142]

Roe advanced subsequently an additional politically-oriented theory regarding ownership and control that implicitly focused on question (2). He hypothesized that public companies with widely dispersed share ownership are less likely to play a key role in "left-wing" social democracies than they are in "right-wing" countries.[143] His logic was that social democracies favor employees over investors, leading those running large firms to cater to employee preferences and give

---

139 For a comparison of investor risk when companies have dominant shareholders and when they have fully dispersed ownership see Cheffins, *supra* note 68, at 356–62.

140 See, for example, Roe, *supra* note 70; ROE, *supra* note 119.

141 Roe was not alone in drawing attention to the governance implications of laws imposing restrictions on financial institutions. See, for example, Joseph A. Grundfest, *Subordination of American Capital*, 27 J. FIN. ECON. 89 (1990). Nevertheless, Roe's work became the dominant influence in the field—John C. Coffee, *The Future as History: Prospects for Global Convergence in Corporate Governance and Its Implications*, 93 NW. UNIV. L. REV. 641, 643, n.4.

142 On the Pujo Committee and the Pecora hearings, see *supra* notes 41, 62 and related discussion; ROE, *supra* note 119, at 33–36, 110–11.

143 Mark J. Roe, *Political Preconditions to Separating Ownership from Control*, 53 STAN. L. REV. 539 (2000); MARK J. ROE, POLITICAL DETERMINANTS OF CORPORATE GOVERNANCE: POLITICAL CONTEXT, CORPORATE IMPACT (2003).

shareholders short shrift. Investors then steer clear of shares, precluding the development of the diffuse share ownership associated with the Berle-Means corporation. According to Roe the United States never fit this pattern, with the class-based economic conflict that gives rise to social democracy never being sufficiently pronounced. This had the effect of "keeping the pressures low that would make diffuse shareholders wary of leaving their money in managers' hands."[144]

A hypothesis first advanced in the late 1990s to explain cross-border differences in stock market development[145] addresses, at least in theoretical terms, all three questions salient to a determination of when ownership will separate from control in large firms. What became known as the "law matters" thesis holds that the extent to which corporate and securities law within a particular country protects minority shareholders does much to dictate whether large business enterprises will have diffuse or concentrated share ownership.[146] This would become the most widely cited and influential explanation for cross-country ownership and control patterns.[147]

To grasp the logic underpinning the law matters thesis, assume a country has laws that regulate closely transactions between companies and their "insiders" (directors and key shareholders), preclude opportunistic conduct by those insiders, and impose comprehensive disclosure requirements on companies that offer shares for sale to the public. With such rules in place, blockholders should lack scope to extract private benefits of control and thus may well be prepared to exit. Concomitantly, investors, aware that the law circumscribes exploitation of outside shareholders and knowing disclosure regulation will help to address informational asymmetries associated with public offerings of shares, should feel "comfortable" buying stocks on offer.[148] With few opportunities being available to take advantage of minority shareholders, those investors buying shares would have little incentive to forsake the benefits of diversification and accumulate dominant stakes in a small portfolio of public corporations. Diffuse share ownership thus will be the norm.

The law matters thesis appears to fit the facts well in the United States. It has a stock-market-oriented corporate economy where large firms typically have diffuse share ownership accompanied by a legal regime offering substantial protection for investors.[149] But did the configuration of corporate and securities law actually help to prompt the separation of ownership and control that occurred? The law matters thesis implies that having legal rules in place that provide significant stockholder protection is a precondition for the blockholder exit and investor demand that will result in diffuse share ownership in large firms.[150] Given that a separation of ownership and control became the standard arrangement in large American public companies during the middle decades of the twentieth century, it follows that the law should have been providing robust protection for shareholders beforehand.

---

[144] ROE, *supra* note 143, at 104.

[145] See, for example, Rafael La Porta, Florencio López-de-Silanes, Andrei Shleifer & Robert Vishny, *Law and Finance*, 106 J. POL. ECON. 1113 (1998).

[146] CHEFFINS, *supra* note 127, at 6, 33–34.

[147] Mark J. Roe, *Corporate Law's Limits*, 31 J. LEGAL STUD. 233, 236–37 (2002); Luca Enriques, *Do Corporate Law Judges Matter? Some Evidence from Milan*, 3 EUR. BUS. ORG. L. REV. 756, 766–67 (2002).

[148] Brian R. Cheffins, *Law as Bedrock: The Foundations of an Economy Dominated by Widely Held Public Companies*, 23 OXFORD J. LEGAL STUD. 1, 6, (2003).

[149] Bernard Black, *The Core Institutions that Support Strong Securities Markets*, 55 BUS. LAW. 1565, 1568–69 (2000); FRANK B. CROSS & ROBERT A. PRENTICE, LAW AND CORPORATE FINANCE 51, 128, 216–17 (2007).

[150] Brian R. Cheffins, *Does Law Matter?: The Separation of Ownership and Control in the United Kingdom*, 30 J. LEGAL STUD. 459, 465 (2001).

Delaware, which by 1930 had emerged clearly as the most popular state of incorporation for large firms, offered mediocre protection to shareholders throughout the first half of the twentieth century.[151] Nevertheless, federal reform occurring in the mid-1930s potentially lends credence to a law matters explanation of the separation of ownership and control in the United States. As part of Roosevelt's New Deal a set of laws was introduced that plausibly would have made investors more "comfortable" about buying shares at prices sufficiently generous to encourage exit by dominant shareholders. The federal Securities Act of 1933 required disclosure of material financial information about public offerings companies made.[152] The Securities Exchange Act of 1934 established the Securities and Exchange Commission (SEC), prohibited various forms of market manipulation, and imposed substantial periodic disclosure requirements on publicly traded companies.[153]

The federal securities laws enacted in the 1930s have been widely hailed as measures that restored investors' faith in stocks after the 1929 stock market crash.[154] Moreover, the timing fits well with the separation of ownership and control chronology already sketched out, in that blockholders were considerably more prominent in the early 1930s than they would be a quarter century later.[155] Perhaps tougher laws, in the form of federal securities regulation, intensified the divorce between ownership and control that was occurring. Management professors Allen Kaufman and Lawrence Zacharias have suggested, for instance, "New Deal securities legislation in effect authorized federal officials to reinforce the shareholder's ownership role under state laws and to reduce the risks of separating ownership from control."[156]

Adolf Berle was sympathetic to the idea that law had contributed to an environment where investors could be confident about how public companies would be run. He noted in 1959 that corporate America had "in recent years been (on the whole) relatively free from the excesses which often make concentrated power odious."[157] This, he said, was "not because historical chance had located American economic power in a collection of saints" but rather because "(c)hecks . . . appeared in the form of periodic political interventions demanded by American public opinion."[158] Berle did not specifically cite the federal securities laws of the 1930s in making this point. He did so, however, in a 1962 law review article:

> I gladly concede that the dishonest conflict of interest between management and shareholder ownership—that is, abuse by management of a position in which it can divert a part of the profit and income stream to itself—has not been accentuated. . . . By law and stock-exchange regulation, management is now obliged to

---

151 Brian R. Cheffins, Steven A. Bank & Harwell Wells, *Questioning "Law and Finance": US Stock Market Development, 1930–70*, 55 BUS. HIST. 598, 604–08 (2013).

152 48 Stat. 74.

153 48 Stat. 881.

154 Cheffins, Bank & Wells, *supra* note 151, at 610.

155 *Supra* notes 74–76, 80–95 and related discussion.

156 Allen Kaufman & Lawrence Zacharias, *From Trust to Contract: The Legal Language of Managerial Ideology*, 66 BUS. HIST. REV. 523, 543 (1992).

157 BERLE, *supra* note 84, at 22.

158 *Id.*

> file and publish annual accounts of its trust, and quarterly interim reports of its progress. . . . In all respects the businessmen-managers now operate under the glare of perpetual publicity. . . . While human nature probably has not changed much, community standards do develop, and they have. These have been implemented by institutions tending to enforce them; [including] the Securities and Exchange Commission. . . ."[159]

While a plausible case can be made that federal securities law contributed to the diffusion of share ownership that underpinned managerial capitalism, the evidence is not clear cut. If the New Deal reforms were indeed decisive, their introduction should have elicited a reasonably rapid boost to investor confidence that created sufficiently robust demand for shares at prices generous enough to induce blockholder exit. In fact, stock markets in the United States were in the doldrums for at least two decades following federal intervention. The number of shareholders flatlined, public offering activity was below historical norms, and the number of companies traded on national stock exchanges stagnated.[160] This hiatus suggests that even if the enactment of federal securities law contributed to the unwinding of large stock ownership stakes between 1932 and the zenith of managerial capitalism in the 1950s and 1960s, there were additional causes. Two variables not accounted for thus far stand out.

The Public Utility Holding Company Act of 1935 (PUHCA),[161] a legislative measure designed to simplify the corporate structure of the utilities industry, unwound control blocks in a sector where they were particularly prevalent. During the opening decades of the twentieth century it was uncommon for a public company to have a dominant corporate shareholder in a pyramidal arrangement.[162] The arrangement was standard, however, in the utility sector, with numerous publicly traded utility companies having another company—typically itself a utility company—as a dominant shareholder. For instance, 14 of the 52 utility companies in Berle and Means's sample of the 200 largest non-financial companies had pyramidal ownership features, a considerably higher proportion than for other types of companies.[163] Though legal challenges blunted the full force of PUHCA until the 1940s, by the early 1950s reorganizations under the legislation meant the end of the road for the corporate pyramid in the one economic sector where it truly flourished.[164]

Merger activity also likely helped to foster the separation of ownership and control in the middle decades of the twentieth century, at least from the late 1940s onward. Depending

---

159 Adolf A. Berle, *Modern Functions of the Corporate System*, 62 COLUM. L. REV. 433, 437 (1962).

160 GEISST, *supra* note 138, 27–35; Cheffins, Bank & Wells, *supra* note 151, 600–03, 610; Janette Rutterford & Dimitris P. Sotiropoulos, *The Rise of the Small Investor in the United States and United Kingdom, 1895 to 1970*, 18 ENTERPRISE & SOC'Y. 485, 516 (2017).

161 49 Stat. 803.

162 Steven A. Bank & Brian R. Cheffins, *The Corporate Pyramid Fable*, 84 BUS. HIST. REV. 435, 450–52 (2010). Railroad financiers Oris Paxton Van Sweringen and Mantis James Van Sweringen were, as "noteworthy pyramiders," an exception: ALLEN, *supra* note 45, at 248, 299–300.

163 Bank & Cheffins, *supra* note 162, at 453. See also Eugene Kandel, Konstantin Kosenko, Randall Morck & Yishay Yafeh, *The Great Pyramids of America: A Revised History of US Business Groups, Corporate Ownership and Regulation, 1930–1950*, ECGI Finance Working Paper No. 419, Table 1 (2013).

164 Bank & Cheffins, *supra* note 162, at 455–57.

on the financing method, mergers can foster diffusion of share ownership among companies conducting acquisitions.[165] If an acquiring company issues new voting shares to carry out a share-for-share exchange with the target company's shareholders, executing the merger will inevitably dilute to some degree a blockholder's stake in the acquiring company. The result will be the same if the target shareholders are paid in cash raised from a public offering of voting shares by the acquirer, assuming the dominant stockholder does not buy a percentage of the shares matching current holdings.

Merger activity was negligible in the 1930s and the first half of the 1940s but increased during the second half of the 1940s and the 1950s.[166] This surge may well have helped to foster ownership dispersion. A 1959 *Business Week* article on Adolf Berle and share ownership entitled "Where Managers Get Their Power" illustrates contemporary awareness of the impact mergers could have on ownership structure.[167] The article traced the history of a hypothetical firm launched in the late nineteenth century that made metal animal traps. The hypothetical company went public in the early 1940s as American Metalworking to raise capital to meet wartime demand. Descendants of the founders still had a controlling interest. As the 1950s drew to a close the company was a diversified enterprise known as American Products Inc. with 100,000 shareholders of which no individual owned more than 1 percent of the stock. What happened? For the hypothetical firm "(p)ostwar growth was a whoosh," with the firm carrying out a dozen acquisitions financed partly by profits but also by a series of public offerings of securities that presumably greatly diluted the stake held by the founders' descendants. To the extent that the American Metalworking hypothetical captured reality for US companies, merger activity would have contributed to the separation of ownership and control that was an integral feature of managerial capitalism.

Managerial Capitalism in Operation

Now that we have a sense of how and why managerial capitalism moved to the forefront, we will examine how it functioned in practical terms during its zenith in the 1950s and 1960s. We will consider initially how the interests of a corporation's executives can diverge from those of the stockholders when ownership is separated from control. We will then ascertain how substantial the divergence was in practice during managerial capitalism's heyday. We will see that even though public company executives were not always fully faithful agents of the shareholders, managerial waywardness overall was modest. Why was this the case? The final section of the chapter addresses this question by examining constraints on managerial discretion.

[165] CHEFFINS, *supra* note 127, at 69–72.

[166] For merger data, see PETER O. STEINER, MERGERS: MOTIVES, EFFECTS, POLICIES 4, 6 (1975); Klaus Gugler, Dennis Mueller & B. Burçin Yurtoglu, *The Determinants of Merger Waves*, unpublished working paper, 41 (Fig. 1) (2006), available at http://www.econstor.eu/bitstream/10419/51061/1/512793220.pdf (accessed Feb. 15, 2018).

[167] *Where Managers Get Their Power*, BUS. WK., Sept. 12, 1959, 186.

THE "CORE FISSURE" IN US CORPORATE GOVERNANCE

Since a Berle-Means corporation lacks dominant shareholders management will necessarily own only a small percentage of the outstanding shares.[168] The executives in turn will, as shareholders, receive only a small proportion of the returns derived from the profit-enhancing activities they engage in on behalf of the company. They correspondingly will have an incentive to further their own interests at the expense of other investors. As Berle and Means mused, "if all profits are earmarked for the security holder, where is the inducement for those in control to manage the enterprise efficiently?"[169]

Despite the meaningful risk in companies with widely held shares that executives will not faithfully serve the shareholders' interests, there will among the shareholders be a bias against taking corrective action.[170] The disciplining of management is a classic collective good with all shareholders benefitting whether or not they contribute to the discipline. Investors will be tempted to "free ride" in the hope others will intervene. With all shareholders thinking similarly, there is a strong likelihood nothing will happen. That in turn potentially affords executives with substantial latitude to act in an ill-advised or self-serving manner and impose, in economic parlance, "agency costs" on investors.[171]

Given that it would become the norm for large US corporations to lack dominant stockholders, and given the scope for abuse of managerial discretion when share ownership is diffuse, the separation of ownership and control was destined to become "the core fissure" in American corporate governance.[172] As early as 1932 Berle and Means were asking readers of *The Modern Corporation and Private Property* "(b)ut have we any justification for assuming that those in control of a modern corporation will also choose to operate it in the interests of their owners?"[173] The danger, they noted, was that "(i)n the operation of the corporation, the controlling group . . . can serve their own pockets better by profiting at the expense of the company than by making profits for it."[174] They concluded their book by indicating that self-interest needed to be curbed "if the corporate system is to survive," reasoning "that 'the control' of the great corporations should develop into a purely neutral technocracy."[175]

As managerial capitalism reached its ascendancy following World War II, there was widespread awareness of the "core fissure" between managers and shareholders. According to a 1948 study of the managerial enterprise, with firms where executives were in control due to passive shareholders there were "many points of personal contact" that could "be utilized for personal gain," meaning that when "professional men join managerial enterprise their

[168] George J. Stigler & Claire Friedland, *The Literature of Economics: The Case of Berle and Means*, 26 J.L. & ECON. 237, 238 (1983).

[169] BERLE & MEANS, *supra* note 71, at 301.

[170] CHEFFINS, *supra* note 127, at 126–27.

[171] The pioneering work on managerial agency costs was Michael C. Jensen & William H. Meckling, *Theory of the Firm: Managerial Behavior, Agency Costs and Ownership Structure*, 3 J. FIN. ECON. 305 (1976).

[172] Mark J. Roe, *The Inevitable Instability of American Corporate Governance*, 1 CORP. GOV. L. REV. 1, 2 (2005).

[173] BERLE & MEANS, *supra* note 71, at 113.

[174] *Id.* at 114. Berle and Means acknowledged that "those in control" could be those with a large block of stock as well as corporate executives but indicated that the "adverse interest" to the interests of stockholders was more potent when a corporation was management controlled (at 114–15).

[175] *Id.* at 312.

professional ethics are subject to great strain."[176] J.A. Livingston, a journalist, expressed concern in a 1958 book on the American stockholder that executives had in practical terms "power to overpay themselves" that could ultimately result in epidemic "self-engorgement," with corporate power becoming "synonymous with grab-bag morality."[177] The editor of a 1959 volume Berle referred to as "the best body of material on the American corporate system yet offered"[178] said "the independence of corporate management from any well-defined responsibility to anyone ... carries with it the possibilities of abuse."[179] A 1964 economic analysis of managerial capitalism maintained managers and shareholders were "sufficiently distinct, and the managers sufficiently autonomous, for the existence of a harmony of interests not to be regarded as axiomatic."[180]

HOW MUCH "PERSONAL GAIN"?

While during the managerial capitalism era there was full awareness of the dangers associated with the "core fissure" between managers and shareholders, the retrospective verdict has been that those running large firms in the mid-twentieth century did not stray far. David Skeel, in a 2005 book where he drew upon the Greek myth of the ill-fated Icarus to characterize as "Icaran" historically noteworthy US executives who took bold and ultimately ill-advised risks, said of "the decades after the nation climbed out of the Depression. . . . For a time, at least, Icarus had been tamed."[181] The chapter dealing with history in a study of corporate scandals published the same year moved directly from McKesson & Robbins, a pharmaceutical wholesaler that misled investors in the late 1930s by fabricating assets and falsely inflating revenues, to a mid-1980s debacle involving savings and loan associations ("thrifts") where egregious managerial recklessness ultimately necessitated a massive financial rescue operation.[182] Sociologists Mark Mizruchi and Howard Kimeldorf cautioned in an article also published in 2005 against romanticizing the post-World War II corporation but nevertheless said "corporate malfeasance on the scale of today's Enron [a scandal ridden corporation from the early 2000s] was neither imaginable nor, in most cases, possible."[183]

---

[176] KNAUTH, *supra* note 102, at 184, 186.

[177] J.A. LIVINGSTON, THE AMERICAN STOCKHOLDER 222 (1958).

[178] Adolf A. Berle, *Foreword, in* THE CORPORATION, *supra* note 87, at ix, xv.

[179] Mason, *supra* note 87, at 11.

[180] ROBIN MARRIS, THE ECONOMIC THEORY OF "MANAGERIAL" CAPITALISM 15 (1964). See also William L. Baldwin, *The Motives of Managers, Environmental Restraints, and the Theory of Managerial Enterprise*, 78 Q.J. ECON. 238, 238 (1964) (indicating theories of managerial enterprise assumed "managerial goals may differ from those of stockholders").

[181] DAVID SKEEL, ICARUS IN THE BOARDROOM: THE FUNDAMENTAL FLAWS IN CORPORATE AMERICA AND WHERE THEY CAME FROM 106 (2005).

[182] KENNETH R. GRAY, LARRY A. FRIEDER & GEORGE W. CLARK, CORPORATE SCANDALS: THE MANY FACES OF GREED 37–40 (2005). On the McKesson scandal, see KNEE, *supra* note 59, 44; THOMAS A. KING, MORE THAN A NUMBERS GAME: A BRIEF HISTORY OF ACCOUNTING 66–67 (2006). On the S&L crisis, see SKEEL, *supra* note 181, at 132–35.

[183] Mizruchi & Kimeldorf, *supra* note 5, at 216. See also Black & Carbone, *supra* note 9, at 388 ("a high degree of corporate honesty").

Contemporaries generally concurred with the retrospective verdict that the public company executives of the 1950s and 1960s were unlikely to exploit counterproductively the discretion available to them. Retail investors demonstrated their faith in those running public companies by flocking to the stock market. The number of individuals who owned shares increased from 6.5 million in 1952 to 30 million in 1970.[184] Their faith was repaid, with public companies thriving during buoyant economic times. "Prosperity was the dominant theme of the postwar era,"[185] with labor productivity and living standards both improving markedly.[186] The US economy grew smartly at a rate of 3.7 percent annually between 1948 and 1973.[187] Large public companies contributed fully, with increases in sales revenue of *Fortune* 500 corporations consistently outpacing this robust growth rate.[188] Share prices rose rapidly in turn. The S&P 500 increased more than 650 percent between January 1950 and December 1968.[189]

Amidst considerable corporate success, the dominant image of public company leadership during the managerial capitalism era was that executives were exercising corporate power in a self-restrained and socially responsible manner.[190] Adolf Berle subscribed to this view, despite having expressed concerns in 1932 that those controlling managerial enterprises would abuse the discretion available to them. In 1959 he observed "(c)onsiderable progress has been made in eliminating the spasms of dishonesty or near dishonesty which too often disgraced our system in the past decades."[191] He noted similarly in 1962 that major corporate scandals were "happily, rare."[192]

Similar views were expressed throughout the heyday of managerial capitalism. Robert Gordon said in a 1945 study of leadership in large corporations "(t)oday, executives are not likely to use extensively the criterion of maximum financial gain for themselves."[193] Harvard Business School research from 1951 on executives indicated "membership in the top management group . . . implied an intense loyalty to the company."[194] According to a 1955 study of big corporations, such firms were "moving steadily toward responsible behavior."[195] A 1964 text on management by Franklin Moore indicated "(b)usiness leaders in the United States almost all talk and practice high ethical codes."[196] A lengthy 1966 *New York Times* essay that bemoaned

---

184 Rutterford & Sotiropoulos, *supra* note 160, at 524.

185 Wyatt Wells, American Capitalism, 1945–2000: Continuity and Change from Mass Production to the Information Society 27 (2003).

186 John D. Wisman, *Did US Labor's Post-World War II Success Lead to Its Subsequent Woes?*, 32 Int'l. J. Social Econ. 901–02 (2005).

187 Nitin Nohria, Davis Dyer & Frederick Dalzell, Changing Fortunes: Remaking the Industrial Corporation 38 (2002).

188 *Id.*

189 During the 1950s and 1960s, the S&P 500 peaked at 109.37 in December 1968. It opened at 16.66 in January 1950. See *S&P 500/Historical Data*, available at https://finance.yahoo.com/quote/%5EGSPC/history/ (accessed Mar. 14, 2018).

190 Gabriel Kolko, Wealth and Power in America: An Analysis of Social Class and Income Distribution 55 (1962) (the author of this study dissented from the consensus).

191 Berle, *supra* note 84, at 3.

192 Berle, *supra* note 159, at 438, n.9.

193 Gordon, *supra* note 69, at 327.

194 Edmund P. Learned, David N. Ulrich & Donald R. Booz, Executive Action 48 (1951).

195 Maurer, *supra* note 3, at 287.

196 Moore, *supra* note 102, at 287.

the growing power of big business nevertheless observed "Americans seem vaguely contented with this development," noting that "(t)he big story is not really one of callous exploitation or crass irresponsibility" and suggesting that "articulate segments of the American public seem at times to show more faith in United States Steel than the United States Senate."[197] Paul Baran and Paul Sweezy, two Marxist economists, conceded the same year that while turn-of-the-twentieth-century tycoons were "interested in self-enrichment.... The modern manager is dedicated to the advancement of the company: he is a company man."[198]

Public company executives' reputation for propriety continued as the 1970s began. While Harvard Business School professor Myles Mace argued in a 1971 study of boards that director oversight of management was largely ineffective, he acknowledged that most chief executives "completely aware of their powers of control, chose to exercise their powers in a manner which was moderate and acceptable to their peers on the board."[199] John Kenneth Galbraith struck a similar chord in commenting on executive pay, which barely budged in inflation-adjusted terms from 1950 through to the 1970s and which was modest in comparison with present-day standards.[200] Writing in 1972 he said "(m)anagement does not go out ruthlessly to reward itself—a sound management is expected to exercise restraint."[201] Correspondingly, "(t)here are few corporations in which it would be suggested that executive salaries are at a maximum."[202]

The reputation for propriety aligned with the personality traits ascribed to public company executives in the 1950s and 1960s. The managerial archetype of this era was a bureaucratically-oriented "organization man" who subordinated personal aspirations to foster the pursuit of corporate goals (women were conspicuous by their absence from the executive suite).[203] Career patterns reinforced loyalty to the corporation. Most top executives at large corporations joined their corporate employers early in their careers and then as "company men" worked their way up through the managerial ranks before becoming senior executives and perhaps ultimately the chief executive.[204] *Forbes* emphasized the connection between continuity and reliability when describing the prototypical corporate executive in 1957:

> The lone wolf captain of industry, in short, has given place to the gregarious and responsibility delegating modern executive. This is the age of the Great Manager....

---

[197] Andrew Hacker, *A Country Called Corporate America*, NY Times, July 3, 1966, Sunday Magazine, 9.

[198] Paul A. Baran & Paul M. Sweezy, Monopoly Capital: An Essay on the American Economic and Social Order 30–31 (1966).

[199] Myles L. Mace, Directors: Myth and Reality 79 (1971).

[200] Carola Frydman & Raven E. Saks, *Executive Compensation: A New View from a Long-Term Perspective, 1936–2005*, 23 Rev. Fin. St. 2099, 2107 (2010); Steven A. Bank, Brian R. Cheffins & Harwell Wells, *Executive Pay: What Worked?*, 42 J. Corp. L. 59, 64–65 (2016).

[201] J.K. Galbraith, The New Industrial State 127 (2d ed. 1972).

[202] *Id.*

[203] Amanda Bennett, The Death of the Organization Man 13–14 (1990). The term "organization man" was coined in this context by William Whyte, The Organization Man (1956). In Mabel Newcomer's 1955 study of the background of chief executives and board chairmen none of the 863 individuals comprising her 1950 sample were women—Newcomer, *supra* note 83, at 42.

[204] Maurer, *supra* note 3, at 96–97; *From the Bottom Up*, Forbes, Nov. 15, 1957, 35; David M. Kotz, The Rise and Fall of Neoliberal Capitalism 30 (2015).

> The head of the giant corporation today is quite the antithesis of the order-barking, sweeping decision-maker of yesteryear. He is more aptly described as the man who keeps the machinery oiled, makes sure its working parts are kept going at top efficiency and that the machine itself is completely up-to-date.[205]

The *New York Times* observed similarly in a 1967 essay on corporate presidents, the term often used then (albeit with diminishing frequency over time) to refer to chief executive officers,[206] "(t)he American preference is for glamour or controversy, characteristics not normally associated with corporation executives.... The corporation executives are not very interesting people.... One is impressed with a certain air of reserve, indeed caution, they possess about themselves and world in which they travel."[207]

The US economy was not as "neatly buttoned-up" as the foregoing might suggest.[208] After all, "(c)apitalism has always had its skates on."[209] The most noteworthy departures from the "organization man" creed were executives constructing highly diversified conglomerate empires by buying up companies operating in a wide range of market sectors. *Business Week* said in 1968

> No creation of the US economy reflects the vigor, imagination, and sheer brass of the 1960s more than the conglomerate corporations. Wheeling and dealing with panache and merging with seeming haste all over the lot, they have shattered the cautious business clichés that have prevailed since the Depression.[210]

Likewise, John Brooks, in a 1973 book on the buoyant stock market of the 1960s, said of conglomerators such as James Ling, founder of Ling-Temco-Vought, and Charles Bluhdorn, impresario of Gulf-Western Industries, they "were all uninhibited free enterprisers, anti-organization men, throwbacks to the 19th century age of individualism in American business."[211]

The 1950s and 1960s were also by no means entirely bereft of unethical managerial behavior. In the mid-1950s financier Lowell Birrell used complex corporate merger transactions as a platform to loot a dozen corporate treasuries of millions of dollars before fleeing to Cuba.[212] Alexander Guterma, who for a period in the 1950s headed three New York Stock Exchange (NYSE) listed companies at the same time, engaged in self-serving related party

[205] *Not to Pioneer, supra* note 85.

[206] For data on the switch from the term "president" to "chief executive officer," see David W. Allison & Blyden B. Potts, *Title Wave: The Diffusion of the CEO Title throughout the US Corporate Network*, Center for Research on Social Organization Working Paper Series #576 20 (1999); John D. Keiser, *Chief Executives from 1960–1989: A Trend toward Professionalization* 10 J. LEADERSHIP & ORG. STUD. 52, 58 (2004).

[207] Andrew Hacker, *The Making of a (Corporation) President*, NY TIMES, Apr. 2, 1967, Sunday Magazine, 26.

[208] Raymond J. Saulnier, *The Shape of Things*, NY TIMES, June 25, 1967, Books, 2 (reviewing JOHN KENNETH GALBRAITH, THE NEW INDUSTRIAL STATE (1967)).

[209] *The Creed of Speed*, ECONOMIST, Dec. 5, 2015, 23.

[210] *Conglomerates*, BUS. WK., Nov. 30, 1968, 74.

[211] JOHN BROOKS, THE GO-GO YEARS 173 (1973).

[212] BLACK, *supra* note 8, at 88–123.

transactions and stock price manipulation and was imprisoned in 1960 for failing to file with the SEC required financial reports.[213] In the late 1950s, Earl Belle, a youthful director of publicly traded Cornucopia Gold Mines, used manipulative techniques to boost the company's share price before absconding to Brazil with nearly $1 million in company funds.[214] Edward Gilbert, after relying on family backing to gain control of hardwood manufacturers E.L. Bruce & Co., stole in 1962 $2 million from the corporate till and fled to Brazil when a bid to acquire a larger company foundered.[215] There were instances, disclosed as part of investigations of improper corporate payments in the 1970s,[216] where public companies set up slush funds in the 1960s from which they would make illicit political contributions and other secret disbursements.[217]

Though conglomerators and rogues were features of corporate capitalism in the 1950s and the 1960s, they were exceptions to the rule. The editors of *Fortune*, commenting on the "conglomerate commotion," said that while the conglomerates might seem to be the ideal home for "a new breed of young, ambitious, creative free-form managers," "only a small percentage of managers can be daring entrepreneurs."[218] Likewise, with corporate scandals, *Fortune*'s editors acknowledged "horrifying case histories . . . show conclusively, that investors . . . can still be flimflammed and bamboozled by unscrupulous insiders who put their mind to it" but cautioned readers that it took "more than several blackbirds to prove there is a national scandal," and offered reassurance that "the overwhelming majority of the financial community observes . . . a high code of ethics."[219]

Others agreed that "the scoundrels" operated on the fringes of the market.[220] A 1962 analysis of enforcement by securities regulators said "(t)he ethics currently practiced by the vast majority of those whose business is Wall Street is exemplary."[221] A 1965 study of institutional shareholders acknowledged the misdeeds of Birrell, Belle, and Gilbert but nevertheless concluded "(t)he vast majority of professional managers are undoubtedly faithful to the responsibilities imposed by their stewardship."[222]

There were other instances of unethical managerial behavior during the heyday of managerial capitalism but there tended to be extenuating circumstances. Between 1956 and 1960 insurgents seeking to be elected by shareholders to boards of public companies made allegations of management dishonesty and fraud in nearly 10 percent of those contests.[223] Complaints about

---

213 *Id.* at 124–67; T.A. Wise and the Editors of Fortune, The Insiders: A Stockholder's Guide to Wall Street 142–52 (1962).

214 Black, *supra* note 8, at 168–92.

215 Brooks, *supra* note 211, at 58–80.

216 Chapter 3, notes 146, 152, 155 and related discussion.

217 Henry Weinstein, *Northrop: Fame in Aircraft, Shame in Politics*, NY Times, May 18, 1975, F1; Michael C. Jensen, The Financiers 242–44 (1976) (focusing on a political "slush fund" the 3M Company had); Robert D. Hershey, *Files of SEC Show Slush Funds in Use Decades before Watergate*, NY Times, May 18, 1977, 1.

218 Editors of Fortune, Conglomerate Commotion 81, 84 (1970).

219 T.A. Wise and the Editors of Fortune, *supra* note 213, at xiv, 186, 187.

220 Sobel, *supra* note 50, at 328, 331.

221 Black, *supra* note 8, at 4.

222 Daniel J. Baum & Ned B. Stiles, The Silent Partners: Institutional Investors and Corporate Control 7 (1965).

223 Douglas V. Austin, Proxy Contests and Corporate Reform 6, 14, 26 (1965).

weak performance and managerial inefficiency were nevertheless considerably more prevalent.[224] Charges by Chrysler shareholders in 1960 that senior executives had been concluding contracts with suppliers in which those executives had a personal stake led to an audit that revealed William Newberg, Chrysler's newly appointed president, had a substantial financial interest in two supplier companies.[225] The Chrysler board responded promptly to the revelations, firing Newberg, who was then ostracized by the auto industry, and the company's market share, profits, and share price rose substantially under new management.[226]

A price-fixing conspiracy in the electrical industry surfacing in 1960, which resulted in jail sentences for seven executives and $2 million in fines levied against 29 corporations, was characterized by *Fortune* as a case that had "focused attention on American business practices as nothing else has in many years."[227] The *Christian Science Monitor* suggested "(t)he organization man stands indicted in the eyes of the world."[228] Nevertheless, coverage of the case in the mass media generally was not extensive,[229] perhaps because the highest-ranking corporate officials in the companies were not directly implicated.[230] There was also little outrage among investors. When some stockholders of industry leader General Electric used the price-fixing scandal to justify proposing anti-management resolutions at a shareholder meeting, those stockholders were booed by the majority attending and the proposals were resoundingly defeated.[231]

OTHER GOALS?

A dearth of dishonest and underhanded behavior during the heyday of managerial capitalism did not necessarily mean senior executives devoted themselves exclusively to promoting shareholder interests. Robert Gordon flagged up additional potential forms of managerial waywardness in his 1945 study of large corporations. While acknowledging executives of large corporations would not seek to maximize personal financial benefits, he said for them there was "considerable opportunity to follow other goals":

> They may very well adopt, at least in part, such criteria as personal position and power, the desire to see the firm larger, or even more socially desirable goals such as the

---

[224] *Id.* at 14, 20.

[225] Carter F. Henderson & Albert C. Lasher, 20 Million Careless Capitalists 23–24 (1967).

[226] Baum & Stiles, *supra* note 222, at 8; Henderson & Lasher, *supra* note 225, at 24–25; Allen Severson, *The Dodge That (Almost) Ate Detroit: Chrysler's Disastrous 1962 Downsizing*, Jan. 11, 2009, available at http://ateupwithmotor.com/model-histories/chrysler-downsizing-disaster-1962/ (accessed June 14, 2018).

[227] Richard Austin Smith, *The Great Electrical Conspiracy*, Fortune, May 1961, 161, 224.

[228] Nate White, *Indictment of the Organization Man*, Christian Sci. Monitor, Feb. 8, 1961, 7.

[229] Alan M. Dershowitz, *Increasing Community Control over Corporate Crime: A Problem in the Law of Sanctions*, 71 Yale L.J. 280, 288–89 (1961). See, though, Theodore P. Kovaleff, Business and Government during the Eisenhower Administration: A Study of the Antitrust Policy of the Antitrust Division of the Justice Department 119 (1980) (indicating that the electrical cases did generate numerous headlines).

[230] Chapter 1, notes 231–32 and accompanying text; Richard Eells, The Government of Corporations 241–42 (1962).

[231] Alfed R. Zipster, *GE Stockholders Back Cordiner*, NY Times, Apr. 27, 1961, 1; Michael D. Reagan, *What 17 Million Shareholders Share*, NY Times, Feb. 23, 1964, Sunday Magazine, 11.

welfare of workers, consumers or other broad groups. Perhaps more important, they may seek to some extent to play safe and to avoid some of the change and uncertainty which result from assiduous pursuit of every possible opportunity to increase profits further.[232]

Empirical analysis testing whether managerial capitalism era executives in fact did "play safe" to a counterproductive degree is lacking.[233] Nevertheless, a 1964 text on management suggested "(m)any top men, for example, don't like to take chances because if something goes wrong, they may lose their jobs.... So they sometimes avoid doing desirable things that involve risk."[234] In 1970 a head of personnel said, having conferred with peers, "(t)he preference is that the corporate ship be moved steadily through the waters and that it not be propelled by inquisitive, challenging, imaginative leadership."[235] *Forbes* observed the same year that because a top executive of a large company was unlikely to own many shares in the firm he ran, "the risk is his job, not his fortune. Thus, as a company grows larger, the tendency is to conserve what *is* rather than to realize what *might be*."[236]

While Gordon suggested that the danger of executives would "play safe" was greater than the risk they would pursue "socially desirable goals," in the 1950s and 1960s the latter managerial predilection received wider attention. Executives certainly did not sacrifice shareholder returns wholesale to advance the interests of other constituencies affected by corporate behavior. For instance, a *New York Times* review of a 1968 reissue of Berle and Means's *The Modern Corporation and Private Property* argued managers conducted themselves as if they were pursuing "all the profits that can be pursued out of the market," and said that on "the political role of harmonizing the interest groups" there was "far from general acceptance."[237]

While managerial capitalism era corporate executives were not forsaking their shareholders, there nevertheless was abundant anecdotal evidence suggesting acceptance of a wider conception of corporate purpose. Berle and Means, having largely discarded the skepticism of management that informed *The Modern Corporation and Private Property*,[238] both acknowledged the point during the managerial capitalism era. Berle, for instance, said "big businessmen" were akin to "civil servants" with "direct responsibility ... to four groups," namely the communities where their companies bought and sold, the employees, and "the security holders to whom the companies pay interest and dividends."[239] He added that "corporate administrators" expected "their ultimate situation to be better" if they did not pursue

---

[232] GORDON, *supra* note 69, at 327–28.

[233] MARRIS, *supra* note 180, at 63.

[234] MOORE, *supra* note 102, at 92.

[235] Joseph R. Joyce, *Why Settle for "So So"?*, THE PERSONNEL ADMINISTRATOR, Jan.–Feb., 1970, quoted in AUREN URIS, THE FRUSTRATED TITAN: EMASCULATION OF THE EXECUTIVE 37 (1972).

[236] *Numbers—Or Most Giants Are Happy Giants*, FORBES, May 15, 1970, 176 (emphasis in original).

[237] Robert Lekachman, *The Corporation Gap*, NY TIMES, Sept. 15, 1968, Book Reviews, 8. See also Wells, *supra* note 6, at 330.

[238] C.A. Harwell Wells, *The Cycles of Corporate Social Responsibility: An Historical Retrospective for the Twenty-first Century*, 51 KANSAS L.J. 77, 102–03 (2002).

[239] BERLE, *supra* note 84, at 8.

"the last dollar of profit."[240] Means, for his part, argued "(t)he modern corporation is . . . an institution for interrelating interests of security holders, workers, consumers and management. . . . There is considerable evidence that the larger corporations are accepting some degree of social responsibility as a step toward their own long-run status and survival."[241] According to Means the executives in charge were engaged in "unbiased arbitration between the parties at interest."[242]

Berle and Means were by no means alone when they emphasized the balancing in which public company executives engaged as managerial capitalism flourished, even if their characterization of managerial priorities could seem quixotic to more recent observers. Economist Paul Krugman felt he had to reassure *New York Times* readers in 2002 that he was not exaggerating when he said of the 1950s and 1960s, "(t)op executives behaved more like public-spirted bureaucrats than captains of industry."[243] In fact, as corporate law scholar Harwell Wells has said of the status of corporate social responsibility in mid-twentieth century corporations, "a surprisingly wide swathe of individuals" including "senior executives themselves, shared a set of assumptions about the corporation that varied both from what was believed earlier in the century and what is believed today."[244]

The chief executive of Sears, a major retailer, indicated "the four parties to business" were, "in order of importance" customers, employees, the community, and shareholders.[245] Healthcare and medical giant Johnson & Johnson provided a similar ranking, saying its "first responsibility" was to medical staff and patients.[246] Management theorist Peter Drucker identified in 1954 a "trend among managers to think of themselves almost as public servants, not as men driven by a ruthless craving for profits."[247] Economist Carl Kaysen said in 1957 of management in the modern corporation "(t)here is no display of greed or graspiness; there is no attempt to push off onto the workers or the community a large part of the social costs of the enterprise."[248] Sociologist Ralf Dahrendorf argued the same year "(n)ever has the imputation of a profit motive been further from the real motives of men than it is for the modern bureaucratic manager."[249] Richard Eells, in his 1962 book *The Government of Corporations,* acknowledged "the case for (the) stockholder constituency" was "probably the foundation stone of the most widely received dogmas about corporate governance" (he was a very early adopter of this term) but indicated "(c)orporate governors . . . try to 'balance the interests' of competing groups."[250]

---

[240] Adolf A. Berle, *The Impact of the Corporation on Classical Economic Theory*, 79 Q.J. ECON. 25, 34 (1965).

[241] GARDINER C. MEANS, THE CORPORATE REVOLUTION IN AMERICA: ECONOMIC REALITY VS. ECONOMIC THEORY 65 (1962).

[242] *Id.* at 169.

[243] Paul Krugman, *For Richer*, NY TIMES, Oct. 20, 2002, E62.

[244] Wells, *supra* note 6, at 331.

[245] RICK WARTZMAN, THE END OF LOYALTY: THE RISE AND FALL OF GOOD JOBS IN AMERICA 95 (2017).

[246] *Id.*

[247] Peter F. Drucker, *The Responsibilities of Management*, HARPER'S, Nov. 1954, 67, 67.

[248] Kaysen, *supra* note 86, at 314.

[249] RALF DAHRENDORF, CLASS AND CLASS CONFLICT IN INDUSTRIAL SOCIETY 46 (1957).

[250] EELLS, *supra* note 230, at 69, 253. On his being a pioneer user of the term "corporate governance," see LAURA F. SPIRA & JUDY SLINN, THE CADBURY COMMITTEE: A HISTORY xx (2013).

To the extent that public company executives actually sought to balance the interests of various corporate constituencies in the 1950s and 1960s, the success public companies were enjoying would have made this easier. As Louis Galambos and Joseph Pratt said of this era in a 1988 analysis of US business during the twentieth century

> (T)he managers of the nation's leading firms sought to satisfy the several groups of clients with whom they had to deal. They paid higher wages and new fringe benefits to labor.... They paid regular dividends to shareholders.... They gave their customers reliable products and services.... So long as American firms dominated the domestic market and held a strong position in foreign markets, those sorts of policies sufficed.[251]

Despite corporate success there were, during the heyday of managerial capitalism, critics of whatever trading off of profits in favor of "balance" was occurring. Management consultant Theodore Levitt, a "vigorous dissenter among the chorus of voices urging management to reach out for more responsibility,"[252] warned in the *Harvard Business Review* in 1958 that "as the profit motive becomes increasingly sublimated, capitalism will become only a shadow—the torpid remains of the creative dynamism which was and might have been."[253] Friedrich Hayek, a distinguished economist, argued at a 1960 conference on the future of the company that executives had strayed too far from money-making toward do-goodism and that corporations should be given back to the stockholders.[254] Henry Manne, a corporate law academic, indicated in 1962 "a great many executives of large corporations today have accepted the mantle of 'statesman,'" but cautioned "(i)t is an easy step from inefficiency in purely business terms to lower returns because of time and resources spent on non-profit-motivated activities."[255]

While in the 1950s and 1960s there was awareness of the core fissure in US corporate governance between managers and shareholders, and while concerns were expressed about potentially deleterious effects, there was little passion for substantial change. Eugene Rostow, dean of Yale Law School, said in 1959 about "endocratic" corporations (firms "where no stockholders own more than a few percent of the stock (and) the directors normally control... the electoral process"), "(i)n reviewing the literature... about possible programs for their reform, one is struck by the atmosphere of relative peace. There seems to be no general conviction abroad that reform is needed."[256] Why the lack of appetite for change? In the same way that the success of the US economy and its leading companies muted concerns about managers trading off profits to promote corporate responsibility, good outcomes tempered doubts regarding managerial control generally. As Galambos and Pratt asked rhetorically

---

[251] GALAMBOS & PRATT, *supra* note 14, at 180.

[252] *In This Issue*, HARV. BUS. REV., Sept.–Oct. 1958, 5, 5.

[253] Theodore Levitt, *The Dangers of Social Responsibility*, HARV. BUS. REV., Sept.–Oct. 1958, 41, 46.

[254] J.A. Livingston, *Will Do-Goodism Prompt Federal Control?*, WASH. POST, Apr. 20, 1960, B8.

[255] Henry G. Manne, *The "Higher Criticism" of the Modern Corporation*, 62 COLUM. L. REV. 399, 415 (1962). For a summary of the views of other critics of balancing of interests by management, see Shorey Peterson, *Corporate Control and Capitalism*, 79 Q.J. ECON. 1, 7–8 (1965).

[256] Eugene V. Rostow, *To Whom and for What Ends Is Corporate Management Responsible?, in* THE CORPORATION, *supra* note 87, at 46, 59.

in their 1988 book "(w)ho could seriously complain about the results achieved by US businesses between 1945 and the late 1960s?"[257] Corporate success in turn reflected positively on management. Galambos and Pratt said "(i)n the thriving postwar economy the corporate style of control would appear to be more of a boon than a social problem."[258] *Time* indeed proclaimed in 1960 "(n)o one doubts the superiority of American business management."[259] Given the circumstances, there was "little incentive between 1945 and 1970 to tinker with what seemed to be smoothly running machinery."[260]

Even Berle and Means were caught up in the mood of the times. In 1932 they were sufficiently concerned about the possibility of managerial abuse of power to suggest that the corporate system might not survive, at least not without "balancing a variety of claims by various groups in the community and assigning each a portion of the income stream on the basis of public policy rather than private cupidity."[261] Following World War II they were much more sanguine about big business. Berle said in 1954 that "very large corporations" could "fairly claim the greatest share of the credit" for the "triumph of American capitalism."[262] Means was similarly won over, indicating in 1962 "I am strongly in favor of big business and what it can contribute to our society," even if the power of large unregulated industrial corporations could be a cause for concern.[263]

While corporate prosperity suppressed concerns about weak checks on managerial power, the core governance fissure between managers and shareholders had not gone away. Instead, the adverse effects were merely in abeyance. As we will see in Chapter 3, when managerial capitalism was on the wane large US business enterprises were being run in ways prone to store up trouble for the future. Tendencies to postpone rather than make decisions would ultimately emerge as a cause for serious concern. Being bold was not necessarily the answer either, as various freewheeling conglomerates of the 1960s foundered in the 1970s.[264] The fact remains that in the 1950s and 1960s egregious corporate misconduct was a rarity and public companies were enjoying considerable success along multiple dimensions. Public company executives correspondingly were not abusing the discretion available to them to the extent that might have been anticipated. The remainder of this chapter considers why.

What Constrained Management?

In 1959 Adolf Berle said the fact that American corporations had recently been relatively free from managerial excesses was not attributable to the arrival of saints.[265] Robert Eagly struck

---

[257] GALAMBOS & PRATT, *supra* note 14, at 180, 182.

[258] *Id.* at 128.

[259] *Judging the Giant*, TIME, Feb. 22, 1960, 91.

[260] NOHRIA, DYER & DALZELL, *supra* note 187, at 168. See also MARK S. MIZRUCHI, THE FRACTURING OF THE AMERICAN CORPORATE ELITE 204 (2013).

[261] BERLE & MEANS, *supra* note 71, at 312–13.

[262] BERLE, *supra* note 101, at 28.

[263] MEANS, *supra* note 241, at 155.

[264] Chapter 3, notes 108–21 and related discussion.

[265] *Supra* note 158 and related discussion.

a similar chord in an essay published the same year in which he said "a new motivational ethos" did not explain why the nature of American capitalism had been transformed since 1900.[266] Eagly cited instead "the changing institutional environment within which big business operates."[267]

As with Eagly, Norton Long, a political scientist also writing in 1959, recognized that the environment within which public companies operated did much to explain how corporate executives were conducting themselves. Long accepted that the typical public company executive "has a concern for harmony and the avoidance of trouble that sets him apart from his predecessors," and noted "present managerial behaviors give rise to doubt as to unrestrained corporate power"[268] The explanation for this state of affairs, according to Long, was that "management is surrounded by a network of constraints and fears," but he acknowledged the network's operation was "as yet an unwritten chapter in industrial sociology."[269] With the benefit of hindsight, the relevant variables can be identified and their significance assessed. We will consider internal constraints affecting public company executives first and then turn to external limitations on managerial discretion.

INTERNAL CONSTRAINTS

For public company executives the key "internal" corporate constraints are the board of directors and the shareholders. During the heyday of managerial capitalism neither played a pivotal role in keeping management in check. With large American corporations of the 1950s and 1960s, "their chief internal characteristic was the almost unlimited discretion of their managers to set the goals and priorities that their organizations pursued."[270] Executives thus were left with "almost complete autonomy in making the key strategic and resource allocation decisions that affected the fortunes of the enterprises they managed."[271]

Boards

Boards do not run public companies despite being legally empowered to do so under state corporate law. Executives the directors appoint do so.[272] From a governance perspective, the obvious role for boards to play is to keep the executives in charge in check, with directors independent from management being the logical candidates to foster accountability due to their objectivity.[273] A "monitoring" model of the board gained wide currency in the 1970s.[274]

---

[266] Eagly, *supra* note 1, at 567.

[267] *Id.*

[268] Norton E. Long, *The Corporation, Its Satellites, and the Local Community, in* THE CORPORATION, *supra* note 87, at 202, 205, 209.

[269] *Id.* at 209.

[270] MARINA V.N. WHITMAN, NEW WORLD, NEW RULES: THE CHANGING ROLE OF THE AMERICAN CORPORATION 4 (1999).

[271] NOHRIA, DYER & DALZELL, *supra* note 187, at 162.

[272] Chapter 1, notes 26–27, and related discussion.

[273] BRIAN R. CHEFFINS, COMPANY LAW: THEORY, STRUCTURE AND OPERATION 605 (1997).

[274] Chapter 3, notes 265–66 and accompanying text.

The idea that the board could and should act as a managerial "watchdog" was by no means unfamiliar, however, during the heyday of managerial capitalism.[275]

In 1940, in the aftermath of the McKesson & Robbins accounting fraud revelations, the NYSE acknowledged that it was anomalous for executives to hold all directorships in a listed corporation.[276] In 1956 the NYSE required companies listed on the Exchange to have at least two independent directors on the board.[277] By the second half of the 1950s a consensus was developing amongst experts on boards that ideally a majority of directors of a public company should be individuals not holding executive posts.[278] This "outside board" model was simultaneously becoming increasingly prevalent in practice.[279] Numerous examples of insider-dominated boards remained.[280] Before the 1950s ended, however, executive directors were outnumbered on the board in a majority of leading manufacturing companies and in most large firms outside the industrial sector.[281]

Despite growing outside director representation, as *Business Week* noted in 1957, mid-twentieth century boards took "volleys of abuse."[282] Where outside directors are in the majority executives theoretically cannot use their voting power to dictate the outcome of board deliberations. Nevertheless, the consensus in the 1950s and 1960s was that only a crisis would preclude boards from deferring to the management team.[283] Peter Drucker said in the mid-1950s the board of directors was "a tired fiction" and "a shadow king."[284] In 1958 E.E. Smith, a professor of business administration, characterized the board as "dead as a dodo."[285] Franklin Moore, in his 1964 text on management, said "most boards don't review the executives' stewardship very critically."[286]

What Berle referred to in 1959 as "obsolete processes of selection" of directors[287] lent credence to the skeptics' assessment. Under state corporate law, the shareholders had the right to elect the directors.[288] Practically speaking, however, the choice shareholders had was limited on the vast majority of occasions to voting on a single slate of nominees selected by

---

[275] MELVIN T. COPELAND & ANDREW R. TOWL, THE BOARD OF DIRECTORS AND BUSINESS MANAGEMENT 146 (1947) ("One of the most common theories about directors . . . is that a main task of directors is to serve as watchdogs, policing the executives. . . . ").

[276] *Supra* note 182 and related discussion; J. George Fredrick, *New Jobs for Directors*, FORBES, Jan. 15, 1940, 12.

[277] Brian R. Cheffins, Steven A. Bank, and Harwell Wells, *Shareholder Protection across Time*, 68 U. FLA. L. REV. 691, 744 (2017).

[278] NEWCOMER, *supra* note 83, 29–30 (describing the views of the "majority of those writing on the subject"); THE DIRECTOR LOOKS AT HIS JOB 82 (Courtney C. Brown & E. Everitt Smith eds., 1957); William Clark, *Corporate Authority: Where Is Dividing Line?*, CHI. TRIB., Jan. 8, 1959, D5.

[279] John Chamberlain, *Why It's Harder and Harder to Get a Good Board*, FORTUNE, Nov. 1962, 108.

[280] *Managers Fade as Directors*, BUS. WK., June 27, 1959, 72.

[281] *Id.* (citing a survey of 925 companies); MACE, *supra* note 199, at 111–12 (data for manufacturing companies for 1953, 1958, 1961, and 1966); Chamberlain, *supra* note 279 (citing a study by *Fortune*).

[282] *Directors Peer into the Mirror*, BUS. WK., Dec. 21, 1957, 57.

[283] MAURER, *supra* note 3, at 201; DIRECTOR LOOKS, *supra* note 278, at 46; J.M. JURAN & J. KEITH LOUDEN, THE CORPORATE DIRECTOR 293 (1966).

[284] PETER DRUCKER, THE PRACTICE OF MANAGEMENT 154 (1955).

[285] Quoted in HAROLD KOONTZ, THE BOARD OF DIRECTORS AND EFFECTIVE MANAGEMENT 221 (1967).

[286] MOORE, *supra* note 102, at 62.

[287] BERLE, *supra* note 84, at 108.

[288] KOONTZ, *supra* note 285, at 76.

the incumbent board.[289] These nominees were in turn almost inevitably endorsed by huge majorities as shareholders refraining from attending stockholder meetings in person sent in proxy documentation authorizing the voting of their shares by those already running the company.[290] With this arrangement, caustically described as a "communist ballot"[291] and "a total farce,"[292] being nominated by the board was the key to becoming and remaining a director.[293]

By the 1980s it would become commonplace for boards of public companies to delegate the task of selecting board candidates to a nomination committee comprised of independent directors.[294] Such committees were a rarity, however, in the 1950s and 1960s.[295] The matter was instead dealt with by the chief executive,[296] perhaps in consultation with existing directors.[297] This occurred despite awareness that it was less than ideal for chief executives to recruit only directors they would be happy to work with.[298]

Boards that are not prepared to monitor executives rigorously can still theoretically seek to shape managerial behavior through the provision of appropriate financial incentives. The setting of executive pay falls within the scope of the managerial powers that state corporate law vests in boards.[299] If boards use the discretion available to them to structure executive compensation so as to reward those in charge when shareholders do well and to penalize the executives when corporate performance is poor, senior management will have a strong financial incentive to focus closely on shareholder interests.[300] However, the general view in the 1950s and 1960s was that public companies did little to tie executive compensation to shareholder returns, at least independent of other measures of corporate performance.[301] Empirical studies conducted in the 1970s corroborated this assessment.[302] More recent research indicates chief executives during the 1950s and 1960s did benefit financially when the market value of their firms increased but that the correlation was modest compared to arrangements in the 1990s and 2000s.[303]

---

289 STANLEY C. VANCE, THE CORPORATE DIRECTOR: A CRITICAL EVALUATION 4 (1968).

290 Mortimer M. Caplin, *Proxies, Annual Meetings and Corporate Democracy: The Lawyer's Role*, 37 VA. L. REV. 653, 654–55 (1951).

291 LIVINGSTON, *supra* note 177, at 46.

292 Rostow, *supra* note 256, at 54.

293 MOORE, *supra* note 88, at 9.

294 See Chapter 4, note 256 and related discussion.

295 JURAN & LOUDEN, *supra* note 283, at 218; Brian R. Cheffins, *Delaware and the Transformation of Corporate Governance*, 40 DEL. J. CORP. L. 1, 33, 39 (2015).

296 MACE, *supra* note 199, at 188; KOONTZ, *supra* note 285, at 227.

297 JURAN & LOUDEN, *supra* note 283, a 217–18.

298 DIRECTOR LOOKS, *supra* note 278, at 53–54; KOONTZ, *supra* note 285, at 227.

299 Bank, Cheffins & Wells, *supra* note 200, at 80.

300 Brian R. Cheffins, *Introduction*, THE HISTORY OF MODERN US CORPORATE GOVERNANCE ix, xvi (Brian R. Cheffins ed., 2011).

301 Wilbur G. Lewellen, *Management and Ownership in the Large Firm*, 24 J. FIN. 299, 300 (1969).

302 David H. Ciscel, *Determinants of Executive Compensation* (1974) 40 S. ECON. J. 613 (data for 1969–1971); K.R. Srinivasa Murthy & Malcolm S. Salter, *Should CEO Pay Be Linked to Results?*, HARV. BUS. REV., May–June 1975, 66 (data from the 1960s).

303 Carola Frydman & Dirk Jenter, *CEO Compensation*, 2 ANN. REV. FIN. ECON. 75, 84–85 (2010).

Shareholders

Richard Eells, in his 1962 analysis of corporate "government," specifically identified shareholder control as an internal mechanism that could stifle the counterproductive exercise of managerial power.[304] Well-attended shareholders' meetings in the late 1950s and early 1960s—a total of 500,000 stockholders went to annual meetings in 1962 alone while in 2016 only 150 went to the annual meeting of banking giant Bank of America[305]—created the impression that shareholders might be taking a close interest in corporate affairs.[306] In fact, shareholders were a governance afterthought during the managerial capitalism era. Ira Millstein, a distinguished corporate lawyer who started practicing in the 1950s, said in 2017 "(t)he major unintended consequence of managerial capitalism" was "little accountability to the owners."[307]

In the 1950s executives of various large public companies sought to generate positive public relations by using tours, exhibits, souvenirs, and lunches to woo shareholders to annual meetings.[308] Corporate enthusiasm soon dissipated, however, with these meetings increasingly being thought of as an exercise to be endured.[309] There were fears of awkward questioning by publicity-seeking corporate "gadflies" and unruly behavior that could yield a circus-like atmosphere.[310] Also, only very rarely would anything formally turn on the deliberations because the vast majority of votes on resolutions were cast in advance through written proxy documentation shareholders submitted, most often backing the stance management recommended.[311]

Stockholder input was no more meaningful in other contexts. Eells, having identified shareholders as a potential constraint on management, viewed the limitation as more theoretical than actual. He said that "attempts . . . to activate shareholder control of management have had insignificant results" and that "(t)he controls of the corporate electorate—the stockholders—over board and management are severely limited in the large public-issue corporation."[312] Others concurred. Shareholders in the managerial capitalism era were described as "passive,"[313] and "an apathetic bunch"[314] that played "no active role at all."[315]

---

304 EELLS, *supra* note 230, at 23.

305 *Are Annual Meetings Really Necessary?*, FORBES, May 15, 1962, 31; Christina Rexrode, *A Ninth-Grader Turned Activist*, WALL ST. J., Apr. 29, 2016, C1.

306 *The Small Shareowner—The New Corporate VIP*, FORBES, Sept. 1, 1957, 15.

307 IRA M. MILLSTEIN, THE ACTIVIST DIRECTOR: LESSONS FROM THE BOARDROOM AND THE FUTURE OF THE CORPORATION 28 (2017).

308 Vartanig G. Vartan, *Spring Stirs Stockholders*, CHRISTIAN SCI. MONITOR, Apr. 13, 1956, 14; *Giving Stockholders Their Day*, BUS. WK., June 29, 1957, 176 (noting, though, that a majority of public companies did not seek to woo their shareholders).

309 *More Voices Raised at Annual Meetings*, BUS. WK., May 28, 1960, 165.

310 *Stockholders Criticized*, CHRISTIAN SCI. MONITOR, Oct. 20, 1964, 11; Myron Kandel, *It's Open Season for Stockholders*, BOS. GLOBE, Jan. 24, 1965, 61.

311 Burton Crane, *Although Votes Are Not Equal, Small Holders Play a Big Role*, NY TIMES, Mar. 18, 1962, Business, 1.

312 EELLS, *supra* note 230, at 23, 199.

313 BERLE, *supra* note 84, at 74.

314 Peter B. Greenough, *Stockholders Lax as Voters*, BOS. GLOBE, Mar. 19, 1964, 20.

315 MAURER, *supra* note 3, at 264.

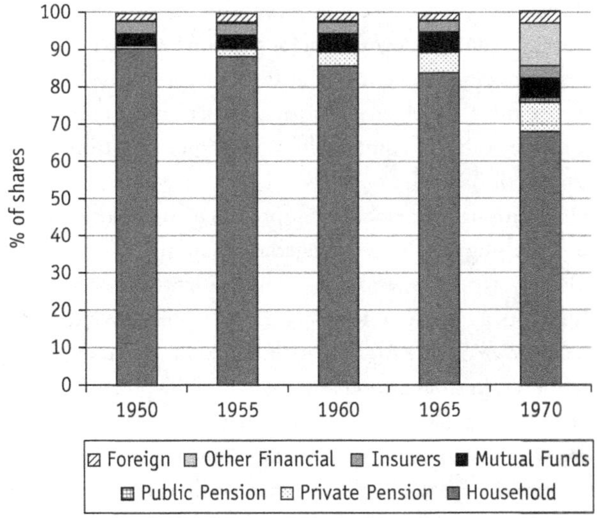

FIGURE 2.1 US Corporate Stock Held by Households and Institutions, 1950–1970.
Source: MARY O'SULLIVAN, CONTESTS FOR CORPORATE CONTROL: CORPORATE GOVERNANCE AND ECONOMIC PERFORMANCE IN THE UNITED STATES AND GERMANY 156 (2000).

It was hardly surprising the prospects for meaningful shareholder governance involvement were bleak in the 1950s and 1960s. "Household" investors—primarily individuals buying and selling securities for their own personal account—collectively owned most of the shares in publicly traded companies (Figure 2.1).[316] Private shareholders, caustically labeled in 1967 "20 Million Careless Capitalists,"[317] typically lack the aptitude, resources, and firm-specific information needed to intervene productively in corporate affairs.[318] Retail investors have little incentive to step forward in any case, given the hassle involved and given that the typical private shareholder owns a tiny stake and thus will only benefit trivially from any share price increase associated with a successful intervention.[319]

While private stockholders dominated share ownership throughout the 1950s and 1960s, institutional investors were growing in importance. The number of account holders in mutual funds, which were heavily concentrated in equities, rose from 296,000 in 1940 to 4.9 million in 1960 and doubled again by the end of the decade.[320] Assets under management grew from $450 million to $17 billion and again to $48 billion over the same period.[321]

---

[316] For data on stock ownership from a different source than Figure 2.1 but revealing a similar pattern see Jeffrey N. Gordon, *The Rise of Independent Directors in the United States, 1950–2005: Of Shareholder Value and Stock Market Prices*, 59 STAN. L. REV. 1465, 1568 (2007). "Households" is the residual term used by the Federal Reserve, which compiles data on holders of corporate stock, to categorize owners of shares. See Marcel Kahan & Edward Rock, *Embattled CEOs*, 88 TEX. L. REV. 989, 996, n.24 (2010).

[317] HENDERSON & LASHER, *supra* note 225.

[318] Cheffins, *supra* note 300, at xix.

[319] *Id.*

[320] MATTHEW P. FINK, THE RISE OF MUTUAL FUNDS: AN INSIDER'S VIEW 56, 58 (2008).

[321] *Id.* at 56, 63.

With pension funds, the number of employees covered grew substantially, hitting 16.5 million by 1958, due largely to unions negotiating for pension benefits in collective bargaining.[322] Pension funds also increasingly invested in shares. The proportion of pension fund assets invested in stocks rose from 14 percent in 1950 to 56 percent in 1966, which contributed to an increase in the market value of equity held by pension funds from $774 million to $36.2 billion over the same period.[323]

The growth of institutional ownership prompted suggestions that mutual funds and pension funds were a promising source of managerial discipline. John Kenneth Galbraith, in a review of Adolf Berle's 1959 *Power without Property*, identified the accumulation of shares by institutional investors as "the one looming threat to the autonomy of the professional managers."[324] The *Christian Science Monitor* maintained in 1966 that "(t)he growing share of institutional shareholders in stock ownership has raised the possibility of making corporate democracy more real."[325] A 1968 text on boards cited the substantial increase in stakes held by institutional investors as a force likely to prompt beneficial change in the boardroom.[326]

Institutional shareholders, setting a pattern that would prevail over the next few decades, failed to step forward in the manner predicted and hoped for. *Business Week* acknowledged in 1955 institutional share ownership was a "change that has come a long way and is gathering speed all of the time." There was, however, an important caveat: "(o)fficers of institutional investors insist that their ownership won't seek control, regardless of how great their holdings in American business become."[327] That certainly held true throughout the remainder of the 1950s and the 1960s. Berle said in 1959 there was "ample evidence" institutional shareholders "do not wish to use the voting power of the stock they have accumulated" and indicated "(w)hen they seriously dislike the managements of corporations . . . their policy is to sell."[328] Nonintervention in turn served "to insulate the corporate managements."[329] A 1965 study of institutional shareholders concurred with Berle, characterizing them as "silent partners" and indicating "(f)or the most part, institutions are investors not controllers."[330]

EXTERNAL CONSTRAINTS

While internal constraints were not a potent check on public company executives in the 1950s and 1960s, external constraints were more meaningful. With two sources of managerial discipline, namely the threat of displacement by way of takeover and pressure from competitors, their potential was recognized but neither was as important a check on executives

---

322 Paul P. Harbrecht, Pension Funds and Economic Power 6–7 (1959).

323 Robert M. Soldofsky, Institutional Holdings of Common Stock, 1900–2000: History, Projection and Interpretation 183–84 (1971). See also Harbrecht, *supra* note 322, at 104.

324 J.K. Galbraith, *The Self-Appointed Tenants in the Executive Suite*, NY Times, Sept. 6, 1959, Book Review, 3.

325 David R. Francis, *Large Shareholders Press for Voice in Management*, Christian Sci. Monitor, Nov. 18, 1966, 20.

326 Vance, *supra* note 289, at 5–6.

327 *Today's Management: Under New Ownership Tomorrow?*, Bus. Wk., June 18, 1955, 140.

328 Berle, *supra* note 84, at 55.

329 *Id.* at 56.

330 Baum & Stiles, *supra* note 222, at 68.

as they would be subsequently. In contrast, two other external constraints were more potent than they would be as the twentieth century drew to a close. These were organized labor and government regulation, with the significance of the latter constraint being reinforced by concerns that public antipathy toward business could readily translate into new and unwelcome forms of state intervention.

The Market for Corporate Control

When institutional shareholders of the managerial capitalism era were dissatisfied with how a company was being run and sold their shares in response, this was referred to as exercising the "Wall Street Rule." [331] While institutional investors were biased in favor of passivity, exiting in this fashion could serve to activate a potentially significant external constraint on management. Henry Manne, in a 1965 article in which he coined the term "market for corporate control," noted that when there was downward pressure on a company's share price this would make the company a more attractive takeover target for those who believed they could run the company more effectively.[332] This possibility, according to Manne, provided "some assurance of competitive efficiency among corporate managers and thereby affords strong protection to the interests of vast numbers of small, non-controlling shareholders."[333]

Even prior to Manne's 1965 identification of the market for corporate control there was awareness that the prospect of an unwelcome takeover bid was a potentially significant disciplinary mechanism for executives. *Business Week* noted in 1955 "(t)here's little doubt that the corporate air is tinged with fear of what incumbent management likes to call 'raids.' "[334] Livingston, in his 1958 book on the American stockholder, said that with savvy investors exiting and driving the stock price of a poorly run company downward, "(u)ltimately, the stock may get low enough for some self-serving knight in financial armour to buy it up and try to take over.... Thus, the market-place vote has power."[335] *Time* suggested in 1960 that "(t)he one man who is still a threat to unbridled corporate power is the raider."[336]

Livingston said that because of the potential for a change of control when share prices fell, "(n)o management can be complacent."[337] This overstates matters because only a small proportion of potential targets actually faced "raids" in the 1950s and 1960s. For those minded to try to secure control of a public company by acquiring a majority of the shares the traditional tactic of buying stock on the open market was being replaced by the tender offer, which involves an acquirer inviting target company shareholders to agree to sell ("tender") their shares to the acquirer in return for cash, shares, or a combination of the two.[338] Tender offers launched against the wishes of the target's board remained, however, a fairly rare event until

---

[331] *Id.* at 67.

[332] Henry G. Manne, *Mergers and the Market for Corporate Control*, 73 J. POL. ECON. 110, 112–13 (1965).

[333] *Id.* at 113.

[334] *Jitters over Company "Raids,"* BUS. WK., Apr. 16, 1955, 133.

[335] LIVINGSTON, *supra* note 177, at 67.

[336] *Judging the Giant*, *supra* note 259.

[337] LIVINGSTON, *supra* note 177, at 46.

[338] John Armour & Brian Cheffins, *Stock Market Prices and the Market for Corporate Control* [2016] U. ILL. L. REV. 761, 784–85.

the mid-1960s. The number attracting press coverage averaged only three per year between 1950 and 1964.[339] Somewhat more common was a proxy contest for board control, where the insurgent would put forward a rival slate of directors to those proposed by the incumbent management team. An average of just over 12 such contests received newspaper coverage annually between 1950 and 1964.[340]

The number of hostile tender offers attracting press coverage leapt to 23 in 1965 and in 1969, 148 companies were targeted.[341] *Fortune* even suggested in 1969 that fear of an unwelcome bid was "epidemic in perhaps three out of five big corporate headquarters."[342] Still, control contests had hardly become an everyday occurrence for public companies, given there were in the late 1960s nearly 6,000 companies with shares listed for trading on stock exchanges in the United States.[343] Moreover, despite *Fortune*'s claim about widespread concern, the largest public companies were virtually immune from tender offers due to their size because for prospective raiders accumulating the funds required to buy up a majority stake was unrealistic.[344] For instance, in a 1969 interview with General Electric board chairman Fred Borch *Forbes* observed "(y)ou're saying that you're too big to be taken over.... *You* have the luxury of devoting your time to business, not to fighting takeovers."[345] Borch replied "Right."[346] Peter Drucker affirmed the point when writing about takeovers in 1986, saying "in the 1960s and early 1970s, the managements of big, publicly-owned companies were widely-believed to be impregnable; nothing short of bankruptcy could threaten, let alone dislodge, them."[347] Ultimately, then, while steps taken by "raiders, renovators, and nascent empire-builders" meant some "noticeably inefficient" managers could lose office,[348] in the 1950s and 1960s other external constraints did more to rein in management than the market for corporate control.

Competitors

Theoretically competition from rival firms can impinge substantially on managerial autonomy.[349] A firm that is not run well enough to offer a marketable product or service at an attractive price can quickly alienate customers and lose market share. This is a predicament management will want to avoid because, if the situation deteriorates far enough, the business will go bankrupt and the executives in charge will take a major reputational "hit." At the same time, though, a firm that has accumulated substantial market power that becomes

---

339 Derived from data generated for *id.* at 783 (Figure 3).

340 *Id.*

341 *Id.*; DOUGLAS AUSTIN & JAY FISHMAN, CORPORATIONS IN CONFLICT—THE TENDER OFFER 12 (1970) (table 2); MARGARET M. BLAIR & GIRISH UPPAL, THE DEAL DECADE HANDBOOK 54 (1993).

342 EDITORS OF FORTUNE, *supra* note 218, at 93 (excerpt from February 1969 article).

343 Cheffins, Bank & Wells, *supra* note 151, at 603.

344 William L. Baldwin, *The Motives of Managers, Environmental Restraints, and the Theory of Managerial Enterprise*, 78 Q.J. ECON. 238, 252 (1965).

345 *"Don't Call Us a Congeneric,"* FORBES, Feb. 15, 1969, 53 (emphasis in original).

346 *Id.*

347 Peter F. Drucker, *Corporate Takeovers—What Is to Be Done?*, PUBLIC INT., Winter 1986, at 3, 5.

348 William Letwin, *The Past and Future of the American Businessman*, DAEDALUS, Winter 1969, at 1, 17.

349 CHEFFINS, *supra* note 127, at 118, 120.

afflicted with weak management may be able to sustain its dominance for a considerable period of time. It follows that "managerial slack is first and foremost an issue for firms in non-competitive industries."[350]

The notion that competitive pressure functions as a disciplinary mechanism in the corporate context was a familiar one during the managerial capitalism era. Economist and corporate executive Oswald Knauth emphasized in 1953 that, for a business, meeting the customer's conditions was "fundamental."[351] Moore, in his 1964 text on management, noted that a badly run firm was likely to fail and said "(m)anagers are always on a treadmill" as "(c)ompetitors keep eroding your income."[352] The 1965 study of institutional investors that characterized them as "silent partners" explained a general absence of "corporate plundering" partly on the basis that "(w)here competition exists, as it does throughout most of the economy, the desire to excel undoubtedly serves to prevent corporate abuse."[353]

While there was awareness during the managerial capitalism era that pressure from rivals could make life difficult for public company executives, the "where competition exists" caveat that the "silent partners" study offered was a significant one. While that study suggested meaningful competition was the norm, the general assumption among academics analyzing the managerial capitalism era retrospectively has been that it was commonplace for a small number of companies to dominate an industry on an oligopolistic basis.[354] Under such circumstances, the leading firms likely competed with each other for market share through advertising and product innovation but management felt secure enough to refrain from using pricing strategies to retain or build market share.[355] As John Kotter, a Harvard management professor, said in 1988 about automotive giant General Motors (GM), "(o)ne doubts if the people who ran GM during the 1950s and 1960s thought they were living in an era of stability and benign competition. But compared to recent years, they surely were."[356]

Numerous academics in the 1950s and 1960s suggested that in a wide range of industries oligopolistic market structures compromised substantially the threat rivals posed for large firms. These included Berle, Means, and Galbraith.[357] Carl Kaysen agreed as well, saying "the possession of a substantial degree of market power is characteristic of the modern

---

[350] Xavier Giroud & Holger M. Mueller, *Does Corporate Governance Matter in Competitive Industries?*, 95 J. FIN. ECON. 312, 312 (2010).

[351] Oswald W. Knauth, *Group Interest and Managerial Enterprise*, 1 J. INDUST. ECON. 88, 91 (1953).

[352] MOORE, *supra* note 102, at 28.

[353] BAUM & STILES, *supra* note 222, at 9.

[354] See, for example, Wells, *supra* note 6, at 317–18; George David Smith & Davis Dyer, *The Rise and Transformation of the American Corporation*, *in* AMERICAN CORPORATION, *supra* note 17, at 28, 51; DOUGLAS M. EICHAR, THE RISE AND FALL OF CORPORATE SOCIAL RESPONSIBILITY 188, 218 (2015). For an exception, see Stacy Mitchell, *The Rise and Fall of the Word Monopoly in American Life*, ATLANTIC.COM, June 20, 2017, available at https://www.theatlantic.com/business/archive/2017/06/word-monopoly-antitrust/530169/ (accessed May 24, 2018).

[355] See, for example, REICH, *supra* note 6, at 29; KOTZ, *supra* note 204, at 29; MIZRUCHI, *supra* note 260, at 100–01.

[356] JOHN P. KOTTER, THE LEADERSHIP FACTOR 6 (1988). See also Wisman, *supra* note 186, at 901.

[357] GALBRAITH, *supra* note 10, at 45–46; BERLE, *supra* note 84, at 89; MEANS, *supra* note 241, at 162–65.

corporation."[358] It followed that competitive pressure would often not be a robust managerial constraint.

There was, however, a division of opinion regarding the extent to which market power insulated dominant firms. Various observers argued that profits were never assured, and suggested "(e)ven the biggest of businessmen probably feel much less secure in their oligopoly positions than the theorist often assumes they should."[359] Berle himself acknowledged in 1962 "(n)o herd of behemoths has yet occupied, or ought ever to occupy the whole living space of new ideas and possibilities."[360]

Market competition is an abstract construct that cannot be observed directly, so measuring it statistically is challenging.[361] Those defending the potency of market forces in the 1950s and 1960s could nevertheless cite various examples of eclipsed dominant companies to assert "the top . . . is a slippery place" and "the way to the top has remained open—and the trap door to failure still yawns."[362] For instance, among the largest 100 industrial firms as of 1909, ranked by assets, only 31 still qualified for the top 100 a half century later, and top 10 firms from 1909 such as International Mercantile Marine Co. (a shipping combine), Pullman Co. (a railway car concern), and Central Leather Co. fell out of the top 100 completely.[363]

While there remained a "trap door" for big companies that lost their way, the prospects for continued success were in fact generally good in the 1950s and 1960s. In nearly half of manufacturing industries the two leading firms as of 1950, ranked by sales, remained the leaders as of 1972.[364] Sixty-five of the largest 100 industrial companies as of 1935, again ranked by assets, were on the list a quarter century later.[365] Eight of the top 10 from 1935 were also among that elite group in 1960, with the other two, Bethlehem Steel Corp. and mining firm Anaconda Co., remaining in the top 30.[366]

As for "the top" remaining "open" during the heyday of managerial capitalism, there were various examples of young firms that rose to prominence.[367] One was Polaroid, which as a modestly successful sunglasses company challenged photography market leader Kodak by launching a radical 60-second developing camera in 1948. Another was Hewlett-Packard. The technology firm, founded by Bill Hewlett and Dave Packard in the late 1930s, went

---

[358] Kaysen, *supra* note 86, at 314.

[359] Peterson, *supra* note 255, at 10. See also A.D.H. Kaplan, Big Enterprise in a Competitive System 138, 185, 222 (rev. ed. 1964); *Battle of the Century*, Barron's, Jan. 4, 1965, 45; Henry Hazlitt, *Galbraith's Book Adds to Business Myths*, Chi. Trib, Sept. 26, 1967, 14.

[360] A.A. Berle, *Bigness: Curse or Opportunity?*, NY Times, Feb. 18, 1962, Sunday Magazine, 10.

[361] Frederic L. Pryor, The Future of US Capitalism 266 (2002); William J. Baumol, Alan S. Blinder & Edward N. Wolff, Downsizing in America: Reality, Causes, and Consequences 18 (2003).

[362] *Battle of the Century*, *supra* note 359; *The Blue Chips of Yesteryear: Where Are They Today?*, Forbes, Apr. 15, 1961, 30.

[363] Kaplan, *supra* note 359, at 124, 136, 140.

[364] Dennis C. Mueller, Profits in the Long Run 41, 46, 49 (1996).

[365] Kaplan, *supra* note 359, at 136–37.

[366] *Id.* at 146.

[367] See Isadore Barmash, The Self-Made Man: Success and Stress American Style 14–15 (1969); Allan A. Kennedy, The End of Shareholder Value: Corporations at the Crossroads 20–29 (2000); The Story of American Business from the Pages of the New York Times 133–34 (Nancy F. Koehn ed., 2009).

public in 1957 on its way to great success as the twentieth century drew to a close. There also were McDonald's, which Ray Kroc built into America's largest restaurant chain after buying out the McDonald brothers in 1961, and future retailing powerhouse Wal-Mart, with Sam Walton launching the first Wal-Mart discount store the same year.

Though there were entrepreneurial success stories, major breakouts by young companies were in fact comparatively rare. Companies that dominated in the 1950s and 1960s typically could trace their origins at least back to the late nineteenth or early twentieth centuries.[368] The average age of the largest firms in the United States, measured by market value, correspondingly rose from under 40 in the late 1920s to nearly 70 in the mid-1960s before falling to under 60 in the late 1990s when newish companies such as software giant Microsoft and Intel, a maker of computer chips and microprocessors, moved to the forefront.[369]

How did the dominant firms of the 1950s and 1960s secure and retain the market power that tempered the disciplining of top management? Part of the explanation, advanced most forcefully by Alfred Chandler, was the development of organizational capabilities late-coming rivals could not readily match.[370] In the late nineteenth century, Chandler pointed out, a wave of technological innovation combined with the flourishing of a transport and communications infrastructure oriented around the railway and the telegraph to set the stage for modern large-scale production and distribution. Old industries such as food processing and metal making were transformed, and new ones appeared, such as oil, rubber, chemicals, heavy and light machinery, and electrical equipment for light, power, and transportation. In most such industries, "first movers" quickly came to dominate by capitalizing effectively on rapidly evolving technologies and by investing as and when required in production facilities, distribution networks, and marketing strategies so as to increase output, drive down costs, and build customer loyalty. Managerial staffing was simultaneously scaled up dramatically to coordinate and direct the increasingly complex operations of these innovative enterprises.[371] Industrial leadership was frequently consolidated by vertical integration (the acquisition of suppliers or distributors) and by moving into related markets where already well-honed organizational competencies could be readily and effectively deployed. The challenges associated with replicating the production, distribution, marketing, and management capabilities of the first movers constituted a barrier to entry that limited the number of direct competitors and fostered oligopolistic market structures.[372]

Competitors faced handicaps in addition to first movers developing organizational capabilities that were challenging and costly to mimic. Difficult economic conditions in the 1930s

---

[368] ROBERT SOBEL, THE LAST BULL MARKET: WALL STREET IN THE 1960S, at 48, 50 (1980).

[369] Boyan Jovanovic & Peter L. Rousseau, *Stock Markets in the New Economy*, *in* TECHNOLOGY AND THE NEW ECONOMY 9, 29 (Chong En-Bai & Chi-Wa Yuen eds., 2002).

[370] See, for example, CHANDLER, *supra* note 56, at 594–99; Alfred D. Chandler, *Corporate Strategy, Structure and Control Methods in the United States during the 20th Century*, 1 INDUST. CORP. CHANGE 263, 264–66, 271–73 (1992).

[371] *Supra* notes 110–111 and related discussion.

[372] NEIL H. JACOBY, CORPORATE POWER AND SOCIAL RESPONSIBILITY 137 (1973); Naomi R. Lamoreaux, *Entrepreneurship in the United States, 1865–1920*, *in* THE INVENTION OF ENTERPRISE: ENTREPRENEURSHIP FROM ANCIENT MESOPOTAMIA TO MODERN TIMES 367, 383 (David S. Landes, Joel Mokyr & William J. Baumol eds., 2010).

meant failure was a regular occurrence for smaller enterprises that likely would have posed a competitive threat to incumbents under conventional circumstances.[373] During World War II established firms benefitted from heavy orders by the US military because these incumbents were best positioned to meet demand for critically needed supplies promptly and on a large scale.[374] Due primarily to the procurement practices of the military, as of 1943 the 100 largest US industrial firms controlled 70 percent of the nation's manufacturing output compared to 30 percent in 1939.[375]

Victory in World War II would in turn help large American companies vested with market power to sustain their dominance. The conflict devastated the economies of countries out of which potential major rivals operated.[376] For a decade or more after World War II ended foreign competitors were not considered a meaningful threat by US firms,[377] with some justification. As of 1959, 44 of the largest 50 global companies were American.[378] In 1960 approximately 95 percent of steel, automobiles, televisions, radios, and other consumer products Americans bought were domestically sourced.[379] When General Electric chairman Gerald Phillippe gave a speech in 1964 arguing that America must "discover the new world of competition" for global markets, the *Austin American-Statesman* indicated it was surprised he was "doing so right in the open" because the topic was little discussed.[380]

Regulation was an additional obstacle for potential insurgents in the 1950s and 1960s. Laws governing an industry that dictate entry requirements, pricing policies, and production or service standards can create substantial barriers to entry for those seeking to challenge dominant incumbents.[381] This occurred with some regularity during the mid-twentieth century. Under Franklin Roosevelt, the federal government responded to the Depression by introducing "a vast new public-policy regime of microeconomic stabilization."[382] By the late 1930s firms in the shipping, trucking, stockyard, telephone, telegraph, electric, and gas industries were operating under an administrative system with rates and practices being regulated to achieve declared goals of reasonableness, non-discrimination, and reliable service.[383]

---

373 Margaret B.W. Graham, *Entrepreneurship in the United States, 1920–2000, in* INVENTION OF ENTERPRISE, *supra* note 372, at 401, 409.

374 *Id.* at 412.

375 MANSEL G. BLACKFORD & K. AUSTIN KERR, BUSINESS ENTERPRISE IN AMERICAN HISTORY 337–38 (2d ed. 1990).

376 Louis Galambos, *The US Corporate Economy in the Twentieth Century, in* CAMBRIDGE ECONOMIC HISTORY, *supra* note 64, at 927, 948.

377 Harold Walsh, *Cautious Optimism Noted among Wall Street Experts*, LA TIMES, Nov. 15, 1955, 24; RAKESH KHURANA, SEARCHING FOR A CORPORATE SAVIOR: THE IRRATIONAL QUEST FOR CHARISMATIC CEOs 68 (2002).

378 Carl Kaysen, *Introduction and Overview, in* AMERICAN CORPORATION, *supra* note 17, at 3, 25.

379 REICH, *supra* note 6, at 43.

380 *Competition Finds Friend*, AUSTIN AMERICAN-STATESMAN, Apr. 26, 1964, D2.

381 MICHAEL E. PORTER, COMPETITIVE STRATEGY: TECHNIQUES FOR ANALYZING INDUSTRIES AND COMPETITORS 13 (1980).

382 Richard H.K. Vietor, *Government Regulation of Business, in* CAMBRIDGE ECONOMIC HISTORY, *supra* note 64, at 969, 986.

383 Joseph D. Kearney & Thomas W. Merrill, *The Great Transformation of Regulated Industries Law*, 98 COLUM. L. REV. 1323, 1333–34 (1998).

A legacy extending through World War II and the managerial capitalism era was a market structure affecting a quarter of the economy where regulation strongly influenced decisions about pricing, production, marketing, and the adoption of new technology.[384] Regulator approval was often required to enter the industries in question, markets were frequently segmented by product and geography, and the need for profits was typically weighed explicitly against the public's interest in safe, fair, and reliable service.[385] Such an environment was hardly propitious for potential challengers to dominant incumbents.

Restricted access to finance was a final significant handicap for those minded to challenge market leaders in the 1950s and 1960s. *Business Week* pointed out in 1958 "(t)he need for risk capital has been stressed over and over again in the postwar decade."[386] Nevertheless, those seeking financial backing to take on incumbents were usually not well situated. With first movers typically having fortified their position through extensive investments in production, marketing, distribution, and managerial hierarchies, substantial outlays were needed to catch up.[387] This often was difficult, if not impossible, to orchestrate. John Kenneth Galbraith made the point in 1956 when he explained "the process by which the typical industry passes from the hands of the many to the few" partly on the basis of "a passive but highly effective handicap on the latecomer. In this race the horse with the poorest record, or no record, must carry the greatest weight. Capital must be found in spite of the fact that there are other firms that are a better prospect for the investor."[388] A 1963 study of America's "managed economy" observed similarly "(n)o one—except possibly (billionaire) J. Paul Getty of Texas—is economically free to enter into competition with the dominant giants of American manufacturing."[389]

A 1959 guide to the American financial system pointed out "(t)he most obvious way to raise money is to walk into a bank and borrow it." [390] Commercial banks, however, were conservative allocators of capital during the heyday of managerial capitalism, so this was not an ideal way forward. As economist Joseph Stiglitz subsequently said of the banking industry of the time, "(b)ankers didn't like scandals and bad loans, and so the banking sector provided an important check on US corporate activity."[391] Challenges to incumbents dominating their market niche were one casualty.

It was hardly surprising that caution was a byword for mid-twentieth-century banks. Widespread bank failures occurring during the Depression remained within living memory, and the regulatory regime in place correspondingly prioritized risk reduction and banking stability.[392] The impact on banking culture was profound. A 1958 analysis of bank recruitment

---

[384] WELLS, *supra* note 185, at 43-44; Vietor, *supra* note 382, at 986. *Cf.* REICH, *supra* note 6, at 24 (15 percent).

[385] REICH, *supra* note 6, at 25; Vietor, *supra* note 382, at 987. Competition, however, was not entirely absent in regulated sectors—Galambos, *supra* note 376, at 953.

[386] *Risk Capital Plays It Safer*, BUS. WK., May 17, 1958, 143.

[387] CHANDLER, *supra* note 56, at 35; PORTER, *supra* note 381, at 9, 15.

[388] GALBRAITH, *supra* note 10, at 46–47.

[389] MICHAEL D. REAGAN, THE MANAGED ECONOMY 6 (1963).

[390] MARTIN MAYER, WALL STREET: THE INSIDE STORY OF AMERICAN FINANCE 42 (1959).

[391] JOSEPH STIGLITZ, THE ROARING NINETIES: A NEW HISTORY OF THE WORLD'S MOST PROSPEROUS DECADE 140 (2003).

[392] Brian R. Cheffins, *The Corporate Governance Movement, Banks and the Financial Crisis*, 16 THEORETICAL INQ. L. 1, 19–21 (2015).

practices observed "(i)n contrast to most commercial enterprises which function in a competitive environment, a bank is an institution characterized by dignity and conservatism. There is relatively little pressure in a bank, which partakes of some of the qualities of a juridical or governing body."[393]

Commercial banks, with their conservative attitudes, tended to be inhospitable to smaller companies seeking significant financial backing.[394] *Business Week* said in 1958 "(c)ommercial banks might extend loans—at stiff rates—but they aren't set up to provide permanent capital—and that is just what most little companies need."[395] Or as the 1959 guide to the American financial system said, banks "are certainly not supposed to risk their money on anything the least bit chancy. . . . A man who can raise a million dollars in bank loans is wasting his time; he should be producing movies."[396] The *New York Times* observed in 1961 that for banks and their cousins, savings and loan associations, it was "not a period of pronounced innovation."[397]

In the 1950s and 1960s alternatives to bank finance were viable only in limited circumstances. High taxes on income and wealth introduced during the New Deal and World War II badly hamstrung the private capitalists who traditionally were the principal providers of risk capital for fledgling business ventures.[398] It was theoretically possible to borrow from insurance companies, but according to the 1959 guide to the American financial system "getting money out of them is like pulling teeth out of an enraged water buffalo."[399] Issuing commercial paper—essentially short-term corporate IOUs—was a popular way to raise working capital in the managerial capitalism era, but this option was only available to a select group of companies with the highest credit standing.[400] Similarly, the bond market was not a promising option for companies lacking a strong track record, with nearly 95 percent of bonds issued between the mid-1940s and mid-1960s being rated as investment grade.[401]

Theoretically tapping venture capital funds set up explicitly to raise capital to deploy in early-round financings for fledgling enterprises could have been a promising way forward for those seeking to challenge incumbents. *Forbes* said in 1970 that "by backing new ideas and entrepreneurial people, venture capital is playing a vital role in nourishing American industry," citing examples such as Teledyne, which had evolved into a major conglomerate, and

---

[393] Robert N. McMurray, *Recruitment, Dependency and Morale in the Banking Industry*, 3 ADMIN. SCI. Q. 87, 88 (1958).

[394] *Lending Problem*, BUS. WK., July 30, 1960, 114.

[395] *Risk Capital, supra* note 386, at 145.

[396] MAYER, *supra* note 390, at 42.

[397] *Private Financial Institutions*, NY TIMES, June 25, 1961, MC9.

[398] *Id.*; Walter Sulzbach, *Decline of Equity Financing Revolutionizes Society*, BARRON'S, Mar. 20, 1950, 9; Philip Hamson, *Big Tax Burden Erodes Supply of Risk Funds*, CHI. TRIB., Sept. 22, 1952, C5; *Big Government v. Little Business*, LA TIMES, Aug. 14, 1952, A4; William Clark, *High Taxes Choke Off Venture Capital: Kerr*, CHI. TRIB., Nov. 9, 1958, B11.

[399] MAYER, *supra* note 390, at 42.

[400] Lee Silberman, *Run for Their Money*, BARRON'S, July 25, 1966, 3; *More Companies Borrow Direct*, BUS. WK., May 18, 1968, 80.

[401] THOMAS R. ATKINSON, TRENDS IN CORPORATE BOND QUALITY 50–52 (1967); Richard Sylla, *A Historical Primer on the Business of Credit Ratings*, World Bank Working Paper, available at http://www.etcases.com/media/clnews/1422509293717634043.pdf 17-18 (2001) (accessed Feb. 12, 2018).

Digital Equipment Corp., a vendor of computer systems.[402] Despite venture capital's theoretical importance, however, it only had a minor impact on entrepreneurial activity as managerial capitalism flourished.[403] American Research & Development (ARD), set up in 1946, was the first investment vehicle launched with a mandate to furnish capital to fledgling enterprises.[404] It proved to be very choosy, having provided funding by the mid-1960s to only 80 or so ventures despite having considered thousands.[405] ARD's closest rivals were in serious trouble with the Securities and Exchange Commission as the 1960s ended.[406] New entrants to the sector were simultaneously learning through experience that venture capital investing was not a quick and easy way to get rich.[407]

Investment bank conservatism further restricted access to capital for potential challengers to dominant firms. In the opening decades of the twentieth century, investment bankers would engage with some regularity in "merchant banking" and take investment positions in client ventures.[408] Following the Depression, however, working out of a "sleepy, private" Wall Street,[409] investment banks largely eschewed such strategies.[410] Investment banks focused instead on their brokerage operations, where fixed commissions provided a low-risk revenue stream,[411] and the underwriting of securities.[412] Investment banks would buy securities on their own account as part of their activities as underwriters or as market makers for clients but would exit promptly if at all possible.[413]

Investment bankers cited a desire to avoid potential conflicts of interest to explain their aversion to engaging in merchant banking, saying that if they were putting together their own deal they would struggle to provide objective advice to clients.[414] Investment banks were also reluctant to tie up funds on a long-term basis because ready access to cash was essential for the smooth operation of their underwriting and broking activities and because most were

---

402 *Has the Bear Market Killed Venture Capital?*, FORBES, June 15, 1970, 28.

403 Geoffrey Jones & R. Daniel Wadhawani, *Entrepreneurship*, *in* OXFORD HANDBOOK OF BUSINESS HISTORY 501, 519 (Geoffrey Jones & Jonathan Zeitlin eds., 2008) (offering this verdict for venture capital generally, acknowledging the United States as a partial exception).

404 *Research Venture Gets SEC Blessing*, NY TIMES, Aug. 9, 1946, 31; Paul Heffernan, *Novel Enterprise for Venture Capital Winning Institutional Investment Backing*, NY TIMES, May 1, 1949, F1.

405 J. Richard Elliott, *Capital for Creative Men*, BARRON'S, May 10, 1965, 45.

406 *A Very Special Affair*, FORBES, Oct. 15, 1969, 42.

407 *No Get-Rich-Quick Scheme*, BARRON'S, Feb. 12, 1973, 7.

408 Fred R. Bleakley, *Wall St.'s Merchant Bankers*, NY TIMES, Nov. 19, 1984, D1; David A. Vise, *Investment Bankers Throw Own Money into the Ring*, WASH. POST, Dec. 30, 1984, F1.

409 ROBERT TEITELMAN, BLOODSPORT: WHEN RUTHLESS DEALMAKERS, SHREWD IDEOLOGUES, AND BRAWLING LAWYERS TOPPLED THE CORPORATE ESTABLISHMENT 44 (2016).

410 Bleakley, *supra* note 408; Vise, *supra* note 408.

411 Arthur E. Wilmarth, *The Transformation of the US Financial Services Industry, 1975–2000: Competition, Consolidation, and Increased Risks*, [2002] UNIV. ILL. L. REV. 217, 408.

412 As of 1966, almost 62 percent of securities firms' revenues came from brokerage commissions and 7 percent resulted from underwriting—Samuel L. Hayes, *The Transformation of Investment Banking*, HARV. BUS. REV., Jan./Feb. 1979, 153.

413 Vise, *supra* note 408; JOSEPH WECHSBERG, THE MERCHANT BANKERS 225 (1966) (describing the activities of Lehman Brothers).

414 Vise, *supra* note 408.

partnerships ill-suited to raising large amounts of permanent capital.[415] Becoming a publicly traded corporation was unrealistic because of NYSE rules that imposed stringent restrictions on eligibility for ownership of interests in member brokerage firms.[416]

The activities of Lazard Frères & Co. in the 1950s and 1960s indicated both that it was theoretically possible for investment banks to back firms that could shake up an industry and that a partnership structure was poorly suited for such activities. The firm was led by financier André Meyer, who, by arranging for direct participation in various deals, generated a fortune for himself and made Lazard Frères partners rich.[417] A major Lazard Frères venture involved Avis rental cars, with the investment bank acquiring majority ownership in the early 1960s.[418] Having replaced shaky short-term financing from "15 nervous banks"[419] Avis was soon pushing industry leader Hertz hard with a much publicized "We're Number Two. We Try Harder" advertising campaign.[420] Avis, however, was destined to be a rarity. Practically, Lazard Frères could only rely on accounts of partners representing accrued earnings to finance deals, meaning that throughout the 1960s the firm was financially incapable of ranging far and wide as a merchant banking operation.[421]

Given the general reluctance of investment banks to invest directly in business enterprises during the managerial capitalism era, firms turning to investment bankers to prepare to challenge entrenched incumbents most likely would have restricted themselves to relying on underwriting services as part of a move to the stock market. The initial public offering (IPO), however, constituted only episodically a meaningful platform for companies seeking to bolster their competitive credentials. Despite Hewlett-Packard's 1957 IPO,[422] the 1940s and 1950s were largely a write-off for moves to the stock market. In 1969, which would have been too late for a challenger to go public as part of a plan to displace an incumbent during the heyday of managerial capitalism, there were more IPOs (683) than there were in the 1940s and 1950s combined (447).[423]

As the 1960s began, there was a surge in the number of companies going public, with new issue prices soaring and everyone seeming to make money.[424] The average number of IPOs carried out annually averaged nearly 260 between 1960 and 1962, as compared with 56 per year between 1963 and 1966.[425] The new issue fever of the early 1960s was not a promising departure point, however, for firms seeking to mount a serious challenge to industry leaders.

---

[415] *Id.*; Arnold W. Sametz et al., *Securities Activities of Commercial Banks: An Evaluation of Current Developments and Regulatory Issues*, 2 J. Comparative Corp. L. & Sec. Reg. 155, 162 (1979).

[416] *Will "The Herd" Go Public?*, Forbes, Sept. 1, 1963, 24.

[417] Vise, *supra* note 408.

[418] Cary Reich, Financier: The Biography of André Meyer—A Story of Money, Power, and the Reshaping of American Business 107–13 (1983).

[419] *Townsend of Avis*, Forbes, May 1, 1963, 29.

[420] Reich, *supra* note 418, at 113–20.

[421] *Id.* at 189–90, 224–25.

[422] *Supra* note 367 and accompanying text.

[423] Cheffins, Bank & Wells, *supra* note 151, 602–03; Paul A. Gompers & Josh Lerner, *The Really Long-Run Performance of Initial Public Offerings: The Pre-NASDAQ Evidence*, 58 J. Fin. 1355, 1360 (2003).

[424] Robert Sobel, NYSE: A History of the New York Stock Exchange 1935–1975 264 (1975).

[425] Gompers & Lerner, *supra* note 423, at 1360.

The IPO wave ended abruptly in 1962 due to falling share prices.[426] Within a few years a large proportion of the companies that had issued stock to the public in the midst of the new issue fever had "disappeared from the market altogether or (were) trading at a fraction of the price they (had) commanded."[427]

While restricted access to finance was a final major handicap to those minded to challenge market leaders, difficulties associated with raising capital could simultaneously have been an independent, meaningful check on public company executives. Ambitious management teams with grand plans for growing the businesses they run will require funding to launch new ventures or carry out acquisitions. If access to capital is tight, otherwise freewheeling executives will have to modify, postpone, or even abandon their schemes.

While restricted access to capital can be a meaningful hindrance for public company executives, for big public companies in the 1950s and 1960s the effect would have been modest in practice. With corporations during this era, "the largest among them (were) awash in profits," given their market power and the buoyant economy.[428] Management was unlikely to feel pressure to increase payouts to shareholders because the diffuse retail investors who dominated share ownership were ill-positioned to lobby for this to occur and because the repurchasing of shares, a convenient means of distributing cash to stockholders, was a rarity until the 1980s.[429] Correspondingly, throughout the 1950s and much of the 1960s retained earnings in the corporate sector were robust by historical standards, and concomitantly reliance on debt was modest.[430]

Numerous academics analyzing the managerial capitalism era retrospectively have taken the view that substantial reliance on internal finance enhanced managerial discretion in large companies by insulating executives from the discipline capital markets can impose.[431] This view was widely held as well in the 1950s and 1960s,[432] including by Berle and Drucker.[433] Fredrick Lewis Allen, editor of *Harper's* magazine, said in 1952 of the big corporation in the mid-twentieth century it was "not nearly so dependent upon the purveyors of money . . . as it used to be" and "nobody in Wall Street is the successful corporation head's master" because such firms were largely self-financing.[434] In 1963, the *Wall Street Journal* indicated that General Motors and many other companies were benefitting handsomely "from a high

---

[426] *New Issues Reviving—But with a Difference*, Bus. Wk., Apr. 23, 1966, 120. See also *New Issues Pour into Weak Market*, LA Times, Dec. 21, 1969, J1.

[427] *New Issues Reviving*, *supra* note 426.

[428] *Supra* notes 185–87, 354–58, 364–66 and accompanying text; Mizruchi, *supra* note 260, at 10.

[429] Chapter 4, notes 306–07 and related discussion.

[430] Mary O'Sullivan, Contests for Corporate Control: Corporate Governance and Economic Performance in the United States and Germany 70 (2000) (table 3.1); Linda Brewster Stearns, *Capital Market Effects on External Control of Corporations*, 15 Theory Soc'y. 47, 54–56 (1986).

[431] See, for example, Wells, *supra* note 6, 317–18; Calomiris & Ramirez, *supra* note 17, at 157–59; Whitman, *supra* note 270, at 6; Lawrence E. Mitchell & Dalia T. Mitchell, *The Financial Determinants of American Corporate Governance: A Brief History* in Corporate Governance: A Synthesis of Theory, Research, and Practice 19, 27–28 (H. Kent Baker & Ronald Anderson eds., 2010).

[432] Mizruchi, *supra* note 260, at 111.

[433] Berle, *supra* note 101, at 37–40; Peter Drucker, *The New Society: Revolution by Mass Production*, Harper's, Sept. 1949, 21, cited and quoted by Davis, *supra* note 5, at 73.

[434] Allen, *supra* note 1, at 237, 238.

level of internally generated capital" that had made "many companies much less dependent on outside sources," and illustrated the point by citing a joke making the rounds in Detroit that GM was saving up to buy the federal government.[435] John Kenneth Galbraith argued in 1967 "(f)ew other developments can have more fundamentally altered the character of capitalism" than the ability of large firms to rely on oligopolistic profits to escape dependence on financial institutions.[436]

Harvard economist John Lintner, focusing on data from the 1920s through to 1955, reported in a 1959 paper that sources of finance for large firms had not changed markedly in recent years, implying continued dependence on capital markets.[437] For many large companies, though, internal funds were already the dominant source of funding by the late 1920s.[438] As a result, there was limited scope for change in favor of internal finance following World War II.[439] The upshot was that those running large public companies during the zenith of managerial capitalism would have only sporadically stepped away from what they were planning due to concerns about raising funds externally. In contrast, restricted access to capital likely was a major stumbling block for those contemplating challenging these big public firms.

Unions

The various potential internal and external constraints on public company executives identified thus far each operated subject to important limitations in the 1950s and 1960s. Further analysis, therefore, is necessary to explain why public company executives with substantial discretion available to them exercised "their powers in a manner which was moderate and acceptable."[440] Two additional external constraints, unions and regulation (including the prospect of new regulation), were crucial.

Rick Wartzman, in a 2017 study of labor relations from the early twentieth century through to the present day, says of the 1950s, "(s)ome employers played nice; others were nasty. But because of their ability to act collectively . . . workers were able to counterbalance the inherent strength of corporate America."[441] John Kenneth Galbraith was the most prominent advocate of this point of view at the time. He argued in his 1952 book *American Capitalism* that with large companies possessing considerable market power the discipline competition from rivals imposed on executives was diminished but said that there were other sources of countervailing power helping to keep executives in check.[442] He identified regulation as one, specifically mentioning antitrust law.[443] He also cited organized labor. Galbraith noted that the strongest unions had tended to emerge in markets served by large firms because for

---

[435] *Affluent Companies: Build-Up of Cash Makes Firms Less Dependent on Banks, Stock Issues*, WALL ST. J., Sept. 9, 1963, 1.

[436] GALBRAITH, *supra* note 208, 92–93. See also DOW VOTAW, MODERN CORPORATIONS 105 (1965).

[437] John Lintner, *The Financing of Corporations*, *in* THE CORPORATION, *supra* note 87, at 166.

[438] Berle, *supra* note 56, at 25; O'SULLIVAN, *supra* note 430, at 78–79.

[439] MIZRUCHI, *supra* note 260, at 117.

[440] *Supra* note 199 and related discussion.

[441] WARTZMAN, *supra* note 245, at 82.

[442] GALBRAITH, *supra* note 10, at 125.

[443] *Id.* at 150, 155, 159.

employees the need for a counterweight was greater with powerful businesses and because a union, if successful, "could share in the fruits of the corporation's market power."[444]

Various managerial capitalism era commentators specifically endorsed Galbraith's views on organized labor.[445] Adolf Berle was one. Having characterized union leaders in 1967 as "(a) mong the most spectacular power-holders in the mid-twentieth century United States," he cited Galbraith when arguing that managers tended to accede to union demands because powerful corporations could readily pass the additional costs along to the consumer.[446] Galbraith's argument that unions were a meaningful source of countervailing power with respect to large companies during the mid-twentieth century gained adherents subsequently as well.[447]

Even when Galbraith was not cited specifically, it was standard in the 1950s and 1960s to characterize unions as a significant check on corporate executives. In 1952 Fredrick Lewis Allen argued "(m)anagement is severely limited . . . by the power of labor unions."[448] Harvard law professor Abram Chayes claimed in 1959 that "(u)nion leaders, representing the workers' constituency, have used these lawmaking (collective bargaining) sessions to harness and regularize corporate power in significant respects."[449] The *New York Times* said the same year that among executives there was an "oppressive sense that management has abdicated so many of its traditional powers that it is in danger of being of swallowed up by the monopolistic force of unionism."[450] The 1965 study of institutional investors that characterized them as silent partners cited the fact that unions were a force to be reckoned with as one explanation for the faithful stewardship the vast majority of post–World War II executives had demonstrated.[451]

Given the weakness of unions in the private sector presently—union density (the proportion of workers who are unionized) is under 11 percent[452]—it scarcely seems plausible that organized labor could be a major check on executives of public companies. The circumstances were quite different, however, during the middle decades of the twentieth century. Between the mid-1930s and the mid-1940s union power grew substantially, bolstered by the enactment of federal legislation that put unions on a sound organizational footing and by a dramatic increase in union membership.[453] The public also was favorably disposed toward unions throughout the 1950s and 1960s.[454] Opposing the right to strike was even said "to

---

444 *Id.* at 129.

445 Reagan, *supra* note 389, at 145; David Finn, The Corporate Oligarch 43–44 (1969).

446 Berle, *supra* note 114, at 223, 230.

447 Mizruchi & Kimeldorf, *supra* note 5, 215–16; Smith & Dyer, *supra* note 354, at 50; Thomas A. Kochan, *The American Corporation as an Employer: Past, Present, and Future Possibilities, in* American Corporation, *supra* note 17, at 242, 244.

448 Allen, *supra* note 1, at 239.

449 Abram Chayes, *The Modern Corporation and the Rule of Law, in* The Corporation, *supra* note 87, at 25, 42.

450 A.H. Raskin, *Deep Shadow over Our Factories*, NY Times, Nov. 29, 1959, Sunday Magazine, 20.

451 Baum & Stiles, *supra* note 222, at 7.

452 Chapter 7, note 319 and related discussion.

453 Mizruchi, *supra* note 260, at 81–82, 87–88; Smith & Dyer, *supra* note 354, at 49–50; Mark Blyth, Great Transformations: Economic Ideas and Institutional Change in the Twentieth Century 84 (2002).

454 Michael Goldfield, The Decline of Organized Labor in the United States 34–35 (1987).

risk the appearance of advocating slavery."[455] Big corporations that had begun engaging in collective bargaining correspondingly shied away from trying to drive out organized labor and accepted the legitimacy of trade unions.[456] In turn, mid-twentieth century executives potentially had to bear organized labor in mind to an extent most of their present-day counterparts would have difficulty contemplating.

Subject to laws regulating the employment relationship and the terms set down in individual employment contracts, executives in US companies are empowered to set wage rates, choose the location of plants, decide what to produce, determine the size of the workforce, generate work assignments, and engage in the promotion and demotion of employees.[457] With unionized companies, collective bargaining and arbitration decisions typically restrict managerial discretion in these areas and various others, which in turn can impinge on the ability of companies to respond effectively when market conditions change.[458] By the late 1950s employers were increasingly thinking "industry ha(d) gone too far in 'coddling' unions," resulting in "a straightjacket of union rules [that] saddles them with useless workers and wasteful work practices."[459] The most serious strikes in the 1950s and 1960s involved union efforts to protect members' jobs against the effects of automation.[460]

While unions had countervailing power, the influence of organized labor operated "within a circumscribed scope of affairs and where unions exist."[461] As for the "scope of affairs," key aspects of managerial discretion remained unaffected by union power. Alfred Chandler said unions

> directly affected only one set of management decisions—those made by middle managers relating to wages, hiring, firing and conditions of work. Such decisions had only an indirect impact on the central ones that coordinated current flows and allocated resources for the future.[462]

With the qualification about where unions existed, in the 1950s and 1960s union members never made up a majority of the workforce. Instead, union density peaked at 35 percent in 1954 and declined steadily to 27 percent by 1970.[463] The impact of collective bargaining may have been greater than these figures suggest because the number of employees affected can

---

[455] FRANCIS X. SUTTON ET AL., THE AMERICAN BUSINESS CREED 118 (1956). See also ALLEN, *supra* note 1, at 256 ("the right to strike remains one of the fundamental liberties of industrial society").

[456] KOTZ, *supra* note 204, at 26, 53, 58.

[457] GEORGE A. STEINER, BUSINESS AND SOCIETY 499 (1971); MARK A. ROTHSTEIN ET AL., EMPLOYMENT LAW 13, 26–27, 288–89 (1994).

[458] STEINER, *supra* note 457, at 500.

[459] Raskin, *supra* note 450.

[460] A.H. Raskin, *Automation Has Made Strikes Senseless*, NY TIMES, Oct. 31, 1965, Sunday Magazine, 45; George Strauss, *Union Bargaining Strength: Goliath or Paper Tiger?*, 350 ANNALS AMER. ACAD. POL. SOCIAL SCI., 86, 90 (1963).

[461] REAGAN, *supra* note 389, at 145.

[462] CHANDLER, *supra* note 12, at 493.

[463] GOLDFIELD, *supra* note 454, at 10 (providing annual statistics, 1930–1978). These union density figures use non-agricultural workers as the denominator and include unionized government workers as well as private sector workers.

exceed the number of union members.[464] Nevertheless, the fact that only a declining minority of the workforce was unionized inevitably would have muted the influence organized labor had on mid-twentieth century public company management. Despite the caveats, many executives running large firms would have thought of unions as a potent check on their managerial prerogatives.

Regulation

In 1952 Fredrick Lewis Allen suggested "the big and successful corporation" was "severely circumscribed by government."[465] Regulation indeed was a meaningful constraint for public company executives throughout the 1950s and 1960s. Most obviously, statutory prohibitions and decisions of government officials administering regulatory schemes would have impinged upon managerial discretion. In addition, concerns that additional unwelcome state intervention could be forthcoming provided executives with incentives to stay on the straight and narrow.

During the heyday of managerial capitalism legislative measures and administrative missives that impinged upon public company executives most often targeted single industries. "Cross-industry" regulation was not extensive throughout the 1950s and most of the 1960s.[466] The situation was evolving as the 1960s drew to a close with momentum growing in favor of reforms intended to protect consumers and the environment.[467] Regulatory activity of this nature was stepped up considerably in the 1970s.[468]

In the 1950s and 1960s single industry regulators typically pursued policies that were designed to foster orderly growth along familiar, predictable lines.[469] Regulation of this sort could mute competition from rivals and make life easier for incumbents.[470] The emphasis on stability also acted, however, as a check on those running companies already well established in the industries affected. Executives in the regulated industries tended to become increasingly averse to risk,[471] which would have discouraged freewheeling managerial gambles that could end up as scandals if things went awry.

Commercial banking provides an instructive, if somewhat extreme, example of how regulation designed to foster orderliness discouraged managerial risk-taking during the middle decades of the twentieth century. By virtue of the Banking Act of 1933,[472] supplemented by the Bank Holding Company Act of 1956[473] and other measures, the commercial banking industry was one of the most heavily regulated sectors of the US economy.[474] Commercial

[464] KOTZ, *supra* note 204, at 27.

[465] ALLEN, *supra* note 1, at 239.

[466] GALAMBOS & PRATT, *supra* note 14, at 153.

[467] BENJAMIN C. WATERHOUSE, THE LAND OF ENTERPRISE: A BUSINESS HISTORY OF THE UNITED STATES 182–88 (2017).

[468] Chapter 3, notes 332–33, 335 and related discussion; Vietor, *supra* note 382, at 88–89.

[469] GALAMBOS & PRATT, *supra* note 14, at 143.

[470] *Supra* note 385 and related discussion.

[471] GALAMBOS & PRATT, *supra* note 14, at 143.

[472] Pub. L. No. 73–66, 48 Stat. 162.

[473] Pub. L. No. 84–511, 70 Stat. 134.

[474] Ross N. Dickens & George Philippatos, *The Impact of Market Contestability on the Systematic Risk of US Bank Stocks*, 4 APP. FIN. ECON. 315, 315 (1994).

banking was also more closely scrutinized than would be the case in either the opening or closing decades of the twentieth century.[475]

A 1967 analysis of the banking industry indicated "(t)he most fundamental business decisions in banking—whether and where to open an office for business, whether to close it, what assets to acquire—are made for the firm by its regulators, except with respect to detail."[476] Banks were afforded little scope to carry out business activities unrelated to banking, meaning in this context taking deposits and making loans.[477] At the same time, though, obvious potential competitors, primarily investment banks, were precluded from engaging in core aspects of banking.[478] Federal and state law also ensured banking remained geographically fragmented, which served to protect banks from competition within their own industry.[479] Moore, in his 1964 text on management, contrasted bank executives, characterized as "elevator operators, whose decisions are closely contained," with executives in other industries who were like ship captains because "they can turn in any direction and go fast and slow."[480]

Managerial capitalism era bank executives fit in well with the tight regulatory matrix under which their banks were operating. Dynamic, aggressive leadership was conspicuous by its absence with safety-first managers being in charge.[481] The 1967 analysis of banking made the point by suggesting the sector "would quickly frustrate a Schumpeterian entrepreneur,"[482] a key agent of change in what economist Joseph Schumpeter famously described as the process of creative destruction that can occur in an industry due to the operation of market forces.[483] The result was "boring" banking, characterized by stable profits and a very low failure rate by historical standards.[484]

While regulation in the 1950s and 1960s tended to be industry specific rather than operating on a cross-industry basis, there were notable exceptions. For instance, the federal securities laws introduced in the mid-1930s[485] were applicable generally to corporations with publicly traded securities. Concerns were expressed in the 1950s and the early 1960s that the SEC was too modestly resourced to administer federal securities law effectively.[486] The general feeling, though, was that the SEC helped to keep "the corporate plutocracy under

---

[475] Thomas Phillipon & Ariell Resheff, *Wages and Human Capital in the US Financial Industry, 1909–2006*, 127 Q.J. ECON. 1551, 1578, 1580 (2010).

[476] A. Dale Tussing, *The Case for Bank Failure*, 10 J.L. ECON. 129, 130 (1967).

[477] Helen A. Garten, *Regulatory Growing Pains: A Perspective on Bank Regulation in a Deregulatory Age*, 57 FORDHAM L. REV. 501, 509–10 (1989); Michael Klausner, *An Economic Analysis of Bank Regulatory Reform: The Financial Institutions Safety and Consumer Choice Act 1991*, 69 WASH. U. L.Q. 695, 696, 698–703 (1991).

[478] Garten, *supra* note 477, at 516–17; Klausner, *supra* note 477, at 695.

[479] Cheffins, *supra* note 392, at 20.

[480] MOORE, *supra* note 102, at 31–32.

[481] Tussing, *supra* note 476, at 130–31; Anthony G. Chase, *The Emerging Financial Conglomerate: Liberalization of the Bank Holding Company Act*, 60 GEO. L.J. 1224, 1226 (1972).

[482] Tussing, *supra* note 476, at 131.

[483] JOSEPH SCHUMPETER, CAPITALISM, SOCIALISM AND DEMOCRACY (1942).

[484] Cheffins, *supra* note 392, at 20–21.

[485] *Supra* notes 152–153 and related discussion.

[486] T.A. WISE AND THE EDITORS OF FORTUNE, *supra* note 213, at 184–85; *Protection for Investors*, TIME, July 16, 1956, 84.

control through rules and regulations."[487] Compliance with disclosure rules federal securities law imposed was seen as "a most valuable discipline"[488] on the potentially wayward executive because "(h)e was no longer a secret deal-maker"[489] and "a goldfish has got to be good."[490]

Antitrust law, which targets anticompetitive business activity and abuses of market power, was another form of "cross-industry" regulation affecting executives of large firms during managerial capitalism's heyday.[491] Some contemporaries maintained that antitrust law was largely an afterthought, citing the modest resources made available to antitrust enforcers given the size of the economy and the prevalence of oligopolistic market structures in key industries.[492] Galbraith, for instance, acknowledged that antitrust enforcement curbed "on occasion, the rapacity of individuals and firms who survive in the entrepreneurial mode," but said absent special circumstances "to the large firm the antitrust laws are harmless."[493]

Executives were not as blasé about antitrust as Galbraith suggested. The *Hartford Courant* indicated in a 1949 editorial that the Department of Justice had "big business trembling in its boots" with a stepping up of the tempo of antitrust cases.[494] The *Washington Post* observed in 1957 "(t)he monopoly and antitrust problem continue to occupy a center ring in the political and business circus."[495] It is difficult to gauge with precision the impact of antitrust on the conduct of business in the 1950s and 1960s.[496] Corporate executives nevertheless reputedly did take care not to violate antitrust laws,[497] which imposed a check on managerial decision-making.

Mergers were an area of particular concern for public company management. In 1957, the *Wall Street Journal* reported that "Uncle Sam's trustbusters are stepping up their drive against the specter they call 'creeping economic concentration,'" which "may mean bad news for businessmen planning mergers."[498] In the 1960s, the US Supreme Court created "a phalanx of antimerger precedent" through a series of decisions the only apparent logic of which, according to a dissenting justice, was that the government always won.[499] The *New York Times*, reporting on these trends in 1964, said "(i)t is clear that any executive of a large business has plenty to think about."[500] *Time* indicated the same year that "corporate giants" had been put "on notice that most future growth must come from within rather than by merger."[501]

---

487 Livingston, *supra* note 177, at 20. See also Sobel, *supra* note 50, at 328 (indicating that the work of federal securities regulators "was instrumental in keeping down excesses").

488 Mayer, *supra* note 390, at 243.

489 Finn, *supra* note 445, at 44.

490 Allen, *supra* note 1, at 240.

491 Galambos & Pratt, *supra* note 14, at 153.

492 Louis M. Kohlmeier, *Gentle Trustbusters*, Wall St. J., Mar. 7, 1967, 18; Louis M. Kohlmeier, *Nader Criticizes Antitrust Enforcement; Chance of Congressional Action Seem Slim*, Wall St. J., June 7, 1971, 6.

493 Galbraith, *supra* note 208, at 193, 194.

494 *Is Big Business Too Big?*, Hartford Courant, Sept. 23, 1949, 14.

495 Irston Barnes, *Counting Monopoly's Hydra Heads*, Wash. Post, July 7, 1957, E6.

496 *Nipping Bigness in the Bud*, Economist, Oct. 11, 1969, 45.

497 Robert Sobel, The Age of Giant Corporations: A Microeconomic History of American Business, 1914–1992, at 191 (3d ed. 1993).

498 *Antitrust Hustle*, Wall St. J., Jan. 16, 1957, 1.

499 Arthur Austin, *Antitrust Reaction to the Merger Wave: The Revolution vs. the Counterrevolution*, 66 N.C. L. Rev. 931, 931, 935 (1988); United States v. Von's Grocery Co., 384 U.S. 270, 301 (1966) (Stewart J., dissenting).

500 Anthony Lewis, *Clayton Antitrust Law 50 Years Old and Strong*, NY Times, Oct. 25, 1964, F1.

501 *New Powers for Trustbusters*, Time, July 3, 1964, 89.

Aside from fostering apprehension that contemplated transactions could fall afoul of the law, antitrust provided a lightning rod for debate on big business about which those running large companies would have been mindful. Misbehavior associated with the 1929 stock market crash and the ensuing Depression did much to discredit the business community, confirming preexisting widespread suspicions about the rapacity of large corporations and Wall Street.[502] Sustained corporate prosperity following World War II ultimately reversed much of the negative sentiment.[503] A 1969 Louis Harris poll found that 58 percent of respondents had confidence in those running major companies.[504] Nevertheless, antipathy toward big business, while largely latent, had not been vanquished. In 1962 the *New York Herald Tribune* acknowledged that "(o)n the one hand, Americans love bigness" but said "(o)n the other hand . . . an undercurrent of resentment has run against the big corporations."[505] A 1963 public opinion poll indicated 61 percent of the public feared the power of big business.[506]

Concerns about big business could be readily channeled through debates on antitrust. A 1954 *New York Times* op-ed on antitrust proceedings involving General Motors and the DuPont chemical company noted that while the benefits of large-scale production had been increasingly recognized, "(t)he conviction is still widespread that bigness is a menace."[507] The *Christian Science Monitor* said in 1955 that both the Republican and Democratic parties were part of "(a) big new surge against monopoly in Washington" with politicians being mindful "(t)he growth of giant corporations has been the source of deep and continuing social anxiety."[508] In 1963, the *Baltimore Sun* conjectured that "aggressive self-promotion" by antitrust enforcers had helped to foster "a chronic public mistrust of American business."[509]

In the 1950s and 1960s, the possibility that unease regarding big business could coalesce into potent support for highly intrusive regulation provided incentives for executives running large companies to avoid sparking an adverse public reaction, regardless of the strict legal propriety of actions contemplated. This might seem fanciful to modern observers. To the extent, however, that executives of large public companies had when managerial capitalism was flourishing an ethic of responsibility that contributed to a dearth of wayward executive behavior, concerns about an unwelcome government crackdown operated as a potent motivator.[510]

Again, those running large business enterprises during the middle decades of the twentieth century were not a "collection of saints."[511] The "nice guy cult" that pervaded instead stemmed in large measure from fears on the part of executives that they would be assailed as greedy, domineering, and grasping in the manner their forebears were in the 1930s, with attendant regulatory consequences.[512] For instance, in 1959 Adolf Berle identified "the public consensus . . . over and beyond the accepted and enacted provisions of law" as an "intangible" but

---

[502] GALAMBOS & PRATT, *supra* note 14, at 127.
[503] *Id.* at 128.
[504] PAUL K. LONGMORE, TELETHONS: SPECTACLE, DISABILITY, AND THE BUSINESS OF CHARITY 45 (2016).
[505] Andrew J. Glass, *The Bigger the Better?*, NY HERALD TRIB., Feb. 25, 1962, C1.
[506] Bert C. Goss, *Antitrust Actions—Other Side of the Coin*, BALT. SUN, Jan. 13, 1963, F24.
[507] *Big Business and the Law*, NY TIMES, Dec. 9, 1954, 32.
[508] Richard L. Strout, *Antitrust Drive Simmers*, CHRISTIAN SCI. MONITOR, Feb. 9, 1955, 6.
[509] Goss, *supra* note 506.
[510] MIZRUCHI, *supra* note 260, at 10.
[511] *Supra* note 158 and related discussion.
[512] *Broadside at Management*, BUS. WK., Feb. 20, 1960, 129.

"wholly real" limitation on the exercise of economic power.[513] According to Berle "managers of great corporations" had "a corporate conscience" due primarily to concerns about violating "the public consensus," where a breach would result in a "loss of prestige, public standing and popular esteem" and "the near-certainty of political intervention by the State."[514]

Observations by other contemporaries lend credence to the idea that fears of public opprobrium and heavy-handed intervention substantially constrained public company executives. A 1948 *Christian Science Monitor* editorial on big business said that the large corporation was a "valuable tool" but with the qualification that "when bigness lacks a social consciousness, public opinion demands that the state intervene."[515] When *Fortune* hailed in 1951 "the transformation of American capitalism" an important element was that "(o)ne of the most pressing concerns of almost every large company today is what people are going to think about it."[516] Peter Drucker said likewise in 1954 that "management should always, in every one of its policies and decisions, ask the question: what would the public reaction be if everyone in industry did that?"[517] In 1959 political scientist Norton Long observed that "(i)n a short thirty years we have passed from a corporate order whose managerial style derived from the so-called 'robber barons' . . . to the business-school trained, public-relations-conscious professional of the highly specialized complex corporate bureaucracy of today," a byproduct of which was "a thinness of skin quite uncharacteristic of the earlier race."[518]

The fact that it was not clear how public antipathy toward business might translate into government action compromised at least to some degree executive self-restraint based on public perceptions of business misconduct.[519] Nevertheless, economist Paul Samuelson argued in 1964 that with big business "constantly on the defensive because it knows it lacks political power," the pressure corporations felt could help society economize on the scarce good of altruism.[520] Certainly on the government side it was assumed that concerns about incurring the wrath of the public informed business thinking in ways that could be relied upon to achieve desired results. For instance, President Dwight Eisenhower counted heavily on corporate "statesmanship" and business community self-awareness to execute a political agenda oriented around restraint, patience, and moderation.[521] According to a 1982 study of Eisenhower's political philosophy

> the famous stag dinners to which he invited the leaders of America's great corporations were not just ritual celebrations of success but meetings at which Eisenhower

---

[513] Berle, *supra* note 84, at 90, 113.

[514] *Id.* at 90–91, 114. For additional background on Berle's views on this point, see Olivier Weinstein, *Firm, Property and Governance: From Berle and Means to the Agency Theory, and Beyond*, 2 Accting., Econ. & Law 1, 23–25 (2012).

[515] George Ericson, *Criterion of Corporate Bigness Public Interest*, Christian Sci. Monitor, Dec. 18, 1948, 15.

[516] Editors (Fortune), *supra* note 1, at 85.

[517] Drucker, *supra* note 247, at 70.

[518] Long, *supra* note 268, at 204, 205.

[519] Mason, *supra* note 4, at 8.

[520] *The Ideological Debate Dividing Businessmen*, Bus. Wk., Sept. 12, 1964, 201.

[521] Robert Griffith, *Dwight D. Eisenhower and the Corporate Commonwealth*, 87 Amer. Hist. Rev. 87, 93, 103–05 (1982).

hoped to exchange views with men whose opinions he respected and whose support was indispensable to his broader purposes. He hoped, it seems clear, that such gatherings would also stimulate business leaders to think in broad, cooperative terms and not just according to their more immediate and parochial interests.[522]

Eisenhower's successor, John Kennedy, demonstrated in a 1962 showdown with the steel industry regarding pricing the leverage the government could exercise in the absence of formal legal authority. The *Wall Street Journal* predicted in 1961 that even though the Kennedy administration lacked any legal mechanism to prevent steel companies from raising prices "the pressure of Administration censure ... would make it very difficult for the industry to hold a firm position."[523] So it proved.

The Kennedy administration, mindful of inflationary pressures, was pleased when in March 1962 a potentially debilitating steel industry strike was averted without a wage increase.[524] The following month, however, Kennedy was furious when the chief executive of United States Steel, the industry leader, visited the White House to tell the president that the company planned to raise steel prices 3.5 percent. The next day a number of other companies announced their intention to do the same. According to Kennedy administration insider Arthur Schlesinger the president "was coldly determined to mobilize all of the resources of public pressure and private suasion to force steel to rescind the increase."[525] Kennedy vilified publicly the steel companies that had raised prices. Administration officials quickly announced plans to launch an investigation into price-fixing in the steel industry and to shift defense purchases to companies that had not followed the lead of US Steel. The steel companies that had announced they intended to increase prices promptly retreated.

Berle, likely feeling that his 1959 prediction of political intervention in the event of a violation of the public consensus had been vindicated, argued in a *New York Times* op-ed that Kennedy's challenge to the steel industry demonstrated the power of big business operated subject to "an unwritten 'social contract'" under which the government could "intervene when economic power in private hands threatens the economic community of the United States."[526] The business press, on the other hand, was generally critical of Kennedy. *Barron's* argued that while the Kennedy administration might claim a victory it was "a triumph which will cost the nation dear."[527] *Forbes* editorialized that the administration had engaged in a "frightening demonstration of how the Government can use its might to win an argument

[522] *Id.* at 103–04.

[523] John A. Grimes, *Anti-business Aura*, WALL ST. J., Aug. 17, 1961, 12.

[524] This summary draws upon Joseph T. Salerno, *From Kennedy's "New Economics" to Nixon's "New Economic Policy": Monetary Inflation and the March of Economic Fascism*, *in* REASSESSING THE PRESIDENCY: THE RISE OF THE EXECUTIVE STATE AND THE DECLINE OF FREEDOM 587, 634–38 (John V. Denson ed., 2001); B. MARK SMITH, TOWARD RATIONAL EXUBERANCE: THE EVOLUTION OF THE MODERN STOCK MARKET 181–84 (2001).

[525] Salerno, *supra* note 524, at 635.

[526] Adolf A. Berle, *Unwritten Constitution for Our Economy*, NY TIMES, Apr. 29, 1962, 208.

[527] *The Wrong War*, BARRON'S, Apr. 16, 1962, 16.

regardless of the right or the rights involved."[528] *Business Week* quoted the chief executive of a major machinery company as saying the damage was "irreparable"[529] and predicted that "industry-government relations (would) not be the same for some time."[530]

In fact, the steel price controversy did not alter fundamentally business-government relations, with business leaders continuing to be willing to listen and respond voluntarily in the absence of explicit governmental regulatory authority. Within months of the showdown, the business community was giving Kennedy a fair hearing on issues of common interest, and he had taken on board "the importance of mutual understanding between government officials and businessmen."[531] Corporate willingness to accede to political priorities in the absence of a firm regulatory foundation would soon be evident again under Kennedy's successor, Lyndon Johnson.

In 1966 Johnson issued an appeal to large companies to restrict their capital spending to help to fight inflation. No corporation or corporate executive openly defied the request.[532] The White House even received a "sheaf of letters" from "a blue-ribbon assembly of 150 company presidents and board chairm(e)n" indicating their willingness to help out.[533] Fear of the alternatives, in the form of higher taxes or wage-and-price controls, underpinned the "remarkable" cooperation.[534] Businessmen, no doubt mindful of the steel price showdown, had also "evidently learned the painful lesson that in a confrontation with the White House they are likely to emerge second best."[535] Capital spending by companies did increase subsequently, though Johnson administration officials argued "things would have been 'even worse' without the presidential request."[536] The upshot is that even in the absence of explicit regulation the possibility of public disapproval and unwelcome additional governmental action was a meaningful check on public company executives from the end of World War II to the beginning of the 1970s.

* * *

As financial capitalism transitioned to managerial capitalism, dominant shareholders capable of keeping management in check became the exception to the rule in large public companies, and the meaningful Wall Street banker scrutiny to which numerous large firms had been subjected as the twentieth century opened ended. During the 1950s and 1960s neither boards nor institutional shareholders, who were gaining a foothold as key investors in public companies, substantially limited managerial discretion. Nevertheless, egregious managerial misconduct was conspicuous by its absence. External constraints played a significant role in this regard. Competitors and the market for corporate control were factors

---

528 *Big Stick and Big Steel*, FORBES, May 1, 1962, 11.

529 *What Businessmen Think about It*, BUS. WK., Apr. 21, 1962, 29.

530 *No Room For Ill Will*, BUS. WK., Apr. 21, 1962, 25.

531 *The Olive Branch for Business*, BUS. WK., May 18, 1963, 204.

532 M.J. Rossant, *How Do You Say No to LBJ?*, NY TIMES, Apr. 10, 1966, 148.

533 Hobart Rowen, *Big Business Promises the President to Cut Expansion in Inflation Fight*, WASH. POST, Apr. 15, 1966, A1.

534 Rossant, *supra* note 532; *Guiding the Nation's Reluctant Tigers*, BUS. WK., Apr. 23, 1966, 160.

535 Rossant, *supra* note 532.

536 Hobart Rowen, *Johnson Appeal Fails to Reduce Capital Outlays*, LA TIMES, June 6, 1966, B9.

that public company executives had to bear in mind but barriers to entry were substantial in many industries, and hostile takeovers were something of a rarity. Organized labor and governmental intervention (including the threat thereof) correspondingly stand out as the factors that did the most to keep executives of big companies in check.

Each of the key constraints to which executives were subject in the 1950s and 1960s were in operation in the 1970s, with some operating with greater potency. For instance, competitive pressure intensified as foreign rivals gained ground. Nevertheless, evidence of managerial misbehavior became increasingly conspicuous amidst growing criticism of big business. This would set the scene for a reconfiguration of the constraints to which executives were subject that would contribute to the transformation of the public company that the remainder of the book explores.

3 The 1970s

MANAGERIAL CAPITALISM SUSTAINED . . . BUT "SOMETHING HAPPENED"

THE 1950S AND the 1960s were the heyday of managerial capitalism. During the 1980s and 1990s, the public company moved on from the managerial capitalism era. How do the 1970s fit into the picture? In a decade characterized by economic and political turmoil, post–World War II assumptions about private enterprise and the role of government were sorely tested. Amidst the tumult, managerial capitalism was sustained, but "something happened" that meant its days were very much numbered.

We will begin this chapter by seeing that the 1970s was a managerial capitalism decade but with the caveat that changes were occurring that set the scene for a new regime as the twentieth century drew to a close. We will then consider a striking illustration of how the ground was shifting in the form of credible predictions that the public company, seemingly triumphant in the 1950s and the 1960s, was destined for extinction. After this, we will find out how concerns about American managers losing ground to foreign challengers, difficulties conglomerates encountered, and revelations of illicit payments by major US corporations put managerial capitalism squarely on the back foot. Our survey of the difficulties the public company was facing will in turn set the scene for an analysis of the efficacy of internal and constraints affecting executives in the 1970s. A key theme that will be developed in this context is that erosion of faith in government precluded substantial additional regulation of public companies in circumstances apparently congenial to state intervention.

Continuity and Change

During the 1970s, for public companies there was continuity with the 1950s and 1960s in that managerial capitalism continued to predominate. On the other hand, the 1970s provided the

The Public Company Transformed. Brian R. Cheffins.

platform for change, an "inflection point" for "the postwar industrial system."[1] As the 1970s concluded, the scene had been set in various ways for the freewheeling 1980s and 1990s. Managerial capitalism would then pass into history in decades characterized by deregulatory initiatives, veneration of the market, the prioritization of shareholder value, celebrity chief executive officers (CEOs), financial innovation, and the retreat of unions.

Among those analyzing retrospectively the nature of corporate capitalism in the 1970s, some have emphasized continuity with the 1950s and 1960s and singled out the 1980s as being when the shift away from managerialism began.[2] Indeed, it was widely assumed during the 1970s that managers operating with substantial autonomy remained the linchpin of American corporate capitalism. Harvard Business School professor John Glover observed in the introduction of a 1976 handbook for chief executives that the "typical" sizeable "modern business corporation" was "publicly held" and was theoretically governed by the board of directors but in fact was "run by managers who, altogether, hold at most only a small fraction of its ownership."[3] A 1979 analysis of the question "who controls the large corporation" concluded "(i)t appears that management is firmly in control of corporate enterprise in general."[4] The 1970s, then, was a managerial capitalism decade.

While there was managerial capitalism continuity between the 1950s and 1960s on the one hand and the 1970s on the other, the prevailing retrospective view is that, to borrow from the title of Joseph Heller's 1974 novel about troubled business executive Bob Slocum, "something happened."[5] When Alfred Chandler referred in the epilogue to his 1990 book *Scale and Scope: The Dynamics of Industrial Capitalism* to "a new era of managerial capitalism" following on from the classic version prevailing immediately after World War II, he marked out the end of the 1960s and the 1970s as the beginning of that new era.[6] Others have suggested that in the 1970s a "shifting economic and political climate started to undermine the foundations of managerialism,"[7] that "the managerial equilibrium of the 1950s and 1960s" was "palpably disrupted,"[8] and that managerial capitalism ran "into headwinds."[9]

---

[1] Rakesh Khurana, From Higher Aims to Hired Hands: The Social Transformation of American Business Schools and the Unfulfilled Promise of Management as a Profession 297 (2007).

[2] See, for example, John C. Coffee, *What Caused Enron? A Capsule Social and Economic History of the 1990s*, 89 Cornell L. Rev. 269, 272 (2004); Dalia Tsuk Mitchell, *Status Bound: The Twentieth Century Evolution of Directors' Liability*, NYU J. L. & Bus. 63, 67, n.6; Bruce Scott, Capitalism: Its Origins and Evolution as a System of Governance 515 (2011).

[3] John Desmond Glover, *The Many Roles of the Chief Executive*, Chief Executive's Handbook 3, 5–6 (John Desmond Glover & Gerald A. Simon, eds., 1976).

[4] Thomas M. Jones, *Corporate Governance: Who Controls the Large Corporation?*, 30 Hastings L.J. 1261, 1285 (1979). See also Melvin Aron Eisenberg, The Structure of the Corporation: A Legal Analysis 97 (1976) ("In many if not most (public) corporations de facto control resides with management").

[5] Joseph Heller, Something Happened (1974).

[6] Alfred D. Chandler, Scale and Scope: The Dynamics of Industrial Capitalism 606 (1990).

[7] Khurana, *supra* note 1, at 305.

[8] Frank Dobbin & Jiwook Jung, *The Misapplication of Mr. Michael Jensen: How Agency Theory Brought Down the Economy and Why It Might Again*, 30B Research Sociology Org. 29, 33 (2010).

[9] Lynn A. Stout, *On the Rise of Shareholder Primacy, Signs of Its Fall, and the Return of Managerialism (in the Closet)*, 36 Seattle U. L. Rev. 1169, 1172 (2013).

Characterizations of public company executives of the 1970s reflect the mix of continuity and change. During the 1950s and 1960s the prototypical executive was ostensibly a reserved, bureaucratically-oriented "organization man" who subordinated personal aspirations to foster the pursuit of corporate goals.[10] Some felt little had changed in the 1970s. Irving Shapiro, chief executive and chairman of DuPont, said in 1978 that "most people couldn't name five businessmen" because executives "sought anonymity in the sense that their lives consist of working hard at the office, going to the club to play a round of golf or cards, having a drink and dinner, and then returning to the briefcase full of work."[11] *Business Week* suggested in 1980 that "for the most part, today's corporate leaders are 'professional managers'—business mercenaries who ply their skills for a salary and bonus but rarely for a vision."[12] William Whyte, who coined the term "organization man" in a 1956 book on corporate executives,[13] explained in 1979 his decision not to write a sequel on the basis that there had not been sufficient change to justify the effort and suggested "(t)he hold of the organization is every bit as great as it ever was."[14]

There was change as well as continuity, however, in the executive suite. Arch Patton, an expert on managerial compensation, suggested in 1976 that "executive self-interest has replaced company loyalty to a substantial degree."[15] Psychoanalyst Michael Maccoby, drawing upon interviews with executives at a handful of very large companies, argued in 1977 that "(a)s a description of corporate reality, the other-directed organization man is too narrow and time-bound" because "(t)hose who reach the top in the seventies are more active and adventurous than the stereotype of the fifties," and labeled the new model of executive as "the corporate gamesman."[16] More tangibly, by the end of the 1970s executive pay began a "regime change" away from stagnancy in the 1950s and 1960s (at least in inflation-adjusted terms) in favor of significant growth that would accelerate in the 1980s and 1990s.[17] For instance, the corporate world's first "Millionaire Club" took form in 1977 when the total compensation of the highest paid public company CEOs exceeded $1 million a year for the first time.[18]

Chrysler's 1979 appointment of Lee Iacocca as chief executive was the most eye-catching single indicator of change in the executive suite. Iacocca, previously an executive at Ford, proved his adeptness at making a mark for himself in 1964 by using interviews and judicious leaks to ensure that he was christened "the father of the Mustang" when Ford began manufacturing the successful sports car.[19] With Chrysler, Iacocca was aware that the board of the troubled automaker was desperate to get someone as experienced as him to take up the helm and negotiated a then-largely unprecedented "front-end bonus" of $1.5 million before turning up for work.[20] Within weeks of taking up his post Iacocca organized a conference

---

10 Chapter 2, note 203 and accompanying text.

11 *Today's Executive: Private Steward and Public Servant*, HARV. BUS. REV., Mar.–Apr. 1978, 94, 98.

12 *Managers Who Are No Longer Entrepreneurs*, BUS. WK., June 30, 1980, 74.

13 WILLIAM WHYTE, THE ORGANIZATION MAN (1956).

14 *"Organization Man" Lives On, Author Says*, CHI. TRIB., June 18, 1979, D11

15 Arch Patton, *Executive Compensation: The Past, Present and Future*, FIN. EXEC., July 1976, 24, 30.

16 MICHAEL MACCOBY, THE GAMESMAN: THE NEW CORPORATE LEADERS 35, 36 (1977).

17 Chapter 2, note 200 and related discussion; Carola Frydman & Raven E. Saks, *Executive Compensation: A New View from a Long-Term Perspective, 1936–2005*, 23 REV. FIN. ST. 2099, 2101 (2010).

18 Donald B. Thompson, *Advent of 7-Figure CEO Prompts Questions*, CHI. TRIB., May 31, 1981, N1.

19 *Some Well-Plotted Success Stories*, BUS. WK., Oct. 12, 1974, 129.

20 Steven A. Bank, Brian R. Cheffins & Harwell Wells, *Executive Pay: What Worked?*, 42 J. CORP. L. 59, 98 (2016).

for leading newspaper publishers to preview Chrysler's product line for the next three years, a publicity strategy without an obvious precedent.[21] His 1984 autobiography, published on the back of a revival of Chrysler's fortunes, would sell 7 million copies.[22] Rakesh Khurana, in a 2002 study of "charismatic CEOs" who would in the 1980s and 1990s replace "the professional Organization Man who toiled in anonymity," said "the advent of this new breed of corporate leader" could be traced back to Iacocca's 1979 appointment.[23]

In Heller's novel, a key source of Bob Slocum's unhappiness is that he did not know why he was unhappy.[24] In contrast, with why "something happened" with managerial capitalism, mounting pessimism regarding the large corporation, so successful in the 1950s and 1960s, explains much. We will consider the change of mood first through the prism of credible if ultimately incorrect 1970s predictions of a gloomy future for the public company. We will then see how the post–World War II "core fissure" in public companies arising from the executives in charge having incentives to pursue their own agenda due to a lack of meaningful share ownership moved from afterthought to a source of serious concern.

Were the Public Company's Days Numbered?

During the 1950s and 1960s observers such as Adolf Berle were citing the public company as a crucial element of America's triumphant version of capitalism.[25] The mood was considerably gloomier in the 1970s. Amidst dismal share price news, various observers suggested that the public company's days may even be numbered. For instance, in August 1979 *Business Week* proclaimed by way of a cover story on the stock market "The Death of Equities."[26] The prognosis was that "the US economy probably has to regard the death of equities as a near-permanent condition—reversible some day, but not soon."[27]

The performance of the stock market was a major strike against the public company in the 1970s. Economist James Lorie argued in 1977 based on a study of share price trends extending back to 1926 "from the end of 1972 until now, we have had the great crash (of 1929) without the Great Depression."[28] *Business Week* substantiated its gloomy 1979 take on the future of the publicly traded company by noting that, adjusted for inflation, the Dow Jones Industrial Average had fallen approximately 50 percent since 1973.[29] The dismal returns

---

[21] William H. Jones, *Chrysler Team Seeks Support for Aid*, WASH. POST, Oct. 14, 1979, G1.

[22] LEE IACOCCA & WILLIAM NOVAK, IACOCCA: AN AUTOBIOGRAPHY (1984); Jerry Useem, *Tyrants, Statesmen, and Destroyers (A Brief History of the CEO)*, FORTUNE, Nov. 18, 2002, 82.

[23] RAKESH KHURANA, SEARCHING FOR A CORPORATE SAVIOR: THE IRRATIONAL QUEST FOR CHARISMATIC CEOS 71 (2002). See also Patricia Sánchez Abril, *The Evolution of Business Celebrity in American Law and Society*, 48 AMER. BUS. L.J. 177, 194 (2011).

[24] John Self, *Joseph Heller: Something Happened*, ASYLUM, Feb. 15, 2012, available at https://theasylum.wordpress.com/2012/02/15/joseph-heller-something-happened/ (accessed May 1, 2018).

[25] Chapter 2, note 262 and accompanying text

[26] *The Death of Equities*, BUS. WK., Aug. 13, 1979, 54.

[27] *Id.*

[28] Ronald L. Soble, *The Stock Market Thinks It Is 1929*, LA TIMES, Nov. 7, 1977, D10.

[29] *Death, supra* note 26.

prompted skeptical younger investors to shun the stock market, meaning there were 7 million fewer individuals owning shares in 1979 than in 1970.[30]

Declining faith in big business also ostensibly imperiled the public company. Irving Kristol, a conservative intellectual, wrote in the *Wall Street Journal* in the 1974 "(t)he large corporation looks . . . like a species of dinosaur lumbering its way to extinction," noting in so doing that "corporate executives are just about the only class of people which a television drama will feel free to cast as pure villains."[31] The television typecasting reflected a growing antipathy toward corporations. *Newsweek* suggested in 1976 in an article on "the embattled businessman" that "a kind of chronic distrust" was bursting "into overt hostility."[32]

Polling data confirmed the public's disillusionment with large corporations in the 1970s. The proportion of Americans with "a great deal of confidence" in major companies fell from 55 percent in 1966 to 30 percent in 1973 and to 16 percent in September 1974, rallied somewhat and then fell back to 18 percent in early 1979.[33] Those who believed that business tried to strike a fair balance between profits and the public interest declined from 70 percent in 1968 to 32 percent in 1972, 19 percent in 1974, and 15 percent in 1976 and 1977 before rallying modestly to 19 percent in 1979.[34] Similarly, as of 1978, 56 percent of the American public adjudged "big businessmen" to be "generally immoral and unethical."[35]

Michael Jensen and William Meckling, management professors at the University of Rochester, identified burdensome regulation rather than falling stock prices or antipathy toward business as the potentially fatal threat to the public company. They would achieve much notoriety for a 1976 article on the theory of the firm in which they described the firm as "a nexus for contracting relationships," with market dynamics defining the relationship among a firm, its financial backers, suppliers, customers, creditors, and so on.[36] The article, the most widely cited academic business paper ever,[37] has been singled out as the catalyst for a shift of managerial priorities in favor of shareholders in public companies as the twentieth century drew to a close.[38] Nevertheless, Jensen and Meckling's work on the theory of the firm did not have a major impact initially as it was only well into the 1980s that their 1976 article moved to the academic forefront.[39] A 1978 article of theirs that predicted a dire fate for the corporate sector captured greater attention at the time of writing.

---

[30] *Id.*

[31] Irving Kristol, *The Corporation and the Dinosaur*, WALL ST. J., Feb. 14, 1974, 20.

[32] Michael Ruby, *The Embattled Businessman*, NEWSWEEK, Feb. 16, 1976, 56.

[33] SEYMOUR MARTIN LIPSET & WILLIAM SCHNEIDER, THE CONFIDENCE GAP: BUSINESS, LABOR, AND GOVERNMENT IN THE PUBLIC MIND 48–49 (1983).

[34] *Id.* at 183.

[35] *Id.* at 172.

[36] Michael C. Jensen & William H. Meckling, *Theory of the Firm: Managerial Behavior, Agency Costs and Ownership Structure*, 3 J. FIN. ECON. 305, 310–11 (1976).

[37] RICK WARTZMAN, THE END OF LOYALTY: THE RISE AND FALL OF GOOD JOBS IN AMERICA 266 (2017).

[38] Dobbin & Jung, *supra* note 8, at 53; Chapter 4, notes 331-34 and related discussion.

[39] Chapter 4, note 340 and related discussion; Johan Heilbron, Jochem Verheul & Sander Quak, *The Origins and Early Diffusion of "Shareholder Value" in the United States*, 43 THEORY & SOCIETY 1, 9–10 (2014).

Jensen and Meckling provocatively titled their 1978 article "Can the Corporation Survive?"[40] They suggested not:

> (t)he corporate form of organization . . . is likely to disappear completely. Even if it survives in some form the larger corporations as we know them are destined to be destroyed. Indeed in a few industries we believe their demise is imminent![41]

Jensen and Meckling's prediction was accorded substantial respect. A 1976 working paper version caught the eye of *Forbes*, which published a lengthy interview with the authors.[42] The article itself was awarded the Graham and Dodd plaque for excellence in financial writing by the Financial Analysts Federation.[43]

Jensen and Meckling, in their 1976 article on the theory of the firm, identified "agency costs" corporate executives impose upon dispersed shareholders as a potentially counterproductive byproduct of the separation between share ownership and managerial control in publicly traded companies.[44] Correspondingly, it might have been anticipated that Jensen and Meckling would, in their 1978 piece, have pegged agency costs as the culprit for the forthcoming demise of the public company. Jensen indeed would cite conflicts of interest between owners and managers to substantiate in 1989 a prediction of "The Eclipse of the Public Corporation."[45]

Jensen and Meckling did reference their work on the theory of the firm in their 1976 *Forbes* interview.[46] They only did so, however, to suggest that the corporation, as nothing more than a set of contractual claims, was a fragile contraption vulnerable to governmental action. Jensen and Meckling's core claim in their 1976 interview and 1978 article instead was that the public corporation would fall victim to excessive regulation. They maintained that with firms suffering from "a revocation of rights" due to substantial growth in state intervention, public companies would require state subsidies, twinned with more government control, just to survive.[47] They cited dismal stock market returns as evidence that investors had deduced "private rights are deteriorating at an increasing rate."[48]

Akin to the sentiment famous author and humourist Mark Twain invoked when he refuted an erroneous 1897 newspaper story concerning his demise,[49] the reports of the death of the

---

[40] Michael C. Jensen & William H. Meckling, *Can the Corporation Survive?*, FIN. ANALYSTS J., Jan./Feb. 1978, 31.

[41] *Id.* at 32.

[42] *As We See It*, FORBES, June 15, 1976, 51.

[43] *Michael C. Jensen*, HARVARD BUSINESS School, available at http://www.hbs.edu/faculty/m/Pages/profile.aspx?facId=6484 (accessed February 11, 2018); David Gindis, *A Timely Rhetoric and a Rallying Label: How the Nexus of Contracts Theory Helped Tame the Critics of the Giant Corporation*, unpublished working paper, 17 (2013).

[44] Jensen & Meckling, *supra* note 36, at 311–12, 327–28.

[45] Chapter 4, notes 131, 134 and accompanying text; Michael C. Jensen, *The Eclipse of the Public Corporation*, HARV. BUS. REV., Sept./Oct. 1989, 61, 64.

[46] *As We See It, supra* note 42.

[47] Jensen & Meckling, *supra* note 40, at 37.

[48] *Id.*

[49] On what Twain actually said and when, see Joseph W. Campbell, *Noting the Anniversary of Twain's "Report of My Death" Comment*, MEDIA MYTH ALERT, June 1, 2011, available at https://mediamythalert.wordpress.com/2011/06/01/noting-the-anniversary-of-twains-report-of-my-death-comment/ (accessed February 5, 2018).

public company were very much an exaggeration. Two Goldman Sachs bankers indeed drew the analogy to Twain in a letter to *Business Week*'s editor disagreeing with the thesis of its "The Death of Equities" article.[50] Throughout most of the 1970s, a swooning stock market provided a plausible factual foundation for claims that the days of the public company were numbered. As the 1970s concluded, however, stock prices were moving upward modestly, with better days to come.[51] By the time the eighth anniversary of the "Death of the Equities" article rolled around, the S&P 500 index had tripled.[52] Kristol, for his part, backtracked from his corporate extinction prediction as early as 1977, saying "(t)he large corporation is not going to disappear," because the price in terms of lost efficiency would be too great.[53] Still, while the public company would very much live on, there was ample evidence during the 1970s that the managerially-oriented version that dominated the corporate economy effortlessly in the 1950s and 1960s was considerably troubled. The faltering of managerial capitalism would in turn set the scene for significant changes to the constraints applicable to public company executives and ultimately for managerial capitalism's displacement in the 1980s and the 1990s.

Managerial Capitalism Falters

During the 1950s and 1960s heyday of managerial capitalism there was awareness that neither boards nor shareholders imposed a meaningful check on senior executives. There was, however, little appetite for change amidst general economic prosperity and a dearth of serious corporate scandals.[54] The views expressed by some observers indicated that sentiments did not change materially in the 1970s. Law professor J.A.C. Hetherington said of public companies in 1979 that "(a)part from occasional management frauds, which probably cannot be prevented at acceptable cost under any scheme of corporate governance, the behavior of corporate management generally conforms with investor expectations," adding that "(a)dvocates of reform have been unable to prove the existence of systemic deficiencies in the present arrangements for governance of publicly held firms." [55] Likewise, Edward Herman, in a 1981 study of control of corporate control and power, acknowledged there was "room for a certain amount of 'expense preference' . . . and other modes of sharing in corporate surpluses by active managers" but argued that in very large corporations "(s)elf dealing and privileged information abuses . . . (were) moderate in the mid- and late 1970s."[56]

---

[50] *Readers React to the Death of Equities Cover Story*, Bus. Wk., Sept. 3, 1979, 68.

[51] The S&P 500 stood at 96.77 at the beginning of September 1977 and 109.32 at the beginning of September 1979. See *S&P 500/Historical Data*, available at https://finance.yahoo.com/quote/%5EGSPC/history/ (accessed Mar. 14, 2018).

[52] *Id.* (indicating the S&P 500 stood at 329.81 at the beginning of September 1987).

[53] Irving Kristol, *The US Corporation at the Bicentennial*, Emerging Issues Affecting US Corporations 3, 4 (1977).

[54] Chapter 2, note 256 and related discussion.

[55] J.A.C. Hetherington, *When the Sleeper Awakes: Reflections on Corporate Governance and Shareholder Rights*, 8 Hofstra L. Rev. 183, 187 (1979).

[56] Edward S. Herman, Corporate Control, Corporate Power: A Twentieth Century Fund Study 247, 248 (1981).

In fact, in the 1970s evidence of managerial capitalism's faults was much more prevalent than was the case in the 1950s and the 1960s. The public company was particularly exposed with the 1970s "bear" market in shares because the robust investor returns that would have assuaged doubts in the 1950s and 1960s were absent. A challenging economic environment in which US public companies had to operate was a mitigating factor. Nevertheless, complacency in the face of growing foreign competition, a "crack up" by high-profile conglomerates, and revelations of illicit payments provided evidence that the discretion made available to public company executives was being squandered in material and detrimental respects. Awareness of these trends would not only put managerial capitalism in jeopardy but would foster calls for better "corporate governance," a phrase only very rarely deployed prior to the 1970s.[57]

AMERICAN MANAGEMENT FALLING BEHIND?

The historical verdict on the quality of management in US public companies in the 1970s has been harsh. Business historians did not wait long to cast aspersions on the decade's executives. Louis Galambos and Joseph Pratt argued in a 1988 history of US business during the twentieth century that in the 1970s "(a) business system that had been dramatically successful for a quarter of a century did not rush to make far-reaching adjustments.... From the president of the large corporation to the union worker to the consumer many Americans had become comfortable, even complacent."[58] Harold Livesay observed acerbically in a 1989 article on entrepreneurship that in the 1970s "big American firms were exposed as tubs of inefficiency.... (I)ncapable of competing, bloated house cats rather than ... the Darwinian tigers they imagined themselves to be."[59]

The harsh verdicts continued thereafter. According to a 1996 survey of the development of the US corporation in the twentieth century, in the 1970s "complacent executives shied away from building or innovating their core businesses, allowed organizational capabilities to erode, and then, like a headless herd, moved headlong into uncertain territory. Across the industrial landscape, serious management failures became apparent."[60] A 2001 review of a book about Jack Welch, who became CEO of General Electric in 1981, said when Welch was getting ready to take power "big companies were far more complacent than they are today, with surprisingly little emphasis on such vital measures as competitiveness, profitability and the price of the stock."[61] *Fortune* argued in 2002 "(t)he decade of the 1970s ranked among the worst for American business (but) remained one of the coziest for American businessmen,"[62] adding in 2004 that "(b)y 1980 American management hadn't had a good idea in years."[63]

[57] Brian R. Cheffins, *The Corporate Governance Movement, Banks, and the Financial Crisis*, 16 THEO. INQ. L. 1, 2 (2015).

[58] LOUIS GALAMBOS & JOSEPH PRATT, THE RISE OF THE CORPORATE COMMONWEALTH: UNITED STATES BUSINESS AND PUBLIC POLICY IN THE 20TH CENTURY 201, 202 (1988).

[59] Harold C. Livesay, *Entrepreneurial Dominance in Businesses Large and Small, Past and Present*, 63 BUS. HIST. REV. 1, 14, 15.

[60] George David Smith & Davis Dyer, *The Rise and Transformation of the American Corporation*, in THE AMERICAN CORPORATION TODAY 28, 54 (Carl Kaysen ed., 1996).

[61] Joseph Nocera, *The Customer Is Usually Right*, NY TIMES, Oct. 14, 2001, Book Review, 13.

[62] Useem, *supra* note 22.

[63] Geoffrey Colvin, *A Concise History of Management Hooey*, FORTUNE, June 28, 2004, 166.

One generally searches in vain for such harsh judgments from contemporaries. Only as the 1970s concluded did criticism of public company executives begin in earnest. Perhaps everyone was in denial. *Fortune* argued in relation to the 1970s in 1999, "(a) decade of stock market stagnation was screaming to CEOs that management was failing, though hardly anyone wanted to admit it."[64] More likely, trends that seemed strikingly clear in hindsight were not obvious at the time because a disruptive economic environment in which businesses had to operate obscured managerial shortcomings.[65] As a management consultant who was advocating in 1980 the adoption of "a new spirit of innovation and risk taking" by those running companies conceded, "during the '70s the leaders of American business were forced to deal with a wide range of problems that did not exist a decade ago," and cited "the unstable economic climate business leaders have encountered."[66]

As soon as the 1970s began, challenges beset the American economy. Under the Bretton Woods system of monetary management introduced at the close of World War II countries committed themselves to stable exchange rates oriented around the American dollar, with the United States in turn undertaking that dollars would be convertible to gold.[67] At the start of the 1970s, US gold reserves were dwindling rapidly as growing fears of inflation diminished faith in the dollar as a store of value.[68] In 1971 President Richard Nixon responded by abandoning the gold convertibility commitment, by imposing a 10 percent surcharge on imports, and by introducing wage and price controls to counteract the anticipated inflationary impact of the move away from fixed exchange rates. The wage and price controls were a peacetime first for the United States.[69] It was initially thought that the dollar would not be allowed to float freely for long.[70] However, what became known as the "Nixon shock"[71] was in fact a crucial first step in a permanent move toward floating exchange rates.

Macroeconomic complications multiplied due to a 1973 embargo by Arab oil producers against the United States and other Western countries, which prompted a quadrupling of oil prices and energy shortages.[72] Arguably, the oil crisis "ended the golden age of postwar capitalism."[73] More particularly, the oil price surge precipitated "stagflation" in the mid-1970s, a simultaneous combination of ailments of high inflation, high unemployment, and slow growth most economists of the time thought could not occur.[74] Conditions were sufficiently

---

[64] Geoffrey Colvin, *The Ultimate Manager*, Forbes, Nov. 22, 1999, 185.

[65] Gordon Donaldson, Corporate Restructuring: Managing the Change Process from Within 31 (1994).

[66] James R. Emshoff, Managerial Breakthroughs: Action Techniques for Strategic Change 2, 15, 26 (1980).

[67] David M. Kotz, The Rise and Fall of Neoliberal Capitalism 13 (2015).

[68] Judith Stein, Pivotal Decade: How the United States Traded Factories for Finance in the Seventies 31 (2010).

[69] Galambos & Pratt, *supra* note 58, at 209.

[70] Charles Geisst, Wall Street: A History 304 (1997).

[71] Wartzman, *supra* note 37, at 217; *Tricky Dick and the Dollar*, Economist, Mar. 27, 2010, 82.

[72] Stein, *supra* note 68, at 82–83.

[73] *Id.* at 74.

[74] Robert Sobel, The Age of Giant Corporations: A Microeconomic History of American Business, 1914–1992, at 237 (3d ed. 1993); Henry Kaufman, On Money and Markets: A Wall Street Memoir 259–60 (2000).

troubled for "normally sober businessmen" to imagine "the collapse of the (economic) system or its radical transformation."[75] *Time* even asked readers on the cover of a July 1975 issue "Can Capitalism Survive?"[76]

Conditions improved somewhat in 1977 and 1978. Oil prices stabilized, which helped to control inflation, and fiscal stimulus boosted gross national product and fostered a modest drop in unemployment.[77] Worrying trends persisted, however. The dollar fell substantially against most other leading currencies as the 1970s drew to a close.[78] Productivity, measured in terms of output per hour, grew only 1.4 percent between 1973 and 1979, having increased 3 percent annually in the decades immediately following World War II.[79] Overall, "(b)y the late 1970s . . . the statistics on the performance of the economy were clearly signaling a red alert for the government's macroeconomic policy."[80] A fresh oil crisis in 1979 that caused long line-ups for gas and pushed the annualized inflation rate up to 13.4 percent rounded out "a perfect storm of external economic shocks."[81]

Even with difficult economic conditions acting as a mitigating factor, by the second half of the 1970s criticism of managerial quality in US corporations began to mount. Ralph Nader, Mark Green, and Joel Seligman, three of the most vocal and prominent "advocates of reform" to which Hetherington referred, argued in their 1976 book *Taming the Giant Corporation* that with corporations having grown more complex "checks upon senior management have all but disappeared. The result has often been irrational decisions, hurried decisions, decisions based upon inadequate factual analysis or executive self-favoritism."[82] Less trenchant observers began to weigh in as well. In 1976 *Business Week* suggested "the country's genius for invention is not what it used to be," and argued "no risk, super-cautious management is one of the prime villains."[83] A 1979 article where *Newsweek* considered whether America had "lost its edge" noted "that America's lead in innovation—and the vaunted US technological superiority that it spawned—may be withering."[84] *Business Week* quoted Thomas Murphy, General Motors' (GM) chairman and "perennial optimist," in 1980 as saying "(t)he 1970s were all but a disaster for auto executives as well as other sectors of business. . . . We seem to have spent most of our time not making decisions but postponing them."[85]

Foreign competition, which had been an afterthought due to economic havoc wrought by World War II that largely bypassed the United States,[86] was a key factor casting doubt on the capabilities of American management. As the 1970s got underway, even though a

---

[75] STEIN, *supra* note 68, at 182–83.

[76] *Can Capitalism Survive?*, TIME, July 14, 1975.

[77] STEIN, *supra* note 68, at 205.

[78] KOTZ, *supra* note 67, at 65.

[79] STEIN, *supra* note 68, at 199–200, 244.

[80] GALAMBOS & PRATT, *supra* note 58, at 211.

[81] KHURANA, *supra* note 1, at 297. See also STEIN, *supra* note 68, at 215.

[82] *Supra* note 55 and accompanying text; RALPH NADER, MARK GREEN & JOEL SELIGMAN, TAMING THE GIANT CORPORATION 77 (1976).

[83] *The Breakdown of US Innovation*, BUS. WK., Feb. 16, 1976, 56.

[84] Merrill Sheils, *Innovation: Has America Lost Its Edge?*, NEWSWEEK, June 4, 1979, 58.

[85] *The Penalties of Short-Term Corporate Strategies*, BUS. WK., June 30, 1980, 70.

[86] Chapter 2, notes 376–77 and related discussion.

surcharge on imports was part of the 1971 economic package Nixon introduced, there was only dim awareness of the threat foreign rivals posed for US business.[87] The facts on the ground changed markedly, however, as the 1970s went on. Imports increased from 5 percent of GDP in 1970 to nearly 10 percent by 1980.[88] Leading American companies were also finding themselves under challenge, as indicated by data on worldwide sales of the largest dozen companies in 15 major industries.[89] In 1970, American firms accounted for at least two-thirds of sales in 9 of the industries, including automobiles, banking and pharmaceuticals. By 1980 there were only 3 such industries, namely aerospace, computers, and paper products.

Completion of the process of reconstruction in countries devastated by World War II was inevitably going to erode the global dominance of US companies to some degree.[90] Foreign competitors also were benefitting from a drastic reduction in the cost of moving things around, with a dramatic increase in the use of shipping containers in the late 1960s being perhaps the most striking change.[91] Nevertheless, by the end of the 1970s the rise of foreign competition was sufficiently striking to foster debate in the United States on national competitiveness.[92]

Analyses of America's faltering economic standing betrayed misgivings about the capabilities of those running US businesses. A 1979 *US News & World Report* article focusing on American companies losing ground abroad observed "(o)nce a giant among pygmies in world trade, the US now looks like an aging champion whose dominance is threatened by a growing field of shrewd competitors."[93] In a 1980 article Harvard Business School's Robert Hayes and William Abernathy said factors such as high oil prices and governmental policy errors could not fully explain "a marked deterioration of competitive vigor" in American business, because America was losing its leadership position in a wide range of industries despite a similar economic climate abroad.[94] Hayes and Abernathy argued "American management," while "universally admired" in the two decades following World War II, was a likely culprit, with "an approach . . . ill-suited to a world characterized by rapid and unpredictable change, scarce energy, global competition for markets and a constant need for innovation."[95]

THE CONGLOMERATE CRACK-UP

While apprehension that foreign rivals were besting those in charge of America's largest companies only developed in earnest as the 1970s concluded, other evidence of managerial fallibility

---

87 *Supra* note 69 and related discussion; AMANDA BENNETT, THE DEATH OF THE ORGANIZATION MAN 96 (1990).

88 KOTZ, *supra* note 67, at 36, 79.

89 Lawrence G. Franko, *Global Corporate Competition: Who's Winning, Who's Losing, and the R&D Factor as One Reason Why*, 10 STRATEGIC MGMT. J. 449, 450–53 (1989).

90 *As America Loses Its Sway in World Markets*, US NEWS & WORLD REPORT, Apr. 23, 1979, 45.

91 ROBERT REICH, SUPERCAPITALISM: THE BATTLE FOR DEMOCRACY IN AN AGE OF BIG BUSINESS 60–61 (2007).

92 William E. Kovacic, The Antitrust Paradox *Revisited: Robert Bork and the Transformation of Modern Antitrust Policy*, 36 WAYNE L. REV. 1413, 1443 (1990).

93 *As America Loses*, *supra* note 90.

94 Robert Hayes & William Abernathy, *Managing Our Way to Economic Decline*, HARV. BUS. REV., July–Aug. 1980, 67, 67.

95 *Id.* at 68.

was emerging as the decade began. Conglomerates were at the center of the action. In the context of geology, stone fragments heaped together in a mass constitute a conglomerate.[96] As the 1970s began evidence was accumulating that in the corporate context the conglomerate model was cracking up. The crack-up, in turn, yielded signs of executive misjudgment that cast doubt on managerial capabilities in public companies generally. As historian Louis Hyman has argued, "the conglomerate . . . came in the 1970s to represent the worst excesses of the bloated postwar corporation. . . . Without the failure of the conglomerate, the explanations of 'how a firm should operate' that guided the post-1970s capitalism would not have been possible."[97]

Researchers have studied the efficiency properties of corporate diversification and the conglomerate firm in considerable detail since *Newsday* proclaimed "The Decline and Fall of 'King Cong' " in 1970.[98] The literature is largely inconclusive,[99] including with respect to whether a "conglomerate discount" is systematically built into the prices of highly diversified public companies.[100] This empirical agnosticism runs contrary to received wisdom, with the conglomerate model having been out of favor intellectually for decades.[101] Regardless, however, of whether the conglomerate in fact was, as the *Economist* said in 1991, "almost certainly the biggest collective error ever made by American business,"[102] evidence of its failings that emerged as the 1970s began would cast doubt on the judgment and capabilities of US executives in a manner unknown at the zenith of managerial capitalism.

The 1960s have been described as "the age of the conglomerate in American business."[103] The conglomerate's fortunes peaked late in the decade as it became "the rage on Wall Street."[104] One explanation advanced for the rise of the conglomerate was that ambitious executives in a buying mood knew that the acquisition of a corporation operating in an unrelated sector was less vulnerable to challenge under antitrust law than a horizontal or vertical merger.[105] Managerial capabilities were also cited. Those in charge of conglomerates characterized

---

[96] *Double the Profits, Double the Pride*, TIME, Sept 8, 1967, 100; *Corporate Fact of Life: Merger Use Spreads*, NEWSDAY, Oct. 6, 1967, 33A; Harvey H. Segal, *The Time of the Conglomerates*, NY TIMES, Oct. 27, 1968, Sunday Magazine, 32.

[97] Louis Hyman, *Rethinking the Postwar Corporation: Management, Monopolies, and Markets*, WHAT'S GOOD FOR BUSINESS: BUSINESS AND AMERICAN POLITICS SINCE WORLD WAR II, 195, 196 (Kim Phillips-Fein & Julian Zelizer eds., 2012).

[98] *The Decline and Fall of "King Cong,"* NEWSDAY, Aug. 12, 1970, 84, republishing David Palmer, *Rise and Fall of the Conglomerate Image*, FIN. TIMES, May 28, 1970, 25. On the intensity of the research effort, see Vojislav Maksimovic & Gordon M. Phillips, *Conglomerate Firms, Internal Capital Markets, and the Theory of the Firm*, 5 ANN. REV. FIN. ECON. 224, 226 (2013).

[99] Dobbin & Jung, *supra* note 8, at 44; Stefan Erdorf et al., *Corporate Diversification and Firm Value: A Review of the Recent Literature*, 27 FIN. MKT. PORTFOLIO. MGMT. 187, 210 (2013).

[100] See Maksimovic & Phillips, *supra* note 98, at 227–29; Lynne L. Dallas, *Is There Hope for Change? The Evolution of Conceptions of Good Corporate Governance*, 54 SAN DIEGO L. REV. 491, 518 (2017).

[101] *The Time Is Right for Breaking Up*, NY TIMES, Jan. 13, 2011, B2.

[102] *Ebb Tide*, ECONOMIST, Apr. 27, 1991, 43.

[103] THOMAS K. MCCRAW, AMERICAN BUSINESS, 1920–2000: HOW IT WORKED 137 (2000).

[104] Barton M. Biggs, *Day of Reckoning?*, BARRON'S, Apr. 3, 1967, 47.

[105] Joel Davidow, *Conglomerate Concentration and Section Seven: The Limitations of the Anti-merger Act*, 68 COLUM. L. REV. 1231, 1234 (1968); *Corporate Scapegoats?*, BARRON'S, Mar. 17, 1969, 49; ROBERT TEITELMAN, BLOODSPORT: WHEN RUTHLESS DEALMAKERS, SHREWD IDEOLOGUES, AND BRAWLING LAWYERS TOPPLED THE CORPORATE ESTABLISHMENT 53–54 (2016).

themselves as astute managerial generalists who could, despite lacking extensive knowledge of the markets in which acquired companies were operating, create value-enhancing "synergism" between diverse units through prudent delegation, continual monitoring, well-timed strategic interventions, and judicious money management.[106] This logic prompted the president of chemical giant DuPont to respond drily when asked in 1967 why DuPont lacked ambitious diversification plans, "(r)unning a conglomerate is a job for management geniuses, not for ordinary mortals like us at DuPont."[107]

As the 1970s got underway, evidence was mounting quickly that managerial genius was in fact in short supply among the conglomerates that had been reshaping US business. Disillusionment can be traced back to Litton Industries announcing unexpectedly in 1968 that its earnings had fallen substantially.[108] The announcement was a shock to investors because Litton had an "impeccable" reputation among conglomerates and because "it was shown for the first time that conglomerate management—even the best of it—could lose track entirely of the progress or regress of the far flung enterprises it ostensibly controlled and thus fail utterly of its function."[109]

Litton's shares fell 85 percent in the two years following its disappointing earnings announcement, and numerous other formerly high-flying conglomerates experienced similarly dismal results.[110] This prompted business professor Stanley Vance to argue in a 1971 study of conglomerate management "it would seem that few if any of the current conglomerators will ever be re-elevated into the ranks of management mythology. Rather the prospects are that most of these neoentrepreneurs will qualify better for a management martyrology."[111] *Forbes* concurred, saying "(t)he conglomerates are now deemed a disaster area, and the good has been written off with the bad. And written off not only as troubled, but somehow morally reprehensible."[112] Likewise, a 1973 study of managerial crises by Joel Ross and Michael Kami suggested that while "synergism" was defensible in theory, "most of the conglomerates have failed because they overlooked management fundamentals."[113] Matters did not improve throughout the course of the decade, with *Forbes* saying in 1979 "(a)s far as market fashion is concerned, conglomerates belong to the age of above-the-knee women's skirts. Today most analysts regard them the way Vidal Sassoon (a noted hair stylist) does flattop haircuts."[114]

The high profile 1970 collapse of Penn Central was a poster child for conglomerate mismanagement. While there had been warning signs with conglomerates extending back at least to Litton's 1968 profit warning, Penn Central's crisis, including the bankruptcy of its

---

[106] *Decline and Fall, supra* note 98; Abraham Briloff, *Conglomerates*, Fin. Times, Apr. 8, 1969, 17; Richard J. Barber, The American Corporation: Its Power, Its Money, Its Politics 44–45 (1970).

[107] Editors of Fortune, The Conglomerate Commotion 77 (1970) (republished version of a *Fortune* article from February 1967).

[108] John Brooks, The Go-Go Years 180–81 (1973).

[109] *Id.* at 181.

[110] Stanley Vance, Managers in the Conglomerate Era 6 (1971).

[111] *Id.* at 6–7.

[112] *Multicompanies*, Forbes, Jan. 1, 1971, 105.

[113] Joel E. Ross & Michael J. Kami, Corporate Management in Crisis: Why the Mighty Fail 82 (1973).

[114] *The Spin-Off Gambit*, Forbes, Nov. 12, 1979, 43.

railroad operations, made "it clear the party was truly over."[115] Penn Central was the product of a merger between the Pennsylvania Railroad and the New York Central railway, with discussions of consolidation extending back to the late 1950s climaxing in 1968 when the US Supreme Court gave the green light.[116] Penn Central comprised the merged railroad companies, which each had considerable non-railway holdings, as well as the Pennsylvania Company, a wholly owned subsidiary of the Pennsylvania Railroad that had interests in pipelines, real estate development, and amusement parks.[117] The non-railway assets were viewed positively, with a Penn Central executive asking rhetorically just after the merger was finalized, "(w)hy put money into the railroad, where the return is 3 percent, when we can invest in things making 15 percent to 20 percent?"[118] By 1970 hotels, coal and oil operations and substantial stakes in the Madison Square Garden arena in Manhattan and its anchor tenants, the New York Knicks basketball team and New York Rangers hockey team, were all part of the mix.[119] Penn Central thus was, a "sprawling rail-based conglomerate"[120] akin to "a giant octopus."[121]

In present day terms, "the downfall of the Penn Central is considered ancient history."[122] At the time of its collapse, though, Penn Central was the "biggest single business failure the nation has ever known."[123] Moreover, it was "not any other company" but rather "a household word."[124] Penn Central reputedly seemed prior to its 1970 collapse "to millions of Americans . . . as solid an institution as the US Senate or the New York Yankees."[125] Stuart Saunders, Penn Central's executive chairman, was even on the cover of *Time* in 1968 under the banner "Railroads of the Future."[126] Correspondingly, to the extent Penn Central executives were to blame for the collapse, this was liable to reflect badly on management of large firms more generally. And blamed they were.

Ross and Kami devoted a chapter to Penn Central and said "the management of Penn Central not only violated most fundamentals of management—they invented some new ones."[127] *Business Week* concurred, saying in 1973 that Penn Central was "the most spectacular case of corporate mismanagement in recent history."[128] The *Baltimore Sun*, noting the

---

[115] Robert Sobel, The Rise and Fall of the Conglomerate Kings 166 (1984). The directors of the Penn Central Company, the holding company that owned the railway operations, put the railway subsidiary into bankruptcy but the parent continued to operate—Donald Prell, The Untold Story of the Survival of the Penn Central Company 3–4 (2010).

[116] *Toward the 21st Century Ltd.*, Time, Jan. 26, 1968, 82.

[117] Sobel, *supra* note 115, at 170–71; Joseph R. Daughen & Peter Binzen, The Wreck of the Penn Central 243, 245–46 (1971).

[118] Charles N. Stabler, *The Conglomerates*, Wall St. J., July 25, 1968, 1.

[119] Ross & Kami, *supra* note 113, at 80; Daughen & Binzen, *supra* note 117, at 243–44, 246.

[120] *Penn-Central Tries a Wider Track*, Bus. Wk., May 10, 1969, 132.

[121] Daughen & Binzen, *supra* note 117, at 13.

[122] Prell, *supra* note 115, at 28.

[123] Frank W. Corrigan, *Penn Central: Tale of Two Egos*, Newsday, July 9, 1970, 96.

[124] Jurek Martin, *Avoiding Another Penn Central*, Fin. Times, June 25, 1970, 14.

[125] Michael C. Jensen, The Financiers 160 (1976).

[126] Time, Jan. 26, 1968, cover available at http://content.time.com/time/covers/0,16641,19680126,00.html (accessed Mar. 8, 2018).

[127] Ross & Kami, *supra* note 113, at 46–47.

[128] *The Old Penn Central Gang*, Bus. Wk., Dec. 15, 1973, 22.

following year that "(t)he reverberations from the 1970 failure of the Penn Central Railroad go on and on," described proceedings just brought by the Securities Exchange Commission alleging various violations of federal securities law and suggested "the best that can be said for the railroad's managers . . . is that they were terribly incompetent."[129]

ILLICIT PAYMENTS

To the extent that high-profile conglomerates were tarnishing the reputation of public company executives in the 1970s, International Telephone & Telegraph Corporation (ITT) was Penn Central's closet peer. For ITT the 1960s was a banner decade. In 1959 Harold Geneen took the helm of an $811 million telecommunications company comprised primarily of diffuse foreign holdings. He used an aggressive acquisition program to transform ITT by the late 1960s into a $6.4 billion conglomerate with holdings so diverse "it was almost impossible for Americans to pass a day without using or buying some ITT product."[130] Geneen, who would serve as ITT's chief executive until 1977, appeared on a 1967 *Time* cover featuring conglomerates.[131] He was hailed by *Forbes* at the end of the 1960s as "possibly the greatest corporation executive of his day."[132]

The editor of a 1972 collection of essays on *Great Business Disasters*, in arguing that the early 1970s likely would "in retrospect be considered the watershed years in the history of the American business calamity," drew attention to two public companies in making the point, Penn Central and ITT.[133] The parallel between the two conglomerates was not exact, in that Penn Central fell further. The Penn Central railway assets placed into bankruptcy were nationalized in 1976 as part of a consolidation of railway properties that became known as Conrail.[134] ITT, on the other hand, largely sidestepped the fall in conglomerate share prices as the 1960s drew to a close.[135] It did well enough in the 1970s to be the 13th largest corporation in the United States as of 1980, ranked by revenue.[136] ITT remained "the quintessential conglomerate" at least until a 1995 breakup into three different firms.[137]

Though ITT did not meet the calamitous fate of Penn Central, as the 1970s began widely publicized allegations of political corruption and ethically dubious foreign activities were a public relations disaster for ITT that tarnished the image of conglomerates and big business

---

[129] *Moral Bankruptcy?*, BALT. SUN, May 8, 1974, A22.

[130] JENSEN, *supra* note 125, at 214.

[131] TIME, Sept. 8, 1967, cover available at http://content.time.com/time/covers/0,16641,19670908,00.html (accessed Mar. 8, 2018).

[132] Quoted in ISADORE BARMASH, THE SELF-MADE MAN: SUCCESS AND STRESS AMERICAN STYLE 351 (1969).

[133] Isadore Barmash, *Introduction*, GREAT BUSINESS DISASTERS: SWINDLERS, BUNGLERS AND FRAUD IN AMERICAN INDUSTRY 1, 1 (Isadore Barmash ed., 1972). Reference was also made to business information provider Dun & Bradstreet.

[134] *Supra* note 115 and related discussion; Railroad Revitalization and Regulatory Reform Act, Pub. L. 94-210, 90 Stat. 31.

[135] *Supra* note 110 and accompanying text; JOEL SELIGMAN, THE TRANSFORMATION OF WALL STREET: A HISTORY OF THE SECURITIES AND EXCHANGE COMMISSION AND MODERN CORPORATE FINANCE 430 (1982).

[136] Charles P. Alexander & Adam Zagorin, *The Incredible Shrinking Conglomerate*, TIME, Jan. 28, 1985, 68.

[137] *The Death of the Geneen Machine*, ECONOMIST, June 17, 1995, 86.

more generally.[138] One charge leveled against ITT related to a promise by its Sheraton Hotel operation to pay $400,000 in support of a bid by San Diego to host the 1972 Republican convention. There were rumors of a corrupt link between ITT's pledge and the settlement of an antitrust suit with the US government advantageous to ITT because the corporation would not have to divest itself of the recently acquired Hartford Fire Insurance Company.[139] Another ITT allegation seemed to confirm "the standard leftist stereotype of the multinational US company." [140] ITT was said to have worked with the Central Intelligence Agency to preclude Salvador Allende from prevailing in a closely contested 1970 election in Chile, with ITT fearing that an Allende government would nationalize the ITT-controlled Chile Telephone Co.

In neither instance were the charges proven. There was "more smoke than fire" with the political angle to ITT's antitrust settlement.[141] ITT's involvement in Chile apparently was restricted to backing anti-Allende candidates and publications.[142] Nevertheless, the allegations "left ITT with a cloud over its head, and gave the public a new three-letter symbol for corporate power, cunning and subterfuge."[143] The prevailing attitude toward ITT's troubles among public company executives was "(t)hey made us all look bad."[144]

While proof of the most explosive allegations of ITT bribery and foreign meddling was lacking, evidence soon emerged that other prominent public companies had made illicit political donations. By the 1970s corporate political contributions had been prohibited for some time under federal election laws.[145] The Watergate Special Prosecution Force, established in 1973 to look into a break-in at Democrat National Committee headquarters at Washington, DC's Watergate complex, investigated potential violations relating to the 1972 presidential election.[146] Eighteen companies would ultimately be convicted for illicit donations to Richard Nixon's re-election campaign but the fines were modest because each cooperated under an amnesty program the Special Prosecutor had established.[147] The corporations included American Airlines and Braniff International Airways, and *Fortune* 500 constituents such as Ashland Petroleum, Carnation Co., Diamond International Co., Goodyear, Gulf Oil, Minnesota Mining and Manufacturing (3M), and Northrop Corp.[148]

---

[138] Isadore Barmash, *Conglomerates—Still Trying*, NY TIMES, Nov. 5, 1972, 1 (focusing on ITT's political engagements).

[139] Jack Anderson, *Secret Memo Bares Mitchell-ITT Move*, WASH. POST, Feb. 29, 1972, B11.

[140] Stanley Karnow, *ITT's Chile Caper*, WASH. POST, Mar. 27, 1972, A1.

[141] Robert Sobel, *The Rise and Fall of Geneen's Way*, NEWSDAY, Mar. 20, 1983, 98.

[142] ROBERT SOBEL, ITT: THE MANAGEMENT OF OPPORTUNITY 314–15 (1982).

[143] JENSEN, *supra* note 125, at 211.

[144] *Id.* at 230.

[145] The Taft-Hartley Act of 1947, Pub. L. 80–101, 61 Stat. 136, § 304, barred both labor unions and corporations from making expenditures and contributions in federal elections.

[146] SELIGMAN, *supra* note 135, at 539.

[147] *Id.* at 539–40; LEONARD SILK & DAVID VOGEL, ETHICS & PROFITS: THE CRISIS OF CONFIDENCE IN AMERICAN BUSINESS 17 (1976); Andrew D. Faith, *Watergate Conviction Toll Is 52 Men, 20 Corporations*, BALT. SUN, Jan. 4, 1975, A2 (listing 16 of the corporations that had made illegal contributions and specifying the fines due).

[148] On the *Fortune* 500 list as of 1972, see http://archive.fortune.com/magazines/fortune/fortune500_archive/full/1972/ (accessed Mar. 16, 2018).

Securities and Exchange Commission (SEC) officials, once they were aware of the illicit corporate donations, reasoned that public companies contributing secretly to the Nixon re-election campaign had breached federal securities law by failing to record or disclose the expenditures.[149] Correspondingly, in 1974 the SEC brought proceedings against another company convicted due to the Special Prosecutor's efforts, American Shipbuilding Co., and against George Steinbrenner, the firm's chief executive and owner of baseball's New York Yankees.[150] The proceedings were settled by way of a consent decree.[151] American Shipbuilding Co. did not admit wrongdoing but agreed to appoint a special review committee comprised of outside directors to investigate and report on the company's political contribution record. The SEC reserved the right to reopen proceedings if the Commission was not satisfied with what the committee did. The SEC then trained its sights on other companies with links to the Nixon re-election campaign, and over the next two years struck deals with 12 companies similar to that reached with American Shipbuilding.[152] The *Boston Globe*'s verdict was that "(c)orporate America's dirty linen is getting a thorough public scrubbing as a result of the Watergate scandal."[153]

For the SEC an advantageous feature of the deals struck with companies such as American Shipbuilding was that much of the investigation expense was borne by the corporation itself rather than the Commission. "It was beautiful," maintained Stanley Sporkin, then chief of the SEC's enforcement division.[154] Nevertheless, the SEC still lacked the resources to investigate on a case-by-case basis all plausible instances of undisclosed illicit payments. Accordingly, it launched in 1975 a "voluntary disclosure" program to encourage companies to set the record straight secure in the knowledge that sanctions would not necessarily follow.[155] Under the scheme, a corporation falling under the Commission's jurisdiction would investigate its own dubious payments, ideally under the supervision of its outside directors, and publicly disclose material information uncovered by way of filings with the SEC.[156] The fact that companies were not under an onus to divulge the identity or nationality of the recipients encouraged cooperation.[157] By early 1977, when the SEC wound down the voluntary disclosure program, nearly 400 companies had made illicit payment disclosures pursuant to the scheme.[158]

While under the SEC's voluntary disclosure program companies were not required to divulge the countries in which recipients were located, the extent of illicit payments abroad was a major revelation.[159] For instance, ITT disclosed in 1976 that its employees had made

---

149 Paul E. Steiger, *SEC Enforcers: Are Hit, Run Tactics Good?*, LA TIMES, Oct. 30, 1975, A1; JESSE EISINGER, THE CHICKENSHIT CLUB 71–72 (2017).

150 SELIGMAN, *supra* note 135, at 541.

151 *Id.*; Steiger, *supra* note 149.

152 SELIGMAN, *supra* note 135, at 541; David P. Doherty, *The SEC's Management Fraud Program*, 31 BUS. LAW. 1279, 1280–81 (1976).

153 Robert Lenzer, *Can Scandal Make Business Honest?*, BOS. GLOBE, May 18, 1975, 1.

154 Steiger, *supra* note 149.

155 SELIGMAN, *supra* note 135, at 541.

156 *Id.* at 541–42.

157 *Disclosure of Payments to Foreign Government Officials under the Securities Acts*, 89 HARV. L. REV. 1848, 1852 (1976); *SEC May End Its Disclosures Plan*, FIN. TIMES, Mar. 8, 1977, 6.

158 SELIGMAN, *supra* note 135, at 542.

159 *The Corporate Rush to Confess All*, BUS. WK., Feb. 23, 1976, 22.

$3.8 million in unauthorized foreign disbursements between 1971 and 1975 and the following year acknowledged that in fact improper and questionable payments totaling $8.7 million had been made.[160] Lockheed admitted in 1975 in an SEC follow-up probe that it had paid at least $22 million to foreign public officials to win lucrative aerospace contracts. The aircraft manufacturer's disclosures prompted major political scandals in Italy, Japan, and the Netherlands.[161] Likewise, an SEC investigation resulted in a 1975 admission by United Brands, marketer of Chiquita bananas, that it paid a $1.25 million bribe in Honduras to reduce a recently imposed tax on banana exports. The revelations prompted not only the fining of United Brands but the suicide of the company's chief executive and the dismissal of Honduras' president.[162]

Taken together, in "this brief but passionate era of corporate history"[163] an unprecedented number of public companies had announced largely simultaneously their participation in improper and illegal conduct.[164] President Gerald Ford was moved to declare "corrupt business practices strike at the heart of our moral code and our faith in free enterprise."[165] According to some observers, what Nader, Green, and Seligman called "a corporate crime wave"[166] shocked the public,[167] damaged the reputation of the large corporation,[168] and eroded trust and confidence in business.[169] There were suggestions that the revelations of illicit payments also made shareholders more sensitive to corporate misconduct.[170]

In fact, while the illicit payments saga has been characterized as one of the more sordid chapters in American corporate history,[171] the public response was rather muted. The *New York Times* said in 1975 that "the most curious upshot of the recent disclosures has been the public's ambivalent reaction to them," with Americans generally lacking a strong sense of moral outrage.[172] Consumers continued to buy and use products of the companies implicated.[173] While polling data indicated that confidence in business dropped sharply in the

---

[160] CORRUPTION IN BUSINESS 144–45 (Lester A. Sobel ed., 1977); MARSHALL B. CLINARD & PETER C. YEAGER, CORPORATE CRIME 169–70 (1980).

[161] CORRUPTION, *supra* note 160, at 101–18.

[162] EISINGER, *supra* note 149, at 83–89; CORRUPTION, *supra* note 160, at 121–23; NEIL H. JACOBY, PETER NEHEMKIS & RICHARD EELLS, BRIBERY AND EXTORTION IN WORLD BUSINESS: A STUDY OF CORPORATE POLITICAL PAYMENTS ABROAD 105–07 (1977).

[163] Russell B. Stevenson, *The SEC and Foreign Bribery*, 32 BUS. LAW. 53, 53 (1976) (quoting the SEC chairman).

[164] Robert W. Hamilton, *Corporate Governance in America 1950–2000: Major Changes but Uncertain Benefits*, 25 J. CORP. L. 349, 359 (2000).

[165] Louis M. Kohlmeier, *The Bribe Busters*, NY TIMES, Sept. 29, 1976, Sunday Magazine, 47.

[166] NADER, GREEN & SELIGMAN, *supra* note 82, at 30.

[167] *John J. McCloy on Corporate Payoffs*, HARV. BUS. REV., July/Aug. 1976, 20.

[168] Stewart Fleming, *The Businessman Returns to Favour in Washington*, FIN. TIMES, Oct. 24, 1978, 18; ARCHIE B. CARROLL ET AL., CORPORATE RESPONSIBILITY: THE AMERICAN EXPERIENCE 280 (2012).

[169] Ruby, *supra* note 32 (quoting the president of the Bank of America); William R. Dill, *Private Power and Public Responsibility, in* RUNNING THE AMERICAN CORPORATION 7, 24 (William R. Dill ed., 1978).

[170] Carter F. Bales & Donald J. Goegel, *Going Public with Corporate Power*, MCKINSEY Q., Winter 1979, at 66, 71.

[171] MARSHALL B. CLINARD, CORPORATE CORRUPTION: THE ABUSE OF POWER 121 (1990).

[172] Michael C. Jensen, *Corporate Corruption is Big Business*, NY TIMES, Sept. 14, 1975, 173.

[173] Dill, *supra* note 169, at 24.

1970s, the decline was most precipitous in 1974 when revelations of questionable payments had barely begun.[174]

Most investors similarly seemed to react to the illicit payment scandals with a yawn.[175] Signs of any negative market stock market reaction to questionable payment revelations were slight and short-lived.[176] The fact that the payments, with isolated exceptions, were tiny as a proportion of gross sales revenues likely was a factor.[177] Investors also may have deduced that managers making or authorizing illicit payments were trying to promote the interests of the firms on whose behalf they were acting, agreeing implicitly with various executives who maintained that in some instances ethics had to be sacrificed for the corporate good.[178] As Roy Chapin, chairman of American Motors, said in 1976, "(w)e can do all the moralizing and preaching you want but when you get into these developing countries, you do business their way or you don't get the business."[179]

Even if consumers and investors took revelations of illicit payments in their stride, the controversy nevertheless did contribute to changes the public company was undergoing in the 1970s. Corporate accountability had been thrust into the spotlight in a way it had not been in recent decades.[180] This, as we will see next, had important implications with respect to the constraints under which executives of public companies operated, most obviously for the board of directors.

Internal Constraints

There was during the 1970s evidence of the "core fissure" in US corporate governance between executives and dispersed shareholders that was lacking when managerial capitalism was at its zenith. Sluggish managerial responses to challenges foreign competitors posed, the conglomerate crack-up, and the questionable payments controversy all indicated in a concrete manner that public company executives were performing suboptimally. One byproduct was that the board of directors, a theoretically key internal constraint on management, was put in the center of the action in a novel manner.[181] There also was the potential for regulation, ultimately substantially unrealized, to operate as an external constraint to an unprecedented degree. We will consider now how the matrix of constraints affecting public company executives changed in the 1970s, and changed in ways that set the scene for more profound

---

[174] *Supra note* 33 and related discussion; LIPSET & SCHNEIDER, *supra note* 33, at 48–49, 183.

[175] James P. Meagher, *When in Rome, It Is Known as a* Bustarella, BARRON'S, Jan. 30, 1978, 58; A.A. Sommer, *The Impact of the SEC on Corporate Governance*, CORPORATIONS AT THE CROSSROADS: GOVERNANCE AND REFORM 177, 201–02 (Deborah A. DeMott ed., 1980).

[176] CLINARD & YEAGER, *supra* note 160, at 180; JACOBY, NEHEMKIS & EELLS, *supra* note 162, at 51–56; *Wall St. Winks at Bribery Cases*, NY TIMES, Nov. 12, 1976, 77.

[177] JACOBY, NEHEMKIS & EELLS, *supra* note 162, at 119 (among 34 corporations with revenues exceeding $1 billion during 1974 that disclosed illicit payments, the payments totaled $93.7 million during the years they occurred. Total sales revenues of the corporations amounted to $679 billion during those same years).

[178] SILK & VOGEL, *supra* note 147, at 228–29.

[179] Ruby, *supra* note 32.

[180] *Voice of Public in Business? The SEC Wants to Hear*, LA TIMES, Sept. 25, 1977, H1.

[181] Stanley C. Vance, *Book Review*, DIRECTORS & BOARDS, Winter 1979, at 45, 46.

modifications in the 1980s. We will begin with internal constraints and focus initially on a limitation on managerial discretion that was of secondary importance throughout the 1970s, namely shareholder action.

SHAREHOLDERS

While in the 1950s and 1960s shareholders were characterized as "apathetic" and "passive," a mitigating factor was that they had little to complain about with the stock market performing well.[182] An investor outcry might have been expected during the 1970s, given dismal stock returns and ample evidence of wayward management.[183] Generally, however, the approach shareholders took changed little. Publicized interventions were essentially restricted to investors with a social agenda to promote.

Contemporaries were well aware of the shareholder bias in favor of passivity. Corporate law scholar Melvin Eisenberg said in a 1976 study of the corporation that while it was critical for potentially unaccountable executives to be monitored, "(t)he body of shareholders is too disparate, shifting and clumsy to conduct the type of inquiry involved."[184] Myles Mace, in a 1979 update of a well-known 1971 study of the board of directors,[185] maintained "(t)he hundreds of thousands of stockholders of large widely held companies continue to be unorganized and unorganizable."[186] A 1980 SEC report on hearings the Commission held in 1977 on corporate accountability said of those involved in the proceedings, "(t)he majority of commentators expressed the view that shareholders have little interest in participating in corporate governance."[187]

Throughout the 1970s retail investors continued to own a majority of shares in public companies even though a shift in favor of institutional ownership evident in the 1950s and 1960s continued (Figure 3.1). Despite the balance still favoring retail investors, for those hoping for meaningful stockholder engagement with public company executives institutional investors stood out as the only realistic option. Eisenberg, contrasting "concentrated institutional shareholders" with "highly dispersed individual shareholdings" said only the former gave "some hope of a check—a countervailing force—to management."[188] Similarly, Harold Williams, chairman of the SEC as the 1970s concluded, said that while "individual shareholder participation is not particularly effective," "institutional shareholders have a part in vitalizing accountability."[189]

---

[182] Chapter 2, notes 189, 313–15 and accompanying text.

[183] *Supra* notes 28–29, 58–63, 82–85 and related discussion; DONALDSON, *supra* note 65, at 29.

[184] EISENBERG, *supra* note 4, at 167.

[185] MYLES L. MACE, DIRECTORS: MYTH AND REALITY (1971).

[186] Myles L. Mace, *Directors: Myth and Reality—Ten Years Later*, 32 RUTGERS L. REV. 293, 297 (1979).

[187] SECURITIES AND EXCHANGE COMMISSION, STAFF REPORT ON CORPORATE ACCOUNTABILITY A-4 (1980).

[188] EISENBERG, *supra* note 4, at 61–62.

[189] Harold M. Williams, *Corporate Accountability and Corporate Power*, POWER AND ACCOUNTABILITY: THE CHANGING ROLE OF THE CORPORATE BOARD OF DIRECTORS 9, 28 (1979).

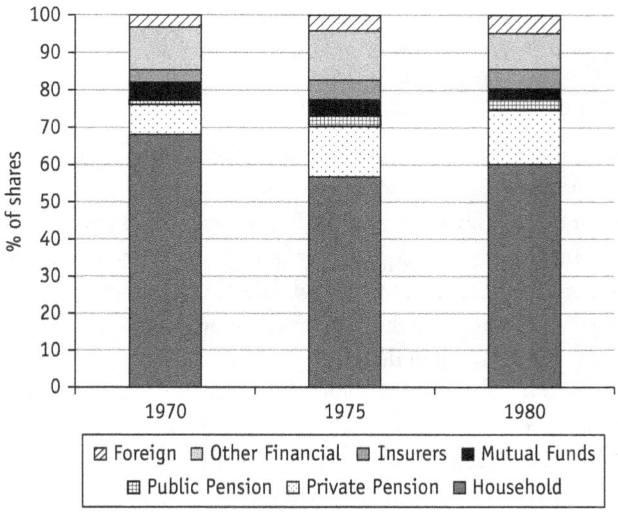

FIGURE 3.1 US Corporate Stock Held by Households and Institutions, 1970–1980.
Source: OECD, OECD ECONOMIC SURVEYS—UNITED STATES 124 (1996).

While institutional investors were seen in the 1970s as the only hope for meaningful shareholder participation in corporate affairs, in practice they remained passive.[190] A management consultant observed in 1978 that "(s)o far, the managers of institutional funds have declined to interfere with management . . . preferring, like the ordinary stockholder, to sell when management fails to produce satisfactory earnings."[191] A 1979 Conference Board study of equity markets that drew heavily on a survey of senior executives confirmed the point, saying "(n)o study respondent expressed the view that institutions try to influence management."[192]

An investor holding sizeable stakes in a small cohort of public companies will, as compared with a fully diversified investor owning dozens of modestly-sized holdings, have stronger incentives to intervene and will have better odds of capturing management's attention.[193] During the 1970s institutional shareholders eschewed, however, accumulating large ownership positions in individual firms. According to a 1978 Senate Subcommittee study of ownership patterns of 122 publicly traded companies that comprised 41 percent of the market value of all outstanding common stock, in only 19 of these companies was there an institutional shareholder that owned 5 percent or more of the shares.[194]

With institutional shareholders forsaking the accumulation of outsized stakes in public companies, institutional investor collaboration was needed to put any meaningful pressure

---

[190] Jones, *supra* note 4, at 1284; HERMAN, *supra* note 56, at 147, 152–53; PHILLIP I. BLUMBERG, THE MEGACORPORATION IN AMERICAN SOCIETY: THE SCOPE OF CORPORATE POWER 12 (1975).

[191] EDWARD MCSWEENEY, MANAGING THE MANAGERS 26 (1978).

[192] VINCENT G. MASSARO, THE EQUITY MARKET: CORPORATE PRACTICES AND ISSUES 15 (1979).

[193] Chapter 6, note 305 and text following (hedge funds); MARK J. ROE, STRONG MANAGERS, WEAK OWNERS: THE POLITICAL ROOTS OF AMERICAN CORPORATE FINANCE 11 (1994).

[194] Staff Study, Subcommittee on Reports, Accounting and Management, *Voting Rights in Major Corporations* 1 (1978).

on management. No such joint efforts were forthcoming. A 1975 study of "the megacorporation" observed that "power resides in the institutions collectively" but offered the caveat "(s)uch power requires an unlikely degree of concerted action among the institutions involved."[195]

With mutual funds, a key type of "mainstream" institutional shareholder, it was understandable that neither cooperation with other investors nor the accumulation of sizeable stakes in particular companies was a priority. In the 1970s there were fears for the future of the entire mutual fund industry as equity assets under management fell substantially due to poor stock market performance and substantial redemptions by investors.[196] Contrary to the general trend for institutional shareholders, the proportion of shares of public companies mutual funds owned actually fell in the 1970s.[197]

The mutual fund industry responded affirmatively to 1970s adversity by developing two new types of funds that would in time revolutionize the industry and have an impact on the US financial system more generally.[198] One was the index fund, which offers diversification at low cost to investors with a passive investment strategy based around mimicking a benchmark index such as the S&P 500. Vanguard launched the first stock market index fund in 1976, with what is now the Vanguard 500 index fund having a mere $11.3 million in assets under management as compared with $250 billion 40 years later.[199]

Money market funds, the first of which started operations in the early 1970s, constituted the other major mutual fund newcomer.[200] Forsaking shares, these funds invested in Treasury bills, commercial paper corporations issued, and other interest-bearing instruments. Money market funds paid out interest (less expenses) to fund investors and functioned similarly to a bank account by offering redeemability through check writing.[201] They quickly found favor, primarily because in a time of high inflation federal banking regulations precluded standard savings accounts from offering interest rates exceeding 5 percent annually.[202] Assets under management increased sharply from less than $2 billion to 1974 to $76 billion in 1980.[203] This contributed to a massive outflow from bank accounts that would ultimately encourage commercial banks to forsake their "boring" banking model of the mid-twentieth century and move into other lines of business to recover lost ground.[204]

Pension funds, unlike mutual funds, did own a greater proportion of public company equity at the end of the 1970s than at the beginning. The percentage of shares of public companies private pension funds owned increased from 8 percent to 14.6 percent from

---

[195] BLUMBERG, *supra* note 190, at 101, 176.

[196] *Leon Levy*, *in* THE WAY IT WAS: AN ORAL HISTORY OF FINANCE: 1967–1987, at 547, 551 (Editors of Institutional Investor, 1988); MATTHEW P. FINK, THE RISE OF MUTUAL FUNDS: AN INSIDER'S VIEW 78 (2008).

[197] OECD, OECD ECONOMIC SURVEYS—UNITED STATES 124 (1996) (4.7 percent in 1970, 4.2 percent in 1975, and 2.8 percent in 1980).

[198] FINK, *supra* note 196, at 79.

[199] Jason Zweig, *Happy Birthday to the Index Fund*, WALL ST. J., Sept. 1, 2016, C1.

[200] FINK, *supra* note 196, 81; Almarin Phillips, *The Metamorphosis of Markets: Commercial and Investment Banking* 1 J. COMP. CORP. L. & SEC. REG. 227, 235 (1978).

[201] FINK, *supra* note 196, at 80; Phillips, *supra* note 200, at 235–36.

[202] FINK, *supra* note 196, at 80.

[203] *Id.* at 82.

[204] Cheffins, *supra* note 57, at 22–23.

1970 to 1980, with the equivalent figures for public pension funds being 1.2 percent and 2.9 percent.[205] Noted management theorist Peter Drucker argued in 1976 that the growth of pension funds as investors meant "the US has 'socialized' the economy" and claimed "(t)he pension funds have become America's 'new tycoons'—surely the most unlikely masters any society ever had."[206] Pension funds did not conduct themselves, however, like corporate "masters" in the 1970s. As Drucker conceded, the fact that the percentage of public company shares pension funds owned was increasing had not resulted in a willingness to act as "owners" prepared to hold management to account, as opposed to being mere "investors" who would sell if they did not like how a company was being run.[207]

While pension funds did not begin acting like "owners" in the 1970s, regulatory reforms affecting pensions would ultimately help to change the environment in which the public company operated. In 1974 Congress enacted the Employee Retirement Income Security Act (ERISA), which established rules regulating private pension plans so as to protect employees' pension rights.[208] A facet of ERISA would have a significant impact on pension fund investment patterns, and would do so in a way that improved the funding prospects of potential rivals to large public companies. ERISA replaced a duty of prudence, or caution, owed at common law under state law that precluded pension fund trustees from investing in speculative securities with a similarly configured statutory standard.[209] Concerns quickly developed that ERISA's prudence duty restricted pension fund investment in companies to securities of well-established "blue chip" firms.[210] Pension funds, it seemed, could not be "a source of venture capital for the Xeroxes of tomorrow" (Xerox's "wizardry was considered as high tech as the iPhone" when it introduced in 1959 what would become very popular photocopiers).[211]

The Department of Labor, in a 1979 interpretative ruling, created a prudence standard "safe harbor" for pension fund trustees insulating them from liability for investments made so long as due consideration was given to factors such as diversification, liquidity, and projected return relative to funding objectives.[212] Adoption brought a "sigh of relief" from venture capitalists, among others, because pension fund trustees now clearly had the scope to look beyond blue-chip companies when investing.[213] That meant, according to one contemporary, "for entrepreneurs who

[205] OECD, *supra* note 197, at 124.

[206] Peter F. Drucker, The Unseen Revolution: How Pension Fund Socialism Came to America 4, 47 (1976).

[207] *Id.* at 82–83.

[208] Pub. L. No. 93-406, 88 Stat. 829.

[209] James D. Hutchinson, *The Federal Prudent Man Rule under ERISA*, 22 Vill. L. Rev. 22, 39–41 (1977); Robert C. Pozen, *The Prudent Person Rule and ERISA: A Legal Perspective*, Fin. Analysts J., Mar.–Apr. 1977, 30, 31, discussing ERISA, §§ 404(a)(1)(B), 514.

[210] Nancy L. Ross, *Widening Pensions' Investing*, Wash. Post, May 15, 1977, 181; Nancy F. Bern, *Fiduciary Responsibility: Prudent Investments under ERISA*, 14 Suffolk U. L. Rev. 1066, 1082–83 (1980).

[211] Ross, *supra* note 210; Steve Lohr & Carlos Tejada, *After Era That Made It a Verb, Xerox, in a Sale, Is Past Tense*, NY Times, Feb. 1, 2018, A1.

[212] 44 Fed. Reg. 37,221 (1979); Bern, *supra* note 210, at 1084.

[213] Nancy L. Ross, *New Law Gives Money Managers Breathing Space*, Wash. Post, July 15, 1979, G4; Donald Moffitt, *New Pension-Fund Regulation Makes It Easier for Trustees to Risk "Alternative" Investments*, Wall St. J., Sept. 10, 1979, 48.

can operate on a shoestring until the big money comes along, the future looks brighter than it has in years."[214] The 1979 reinterpretation of the prudent man rule reinforced for the venture capital (VC) industry a shift in focus from raising money from wealthy families to institutional investors and as such contributed to a "serious turning point" for the industry.[215] Venture capital would in turn prove to be, as the twentieth century drew to a close, a vital source of financial support for various firms seeking to mount challenges to incumbents vested with market power.[216]

Though passivity was the norm for shareholders in the 1970s as it was in the 1950s and 1960s, not all was quiet for management on the shareholder front. Interventions occurred, but not to prompt executives to generate stronger stockholder returns. The shareholder activists instead were seeking to advance a social agenda.

There was considerable social ferment as the 1970s got underway. Opposition to US involvement in the Vietnam War was mounting rapidly. Concerns about pollution were escalating dramatically, as exemplified by millions taking part in Earth Day events in April 1970.[217] Large corporations found themselves in the crosshairs. The *Wall Street Journal* noted in 1970 "(a)ctivists protesting the Vietnam War, pollution and what they charge is industrial irresponsibility are planning to press vigorously their campaigns in coming weeks at a number of shareholder meetings across the country."[218] Companies targeted included Honeywell Inc. due to a munitions program, AT&T because of its "complicity with the war machine," and utility Commonwealth Edison, which had "been waging a running battle with antipollution activists for months."[219]

Throughout the 1970s social activists had the opportunity to put before shareholders proposals on topics such as apartheid in South Africa, equal employment opportunity programs, and an Arab boycott of Israel.[220] An initiative coined Campaign GM was the most publicized instance of public interest lobbying by shareholders, pitting "a leader of American capitalism [General Motors] against the nation's leading consumer advocate," Ralph Nader.[221] Nader rose to prominence in 1965 with the publication of an exposé of General Motors' seemingly cavalier approach to public safety.[222] He subsequently cofounded the Project on Corporate Responsibility (PCR), which chose GM as its first target in 1970.[223] PCR bought a dozen

---

214 David Pauly, *Venture Capital Comes Back*, NEWSWEEK, June 4, 1979, 67.

215 Margaret B.W. Graham, *Entrepreneurship in the United States, 1920–2000, in* THE INVENTION OF ENTERPRISE: ENTREPRENEURSHIP FROM ANCIENT MESOPOTAMIA TO MODERN TIMES 401, 431 (David S. Landes, Joel Mokyr & William J. Baumol eds., 2010). See also Paul A. Gompers, *The Rise and Fall of Venture Capital*, 23 BUS. ECON. HIST. 1, 12–13 (1994); William Lazonick, *The Quest for Shareholder Value: Stock Repurchases in the US Economy*, 74 LOUVAIN ECON. REV. 479, 499 (2008).

216 Chapter 4, notes 523–25 and accompanying text; Chapter 5, notes 412, 439, 442–52 and related discussion.

217 *Millions Join Earth Day Observances across the Nation*, NY TIMES, Apr. 23, 1970, 1.

218 *Activists Intend to Use Annual Meetings as Forums for Protests in Coming Weeks*, WALL ST. J., Apr. 7, 1970, 40.

219 *Id.* For other examples, see Philip I. Blumberg, *The Politicization of the Corporation*, 26 BUS. LAW. 1551, 1552 (1971).

220 Donald E. Schwartz & Elliott J. Weiss, *An Assessment of the SEC Shareholder Proposal Rule*, 65 GEO. L.J. 643–46 (1977).

221 *Campaign GM*, THE CORPORATION IN A DEMOCRATIC SOCIETY 89, 89 (Edward J. Bander ed., 1975).

222 RALPH NADER, UNSAFE AT ANY SPEED: THE DESIGNED-IN DANGERS OF THE AMERICAN AUTOMOBILE (1965).

223 ROBERT A.G. MONKS & NELL MINOW, CORPORATE GOVERNANCE 419 (4th ed. 2008).

shares and requested that the automaker circulate to shareholders prior to GM's 1970 annual meeting nine resolutions to be voted upon.[224] The topics included vehicle emissions, automobile safety, pollution from manufacturing plants, and ownership of car dealerships by minority groups.[225]

General Motors refused to circulate any of the proposals to shareholders.[226] With its hand forced by an SEC decision on the matter, GM ultimately put to a shareholder vote proposals to create a shareholder committee on corporate responsibility and to add three directors to GM's all-male, all-white board.[227] The subtext with PCR's board resolution was that the vacancies created should be filled by an environmentalist, an Afro-American, and a female consumer advocate PCR had identified.[228] The resolutions, as with other public interest proposals shareholders put forward at GM and other companies in the 1970s, were voted down by overwhelming majorities.[229] Many investors indeed found the phrase "social responsibility" to be pretentious and annoying.[230]

Despite shareholders resoundingly defeating the PCR proposals, General Motors' 1970 annual meeting was characterized in the mid-1970s as "the decisive event in the politicization of the corporation"[231] and "perhaps a turning point in American business history."[232] In fact, in the 1980s and 1990s the promotion of shareholder value, not the pursuit of social goals, would become the hallmark of shareholder/public company relations.[233] Still, while Campaign GM was not a decisive turning point in favor of politicization of the corporation, within three years of the automaker's 1970 annual meeting a black community leader, a female bank executive, and an eminent scientist had joined the GM board and GM had set up a public policy committee comprised entirely of outside directors.[234] More generally, social activism by shareholders likely influenced managerial perceptions of the goals companies should be seeking to achieve, if only temporarily. Opinion was divided during the 1950s and 1960s about the extent to which managers were seeking to balance the interests of competing groups rather than prioritize shareholder returns.[235] In the 1970s it seemed to be

---

224 Lewis H. Young, *The Claimants for Influence with the Corporation*, RUNNING THE AMERICAN, *supra* note 169, at 38, 51–52.

225 Donald E. Schwartz, *The Public-Interest Proxy Contest: Reflections on Campaign GM*, 69 MICH. L. REV. 419, 534–37 (1971).

226 *Id.* at 451.

227 *Id.* at 453–57.

228 E.J. Kahn, *We Look Forward to Seeing You Next Year*, NEW YORKER, June 20, 1970, 40.

229 C.A. Harwell Wells, *The Cycles of Corporate Social Responsibility: An Historical Retrospective for the Twenty-first Century*, 51 KANSAS L. REV. 77, 117 (2002).

230 SILK & VOGEL, *supra* note 147, at 56.

231 David Vogel, *The Corporation as Government: Challenges & Dilemmas*, 8 POLITY 5, 28 (1975), quoting Blumberg, *supra* note 219, at 1561.

232 ROBERT HARGREAVES, SUPERPOWER: A PORTRAIT OF AMERICA IN THE 70S, at 164 (1973).

233 Chapter 4, notes 293–305 and related discussion; Chapter 5, notes 192–96, 199 and accompanying text.

234 Schwartz & Weiss, *supra* note 220, at 647.

235 Chapter 2, notes 9, 237–50 and accompanying text.

more widely accepted that those running large corporations had a social arbiter function to perform.[236]

In a widely publicized 1970 essay the *New York Times* published together with numerous photos relating to Campaign GM, noted University of Chicago economist Milton Friedman denounced efforts by corporations to focus on "social responsibilities of business" and to seek to achieve ostensibly desirable social ends.[237] He argued that executives ignoring their primary responsibility to shareholders were "unwitting puppets" of "intellectual forces . . . undermining the basis of a free society."[238] Friedman, however, was widely thought of in the 1970s as a spokesperson for a "rear guard" defending an antiquated ideology.[239] Peter Drucker, for instance, said in 1980, "most businesses look upon shareholders as a constituency that has to be satisficed" with a minimum acceptable return.[240] While "shareholder value" would become talismanic for executives as the twentieth century drew to a close, the phrase was rarely used in the 1970s, and when it was this was not done to convey the message that increasing shareholder returns should be the top corporate priority.[241]

The 1970s, in sum, was not a decade in which shareholders impinged considerably on corporate executives. Instead, in "an age of 'corporate responsibility,' "[242] shareholders remained primarily a theoretical constraint for management. Matters were potentially different with the board of directors, as reflected in the emergence of corporate governance as a serious topic for discussion.

BOARDS

The term "corporate governance," invoked with considerable frequency as the twentieth century concluded, was rarely used before 1970.[243] The 1970s were the turning point.[244] The Penn Central bankruptcy and the questionable payments revelations prompted concerns about managerial accountability largely unknown in the 1950s and 1960s.[245] "Corporate

---

[236] *The Top Man Becomes Mr. Outside*, Bus. Wk., May 4, 1974, 38; Courtney C. Brown, Putting the Corporate Board to Work 51–52, 58–59 (1976); J. Keith Louden, Managing at the Top: Roles and Responsibilities of the Chief Executive 8 (1977).

[237] Milton Friedman, *The Social Responsibility of Business Is to Increase Its Profits*, NY Times, Sept. 13, 1970, Sunday Magazine, 17.

[238] *Id.*

[239] Blumberg, *supra* note 190, at 4. See also Jeffrey N. Gordon, *The Rise of Independent Directors in the United States, 1950–2005: Of Shareholder Value and Stock Market Prices*, 59 Stanford L. Rev. 1465, 1520 (2007) ("seemed far out of the mainstream").

[240] Peter F. Drucker, Managing in Turbulent Times 210 (1980).

[241] Heilbron, Verheul & Quak, *supra* note 39, at 7–9; Blake Edward Taylor, *Reconsidering the Rise of "Shareholder Value" in the United States, 1960–2000*, LSE Economic History Working Paper, No. 214/2015 10-15 (2015).

[242] Herman, *supra* note 56, at 251.

[243] *Supra* note 57 and accompanying text; Brian R. Cheffins, *Corporate Governance since the Managerial Capitalism Era*, 89 Bus. Hist. Rev. 717, 727–28 (2015).

[244] Teitelman, *supra* note 105, at 82–83.

[245] Cheffins, *supra* note 243, at 725–26.

governance" was the catchphrase typically deployed in the debates that ensued, which meant "in the last half of the 1970s the issue caught fire."[246]

Shareholders are typically thought of as major corporate governance players. Due, however, to "a widespread appreciation of the practical obstacles to enlarging the role of share owners in the conduct of corporate affairs,"[247] they were an afterthought as corporate governance first rose to prominence in the 1970s. The board of directors instead held center stage.[248] During the 1970s boards were subjected to considerable criticism but a consensus would develop on how they might be reconfigured so as to enhance managerial accountability. There was disagreement, however, about the merits of regulatory intervention as compared with voluntary reform.

Criticism

The 1970 Penn Central debacle would launch debate in earnest about boards. The Penn Central board, comprised primarily of outside directors, did ultimately dismiss its chairman and "generally blew the whistle on the railroad's disastrous financial condition."[249] Nevertheless, the board became a lightning rod for discontent relating to Penn Central's collapse.

Critics questioned the objectivity of Penn Central's board, noting that two-thirds of the directors were representatives of banks and a majority of those directors were affiliated with banks to which Penn Central was indebted.[250] There also was widespread condemnation of the efforts of the Penn Central board, or lack thereof.[251] A 1971 study of Penn Central's collapse indicated the corporation's "directors seem to have done very little. . . . In most cases all they did was sit."[252] The SEC, in a 1972 report to Congress, said the Penn Central board failed in that the board did not set up procedures to ensure it was kept fully appraised of what was going on with the corporation's railroad operations and did not respond to specific warnings about Penn Central's true condition.[253] Louis Cabot, who quit the Penn Central board just prior to the railroad operations bankruptcy after serving for a year, accepted the SEC's verdict that the board had not done anything meaningful to halt the slide and acknowledged that as a board Penn Central's was "a horrible example."[254]

---

246 Robert S. Hatfield, *The Changing Corporate Environment: Problems and Opportunities, in* THE CHANGING BOARDROOM: MAKING POLICY AND PROFITS IN AN AGE OF CORPORATE CITIZENSHIP 18, 18 (George C. Greanias & Duane Windsor eds. 1982). See also *Running the American Corporation*, BUS. WK., Jan. 22, 1979, 9 ("a growth industry").

247 Business Roundtable, *The Role and Composition of Directors of the Large Publicly Owned Corporation*, 33 BUS. LAW. 2083, 2095 (1978).

248 Irving Kristol, *"Reforming" Corporate Governance*, WALL ST. J., May 12, 1978, 20 ("All serious discussions of the reform of 'corporate governance' tend ineluctably—perhaps too glibly—in the direction of increasing both the power and responsibility of the board of directors").

249 STANLEY C. VANCE, CORPORATE LEADERSHIP: BOARDS, DIRECTORS, AND STRATEGY 166 (1983).

250 DAUGHEN & BINZEN, *supra* note 117, at 264–65.

251 SELIGMAN, *supra* note 135, at 536.

252 DAUGHEN & BINZEN, *supra* note 117, at 17.

253 Sommer, *supra* note 175, at 213.

254 *To Resign or Challenge*, FORBES, May 15, 1976, 104.

Ross and Kami, in their 1973 study of prominent managerial failures, said the fact that "most boards are little more than ineffective window dressing" had "been glossed over for many years, but it took the Penn Central 'incident' to focus attention upon it."[255] Myles Mace observed in 1974 "(i)f we have a few more Penn Centrals there's going to be a growing interest in what boards do and don't do."[256] There would not be a corporate collapse on the same scale in the 1970s. The controversy surrounding illicit payments, both domestic and foreign, nevertheless served to keep the board in the spotlight.

The SEC noted in a 1976 report on the illicit corporate payment saga that outside directors of the companies implicated were consistently kept out of the loop and characterized the situation as "the apparent frustration of our system of corporate accountability."[257] The *New York Times* observed in 1977 that "(t)he talk of bribes, kickbacks, illegal contributions and 'questionable' payments led to the urging of a thorough revamping of corporate boards of directors."[258] Nader concurred in a 1984 article on corporate governance in the *California Management Review*. He said "(p)robably nothing has highlighted the board of directors in capacity more than the bribery scandals of the seventies and the collapse of companies such as the Penn Central," suggesting in so doing "boards either did not know, did not want to know, or did not want to do anything about what they knew."[259]

Dissatisfaction with boards did not relate purely to Penn Central and the illicit payment controversy.[260] There was a consensus emerging in the early 1970s "that the average board of directors was malfunctioning—if indeed it were functioning at all."[261] In 1976 *Business Week* called "the corporate board system ... a serious embarrassment."[262] By 1977 "the fact that many boards—perhaps most—do not perform well (was) not news."[263] The consensus was endorsed in governmental circles, with the chairman of the SEC testifying in 1976 that "(t)op management personnel of far too many corporations certainly have been unresponsive ... to boards of directors."[264]

---

[255] Ross & Kami, *supra* note 113, at 24. See also Neil H. Jacoby, Corporate Power and Social Responsibility 166 (1973) (saying of recent criticism of boards "no single recent event" had "raised sharper questions than.... Penn Central").

[256] John V. Conti, *Boardroom Blues*, Wall St. J., Sept. 17, 1974, 1.

[257] John C. Coffee, *Beyond the Shut-Eyed Sentry: Toward a Theoretical View of Corporate Misconduct and an Effective Legal Response*, 63 Va. L. Rev. 1099, 1128–29 (1977). See also Gordon, *supra* note 239, at 1516.

[258] Fredrick Andrews, *The First Draft of a Corporate Constitution*, NY Times, Apr. 22, 1977, 91.

[259] Ralph Nader, *Reforming Corporate Governance*, Calif. Mgmt. Rev., Summer 1984, at 126, 127. See also Seligman, *supra* note 135, at 539 ("No series of events better illustrated the deficiencies of the corporate board of directors than the SEC questionable payments cases").

[260] Seligman, *supra* note 135, at 537.

[261] Joseph Hinsey, *Corporate Governance: Legal Realities and Trends, in* Changing Boardroom, *supra* note 246, at 37, 38.

[262] Carl Burgen, *Separating the Board from Management*, Bus. Wk., Apr. 26, 1976, 6.

[263] Transcript and Proceedings: Toward a More Effective Board 8 (1977).

[264] Quoted in Harvey J. Goldschmid, *The Governance of the Public Corporation: Internal Relationships, in* Commentaries on Corporate Structure and Governance: The ALI-ABA Symposiums 1977–1978, at 167, 173 (Donald E. Schwartz ed., 1978).

Ideas for Improvement

While concerns were often expressed in the 1970s that boards were part of the problem with potentially wayward public companies, there also was a growing consensus that boards could be an important part of the solution. The idea was that from a governance perspective the board of a public company should oversee and restrain management so as to keep in check the executives responsible running the firm on a day-to-day basis. The Securities and Exchange Commission said in its 1980 report on its 1977 corporate accountability hearings "a new consensus is emerging with the vital monitoring role played by the board of directors."[265] Corporate law scholar Melvin Eisenberg has been credited with providing "the first coherent statement of the monitoring model" of the board in his 1976 book *The Structure of the Corporation*.[266] Nevertheless, during the first half of the 1970s, "auditing the performance of the operating management"[267] and "actively check(ing) management"[268] had already been identified as key tasks for the board.

As for how to prompt boards to fulfill their governance potential as monitors of management, *Business Week* said in 1971 "there are as many suggestions for reform as there are voices."[269] By the end of the decade the situation had changed. The SEC, in its 1980 report, indicated that in addition to broad agreement on the role that the board should play

> the consensus is moving strongly towards greater participation by directors independent of management, currently calling for a board composed of at least a majority of independent directors, with properly functioning independent audit, compensation and nominating committees, as essential to enhanced and effective corporate accountability.[270]

By the end of the 1970s even among public company executives there was general acceptance it was sound practice for outside directors to be well represented on boards and for certain key tasks to be delegated to committees outside directors dominated. In 1972, on the initiative of Fred Borch, General Electric's CEO, the Business Roundtable was established

---

[265] Securities and Exchange Commission, *supra* note 187, Forward, at 2. See also Gordon, *supra* note 239, at 1518; George W. Dent, *The Revolution in Corporate Governance, the Monitoring Board, and the Director's Duty of Care*, 61 Boston U. L. Rev. 623, 632 (1981); Lawrence E. Mitchell, *The Trouble with Boards*, Perspectives on Corporate Governance 17, 46 (F. Scott Kieff & Troy A. Paredes eds., 2010).

[266] Mitchell, *supra* note 265, at 32; Eisenberg, *supra* note 4. See also Elliott J. Weiss & Donald E. Schwartz, *Using Disclosure to Activate the Board of Directors*, Corporations at the Crossroads, *supra* note 175, at 109, 122.

[267] Jacoby, *supra* note 255, at 177.

[268] Harvey J. Goldschmid, *The Greening of the Board Room: Reflections on Corporate Responsibility*, 10 Colum. J.L. Social Problems 15, 24 (1973).

[269] *The Board: It's Obsolete unless Overhauled*, Bus. Wk., May 22, 1971, 50.

[270] Securities and Exchange Commission, *supra* note 187, Forward, at 3. See also at F155 (consensus on a majority of independent directors), F156 (general agreement on the critical nature of audit, compensation, and nomination committees). See, though, Victor Brudney, *The Independent Director—Heavenly City or Potemkin Village?*, 95 Harv. L. Rev. 597, 598–99 (1981) (indicating that the concept of "outside" or "independent" director "does not carry a clear meaning for many of its proponents or the same meaning for all its proponents").

to represent the views of chief executive officers of major corporations on public policy.[271] In 1978 the Business Roundtable issued a statement on "The Role and Composition of Directors of the Large Publicly Owned Corporation" that indicated boards of public companies should typically be composed of a majority of non-management directors and should establish audit, compensation and nomination committees outside directors dominated.[272]

The logic underlying the growing consensus oriented around outside directors and board committees was straightforward. With respect to boardroom monitoring of managerial performance there is an obvious risk of bias on the part of executive directors. So obvious, according to a 1975 *Harvard Business Review* article imploring industry to "clean up the boardroom," "(i)t is almost ridiculous to have to justify the importance of a strong majority of outside directors."[273] Reliance on board committees was thought to be salutary because committees staffed by outside directors could focus on areas where independent judgment was most crucial and ensure that key issues were dealt with in sufficient depth despite outside directors only serving on a part-time basis.[274] By the end of the 1970s, there was general agreement with the SEC and the Business Roundtable that the key committees boards should have were an audit committee to deal with accounting and risk control issues, a compensation committee to address the potentially fraught topic of executive pay, and a nomination committee to identify suitable directors going forward.[275]

Board Reform Implementation

During the 1970s, boards were reconfigured in a manner that moved them toward the consensus view that was developing regarding substantial outside director representation and the deployment of committees. In large manufacturing companies the proportion of executive directors fell from 40 percent in 1970 to 38 percent in 1975 and to 33 percent in 1980.[276] Similarly, among 270 major industrial, transportation, and distribution companies the executive director component dropped from 54 percent in 1970 to 43 percent in 1980.[277] According to Conference Board data relating to large industrial companies 93 percent had an audit committee in 1977 as compared with 19 percent in 1967 and 45 percent in 1972.[278]

---

[271] William E. Rothschild, The Secret to GE's Success 164 (2007); Benjamin C. Waterhouse, Lobbying America: The Politics of Business from Nixon to NAFTA 101–04 (2014) (identifying the original members).

[272] Business Roundtable, *supra* note 247, at 2107–10.

[273] Marvin Chandler, *It's Time to Clean Up the Boardroom*, Harv. Bus. Rev., Sept./Oct. 1975, 73, 74.

[274] Business Roundtable, *supra* note 247, at 2109; Joseph Hinsey, *Reform from Within: An Alternative to Radical Change, in* Commentaries on Corporate, *supra* note 264, 309–10; Brian R. Cheffins, Company Law: Theory, Structure and Operation 622 (1997).

[275] Williams, *supra* note 189, at 19–20; Andrews, *supra* note 258 (discussing conclusions reached by "a thoughtful assortment of prominent figures in business, government, and the professions, gathered by the American Assembly, a Columbia University affiliate, to discuss and debate 'the ethics of corporate conduct'").

[276] Kenneth M. Lehn, Sukesh Patro & Mengxin Zhao, *Determinants of the Size and Composition of US Corporate Boards: 1935–2000*, 38 Fin. Mgmt. 747, 755 (2009). This data is cited by Gordon, *supra* note 239, at 1473.

[277] Barry D. Baysinger & Henry N. Butler, *Corporate Governance and the Board of Directors: Performance Effects of Changes in Board Composition*, 1 J.L. Econ. & Org. 101, 113 (1985).

[278] Data reported by Marshall Small, *The Evolving Role of the Director in Corporate Governance*, 30 Hastings L.J. 1353, 1358 (1979).

The proportion with compensation committees rose from 57 percent to 72 percent and to 90 percent over the same period.[279] Nomination committees staffed by outside directors were a rarity before General Motors set a precedent for their use in 1972.[280] By 1979, however, 29 percent of companies traded on a major stock exchange had such a committee, including 38 percent of companies listed on the New York Stock Exchange (NYSE).[281]

Though in the 1970s boards were being reconfigured in a manner consistent with the developing consensus on how boards should be structured, there was disagreement about the extent to which boards were positioned in practice to enhance managerial accountability. Some were optimistic. A 1977 guide to the chief executive role indicated "(n)o element of management has undergone such change as the board of directors."[282] In a survey of long-serving directors of *Fortune* 500 companies accounting firm Touche Ross conducted in 1978, 89 percent indicated that boards had undergone significant changes over the previous decade.[283] Harold Williams, as chairman of the SEC, remarked in 1979 upon "the very real progress which many boards have made."[284]

Others were skeptical. Law professor Harvey Goldschmid argued in 1978 that with boards "the experimentation has been limited and certainly not broad enough in scope."[285] Similarly, while Myles Mace, a strong critic of boards in his 1971 study,[286] indicated in 1975 that he saw "a desire on the part of directors and executives to strengthen their boards,"[287] by 1979 he was saying "boards of directors operate pretty much as they did ten years ago."[288] Venerable corporate lawyer Ira Millstein said of 1970s boards in 2016 that they were "passive and inert, pliable rubber stamps."[289] Perhaps, as law professor Jeffrey Gordon subsequently suggested, the correct verdict on board reform in the 1970s is a mixed one, "in which managerial elites made significant concessions.... (B)ut the work of genuine change in the habits and practices of the board had barely begun."[290]

There also was a lack of consensus regarding the suitable means for reforming the board. Senator Howard Metzenbaum said in 1980 "(t)here is widespread agreement within and without the business community that reforms are necessary in the governance of the nation's major corporations. There is no agreement, however, on the need for federal legislation to

---

279 *Id.*

280 Rosabeth Moss Kanter, The Change Masters 318 (1983). According to Conference Board data, 7 percent of large industrial companies had a nomination committee as of 1972—Small, *supra* note 278, at 1358.

281 Securities and Exchange Commission, *supra* note 187, at F99.

282 Louden, *supra* note 236, at 117.

283 Touche Ross, *The Touche Ross Survey on the Changing Nature of the Corporate Board*, xii (1978).

284 Williams, *supra* note 189, at 15.

285 Goldschmid, *supra* note 264, at 172.

286 Mace, *supra* note 185.

287 David R. Francis, *Corporations Feel Cleansing Tide of Watergate*, Christian Sci. Monitor, Apr. 21, 1975, 18.

288 Mace, *supra* note 186, at 297.

289 Ira M. Millstein, The Activist Director: Lessons from the Boardroom and the Future of the Corporation 27 (2017).

290 Gordon, *supra* note 239, at 1519. See also Harald Baum, *The Rise of the Independent Director: A Historical and Comparative Perspective*, Max Planck Institute for Comparative and International Private Law Research Paper Series No. 16/20 14 (2016) (endorsing Gordon's verdict).

bring about those essential reforms."[291] Metzenbaum spoke from experience, having recently sought and failed to forge a consensus that could have provided the platform for legislative change.

Metzenbaum, in his capacity as chairman of the Judiciary Committee's Subcommittee on Citizens and Shareholder Rights and Remedies, appointed in early 1978 a diverse advisory committee on corporate governance to consider legislative initiatives.[292] The advisory committee met in June, August, and November, with those attending including John deButts, the chairman of the board of AT&T, Irving Shapiro, CEO and chairman of DuPont, Lewis Gilbert, a veteran shareholder "gadfly," and Mark Green, a close associate of Ralph Nader.[293] One participant in the meetings of Metzenbaum's advisory committee, drawing an analogy to recent peace negotiations between Egypt and Israel, said of the exercise "(i)t was to be the corporate equivalent of Camp David. We were to sit together and hammer out our differences until we could achieve peace."[294] The advisory committee considered draft legislation Senator Metzenbaum's staff had generated, with a key element being a provision obliging all companies with more than 500 shareholders and assets exceeding $1 million in value to have a majority of independent directors on the board.[295] Metzenbaum told the members of the committee at the first of its three meetings "(g)entlemen, if this group can agree on a legislative proposal, I can almost assure you that it will become law."[296]

In 1976 a bill introduced to the Senate in response to the revelations of illicit foreign payments that would have required one-third of the board of a public company to be outside directors and mandated the formation of audit committees comprised of independent directors fell quietly by the wayside.[297] Nevertheless, Metzenbaum's boast about enacting legislation reforming boards was not an idle one. Harold Williams, the SEC chairman, warned in 1978 "(i)f business cannot clean its own house, government will clean the house of business."[298] Law professor David Ruder said of Metzenbaum's committee at a 1979 corporate governance symposium that its "very existence ... should dispell doubts regarding the seriousness of the federal intervention movement."[299]

The consensus Metzenbaum was seeking among members of the corporate governance advisory committee proved to be lacking, which doomed the prospects for immediate legislative dividends. Caspar Weinberger, a future secretary of defense under Ronald Reagan, described Metzenbaum's strategy as being one of proclaiming that legislation was inevitable

---

[291] Howard M. Metzenbaum, *Legislative Approaches to Corporate Governance*, 56 NOTRE DAME L. REV. 926, 926 (1980).

[292] *Id.* at 929; Thomas E. Mullaney, *Governance of US Companies: Proposals on Reform Likely Soon*, NY TIMES, Feb. 24, 1978, D3.

[293] Judith Miller, *At Odds over Corporate Governance*, NY TIMES, Dec. 24, 1978, F1. Not all members who agreed to join the committee attended. On the full membership, see Metzenbaum, *supra* note 291, at 929, n.20.

[294] Miller, *supra* note 293.

[295] *Id.*

[296] *Id.*

[297] *Commissars for Corporations*, WALL ST. J., May 12, 1976, 16; Brenda S. Birkett, *The Recent History of Corporate Audit Committees*, 13 ACCOUNTING HISTORIANS J. 109, 118 (1986).

[298] Quoted in MCSWEENEY, *supra* note 191, at 13.

[299] David S. Ruder, *Corporate Governance: An Analysis of Duties, Attacks, and Responses*, 4 DEL. J. CORP. L. 741, 752 (1979).

so as to orchestrate an agreement on content. "The only flaw," Weinberger noted, "is that the corporate executives who did attend the meetings . . . failed to agree that any bills should be passed."[300] DeButts and Shapiro announced at the November 1978 meeting of the advisory committee that they could not support the draft legislation in front of them.[301]

DeButts and Shapiro likely were mindful that the corporate community they were in effect representing would be very difficult to swing around.[302] The strongly preferred approach to board reform was voluntary adjustment.[303] Guidance was available from the Business Roundtable's 1978 statement on boards.[304] There also was an "important" 1976 guidebook an American Bar Association subcommittee issued that indicated a model board of a publicly traded company would have a majority of outside directors and would establish audit, compensation, and nomination committees outside directors dominated.[305]

Despite the derailment of Metzenbaum's plans for legislative reform the changes that boards underwent in the 1970s were by no means entirely voluntary. Instead, public officials provided a strong nudge, both by statute and administrative fiat. The Federal Corrupt Practices Act of 1977 was Congress's legislative response to the revelations of illicit foreign payments in the mid-1970s.[306] The Act made it a crime to promise payment to a foreign public official to obtain or retain business as well as amending federal securities law to require publicly traded companies to keep accurate books and records and have a suitable system of internal accounting controls in place.[307] While boards were not regulated directly, having a suitably constructed audit committee in place was quickly identified as a vehicle for ensuring that internal controls were appropriate.[308]

On the administrative side, the SEC was active in fostering boardroom change.[309] In 1972 the Commission offered a strong endorsement in principle of the use of audit committees staffed by outside directors, and in 1974 required public companies to disclose whether they had such a committee in place.[310] During the mid-1970s SEC officials resolved a substantial number of cases it brought against public companies, usually in relation to illicit payments, with a settlement where the companies would agree to make board-level changes, such as the appointment of additional outside directors and the creation of an audit committee.[311] In 1976 the SEC urged the NYSE to amend the Exchange's listing rules to make the

---

300 Caspar Weinberger, *How to Put Feds in Control of Everything: A Case Study*, CHI. TRIB., Jan. 28, 1979, A6.

301 Miller, *supra* note 293.

302 *Id.*

303 Metzenbaum, *supra* note 291, at 930.

304 Business Roundtable, *supra* note 247.

305 Mitchell, *supra* note 265, at 35; ABA Subcommittee on Functions and Responsibilities of Directors, Committee on Corporate Laws, *Corporate Directors' Guidebook*, 32 BUS. LAW. 5, 11, 33, 35–36 (1976).

306 P.L. 95-213; 91 Stat. 1494.

307 Federal Corrupt Practices Act, §§ 102, 104.

308 Birkett, *supra* note 297, at 119.

309 *End of the Directors' Rubber Stamp*, BUS. WK., Sept. 10, 1979, 72 ("Most government pressure for more responsible boards . . . has been coming from the SEC").

310 Birkett, *supra* note 297, at 109–10; LOUIS BRAIOTTA, THE AUDIT COMMITTEE HANDBOOK 438–39 (4th ed. 2004).

311 Sommer, *supra* note 175, at 194–99.

establishment of an audit committee comprised of outside directors a condition of listing.[312] The NYSE made the change the following year.[313]

The public hearings the SEC held on corporate accountability in 1977 appeared to set the stage for further intervention. The hearings were "part of the most serious and far-reaching study of corporate conduct in the SEC's 43 year history," with the proposing of new legislation to Congress thought to be a clear possibility.[314] The Commission was keen to solicit a wide variety of opinions.[315] Hearings correspondingly were held in four cities and more than 300 persons and organizations offered input in person or in writing.[316]

Given the Penn Central debacle, the illicit payments controversy, the public's dwindling faith in large corporations, growing acceptance of the idea that a public company's board should monitor top management, and the SEC's hearings, in the late 1970s the timing seemingly was propitious for substantially enhanced regulation of boards. Indeed, a 1978 *Harvard Business Review* article on "the assault on managerial autonomy" said "(n)ot since the early days of the New Deal has the field of corporation law been so astir with proposals to reform the corporation."[317] Edward McSweeney, a management consultant, suggested in 1978 that it was "fairly certain that Congress would . . . enact legislation to restrict management's dominance of board business."[318]

Again, despite the seemingly congenial setting, Senator Metzenbaum's late-1970s legislative initiative came to nothing. Similarly, with the SEC's 1977 hearings on corporate accountability the potential for further dramatic action went largely unfulfilled. SEC chairman Harold Williams was skeptical of federal legislative intervention in the corporate realm and favored voluntary reform.[319] The Commission's staff correspondingly "put on the back burner most of the fundamental issues" the 1977 hearings raised.[320] The SEC focused instead on bolstering disclosure requirements concerning the board of directors. In 1978 the Commission adopted rules requiring a company under the SEC's jurisdiction to describe significant personal and business relationships between the company and its directors, the existence of auditing, nomination, and compensation committees (if any), and the composition of any such committees.[321] The SEC dropped a proposal highly unpopular with business interests that would have required that a public company identify each of the company's existing directors and nominees for the board as "management," "independent," or non-management but affiliated.[322]

---

[312] SELIGMAN, *supra* note 135, at 547; Sommer, *supra* note 175, at 210.

[313] SELIGMAN, *supra* note 135, at 547; Myron Kandel & Philip Greer, *June 30: Day of the Audit Panel for Corporate America*, CHI. TRIB., Jan. 15, 1978, A9.

[314] Joel Seligman, *Reformers Take on the Corporate Dragon*, LA TIMES, Sept. 29, 1977, D7.

[315] *Id.*

[316] Schwartz & Weiss, *supra* note 220, at 135.

[317] Sumner Marcus & Kenneth D. Walters, *The Assault on Managerial Autonomy*, HARV. BUS. REV., Jan./Feb. 1978, 57, 57.

[318] MCSWEENEY, *supra* note 191, at 32.

[319] *Corporate Governance—New Heat on Outside Directors*, FORBES, Nov. 1, 1977, 33; Judith Miller, *SEC Chief a Policy Enigma*, NY TIMES, May 14, 1979, D1.

[320] *SEC Acts to Require Disclosures by Firms on Directors, But Delays Other Decisions*, WALL ST. J., June 8, 1978, 8.

[321] SEC Securities Exchange Act Release No. 34-15384 (Dec. 6, 1978), summarized by BRAIOTTA, *supra* note 310, at 448.

[322] Schwartz & Weiss, *supra* note 220, at 135–36; Burt Schorr, *Agency Enigma*, WALL ST. J., Nov. 20, 1978, 1.

Senator Metzenbaum tried legislative reform again in 1980. He introduced a bill to the Senate that would have mandated an independent director majority on boards of large companies and required the establishment of audit and nomination committees composed solely of independent directors.[323] Again, his efforts fell short.[324] The Corporate Democracy Act of 1980, introduced to the House of Representatives with these features as well as provisions regulating plant closures, enhancing the rights of employees and bolstering the disclosure obligations of public companies,[325] suffered the same fate.[326]

Why was the 1970s regulatory legacy with boards not more substantial? Analysis provided next of the extent to which regulation operated as an external constraint on executives of public companies provides important clues. Growing antipathy toward government is at the center of the story.

External Constraints

During the 1950s and 1960s, regulation and unions were the most potent external constraints on managerial discretion. Both remained significant during the 1970s and, in the case of regulation, its impact grew and there was potential for the trend to continue. At the same time, with unions and regulation the scene was set as the 1970s concluded for a retreat that would become fully evident in the 1980s and 1990s. In contrast, competitors and the market for corporate control were both emerging as more substantial external checks on public company executives than had been the case during the heyday of managerial capitalism.

REGULATION

Throughout much of the 1970s, there was considerable momentum in favor of increased regulation relevant to business activity. This was halted as the decade drew to a close, with substantial erosion of faith in government changing the equation. Skepticism regarding government would also contribute substantially to a deregulatory movement that would from the late 1970s through to end of the twentieth century enhance managerial discretion in industries affected.

Expansion

Jensen and Meckling, in the process of arguing in their 1978 article that overweening government threatened the future of the public company, not surprisingly emphasized the potency of regulatory constraints. They said "(t)he corporate executive's power to make decisions affecting owners of his firm, employees of the firm and consumers of the firm's products

323 The Protection of Shareholders' Rights Act S. 2567, 96th Congress, 2d Sess., 126 Congressional Record S3754.

324 Vance, *supra* note 249, at 143–44 (summarizing the proposed legislation and observing "(p)assage of any legislation comparable to Senator Metzenbaum's proposal is probably a few years away").

325 H.R. 7010, 96th Congress, 2d Sess. For background on the bill's provisions see Mark Green et al., The Case for a Corporate Democracy Act (1979).

326 A.A. Sommer, *Corporate Governance: Its Impact on the Profession*, J. Accountancy, July 1980, 52, 58 ("this legislation is not expected to move swiftly in Congress").

is becoming more constrained every day."[327] Their verdict on the trend with government/business relations in the 1970s would be endorsed retrospectively. Economist Luigi Zingales suggested in a 2011 study of American capitalism that during the decade "business was a four-letter word in Washington," a stance that "helped keep big business power in check."[328] Mark Mizruchi, in a 2013 analysis of how attitudes of businessmen toward the state changed in the decades following World War II, characterized the 1970s as an era when "(g)overnment regulation . . . expanded" in various ways that placed "limits on managers' ability to run their firms."[329]

Between 1967 and 1977 Congress enacted "nearly 100 substantial pieces of legislation affecting the conduct of business."[330] There was also a shift in emphasis. Through to the 1960s, regulation of business was usually industry-specific and oriented around entry qualifications, pricing, and protection of standards in the industries affected.[331] The emphasis shifted in the late 1960s to "social" regulation that crossed industry lines and defined in relation to a particular facet of economic activity the applicable ground rules.[332] To a substantial degree, the legislative output institutionalized influential social activist causes of the era, such as civil rights, consumer protection, and the environment.[333] The publisher of the late 1960s and early 1970s counterculture bible *The Whole Earth Catalog* even suggested "(t)here was a quick assimilation of practically our whole damn culture."[334] Regulatory agencies created to administer the statutory measures included the Equal Employment Opportunity Commission, the National Highway Traffic Safety Administration, the Occupational Safety and Health Administration, the Consumer Product Safety Commission, and the Environmental Protection Agency.[335]

Galambos and Pratt said in 1988 of the laws Congress introduced from the mid-1960s through the mid-1970s "that applied broadly across the economy," "(t)hese regulations reached deeply into the decision-making processes of most businesses, adding a layer of government supervision where managers had traditionally enjoyed great autonomy."[336] The business community very much noticed that government scrutiny had been stepped up. As the 1970s wrapped up chief executives were denouncing in speeches "regulatory madness,"

---

[327] Jensen & Meckling, *supra* note 40, at 31.

[328] Luigi Zingales, A Capitalism for the People: Recapturing the Lost Genius of American Prosperity 80 (2014).

[329] Mark S. Mizruchi, The Fracturing of the American Corporate Elite 204 (2013).

[330] Robert Bleiberg, *Shareholder Constituency? The Liabilities Probably Outweigh the Assets*, Barron's, Aug. 29, 1977, 57.

[331] Chapter 2, note 466 and related discussion.

[332] Herman, *supra* note 56, at 173–74; Mizruchi, *supra* note 329, at 162–63; James Q. Wilson, *The Corporation as a Political Actor, in* American Corporation, *supra* note 60, at 413, 417–18; Douglas M. Eichar, The Rise and Fall of Corporate Social Responsibility 220, 227, 247–48 (2015).

[333] Larry Martz, *The Limits of Power*, Newsweek, Nov. 19, 1979, 86.

[334] *Id.*

[335] Carroll et al., *supra* note 168, at 234; Mansel G. Blackford & K. Austin Kerr, Business Enterprise in American History 405–09 (2d ed. 1990); Richard H.K. Vietor, *Government Regulation of Business, in* The Cambridge Economic History of the United States, Volume III: The Twentieth Century 969, 988 (Stanley L. Engerman & Robert E. Gallman eds., 2000).

[336] Galambos & Pratt, *supra* note 58, at 213.

"the regulation revolution," and "the regulator barons."[337] A constant refrain from the business community was that recent interventions by the state had been counterproductive.[338] Environmental laws and other forms of social regulation were singled out as being disproportionately onerous in relation to the benefits.[339]

Momentum Halted

In the late 1970s, given Congress's recent legislative proclivity, given control of Congress by the usually left-leaning Democrats, and given the election of Democrat Jimmy Carter as president in 1976, a continuation of the trend favoring increased regulation of business seemed a good bet.[340] Jensen and Meckling, in their article on the dismal future of the public company, said "(w)e see no forces likely to curb the gradual encroachment of government."[341] *Barron's* predicted in 1977 that "(w)ith the Democrats now in control of both the legislative and executive branches of government Big Brother is apt to grow increasingly heavy-handed" and cited a "long and horrendous list" of anti-business legislation on the agenda.[342]

"Stricter control of corporate directors" was part of *Barron's* "long and horrendous list."[343] This lent credence to Senator Metzenbaum's claim that if his advisory committee on corporate governance that was at work in 1978 could have agreed on legislation, enactment was likely.[344] In fact, a counter-reaction was developing that would undercut not only Senator Metzenbaum's efforts but the general momentum in favor of regulation of corporate activity.

The 1970s no doubt were bad for big business but it was a dismal decade for government as well. The Watergate political scandal that prompted Richard Nixon's 1974 resignation from office, the collapse of US-backed South Vietnam in 1975, chronic federal budget deficits, and repeated failed efforts to bring inflation under control fostered what *Newsweek* characterized in 1979 as "a growing sense that the country's institutions and leaders were no longer up to managing problems that were simply too complex to grasp."[345] Polling data indicated that antigovernment sentiment grew from 32 percent in 1964 to 50 percent in 1972 and 67 percent in 1980. Over the same time period, anti-business feeling peaked at 61 percent in 1979.[346]

---

[337] Robert J. Myers & Martha Stout Kessler, *Business Speaks: A Study of the Themes in Speeches by America's Corporate Leaders*, J. Bus. Commc'ns, Spring 1980, at 5, 7–8. For additional examples, see Mizruchi, *supra* note 329, at 163–64.

[338] Elliott J. Weiss, *Social Regulation of Business Activity: Reforming the Corporate Governance System to Resolve an Institutional Impasse*, 28 UCLA L. Rev. 343, 349 (1981).

[339] *The Incoherence of Government Policy*, Bus. Wk., June 30, 1980, 66; Wyatt Wells, American Capitalism, 1945–2000: Continuity and Change from Mass Production to the Information Society 100–01 (2003).

[340] Eichar, *supra* note 332, at 260.

[341] Jensen & Meckling, *supra* note 40, at 32.

[342] Bleiberg, *supra* note 330.

[343] *Id.*

[344] *Supra* note 296 and accompanying text.

[345] Martz, *supra* note 333. See also Vietor, *supra* note 335, at 996; Benjamin C. Waterhouse, The Land of Enterprise: A Business History of the United States 223 (2017).

[346] Lipset & Schneider, *supra note* 33, at 33.

Politicians who might have been expected to favor increased state involvement in the economy picked up on and attended to the antigovernment mood that developed in the 1970s. Jimmy Carter railed against the excesses of big government when campaigning for president in 1976 and told Congress soon after coming to office that "(r)egulation, once designed to serve the public, now stifles competition."[347] Carter acknowledged in his 1978 State of Union speech that "(g)overnment cannot solve our problems."[348] Among congressional Democrats many junior members lacked an appetite for business bashing and were aware of growing concerns about intrusive government among their constituents.[349] *Barron's* noted approvingly in 1978 that "Ralph Nader and his cohorts have begun to wear out their welcome on Capitol Hill."[350] The California electorate's strong endorsement of anti-tax Proposition 13 the same year quickly became a potent symbol of a desire for smaller government.[351] Mark Green, serving as director of Congress Watch, a lobbying group associated with Nader, acknowledged in 1979 "(i)t's a dark time for progressive activists."[352]

The business community was a key element of the growing antipathy toward government. Business leaders during the 1950s and 1960s were fearful of crossing federal politicians and tempered their managerial conduct to avoid showdowns.[353] Their 1970s counterparts, confronted with "the tidal wave of regulation" Ralph Nader and other members of the well-organized "public interest movement" had fostered, revamped their approach and adopted a proactive lobbying stance to counteract unwelcome regulatory initiatives.[354] By 1980 more than 80 percent of *Fortune* 500 firms had a public affairs office in Washington, with over half of the offices having been launched in the 1970s.[355] The Business Roundtable also quickly moved to the forefront of the lobbying scene.[356] Mark Green called it in 1979 "the most powerful secret lobby in Washington."[357] The fact that politicians were more likely to talk with chief executives than with lower-ranking corporate officials enhanced the Business Roundtable's clout.[358] Pragmatism also helped. Where enactment of legislation was assured, the Business Roundtable would accept the inevitable and instead seek to shape the contents.[359]

By the end of the 1970s the public interest movement's legislative juggernaut had completely stalled.[360] The fate of proposals to create a Consumer Protection Agency illustrated

[347] *The High Costs of Intervention*, BUS. WK., Apr. 4, 1977, 65; WATERHOUSE, *supra* note 271, at 170, 186 (Carter campaign rhetoric).

[348] KIM PHILLIPS-FEIN, INVISIBLE HANDS: THE BUSINESSMEN'S CRUSADE AGAINST THE NEW DEAL 198 (2009).

[349] *A Winning Streak for Business*, BUS. WK., Feb. 27, 1978, 28.

[350] Robert M. Bleiberg, *As the Worm Turns*, BARRON'S, Oct. 23, 1978, 58.

[351] David Buchan, *Administration Relaxes its Regulatory Grip*, FIN. TIMES, May 6, 1980, Finance and Investment in the US, xii.

[352] *A Fading Ralph Nader Rewrites His Strategy*, BUS. WK., Apr. 9, 1979, 72.

[353] Chapter 2, notes 510–18 and related discussion.

[354] Benjamin Waterhouse, *Corporate Mobilization against Liberal Reform, in* WHAT'S GOOD, *supra* note 97, at 233, 234–35.

[355] Wilson, *supra* note 332, at 422.

[356] WATERHOUSE, *supra* note 271, at 78.

[357] Philip Shabecoff, *Big Business on the Offensive*, NY TIMES, Dec. 9, 1979, Sunday Magazine, 34.

[358] PHILLIPS-FEIN, *supra* note 348, at 151.

[359] *Winning Streak, supra* note 349; *Business' Most Powerful Lobby in Washington*, BUS. WK., Dec. 20, 1976, 60.

[360] Waterhouse, *supra* note 354, at 235.

the reversal in momentum. During the first half of the 1970s arcane parliamentary tactics supported by the threat of a presidential veto were needed to derail legislative proposals on point.[361] In 1978, lobbying by the business community was sufficiently robust to foster the outright defeat of a bill providing for creation of the agency, an outcome that rendered the concept politically unviable.[362] Ralph Nader complained in response that "(t)his Congress is a wholly owned subsidiary" of American business.[363] Business leaders, for their part, were "congratulating themselves on the transformation of their political fortunes."[364] The *New York Times* declared in 1979 "(t)hese are the days of wine and roses—of champagne, even, and orchids— for business interests in Washington."[365]

When placed in this rapidly evolving political context, it is hardly a mystery that Senator Metzenbaum's corporate governance initiative foundered despite scandals affecting business and Democratic control of the executive and legislative branches. AT&T's deButts was a founding member of the Business Roundtable and DuPont's Shapiro became in 1975 the first chair of its task force on regulation.[366] When they agreed to serve on Metzenbaum's advisory committee they likely were prepared to execute that organization's pragmatic strategy of shaping inevitable legislation. Within months the political backdrop had changed, meaning that such a conciliatory approach was unnecessary. According to a *New York Times* source:

> One participant at the meetings suggested that the businessmen had lost interest in the project after it gradually became clear that the chances of any bill on corporate governance being passed was slight because of the more conservative instincts of the new Congress, the growing concern about a possible recession next year and mistrust of big government. "They knew by November that the mood had shifted," he said.[367]

A spokesperson for deButts cast doubt on this version of events, saying AT&T's chief executive was "not that expedient."[368] Regardless, shifting political tides likely do much to explain why changes in the boardroom in the late 1970s would occur primarily on a voluntary rather than a compulsory basis.

Deregulation

The shifting political tides of the late 1970s would not merely call a halt to increased regulation but would also act as a catalyst for a deregulation movement that would expand considerably managerial discretion as the twentieth century drew to a close. Deregulation is often treated as a core element of Ronald Reagan's presidential legacy but the push to deregulate

361 WATERHOUSE, *supra* note 271, at 156–61.

362 *Id.* at 170–71.

363 *Id.* at 170.

364 Fleming, *supra* note 168.

365 Shabecoff, *supra* note 357.

366 WATERHOUSE, *supra* note 271, at 87, 182.

367 Miller, *supra* note 293.

368 *Id.*

was well underway by the time he took office in 1981.[369] Hints of the trend could be found in the mid-1970s. In 1975, the NYSE, under orders from the SEC, abolished fixed commissions for stock trading, which drove down considerably the cost of trading for large investors such as institutional shareholders.[370] Michael Jensen and William Meckling indicated in their 1976 interview with *Fortune* that discussions on possible deregulation of the airline and trucking industries had begun in Washington DC.[371]

Deregulation began in earnest under Jimmy Carter. The 1978 Airline Deregulation Act broadened considerably the discretion airlines had to choose routes and set fares.[372] Other deregulatory moves carried out under Carter included wiping away entry, route, and rate restrictions in the trucking industry, liberalizing rate setting and route selection for railways, loosening controls on natural gas prices, and relaxing interest rate ceilings on bank accounts.[373] A May 1980 *Financial Times* article on regulatory trends in the United States said "taking government out of economic regulation . . . has become almost the new political orthodoxy."[374] Carter, in his August presidential nomination acceptance speech, argued that deregulation carried out under his administration constituted the most important change in governmental relations since the New Deal.[375]

Growing antipathy toward government in the late 1970s fueled the deregulation surge.[376] However, unlike with the halting of the public interest movement's legislative juggernaut, there was considerable ambivalence in the business community about the deregulation push. The Business Roundtable and the US Chamber of Commerce did not stake out a position on the deregulatory reforms occurring under Jimmy Carter.[377] In both the airline and trucking industries, advantageously positioned incumbent firms actively opposed proposals to deregulate, as did organized labor.[378]

The fears of incumbents and unions in the industries that were deregulated were realized. By the end of the 1970s dozens of trucking companies had gone by the wayside under pressure from new low-cost entrants and venerable airlines such as Continental and Eastern were struggling to survive.[379] Unions in both industries faced substantial pressure to grant concessions to increasingly cost-conscious employers.[380] The growth of antigovernment sentiment in the 1970s correspondingly would help to set the scene both for organized labor to recede as a constraint on public company executives and for competitors to grow in importance. As

---

369 Reich, *supra* note 91, at 65; John Steele Gordon, An Empire of Wealth: The Epic History of American Economic Power 392–93 (2004).

370 Gordon, *supra* note 369, at 393.

371 *As We See It*, *supra* note 42.

372 Pub. L. 95-504; 92 Stat. 1705; Richard H.K. Vietor, Contrived Competition: Regulation and Deregulation in America 57 (1994).

373 Vietor, *supra* note 335, at 999–1006.

374 Buchan, *supra* note 351.

375 Stein, *supra* note 68, at 244.

376 *Id.* at 251.

377 Waterhouse, *supra* note 271, at 185.

378 *As We See It*, *supra* note 42; Joseph D. Kearney & Thomas W. Merrill, *The Great Transformation of Regulated Industries Law*, 98 Colum. L. Rev. 1323, 1394 (1998).

379 Reich, *supra* note 91, at 68–69; Wilson, *supra* note 332, at 419; Wells, *supra* note 339, at 108–09.

380 Reich, *supra* note 91, at 69; Wells, *supra* note 339, at 109.

we will see now, on both fronts changes began in the 1970s that would subsequently help to turn the world of the public company executive upside down. Awareness of the new ground rules was only beginning to dawn, however, as the decade ended.

UNIONS

In the 1950s and 1960s organized labor was a meaningful source of countervailing power impinging on the discretion of public company executives.[381] Unions remained a potentially significant check on management in the 1970s. A 1979 analysis of who controlled the large corporation which concluded management did so nevertheless conceded organized labor had significant coercive power and served to "bound the area of corporate decision-making" in pursuit of the interests of union members.[382] Herman, in his 1981 study of control of corporate control and power, acknowledged "external factors affect the making of important corporate decisions" and argued unions "can have profound effects on a variety of corporate decisions."[383] Lawyers Ira Millstein and Salem Katsh, in a 1981 book on limits on the exercise of discretion available to corporations, argued that the process of collective bargaining sharply diminished corporate flexibility and said "(t)he power of unions to constrain corporate behaviour is widely acknowledged."[384]

While unions remained important in the 1970s as a constraint on public company executives, organized labor's grip was loosening.[385] By the end of the 1970s, unions were even said to be "in disarray,"[386] "embattled," and "threatened . . . by a panoply of woes."[387] A more aggressive approach corporate executives began to take in dealing with unions was a key reason organized labor was on the back foot.[388]

As the 1970s got underway, management understood and respected the right of workers to organize and bargain collectively, even if executives would have preferred ideally to run their companies without interference from unions.[389] By the late 1970s this spirit of pragmatic, guarded cooperation with organization labor had faded.[390] A labor relations consensus in place since shortly after the end of World War II accordingly cracked.[391] Companies engaged increasingly in "union avoidance"involving the hiring of consulting firms specializing in combatting union organization drives and the outsourcing of work to nonunion firms.[392] Another tactic managers began to use to "zap" unions was to hire replacement

---

[381] Chapter 2, notes 444–51 and accompanying text.

[382] Jones, *supra* note 4, at 1278–79.

[383] HERMAN, *supra* note 56, at 18.

[384] IRA MILLSTEIN & SALEM KATSH, THE LIMITS OF CORPORATE POWER: EXISTING CONSTRAINTS ON THE EXERCISE OF CORPORATE DISCRETION 151, 236 (1981).

[385] Ralph Gomory & Richard Sylla, *The American Corporation*, DAEDALUS, Spring 2013, at 102, 108.

[386] Fleming, *supra* note 168.

[387] *Embattled Unions Strike Back at Management*, BUS. WK., Dec. 4, 1978, 54.

[388] *Id.*

[389] GEORGE A. STEINER, BUSINESS AND SOCIETY 497 (1971).

[390] *The New Chill in Labor Relations*, BUS. WK., Oct. 24, 1977, 32.

[391] MIZRUCHI, *supra* note 329, at 159–60, 178.

[392] PHILLIPS-FEIN, *supra* note 348, at 206; BENNETT HARRISON & BARRY BLUESTONE, THE GREAT U-TURN: CORPORATE RESTRUCTURING AND THE POLARIZING OF AMERICA 48 (1988).

workers to keep operating during a strike, heretofore a rare practice in post–World War II labor relations.[393]

As well as increasingly forsaking cooperation with unions in favor of confrontation the business community lobbied successfully in the late 1970s against pro-union legislative measures that a Democratic Congress might have been expected to enact. A 1977 defeat in the House of Representatives of a bill regarding picketing that the powerful AFL-CIO union federation backed was an intoxicating "first big victory over labor in many years."[394] A more stunning triumph occurred in 1978 when business lobbying ensured that there were insufficient votes in the Senate to overcome a filibuster of a bill President Carter publicly endorsed that would have amended the National Labor Relations Act in a pro-labor manner.[395] The stance business took on the bill prompted the president of the United Automobile Workers (UAW) to bemoan the fact "(t)he leaders of industry, commerce and finance in the United States have broken and discarded the fragile, unwritten compact previously existing during a past period of growth and progress."[396]

The growing antipathy toward government that helped to derail the public interest movement's legislative juggernaut and Senator Metzenbaum's corporate governance initiative contributed to organized labor's legislative setbacks.[397] There also were labor-specific factors that eroded the influence of unions. In the 1970s union wage hike demands, backed by strikes launched with a frequency unprecedented since the end of World War II, appeared to be contributing to the decade's chronic inflation.[398] This undermined public confidence in unions and likely made it more difficult for organized labor to win elections to unionize workplaces.[399] An increasing proportion of workers were also being employed in the service sector, which was less susceptible to unionization than "smokestack" industries featuring large-scale workplaces geared to mass production.[400] Union density in the workforce fell from 27 percent in 1970 to 22 percent in 1980.[401]

Another difficulty for organized labor was that the market power large corporations had in the 1950s and 1960s which created "slack" that left room for union concessions diminished in the 1970s. For instance, imports were battering numerous unionized firms and, by extension their unions.[402] Employers discovering they could no longer simply pass increased labor costs along to consumers balked at the sort of after-inflation wage increases unions had come to expect in the 1950s and 1960s.[403] Organized labor in turn began to feel it had

---

[393] Reich, *supra* note 91, at 80; Harrison & Bluestone, *supra* note 392, at 21, 51; Peter Perl, *US Unions Losing Clout in Shifting Labor Market*, Wash. Post, Sept. 6, 1987, H1.

[394] Stein, *supra* note 68, at 182–83.

[395] *Id.* at 183–89; Shabecoff, *supra* note 357.

[396] Waterhouse, *supra* note 271, at 129; Jefferson Cowie, *"A One-Sided Class War": Rethinking Doug Fraser's 1978 Resignation from the Labor-Management Group*, 44 Labor Hist. 307, 307 (2003).

[397] *Embattled Unions, supra* note 387; *A Potent New Business Lobby*, Bus. Wk., May 22, 1978, 64.

[398] Phillips-Fein, *supra* note 348, at 153–56; *The US Can't Afford What Labor Wants*, Bus. Wk., Apr. 11, 1970, 104.

[399] Lipset & Schneider, *supra note* 33, at 352–53.

[400] Gerald F. Davis, Managed by Markets: How Finance Reshaped America 80 (2009).

[401] Gerald Mayer, Union Membership Trends in the United States 22 (2004) (calculated using non-agricultural workers as the denominator).

[402] Kotz, *supra* note 67, 80-81; *Embattled Unions, supra* note 387; *Unions Eye Some New Directions*, Christian Sci. Monitor, Sept. 27, 1979, 10.

[403] Reich, *supra* note 91, at 81.

to adjust to respond to the market pressures management was confronting, at least to some degree. The UAW, for example, acknowledged in 1979 that it agreed "to a cheap contract" with Chrysler because the automaker was "threatened with bankruptcy."[404] During the 1970s, then, the competitive pressure large corporations were increasingly under meant organized labor was becoming a less important source of countervailing power for management. Pressure from rivals, however, was simultaneously growing in potency as a check on public company executives.

COMPETITORS

A common assumption during the 1970s was that competitors had only a modest impact on companies with any market power. Eisenberg, in the 1976 book where he advocated the monitoring model of the board, said "the market in which the corporation operates.... (P)ermits substantial inefficiency, since given the structure of most markets, a firm can usually remain in business for a protracted period of time if it has even the most meagre returns."[405] Elliott Weiss, another law professor, claimed in 1978 "(t)he intensity of competition in most major industries has not changed materially since 1959," meaning "imperfections in the market allow managers a great deal of discretion."[406]

The retrospective verdict on the threat rivals posed in the 1970s would be quite different. Alfred Chandler wrote in 2004 that an "intensifying battle for markets" meant that executives of large industrial firms "appreciated that an era of competition demanded different responses than did one of growth."[407] Robert Reich, a Harvard academic who served in the Clinton administration, said in 2007 "in the mid-1970s the large oligopolies that anchored the American system began to teeter."[408] Economist David Kotz argued in 2015 that "(i)n the 1970s . . . regulated capitalism . . . was breaking down," and "this turned big business into small business . . . no longer having the luxury of a stable existence undisturbed by the prospect of bankruptcy."[409]

A 1982 study by economist William Shepherd substantiates these retrospective conjectures. He reported that while in 1958 44 percent of national income was produced in industries that were monopolies, were dominated by a single firm, or constituted tight oligopolies, this figure had fallen to 23 percent by 1980.[410] This meant, according to Shepherd, that "the US economy is now an enormous test case for the functioning of competition in a large-scale industrial economy."[411]

---

[404] Harry Bernstein, *Unionists on Boards Not a New Concept*, LA TIMES, Oct. 27, 1979, C1.

[405] EISENBERG, *supra* note 4, 166.

[406] Elliott J. Weiss, *Governance, Disclosure, and Corporate Legitimacy*, RUNNING THE AMERICAN, *supra* note 169, at 58, 60.

[407] Alfred D. Chandler, *Corporate Strategy, Structure and Control Methods in the United States during the 20th Century*, UNDERSTANDING INDUSTRIAL AND CORPORATE CHANGE 381, 397 (Giovanni Dosi, David J. Teece & Josef Chytry eds., 2004).

[408] REICH, *supra* note 91, at 51.

[409] KOTZ, *supra* note 67, at 80.

[410] William G. Shepherd, *Causes of Increased Competition in the US Economy, 1939–1980*, 64 REV. ECON. STAT. 613, 618 (1982).

[411] *Id.* at 620.

Shepherd attributed the erosion of oligopolistic market structures partly to two agents of change already identified, namely increased pressure from foreign rivals and deregulation.[412] He also cited antitrust enforcement targeting price-fixing and mergers.[413] Growing awareness that foreign competition was posing challenges for American companies was prompting a rethink of antitrust orthodoxy in the 1970s. Under the Reagan administration, antitrust regulation would be relaxed considerably, at least with respect to mergers.[414] This was prefaced in the 1970s by a growing belief that antitrust enforcement needed to be adjusted to reflect global realities.

In 1974 *Business Week* suggested the Sherman Act, the 1890 legislative foundation of antitrust law,[415] might be obsolete. The key reason was that "antitrust action aimed at cutting down corporate size might ... handicap US companies in keeping pace with the growing number of multinational corporations around the world."[416] Such reasoning grew in popularity. *Newsweek* said in 1978 "even zealous trust-busters acknowledge that virtues do exist in the trend toward size. Bigger companies may be necessary if the US is to compete in world markets."[417] Judges adjudicating antitrust cases evidently were susceptible to the logic involved. In 1990 antitrust expert William Kovacic cited growing awareness of foreign competition to explain a series of US Supreme Court and lower court antitrust rulings in the 1970s that were favorable to defendants:

> In 1962, *Brown Shoe*[418] gave primacy to non-efficiency goals when American firms were preeminent and faced few threats from abroad. By 1980, it was far more difficult for courts to discount efficiency and vindicate social aims as American companies struggled to stay abreast of their potent foreign counterparts.[419]

"Threats from abroad," the dialing back of governmental regulation, and antitrust enforcement were not the only factors ramping up competitive pressure on incumbents in the 1970s. Potential challengers to dominant firms also were beginning to be able to secure access to finance more readily. During the 1950s and 1960s heyday of managerial capitalism it seemed that no one other than oil billionaire J. Paul Getty had the wherewithal to mount a challenge to leading industrial firms.[420] With difficult economic conditions in the 1970s meaning that it was often "a credit-short and capital-starved world,"[421] various observers surmised the situation had not changed much. *Forbes* said in 1975 "money is still available for people who

[412] *Id.* at 620, 622–24.

[413] *Id.* at 622–23.

[414] Chapter 4, notes 174–83 and accompanying text.

[415] 26 Stat. 209.

[416] *Is John Sherman's Antitrust Obsolete?*, Bus. Wk., Mar. 23, 1974, 46.

[417] David Pauly, *The Merger Rage*, Newsweek, Oct. 16, 1978, 88.

[418] Brown Shoe v. United States, 370 U.S. 294 (1962).

[419] Kovacic, *supra* note 92, at 1444; see also at 1426–27 (discussing the US Supreme Court cases).

[420] Chapter 2, note 389 and related discussion.

[421] Greta R. Krippner, Capitalizing on Crisis: The Political Origins of the Rise in Finance 59, 82 (2011). See also Glenn Yago, Junk Bonds: How High Yield Securities Restructured Corporate America 20–21 (1991).

want to start a business, but not much of it."[422] Ralph Nader, Mark Green, and Joel Seligman, when identifying "high entry barriers" as the "mortar" of "market power" in their 1976 book *Taming the Giant Corporation,* drew attention to the fact "the large capital outlay initially required, given an imperfect capital market, discriminates against the new firms."[423]

In the 1950s and 1960s those seeking financing to take on entrenched incumbents were handicapped because commercial banks were conservative allocators of capital, because investment banks were reluctant to provide direct financial backing for business enterprises, and because venture capital was having only a narrow impact on entrepreneurial activity.[424] On each of these counts the situation was not radically different in the 1970s. However, commercial banks, investment banks, and the venture capital industry were undergoing changes that would improve considerably access to finance in the 1980s and 1990s. In retrospect, then, "(t)he 1970s constituted a critical period for firms in matters of finance and capital"[425] that would ultimately contribute to a more favorable environment for those seeking to challenge incumbents and, by extension, to more robust market-oriented checks on potentially wayward public company executives.

With commercial banks, a cautious approach to business lending prevalent in the 1950s and 1960s generally continued to predominate in the 1970s. As Martin Mayer said in a best-selling 1974 book on the banking industry,

> In a well-run bank, no more than 1/3 of 1 percent of loans are supposed to go sour. Unlike the venture capitalist, who can cheerfully take his lumps on losers, because the pay-out is big on the winners, the banker has to live and pay his expenses (including his loan losses) on the proceeds of the limited interest charge.[426]

Such conservatism meant commercial bank failures were a rarity in the 1970s despite the poor economy, averaging less than two per year.[427] That track record lent credibility to a reputation for reliability that bankers were keen to cultivate. According to Mayer, "(m)ore than most people these days, bankers believe in living up to one's obligations. Loyalties are expected and given."[428]

The public bought in. While business generally took a reputational battering in the 1970s, banks were well regarded. Survey data indicated public confidence in bankers neared the high level reserved for churches, with banks being perceived of as service institutions operating in the public interest by functioning on a highly ethical basis.[429]

---

[422] *Brother Can You Spare $100 Million?*, FORBES, Nov. 15, 1975, 22.

[423] NADER, GREEN & SELIGMAN, *supra* note 82, at 207.

[424] Chapter 2, notes 394–98, 403–13 and related discussion.

[425] Dirk M. Zorn, *Here a Chief, There a Chief: The Rise of the CFO in the American Firm*, AMER. SOC. REV. 345, 361 (2004).

[426] MARTIN MAYER, THE BANKERS 262 (1974).

[427] John H. Boyd & Mark Gertler, *US Commercial Banking: Trends, Cycles, and Policy*, NBER MACROECONOMICS ANNUAL 1993, at 319, 319 (Olivier Blanchard & Stanley Fischer eds., 1993).

[428] MAYER, *supra* note 426, at 15.

[429] LIPSET & SCHNEIDER, *supra note* 33, at 78, 196, 367.

Mayer attributed the conservatism of banks partly to tight regulation, saying that "for reasons that lie deep in the history of American banking, the assumption behind bank examinations is that every bad loan endangers the interests of the depositors, and the (bank) examiners do not like to see many of them."[430] In the 1980s there would be some moves toward deregulation, beginning in 1980 with liberalization of caps on bank account interest rates.[431] Deregulation was not, however, a feature of banking in the 1970s. The purpose of the Financial Institutions Regulatory and Interest Rate Control Act of 1978,[432] the first major piece of banking legislation to come out of Congress in almost 50 years,[433] was to regulate the banking industry more closely.[434]

Despite continuity with the 1950s and 1960s, to an extent that was perhaps not fully apparent at the time, in the 1970s commercial banking began to break away from restrictive mid-twentieth century arrangements.[435] Whereas in the 1950s fewer than half-a-dozen bank stocks were listed on national stock exchanges, by the early 1970s shares in numerous banks (or more precisely bank holding companies) were being aggressively traded.[436] Bankers who had traditionally kept a low profile correspondingly were "unabashedly wooing analysts and courting investors."[437] Walter Wriston, chief executive of First National City Corp., renamed Citibank in 1974,[438] was championing entrepreneurship by banks and, as the most influential banker of the day, was "a kind of Pied Piper of commercial banking."[439] With bank holding companies being permitted to engage in nonbank commercial activity that was bank related,[440] some began operating in fields such as consumer finance, mortgage banking, and the launching of real estate investment trusts.[441]

The pushing of boundaries by banks in the 1970s extended to increased provision of finance for business. Throughout most of the 1960s it was rare for commercial banks to finance a client's business by buying account receivables, a practice known as "factoring."[442] By the early 1970s this was commonplace.[443] Some commercial banks began to experiment

---

[430] Mayer, *supra* note 426, at 385.

[431] Depository Institutions Deregulation and Monetary Control Act of 1980, Pub. L. No. 96-221, 94 Stat. 132 (1980); Chapter 4, note 395 and accompanying text.

[432] Pub. L. No. 95-630, 92 Stat. 3641.

[433] John B. Wynne & Susan Sturges Spagnola, *The Myth of Bank Deregulation: For Every Action There Is an Equal and Opposite Reaction*, 42 Wash. & Lee L. Rev. 383, 388 (1985).

[434] Alan F. Garrison, *The Financial Institutions Regulatory and Interest Rate Control Act of 1978, Federal Banking Agencies, and the Judiciary: The Struggle to Define the Limitation of Cease and Desist Order Authority*, 44 Wash. & Lee L. Rev. 1357, 1357 (1987).

[435] Simon Johnson & James Kwak, 13 Bankers: The Wall Street Takeover and the Next Financial Meltdown 64–65 (2010).

[436] Mayer, *supra* note 426, at 18–19.

[437] *Beautiful Balloon*, Barron's, Apr. 29, 1974, 54.

[438] *Id.*

[439] Kaufman, *supra* note 74, at 263.

[440] Anthony G. Chase, *The Emerging Financial Conglomerate: Liberalization of the Bank Holding Company Act*, 60 Geo. L. J. 1225, 1236 (1972).

[441] *Merchant Banking: Is the US Ready for It?*, Bus. Wk., Apr. 19, 1976, 54.

[442] Mayer, *supra* note 426, at 279–80.

[443] *Id.* at 281.

with a form of merchant banking, aspiring to pocket fees for steering companies to sources of funds other than what they as banks were lending.[444] Lending practices were also being liberalized, with mergers and acquisitions (M&A) activity being one area affected.[445] When Kohlberg, Kravis and Roberts (KKR) carried out in 1979 the first modern public-to-private buyout of a sizeable public company by acquiring Houdaille Industries,[446] many were skeptical about KKR's ability to finance the debt-driven deal.[447] The willingness, however, of three commercial banks to lend $60 million helped to swing the momentum in KKR's favor.[448]

As for investment banking, it was a clubby affair in the decades immediately following World War II.[449] Corporate customers in need of underwriting services were loyal to a single investment bank and refrained from shopping around for better terms.[450] The fact that the vast majority of investment banks were partnerships reinforced the cliquey nature of the business, as the partners had neither the capital nor the risk appetite for aggressive expansion.[451]

Change was afoot with the investment banking sector in the 1970s.[452] On the underwriting side, public company executives were becoming increasingly financially savvy.[453] They correspondingly became prepared to forsake past loyalties to ensure the distribution of securities to the public on the most advantageous terms available.[454] Investment banks, in their turn, solicited clients much more aggressively.[455] Investment bank leadership reflected the new ethos. Felix Rohatyn, a prominent partner at Lazard Frères, said in 1979 of those running major investment banks "(t)hey're younger and more aggressive. There's a coterie of samurai out there."[456]

Rule changes by the New York Stock Exchange also helped to reshape investment banking in the 1970s. In 1969, the NYSE, under pressure from brokerages needing to raise capital to automate antiquated back-office operations, rescinded a prohibition against public ownership of members.[457] Investment banks responded with alacrity. By the mid-1970s most had been converted from partnerships to corporations and many were publicly held and traded on the stock exchange.[458] With undercapitalized brokerages falling by the wayside with some regularity due to mounting costs, expansion became a priority.[459]

---

444 *Merchant Banking, supra* note 441; *What Banking Needs*, Bus. Wk., Apr. 19, 1976, 150.

445 *Infra* note 514 and related discussion (takeovers).

446 Brian R. Cheffins & John Armour, *The Eclipse of Private Equity*, 33 Del. J. Corp. L. 1, 18 (2008).

447 George P. Baker & George David Smith, The New Financial Capitalists: Kohlberg Kravis Roberts and the Creation of Corporate Value 67 (1998).

448 *Id.* at 67–68; George Anders, Merchants of Debt: KKR and the Mortgaging of American Business 29–32 (1992).

449 Geisst, *supra* note 70, at 306; *Leon Levy, supra* note 196, at 552.

450 *John Whitehead, in* Way It Was, *supra* note 196, at 43, 46.

451 Chapter 2, notes 415, 421 and related discussion.

452 Jolie Solomon, *Dialing for More Deals*, Newsweek, Dec. 27, 1993, 34.

453 Samuel L. Hayes, *The Transformation of Investment Banking*, Harv. Bus. Rev., Jan./Feb. 1979, 153, 155–56.

454 Geisst, *supra* note 70, at 319; *Leon Levy, supra* note 196, at 551–52.

455 Geisst, *supra* note 70, at 319; Hayes, *supra* note 453, at 157–60.

456 *Ira Harris: Chicago's Big Dealmaker*, Bus. Wk., June 25, 1979, 70.

457 Alan D. Morrison & William J. Wilhelm, Investment Banking: Institutions, Politics, and Law 237–38 (2007).

458 Jensen, *supra* note 125, at 313; *What Banking, supra* note 444.

459 Geisst, *supra* note 70, at 306; Hayes, *supra* note 453, at 153.

The NYSE's 1975 abolition of rules requiring the charging of fixed commissions on trades also shook up investment banking.[460] Forty years later, a *Wall Street Journal* columnist said the change "may well have been the most momentous day on Wall Street" since the founding of the New York Stock Exchange in 1792, as it blew a "cozy world to smithereens."[461] Brokerage departments suddenly had to become major discounters to keep market share as institutional shareholders shopped for bargains.[462]

Despite the changes beginning to affect commercial and investment banking, in the 1970s large, well-established companies retained important advantages in raising finance as compared with potential rivals. Throughout most of the decade, public bond markets were effectively "closed to all but blue-chip borrowers."[463] A rush for quality by investors during what typically were challenging economic times left hundreds of public companies lacking high bond ratings out of luck.[464] Similarly, while increasingly intense competition between a small number of investment banks specializing in dealing in commercial paper helped to foster substantial growth in the market for this source of short-term corporate financing, investors would only buy the paper of top-rated issuers.[465] As of 1975, according to *Business Week*, for companies that had debt rated lower than Baa, the lowest rating still in the investment grade category, "neither the public nor the private markets (were) a reasonable source of financing any more" and "the likelihood of new, potentially innovative companies finding risk capital (was) grim."[466]

Despite potential rivals continuing to have difficulties securing financial backing to challenge incumbents during the 1970s, two important counter-trends were emerging as the decade drew to a close. The first related to non-investment grade, high-yield "junk" bonds. As far back as the late 1940s a small proportion of the public bond market was comprised of speculative "fallen angels" issued by investment grade companies that subsequently dropped out of that class.[467] Through the 1950s, 1960s, and most of the 1970s, however, there was no market for bonds that were "junk" at the time of issuance.[468]

In 1977, Lehman Brothers Kuhn Loeb broke with tradition by underwriting several issues of low-grade, high-yielding corporate bonds.[469] Its investment banking partners concluded, however, that "the business was too dicey for" their "high-class firm."[470] Other major

---

[460] *Supra* note 370 and related discussion.

[461] Jason Zweig, *Lessons of May Day 1975 Ring True Today*, WALL ST. J., May 1, 2015, C1.

[462] *E. John Rosenwald, in* WAY IT WAS, *supra* note 196, at 537, 539.

[463] *Merchant Banking*, *supra* note 441.

[464] Eugene N. White, *Banking and Finance in the Twentieth Century*, CAMBRIDGE ECONOMIC, *supra* note 335, at 743, 788; *The Crushing Burden of Corporate Debt*, BUS. WK., Oct. 12, 1974, 54; John P. Birkelund, *Who Would Finance a Xerox Today?*, NY TIMES, July 25, 1976, 88.

[465] *Why a Rush into Commercial Paper*, BUS. WK., July 3, 1978, 82.

[466] *The Big Squeeze on US Companies*, BUS. WK., Sept. 22, 1975, 50; Moody's Investor Service, *Moody's Rating System in Brief*, available at https://www.moodys.com/sites/products/ProductAttachments/Moody's%20Rating%20System.pdf (accessed May 25, 2018).

[467] White, *supra* note 464, at 788; CHARLES R. GEISST, THE LAST PARTNERSHIPS: INSIDE THE GREAT WALL STREET MONEY DYNASTIES 266 (2001).

[468] CONNIE BRUCK, THE PREDATORS' BALL: THE INSIDE STORY OF DREXEL BURNHAM AND THE RISE OF THE JUNK BOND RAIDERS 44–45 (1988).

[469] *Id.* at 44.

[470] *Id.* at 48. See also GEISST, *supra* note 467, at 79.

investment banks, concerned that their reputations might be tarnished by bringing the debt of "shlock" companies to market, felt they had better things to do.[471] Drexel Burnham, which had only a modest investment banking operation at the time, stepped into the breach.[472] It quickly emerged as the market leader with a junk bond group led by Michael Milken that would become a powerhouse in the 1980s and ignite a "debt revolution."[473] One important byproduct, as identified by a 1986 congressional report, was that "capital could be raised by firms which might otherwise not secure it, or would do so at considerably greater cost."[474]

The second counter-trend concerned venture capital. It was well understood in the 1970s that VC backing could give a boost to those seeking to challenge incumbents. The *Boston Globe* said in 1971 venture capital was "the stuff of which business dreams are made."[475] In 1975 *Forbes* characterized venture capital as "a business that is helping mount attacks on some of our biggest corporations."[476]

While theoretically venture capital could "be inspirational for the myriad of embryonic entrepreneurs,"[477] throughout most of the 1970s it was in the doldrums. *Forbes* suggested in 1973 that with venture capital "less active" than "almost dead," "the ambitious entrepreneur" might need to go to one of a number of big corporations gearing up to invest in fledgling ventures even though these large firms could be thought of as "the very antithesis of the entrepreneurial spirit."[478] Two years later, having indicated financing likely would be available for ideas with the potential to "change the world," *Forbes* simultaneously felt the need to reassure readers that the VC business was not "dead."[479] The *Los Angeles Times*, in a 1976 story alerting readers to the possibility that venture capital was "drying up," described "the current investment climate as 'horrible' for businesses seeking to market new products."[480] That year, for instance, Steve Jobs and Steve Wozniak struggled to obtain financial backing for the computer prototype that would be Apple Computer's first hit with consumers.[481]

Reasons cited for venture capital's problems in the 1970s included the tax treatment of profits generated, with the maximum tax rate for capital gains on the sale of investments having been increased from 28 percent to 49.5 percent in 1969.[482] There also were fears among pension fund trustees that the introduction of the federal "prudent man" investing standard in ERISA in 1974 precluded participation in a risky area such as venture capital.[483] "(V)enture capital money (was) scarce" as well because of a discouraging track record, with

---

[471] GEISST, *supra* note 467, at 268.

[472] BRUCK, *supra* note 468, at 42, 47.

[473] GEISST, *supra* note 467, at 269–70. See also BRUCK, *supra* note 468, at 47–48.

[474] CONGRESSIONAL RESEARCH SERVICE, CORPORATE MERGERS AND HIGH YIELD [JUNK] BONDS: RECENT MARKET TRENDS AND REGULATORY DEVELOPMENTS 4 (1986).

[475] Donald White, *Greater Boston's Venture Capitalists*, BOS. GLOBE, July 11, 1971, A41.

[476] *Brother Can You Spare $100 Million*, FORBES, Nov. 15, 1975, 22.

[477] Donald White, *Golden Age Dawning for Venture Capitalists?*, BOS. GLOBE, June 21, 1972, 65.

[478] *Corporate Sugar Daddies*, FORBES, Oct. 15, 1973, 102.

[479] *Brother Can, supra* note 476.

[480] Margaret A. Kilgore, *Public Urged to Invest in Technology*, LA TIMES, Apr. 13, 1976, D7.

[481] NITIN NOHRIA, DAVIS DYER & FREDERICK DALZELL, CHANGING FORTUNES: REMAKING THE INDUSTRIAL CORPORATION 244 (2002).

[482] *Death, supra* note 26.

[483] *Supra* note 210 and accompanying text; Ross, *supra* note 213.

numerous VC-backed firms struggling in the difficult 1970s economic milieu.[484] To illustrate the point *Forbes* cited in 1975 the example of courier company Federal Express, which had raised $90 million worth of venture capital since 1972, only to accumulate $29 million in operating losses and narrowly escape bankruptcy twice.[485]

By the end of the 1970s the picture looked considerably different, with the venture capital sector "blossoming."[486] In 1978, investment in venture capital surged.[487] In 1979 the amount raised roughly equaled that for 1969 to 1977 inclusive.[488] The 1979 interpretative ruling the Department of Labor issued indicating ERISA's prudence standard did not preclude pension funds from investing in risky asset classes played a significant role as "the institutionalization of venture capital" moved into full swing.[489]

Federal tax reforms in 1978 that reversed the 1969 capital gains tax hike have been widely cited as an additional catalyst for venture capital "blossoming" as the 1970s ended.[490] It is doubtful whether the capital gains tax reduction was pivotal, given that by the late 1970s a majority of venture capital funding was being provided by tax-exempt sources that included charitable endowments and foreign corporations as well as pension funds.[491] On the other hand, improving returns, averaging nearly 15 percent annually for venture capital funds in the late 1970s,[492] were a major draw.[493] A dramatic turnaround by Federal Express, culminating in a highly successful 1978 initial public offering, particularly impressed institutional investors.[494] Apple Computer, which ultimately was able to raise $3.5 million in venture capital as well as obtain the backing of a wealthy retired executive from Intel,[495] also became well known as a venture capital success story because there was intense speculation about it going public for months before a wildly successful 1980 IPO.[496]

With competitors, the upshot was that during the 1970s incumbents with market power retained significant advantages. Circumstances were changing, however. Foreign rivals were growing in prominence, deregulation was beginning to erode barriers to entry, and for challengers access to finance was beginning to improve. The 1970s correspondingly set the scene

---

[484] Ronald L. Soble, *Venture Capital Holding Out*, LA TIMES, Mar. 23, 1975, I1; *Good Ideas and Big Money Aren't All You Need*, FORBES, Nov. 15, 1975, 30; Alexander L. Taylor, Michael Moritz & Frederick Ungeheuer, *Boom Time in Venture Capital*, TIME, Aug. 10, 1981, 58.

[485] *Good Ideas*, *supra* note 484. See also William A. Sahlman, *The Structure and Governance of Venture-Capital Organizations*, 27 J. FIN. ECON. 473, 484, 487 (1990).

[486] Pauly, *supra* note 214.

[487] Peter A. Brooke, *Stockbroker Analyzes the Venture Capital Scene*, HARTFORD COURANT, Jan. 28, 1979, G4.

[488] Pauly, *supra* note 214.

[489] *Supra* notes 214–15 and accompanying text; Gompers, *supra* note 215, at 13.

[490] Graham, *supra* note 215, at 431; GORDON, *supra* note 369, at 395; Carrie Dolan, *How High-Tech Ideas Often Become Reality in Silicon Valley*, WALL ST. J., Aug. 2, 1983, 1.

[491] STEIN, *supra* note 68, at 201; Gompers, *supra* note 215, at 10, 12.

[492] Gompers, *supra* note 215, at 21.

[493] Ross, *supra* note 213.

[494] Brooke, *supra* note 487; Robert J. Flaherty, *Breathing under Water*, FORBES, Mar. 1, 1977, 36.

[495] Gompers, *supra* note 215, at 9; NOHRIA, DYER & DALZELL, *supra* note 481, at 244-45; Sahlman, *supra* note 485, at 481.

[496] Gompers, *supra* note 215, at 9; *Public Might Get a Crack at Apple*, WALL ST. J., June 30, 1980, 17; Michael Schrage, *Nation's High-Tech Engine Fueled by Venture Capital*, WASH. POST, May 20, 1984, G1.

for a late twentieth century intensification of competitive pressure that would impinge substantially upon the discretion available to public company executives.

THE MARKET FOR CORPORATE CONTROL

During the 1950s and 1960s, there was awareness that the prospect of an unwelcome takeover was a potentially significant disciplinary mechanism for executives, as evidenced by the coining of the term "the market for corporate control" in the mid-1960s.[497] Nevertheless, hostile transfers of corporate control, whether by way of the acquisition of a majority of shares or a proxy contest for a majority of directorships, were hardly a daily occurrence and were a rarity for large companies.[498] In contrast, in the 1980s, often referred to as the Deal Decade, there were numerous headline-grabbing hostile takeover contests with bidders relying regularly on aggressive, innovative financial and legal techniques to offer generous premiums to shareholders to secure voting control.[499] In this often hectic milieu, the market for corporate control was a potent form of managerial discipline. The 1970s provided the transition between these two eras. Limitations of the 1950s and the 1960s were cast aside without the full panoply of takeover weapons being deployed in the manner they would be in the 1980s.

During the 1970s, for those minded to execute a hostile takeover securing voting control by way of a tender offer to a target company's shareholders emerged as the preferred tactic, displacing the achievement of boardroom dominance by soliciting enough proxies to elect a majority of directors.[500] *Forbes* referred to the latter technique in 1979 as "a relic of the past."[501] As the 1970s began, however, tender offers were an afterthought as potential acquirors lacked the cash required to make realistic bids.[502] Matters then changed. The authors of *Tender Offers for Corporate Control* said between their 1973 and 1977 editions there had been "a torrent of tender offers, many contested by target managements."[503] The trend accelerated as the 1970s drew to a close. The *Wall Street Journal* referred in 1977 to a "tender-offer craze."[504] The *New York Times* said in 1978 "(t)akeover fever has gripped the land."[505]

The cheapness of prospective targets, prompted by the mid-1970s stock market swoon, did much to foster the acceleration in takeover activity.[506] The *Wall Street Journal* said in

---

497 Chapter 2, notes 332–37, 342 and related discussion.

498 Chapter 2, notes 338–40, 343–48 and accompanying text.

499 Chapter 4, notes 51–58, 373, 381–82, 473 and related discussion.

500 Jones, *supra* note 4, at 1284; McSweeney, *supra* note 191, at 51–52; Joel Seligman, *The Breakdown in Corporate Democracy*, LA Times, Oct. 20, 1976, C7 (indicating there had not been a proxy contest for board control since 1967).

501 Richard Phalon, *Return of the Proxy Fighter*, Forbes, Nov. 12, 1979, 37.

502 Jonathan R. Laing, *Poor Performance and Personality Clashes Encourage More Corporate Proxy Contests*, Wall St. J., May 14, 1971, 32; *Joseph Flom, in* Way It Was, *supra* note 196, at 693, 695.

503 Edward R. Aranow, Herbert A. Einhorn & George Berlstein, Tender Offers for Corporate Control vi (1977).

504 Wayne E. Green, *Takeover Fights Pose an Ethical Question for Banks and Brokers*, Wall St. J., Dec. 12, 1977, 1.

505 Robert J. Cole, *Booming Takeovers: What Good Do They Do?*, NY Times, Jan. 8, 1978, 16.

506 *Supra* notes 28–29 and related discussion; McSweeney, *supra* note 191, at 52; Robert Lenzer, *Unfriendly to Whom?*, Barron's, Sept. 22, 1975, 55; Charles J. Elia, *Take-Over Offers Are Attracting More Rivals with the Original Bidders Often Losing Out*, Wall St. J., Feb. 6, 1976, 27.

1974 "(p)rices . . . are so low (that) even some large corporations are vulnerable."[507] *Barron's*, reporting in 1975 on substantial premiums that bidders were putting on the table to entice shareholders in target corporations, said "sometimes it seems that the only way to make money in the stock market is to be lucky enough to own shares for which someone is making a tender offer."[508] Even with stock prices having rallied somewhat, Felix Rohatyn suggested in 1978 a key reason for surging merger activity was "the stock market's 'pathetic' price level."[509] The *Washington Post* indicated in 1980 "(s)tocks—whole companies—are one of the cheapest things you can buy in America today."[510]

Improved access to finance also contributed to the growth of takeovers. In the 1960s, conglomerates, which were at the forefront of acquisition activity, tended to offer to exchange their equity or bonds they issued for shares in their targets.[511] In contrast, in the 1980s bidders typically paid cash, and raised $667 billion from outside investors between 1987 and 1989 alone to buy out target company shareholders.[512] The switch occurred when "the takeover game" picked up in the mid-1970s as "(t)here were fewer deals for stock, and many more for cash."[513] Bidders were able to raise the sums required to make sizeable tender offers because large banks, sometimes supplemented by institutional investors prepared to act as lenders, became increasingly open to the idea of financing takeovers.[514]

The fact that bidders could turn to large banks to obtain backing for tender offers reflected an acceptance of takeovers in elite business circles lacking previously. Joseph Flom, a star M&A practitioner with Skadden Arps, a leading New York law firm, told *Newsweek* in 1978 about hostile takeovers "(i)n the late '60s, people in polite society didn't do this" but indicated that they had become accepted practice.[515] Flom observed subsequently regarding takeover bids that "once the log jam was broken . . . everybody was starting to do these things."[516]

Hostile takeovers entered "polite society" in 1974 when International Nickel Co. of Toronto (later known as Inco Ltd.) sought to acquire battery-maker ESB Inc., was rebuffed, and subsequently won control by offering an enormous premium to ESB's shareholders.[517] This was in the merger world "a very big event," namely "the first blue-chip raid."[518] Before

---

[507] *Company Executives Shore Up Defenses against Take-Overs*, WALL ST. J., Oct. 21, 1974, 1.

[508] *Take the Money and Run*, BARRON'S, Dec. 8, 1975, 55.

[509] Cole, *supra* note 505.

[510] Morton Mintz, *Playing the Takeover Game*, WASH. POST, Apr. 18, 1980, A1.

[511] Cheffins & Armour, *supra* note 446, at 40, 47; JONATHAN BARRON BASKIN & PAUL J. MIRANTI, A HISTORY OF CORPORATE FINANCE 274–78 (1997).

[512] Peter Tufano, *Financing Acquisitions in the Late 1980s: Sources and Forms of Capital*, *in* THE DEAL DECADE: WHAT TAKEOVERS AND LEVERAGED BUYOUTS MEAN FOR CORPORATE GOVERNANCE 289, 289 (Margaret M. Blair ed., 1993).

[513] RICHARD PHALON, THE TAKEOVER BARONS OF WALL STREET: INSIDE THE BILLION DOLLAR MERGER GAME 67 (1981). See also *Saul Steinberg*, *in* WAY IT WAS, *supra* note 196, at 67, 73.

[514] John W. Shultz, *Capital Shrink*, BARRON'S, Oct. 15, 1979, 59; Srully Blotnick, *Hidden Profits*, FORBES, Nov. 26, 1979, 208.

[515] Pauly, *supra* note 417. See also Robert Metz, *The Etiquette of Takeovers*, NY TIMES, Mar. 27, 1980, 86.

[516] *Joseph Flom*, *supra* note 502, at 695.

[517] Metz, *supra* note 515; see also TEITELMAN, *supra* note 105, at 71–72.

[518] Harry Anderson, *The Marriage Brokers*, NEWSWEEK, July 27, 1981, 52 (quoting Steve Friedman of Goldman Sachs). See also *Rise of the Blue-Chip Raiders*, BUS. WK., Aug. 17, 1974, 65.

International Nickel, "the unfriendly takeover was perceived as . . . all right for on-the-make conglomerates, maybe, but not a done thing for . . . outfits . . . in the Olympian reaches of the top 500 corporations."[519] Though large companies would not begin to bid in earnest until the 1980s,[520] International Nickel's 1974 move represented a basic change in attitude. Executives of other large public companies concluded, according to Flom, that "(i)f it's good enough for them, why isn't it good enough for me?"[521]

The pattern was similar in the investment banking community. Mindful of a norm among major investment banks against participating in hostile takeovers Morgan Stanley hesitated when International Nickel, a long-time client, asked for help raising money to carry out its ESB bid.[522] As Flom observed in the late 1980s, "(i)n the 1960s, the 'respectable' banking houses wouldn't touch any hostile takeovers."[523] When Morgan Stanley opted to work with International Nickel, other investment bankers reasoned "if the House of Morgan could participate in a raid, why couldn't everyone else?"[524] Carrying out work of this sort fit in well in the newer, faster world of investment banking that was emerging in the 1970s,[525] and indeed helped to transform the investment banking sector. *Business Week* said in 1979 that the M&A departments investment banks were building had

> irrevocably altered the way investment bankers do business, as well as the public's perception of them. For, along with the profits, the frenetic activity of those departments has led to a change of image at banking houses—from the traditional picture of gray eminences dispassionately advising corporations on their financial structure and aiding them in underwriting their equity and debt, to street fighters willing to plot hostile takeovers and hustlers who, as one chief executive charges, "go up and down the country peddling companies to make a buck."[526]

In various ways, then, the takeover activity of the 1970s had set the scene for the hectic dealmaking that would put public company executives under substantial pressure in the 1980s.

* * *

As the 1970s reached the midpoint it appeared that the constraints within which public company executives would operate would change considerably. As this chapter has shown, the 1970s indeed did provide the staging post for a substantial reorientation of the environment in which public company executives would run their firms. The trend, however, would take matters in a considerably different direction than would have been anticipated at the time.

---

519 PHALON, *supra* note 513, at 67.

520 Chapter 4, notes 61–64 and related discussion.

521 Pauly, *supra* note 417.

522 DAVID SKEEL, ICARUS IN THE BOARDROOM: THE FUNDAMENTAL FLAWS IN CORPORATE AMERICA AND WHERE THEY CAME FROM 111 (2005).

523 *Joseph Flom*, *supra* note 502, at 695.

524 Metz, *supra* note 515.

525 *Supra* notes 452–56 and related discussion.

526 *Ira Harris*, *supra* note 456.

Between the mid-1960s and the mid-1970s, "public interest movement" reforms relating to topics such as the environment, consumers, and occupational health and safety bolstered considerably regulation of the corporate sector. Further state intervention seemed to be on the way. During the opening half of the 1970s, the Penn Central debacle, the controversy concerning illicit payments, and dismal stock market returns eroded considerably the credibility of big business. Jimmy Carter's election in 1976 appeared to create a "perfect storm" for executives fearful of additional regulation, as the executive and legislative branches were under control of the normally pro-regulation Democrats.

The regulatory "perfect storm" never happened, largely because faith in government diminished in tandem with the declining credibility of business. Advocates of additional regulation, having enjoyed considerable success in the late 1960s and early 1970s, found the ground had shifted beneath their feet as the 1970s drew to a close. Indeed, robust counter-momentum was developing, as manifested by deregulation of stockbroking commissions and the airline and trucking industries. These reforms created greater scope for competition from rivals, which would in turn impinge upon executive discretion. Ronald Reagan's landslide election victory in 1980 emphatically affirmed the turning of the tide and marked the beginning of a decade where market forces would influence public companies in a way that would have been scarcely imaginable to executives during the heyday of managerial capitalism.

4 The 1980s

MANAGERIAL CAPITALISM TAKEN OVER

DURING THE 1950S and 1960s heyday of managerial capitalism, executives running large public companies typically conducted themselves in a bureaucratic, reserved manner in accordance with an "organization man" stereotype. They did so in spite of ample discretion generally being available to them, unions, regulation, and worries about additional regulation aside. Neither boards nor shareholders acted as a substantial check, absent a crisis. Those in charge of large corporations were aware of the possibility that their firms could be laid low by rivals and that a declining share price could elicit an unwelcome takeover offer but in practice insulation from these market forces was substantial. Matters were beginning to change in the 1970s but public company executives continued to operate on a sufficiently autonomous and low-key basis to mean that capitalism remained "managerial." The 1980s constituted a new era. Entrepreneurial rather than managerial skills were increasingly highly prized and the comfort zone that had existed for public company executives was substantially eroded, primarily but not exclusively due to takeover activity.

The 1980s was "the Deal Decade,"[1] with takeover-related activities preoccupying executives, commentators, and the public to an unprecedented extent. Merger and acquisition (M&A) activity would, in statistical terms, be more robust at various points during subsequent decades. For public company executives and their firms, however, the disruptive effect during the 1980s would remain without peer. Public companies were confronted to a unique

[1] THE DEAL DECADE: WHAT TAKEOVERS AND LEVERAGED BUYOUTS MEAN FOR CORPORATE GOVERNANCE (Margaret M. Blair, ed., 1993); Jeffrey N. Gordon, *The Rise of Independent Directors in the United States, 1950–2005: Of Shareholder Value and Stock Market Prices*, 59 STANFORD L. REV. 1465, 1521 (2007). See also *The Best and Worst Deals of the 1980s*, BUS. WK., Jan. 15, 1990, 52 ("Decade of the Deal").

extent by uninvited acquirers prepared to make generous offers directly to the shareholders to gain control. Executives who had enjoyed considerable autonomy from stockholders correspondingly found themselves under a novel, heavy onus to respond to shareholder preferences. Managerial capitalism had been taken over.

While the managerial capitalism era ended in the 1980s, the manner in which this occurred was to a significant extent transitory. Takeovers did much to displace managerial capitalism but their impact on public company executives was rather fleeting. The hostile takeover receded into the background as the 1980s ended, ultimately rendering the market for corporate control a constraint on public company executives of secondary importance. A possible byproduct could have been the restoration of the substantial executive autonomy associated with managerial capitalism. Instead, constraints partially obscured by takeovers in the 1980s would move to the forefront as the 1990s got underway, and do so in a way that foreclosed the return of managerial capitalism.

With takeovers playing a pivotal (if transitory) role in reconfiguring managerial discretion in the 1980s, we will consider this external constraint in some detail. Doing so will set the scene for analysis of other constraints of which public company executives would have been mindful. We will begin, however, by finding out how expectations regarding the contribution executives could and should make to corporate success intensified as the managerial capitalism era drew to a close. We return to the public company executive to conclude the chapter, considering in so doing how a dizzying decade turned life upside down in the executive suite and presaged unprecedented CEO prominence and prosperity in the 1990s.

Don't Just Manage—Lead!

Managerial capitalism predominated in corporate America during the middle decades of the twentieth century. In the 1970s "something happened."[2] Revelations of illicit payments tarnished the reputation of numerous prominent corporations and the crack-up of conglomerates built in the 1960s together with mounting foreign competition cast doubt on the capabilities of public company executives.[3] Nevertheless, consistent with the tenets of managerial capitalism leaders of large companies remained largely anonymous career-oriented professionals with extensive (if diminishing) scope to operate independent of market forces.

In the 1980s the decisive break with managerial capitalism occurred. Numerous commentators considering the decade retrospectively concur that managerial capitalism was a casualty.[4] As Rakesh Khurana observed in a 2007 study of the development of management education, "(t)he social and political context that had favoured managerialism . . . and . . . had virtually

---

[2] Chapter 3, note 5 and accompanying text.

[3] Chapter 3, notes 93–95, 97, 163–69 and related discussion.

[4] See, for example, Gerald F. Davis & Henrich R. Greve, *Corporate Elite Networks and Governance Changes in the 1980s*, 103 Amer. J. Soc., 1, 8 (1997); Martin Gelter, *The Pension System and the Rise of Shareholder Primacy*, 43 Seton Hall L. Rev. 909, 915, 917 (2013); Benjamin C. Waterhouse, Lobbying America: The Politics of Business from Nixon to NAFTA 236 (2014); Johan Heilbron, Joachim Verheul & Sander Quak, *The Origins and Early Diffusion of "Shareholder Value" in the United States*, 43 Theo. Soc. 1, 3 (2014).

guaranteed managerial autonomy . . . was rapidly dismantled during the 1980s," meaning "a new type of American capitalism had emerged."[5]

Contemporaries were well aware that a new form of capitalism was taking shape in the public companies of the 1980s. Peter Drucker, the noted managerial theorist, argued in 1986 that "corporate capitalism," where large American companies "were run by autonomous managements," had been "finished off."[6] Corporate lawyer Martin Lipton, arguing in 1987 "(m)anagement has in many cases lost its independent ability to determine the destiny of the company," suggested that the United States had embarked on an era of "finance capitalism."[7] *Newsweek* columnist Robert Samuelson, having said in 1986 that "ours is an age of bureaucratic capitalism,"[8] changed course in 1989 and said the 1980s had "shattered" the "appealing vision" of management being "a sweeping set of business skills that would make capitalism less chaotic and cruel."[9] Economist Harvey Segal, in his 1989 book *Corporate Makeover*, suggested "managerial capitalism is clearly breaking down."[10]

The displacement of managerial capitalism did not mean that public company executives were relegated to irrelevance. Instead, expectations of what they could and should be seeking to achieve were ratcheting upward. The prototypical managerial capitalism era public company executive was a pragmatic "organization man." In the 1980s executives were supposed to offer more. Those in charge of large corporations, the thinking went, should be aiming not merely to manage their firms but to lead them as well. Leadership would become in the corporate context a "rallying cry" of the 1980s, with chief executive officers (CEOs) being "encouraged to see themselves more as predators in a jungle . . . searching and destroying."[11]

Leadership was thought to be in short supply in the executive suites of US public companies as the 1980s began. *Business Week* devoted a June 1980 issue to describing and analyzing an economic decline America appeared to be experiencing. A dearth of leadership and entrepreneurial drive among top corporate executives was identified as a cause of the malaise:

> (F)or the most part, today's corporate leaders are 'professional managers'—business mercenaries who ply their skills for a salary and bonus but rarely for a vision. And those skills are generally narrow and specialized. Just as the general practitioner who made house calls is a dim memory, so is the hands-on corporate leader.[12]

The *New York Times* concurred in 1981, saying "the freewheeling entrepreneur, the Henry Ford or the Andrew Carnegie, seems to have fallen in short supply, at least among the

---

[5] Rakesh Khurana, From Higher Aims to Hired Hands: The Social Transformation of American Business Schools and the Unfulfilled Promise of Management as a Profession 302, 303 (2007).

[6] Peter F. Drucker, *A Crisis of Capitalism*, Wall St. J., Sept. 30, 1986, 32.

[7] Martin Lipton, *New Laws Are Needed to Combat Abuses*, NY Times, Feb. 15, 1987, E5.

[8] Robert J. Samuelson, *How Companies Grow Stale*, Newsweek, Sept. 8, 1986, 45.

[9] Robert J. Samuelson, *The Message of the Market*, Newsweek, Oct. 30, 1989, 64.

[10] Harvey H. Segal, Corporate Makeover: The Reshaping of the American Economy 27 (1989).

[11] Anthony Sampson, Company Man: The Rise and Fall of Corporate Life 206 (1995).

[12] *Managers Who Are No Longer Entrepreneurs*, Bus. Wk., June 30, 1980, 74, 78.

denizens of big corporations. . . . (T)he current emphasis is more on safeness, certain profitability, than on boldness, ingenuity, innovation—old American trademarks."[13]

Growing admiration of entrepreneurial flair underscored the ostensible dearth of executive vitality in the large public company and contributed to the ditching of managerial capitalism in the 1980s.[14] Tom Peters and Bob Waterman's *In Search of Excellence*, a 1982 study of 43 "excellent" companies, was "the original management blockbuster" and managerial tome of the moment, selling more than 6 million copies.[15] Peters and Waterman hailed "the virtues of outward looking styles of management founded not on systematic control and painstaking analysis, but on entrepreneurial flair and leadership skills which united the workforce."[16] Others weighed in similarly. A prominent venture capitalist proclaimed entrepreneurs in 1984 to be "the rock stars of business."[17] A guest columnist for the *Los Angeles Times* elaborated in 1986:

> The worship of the entrepreneurial spirit has reached a religious fervour in corporate America. Books about entrepreneurs are passed through executives suites like bibles, board chairmen spout entrepreneurial aphorisms and assign senior talent to head new ventures in an effort to infuse their staid corpocracy with the atmosphere of risk-and-reward. Several business magazines have declared this to be the decade of the entrepreneur.[18]

Fewer than one-third of Peters and Waterman's "excellent" companies operated in the high-tech sector.[19] Nevertheless, firms of this sort exemplified the entrepreneurial virtues large, well-established public companies were thought to lack. Microsoft, which Bill Gates cofounded in 1975 and moved to Seattle in 1979, was a prime example. Microsoft went public in 1986, with Gates becoming high-tech's first billionaire on the strength of the company's dominance of the personal computer operating system market.[20] Microsoft was at this time thought of as the antithesis of a large corporate bureaucracy. Gates himself, while a self-confessed "wonk," also was "something of a ladies' man and a fiendishly fast driver who has racked up speeding tickets even in the sluggish Mercedes diesel he bought to restrain himself."[21] A 1987 *Los Angeles Times* profile of Microsoft quoted the company's product

---

[13] Steve Lohr, *Overhauling America's Business Management*, NY Times, Jan. 4, 1981, Sunday Magazine, 4.

[14] Adrian Wooldridge, Masters of Management 173 (2011); Bo Carlsson *et al. The Evolving Domain of Entrepreneurship Research*, 41 Small Bus. Econ. 913, 919–20 (2013).

[15] Tom Peters & Bob Waterman, In Search of Excellence (1982); John Micklethwait & Adrian Wooldridge, The Witch Doctors: What the Management Gurus Are Saying, Why It Matters and How to Make Sense of It 89 (1997); Walter Kiechel, *The Management Century*, Harv. Bus. Rev., Nov. 2012, 63, 72.

[16] Michael Dixon, *Management Education & Training*, Fin. Times, July 16, 1984, Management Education, 21.

[17] William M. Bulkeley, *In Venture Capitalism, Few Are as Successful as Benjamin Rosen*, Wall St. J., Nov. 28, 1984, 1.

[18] Daniel Burstein, *Big Business v. the Entrepreneur*, LA Times, Dec. 5, 1986, B5.

[19] Peters & Waterman, *supra* note 15, 20 (14 of 43).

[20] Nitin Nohria, Davis Dyer & Frederick Dalzell, Changing Fortunes: Remaking the Industrial Corporation 248 (2002).

[21] Bro Uttal & David Kirkpatrick, *Inside the Deal That Made Bill Gates $350,000,000*, Fortune, July 21, 1986, 23.

manager as saying "IBM is basically composed of middle-aged to older people," and went on to observe

> This is no compliment coming from Microsoft, where the average age is 28 and where the chairman—hacker, Harvard drop-out and PC pioneer William H. (Bill) Gates—became a billionaire at 31. Cocky? Without a doubt. . . . (But) Microsoft's swagger is understandable.[22]

Silicon Valley, the southern portion of the San Francisco Bay area nicknamed by a local journalist in 1971 to reflect the success of the region's memory-chip makers,[23] was an even more potent symbol of entrepreneurship in the 1980s. Journalists breathlessly sought to enlighten readers about the Valley's robust entrepreneurial culture. A 1984 Associated Press report indicated Silicon Valley, where "new technology is outmoded in 18 months," was an "electronic wonder child . . . where new companies . . . multiply like Medflies" and constituted "a throwback to something that made this country No. 1 in the first place. Enterprise. Free enterprise."[24] The West Coast reporter for the *Baltimore Sun* told readers in 1988

> The lifeblood of Silicon Valley, its entrepreneurial spirit, has created a different set of rules by which a company's success is measured—and an employee's too. . . . (T)here is less respect for . . . the person who hangs on for 20 years. Nobody bothers with that here. You are measured instead by your income, your equity position and your technical contributions.[25]

Apple Computer Inc., launched by Steve Jobs and Steve Wozniak in a garage in the mid-1970s,[26] epitomized the Silicon Valley ethos. As the company geared up for a highly successful 1980 initial public offering (IPO), the *Los Angeles Times* observed "Apple is merchandise that comes with an appealing, American-dream type story," and indicated Jobs was "deft with the kind of arresting analogy that entrances securities analysts and the investing public."[27] John Sculley, the Pepsi president whom Jobs lured in 1983 to manage Apple, said the following year "(w)e don't find role models for Apple at the Harvard Business School."[28]

Sculley and Jobs would soon fall out, prompting Apple's board in 1985 to dismiss Jobs as chairman. Jobs nevertheless continued to have numerous admirers. Robert Sobel, a prolific

---

[22] Victor R. Zonana, *Cocky Microsoft Set to Challenge Software Rivals on Their Own Turf*, LA TIMES, Aug. 23, 1987, D1.

[23] JOHN MICKLETHWAIT & ADRIAN WOOLDRIDGE, THE COMPANY: A SHORT HISTORY OF A REVOLUTIONARY IDEA 140 (2003).

[24] Sid Moody, *Heart of High-Tech*, LA TIMES, July 8, 1984, 3.

[25] Ellen Uzelac, *Entrepreneurs' Heaven on Earth*, BALT. SUN, Sept. 18, 1988, F1.

[26] James Flanigan, *Apple Computer Looks Tasty but Its Market Needs Ripening*, LA TIMES, Oct. 19, 1980; Nik Rawlinson, *History of Apple: The Story of Steve Jobs and the Company He Founded*, MACWORLD, Apr. 25, 2017, https://www.macworld.co.uk/feature/apple/history-of-apple-steve-jobs-mac-3606104/ (accessed Jan, 20, 2018).

[27] Flanigan, *supra* note 26.

[28] Michael Rogers, *It's the Apple of His Eye*, NEWSWEEK, Jan. 30, 1984, 54.

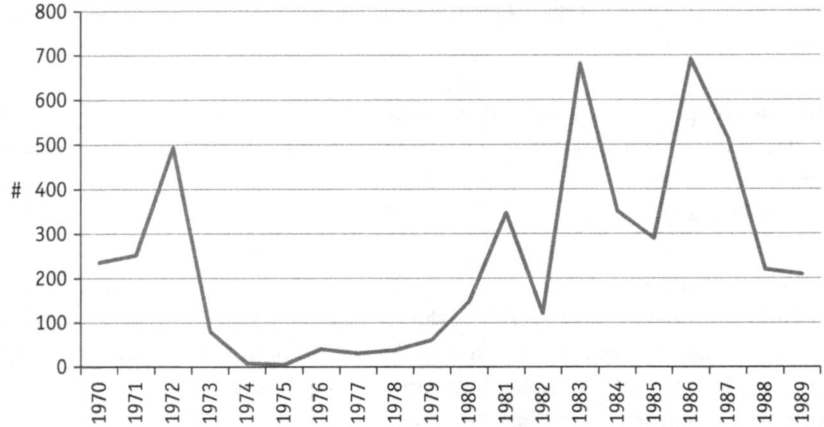

FIGURE 4.1 Number of IPOs, 1970–1989.
Source: NITIN NOHRIA, DAVIS DYER & FREDERICK DALZELL, CHANGING FORTUNES: REMAKING THE INDUSTRIAL CORPORATION 251 (2002).

author of popular business history, wrote at the time Jobs departed that the term "entrepreneur" "pretty well describes Steve Jobs" and observed presciently "(t)he first act of his career is over. There will be others."[29] Tom Peters, in a 1989 newspaper column canvassing the top 10 business stories of the 1980s, offered "plaudits to Steve Jobs," whose "youth, energy and successful challenges to the establishment" helped to erase "entrepreneur from the dirty word list and put professional manager there instead."[30]

Trends concerning IPOs reflected the 1980s enthusiasm for entrepreneurial skills. IPO activity surged as the decade got under way, following a 1970s slump (Figure 4.1). Apple's 1980 IPO was a forerunner, with robust investor demand yielding a number of "newly minted Midases," including Jobs.[31] A 1985 study of America's "future rich" said of entrepreneurs in that era "the equity markets couldn't have been more enthusiastic," with "the stock market thirst for equity in as yet unproven hi-tech companies (being) so strong that many founders began taking them public before their enterprise had begun selling a product and long before it showed any hope of turning a profit."[32]

Tech stocks performed poorly as 1984 got underway, which helped to curtail the IPO surge temporarily.[33] Enthusiasm returned in 1986, the peak year for IPOs during the 1980s, with Microsoft being at the center of a "really hot" market.[34] *Fortune*, having told readers "(g)oing public is one of capitalism's major sacraments, conferring instant superwealth on a few talented and lucky entrepreneurs," said "of the more than 1,500 companies that have

---

[29] Robert Sobel, *Reaching for the Brass Ring in Business*, NEWSDAY, Nov. 10, 1985, K1.

[30] Tom Peters, *Deserving Decoration in the "Me" Decade*, BALT. SUN, Dec. 25, 1989, 4.

[31] Chapter 3, note 496 and accompanying text; JACQUELINE THOMPSON, FUTURE RICH: THE PEOPLE, COMPANIES, & INDUSTRIES CREATING AMERICA'S NEXT FORTUNES 87 (1985).

[32] THOMPSON, *supra* note 31, at 38.

[33] Lawrence J. Tell, *Bleeding Edge of Technology*, BARRON'S, Apr. 23, 1984, 20; Jack Egan, *Wall Street Cranks Out the Shares*, US NEWS & WORLD REPORT, May 20, 1991, 57.

[34] *Timing Is Everything When You Go Public*, BUS. WK., Nov. 3, 1986, 120.

undergone this rite of passage in the past five years, few have enjoyed a more frenzied welcome from investors than Microsoft."[35] Oracle Systems Corporation, destined to become a software powerhouse under the leadership of its hard-driving founder Larry Ellison,[36] went public the day before Microsoft and was also enthusiastically received by investors as shares priced at $15 for its public offering closed at $20.50 after the first day of trading.[37]

Larger companies that were already public became keen to join the 1980s entrepreneurship bandwagon,[38] with the term "intrapreneurship" becoming shorthand for the entrepreneurial ethos in big companies.[39] A *Los Angeles Times* business columnist claimed in 1983 "entrepreneurship is suddenly in fashion at the smarter big companies."[40] The *New York Times* hailed in 1985 "A New Breed of CEO," saying "today's CEOs. . . . (D)etest bureaucracy."[41] *Time* noted the same year

> Now some big companies are fighting back. They are trying to create the spirit, zest and rewards of entrepreneurship right in their corridors, shop floors and laboratories. They are giving employees the resources and freedom to pursue their own ideas, cutting back on traditional red tape, endless meetings and other obstacles that can slow down innovation.[42]

For those running large firms, then, just being an effective and loyal "organization man" seemingly no longer sufficed in the way it had during the heyday of managerial capitalism.

Big companies were by no means fully committed to an entrepreneurial ethos in the 1980s. In 1986, a guest columnist for the *Los Angeles Times* who acknowledged that the 1980s were being called "the decade of the entrepreneur" nevertheless argued that "big business is cheating on its professed love affair with entrepreneurs. It is cheating too, on its commitment to intrapreneurship."[43] He explained this was due to "the fundamental clash of cultures between the entrepreneur's world and the environment of a large, established business."[44] He illustrated the point by citing General Motors' (GM) then recent decision to buy out "honest-to-goodness rags-to-riches entrepreneur" Ross Perot for $700 million, paying in so doing a hefty premium compared to the prevailing stock market price.[45] This occurred just two years

[35] Uttal & Kirkpatrick, *supra* note 21.

[36] Brenton R. Schendler, *Oracle Corp.'s Ellison Spurs Its Fast Growth with Aggressive Style*, Wall St. J., May 31, 1989, A1.

[37] John Letzing, *In 1986, Sun Led the Way for Future Tech Giants*, MarketWatch, Oct. 19, 2009, available at http://www.marketwatch.com/story/sun-was-first-to-go-public-is-first-to-disappear-2009-10-19 (accessed Dec. 18, 2017).

[38] Michael E. McGill, American Business and the Quick Fix 57 (1988).

[39] Gifford Pinchot, Intrapreneuring, or Why You Don't Have to Leave the Corporation to Become an Entrepreneur (1985).

[40] James Flanigan, *Scrooge-Like Entrepreneurs Play Key Role*, LA Times, Dec. 25, 1983, 11.

[41] N.R. Kleinfeld, *A New Breed of CEO Enters the Public Eye*, NY Times, Dec. 1, 1985, Sunday Magazine, 76.

[42] John S. DeMott & Rosemary Byrnes, *Here Come the Intrapreneurs*, Time, Feb. 4, 1985, 36.

[43] Burstein, *supra* note 18.

[44] *Id.*

[45] *Id.* See also Jeff Gramm, Dear Chairman: Boardroom Battles and the Rise of Shareholder Activism 116 (2015).

after GM acquired Electronic Data Systems, the data services firm Perot founded, so Perot could bring welcome energy to GM's boardroom and beneficially upend the automaker's bureaucratic culture.[46]

By 1989, intrapreneurship was being referred to as a mere "fad."[47] The *Washington Post* suggested that big business was abandoning its effort "to co-opt entrepreneurism," which was a signal that "the Cult of the Entrepreneur" might be drawing to a close.[48] Regardless, the emphasis on entrepreneurial values was part of a larger sustained pattern, namely the discrediting of the bureaucratic, cautious managerial ethos that the large public company epitomized during the middle decades of the twentieth century. We turn next to a pivotal catalyst in the process, namely M&A activity sufficiently robust to result in the 1980s being referred to as "the Deal Decade."

The Deal Decade

Throughout this book changes affecting public companies are analyzed primarily by reference to internal and external constraints relevant to corporate executives. External constraints operating during the 1980s will be discussed generally later in this chapter. One, however, merits analysis at this point, this being "the market for corporate control." The focus will be on corporate acquisitions where the parties seeking control anticipated they could add value by putting in place different managerial arrangements. The hostile takeover, involving an uninvited and at least initially unwelcome approach, was a particularly dramatic example of such an acquisition.

Peter Drucker recognized in 1986 the pivotal role the market for corporate control was playing in reshaping the public company, saying "(t)he new wave of hostile takeovers has already profoundly altered the contours and landmarks of the American economy. It has become a dominant force—many would say the dominant force—in the behavior and actions of American management."[49] Law professor Ron Gilson offered a similar verdict retrospectively in 2006, maintaining "(t)he mechanism that transmitted changes . . . during the 1980s is clear: the hostile takeover."[50] One implication was that M&A activity did not simply operate in isolation as a source of managerial discipline but instead influenced the operation of various constraints relevant for executives of public companies, both internal and external. The basic parameters of the Deal Decade correspondingly merit examination before we turn to these other constraints. A helpful departure point is to consider takeovers separately from a debt-driven acquisition variant referred to as the "leveraged buyout" (LBO). We will also consider why an era where the market for corporate control was a constraint on public company executives of first order importance ended abruptly as the 1980s concluded.

---

[46] GRAMM, *supra* note 45, at 96, 106.

[47] Christopher Lorenz, *The Rise and Fall of Business Fads*, FIN. TIMES, June 21, 1989, p. 24.

[48] Steve Pearlstein, *Capitalism's Brave New World*, WASH. POST, July 2, 1989, H1.

[49] Peter F. Drucker, *Corporate Takeovers—What Is to Be Done?*, PUBLIC INT., Winter 1986, at 3, 3. See also John C. Coffee, *Shareholders Versus Managers: The Strain in the Corporate Web*, (1986) 85 MICH. L. REV. 1, 8 (1986).

[50] Ronald J. Gilson, *Catalysing Corporate Governance: The Evolution of the United States System in the 1980s and 1990s*, 24 CO. & SEC. L.J. 143, 150 (2006).

TAKEOVERS

Takeover activity functioned as a check on managerial discretion during the 1980s to a greater extent than at any point before or after. Contemporaries were thoroughly caught up in proceedings. By 1985 the financial press was "bulging with the latest examples of a world seemingly gone mad with corporate takeover fever."[51] *Business Week* indicated in 1986 that "fear and anxiety" were "lurking in executive suites all over the U.S. . . . (N)ow everybody's hearing the menacing music from [the 1975 shark movie blockbuster] *Jaws*."[52] Indeed, due to takeovers "American business became the subject of public interest," with the protagonists becoming "heroes, villains, larger-than-life figures whose antics kept the nation enthralled."[53]

During the 1980s an unprecedentedly large number of public companies found they were targets in takeover contests. The aggregate market value of the targets also increased dramatically (Figure 4.2). While size had formerly functioned as a potent obstacle to uninvited bids for control,[54] this was rarely the case in the 1980s. *Newsweek* told readers in 1988 that "on today's Wall Street few companies, no matter how big or venerable, are off limits."[55] The *Wall Street Journal* made the same point with greater rhetorical flourish, acknowledging that while IBM, oil giant Exxon, and likely General Motors had little to fear "(t)he marauding huns of the takeover game are besieging ever larger corporate kingdoms" and leaving executives to wonder "who, if anyone, is safe."[56] In the 1980s, nearly 30 percent of companies in the *Fortune* 500 received tender offers where control was sought, with a substantial proportion

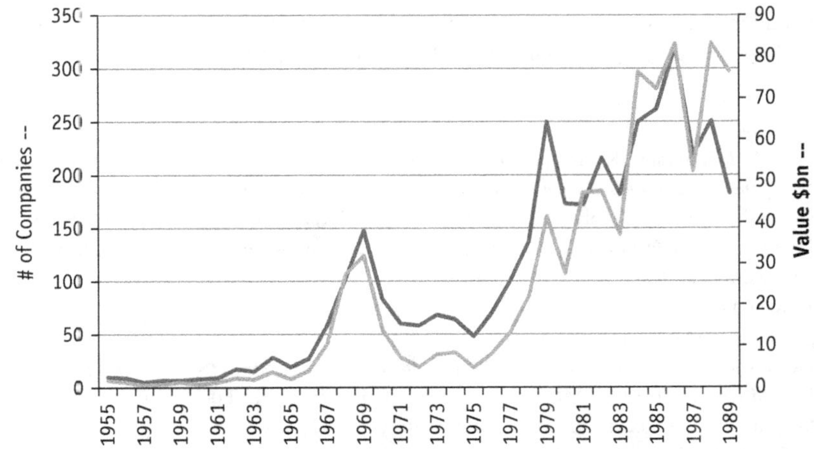

FIGURE 4.2 Public Company Takeover Bid Targets, 1955–1989 (# and aggregate value, $1987). *Source:* MARGARET M. BLAIR & GIRISH UPPAL, THE DEAL DECADE HANDBOOK 54 (1993).

---

51 Fred R. Bleakley, *The Power and the Perils of Junk Bonds*, NY TIMES, Apr. 14, 1985, F1.

52 *More than Ever, It's Management for the Short Term*, BUS. WK., Nov. 24, 1986, 92.

53 ROBERT SLATER, THE TITANS OF TAKEOVER 3 (1987).

54 Chapter 2, notes 344–47, Chapter 3, notes 498, 502 and related discussion.

55 *Time Inc. Feels the Heat*, NEWSWEEK, Oct. 3, 1988, 40.

56 Randall Smith, *In Takeover-Ridden Times, Mighty Fortresses Are Some Firms*, WALL ST. J., Oct. 28, 1988, C1.

clearly being hostile.[57] With the 100 largest industrial companies, between 1981 and 1989 there were 32 tender offers launched to obtain voting control, 17 hostile.[58]

Larger public companies emerged as predators as well as prey with hostile takeovers in the 1980s. A 1974 bid by International Nickel to obtain control of ESB Inc. broke a taboo against big public firms carrying out hostile takeover offers.[59] In practice for the remainder of the 1970s the companies that made "hostile bids were typically outside the corporate mainstream."[60] By the early 1980s, though, companies, of whatever size, that refrained as a matter of principle from making an unfriendly takeover offer had become a rarity.[61] As of 1985, mainstream corporate strategizing typically encompassed the possibility of launching a bid.[62] With the decade drawing to a close, there was amongst "blue-chip corporations ... a no-holds barred attitude" with the launching of takeovers.[63] Winthrop Knowlton, the former CEO of Harper & Row publishers, and Ira Millstein, a prominent Wall Street lawyer, maintained in 1988 "(g)ood or bad, friendly or unfriendly, takeovers are now a fact of corporate life."[64]

While mainstream public companies became prominent takeover practitioners in the 1980s, the limelight tended to be on iconoclastic corporate "raiders." The best-known even "became household words in the 1980s."[65] As of the mid-1980s the names of T. Boone Pickens, Carl Icahn, Saul Steinberg, Irwin Jacobs, and Sir James Goldsmith were "spoken with a shudder in board rooms from Pittsburgh to Bartlesville [Oklahoma]. They are the new buccaneers of capitalism, making millions by taking over, or just threatening to take over, America's largest corporations."[66] The raiders were financial entrepreneurs who operated independent of corporate affiliations or, as with Pickens, through the medium of a modestly-sized public firm (Mesa Petroleum).[67]

The raiders had an aggressive style public company management found off-putting. Reputedly they would "snap at their prey like a school of bluefish in a feeding frenzy."[68] The

---

[57] Gerald F. Davis & Suzanne K. Stout, *Organization Theory and the Market for Corporate Control: A Dynamic Analysis of the Characteristics of Large Takeover Targets, 1980–1990*, 37 Admin. Sci. Q. 605, 605 (1992) (77 of 144 hostile); Dirk Zorn et al., *Managing Investors: How Financial Markets Reshaped the American Firm*, The Sociology of Financial Markets, 269, 273–74 (Karin Knorr Cetina & Alexandru Preda eds., 2005) (one-third hostile).

[58] Nohria, Dyer & Dalzell *supra* note 20, at 179.

[59] Chapter 3, notes 517–21 and related discussion.

[60] Leo Herzl & John R. Schmidt, *Hostile Bids "Undermine the Ability to Plan,"* Fin. Times, Aug. 2, 1982, 10.

[61] *Id.*; Jeff Madrick, Taking America: How We Got from the First Hostile Takeover to Megamergers, Corporate Raiding and Scandal 194–95 (1987).

[62] Daniel F. Cuff, *The Rising Tide of Mergers*, NY Times, June 28, 1985, D1.

[63] *A New Strain of Merger Mania*, Bus. Wk., Mar. 21, 1988, 122.

[64] Winthrop Knowlton & Ira Millstein, *Can the Board of Directors Help the American Corporation Earn the Immortality It Holds So Dear?*, *in* The US Business Corporation: An Institution in Transition 169, 180 (John R. Meyer & James M. Gustafson eds., 1988). On Knowlton, see Jeffrey Sonnenfeld, The Hero's Farewell: What Happens When CEOs Retire 163–65 (1988).

[65] Charles R. Geisst, Wall Street: A History 339 (1997).

[66] *Greenmail: Who's the Villain?*, NY Times, Mar. 8, 1985, A34.

[67] David A. Vise, *Mesa Petroleum Sets Corporate Restructuring*, Wash. Post, Aug. 27, 1985, E1; Barrie A. Wigmore, Securities Markets in the 1980s, Volume 1: The New Regime 302, 360 (1997) (Mesa was an "insignificant player in the oil patch").

[68] Aloysius Ehrbar & Lorraine Carson, *Have Takeovers Gone Too Far?*, Fortune, May 27, 1985, 20.

raiders' rhetoric reflected their abrasive approach. Pickens, who focused on oil companies with his forays, said of top management in the sector "(t)hey are bureaucrats and caretakers. They have learned to move up through the bureaucracy with a minimum of personal risk. It is a special talent."[69] Pickens did not think matters were much different in other industries, saying "(n)ot all chief executives in America are incompetent; only 80 percent of them are."[70] Icahn, for his part, characterized top management in US public companies as a "corpocracy" of which he offered a dismissive description in a 1986 interview with *Newsweek*

> What I've always said is that the only way you get these top executives off the golf courses is when I file [with the Securities and Exchange Commission] a 13D on them (required when someone has bought more than 5 percent of a company's stock). Then I sometimes think they're better off on the golf course than in the office, where they're either buying the wrong companies, or worse than that, bothering (the people doing the real work) with a lot of bureaucracy and a lot of paperwork.[71]

Joe Nocera, a leading business journalist, said in the late 2000s of Pickens "his famous raids . . . struck me then—and strike me now—as one of the most important moments in modern business history."[72] Nevertheless, the raiders' impact was limited in two important ways. First, they were only at the center of the action briefly. A 1986 book, *The Raiders of Wall Street*, claimed "(t)oday's raiders are individuals. They are the opposite of the faceless corporations that dominated takeovers only a few years ago. . . . They are modern buccaneers."[73] It in fact was only in late 1983 that one of these buccaneers, namely Pickens, first targeted one of America's true corporate giants, the Gulf Oil Company, which was more than 75 times larger than Pickens' Mesa Corp.[74] Following judicial stymying of forays involving Amoco and Unocal in 1985, Pickens geared down considerably.[75] His subsequent raids were "timid intrusions," meaning that by 1988 he was no longer feared in corporate boardrooms.[76] The pattern was similar with other prominent raiders. A late 1980s retreat left the hostile takeover field clear for corporate buyers prepared to execute takeovers.[77]

---

69 Robert Sobel, Dangerous Dreamers: The Financial Motivators from Charles Merrill to Michael Milken 123 (1993).

70 Leigh B. Trevor, *Hostile Takeovers: A US Falkland Islands Where the Argentines Always Win*, Hostile Takeovers: Issues in Public and Corporate Policy 16, 20 (David L. McKee ed., 1989).

71 *Confessions of a Raider*, Newsweek, Oct. 20, 1986, 51.

72 Joe Nocera, Good Guys & Bad Guys: Behind the Scenes with the Saints and Scoundrels of American Business (and Everything in Between) 6 (2008).

73 Eric W. Allison, The Raiders of Wall Street 13 (1986).

74 *Gulf Oil Is Boone Pickens' Biggest Target Yet*, Bus. Wk., Oct. 24, 1983, 48; Mark Potts, *Pickens' Raids*, Wash. Post, Oct. 30, 1983, G1; Allen Kaufman & Lawrence Zacharias, *From Trust to Contract: The Legal Language of Managerial Ideology, 1920–1980*, 66 Bus. Hist. Rev. 523, 560 (1992).

75 Ian Hargreaves, *The Art of Living Dangerously*, Fin. Times, May 23, 1985, 26; *The World According to Pickens*, Barron's, Sept. 23, 1985, 65.

76 George Getschow & Bryan Burrough, *Pickens, Acting Bitter, Finds Takeover Game Isn't Much Fun Now*, Wall St. J., Apr. 5, 1988, 1.

77 Bryan Burrough, *Companies Take Over the Takeover Game from Flashy Raiders*, Wall St. J., Jan. 25, 1988, 1; Caroline E. Mayer, *New Players Join the Takeover Game*, Wash. Post, Jan. 31, 1988, K1; Martin Lipton, *Why Takeovers Are Taking Off Again*, NY Times, Apr. 1, 1988, A35.

Second, the raiders only rarely acquired control of the companies they targeted.[78] Pickens did not make a single takeover,[79] even with his lawyer warning that Pickens would lose credibility as a raider if he failed to buy a company.[80] Icahn only took control of two US public companies throughout the entire 1980s, railroad car supplier ACF Industries and the airline TWA.[81] This was the same number as Goldsmith, a flamboyant English-French financier who bought Diamond International, a forest products and packaging company, and Crown Zellerbach, a large forestry company.[82]

A raider could, without actually successfully executing a takeover, still have a meaningful impact as a provocateur. By acquiring a sizeable stake in a putative target, a raider could be the catalyst for an acquisition by a mainstream corporate buyer that might not have occurred without the raider finding the target and forcing the target's senior executives and board to consider sacrificing corporate independence.[83] As and when there was news of a raider's stake-building, the targeted company's shares tended to gravitate toward investors seeking a quick lucrative sale, such as professional arbitrageurs.[84] Having put a target "in play" the raider could then make a profitable exit by selling into the market after the share price had gone up due to the proposed bid, by agreeing with a harried management team to a share buy-back on favorable terms not offered to other shareholders ("greenmail") or by accepting a tender offer made by a corporate buyer at a price incorporating a takeover premium.[85] New York financier Saul Steinberg profited to the tune of $60 million when Walt Disney Corp. agreed in 1984 to repurchase the 11 percent stake he had acquired.[86] This tidy greenmail sum paled in comparison, though, to the profit of $760 million Pickens made when in 1984 Chevron Corp., an oil company similar in size to Gulf that was treated as a rescuing "white knight," acquired Gulf.[87]

Chevron's acquisition of its rival Gulf Oil fell into line with a trend that might be unanticipated with 1980s takeovers. Despite the publicity the raiders attracted, the assets of companies acquired by way of hostile takeovers usually ended up in the hands of a direct competitor. Of the 62 US companies that were targets of hostile bids exceeding $50 million in value between 1984 and 1986, on 34 occasions the takeover was strategic, in the sense that the bidder was in the same industry and anticipated rolling into its business a majority of the

---

[78] WIGMORE, *supra* note 67, at 360–61.

[79] *Id.* at 361.

[80] BRETT COLE, M&A TITANS: THE PIONEERS WHO SHAPED WALL STREET'S MERGERS AND ACQUISITIONS INDUSTRY 146 (2008).

[81] ALLISON, *supra* note 73, at 55–56, 64–74; *Carl Icahn, Raider Unbowed*, BUS. WK., Nov. 26, 1990, 146.

[82] ALLISON, *supra* note 73, 189–202.

[83] WIGMORE, *supra* note 67, 359–60.

[84] *Id.* at 355.

[85] *Id.* at 350–53.

[86] Fred B. Bleakley, *Outrage over Disney Buyout*, NY TIMES, June 13, 1984, D1; Kenneth B. Noble, *Time Is Money; Fear Is Lots of Money*, NY TIMES, Aug. 26, 1984, E8.

[87] WIGMORE, *supra* note 67, at 354; ALLISON, *supra* note 73, at 144; Ken Wells & Carol Hymowitz, *Gulf's Managers Find Merger into Chevron Forces Many Changes*, WALL ST. J., Dec. 5, 1984, 1; NILS LINDSKOOG, LONG-TERM GREEDY: THE TRIUMPH OF GOLDMAN SACHS 36 (2d ed. 1998).

target's assets.[88] On seven other occasions the bidder dismantled the target but most of the assets were sold to strategic, same industry buyers.[89]

LEVERAGED BUYOUTS

Corporate raiders aside, what were known as leveraged buyouts "were perhaps the most conspicuous element of the merger boom of the 1980s."[90] The term "leveraged buyout," which was first used regularly in the mid-1970s,[91] reflected the fact such acquisitions were usually financed heavily by debt backed by the assets and cash flow of the business being acquired.[92] Following a precedent set by LBO pioneers Kohlberg, Kravis and Roberts (KKR) in 1978, 1980s buyout firms usually established and ran stand-alone funds to which investors would commit capital and which would become the controlling shareholder in enterprises acquired.[93] Executives destined to run the acquired businesses would also most often take up a substantial percentage of the shares, usually financed at least partly by their own capital.[94]

Leveraged buyouts encompass both the purchasing of divisions of publicly traded firms and the acquisition and "taking private" of entire public companies.[95] A milestone divisional buyout involved greeting card maker Gibson Greetings Inc., sold in 1982 by RCA Corporation for $80 million with $79 million having been borrowed.[96] After Gibson Greetings' buyers took the company public with a $280 market valuation just 18 months later, "(s)uddenly everyone wanted to try this 'LBO thing.'"[97] Buyouts of divisions grew in number and size in the 1980s through until 1986, when 144 occurred at an average value of $181 million.[98] Divisional buyout activity then leveled off as the decade concluded.[99]

Divisional buyouts were an important part of a 1980s trend of "deconglomeration," one of "the hottest buzzwords in the executive suite" at the time.[100] Unease that had built up in the 1970s regarding highly diversified public companies, exemplified by conglomerates assembled in the 1960s,[101] continued to mount in the 1980s. For instance, a key message of Peters and Waterman's popular 1982 management tome *In Search of Excellence* was that "excellent" companies would "stick to their knitting," "stay reasonably close to businesses they know,"

---

[88] Sanjai Bhagat, Andrei Shleifer & Robert W. Vishny, *Hostile Takeovers in the 1980s: The Return to Corporate Specialization*, BROOKINGS PAPERS ON ECONOMIC ACTIVITY: MICROECONOMICS 1, 12, 44, 48 (1990).

[89] *Id.* at 48.

[90] Guy Halverson, *Slow Economy Means Fewer Deals*, CHRISTIAN SCI. MONITOR, Dec. 20, 1989, 9.

[91] GEORGE ANDERS, MERCHANTS OF DEBT: KKR AND THE MORTGAGING OF AMERICAN BUSINESS 8 (1992).

[92] Winston Williams, *Frenzy and Style in the Merger Boom*, NY TIMES, Jan. 15, 1984, F1.

[93] Brian Cheffins & John Armour, *The Eclipse of Private Equity*, 33 DEL. J. CORP. L. 1, 12–13, 18–19 (2008).

[94] *Id.* at 12–13; Michael C. Jensen, *Eclipse of the Public Corporation*, HARV. BUS. REV., Sept.–Oct., 1989, 61, 68.

[95] Cheffins & Armour, *supra* note 93, at 9.

[96] ANDERS, *supra* note 91, at 37.

[97] BRYAN BURROUGH & JOHN HELYAR, BARBARIANS AT THE GATE: THE FALL OF RJR NABISCO 140 (1990). See also Clemens P. Work & Manuel Schiffres, *Leveraged Buyouts—Are They Growing Too Risky?*, US NEWS & WORLD REPORT, Nov. 18, 1985, 49.

[98] Jensen, *supra* note 94, at 65 (providing annual data, 1979–1988, with value calculated in 1988 dollars).

[99] *Id.* at 65.

[100] Coffee, *supra* note 49, at 52–53.

[101] Chapter 3, notes 111–14 and related discussion.

and avoid major diversification moves that would cause management to lose its "feel" by jumping into new activities.[102] Oil companies provided an exemplary case study of diversification going awry. They squandered cash flow generated by a dramatic rise of oil prices in the 1970s with value-destroying acquisitions of mines, department store chains, financial institutions, entertainment properties, and various other non-petroleum assets that were supposed to hedge against the risk that oil reserves would soon be depleted.[103]

Underpinned by general antipathy toward diversification there was by the mid-1980s a "riot of voluntary restructuring."[104] Dramatic growth in divestitures of divisions and subsidiary companies ensued (Figure 4.3). The proportion of *Fortune* 500 companies operating in one industry duly increased from 25 percent in 1980 to 42 percent to 1990.[105]

Leveraged divisional buyouts such as RCA's sale of Gibson Greetings proved to be an "extremely practical" technique for diversified companies to sell off businesses.[106] Between 1985 and 1989, leveraged buyouts accounted for nearly two-fifths of the value of divestitures public corporations carried out.[107] Michael Adler, professor of finance at the Columbia Business School, told the *New York Times* for an article arguing that LBOs were "altering

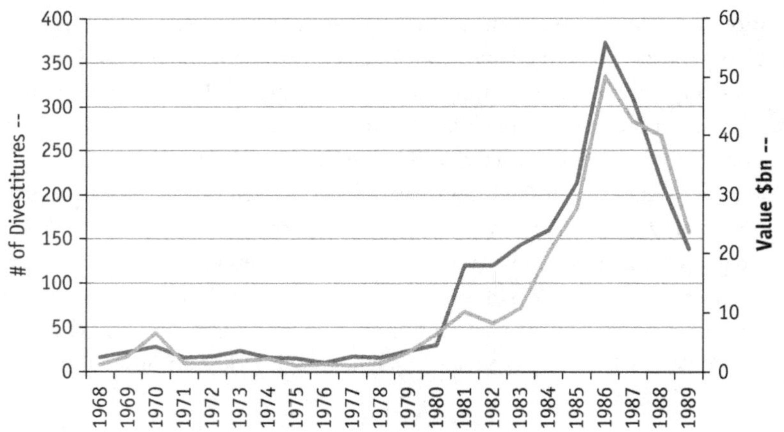

FIGURE 4.3 Divestitures of Subsidiaries & Divisions, 1955–1989 (# and aggregate value, $1987).
Source: MARGARET M. BLAIR & GIRISH UPPAL, THE DEAL DECADE HANDBOOK 53 (1993).

[102] PETERS & WATERMAN, *supra* note 15, 15, 292–305; Richard Lambert, *What Makes the Winners Tick*, FIN. TIMES, Jan. 31, 1983, 12.

[103] WALTER ADAMS & JAMES W. BROCK, DANGEROUS PURSUITS: MERGERS AND ACQUISITIONS IN THE AGE OF WALL STREET 35–36 (1989).

[104] *Splitting Up*, BUS. WK., July 1, 1985, 50.

[105] Gerald F. Davis, Kristina A. Diekmann & Caroline H. Tinsley, *The Decline and Fall of the Conglomerate Firm in the 1980s: The Deinstitutionalization of an Organizational Form*, 59 AMER. SOC. REV. 547, 562 (measured to the two-digit level using the Standard Industrial Classification system).

[106] William J. Golden & Arthur D. Little, *Leveraged Buyouts as a Corporate Development Tool*, J. BUS. STRATEGY, Summer 1985, at 7, 7.

[107] MARGARET M. BLAIR & GIRISH UPPAL, THE DEAL DECADE HANDBOOK 53 (1993) (providing data indicating the value of divestitures executed by buyout totaled $60.3 billion between 1986 and 1989 while the value of all divestitures was $156.1 billion).

(the) face of corporate America," "(l)everaged buyouts are the way the market is now unraveling the big conglomerate wave of the last two decades."[108]

Numerically during the 1980s divisional divestitures executed as leveraged buyouts outpaced buyouts where a public company was taken private.[109] On the other hand, the aggregate value of the public-to-private buyouts that were carried out was nearly double that of divestiture buyouts.[110] Public-to-private buyouts were also more likely to capture attention because removing a company from the stock market was a more dramatic event than the offloading of a division. The *New York Times* indicated in 1986 that leveraged buyouts had "revolutionized the way companies are bought and sold."[111] The *Baltimore Sun* said in 1989 that public-to-private buyouts were the "most powerful trend in determining control of US business."[112]

According to one estimate, the value of shares of all companies taken private by way of a leveraged buyout throughout the 1980s amounted to no more than a modest 8 percent of the total market value of equity holdings in US companies.[113] Some indeed suggested public-to-private buyouts attracted attention out of proportion to the number of firms actually affected.[114] However, controversy, in the form of intense criticism of and praise for public-to-private buyouts, guaranteed the transaction the spotlight.

With the critics, a *Chicago Tribune* columnist went so far as to say that due to the LBO "nightmare" "(a) systematic destruction of traditional American business is underway."[115] One source of concern was that, with key executives of a public company target often continuing to run the business after it was taken private, public-to-private buyouts provided ample scope for problematic self-dealing. Some suggested that the LBO was the "ultimate insider trade"[116] where, in effect, "corporate managers do their own raiding."[117] High prices realized with post-LBO asset sales were cited as evidence that public shareholders were being shortchanged, even though these investors would in all likelihood have been cashed out at a premium to the prevailing stock market price.[118]

The leveraged nature of going-private transactions also caused alarm in the 1980s. Some expressed concerns about preexisting bondholders who were "dunked . . . into icy water" due

---

[108] Leslie Wayne, *Buyouts Altering Face of Corporate America*, NY Times, Nov. 23, 1985, 1.

[109] Blair & Uppal, *supra* note 107, at 11 (setting out data indicating that between 1980 and 1989 there were 559 divestiture buyouts and 468 public-to-private buyouts); Michael Useem, Executive Defense: Shareholder Power and Corporate Reorganization 256 (1993) (providing annual data for 1980 and 1990 indicating somewhat higher divestiture and public-to-private totals but revealing the same pattern).

[110] Blair & Uppal, *supra* note 107, at 11 (setting out data indicating that between 1980 and 1989 the total value of divestiture buyouts was $99.8 billion as compared with $170.3 billion for public-to-private buyouts); Useem, *supra* note 109, at 256 (citing higher amounts but again revealing the same pattern).

[111] James Sterngold, *Lure of Leveraged Buyouts*, NY Times, Sept. 8, 1986, D1.

[112] Thomas Easton, *Leveraged Buyouts: Economic Boon or Menace?*, Balt. Sun, May 24, 1989, G1.

[113] Henry N. Goldstein, *Junk Bonds and Corporate America: Revisiting the Yago/Brock Debate*, 9 Critical Rev. 403, 406 (1995).

[114] Useem, *supra* note 109, at 34.

[115] William Neikirk, *LBO: Nightmare on Wall Street?*, Chi. Trib., Aug. 20, 1989, Business, 3.

[116] *Doubts on Buyouts*, LA Times, Oct. 22, 1988, A8.

[117] Michael Kinsley, *The Buyout Boom*, Wash. Post, Nov. 3, 1988, A27.

[118] Benjamin J. Stein, *Where Are the Shareholders' Yachts?*, Barron's, Aug. 18, 1986, 66.

to the massive fresh debt obligations target companies would have to shoulder.[119] Others worried about debt burdening the companies being taken private. One fear was that the companies would cut "crucial corners to keep up their payments."[120] Another was that defaults might occur on a sufficiently wide scale to jeopardize the stability of the financial system.[121]

On the other side of the ledger LBO advocates hailed public-to-private buyouts as "an elixir, a cure-all for corporate America."[122] An accountant specializing in M&A claimed, for instance, that "(a) leveraged buyout is like taking the corporation to the health club and getting it into better shape."[123] LBO boosters suggested that managerial waywardness would be curbed because servicing the substantial debt involved meant "pressure to repay creditors makes cash as valuable as fresh water on a lifeboat."[124] At the same time, executives would have the freedom to run their company without offering explanations to securities analysts or the financial press for tough choices made.[125] Moreover, according to LBO advocates, management's substantial ownership stake would provide those in charge with a potent incentive to bolster the value of the firm that public company executives owning a tiny percentage of shares would inevitably lack. The president of Merrill Lynch Capital Partners made the point in a 1988 interview, pointing out that while the manager of a publicly traded firm still gets paid if "he walks out of the office and leaves the light on," "(i)n the aftermath of an LBO when 20 cents of every dollar saved goes into his pocket, he is much more likely to turn off that light."[126]

Michael Jensen, the financial economist who predicted in the late 1970s that excessive regulation would spell the end of the public company,[127] was such a strong believer in public-to-private buyouts that he proclaimed "The Eclipse of the Public Corporation" in a 1989 *Harvard Business Review* article.[128] Jensen conceded that the publicly traded company remained "a viable option in some areas of the economy, particularly for growth companies whose profitable investment opportunities exceed the cash they generate internally."[129] He said, however, that "the public corporation is not suitable" in other economic sectors, particularly "where long-term growth is slow (and) where internally generated funds outstrip the opportunities to invest them profitably."[130]

To make his case, Jensen cited flaws afflicting the public corporation, namely "widespread waste and inefficiency" and an "inability to adapt to changing economic circumstances."[131]

---

[119] Benjamin J. Stein, *A New Low?*, BARRON'S, Nov. 14, 1988, 68. See also Walter Adams & James W. Brock, *Merger Mania Makes Economy Its Victim*, LA TIMES, May 1, 1988, D3.

[120] Peter T. Kilborn, *Takeovers: A Friendly Climate*, NY TIMES, Nov. 6, 1988, 1.

[121] Daniel F. Cuff, *Perils of Leveraged Buyouts*, NY TIMES, May 14, 1984, D1; *Wall Street's Risky Takeover Binge*, CHI. TRIB., Nov. 13, 1988, D2.

[122] ROGER LOWENSTEIN, ORIGINS OF THE CRASH: THE GREAT BUBBLE AND ITS UNDOING 12 (2004).

[123] Wayne, *supra* note 108.

[124] *Life after Debt: How LBOs Do It*, FORTUNE, Mar. 13, 1989.

[125] David Pauly, *The Pleasures of Privacy*, NEWSWEEK, Mar. 19, 1984, 73.

[126] *Have Leveraged Buyouts Gone Too Far?*, US NEWS & WORLD REPORT, Dec. 12, 1987, 73.

[127] Chapter 3, notes 40–41 and related discussion.

[128] Jensen, *supra* note 94.

[129] *Id.* at 64.

[130] *Id.*

[131] *Id.* at 65.

He also drew attention to the disciplinary properties of debt and the strong relationship between pay and performance for managers in companies taken private by LBOs.[132] Jensen argued additionally that buyout firms—he used the term "LBO associations"—would be more effective monitors of management than the "powerless" institutional shareholders in public companies because LBO associations took "the bulk of their compensation as a share in the companies' increased value."[133] In sum, business enterprises taken private by LBO funds would displace the public company because "the new organizations ... eliminate much of the loss created by conflicts between owners and managers, without eliminating the vital functions of risk diversification and liquidity once performed exclusively by public equity markets."[134]

Jensen's article received substantial coverage in the business media.[135] This was due partly to a then-recent public-to-private transaction large enough to indicate that there may not be a company too large to be removed from public markets by way of a LBO. The transaction involved RJR Nabisco, a food and tobacco concern that was the 19th largest industrial enterprise in the United States.[136] As 1988 drew to a close, a KKR-led investment syndicate including Morgan Stanley, Drexel Burnham, and Merrill Lynch won a bidding war to purchase RJR Nabisco for nearly $25 billion, incorporating in so doing almost a 100 percent stock price premium as compared with recent market valuations.[137] KKR, which threw its hat into the ring despite preferring to avoid hostile offers,[138] prevailed over a bid made by RJR Nabisco CEO F. Ross Johnson, backed by investment banks Salomon Brothers Inc. and Shearson Lehman Hutton Inc. The deal closed in early 1989.[139]

The RJR Nabisco acquisition was nearly four times larger than any other leveraged buyout of the 1980s.[140] It also dwarfed the largest previous takeover, Chevron's $13.3 billion acquisition of Gulf in 1984.[141] A *Los Angeles Times* business columnist labeled the transaction as "a historic shift in ownership and control of American industry."[142] *Barron's* said "(t)he RJR LBO probably represented a watershed in corporate finance. No longer were deals the size of US treasury refinancings or the gross national products of small countries beyond the capability of Wall Street."[143] *Time* speculated as the RJR bidding war was underway "is any

---

[132] *Id.* at 68–70.

[133] *Id.* at 66, 68, 70.

[134] *Id.* at 64.

[135] See, for example, George Melloan, *Reading the Tea Leaves on Corporate Privatizations*, WALL ST. J., Sept. 19, 1989, A31; Christopher Farrell, *The LBO Isn't a Superior New Species*, BUS. WK., Oct. 23, 1989, 126; David Warsh, *The Case for Turning Over Business to the Leveraged Buyout Specialists*, WASH. POST, Oct. 25, 1989, C3.

[136] *History of the RJR Nabisco Takeover*, NY TIMES, Dec. 2, 1988, D15.

[137] *Going, Going, Going, Going... Gone*, NEWSDAY, Dec. 4, 1988, 96; BRUCE WASSERSTEIN, BIG DEAL: 2000 AND BEYOND 136–38 (2000).

[138] BURROUGH & HELYAR, *supra* note 97, at 151–52; Janice Castro, Thomas McCarroll & Frederick Ungeheuer, *Big-Time Buyouts: Duel of the Takeover Titans*, TIME, Nov. 7, 1988, 94.

[139] BURROUGH & HELYAR, *supra* note 97, at 505–06.

[140] BLAIR & UPPAL, *supra* note 107, at 12.

[141] Castro, McCarroll & Ungeheuer, *supra* note 138.

[142] James Flanigan, *Buyouts Move Into New, More Risky Territory*, LA TIMES, Oct. 26, 1988, A1.

[143] Randall W. Forsyth, *Year of the Deal*, BARRON'S, Jan. 2, 1989, 20.

company safe? Is DuPont doable? Can General Electric be hot-wired?"[144] A *Washington Post* columnist suggested as the RJR Nabisco deal closed "almost no corporation is now secure."[145] Such conjectures lent credence to Jensen's claim that the public company's eclipse was nigh.

END OF AN ERA

As was the case when Michael Jensen speculated in the late 1970s that over-regulation was jeopardizing the future of the public company just as growing antipathy toward government was fostering deregulatory momentum,[146] the timing of his 1989 eclipse prediction was unfortunate. The RJR Nabisco deal proved to be the crest of a wave. As 1990 opened, the LBO boom had come to a shuddering halt, with *Business Week* proclaiming in February of that year "Leveraged Buyouts Fall to Earth."[147] Public-to-private transactions were a rarity for the rest of the decade (Figure 4.4). By the mid-1990s "large LBOs of public companies were a forgotten species."[148] Correspondingly, the mechanism Jensen identified as the catalyst for the public company's demise was at least temporarily in abeyance.

The public-to-private LBO bust coincided not only with the end of the 1980s but with the end of the takeover boom more generally that had characterized the decade. Speculation began as early as the mid-1980s that takeovers were on the ropes. This was prompted by entrepreneurial corporate raiders such as T. Boone Pickens and Carl Icahn gearing down and

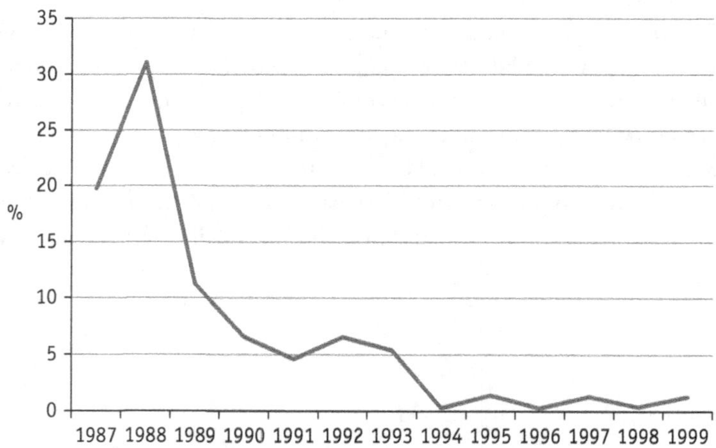

FIGURE 4.4 LBOs as a Proportion of Completed M&A Transactions, 1987–1999.
Source: ROY C. SMITH & INGO WALTER, GOVERNING THE MODERN CORPORATION: CAPITAL MARKETS, CORPORATE CONTROL, AND ECONOMIC PERFORMANCE 34 (2006).

---

[144] Castro, McCarroll & Ungeheuer, *supra* note 138.

[145] Hobart Rowen, *It's Time to Stop LBO Nonsense*, WASH. POST, Feb. 5, 1989, H1.

[146] Chapter 3, notes 47–48, 341, 347–52, 372–76 and accompanying text.

[147] Judith H. Dobrzynkski, *Leveraged Buyouts Fall to Earth*, BUS. WEEK, Feb. 12, 1990, 62.

[148] ROY C. SMITH, THE WEALTH CREATORS: THE RISE OF TODAY'S RICH AND SUPER-RICH 130 (2001).

by a buoyant stock market supposedly making targets too expensive.[149] Also, when the Dow Jones Industrial Index fell nearly 23 percent on October 19, 1987 ("Black Monday") market jitters briefly "chastened the mergers-and-acquisitions crowd."[150] Dealmaking, however, soon marched on. The *Christian Science Monitor* said in late 1988 "Wall Street is abuzz with rumours. Stocks are jumping. Everybody wonders which titanic company will be the next mega-billion-dollar takeover candidate.... We're living in a heady period."[151]

Matters were different once the 1980s were actually over. As *Time* noted in February 1990 "Wall Street's merger machine has run out of gas."[152] M&A activity would surge later in the 1990s but the freewheeling 1980s ethos did not return. As a 2013 study of takeovers focusing primarily on the Deal Decade said "(t)he M&A boom of the 1980s stopped abruptly at the end of the decade, almost to the day. The classic hostile acquirer ... was uprooted and tossed to the side."[153] With "raiders" and hostile bids marginalized, corporations carrying out "friendly" strategically motivated acquisitions set the tempo in the 1990s.[154]

Why did the 1980s M&A party end? Corporate law academic Jeffrey Gordon noted correctly in 1991, "(m)any forces have played a role in this reversal."[155] There was, for instance, "the sudden disappearance of money" that made it much harder to raise cash to pay out target shareholders.[156] Lending by commercial banks, which accounted for most of the debt financing for hostile takeovers in the 1980s, contracted markedly as the decade ended with fears of a recession taking hold.[157] Also, the market for "junk bonds," which many observers credited, perhaps too generously,[158] for supercharging the 1980s market for corporate control,[159] became temporarily "comatose."[160] Formerly enthusiastic debt investors took fright

[149] *Supra* notes 75–77 and related discussion; *Twilight for the Lone Raider*, BUS. WK., Jan. 27, 1986, 38; George Anders & Phillip L. Zweig, *Friendly Takeover Offers Prevail amid Insider Scandal*, WALL ST. J., Feb. 25, 1987, 6; *Accountants Await Mirror Reflections by Treasury*, FIN. TIMES, June 16, 1987, Survey of US Finance and Investment, 12.

[150] Elliott D. Lee, *Takeover Pace Is Seen Picking Up in 1988*, WALL ST. J., Jan. 4, 1988, B8.

[151] Mark Clayton, *Behind US Merger Boom—Debt Bomb?*, CHRISTIAN SCI. MONITOR, Oct. 28, 1988, 1.

[152] John Greenwald et al., *Predator's Fall*, TIME, Feb. 26, 1990, 46.

[153] JOHN WEIR CLOSE, A GIANT COW-TIPPING BY SAVAGES: THE BOOM, BUST AND BOOM CULTURE OF M&A 160–61 (2013).

[154] *Infra* note 226 and related discussion; Chapter 5, note 147 and accompanying text.

[155] Jeffrey N. Gordon, *Corporations, Markets, and Courts*, 91 COLUM. L. REV. 1931, 1931 (1991). See also Marcel Kahan & Edward B. Rock, *How I Learned to Stop Worrying and Love the Pill: Adaptive Responses to Takeover Law*, 69 U. CHI. L. REV. 871, 879 (2002) ("This downturn was attributed to several causes").

[156] CLOSE, *supra* note 153, at 163.

[157] WASSERSTEIN, *supra* note 137, 154–55; Glenn Yago, *Ownership Change, Capital Access, and Economic Growth*, 7 CRITICAL REV. 205, 212 (1993); Robert Comment & G. William Schwert, *Poison or Placebo? Evidence on the Deterrence and Wealth Effects of Modern Antitakeover Statutes*, 39 J. FIN. ECON. 3, 8 (1995).

[158] Kurt Eichenwald, *Junk Bonds Still Have a Bad Name*, NY TIMES, Sept. 25, 1988, E7; GLENN YAGO, JUNK BONDS: HOW HIGH YIELD SECURITIES RESTRUCTURED CORPORATE AMERICA 7, 36 (1991).

[159] SEGAL, *supra* note 10, 85; ROBERT A.G. MONKS & NELL MINOW, POWER AND ACCOUNTABILITY 41 (1991); MARK S. MIZRUCHI, THE FRACTURING OF THE AMERICAN CORPORATE ELITE 211 (2013).

[160] Jonathan Peterson, *Junk Bonds: A Financial Revolution That Failed*, LA TIMES, Nov. 22, 1990, A1. See also Floyd Norris, *As Defaults Keep Rising, A Market Dies*, NY TIMES, Sept. 9, 1990, F1; Arthur E. Wilmarth, *The Transformation of the US Financial Services Industry, 1975–2000: Competition, Consolidation, and Increased Risks* [2002] UNIV. ILL. L. REV. 217, 232.

with numerous companies struggling to avoid defaulting on outstanding high-yield bonds and with investment bank Drexel Burnham Lambert shutting its doors shortly after the 1989 indictment of its junk bond guru Michael Milken for racketeering and securities fraud.[161]

A changing legal environment also contributed to the end of the Deal Decade. During the first half of the 1980s, the legal context was congenial for hostile takeovers. Martin Lipton, a leading M&A lawyer, said in 1982 "(d)efense is extremely difficult. It's so much easier to be a raider."[162] Lipton, described in 1989 as "legendary counselor to companies that fear becoming raider-bait,"[163] was working on changing the situation. He invented in 1982 the shareholder rights plan, or "poison pill," that was designed to make a hostile acquisition prohibitively expensive by giving a target company's shareholders the right to buy more stock at a substantial discount when a prospective bidder acquired a prescribed percentage of shares.[164] The initial response to Lipton's creativity was, however, tepid. As of early 1985, fewer than 5 percent of publicly traded *Fortune* 500 companies had a poison pill in place, with scores of companies waiting for clear judicial approbation before deciding what to do.[165]

A 1982 ruling of the US Supreme Court in *Edgar v. MITE Corp.*[166] also helped to ensure during the first half of the 1980s "the regulatory climate was ripe for . . . an active market for corporate control."[167] The Williams Act of 1968 extended the coverage of federal securities law to takeovers by prohibiting fraud and deception in relation to bids, by requiring bidders to disclose their plans for their targets, and by regulating how long a tender offer to buy shares had to remain open for acceptance by target company shareholders.[168] Between 1968 and 1982 Illinois and 36 other states enacted anti-takeover laws that required an offeror to make a filing in a state so long as there were target company shareholders in that state, and gave state regulators various grounds to shut down tender offers that otherwise fulfilled the requirements of the Williams Act.[169] In *MITE* the Supreme Court held that the Illinois legislation frustrated the objectives of the Williams Act and imposed an unconstitutionally severe burden on interstate commerce.[170] The ruling invalidated the Illinois law and its brethren in other states.[171]

---

[161] Wasserstein, *supra* note 137, 150–55; Robert N. McCauley, Judith S. Rudd & Frank Iacono, Dodging Bullets: Changing US Corporate Capital Structure 46–51 (1999).

[162] Leslie Wayne, *The Corporate Raiders*, NY Times, July 18, 1982, Sunday Magazine, 18.

[163] Judith H. Dobrzynski, *If Stockholders Bang on Boardroom Doors, Open 'Em*, Bus. Wk., Dec. 3, 1990, 149.

[164] Martin Lipton, *Twenty-Five Years after* Takeover Bids in the Target's Boardroom: *Old Battles, New Attacks and the Continuing War*, 60 Bus. Law. 1369, 1372 (2005); Robert Teitelman, Bloodsport: When Ruthless Dealmakers, Shrewd Ideologues, and Brawling Lawyers Toppled the Corporate Establishment 168–69 (2016).

[165] Ford S. Worthy & Philip Mattera, *What's Next for the Raiders*, Fortune, Nov. 11, 1985, 20; Brian R. Cheffins, *Delaware and the Transformation of Corporate Governance*, 40 Del. J. Corp. L. 1, 32–33 (2015).

[166] 457 U.S. 624 (1982).

[167] Gerald F. Davis, Managed by the Markets: How Finance Reshaped America 84 (2009).

[168] Pub. L. No. 90-439, 82 Stat. 454; Mark J. Roe, *Takeover Politics, in* Deal Decade, *supra* note 1, 321, 332.

[169] Roe, *supra* note 168, at 335, 338; Martin Lipton & Paul K. Rowe, *Pills, Polls and Professors: A Reply to Professor Gilson*, 27 Del. J. Corp. L. 1, 8 (2002).

[170] 457 U.S. 624, 634-40, 643-46 (1982).

[171] Roe, *supra* note 168, at 335.

Early 1980s changes to antitrust policy also provided "a catalyst to bring about a wholesale reshuffling of the industrial deck."[172] The Reagan administration moved into the White House in 1981 pledging to "get government off people's backs."[173] Relaxation of antitrust enforcement, particularly in relation to mergers, was a step taken in this direction.[174] One antitrust scholar argued in 1990 that "(t)he dramatic shift in antitrust orthodoxy from the expansionism of the 1960s and early 1970s to the permissiveness of the 1980s is one of the most striking developments in post–World War II economic regulation."[175]

Antitrust enforcement did not cease under Reagan as some critics charged.[176] The Department of Justice launched more criminal prosecutions under antitrust law between 1981 and 1988 than had been brought between 1890 and 1980.[177] Nevertheless, there was a new, more relaxed stance with mergers, as evidenced by the Reagan administration giving the green light in 1981 to a $1.9 billion tie-up between food giants Nabisco and Standard Brands and to DuPont's $6.8 billion acquisition of oil company Conoco.[178] Irving Shapiro, who had just stepped down as DuPont's CEO and chairman of the board, said that under previous administrations "(a)nything this size would have been unacceptable."[179]

William Baxter, who headed up the Department of Justice's Antitrust Division from 1981 to 1983, formalized in 1982 the new approach to mergers by replacing merger guidelines from 1968 with new standards that defined the relevant market for analysis in a considerably more relaxed manner.[180] Baxter, a Stanford-based academic, shared with an antitrust school of thought commonly associated with the University of Chicago concerns that antitrust enforcement was hindering US companies competing with foreign rivals and a belief that many business practices antitrust law impugned actually increased competition beneficially.[181] Throughout the remainder of the Reagan administration horizontal mergers between industry leaders that would have been "completely taboo before the 1980s" were often cleared.[182] Reagan antitrust officials indeed were generally pleased to see companies growing by way of same industry acquisitions as opposed to engaging in potentially misguided diversification.[183]

---

[172] DAVIS, *supra* note 167, at 84.

[173] *The New Look in Antitrust*, BUS. WK., Jan. 19, 1981, 120.

[174] ROY C. SMITH & INGO WALTER, GOVERNING THE MODERN CORPORATION: CAPITAL MARKETS, CORPORATE CONTROL, AND ECONOMIC PERFORMANCE 31 (2006); DOUGLAS M. EICHAR, THE RISE AND FALL OF CORPORATE SOCIAL RESPONSIBILITY 268–69 (2015).

[175] William E. Kovacic, The Antitrust Paradox *Revisited: Robert Bork and the Transformation of Modern Antitrust Policy*, 36 WAYNE L. REV. 1413, 1417 (1990).

[176] Lawrence A. Sullivan & Wolfgang Fikentscher, *On the Growth of the Antitrust Idea*, 16 BERKELEY J. INT'L. L. 197, 206 (1998). See also ADAMS & BROCK, *supra* note 103, at 27 ("declining to enforce the antitrust laws").

[177] William E. Kovacic, *The Modern Evolution of US Competition Policy Enforcement Norms*, 71 ANTITRUST L.J. 377, 420 (2003).

[178] WIGMORE, *supra* note 67, at 309.

[179] *Id.*

[180] *Id.* at 310–11.

[181] Beth Brophy, *Actions Speak Louder than Words*, FORBES, May 11, 1981, 55; Arthur Austin, *Antitrust Reaction to the Merger Wave: The Revolution vs. the Counterrevolution*, 66 N.C. L. REV. 931, 947 (1988).

[182] Gregg A. Jarrell, James A. Brickley & Jeffry M. Netter, *The Market for Corporate Control: The Empirical Evidence since 1980*, 2 J. ECON. PERSPECTIVES 49, 50 (1988).

[183] *Splitting Up*, *supra* note 104.

The change in policy under Reagan helped to foster a substantial growth of horizontal acquisitions relative to other varieties as M&A activity accelerated (Figure 4.5).[184] There also was a significant knock-on effect for the market for corporate control. The assets of firms acquired by way of hostile takeovers usually ended up in the hands of firms in the same industrial sector.[185] Antitrust enforcement of the type engaged in from the 1950s through the 1970s probably would have precluded much of this type of dealmaking. The relaxation of antitrust scrutiny of mergers under Reagan correspondingly stimulated the hostile takeover element of the market for corporate control.[186]

The Reagan administration provided a congenial atmosphere for the Deal Decade not only by changing antitrust policy but also by acting as a roadblock to new federal restrictions on takeover bids. The President's Council of Economic Advisers, in a chapter on takeovers in its 1985 report, noted that "(t)o the extent that government regulations impose costs on bidders . . . fewer takeover attempts will be made" and concluded "(f)urther Federal regulation of the market for corporate control would be premature, unnecessary and unwise."[187] The Reagan administration concurred, indicating it would veto any legislation Congress passed regulating takeovers, a stance that helped to stymie federal legislative reform where dozens of bills were being proposed.[188]

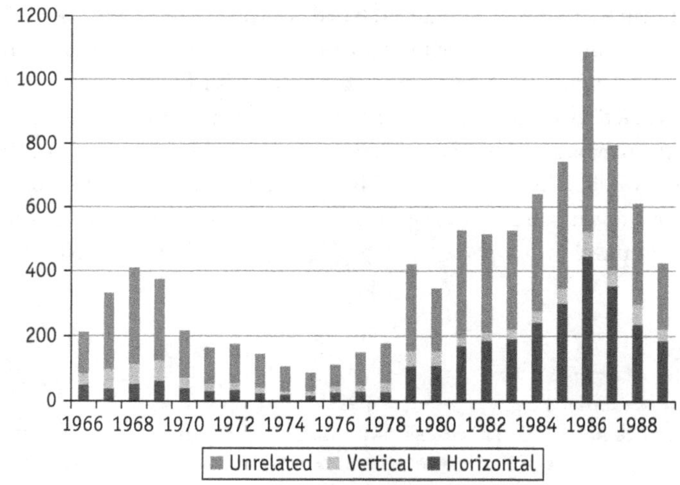

FIGURE 4.5 Horizontal, Vertical, and Unrelated Acquisitions of US Companies, 1966–1989.
Source: MARGARET M. BLAIR & GIRISH UPPAL, THE DEAL DECADE HANDBOOK 63 (1993).

[184] See also Zorn et al., *supra* note 57, at 285 (providing data on acquisition patterns involving a sample of companies from the *Fortune* 500).

[185] *Supra* notes 88–89 and accompanying text. See also Bhagat, Shleifer & Vishny, *supra* note 88, at 51, 55.

[186] DAVID SKEEL, ICARUS IN THE BOARDROOM: THE FUNDAMENTAL FLAWS IN CORPORATE AMERICA AND WHERE THEY CAME FROM 119–20 (2005).

[187] ECONOMIC REPORT OF THE PRESIDENT/ANNUAL REPORT OF THE COUNCIL OF ECONOMIC ADVISERS 191, 216 (1985).

[188] Heilbron, Verheul & Quak, *supra* note 4, at 14; CONNIE BRUCK, THE PREDATORS' BALL: THE INSIDE STORY OF DREXEL BURNHAM AND THE RISE OF THE JUNK BOND RAIDERS 260 (1988); Gerald F. Davis & Tracy A. Thompson, *A Social Movement Perspective on Corporate Control*, 39 ADMIN. SCI. Q. 141, 159 (1994).

The Securities and Exchange Commission (SEC) followed the Reagan administration's cue and generally adopted a hands-off stance to takeovers. There was tinkering with Williams Act-related rules on tender offers.[189] However, the SEC rejected in 1986 further consideration of proposals to impose significant restrictions on otherwise permissible takeovers tactics, including recommendations for reform by a high-powered advisory committee the SEC set up in 1983.[190]

While takeover opponents found Washington, DC to be inhospitable, by the late 1980s states were in a position to be more accommodating. Due to the striking down of Illinois' anti-takeover legislation in *Edgar v. MITE Corp.* during the mid-1980s only five states passed anti-takeover legislation.[191] One was Indiana, which enacted a law providing that when an entity acquired "control shares" by purchasing a large equity stake in an Indiana-incorporated public company that entity could not vote its shares unless other shareholders in the Indiana corporation approved.[192] In a 1987 case, *CTS Corp. v. Dynamics Corp. of America*,[193] the Supreme Court held this law was constitutional. Within two years, 37 states had put in place anti-takeover laws restricting bids for in-state companies, quite often with a provision similar to Indiana's but frequently incorporating other measures.[194]

Delaware was the most important state adopting anti-takeover legislation post-*CTS*. At the time, nearly half of all public companies were incorporated in the state, including more than half of all *Fortune* 500 enterprises.[195] Delaware enacted in 1988 what was referred to as a "business combination" provision as part of the Delaware General Corporation Law.[196] This measure focused on bidders who failed to acquire with a tender offer 85 percent or more of the shares of the target. A bidder coming up short was precluded from buying out the remaining shareholders for three years unless the target's board gave advance clearance or the board gave its approval after the fact with the backing of two-thirds of the votes of disinterested shareholders. Many at the time believed the new anti-takeover laws from Delaware and other states "dramatically shifted the balance of power between corporate hunters and their prey."[197] They in fact were not "absolute show-stoppers" but did help to throw the brakes on the market for corporate control.[198]

---

189 Alan R. Palmiter, *The CTS Gambit: Stanching the Federalization of Corporate Law*, 69 Wash. Univ. L.Q. 445, 474–75 (1991).

190 John Brooks, The Takeover Game 261–67 (1987); Gregg Jarrell, Annette Poulsen & John Pound, *Regulating Hostile Takeover Activity: An Interpretive History of the US Experience*, *in* Takeovers and Corporate Control: Towards a New Regulatory Environment 19, 19–20 (Peter Dodd & Robert R. Officer eds., 1987).

191 *Supra* notes 170–71 and related discussion; Useem, *supra* note 109, at 171.

192 CTS Corp. v. Dynamics Corp. of Am., 481 U.S. 69, 73 (1987).

193 481 U.S. 69 (1987).

194 Useem, *supra* note 109, at 170–72.

195 Paul M. Barrett, *Delaware Moves Closer to Adopting Law to Deter Hostile Takeovers*, Wall St. J., Dec. 9, 1987, 41 (reporting that 45 percent of NYSE companies were incorporated under Delaware law); Doug Bandow, *Curbing Raiders Is Bad for Business*, NY Times, Feb. 7, 1988, F2.

196 Del. Code Ann., tit. 8, § 203 (2018); McCauley, Rudd & Iacono, *supra* note 161, at 117.

197 David Rosenthal, *Erecting Bastions against Buyouts*, Balt. Sun, Mar. 29, 1989, C1.

198 Roe, *supra* note 168, at 339. See also Guhan Subramanian, *The Influence of Antitakeover Statutes on Incorporation Choice: Evidence on the "Race" Debate and Antitakeover Overreaching*, 150 U. Pa. L. Rev. 1795, 1862 (2002).

Delaware court cases also tilted the takeover playing field in favor of management and against raiders. In January 1985, the Delaware Court of Chancery upheld a poison pill that Household International, a widely diversified conglomerate, had adopted.[199] Michael Jensen, who testified in the case that the pill was likely to have an adverse impact on shareholders,[200] condemned the ruling in the press as "an absolutely incredible change in the contractual relationship between a corporation and its shareholders."[201] The plaintiffs appealed to the Delaware Supreme Court. Before handing down its judgment in that case, that court ruled against T. Boone Pickens' Mesa Corp. as part of a bid to acquire oil company Unocal Corp.[202]

Unocal's board made a self-tender offer for a proportion of its stock at a price higher than that which Pickens had bid but made the offer explicitly discriminatory by indicating shares Mesa tendered would not be accepted.[203] Mesa sued, challenging the self-tender offer on the basis that the board had violated fiduciary duties owed to Mesa and other Unocal shareholders. The Delaware Supreme Court acknowledged on appeal that there was an "omnipresent specter" of potentially self-interested entrenchment when a board adopted defensive measures in the takeover context.[204] Correspondingly, the court declined to assess Unocal's defensive tactics purely by reference to the "business judgment rule," a board-friendly standard under which directorial decisions are protected from challenge so as long as there was no conflict of interest and the board was tolerably well-informed.[205]

The Delaware Supreme Court said that in the takeover context a board taking defensive steps would need to show there were reasonable grounds for believing that there was a danger to corporate policy and that the effectiveness of the defensive tactic was reasonable in relation to the threat posed.[206] The court ruled that with Unocal this standard was met because features of Mesa's tender offer were potentially coercive for Unocal shareholders and because of Pickens's national reputation as a "greenmailer."[207] Mesa ultimately did sell back to Unocal the 14 percent stake it had accumulated but at an estimated pretax loss of $100 million, once expenses were taken into account.[208] Armand Hammer, the chief executive of Occidental Petroleum, told shareholders that the outcome would "send a signal to all future raiders."[209]

Following on the heels of *Unocal*, the Delaware Supreme Court deployed the reasonable-in-relation-to-the-threat-posed standard of review to deny the appeal against the Court of Chancery's ruling upholding Household International's poison pill.[210] This decision likely

[199] Moran v. Household Int'l, Inc., 490 A.2d 1059 (Del. 1985); Peter W. Bernstein, *Takeover Tangles*, FORTUNE, Mar. 4, 1985, available at http://archive.fortune.com/magazines/fortune/fortune_archive/1985/03/04/65653/index.htm (accessed Dec. 17, 2017).

[200] *Moran*, 490 A.2d at 1067–68.

[201] *Nasty Pills Popping Up on Wall Street*, ECONOMIST, Feb. 16, 1985, 79.

[202] Unocal Corp. v. Mesa Petroleum Co., 493 A.2d 946 (Del. 1985).

[203] ALLISON, *supra* note 73, at 155.

[204] *Unocal*, 493 A.2d at 954.

[205] *Id.* at 955.

[206] This characterization comes from Paramount Commc'ns, Inc. v. Time, Inc., 571 A.2d 1140, 1152 (Del. 1989).

[207] *Unocal*, 493 A.2d at 955–56.

[208] ALLISON, *supra* note 73, at 153, 156.

[209] William Hall, *Unocal Chief Proves Attack Is the Best Defence*, FIN. TIMES, May 23, 1985, 33.

[210] Moran v. Household Int'l., Inc. 500 A.2d 1346, 1348, 1350, 1354 (Del. 1985).

had a greater practical impact than *Unocal*.[211] The judicial blessing of the poison pill was characterized as a "seminal event"[212] that "unleashed a flood of poison pill adoptions."[213] As of 1986, 35 percent of publicly traded *Fortune* 500 companies had implemented a pill, and 60 percent had done so by the end of 1989.[214]

While the 1985 rulings in *Unocal* and *Household* made it clear that boards of Delaware companies were not required to be passive in the event of an unwelcome tender offer, hostile takeover bids did continue throughout the remainder of the 1980s. The Delaware Supreme Court even acknowledged in 1989 that a continuing "spate of takeover litigation . . . readily demonstrates such 'poison pills' do not prevent rival bidders from expressing their interest in acquiring a corporation."[215] A 1987 *Chicago Tribune* report on "Takeover Inc." suggested that despite poison pills, "(o)nce Wall Street puts a stock in play a corporate board . . . hardly can say no to the highest offer."[216] This logic was tested in 1989 with Delaware litigation involving Time Inc. and Paramount Communications.

Paramount, a media and entertainment powerhouse, responded to news of an agreed-upon but not finalized merger between its peers Time Inc. and Warner Communications Inc. by making a hostile tender offer to Time's shareholders on terms that were considerably more generous.[217] An investment banker argued the Time/Warner deal was "dead. There's no going back. You can't go back and value Time at around $120 when you've got (Paramount's) $175 a share bid on the table. Forget it."[218] Nevertheless, Time pressed ahead with a restructured Time/Warner merger scheme rather than consider the last-minute Paramount bid. Paramount sued.

Time prevailed initially in the Delaware Court of Chancery, prompting the headline "Ruling Gives Managers Another Ace in the Hole" in the *Los Angeles Times*.[219] The Delaware Supreme Court affirmed the lower court ruling, applying the *Unocal* standard of review in so doing.[220] Some legal experts argued the decision would not serve as a major precedent.[221] To other observers, however, the case was pivotal. Robert Monks and Nell Minow, operators of a shareholder advisory service, claimed the case was "probably the greatest incursion in US business history into the rights of shareholders."[222] The *Economist* said in 1993 "Time's bosses

---

[211] Martin Lipton, *Pills, Polls and Professors Redux*, 69 U. CHI. L. REV. 1037, 1047 (2002).

[212] COLE, *supra* note 80, at 155 (quoting Morris Kramer, a lawyer at Wall Street firm Skadden Arps).

[213] Michael C. Jensen, *Takeovers: Their Causes and Consequences*, 2 J. ECON. PERSP. 21, 43 (1988).

[214] Gerald F. Davis, *Agents without Principles? The Spread of the Poison Pill through the Intercorporate Network*, 36 ADMIN. SCI. Q. 583, 587 (1991). For additional data on poison pill adoptions, see Mark R. Wingerson & Christopher H. Dorn, *Institutional Investors in the US and the Repeal of Poison Pills: A Practitioner's Perspective* [1992] COLUM. BUS. L. REV. 223, 236.

[215] Barkan v. Amsted Indus., Inc., 567 A.2d 1279, 1287 (Del. 1989).

[216] *Takeover Inc.*, CHI. TRIB., Sept. 20, 1987, F1.

[217] TEITELMAN, *supra* note 164, at 297; Paul Richter, *Thinking Big*, LA TIMES, June 8, 1989, D1; Charles Storch, *Paramount, Warner, Time in Their Corners*, CHI. TRIB., June 9, 1989, A1.

[218] John Cassidy, *Raiders of the Time Machine*, SUNDAY TIMES, June 11, 1989.

[219] Bill Sing, *Ruling Gives Managers Another Ace in the Hole*, LA TIMES, July 15, 1989, 59, discussing Re Time Inc. Shareholders Litigation (Paramount Commc'ns, Inc. v. Time Inc.), [1989 Transfer Binder] Fed. Sec. L. Rep. ¶ 94514 (Del. Ch. July 14, 1989), aff'd. 565 A.2d 280 (Del. 1989).

[220] Paramount Commc'ns, Inc. v. Time, Inc., 571 A.2d 1140, 1152 (Del. 1989).

[221] John Schwartz, *How to Drive Off a Raider*, NEWSWEEK, Aug. 7, 1989, 43.

[222] MONKS & MINOW, *supra* note 159, at 93.

were free 'to just say no' to unwanted offers. Paramount's bid failed, Time's shareholders lost a fortune and hostile bids all but disappeared."[223]

Paramount did not deal a decisive blow against hostile takeovers. A majority of public companies, after all, were not incorporated in Delaware.[224] Moreover, "the sudden disappearance of money" due to debt markets tightening contributed substantially to the demise of the Deal Decade.[225] Roy Smith, in *The Money Wars*, a 1990 study of 1980s takeovers, likely was correct when he cited the Time/Paramount litigation to make the point that "by the end of 1989 both the market and legal atmosphere were tilting back towards large, old-fashioned industrial deals," namely "friendly mergers."[226] Regardless of precisely why the Deal Decade ended, however, the freewheeling dealmaking that occurred had a major impact on public companies in the 1980s, including those not directly involved as a bidder or a target. Canvassing the internal and external constraints impinging upon the discretion potentially available to executives of public companies illustrates the point clearly. We consider now how these constraints operated in the 1980s.

Internal Constraints

In a publicly traded company the board of directors and shareholder action constitute the primary "internal" constraints on managerial autonomy. Extrapolating from trends from the 1970s, boards should have been at the center of the action in the 1980s. During the 1970s, as debates about "corporate governance" grew in intensity, expectations of what directors could and should do to foster managerial accountability increased substantially and boards were reconfigured in ways that suggested these expectations would be fulfilled, at least partially.[227] The scene was much quieter on the shareholder front. Efforts at activism focused on social issues rather than promotion of shareholder value, and a balancing of interests between stockholders and other corporate constituencies was thought by many to be the proper course for executives to adopt.[228]

In the 1980s, matters would develop dramatically differently than events from the 1970s implied. Changes regarding boards were modest. In contrast, shareholders would move to center stage to an extent unknown during the managerial capitalism era, albeit primarily as a collateral feature of the market for corporate control rather than due to affirmative stockholder pressure.

---

[223] *Of Paramount Importance*, ECONOMIST, Dec. 18, 1993, 74.

[224] *Supra* note 195 and accompanying text; Cheffins, *supra* note 165, at 63–64.

[225] *Supra* notes 156–161 and accompanying text.

[226] ROY C. SMITH, THE MONEY WARS: THE RISE AND FALL OF THE GREAT BUYOUT BOOM OF THE 1980S 326 (1990).

[227] Chapter 3, notes 244, 246, 248, 282-84 and related discussion.

[228] Chapter 3, notes 218–36, 242 and accompanying text.

BOARDS

As the 1980s began, corporate governance was "on the public policy agenda."[229] Bills were introduced to Congress that would have required publicly traded companies to have an independent director majority on boards and to establish audit and nomination committees composed solely of independent directors.[230] Harold Williams, the SEC chairman, was said to be pushing "the corporate governance thing as far as he can, given the statute they have to work under."[231] The bills, however, stalled, and an SEC staff report issued in 1980 indicated that the Commission should refrain for the time being from promulgating rules on how corporations governed themselves.[232]

A political shift to the right, exemplified by Ronald Reagan's election to the presidency in 1980, closed the door firmly on 1970s-style corporate governance reform at the federal level.[233] Senator Howard Metzenbaum, who introduced one of the bills to Congress in 1980 that would have mandated the configuration of public company boards,[234] acknowledged the following year that with Congress having become more conservative enactment of legislation of a similar sort was unlikely for the foreseeable future.[235] Similarly, the SEC was unlikely to pursue corporate governance reform with great vigor under John Shad, Reagan's choice as chairman to succeed Williams. Shad said in 1981 that his predecessor "was identified very much with corporate governance, and I hope to be identified with capital formation."[236]

A governance reform initiative the American Law Institute (ALI) launched in the late 1970s that put restructuring of the board squarely on the agenda illustrated the board reform backtracking trend that was occurring more generally. The ALI, a private organization composed of practicing lawyers, academics, and judges that produces scholarly work to clarify and modernize the law, committed itself in principle in 1978 to undertake a project on corporate governance.[237] The ALI's corporate governance "reporters"—academic members of the ALI drafting on its behalf—released their first public output, Tentative Draft No. 1, in 1982.[238] Board structure was one of the key issues Tentative Draft No. 1 canvassed, stipulating in so doing that corporate law should require boards of large corporations to have a majority of independent directors and to establish audit and nomination committees made up entirely of independent directors.[239]

---

229 Francis W. Steckmest, Corporate Performance: The Key to Public Trust 167 (1982).

230 Chapter 3, notes 323, 325 and accompanying text.

231 Laurie Cohen, *Industry Hopes Reagan Will Keep SEC Chief*, Chi. Trib., Nov. 19, 1980, E3.

232 Chapter 3, notes 324, 326 and related discussion; SEC Division of Corporation Finance, Staff Report on Corporate Accountability (1980); *Corporate Governance Faulted in Study by SEC Staff, but Action Isn't Advocated*, Wall St. J., Sept. 5, 1980, 4.

233 John C. Boland, *Nader Crusade*, Barron's, Oct. 12, 1981, 61.

234 Chapter 3, note 323 and related discussion.

235 Barbara Bry *Activists, Executives Clash on How Firms Should Be Run*, LA Times, Jan. 12, 1981, E1.

236 Stan Crock, *SEC's Shad Shows Pro-business Tilt but Says He Won't Be a Pushover*, Wall St. J., Sept. 16, 1981, 29. See also Teitelman, *supra* note 164, at 84.

237 Brian R. Cheffins, *The History of Corporate Governance, in* The Oxford Handbook of Corporate Governance 46, 49 (Mike Wright et al. eds., 2013).

238 American Law Institute, Principles of Corporate Governance and Structure: Restatement and Recommendations—Tentative Draft No. 1 (1982).

239 *Id.*, part III, ch. 1, Introductory Note, §§ 3.03, 3.05(a)(1), 3.06(a)(1).

Tentative Draft #1 prompted robust pushback from the business community, partly due to objections to the perceived rigidity of the proposals regarding the board.[240] Academics analyzing corporate law from a new, market-oriented "law and economics" perspective provided energetic intellectual cover.[241] Berle and Means's separation of ownership and control characterization of the public company became "the master problem for research" for corporate law academics during the middle decades of the twentieth century.[242] The normative inference typically drawn was that powerful executives would shortchange vulnerable shareholders unless sufficiently robust regulation was in place.[243] In the 1980s however, a "contractarian" theory of the corporation that used economic analysis as its departure point challenged the view that public company shareholders were being taken advantage of.[244] In a 1976 article on the theory of the firm Michael Jensen and William Meckling offered using what they referred to as agency cost theory an intellectually elegant account of potentially potent market-oriented limitations on the exercise of managerial discretion, characterizing the corporation is so doing as a nexus of contracting relationships.[245] "Contractarian" corporate law academics, taking their cue from this intellectual departure point, emphasized that market dynamics defined relationships among a corporation's managers, shareholders, and other corporate constituencies, and did so in a way that cast doubt on the need for substantial state intervention in public company governance.[246] The ALI's proposals in favor of regulating board structure were assailed accordingly.[247]

The ALI was initially taken aback by the firestorm Tentative Draft No. 1 elicited.[248] Those taking responsibility for the corporate governance project on the ALI's behalf made various concessions, including recasting in the next tentative draft most of the proposed mandatory stipulations regarding board structure as mere recommendations.[249] This reformulation of

---

[240] Kenneth R. Andrews, *Corporate Governance Eludes the Legal Mind*, 37 U. MIA. L. REV. 213, 213–14, 217 (1983); STATEMENT OF THE BUSINESS ROUNDTABLE ON THE AMERICAN LAW INSTITUTE'S PRINCIPLES OF CORPORATE GOVERNANCE AND STRUCTURE: RESTATEMENT AND RECOMMENDATIONS 17–19, 28–31 (1983).

[241] Jonathan R. Macey, *The Transformation of the American Law Institute*, 61 GEO. WASH. L. REV. 1212, 1226–28 (1993).

[242] Roberta Romano, *Metapolitics and Corporate Law Reform*, 36 STAN. L. REV. 923, 923 (1984). See also Chapter 2, note 99 and related discussion.

[243] BRIAN R. CHEFFINS, THE TRAJECTORY OF (CORPORATE LAW) SCHOLARSHIP 44 (2004).

[244] Cheffins, *supra* note 237, at 51.

[245] Michael C. Jensen & William H. Meckling, *Theory of the Firm: Managerial Behavior, Agency Costs and Ownership Structure*, 3 J. FIN. ECON. 305, 310–11 (1976). See also Chapter 3, note 36 and accompanying text; Eugene F. Fama, *Agency Problems and the Theory of the Firm*, 88 J. POL. ECON. 288 (1980).

[246] CHEFFINS, *supra* note 243, at 44–45.

[247] See, for example, Daniel R. Fischel, *The Corporate Governance Movement*, 35 VAND. L. REV. 1259 (1982); Frank H. Easterbrook, *Managers' Discretion and Investors' Welfare: Theories and Evidence*, 9 DEL. J. CORP. L. 540 (1984); NICHOLAS WOLFSON, THE MODERN CORPORATION: FREE MARKETS VERSUS REGULATION 83–98 (1984).

[248] Bayless Manning, *Principles of Corporate Governance: One Viewer's Perspective on the ALI Project*, 48 BUS. LAW. 1319, 1325 (1993).

[249] AMERICAN LAW INSTITUTE, PRINCIPLES OF CORPORATE GOVERNANCE AND STRUCTURE: ANALYSIS AND RECOMMENDATIONS—TENTATIVE DRAFT NO. 2 (1984) §§ 3.04, 3.06. The draft continued to stipulate that corporate law statutes should provide that large public companies set up an audit committee staffed by independent directors—§ 3.03.

proposals regarding boards was retained in the *Principles of Corporate Governance* the ALI ultimately issued in 1994.[250]

A point critics of the ALI's initial corporate governance proposals stressed was that it was unnecessary and unwise to mandate the configuration of boards and board committees because public companies were taking on their own initiative important steps to improve board effectiveness and would continue to innovate in a beneficial manner.[251] In the 1970s numerous public companies indeed voluntarily restructured their boards in a manner that raised the profile of independent directors.[252] In the 1980s, "the 1970s trend ... continued, although more slowly."[253] As Michael Useem, a University of Pennsylvania management professor, indicated based on annual data on the ratio of inside and outside directors on the boards of larger US companies, "(d)uring the 1980s ... company board composition displayed only modest overall movement toward greater independence."[254] To the extent the trend in favor of appointing outside directors continued, judicial decisions arising from takeovers deserve part of the credit. The Delaware Supreme Court's rulings in the *Unocal, Household International,* and Time/Paramount cases created incentives for public companies to have boards with a majority of independent directors because they each indicated that courts would look more favorably on the deployment of takeover defenses if the board was structured in this manner.[255]

The direction of travel was the same with board committees as with independent director representation, with their adoption increasing in the 1980s but only modestly. According to Conference Board data, the proportion of larger companies with an audit committee increased from 88 percent in 1981 to 97 percent in 1989. The equivalent figures for compensation committees and nomination committees were 78 percent/82 percent and 43/49 percent respectively.[256]

How much did boards change in practice? The *New York Times* said in a 1983 article on boards this was "a question that is impossible to answer since most board actions take place behind closed doors."[257] Numerous conjectures nevertheless were offered, with the verdict being mixed.

---

250 American Law Institute, Principles of Corporate Governance and Structure: Analysis and Recommendations (1994) §§ 3.05, 3A.01. 3A.04.

251 See, for example, Statement of the Business Roundtable, *supra* note 240, at 17; Bryan F. Smith, *Corporate Governance: A Director's View,* 37 U. Mia. L. Rev. 273, 279–82 (1983); Donald V. Seibert, *Keynote Address: The Dynamics of Corporate Governance,* 9 Del. J. Corp. L. 515, 515–16, 520 (1984).

252 Chapter 3, notes 276–81 and related discussion.

253 George Melloan, *A Good Director Is Getting Harder to Find,* Wall St. J., Feb. 9, 1988, 39.

254 Useem, *supra* note 109, at 189. *Cf.* Gordon, *supra* note 1, at 1473–76 (indicating the trend in the 1980s was similar to that in other decades).

255 Cheffins, *supra* note 165, 36–38; Unocal Corp. v. Mesa Petroleum, 493 A.2d 946, 955 (Del. 1985); Moran v. Household Int'l., Inc., 500 A.2d 1346, 1348, n.2, 1356 (Del. 1985); Paramount Commc'ns, Inc. v. Time, Inc., 571 A.2d 1140, 1154 (Del. 1989).

256 Jeremy Bacon, Membership and Organization of Corporate Boards 33 (1990).

257 Leslie Wayne, *Who's Playing the Board Game?,* NY Times, Oct. 9, 1983, F4. See also Knowlton & Millstein, *supra* note 64, at 169 ("there is little useful material available today on what American corporate directors actually do").

Board reform optimists included the president of an executive search firm who described in 1984 "a new willingness on the part of boards of directors to take a harder look at the management of companies under their governance."[258] *Business Week* claimed in 1987 that "management is being assailed from all sides," with part of the explanation being "(o)utside directors are asserting themselves."[259] Prominent Wall Street lawyer Arthur Fleischer, in a 1988 coauthored study that focused on the board of directors to ascertain "the changing shape of corporate power," argued that boards were no longer what the chairman of US Steel from the 1940s described as "parsley on the fish."[260] Instead there had been a "revolution in the directors' role," where independent directors who "first achieved supremacy in number . . . now . . . have achieved supremacy in power."[261]

M&A activity, according to Fleischer and his coauthors, had "radically transformed the directors' role in the power structure of the American corporation" because often "the boardroom is where the battles are fought and concluded."[262] The RJR Nabisco buyout by KKR in 1988 illustrated in the M&A context how directors could exert authority independent of management. The board, instead of nodding through the buyout proposal CEO F. Ross Johnson put forward, conducted an open bidding process and accepted KKR's rival bid.[263] The *Los Angeles Times* hailed the "stubborn independence" of the outside directors and a senior investment banker observed subsequently that "(t)he RJR board was a model of how directors should act."[264]

Smith v. Van Gorkom, a 1985 Delaware Supreme Court decision Fleischer and his coauthors discussed at length,[265] was characterized as a "turning point" in director attitudes toward boardroom responsibilities.[266] In that case outside directors of a public company were held to have failed to scrutinize sufficiently diligently a merger proposal the company's CEO had negotiated. They ended up paying damages out of their own pocket, something outside directors do only very rarely.[267] A Delaware Supreme Court justice told the *Chicago Tribune* in 1989 that the case showed "(t)he director who believes his role is to come to the meeting once a month and never challenge (management) or ask the hard questions, those directors are going to end up with a problem."[268]

Though 1980s boards were praised by some, there also were strong critics. In 1984 *Barron's* labeled the board "an imperfect institution," with "the fox policing the chicken coop" due to CEOs usually picking their own boards by selecting nominees confident the shareholders

---

[258] Thomas J. Neff, *Learn to Respect Your Board Before It's Too Late*, WALL ST. J., May 14, 1984, 26.

[259] *The Battle for Corporate Control*, BUS. WK., May 18, 1987, 102.

[260] ARTHUR FLEISCHER, GEOFFREY C. HAZARD & MIRIAM Z. KLIPPER, BOARD GAMES: THE CHANGING SHAPE OF CORPORATE POWER 3 (1988).

[261] *Id.* at 3, 11.

[262] *Id.* at 3.

[263] *Supra* notes 138–39 and related discussion.

[264] Paul Richter & Jonathan Peterson, *RJR Deal May Set New Standards for Outside Directors*, LA TIMES, Dec. 3, 1988, C1; Jack Egan et al., *Time vs. Its Shareholders*, US NEWS & WORLD REPORT, July 3, 1989, 38.

[265] 488 A.2d 858 (1985); FLEISCHER, HAZARD & KLIPPER, *supra* note 260, Prologue.

[266] Fran Hawthorne, *Outside Directors Feel the Heat*, INST. INVESTOR, Apr. 1989, 58, 60.

[267] Bernard Black, Brian Cheffins & Michael Klausner, *Outside Director Liability*, 58 STAN. L. REV. 1055, 1060, 1064, 1067 (2006).

[268] Pat Widder, *Time Inc. Case Another Test for Outside Directors*, CHI. TRIB., July 9, 1989.

would endorse the nominations.[269] A *Wall Street Journal* columnist similarly suggested in 1989 that the fact "shareholders blindly ratify candidates selected by management" explained why "directors of large public corporations often feel their loyalty is to management."[270] Economist Harvey Segal concurred in a study of corporate restructuring published the same year, saying most "outside directors tend obediently to endorse whatever the insiders on a board propose. They are highly paid boardroom appurtenances."[271] Roy Smith, in his study of 1980s takeovers, indicated similarly that most board members "were well plied with perks and comforts" and "only start to think for themselves when a takeover situation comes along and their lawyers are telling them what to do."[272]

Even observers inclined to offer encouraging words about boards often felt compelled to acknowledge qualifications. In 1988 Winthrop Knowlton and Ira Millstein said changes occurring with boards since the 1960s were "useful, on balance" and meant boards were a "more serious, knowledgeable and hardworking group than before."[273] An important caveat, however, was that with directors "their gut feeling is that their role is exceedingly limited.... While they can criticize CEOs, punish them, and even remove them, there is immense unwillingness to do."[274]

The tone was similar in *Pawns and Potentates*, a 1989 study based on interviews with approximately 75 past and present directors.[275] Harvard Business School professor Jay Lorsch and coauthor Elizabeth MacIver concluded that while directors were not the pawns of management in the way they had been 15 or 20 years previously, directors also were not the potentates that corporate law contemplated when vesting the board with managerial authority.[276] Referencing a 1971 study by Myles Mace that was critical of boards of that era,[277] Lorsch and MacIver said "(c)orporate boards are very different from the old elitist corps of overseers with limited responsibility."[278] Instead, "America's boards are made up of, by and large, responsible and dedicated directors who take their duties seriously."[279] On the other hand, Lorsch and MacIver found "(m)any directors still feel they are serving at the pleasure of the CEO-chairman."[280] Another limitation was that "(w)hile few CEOs abuse their power, the norms of polite boardroom behavior discourage directors from openly questioning or challenging the CEO's performance."[281] Boards, it seems, changed in the 1980s but not

---

269 Roberta Reynes, *Musical Chairs*, BARRON'S, Sept. 3, 1984, 64.

270 Mark S. Nadel, *More Power to the Stockholders*, WALL STREET J., June 26, 1989, A8.

271 SEGAL, *supra* note 10, at 168.

272 SMITH, *supra* note 226, at 127.

273 Knowlton & Millstein, *supra* note 64, at 182.

274 *Id.*

275 For a list of those interviewed, see JAY W. LORSCH & ELIZABETH MACIVER, PAWNS AND POTENTATES: THE REALITY OF AMERICA'S CORPORATE BOARDS 31–35 (1990).

276 Jay Lorsch & Jack Young, *Pawns or Potentates: The Reality of America's Corporate Boards*, EXECUTIVE, Nov. 1990, 85, 85.

277 MYLES L. MACE, DIRECTORS: MYTH AND REALITY (1971).

278 LORSCH & MACIVER, *supra* note 275, at 4.

279 *Id.* at 30.

280 *Id.* at 17.

281 *Id.* at 96.

sufficiently to be a substantially more potent constraint on corporate executives than they were during the 1970s.

SHAREHOLDERS

The 1970s were a grim decade for shareholders. Share prices were stagnant (Figure 4.6) and it was an "age of 'corporate responsibility'" where it was very much open to question whether increasing shareholder returns was management's top priority.[282] The 1980s was a much different proposition.

While shares offered disappointing returns in the 1970s, beginning in 1982 there was a bull market of historic proportions that would endure until the end of the 1990s.[283] October 1987's Black Monday crash shook the faith of numerous investors and prompted cost-cutting by various Wall Street banks.[284] Still, the fact that share prices began recovering quickly (Figure 4.6) convinced many that the stock market was "bullet-proof" and thereby helped to provide the foundation for the continuation of the bull market in the 1990s.[285] Moreover, 1980s shareholders were not a mere afterthought as they sometimes seemed to be in the managerial capitalism era. Instead, as the decade proceeded shareholders moved up the managerial priority list. By the end of the decade promotion of shareholder value was being cited regularly as a core corporate objective. We will consider initially the chronology involved and then assess why the switch occurred.

FIGURE 4.6 S&P 500 Index, 1973–1991 (Opening Prices, monthly).
Source: S&P 500—Historical Data, Yahoo! Finance, available at https://uk.finance.yahoo.com/quote/%5EGSPC/history?p=%5EGSPC (accessed May 26, 2018).

---

[282] Chapter 3, notes 235–36, 239–42 and related discussion.

[283] Chapter 1, note 292 and accompanying text.

[284] John Crudele, *Wall Street Has a Difficult Task in Luring Back Mom and Pop Investors*, LA TIMES, Aug. 7, 1988, D2; MAGGIE MAHAR, BULL: A HISTORY OF THE BOOM, 1982–1999, at 66–68, 73–74 (2003).

[285] ALEX BERENSON, THE NUMBER: HOW THE DRIVE FOR QUARTERLY EARNINGS CORRUPTED WALL STREET AND CORPORATE AMERICA 82 (2003).

Shareholders Move Up the Priority List

As the 1980s got underway, "the age of corporate responsibility" that prevailed in the 1970s continued to hold sway. Rosabeth Moss Kanter, a sociology professor who subsequently took up a post at Harvard Business School, argued in 1983 that executives were "now operating in open systems facing multiple constraints—retaining their jobs as long as . . . they can manage a wide variety of demands 'external' to the organization."[286] To make the case this was "now a mainstream part of elite corporate thought," she cited a 1981 statement on point by the Business Roundtable, the association of CEOs of major corporations.[287] The Business Roundtable said "(m)ore than ever, managers are expected to serve the public interest as well as private profit" and cited three "constituencies" in addition to shareholders—customers, employees, and society at large—that responsible management would take into account.[288]

Survey evidence lent credence to Kanter's assessment of managerial priorities. A 1983 American Management Association survey of nearly 900 executive managers indicated shareholders ranked 14th in terms of importance among 16 "organizational stakeholders."[289] Jay Lorsch, together with Harvard Business School colleague Gordon Donaldson, interviewed top executives at a dozen leading corporations for a 1983 study and found that while "(i)t is commonly believed that the primary goal of these corporate managers is the maximization of shareholder wealth," their respondents' top priority in fact was "the survival of the corporation in which they invested themselves psychologically and professionally."[290] Their interviews also revealed that "none of the executives was very concerned about the current market value of his company's stock. . . . (W)hat really mattered was the long-term health of the company."[291]

While the 1970s emphasis on balancing the interests of corporate constituencies continued to prevail in the early 1980s, prioritization of shareholders was beginning to gain momentum. Not until 1983 did more than two public corporations use the term "shareholder value" in an annual report to shareholders.[292] By 1985, the number was over 50, and shareholder value was mentioned in the annual reports of 30 percent of public companies as the decade concluded.[293] In a 1985 survey of CEOs 51 percent said creating shareholder value was their top priority, with only 18 percent indicating becoming the market leader in their industry was the primary objective.[294]

Business publications reflected the growing attention shareholder interests were attracting. The term "shareholder value" was rarely mentioned in the daily *Wall Street Journal* prior

---

[286] ROSABETH MOSS KANTER, THE CHANGE MASTERS 48 (1983).

[287] *Id.* at 49.

[288] *Id.*

[289] Barry Z. Posner & Warren H. Schmidt, *Values and the American Manager: An Update*, 26 CALIF. MGMT. REV. 202, 204, 206 (1984).

[290] GORDON DONALDSON & JAY W. LORSCH, DECISION MAKING AT THE TOP: THE SHAPING OF STRATEGIC DIRECTION 7 (1983).

[291] *Id.* at 21.

[292] Blake Edward Taylor, *Reconsidering the Rise of "Shareholder Value" in the United States*, London School of Economics Economic History Working Paper No. 214/2015, 18.

[293] *Id.* at 12–13.

[294] Pat Choate & J.K. Lenger, *The Quest of a Quick Return*, HARTFORD COURANT, July 13, 1986, B1.

to 1980 and was only referred to in 10 articles between 1980 and 1982. Usage increased to 13 articles in 1983, 26 in 1984, 76 in 1985, and 113 in 1986.[295] With the bimonthly *Harvard Business Review* the pattern was similar. "Shareholder value" was first mentioned in 1955, referred to again in 1981, and then mentioned nine times between 1986 and 1989.[296]

There was awareness at the time of changes afoot. Joe Nocera subsequently said that when he began his journalism career in the early 1980s writing about oilman and corporate raider T. Boone Pickens and heard Pickens's "ideas about the primacy of the shareholder . . . it felt to me as though I were hearing a foreign language for the first time. Shareholders owned companies? Really? As I listened I felt some dismay . . . but I also felt a growing sense of excitement."[297] A 1986 report by an Energy and Commerce subcommittee on takeovers suggested that "(w)hile the corporate reformers of the 1970s urged that 'accountability' meant being a good corporate citizen answerable to society as a whole, observers might now suggest that 'accountability' in the 1980s means keeping stock prices high for stockholders."[298] Knowlton and Millstein argued in 1988 that the US corporation was undergoing "a vast and necessary transition" at the core of which was "a heightened awareness of the need to serve shareholders better."[299] The *Chicago Tribune*'s financial editor said the same year shareholder was "king now," with the caveat that change could occur if the economy suffered a downturn.[300] In a 1990 book referred to by one reviewer as "the middle manager's diary of the 1980s"[301] *Wall Street Journal* reporter Amanda Bennett endorsed the proposition "(w)e are moving away from a soft capitalism with its concepts of sharing and stakeholders to a hard, market-driven system of profit maximization."[302] Alfred Rappaport, a shareholder value pioneer amongst academics,[303] said the same year "(t)he shareholder-value movement is in its infancy."[304] He conceded, however, that the shareholder value was "(a)lready a corporate buzzword."[305]

The repurchasing of shares was a tactic public companies began to engage in regularly that showed how priorities were changing. In 1982 the *Chicago Tribune* told readers "a growing number of corporations are making what seems a strange purchase: They're buying back their own previously issued shares."[306] Louis Lowenstein, a Columbia law professor critical

---

295 Heilbron, Verheul & Quak, *supra* note 4, at 10–12.

296 *Id.* at 16.

297 Nocera, *supra* note 72, at 4.

298 Chairman of the Subcommittee on Telecommunications, Consumer Protection, and Finance, Corporate Takeovers: Public Policy Implications for the Economy and Corporate Governance 77 (1987).

299 Knowlton & Millstein, *supra* note 64, at 169.

300 William Neikirk, *Too Much Mania and Too Little Fear*, Chi. Trib., Oct. 26, 1988, A3.

301 Bill Barnhart, *A Birth Announcement for the Anti-organization Man*, Chi. Trib., Mar. 25, 1990, C3.

302 Amanda Bennett, The Death of the Organization Man 22 (1990) (quoting futurist R. Morton Darrow).

303 James Kristie, *Timeline: The Evolution of 20th Century Corporate Governance*, Directors & Boards, Fall 1997, at 37, 43, citing Alfred Rappaport, Creating Shareholder Value: The New Standard for Business Performance (1986).

304 Alfred Rappaport, *The Staying Power of the Corporation*, Harv. Bus. Rev., Jan.–Feb. 1990, 96, 99.

305 *Id.* at 99.

306 Mary Holm Ansley, *When Firms Buy Back Shares It's Mainly a Value Judgment*, Chi. Trib., Jan. 6, 1982, C1.

of share buy-backs, analogized the practice to "a lizard lunching on its own tail. It seems unnatural."[307] Nevertheless, share repurchases grew considerably in popularity in the remaining years of the 1980s (Figure 4.7).

The SEC's 1982 adoption of a rule that clarified what steps repurchasing firms needed to take to avoid being accused of engaging in illegal share price manipulation under federal securities law helped to encourage buy-backs.[308] Share repurchases, however, also grew in popularity due to executives focusing more closely on shareholder interests. The *New York Times*, having told readers in 1984 that "on its most basic level, a high stock price is what a corporation is all about—maximizing shareholder value—and it is perhaps the best measuring stick of corporate performance," identified share buy-backs as a key tactic companies would adopt to achieve the desired result.[309] The *Times* reasoned "share repurchases usually lead to higher stock prices—if for no other reason than that a company's management has signaled investors that its future is rosier than its stock price shows, and it is willing to underscore this belief with its own money."[310] The following year *Fortune* said "(s)tock buybacks by financially strong corporations in recent years . . . have been a bonanza for shareholders who held on to their shares," citing research it had conducted indicating that stockholders in companies that had carried out buy-backs had substantially higher returns than investors in companies that had not.[311] This finding was confirmed subsequently by empirical analysis showing that public companies that carried out share repurchases in the 1980s not only

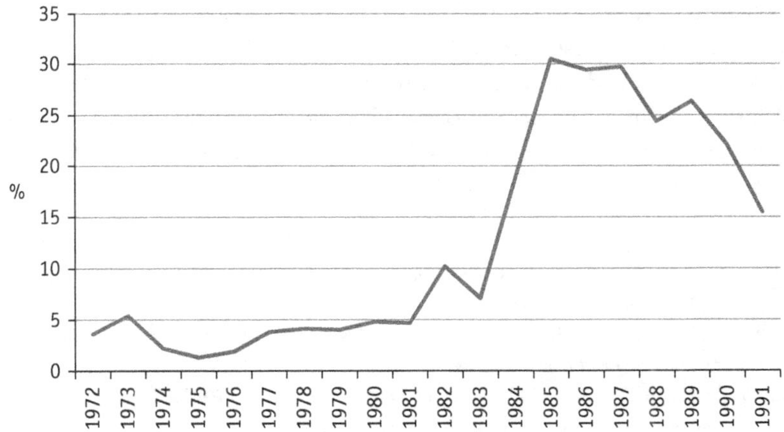

FIGURE 4.7 Share Buy-Back/Earnings, US Public Companies, 1972–1991.
Source: Gustavo Grullon & Roni Michaely, ***Dividends, Share Repurchases, and the Substitution Hypothesis***, 57 J. FIN. 1649, 1655 (2002).

---

[307] LOUIS LOWENSTEIN, SENSE & NONSENSE IN CORPORATE FINANCE 145 (1991).

[308] Gustavo Grullon & Roni Michaely, *Dividends, Share Repurchases, and the Substitution Hypothesis*, 57 J. FIN. 1649, 1676–82 (2002).

[309] Leslie Wayne, *A Look at New Corporate Tactics*, NY TIMES, Feb. 26, 1984, F6.

[310] *Id.*

[311] Kenneth Labich & Wilton Woods, *Is Business Taking On Too Much Debt?*, FORTUNE, July 22, 1985, 82.

experienced a share price boost at the time the buy-back was announced but also outperformed the market for a number of years thereafter.[312]

Paring back the workforce through "downsizing" was another practice rarely engaged in prior to the 1980s that plausibly could be attributed to shareholders moving up the pecking order. During each year in the 1980s more than 10 percent of large corporations made at least one downsizing announcement.[313] Throughout the decade, *Fortune* 500 companies cut 3.5 million jobs.[314] For many such firms, letting workers go on a mass scale was a radical change.[315] As the *Los Angeles Times* said in 1987, "(c)ompanies that once stood for lifetime employment—Eastman Kodak, IBM, DuPont—have forced employees into early retirement."[316]

Various observers have argued that downsizing commenced in earnest in the 1980s as a result of changing managerial priorities, with executives proceeding in order to bolster shareholder value.[317] The actual process was messier. US corporations began downsizing in earnest during tough economic times at the beginning of the 1980s,[318] which was still an age of broadly cast corporate responsibility.[319] Nor were 1980s executives or investors particularly enthusiastic about the practice. In 1987, *Business Week* said of chief executives laying off staff in an article on "The Changing Role of the CEO," "(m)any of them hate it."[320] CEOs knew they were having "to rewrite the social contract they have long had with their employees," namely for staff "an unwritten rule in Corporate America that ... the economy willing, the corporation would take care of them."[321]

To the extent that managers were trying to please shareholders by engaging in downsizing, the investor reception was at best mixed. Share prices often fell after 1980s downsizing announcements.[322] Investors tended to draw negative inferences about future cash flows when executives indicated it was necessary to lay off employees.[323] Stock market reactions to downsizing became more positive as executives became increasingly adept at contextualizing lay-off announcements with references to the need to "bite-the-bullet" and to the benefits

---

312 David Ikenberry, Josef Lakonishok & Theo Vermaelen, *Market Underreaction to Open Market Share Repurchases*, 39 J. Fin. Econ. 181 (1995).

313 Jiwook Jung & Frank Dobbin, *Finance and Institutional Investors, in* The Sociology of Finance 52, 67 (Karin Knorr Cetina & Alex Preda eds., 2012).

314 Robert L. Bartley, The Seven Fat Years and How to Do It Again 140 (1995).

315 Bennett, *supra* note 302, at 114.

316 James Flanigan, *Bears Don't Scare the Lean, Mean*, LA Times, Dec. 18, 1987, 2.

317 Jung & Dobbin, *supra* note 313, at 67; Linda Brewster Stearns, *Book Review*, 39 Admin. Sci. Q. 174, 175, (1994); Adam Goldstein, *Revenge of the Managers: Labor Cost-Cutting and the Paradoxical Resurgence of Managerialism in the Shareholder Value Era, 1984 to 2001*, 77 Amer. Sociological Rev. 268, 270–71 (2012).

318 Bennett, *supra* note 302, at 117.

319 *Supra* notes 286–91 and related discussion.

320 *The Changing Role of the CEO*, Bus. Wk., Oct. 23, 1987, 13. See also Bennett, *supra* note 302, at 117.

321 *Changing Role*, *supra* note 320.

322 Dan L. Worrell, Wallace N. Davidson III & Varinder M. Sharma, *Layoff Announcements and Stockholder Wealth*, 34 Acad. Mgmt. Rev. 662 (1991).

323 David W. Blackwell, M. Wayne Marr & Michael F. Spivey, *Plant-Closing Decisions and the Market Value of the Firm*, 26 J. Fin. Econ. 277, 278 (1990).

that would arrive from an efficiency-driven rationalization of resources.[324] This only occurred with any regularity, however, as the 1980s concluded.[325]

Explaining the Reorientation

Why did the 1980s reorientation of managerial priorities in favor of stockholders occur? Changes with institutional shareholders constitute one plausible explanation. Rapid growth in share ownership by institutional investors elicited much discussion in the 1970s.[326] The trend in favor of institutional ownership continued in the 1980s, with the proportion of shares held by pension funds, mutual funds, and insurers collectively rising from 26 percent to 36 percent between 1980 and 1990.[327] Institutional ownership was even more pronounced in larger companies, with the proportion of stock owned by institutions in the 1,000 largest public corporations being 49 percent in 1988.[328] Unlike in the 1970s, mutual funds reinforced the trend, with the number of shareholder accounts increasing from 12 million worth $135 billion in 1980 to 58 million worth nearly $1 trillion in 1990.[329] The growth in institutional holdings theoretically meant, as *Business Week* said in 1987, "mutual funds and other institutional owners ha(d) muscles to flex."[330]

Another possible explanation for shareholders becoming a higher priority for 1980s public company executives is intellectual in nature, oriented around Jensen and Meckling's articulation of agency cost theory in their 1976 article on the theory of the firm.[331] Sociologists Jiwook Jung and Frank Dobbin have argued that "(t)he shareholder value movement, fueled by the growth of institutional shareholding, found its voice in a budding financial theory in economics—agency theory" and that "(u)nder the tutelage of newly empowered institutional investors executives pursued shareholder value with the tools of agency theory."[332] Bruce Scott, in a 2011 book on the history of the development of capitalism, says of agency cost theory that it "soon became the rationale for, if not the driving force, behind the broader theory of shareholder capitalism" and "became solidified in managerial practices."[333] Economist William Lazonick, in seeking to explain why share buy-backs rose to prominence

---

[324] Richard E. Caves & Matthew B. Kreps, *Fat: The Displacement of Nonproduction Workers from US Manufacturing Industries*, 2 BROOKINGS PAPERS ON ECON. ACTIVITY: MICROECONOMICS 227, 272 (1993); DAN KRIER, SPECULATIVE MANAGEMENT 182 (2005).

[325] KRIER, *supra* note 324, at 260–61.

[326] Chapter 3, notes 188–89, 205–6 and accompanying text.

[327] MARY O'SULLIVAN, CONTESTS FOR CORPORATE CONTROL: CORPORATE GOVERNANCE AND ECONOMIC PERFORMANCE IN THE UNITED STATES AND GERMANY 156 (2000).

[328] USEEM, *supra* note 109, at 32. See also John C. Coffee, *Liquidity versus Control: The Institutional Investor as Corporate Monitors* 91 COLUM. L. REV. 1277, 1291 (1991).

[329] Chapter 3, note 197 and related discussion; RICHARD D. CRAWFORD & WILLIAM W. SIHLER, THE TROUBLED MONEY BUSINESS: THE DEATH OF AN OLD ORDER AND THE RISE OF A NEW ORDER 125 (1991).

[330] *Mutual Fund Managers Should Make Trouble*, BUS. WK., Feb. 23, 1987, 156. See also Choate & Lenger, *supra* note 294; *'88 Looks Like Year of Institutional Investors*, CHI. TRIB., July 10, 1988, G3.

[331] Jensen & Meckling, *supra* note 245; Chapter 3, note 38 and related discussion.

[332] Jung & Dobbin, *supra* note 313, at 57, 69.

[333] BRUCE R. SCOTT, CAPITALISM: ITS ORIGINS AND EVOLUTION AS A SYSTEM OF GOVERNANCE 560 (2011).

in the mid-1980s, has argued similarly "(t)his disgorging of the corporate cash flow manifests a decisive triumph of agency theory and its shareholder value ideology."[334]

It is understandable that intellectual trends have been identified as a catalyst for the shift of managerial priorities during the 1980s. Theoretically based arguments were indeed made in the 1980s by "contractarian" corporate law scholars that managers should put shareholder value front and center.[335] They reasoned that corporate law appropriately privileged shareholders as compared to other constituencies affected by corporate activity. This was because shareholders, as "residual claimants" (the ultimate beneficiaries of corporate success or lack thereof), had strong incentives to encourage maximum corporate achievement in a manner that benefitted other corporate constituencies, and because shareholders could not contract for protection nearly as readily as "fixed" claimants such as employees and creditors.[336]

While there were corporate law academics in the 1980s prepared to defend the view that management should prioritize shareholders, "(i)t would be a stretch to suggest that agency theory was the cause of the shareholder value logic that engulfed the corporate world beginning in the 1980s."[337] If agency cost theory was a catalyst for managers prioritizing shareholders, it should have achieved prominence in academic circles earlier than it in fact did.[338] Jensen and Meckling's 1976 article ultimately was very widely cited.[339] Nevertheless, in the field of financial economics from which it arose it did not have a marked influence until the 1980s drew to a close.[340] By that point shareholder value was "(a)lready a corporate buzzword."[341] Agency cost theory thus might have provided a convenient ex post rationale for executives giving shareholders precedence but it did not get the shareholder primacy ball rolling.

As for the growing clout of institutional investors, if this was the primary reason shareholders moved up the priority list for public company executives in the 1980s one would have expected to find that the strong bias in favor of institutional passivity that prevailed during the 1950, 1960s, and 1970s would have been eroding.[342] In fact, institutional shareholders remained quiescent.[343] The *Los Angeles Times* said in 1986 "most shareholders, even

---

[334] William Lazonick, *The Quest for Shareholder Value: Stock Repurchases in the US Economy*, 74 LOUVAIN ECON. REV. 479, 485 (2008). For other examples, see Taekjin Shin, *The Shareholder Value Principle: The Governance and Control of Corporations in the United States*, 7 SOCIOLOGY COMPASS 829, 832–33 (2013); Lynne L. Dallas, *Is There Hope for Change? The Evolution of Conceptions of Good Corporate Governance*, 54 SAN DIEGO L. REV. 491, 510-12 (2017); ALEXANDER STYHRE, THE MAKING OF SHAREHOLDER WELFARE SOCIETY: A STUDY IN CORPORATE GOVERNANCE 141–42 (2018).

[335] Brian R. Cheffins, *Introduction, in* THE HISTORY OF MODERN US CORPORATE GOVERNANCE xiv–xv (Brian R. Cheffins ed., 2011).

[336] CHEFFINS, *supra* note 243, at 48.

[337] MIZRUCHI, *supra* note 159, at 207.

[338] Taylor, *supra* note 292, at 5–6.

[339] Chapter 3, note 37 and related discussion; Boris Durisin & Fulvio Puzone, *Maturation of Corporate Governance Research, 1993–2007: An Assessment*, 17 CORP. GOV. INTERNATIONAL REV. 266, 270–72 (2009); Olivier Weinstein, *Firm, Property and Governance: From Berle and Means to the Agency Theory, and Beyond*, 2 ACCTING., ECON. & LAW 1, 35 (2012).

[340] Heilbron, Verheul & Quak, *supra* note 4, at 9–10.

[341] *Supra* note 305 and related discussion.

[342] Chapter 2, notes 327–30 and accompanying text; Chapter 3, notes 190–92, 195 and related discussion.

[343] IRA M. MILLSTEIN, THE ACTIVIST DIRECTOR: LESSONS FROM THE BOARDROOM AND THE FUTURE OF THE CORPORATION 53 (2017).

sophisticated money managers" were "inattentive to their rights as corporate owners."[344] Michael Jensen, in making the case in 1989 that the public company could be eclipsed, argued "institutional investors are remarkably powerless" and "almost completely uninvolved in the major decisions and long-term strategies of the companies" in which they held shares.[345] Harvey Segal, in his 1989 book on corporate restructuring, dismissed the idea that the substantial ownership stakes institutions held meant they had effective control of the companies, pointing out that "most institutions are still passive investors."[346] *Business Week* told readers the same year "institutions are sloppy with their votes" and "don't question management's choices of directors," and said on other issues "management gets the benefit of the doubt."[347]

Institutional shareholders were not entirely passive during the 1980s, but activism occurring was narrowly focused. In 1984 greenmail payments by Disney to Saul Steinberg and by Texaco to Texas' Bass family, potentially hostile suitors with a 12 percent ownership stake in the oil company, outraged Jesse Unruh, who as state treasurer of California oversaw the huge California Public Employees Retirement System (CalPERS).[348] Unruh said "(i)n most cases we were voting blindly with company management, because nobody knew what else to do. The raiders and the companies were playing footsie back and forth without regard to what we thought."[349] Unruh responded by joining with New York City Comptroller Harrison J. Goldin and Roland Machold, the New Jersey government's head investment manager, to set up in 1985 the Council of Institutional Investors (CII), an association of public pension funds that had by 1988 62 members representing $300 billion in assets.[350]

Despite the CII being the progeny of public pension funds rather than institutional investors generally, investment banker Joseph Fogg told *Harvard Business Review* readers in 1985 "(f)inally, the sleeping giants, the institutional shareholders ... are awakening. The recent formation of the Council of Institutional Investors ... signals a potent new countervailing lobbying power to the heretofore more organized management-oriented interests."[351] The CII indeed wanted to extend its reach to bring private pension funds, typically set up by corporations, into the fold.[352] This initiative failed, partly due to concerns among operators of private pension funds that the CII was influenced by anti-management bias reminiscent "of the campus radicalism of the late 1960s and early 1970s."[353]

More generally, private pension funds, as with mutual funds and insurance companies, refrained from challenging executives of the public companies in which they owned shares,

---

[344] Michael E. Hiltzik, *Investors Relinquish Key Rights*, LA TIMES, May 18, 1986, 1.

[345] Jensen, *supra* note 94, at 65.

[346] SEGAL, *supra* note 10, at 202.

[347] *Moneymen May Stop Deep-Sixing Proxies*, BUS. WK., Mar. 20, 1989, 142.

[348] *Supra* note 86 and accompanying text; Bleakley, *supra* note 86; Deborah Whitefield, *Unruh Calls for Pension Funds to Flex Muscles*, LA TIMES, Feb. 3, 1985, C3.

[349] Clemens P. Work, *As Big Investors Take On Top Management*, US NEWS & WORLD REPORT, Mar. 11, 1985, 75.

[350] Nancy J. Perry & Mark Alpert, *Who Runs Your Company Anyway?*, FORTUNE, Sept. 12, 1988, 140.

[351] Joseph C. Fogg, *Takeovers: Last Chance for Self-Restraint*, HARV. BUS. REV., Nov./Dec. 1985, 30, 31.

[352] David A. Vise, *Bill of Rights Seeks to Boost Power of Shareholders*, WASH. POST, Apr. 13, 1986, F1.

[353] *Id.* Unruh for his part vociferously denied that the CII was "anti-management"—Fred R. Bleakley, *A Trustee Takes On the Greenmailers*, N.Y TIMES, Feb. 10, 1985, 143.

leaving the field to public pension funds.[354] Even public pension funds pursued a circumscribed agenda. The CII issued in 1986 a Shareholder Bill of Rights that emphasized equal treatment of shareholders and the need for shareholder approval of fundamental corporate actions.[355] In the late 1980s Goldin led a group of large pension fund managers that complained to Exxon about the oil company responding tardily following a major Alaska oil spill.[356] Otherwise, public pension activism in the 1980s was restricted to takeovers, without substantial effect.

When public pension funds stepped forward in the 1980s regarding takeovers, they typically relied on the shareholder proposal, the governance mechanism that was the centerpiece of Campaign GM in the early 1970s, to challenge takeover defenses.[357] Between 1987 and 1989, of 199 corporate governance-related shareholder proposals filed with public companies that received more than 20 percent support, 154 had this objective.[358] Public pension funds filed most of these proposals.[359] Very few passed, and during the same period shareholders voted in favor of the vast majority of anti-takeover amendments management proposed to change corporate charters.[360] The results, as the *Baltimore Sun* indicated in 1989, "hardly qualify as institutional muscle."[361]

Takeovers and Managerial Priorities

If neither intellectual conjectures nor institutional activism played the decisive role in moving shareholders up the priority list of managers of public companies in the 1980s then what did? The surge in takeover activity was the key.[362] The fact that the market for corporate control only operated at a 1980s-level of intensity during that decade tends to obscure as time passes the crucial part takeovers played in moving shareholders front and center. Academic theorizing and institutional shareholder input were secondary considerations. In contrast, takeover activity, and particularly the willingness of fund managers acting on behalf of institutional investors to cash in when a target company was "in play," was crucial in bringing shareholders to the forefront.

The number of hostile takeovers increased substantially during the 1980s (Figure 4.2). Moreover, their impact extended well beyond hostile bids actually launched or completed.[363]

---

354 Harwell Wells, *A Long View of Shareholder Power: From the Antebellum Corporation to the Twenty-First Century*, 67 U. Fla. L. Rev. 1033, 1092 (2015).

355 Vise, *supra* note 352. The Bill of Rights is set out in full in Monks & Minow, *supra* note 159, at 214–16.

356 David Pauly, *Wall Street's New Musclemen*, Newsweek, June 5, 1989, 46.

357 Wells, *supra* note 354, 1092–93; Chapter 3, note 224 and related discussion.

358 Edward B. Rock, *The Logic and (Uncertain) Significance of Institutional Shareholder Activism*, 79 Geo. L.J. 445, 482–83 (1991).

359 Wells, *supra* note 354, at 1093.

360 *Id.*; Rock, *supra* note 358, at 487.

361 Rosenthal, *supra* note 197.

362 See, for example, Khurana, *supra* note 5, at 302; Neil Fligstein & Taek-Jin Shin, *The Shareholder Value Society: A Review of the Changes in Working Conditions and Inequality in the United States, 1976 to 2000, in* Social Inequality 401, 402–03 (Kathryn Neckerman ed., 2004); Greta R. Krippner, Capitalizing on Crisis: The Political Origins of the Rise of Finance 8–9 (2011).

363 Chairman of the Subcommittee on Telecommunications, Consumer Protection, and Finance, *supra* note 298, at 14, 29.

This was because executives were eager to avoid ever being caught in the firing line. The robust M&A activity of the 1980s caused the managerial "fear quotient" to increase markedly.[364] The desire to sidestep an unwelcome bid in turn put apprehensive public company executives under an onus to prioritize shareholders they might have formerly felt they could take for granted. Mark Mizruchi, Linda Brewster Stearns, and Christopher Marquis wrote, for example, in 2006 that "the merger wave of the 1980s was accompanied by the development of a new worldview, in which the most important goal of managers was to increase the firm's stock price, and the vulnerability of managers, as well as the pressure to 'eat or be eaten,' became a taken-for-granted characteristic of the environment."[365]

Contemporaries were well aware that takeovers were changing managerial predilections and pushing shareholders up the priority list. "Suddenly," *Forbes* reported in 1984, "corporate America, too, is aware of a new force that could become its enemy—its own shareholder base. Indeed, more than ever, corporate managements realize that in order to remain the masters of their own destiny they must create the same values that shareholders could achieve through a breakup or acquisition of their companies."[366] *Business Week* said in 1985, "(c)ompanies are paying more attention to shareholders, particularly catering to the institutional holders so critical in a takeover battle. They are reorganizing their balance sheets, repurchasing their shares, and doing all they can to make stock prices reflect asset values and cash flows."[367] The *New York Times* concurred, saying "current corporate catchwords are 'restructuring' and 'maximizing shareholder value.' It turns out that the best defense against corporate raiders is to beat them at their own game of trying to drive up a stock price."[368] A *Chicago Tribune* columnist suggested in 1987 "(t)he prospect of a takeover is a discipline on corporate managers, who otherwise would have considerable latitude to treat their shareholders' interests as a minor distraction. It impels managers to use their assets as profitably as possible."[369] Knowlton and Millstein observed in 1988 takeovers were "providing a mighty goad to corporate self-examination as to whether use of the corporation's assets is being maximized in the best interests of the shareholders. Any corporation that doesn't engage in this self-analysis (i.e. 'think like a raider') will undoubtedly receive assistance—wanted or unwanted—in the marketplace for corporate control."[370]

Alfred Rappaport, the academic shareholder value pioneer, argued forcefully that takeovers played the pivotal role in moving stockholders up the priority list. He said in 1990 "(i)t is impossible to overstate how deeply the market for corporate control has changed the attitudes and practices of US managers."[371] Indeed he explicitly attributed the passing of the managerial capitalism era to "the rise of the unsolicited tender offer," explaining that due to

---

364 *America's Leanest and Meanest*, BUS. WK., Oct. 5, 1987, 78.

365 Mark S. Mizruchi, Linda Brewster Stearns & Christopher Marquis, *The Conditional Nature of Embeddedness: A Study of Borrowing by Large US Firms*, 71 AMER. SOC. REV. 310, 329 (2006).

366 Fred R. Bleakley, *Mergers & Divestitures: Restructuring Corporate America*, FORBES, Feb. 27, 1984, Advertising Supplement, 2.

367 *Getting Rough with the Raiders*. BUS. WK., May 27, 1985, 34.

368 Cuff, *supra* note 62.

369 Stephen Chapman, *Boesky, Takeovers and the Value of Rewarding Greed*, CHI. TRIB., May 1, 1987, 23.

370 Knowlton & Millstein, *supra* note 64, at 180.

371 Rappaport, *supra* note 304, at 100.

takeovers "managers who can't or don't want to understand the new realities will have to—or be replaced by managers who do."[372]

While with respect to reorienting managerial priorities direct interventions by institutional shareholders was a sideshow compared with the market for corporate control, to put the role of institutional investors into proper context it is necessary to circle back and acknowledge their enthusiasm for takeover activity. A.A. Sommer, a former SEC commissioner, said in 1987 institutions "yearn for the windfall of a takeover" and "leap at the prospect of a takeover bonanza."[373] This was a relatively novel stance for institutional shareholders. Martin Lipton suggested in 1983 the fact institutional investors were willing, enthusiastic even, to act "other than was desired by management" was "a fundamental change in the attitudes of institutional investors, who a decade ago almost invariably and uniformly supported management."[374] The new shareholder "fickleness," executives knew, left "their companies victim to raiders."[375] Indeed, the *Los Angeles Times* told readers in 1986 "(e)xecutives hold institutional investors largely responsible for the wave of hostile takeovers, contending that they sell firms to the highest bidder for the sake of a quick profit."[376]

More robust competition between money managers to obtain and retain mandates to invest on behalf of institutional clients did much to foster the enthusiasm for takeovers. During the 1980s, asset managers found themselves increasingly being evaluated continuously by reference to the performance of market indices and to their competitors.[377] Improved technology had increased the level of scrutiny. The personal computer began to feature heavily in the investing realm in the 1980s.[378] That made it "possible to make precise, rapid comparison of present returns ... where before it was technically impossible."[379] In turn, according to William McGowan, chairman and chief executive of telecommunications firm MCI Communications, "every money manager is now measured through a computer against every other manager and against every index. And he's got to perform."[380]

With performance-related rivalry between money managers intensifying, opportunities to sell out at a substantial premium because a bidder offered a generous price to secure control without the backing of management could provide a valuable competitive edge.[381] As the managing director of a firm that invested $3 billion on behalf of institutional clients said of takeovers in 1988, "(w)henever we can get a 40 percent increase in stock value,

---

[372] *Id.*

[373] A.A. Sommer, *Let the Holders Vote on a Device to Defeat Raiders*, LA TIMES, Jan. 18, 1987, D3.

[374] Randall W. Forsyth, *The New Proxy Wars*, BARRON'S, Apr. 25, 1983, 63.

[375] *Battle for Corporate, supra* note 259.

[376] Hiltzik, *supra* note 344.

[377] *Will Money Managers Wreck the Economy?*, BUS. WK., Aug. 13, 1984, 86.

[378] John Armour & Brian Cheffins, *Stock Market Prices and the Market for Corporate Control* [2016] U. ILL. L. REV. 761, 802.

[379] FLEISCHER, HAZARD & KLIPPER, *supra* note 260, 6. See also *Will Money, supra* note 377.

[380] RALPH NADER & WILLIAM TAYLOR, THE BIG BOYS: POWER & POSITION IN AMERICAN BUSINESS 517 (1986).

[381] *Will Money, supra* note 377; Thomas C. Franco, *Institutional Ownership in the US: An Overview, in* SHAREHOLDER ACTIVISM: THE EMERGING ROLE OF INSTITUTIONAL INVESTORS, Corporate Law Practice Course Handbook Series, No. 575, 285, 287 (1987).

we're delighted."[382] Without this sort of enthusiasm for takeover bids, the Deal Decade likely would have operated at a lower intensity level than it in fact did. Shareholders correspondingly probably would not have moved up the managerial priority list in as forthright a manner as they did.

External Constraints

Michael Useem, based on interviews with executives at seven large US corporations conducted between 1989 and 1991, observed "omnipotence was rarely felt to be a characteristic of the executive suite. Instead, senior managers complained of a host of limitations on their powers."[383] We have considered to this point the extent to which "internal" constraints, namely boards and shareholders, and an important "external" constraint, the market for corporate control, impinged upon managerial discretion in the 1980s. We will consider now additional external constraints. Some declined in importance in the 1980s, namely regulation and unions. On the other hand, executives of large corporations accustomed to their firms benefitting from a substantial market power buffer were finding competitive pressure from rival firms intensifying.

REGULATION

Admiration for entrepreneurial proclivities was growing as the 1980s began.[384] Ronald Reagan was attuned to this change of sentiment and his administration correspondingly advocated policies designed to foster economic growth through the reduction of governmental interference with business.[385] A cornerstone of the Reagan administration's approach was its "four square commitment to deregulation."[386] This stance created potential for executives to exercise discretion previously unavailable. Robert Goizueta, the newly appointed chairman and CEO of Coca-Cola, told the business community in 1981, "(i)f we fail, we can't put our shortcomings on the back of government any longer."[387] Robert Reich, who would subsequently serve in the Clinton administration, claimed in 1985 that "(n)ot since the '20s has big business been so unconstrained."[388] Reich noted that economist John Kenneth Galbraith had in the 1950s written "reassuringly of the 'countervailing power' in the American system" but cited cutbacks to regulation when telling readers that "in the America of the eighties, these counterweights have been all but removed."[389]

---

[382] Anise C. Wallace, *Takeover Spree Starts a Speculative Frenzy*, NY TIMES, Oct. 25, 1988, D1.

[383] USEEM, *supra* note 109, at 5, 216.

[384] *Supra* notes 16–18, 21–30 and related discussion.

[385] STECKMEST, *supra* note 229, at 5.

[386] SKEEL, *supra* note 186, at 120.

[387] Carl Cannon, *Goizueta: Reagan Has Given Business a Chance*, LA TIMES, Sept. 30, 1981, G1. See also STECKMEST, *supra* note 229, at 5.

[388] Robert B. Reich, *The Executive's New Clothes*, NEW REPUBLIC, May 13, 1985, 23.

[389] *Id.*

Bruce Scott argues in his 2011 history of capitalism "(l)aissez faire capitalism emerged again in the 1980s as the US economy was deregulated back toward its free state of the late 19th century."[390] This overstates the extent to which executives operated free from regulatory restraints due to Reagan policies. With respect to dismantling existing restrictions, the legislative legacy was modest compared to the reform of airlines, railways, and trucking occurring when Jimmy Carter was president.[391] The Garn-St. Germain Depository Institutions Act of 1982[392] and the Cable Television Act of 1984[393] were the only major industry-specific deregulatory measures promulgated under Reagan.[394] The 1982 depository institutions legislation gave commercial banks increased scope to market to depositors accounts offering competitive rates of interest but left untouched federal restrictions on interstate banking and provisions in the Glass Steagall Act of 1933 that separated commercial banking from investment banking.[395]

The Environmental Protection Agency (EPA), the Occupational Health and Safety Administration (OHSA), and the Consumer Protection Safety Commission, governmental organizations charged with implementing social regulation introduced from the mid-1960s through to the mid-1970s, would have had no role to play in a true laissez-faire economy. They remained, however, "alive and well" throughout the Reagan years.[396] There were funding cuts initially but by the end of Reagan's second term as president the budgets of both the EPA and OHSA had gone up in inflation-adjusted terms, 131 percent in the case of the EPA.[397] More generally, as was the case with each administration extending back at least to Nixon, the number of prescriptive measures in the code of federal regulations increased under Reagan.[398] The end result was hardly a laissez-faire idyll.

Reagan himself had anticipated that deregulation might not yield radical change, saying just before he took office that "(g)overnment is like an ocean liner, not a speedboat."[399] Still, government did impinge less on business by the end of the 1980s than it did in the 1950s, 1960s, and 1970s. Relaxation of antitrust policy, for instance, offered executives greater scope to carry out mergers, especially with rivals.[400] The Reagan administration believed that the country's entrepreneurial spirit would be fostered if people could keep more of

---

[390] SCOTT, *supra* note 333, at 574.

[391] Chapter 3, notes 372–73 and related discussion.

[392] Pub. L. No. 97-320, 96 Stat. 14 (1982).

[393] Pub. L. No. 98-549, 98 Stat. 2779 (1984).

[394] Richard H.K. Vietor, *Government Regulation of Business, in* THE CAMBRIDGE ECONOMIC HISTORY OF THE UNITED STATES, VOLUME III: THE TWENTIETH CENTURY 969, 1009 (Stanley L. Engerman & Robert E. Gallman eds., 2000).

[395] SIMON JOHNSON & JAMES KWAK, 13 BANKERS: THE WALL STREET TAKEOVER AND THE NEXT FINANCIAL MELTDOWN 73–74 (2010). For a summary of the 1982 changes, see Joseph Jude Norton, *The 1982 Banking Act and the Deregulation Scheme*, 38 BUS. LAWYER 1627, 1633–34 (1983); Gillian Garcia, *The Garn-St. Germain Depository Institutions Act of 1982*, Federal Reserve History, available at http://www.federalreservehistory.org/Events/DetailView/45 (2013) (accessed April 15, 2018).

[396] WATERHOUSE, *supra* note 4, at 196.

[397] Vietor, *supra* note 394, at 1010.

[398] *Grudges and Kludges*, ECONOMIST, Mar. 4, 2017, 30 (citing data compiled by the Mercatus Center).

[399] Ronald Reagan, *Government & Business in the '80s*, WALL ST. J., Jan. 9, 1981, 18.

[400] *Supra* notes 184–186 and related discussion.

what they earned and correspondingly orchestrated substantial cuts in income tax rates, including reducing the top rate from 70 percent to 50 percent in 1981 and again to 28 percent in 1986.[401] Reagan also achieved deregulatory results by appointing agency and department heads who shared his bias against governmental burdens and prioritized lowering compliance costs.[402] *Newsweek* said of the change of tone in 1984,

> business seems encouraged by a change in the regulatory climate. It's not that the absolute level of regulation is expected to decline, but that the rule making has become less capricious. Executives no longer worry, for example, that a single change in the federal air-quality standards might render hundreds of millions of dollars of investment obsolete.[403]

Ultimately, while it was not the case that government regulation had been "all but removed" in the 1980s it was a less potent fetter on managerial discretion than it had been in living memory.

UNIONS

Unions, a meaningful source of countervailing power during the managerial capitalism era, suffered setbacks in the 1970s but remained a potentially significant constraint for many public company executives.[404] Unions declined further in importance in the 1980s. The *Washington Post* said in 1989 the 1980s "has been a decade of despair for many in the labor movement" and that "(o)rganized labor is in trouble as it marks the end of one of its worst decades in postwar history."[405] Mark Mizruchi, in a 2013 study of changes affecting American business elites from the 1950s through to the 1980s, argued that by the mid-1980s organized labor "had been largely quieted" and by the end of the decade "was in disarray, a shrunken and weakened movement fighting for its life."[406] Organized labor thus had been marginalized as a constraint on public company executives to an extent that would have been difficult to envisage even a decade or two earlier.

Ronald Reagan's robust response when the Professional Air Traffic Controllers Organization (PATCO) commenced an illegal strike in 1981 would prove to be a potent symbol of union decline.[407] He fired the employees who left work, disbanded the union, and authorized subsequently the hiring of new air traffic controllers.[408] The public, according

---

401 Wyatt Wells, American Capitalism, 1945–2000: Continuity and Change from Mass Production to the Information Society 115–16 (2003); Anthony J. Mayo & Nitin Nohria, In Their Time: The Greatest Business Leaders of the Twentieth Century 292 (2005).

402 Waterhouse, *supra* note 4, at 195.

403 Harry Anderson, *A Surprising Surge in Productivity*, Newsweek, Feb. 6, 1984, 62.

404 Chapter 3, notes 382–87 and accompanying text.

405 Frank Swoboda, *Organized Labor Toughens Its Stance*, Wash. Post, Sept. 3, 1989, H1.

406 Mizruchi, *supra* note 159, at 190–91, 197.

407 Wells, *supra* note 401, at 131; James Strong, *Labor's Miseries Traceable to PATCO Strike Fiasco*, Chi. Trib., Jan. 6, 1984, F4.

408 Michael K. Burns, *10 Years after PATCO Strike, A Legacy of Labor Bitterness*, Balt. Sun, Aug. 4, 1991, E4.

to opinion polls, supported Reagan's tough stance by a two-to-one margin, which stunned union leaders.[409]

Though the PATCO showdown involved government employees, corporate executives treated it as an endorsement of the use of replacement workers to keep operating during a work stoppage.[410] This practice, which employers began to deploy tentatively in the 1970s, was commonplace by the late 1980s.[411] In this new environment unions suffered defeats with most of the major strikes they launched.[412] Unions in turn cut back on work stoppages, meaning strike activity was much rarer during the 1980s than it was in the 1950s, 1960s, and 1970s (Figure 4.8). Management pressed its advantage, resulting in many freshly negotiated collective agreements providing for wage freezes and concessions involving the giving back of previously won benefits.[413]

Various factors in addition to PATCO put unions on the back foot in the 1980s. Once Reagan appointees formed a majority on the National Labor Relations Board the board

FIGURE 4.8 Strike Activity, 1950–1990 (# involving 1000 or more workers).
Source: Bureau of Labor Statistics, *Work Stoppages Involving 1,000 or More Workers, 1947–2017*, available at https://www.bls.gov/news.release/wkstp.t01.htm (accessed Apr. 6, 2018).

---

[409] Strong, *supra* note 407; KIM MCQUAID, UNEASY PARTNERS: BIG BUSINESS IN AMERICAN POLITICS, 1945–1990, at 183 (1994).

[410] Burns, *supra* note 408.

[411] Chapter 3, note 393 and related discussion; EUGENE F. FINKIN, SUCCESSFUL CORPORATE TURNAROUNDS: A GUIDE FOR BOARD MEMBERS, FINANCIAL MANAGERS, FINANCIAL INSTITUTIONS AND OTHER CREDITORS 188 (1987); Peter Perl, *US Unions Losing Clout in Shifting Labor Market*, WASH. POST, Sept. 6, 1987, H1.

[412] Kathy Sawyer, *Organized Labor Lost Big in 1983, And New Year Promises Little More*, WASH. POST, Jan. 8, 1984, G2; Jay S. Siegel, *Labor Must Face Changing Society*, CHI. TRIB., Sept. 2, 1989, 11.

[413] John D. Paulus & Robert S. Gay, *Is America Helping Herself? Corporate Restructuring and Global Competitiveness*, *in* MORGAN STANLEY WORLDWIDE ECONOMIC REVIEW 14, 19 (1987); MICHAEL GOLDFIELD, THE DECLINE OF ORGANIZED LABOR IN THE UNITED STATES 43–46 (1987); BENNETT HARRISON & BARRY BLUESTONE, THE GREAT U-TURN: CORPORATE RESTRUCTURING AND THE POLARIZING OF AMERICA 39–42 (1988).

issued numerous rulings overturning pro-labor precedents.[414] Union density in the workforce continued to fall, from 22 percent in 1980 to 16 percent in 1989.[415] The decline was even more precipitous among private sector employers (20 percent to 12 percent).[416] Structural changes in the economy hit union participation. Services, a lightly unionized sector of the economy, accounted for the entire net increase in employment that occurred in the 1980s.[417] Efforts by organized labor to gain a foothold in the rapidly growing tech sector proved largely fruitless.[418] Employers in "blue collar" industries that had traditionally been union bastions increasingly shifted production from the "Rust Belt" states to "Sun Belt" states in the south and west, areas of the country with a tradition of antipathy toward organized labor.[419]

An additional factor that put unions on the back foot in the 1980s was the growing competition unionized firms were facing from rivals.[420] Feeling the pressure from market forces, employers felt compelled to play "hardball" in labor negotiations and unions often buckled, settling on terms unthinkable a few years beforehand.[421] As Audrey Freedman, a labor economist explained to the *Baltimore Sun* in 1983, "(i)ndustries that previously had the power to pass on high labor costs in higher prices don't have that power any more. . . . You now have competition with a capital C and we are now seeing an attempt to keep wages at the market level."[422] Though heightened competition from rivals indirectly weakened the constraints unions imposed on management, as we will see next, this trend would simultaneously reduce the discretion executives of large companies were accustomed to having.

COMPETITORS

While regulation and organized labor receded in importance as external constraints on executive discretion in US public companies in the 1980s, the pressure competitors brought to bear grew in significance. The evidence on the extent to which competitive pressure intensified is not entirely clear-cut but on balance indicates that losing out to rival firms was a considerably greater source of concern for public company executives at the end of the decade than at the beginning. After considering this evidence, we will turn to the reasons things changed, focusing primarily on challengers having better access to finance.

---

414 MIZRUCHI, *supra* note 159, at 190; MARK BLYTH, GREAT TRANSFORMATIONS: ECONOMIC IDEAS AND INSTITUTIONAL CHANGE IN THE TWENTIETH CENTURY 182–83 (2002).

415 GERALD MAYER, UNION MEMBERSHIP TRENDS IN THE UNITED STATES 22 (2004) (calculated using non-agricultural workers as the denominator).

416 Unionstats.com, *Union Membership and Coverage Database from the CPS*, available at http://unionstats.gsu.edu/ (accessed Apr. 6, 2018).

417 WELLS, *supra* note 401, at 133.

418 *Id.*; David Pauly, *High Tech's Challenge*, NEWSWEEK, Sept. 5, 1983, 53.

419 Ian Hargreaves, *Unions Seem Powerless to Hold Grip on Workers*, FIN. TIMES, June 16, 1981, US Finance and Investment, iv; *The Rise and Fall of Big Labor*, NEWSWEEK, Sept. 5, 1983, 50; Ralph Gomory & Richard Sylla, *The American Corporation*, DAEDALUS, Spring 2013, at 102, 108.

420 This continued a pattern from the 1970s. See Chapter 3, notes 402–4 and accompanying text.

421 Lorraine Branham, *A Bumpy Ride for Labor*, BALT. SUN, Dec. 25, 1983, K1; Robert M. Bleiberg, *"More" Is Less and Less*, BARRON'S, Feb. 24, 1986, 66; JOHN EHRMAN, THE EIGHTIES: AMERICA IN THE AGE OF REAGAN 107 (2005).

422 Branham, *supra* note 421.

The Pressure Mounts

Management professor Glenn Yago suggested in 1993 "(i)n the 1980s, bigness ceased to be an advantage in corporate America."[423] Gary Hamel and C.K. Prahalad, experts on management strategy, elaborated on this in their 1994 book *Competing for the Future.* They said that while "the watchword for management in top companies" had for decades been "steady as she goes," "few companies that began the 1980s as industry leaders ended the decade with their leadership intact and undiminished."[424] They cited IBM, Texas Instruments, Boeing, Bank of America, Sears, Westinghouse, DuPont, and Pan Am as examples of leading firms that "saw their success eroded or destroyed."[425] "Few firms, they said, "seemed to be in control of their own destiny."[426]

Available data provides a somewhat mixed picture, but on balance suggests that for larger companies pressure from rivals indeed ramped up in the 1980s. Contrary to what would be expected if competition was proliferating the collective market share of the biggest firms in the manufacturing, wholesale, and retail sectors increased between 1982 and 1992, likely because of horizontal mergers occurring with greater frequency due to relaxed antitrust scrutiny of such transactions.[427] On the other hand, annual turnover of companies in the *Fortune* 500 was considerably higher in the 1980s than it was in the 1950s, 1960s, or 1970s, implying the relative stability of these decades had come to an end.[428] Likewise, the fact the assets of *Fortune* 500 companies fell throughout the 1980s as a proportion of those of the entire nonfinancial private sector suggests the market power of large companies declined as the decade proceeded.[429]

While the statistical evidence is somewhat mixed, by the second half of the 1980s there was a general consensus that pressure from market rivals was intensifying markedly. Harvard Business School academic D. Quinn Mills said in his 1985 book *The New Competitors* "(t)his is the age of the new competition, of the toppling of many old and established companies and the building of great new ones, an age in which adaptation is the greatest virtue."[430] *Business Week* told readers in 1986 "(t)he large US corporation is not the unassailable citadel it once was."[431] Tom Peters declared in 1988 "(n)o company" was "safe" or could "take anything in its market for granted."[432] John Kotter, another Harvard Business School professor, argued the same year that a "new competitive intensity" had "turned a few cozy oligopolistic arenas into

---

423 Yago, *supra* note 157, at 205.

424 Gary Hamel & C.K. Prahalad, Competing for the Future 5 (1994). See also Marina v.N. Whitman, New World, New Rules: The Changing Role of the American Corporation 8 (1998).

425 Hamel & Prahalad, *supra* note 424, at 5–6.

426 *Id.* at 6.

427 *Supra* note 184 and related discussion; Fredric L. Pryor, *New Trends in US Industrial Concentration*, 18 Rev. Indust. Org. 301, 308–09, 316–17 (2001).

428 Whitman, *supra* note 424, at 9; Dane Stangler & Sam Arbesman, *What Does Fortune 500 Turnover Mean*, Ewing Marion Kauffman Foundation Working Paper 5–8 (2012).

429 Lawrence J. White, *Aggregate Concentration in the United States*, 16 J. Econ. Persp. 137, 144–45 (2002).

430 D. Quinn Mills, The New Competitors: A Report on American Managers 19 (1985).

431 *American Business Has a New Kingpin: The Investment Banker*, Bus. Wk., Nov. 24, 1986, 77.

432 Tom Peters, *Facing Up to the Need for a Management Revolution*, Calif. Mgmt. Rev., Winter 1988, at 8, 15.

battlefields" and had created "a level of turbulence that is sometimes extraordinary, especially when compared with the 1950s and 1960s."[433]

The growth in competitive pressure occurring in the 1980s had a strong foreign dimension.[434] By the end of the 1970s the success foreign corporations were enjoying, seemingly at the expense of US companies, was casting doubt on the capabilities of American executives.[435] The foreign challenge grew in prominence in the 1980s, with imported goods accounting for 19 percent of all products sold in the United States in 1986 as compared with 13.4 percent in 1980.[436]

There was during the 1980s widespread awareness that foreign competition was putting pressure on American corporations and their executives. *Barron's*, in a survey of events occurring in 1982, labeled the Japanese worker "(t)he most feared person in the world."[437] Nor was the competitive challenge restricted to Japanese companies. The *Financial Times* referred in 1986 to "(d)estruction and creation, endless and incessant: the tempo of management becomes quicker and quicker as competition emerges from countries regarded two decades ago as subjects only for the *National Geographic* magazine."[438]

The growth in competitive pressure on larger American firms in the 1980s also had a substantial domestic component. Entrepreneurial values were being hailed,[439] which provided a congenial setting for the growth of companies that could and would challenge incumbents. *Fortune*, in a 1988 article on America's fastest growing companies, christened "the billion-dollar kids," observed somewhat breathlessly

> Innovative, opportunistic, above all entrepreneurial, they are romping through the ranks of the *Fortune* 500 like grade-schoolers at a Saturday afternoon picnic. The speed of their ascent is mind-boggling. At the beginning of the decade most members of this Shirley Temple set were mere startups, and a few didn't exist. Suddenly in American business, a childhood fantasy is coming true: You don't have to wait to grow big.[440]

As *Fortune* acknowledged with the companies it focused on in its 1988 article, "(w)hen the rocket lifts off, a lot of companies can't hang on."[441] This was the case, for example, with Businessland, a pioneering California-based computer retailer that called it quits in 1991.[442] Other "billion-dollar kids," however, did mount successful challenges to major American companies. For instance, Compaq made its way into the *Fortune* 500 in 1986 faster than

---

433 John P. Kotter, The Leadership Factor 6 (1988).

434 *Id.* at 5–6; Frederic L. Pryor, Economic Evolution and Structure: The Impact of Complexity on the US Economic System 90 (1996).

435 Chapter 3, notes 93–95 and related discussion.

436 *America's Leanest*, *supra* note 364 (citing data compiled by economist Paul Krugman).

437 Jaye Scholl, *1982: A Year to Remember*, Barron's, Dec. 27, 1982, 62.

438 *Incessantly Destroying the Old, Relentlessly Creating the New*, Fin. Times, July 24, 1986, Work: Financial Times Special Report, 5.

439 *Supra* notes 16–18, 21–30 and related discussion.

440 Stuart Gannes & Edward Pruitt, *America's Fastest Growing Companies*, Fortune, May 23, 1988, 28.

441 *Id.*

442 Laurence Hooper, *JWP to Buy Businessland for Cash, Stock*, Wall St. J., June 5, 1991, A4.

any other company ever by manufacturing a portable computer that outsold IBM's seven to one though IBM was one hundred times Compaq's size.[443] Reebok, having capitalized on a 1980s aerobics craze, moved so successfully into the athletic footwear market that there was speculation that rival Nike had "hit the wall" just a few years after Nike had successfully challenged West German shoe giants Adidas and Puma.[444] Phil Knight, Nike founder and chief executive confessed "(w)e got a little arrogant. Then everything changed."[445]

These were by no means isolated examples. Apple Computers, for instance, offered its own potent challenge to IBM during the 1980s. While Compaq and dozens of rivals manufactured computers with IBM licensed operating systems, Apple opted to use its own proprietary operating system and sought to distinguish itself in a crowded market with a Macintosh PC characterized by ease of use and high-level graphic capabilities.[446] In the retailing sector, department store chains such as Sears and Woodward & Lothrop were left reeling. "Category killer" specialty discount stores such as Tower Records, Circuit City, and Home Depot "suck(ed) up market share like crazy" by carrying all brands of a major type of good, by hiring knowledgeable staff, by engaging in potent marketing, and by taking advantage of immense buying power to drive down prices.[447]

There was a tendency as the 1980s drew to a close to assume that the growing competitive pressure previously cozy incumbents were facing was pushing the American economy in the right direction. *Business Week* said in 1987 there was "a new, hard nosed approach to business in the US" with "the leanest and meanest" offering "America's best shot at turning back a tide of foreign competition."[448] The *Los Angeles Times* indicated the same year that "major US corporations" were "in fit shape" and that "US industry has reshaped itself to meet the requirements of a new global reality."[449] Louis Galambos and Joseph Pratt offered a similar verdict in their 1988 analysis of US business during the twentieth century. They said "as competition became more intense, many companies found they had to be more nimble in taking advantage of market opportunities and new technologies" and suggested "(r)econstruction along these lines seems to have succeeded in making US companies more efficient and innovative."[450]

With a mild recession occurring as the 1990s got underway, criticism of 1980s economic trends replaced late 1980s optimism.[451] For instance, Bill Clinton, in his successful 1992 presidential campaign, repeatedly characterized the 1980s as a lost decade economically.[452] Later

---

[443] Barbara Bradley, *The Dull Dizzy Rise of Compaq*, CHRISTIAN SCI. M., May 27, 1986, 25.

[444] John Heins, *Looking for That Strong Finish*, FORBES, May 4, 1987, 74.

[445] *Id.*

[446] *Apple's New Crusade*, BUS. WK., Nov. 26, 1984, 146; ALFRED D. CHANDLER, INVENTING THE ELECTRONIC CENTURY: THE EPIC STORY OF THE CONSUMER ELECTRONICS AND COMPUTER INDUSTRIES 145–46 (2001).

[447] EHRMAN, *supra* note 421, at 124.

[448] *America's Leanest, supra* note 364.

[449] Flanigan, *supra* note 316.

[450] LOUIS GALAMBOS & JOSEPH PRATT, THE RISE OF THE CORPORATE COMMONWEALTH: UNITED STATES BUSINESS AND PUBLIC POLICY IN THE 20TH CENTURY 232, 233 (1988).

[451] On economic trends in the early 1990s, see Chapter 5, notes 37–39 and related discussion. For a summary of the views of leading critics, see MYRON H. ROSS, A GALE OF CREATIVE DESTRUCTION: THE COMING ECONOMIC BOOM, 1992–2020, at 11–30 (1989).

[452] RICHARD B. MCKENZIE, WHAT WENT RIGHT IN THE 1980S i (1994).

in the 1990s, however, with the US economy flourishing,[453] the surge in competitive pressure with which the 1980s had become associated was again cast in a favorable light. Robert Kuttner, an economist often skeptical of the veracity of market forces, conceded in 1997 "(l)arge corporations . . . emerged from the trauma of the 1970s and 1980s as lean and mean competitors."[454] George Baker and George David Smith, management professors at Harvard and NYU respectively, said in 1998 that by 1990 "America's entrepreneurial resilience was no longer in doubt" and "even . . . rust-belt corporations were regaining much of the vitality" as various "corporate excesses . . . had been brought to heel."[455]

Why Did Competition Intensify?

During the 1980s "category killer" retailers were not the only competitors putting heretofore dominant department store chains on the back foot. Wal-Mart, named company of the decade by Tom Peters, was another potent threat.[456] Wal-Mart gained ground rapidly due to its customer-friendly reputation, its ability to drive hard bargains with suppliers well aware of the retailer's success, and its pioneering use of information technology for tracking inventory and analyzing sales data.[457] Technological change fostered challenges to entrenched incumbents elsewhere in the economy as well.[458] Nimble up-and-coming industrial firms could match economies of scale incumbents enjoyed more readily than had formerly been the case because miniaturization had reduced optimal factory size dramatically and because computer-aided engineering had cut the length of design-to-manufacture cycles.[459]

Other factors that contributed to the increase in competitive intensity in the 1980s have already been discussed. One was the continuing rise of foreign rivals.[460] Deregulation also was a catalyst, at least in the industries specifically targeted.[461] A *Business Week* columnist said in 1987 "(d)eregulation . . . has exposed managerial complacency and inefficient practices caused by years of shelter from market forces."[462] The *Washington Post*, assessing the economic record of "Reaganomics" during the summer of 1988, observed that "(d)eregulation . . . sharply increased competition and held down prices in areas such as trucking, airlines and railroads."[463]

Improved access to finance was a final factor during the 1980s that provided a substantial boost to firms minded to challenge entrenched incumbents.[464] In the 1950s and 1960s

---

453 Chapter 5, notes 52–53, 64–66 and related discussion.

454 Robert Kuttner, *Foreword, in* BENNETT HARRISON, LEAN & MEAN: WHY LARGE CORPORATIONS WILL CONTINUE TO DOMINATE THE GLOBAL ECONOMY xiii (1997).

455 GEORGE P. BAKER & GEORGE DAVID SMITH, THE NEW FINANCIAL CAPITALISTS: KOHLBERG KRAVIS ROBERTS AND THE CREATION OF CORPORATE VALUE 24–25 (1998).

456 Peters, *supra* note 30.

457 *Id.*; EHRMAN, *supra* note 421, at 124.

458 *The Rise and Rise of America's Small Firms*, ECONOMIST, Jan. 21, 1989, 89; J. Fred Weston & Kwang S. Chung, *Takeovers and Corporate Restructuring: An Overview*, BUS. ECON., Apr. 1990, 6, 7.

459 Peters, *supra* note 432, at 14.

460 *Supra* notes 434–38 and related discussion.

461 KOTTER, *supra* note 433, at 5–6.

462 Judith H. Dobrzynski, *Why Nothing Seem to Make a Dent in Dealmaking*, BUS. WK., July 20, 1987, 75.

463 Robert Munn, *Don't Knock Reaganomics*, WASH. POST, July 24, 1988, 41.

464 Yago, *supra* note 157, 205–06.

capital was allocated conservatively. This helped to insulate powerful incumbents from market competition but typically did not impinge substantially on managerial discretion in these dominant firms because they were generating substantial retained earnings.[465] In the 1970s, commercial banks, investment banks, and the venture capital (VC) industry liberalized access to capital to some degree but the basic pattern remained unchanged.[466] In contrast, in the 1980s access to finance expanded considerably and did so in a way that was potentially liberating for ambitious executives, whether from companies that were already large or from fledgling businesses aiming to grow. The change was particularly dramatic for smaller enterprises because the luxury of falling back on retained earnings was unlikely to be available to them. Executives of such firms could increasingly count on having the financial wherewithal required to challenge entrenched incumbents, on the assumption they could run a sufficiently tight ship to ensure there was sufficient cash flow to service borrowing undertaken.[467]

As the 1980s went on, contemporaries frequently remarked upon how much easier it had become for companies to raise finance. Ira Harris, a Chicago investment banker, warned in 1985 "(i)t's getting a little nutty. We've seen the greatest addition to outstanding corporate debt this country has ever seen."[468] The *Los Angeles Times* said in 1989 of the 1980s "(o)ld rules about prudent limits on borrowing gave way as new free-spending managers, like aircraft test pilots, launched venture after venture to test the outer limits of indebtedness."[469] The editor of *Grant's Interest Rate Observer* suggested more pithily the same year that "the 1980s are to debt what the 1960s were to sex."[470]

Junk bonds, which first became a meaningful part of American corporate finance in the late 1970s,[471] were a core element of the new corporate finance regime. The *Chicago Tribune* said in 1989 "in the space of about a decade the high-yield junk bond market has become so broad, so deep and so liquid that it has altered the way companies are financed and the way corporations look at debt."[472] Junk bonds achieved notoriety in large measure due to their use in the market for corporate control. According to a 1991 study of junk bonds, "it was assumed—until junk bonds came along—that only a bigger company could muster the resources to buy up all the shares [in a public company]. Junk bonds changed all that. . . ."[473] Crucially, though, for present purposes, the impact of junk bonds on corporate America was pronounced outside the takeover realm too, as "the market for junk debt empowered entrepreneurs."[474]

A 1986 congressional report noted junk bonds had only been deployed to finance takeovers for a couple of years. Prior to that, the junk bond market was "used primarily to raise

---

[465] Chapter 2, notes 386–89, 428–30 and related discussion.

[466] Chapter 3, notes 425–26, 442–48, 463–66, 478–81, 486–88 and accompanying text.

[467] *The Bills Are Coming Due*, Bus. Wk., Sept. 11, 1989, 84.

[468] Herb Greenberg, *Junk-Bond Junkies*, Chi. Trib., Oct. 20, 1985, D1.

[469] Paul Richter, *In Decade of the Big Deals, Rules Were Rewritten*, LA Times, Dec. 17, 1989, D1.

[470] James Grant, *Michael Milken, Meet Sewell Avery*, Forbes, Oct. 23, 1989, 60.

[471] Chapter 3, notes 469–74 and related discussion.

[472] Pat Widder, *Corporate Makeovers*, Chi. Trib., June 25, 1989, E1.

[473] Fenton Bailey, The Junk Bond Revolution: Michael Milken, Wall Street & The Roaring Eighties 73–74 (1991).

[474] *Junk Bonds Finally Face the Acid Test*, Bus. Wk., Nov. 16, 1987, 64.

funds for the general operations of companies whose credit ratings were below investment grade."[475] Throughout the 1980s, in fact, the market for corporate control was something of a sideshow for junk bonds. Nearly four-fifths of the $215 billion of high yield debt raised during the decade was used to expand or rebuild firms, rather than for acquisitions.[476] Felix Rohatyn, a prominent Lazard Frères investment banker who bemoaned in the 1980s debt market excesses,[477] nevertheless acknowledged subsequently that "(t)he junk bond was ... particularly appealing to new entrepreneurs who previously would not have had access to the capital markets."[478]

It was no accident that growth of the junk bond market was a boon for the sort of firms likely to be formulating challenges to incumbents. Michael Milken, the junk bond impresario at Drexel Burnham Lambert, said that the most pleasurable part of his work was arranging financing for ambitious small- and medium-sized enterprises seeking to step up.[479] Drexel put in place junk bond financing for challengers that enjoyed substantial success in a variety of industries, including cable television (Cablevision, Turner Broadcasting, and Viacom), manufacturing (Duracell), retailing (Barnes & Noble and Calvin Klein) and telecommunications (MCI and McCaw Cellular).[480] Drexel junk bonds also financed casino development. Steve Wynn, who would revive the Las Vegas Strip with hotels built at the end of the 1980s and at the beginning of the 1990s, said of Milken in 1988 "I love him. He is my favorite living human, he and my wife."[481]

Drexel Burnham Lambert's dominance of junk bonds tailed off to some degree during the 1980s, with its market share dropping from 68 percent in 1984 to 50 percent in 1988.[482] This was because "Wall Street firms that at first laughed at Mr. Milken and his unorthodox tool" changed gears and set up their own junk bond shops to tap into the lucrative market for high-yield corporate debt.[483] *Forbes* described evocatively in 1985 how elite investment bank Morgan Stanley made the move:

> The image of Morgan Stanley & Co. is as remote from that of junk bonds as Chanel No. 5 is from underarm deodorant. So when Morgan, snootiest of investment banking houses, announced a major move into the junk bond business dominated by the arriviste firm of Drexel Burnham Lambert, it was like the lord of the manor taking up mud wrestling. The lure was irresistible, however.[484]

---

[475] Congressional Research Service, *Corporate Mergers and High Yield (Junk) Bonds: Recent Market Trends and Regulatory Developments* 1 (1986).

[476] Yago, *supra* note 157, at 216.

[477] Felix Rohatyn, *Institutional "Investor" or Speculator?*, Wall St. J., June 24, 1988, 18.

[478] Felix Rohatyn, Dealings: A Political and Financial Life 166 (2010).

[479] Robert Sobel, When Giants Stumble 173 (1999).

[480] *Id.* at 172.

[481] David Vise, *Michael Milken: A Dream-Maker's "Nightmare,"* Wash. Post, Nov. 20, 1988, H1. See also Tom Gorman, *Casino Mogul Wynn Is Biggest Player around Las Vegas*, LA Times, Aug. 12, 1993, WA6. Steve Wynn and his wife would divorce in 2010 and she would subsequently become the largest shareholder in the resort empire Wynn led after he sold his stake in response to allegations of sexual misconduct. See James B. Stewart, *The Other Wynn Holds a Stake. And Has a Say*, NY Times, May 11, 2018, B1.

[482] Sarah Bartlett, *A Corporate Milestone*, NY Times, Oct. 26, 1988, A1.

[483] James Sterngold, *"Junk Bond" Revolution Will Outlive Its Creator*, NY Times, Mar. 30, 1989, D23.

[484] Allan Sloan, *Red Faces at Morgan Stanley*, Forbes, July 29, 1985, 43.

For investment banks such as Morgan Stanley the move into the junk bond market was part of a broader revamping of their business model that expanded access to finance for corporate clients. During the managerial capitalism era investment banking was a clubby affair, with corporate customers being loyal to a single investment bank and refraining from shopping around for better terms.[485] This sort of arrangement was under challenge in the 1970s.[486] Before the 1980s concluded long-term investment banking relationships had become largely passé, displaced by "transactional" arrangements where "(w)hatever investment house had the best idea for a deal won the business—and the fees—until the next proposal came along."[487]

In this new transactionally-oriented world of corporate finance, investment banking firms "began hand-to-hand combat to win clients."[488] Having suggested "contemporary investment bankers bear about as much resemblance to their 1960s counterparts as the [supersonic jet] Concorde does to the Wright Bros. plane," *Business Week* warned in 1986 that "in their increasingly aggressive pursuit of self-interest the investment banks clearly are antagonizing their traditional corporate clients."[489] In fact, the change from relationship to transactional investment banking was a two-way street. Corporate executives increasingly looked to shop around as and when required to obtain financing under as favorable circumstances as possible.[490] With companies contemplating challenging dominant players in a market sector, the new approach could make available strategic choices financial constraints would have previously foreclosed. Sanford Sigoloff, chief executive of retailer Wickes Companies, made the point to *Business Week*, saying "(t)here are a lot of new opportunities available for smart CEOs who understand the changing financial markets."[491]

A 1982 rule change by the Securities and Exchange Commission that provided for what was known as shelf registration accelerated the switch from relationship to transactional investment banking.[492] Prior to 1982 a company seeking to issue new securities to the public would register with the SEC and then wait a mandatory three week "cooling-off" period before proceeding. During this period, under the tutelage of the company's investment bank acting as lead underwriter, buyers would be found for the securities, meaning the investment bank would not have to commit any of its own funds.[493] Under the shelf registration procedure introduced in 1982 experienced issuers that filed properly prepared preliminary papers in anticipation of issuing new securities could proceed for a period of up to two years after filing and do so without regard for the cooling-off period.[494] A company could register without listing its underwriters, which set the scene for intense post-shelf registration competition

---

[485] Chapter 2, notes 408–10 and related discussion; Chapter 3, notes 449–51 and accompanying text.

[486] Chapter 3, notes 452–56, 460–62 and related discussion.

[487] Karen W. Arenson, *How Wall Street Bred an Ivan Boesky*, NY Times, Nov. 23, 1986, F1.

[488] Michael Blumstein, *Creating New Financial Products*, NY Times, Aug. 8, 1982, F6.

[489] *American Business, supra* note 431.

[490] Geisst, *supra* note 65, at 332.

[491] *Changing Role, supra* note 320.

[492] Sobel, *supra* note 69, at 124; Krier, *supra* note 324, at 35–36.

[493] Charles R. Geisst, The Last Partnerships: Inside the Great Wall Street Money Dynasties 205 (2001).

[494] 17 C.F.R. 230.415 (2018).

among investment bankers for the right to "buy the deal."[495] One investment banker said "(w)e're moving from the traditional concept of marriage to one-night stands."[496]

Corporate clients were favorably disposed toward the new transactional approach to underwriting shelf registration precipitated, with the streamlined process facilitating the issuance of securities at an opportune time.[497] The adjustment was more fraught for investment banks. Not only did they have to compete for underwriting business in an unfamiliar manner but they also needed capital in a way they had not previously because they knew clients would expect to receive up front the funds generated by an offering, leaving the investment banks to find buyers of securities issued at their own risk.[498] The introduction of the shelf registration rule correspondingly encouraged those investment banks that had continued to operate as partnerships through to the 1980s to bolster their financial wherewithal by incorporating and carrying out a public offering of shares or by becoming a division of a deep-pocketed corporate buyer.[499]

Changes investment banks made to compete for shelf registration business did not occur in isolation. Financial innovation was a hallmark of the new investment banking world of the 1980s. According to Rohatyn, "(i)n the wake of Drexel's success, the entire financial industry tried to come up with ways to provide increased credit for clients. New instruments were invented."[500] The *Wall Street Journal* made the same point in 1987, saying that "(a)ided by computers and mathematical whizzes lured away from universities, Wall St. created exotic financing vehicles that allowed corporations to raise money in new ways."[501] The *Wall Street Journal* specifically mentioned as an example securitization, the packaging of business loans into securities for sale to investors, a process that began growing in popularity in the late 1970s.[502]

Commercial banks, as with investment banks, were changing their business model in the 1980s in ways that liberalized access to capital for ambitious corporate executives. Commercial banks by no means entirely abandoned the conservative, cautious mindset that prevailed in the middle decades of the twentieth century.[503] A 1990 study of an evolving banking sector offered the caveat "(c)hange, in many ways, is antithetical to banking, which is an industry fundamentally tied to confidence."[504] Moreover, with most banking regulation being left untouched by the Reagan administration's deregulatory efforts,[505] if American

---

495 Ken Auletta, Greed and Glory on Wall Street: The Fall of the House of Lehman 139 (1986).

496 Sobel, *supra* note 69, at 124.

497 Geisst, *supra* note 65, at 332; Crawford & Sihler, *supra* note 329, at 87.

498 Crawford & Sihler, *supra* note 329, at 87; Geisst, *supra* note 493, at 206.

499 Auletta, *supra* note 495, at 140; Clemens P. Work, *The House of Morgan Goes Public*, US News & World Report, Feb. 10, 1986, 48; Myron Magnet & Margaret A. Elliot, *The Decline and Fall of Business Ethics*, Fortune, Dec. 8, 1986, 65.

500 Rohatyn, *supra* note 478, at 168.

501 Steve Swartz & Bryan Burrough, *Crash Could Weaken Wall Street's Grip on Corporate America*, Wall St. J., Dec. 29, 1987, 1.

502 Henry Kaufman, On Money and Markets: A Wall Street Memoir 53–54 (2000).

503 Chapter 2, notes 391, 394–97 and accompanying text; Chapter 3, note 426 and related discussion.

504 Jeremy F. Taylor, The Process of Change in American Banking: Political Economy and the Public Purpose 13 (1990).

505 *Supra* note 395 and accompanying text.

bankers had sought to engage in investment banking practices "universal" banks elsewhere in the world undertook, the bankers "would have had to run their banks from jail."[506]

While commercial banking was not entirely turned on its head in the 1980s, the status quo was also not a realistic option. A banker at Chase Manhattan, a large New York-headquartered financial institution, observed in 1987, "(t)he most unaffordable luxury in today's banking environment is traditionalist thinking. A corporate culture that remains rooted in the business as usual philosophy must be revised to adjust to the new world of the financial services industry."[507] The *Financial Times* reasoned similarly that year in a survey of American banking, saying "US commercial banks are facing probably the greatest upheaval in the history of their industry since the 1930s. Increased competition, combined with falling profits and deteriorating asset quality have contributed to a sense of unease."[508] Rivals for commercial banks were not restricted to the banking sector but also included "non-banks" entering into parts of the banking business without exposing themselves to the full panoply of banking regulation.[509] Examples included brokerage firms, insurance companies, and finance companies affiliated with large non-financial enterprises such as General Electric, General Motors, and Sears.[510]

Banks, despite their continuing bias toward caution, took steps to adjust to the new conditions. The *Los Angeles Times* said in 1987 "(a)fter decades of being virtually somnambulant, the banking industry is waking up."[511] A 1990 study of the approach CEOs of major banks were taking to address the challenges their industry faced even suggested "(b)anking is one of the more, if not the most, dynamic industries in American today."[512]

One change commercial banks made to respond to the increased competition they were facing was to relax credit standards and lend to riskier categories of borrower, including in the corporate sector.[513] Often the debt would not end up on the banks' own balance sheets because they were increasingly engaging in securitization that entailed turning around and selling their loans in pieces to other financial institutions.[514] Still, risky business loans could pose dangers. Continental Illinois, one of the 10 largest banks in the country, nearly collapsed in 1984 due in part to loan participations with an Oklahoma bank that had cut corners amidst intense competition to lend to oil, gas, and coal producers.[515]

---

506 Mark J. Roe, Strong Managers, Weak Owners: The Political Roots of American Corporate Finance 190 (1994).

507 Eric N. Compton, The New World of Commercial Banking 45 (1987).

508 William Hall, *Enter the Super-Regionals*, Fin. Times, June 16, 1987, US Finance and Investment, 11.

509 Susan Dentzer, *A Bank's a Bank—Or Is It?*, Newsweek, Nov. 12, 1984, 83.

510 Nathaniel C. Nash, *In the Darwinian Age of Global Finance, Only Megabanks May Survive*, NY Times. June 26, 1988, E6; Michael Klausner, *An Economic Analysis of Bank Regulatory Reform: The Financial Institutions Safety and Consumer Choice Act 1991*, 69 Wash. U. L.Q. 695, 727 (1991).

511 Douglas Frantz, *Banking: Technology Creates Need for Versatility*, LA Times, Sept. 20, 1987, R11.

512 Richard B. Miller, American Banking in Crisis: Views From Leading Financial Services CEOs 39 (1990).

513 Wilmarth, *supra* note 160, at 313; Lowell L. Bryan, *A Blueprint for Financial Reconstruction*, Harv. Bus. Rev., May/June 1991, 73, 77.

514 Bartlett, *supra* note 482; Bryan, *supra* note 513, at 76.

515 Timothy A. Canova, *The Transformation of US Banking and Finance: From Regulated Competition to Free-Market Receivership*, 60 Brook. L. Rev. 1295, 1328 (1995); Federal Deposit Insurance Corporation, History of the Eighties: Lessons for the Future, Volume I 44 (1997).

Financing takeovers was one type of higher-risk corporate lending in which commercial banks engaged in the 1980s.[516] *Forbes*, seeking to explain to readers in 1985 why no company was safe from a takeover, said "(w)ithout cooperation from the banks, all this would not have evolved. Banks practically throw money at takeover deals because acquisition loans carry high rates and fat fees at a time when bank profits are under pressure."[517] Commercial banks had traditionally shunned takeover lending.[518] Their stance was much different by the early 1980s as they relaxed their approach to lending markedly to underwrite M&A activity.[519] By 1985, according to *Business Week*, banks stood "ready to provide copious quantities of debt financing for any deal that makes a shred of sense on paper."[520] Banks paused to some degree due to complaints by corporate clients that feared becoming targets.[521] Nevertheless, between 1980 and 1988 banks provided 73 percent of the debt financing underpinning tender offers as compared with 10 percent for junk bonds.[522]

For businesses seeking to challenge incumbents venture capital was an additional potential source of financing that grew in significance in the 1980s. Venture capital was indeed cited, often enthusiastically, as a key resource available to ambitious entrepreneurs. A *Hartford Courant* columnist said in 1983 "(a)nyone who insists it is impossible to get money to start a business these days does not know what is going on in the world of venture capital."[523] *Time* added, somewhat breathlessly, in 1986, "America's celebrated capacity for ceaseless business fertility owes much to a special class of high-risk, high-reward investors known as venture capitalists. In Old Testament fashion, they scatter bread upon the entrepreneurial waters, financing chancy new products in hopes of reaping long-term rewards."[524] Tom Peters, explaining in 1988 why for management "(p)redictability is a thing of the past," said "(n)ew competitors financed by venture capital . . . spring up like mushrooms."[525]

New funds committed to venture capital firms grew rapidly in the early 1980s, with fresh investment in the sector growing from $700 million in 1980 to $1.4 billion in 1982 and a then-record $3.4 billion in 1983.[526] The *Christian Science Monitor* said of the trend in 1982 "(e)ntrepreneurs are encouraged by this" and quoted a venture capital journalist as saying "(t)hey are coming out of the woodwork like crazy, driven by the perception of available money."[527] Fundraising fell off from the 1983 peak during the mid-1980s when VC returns declined due to a shakeout prompted by over-investment in computer disc drives

---

516 Franklin R. Edwards, The New Finance: Regulation & Financial Stability 38 (1996).

517 Allan Sloan, *Why Is No One Safe?*, Forbes, Mar. 11, 1985, 134.

518 Patricia M. Scherschel, *Helping Fund a Takeover? You Could Get Burned*, US News & World Report, May 13, 1985, 75.

519 Wigmore, *supra* note 67, at 302.

520 *Playing with Fire*, Bus. Wk., Sept. 16, 1985, 78.

521 Arenson, *supra* note 487.

522 Yago, *supra* note 157, at 212.

523 Thomas J. O'Connor, *Venture Capital Is Plentiful*, Hartford Courant, Aug. 21, 1983, C2.

524 George Russell, Cristina Garcia & Frederick Ungeheuer, *Venture: An Exciting Game of Adventure for Well-Heeled Investors*, Time, June 16, 1986, 56.

525 Peters, *supra* note 432, at 14.

526 Cynthia A. Beltz, *Introduction*, *in* Financing Entrepreneurs 1, 14 (Cynthia A. Beltz ed., 1994).

527 Francine Kiefer, *Venture Capital Running Strong for Fledgling Businesses*, Christian Sci. Monitor, July 30, 1982, 11.

and personal computers.[528] New capital committed to VC firms nevertheless amounted to $13 billion between 1984 and 1987, including $4.2 billion in 1987, the peak for the decade.[529] Fund-raising fell off again in 1988 and 1989 as VC returns took a hit when a chilly market for initial public offerings prompted by the October 1987 stock market crash made profitable exits much more difficult.[530] Nevertheless, assets under management by VC firms increased each year through the 1980s, with the total being $4.5 billion in 1980, $19.6 billion in 1985, and $33.4 billion in 1989.[531]

While the growth of the venture capital industry eased restrictions on access to finance for fledgling businesses, many credible, ambitious entrepreneurs would not have benefitted. According to a 1990 study of innovation and small firms "(a)lthough the venture capital market has been growing at rapid rates in recent years it still affects only a miniscule portion of all firms, large or small."[532] In the 1980s, no more than 1 percent of start-up companies in the United States accessed venture capital funding.[533] Moreover, most VC-backed companies operated in high-technology industries.[534] As the *US News & World Report* said in 1987 "(f)irst-time entrepreneurs have their best chances of winning attention—and funding—in hot high-tech niches."[535] Venture capital thus was not a universally available tonic. Nevertheless, the expansion of the venture capital industry in the 1980s, combined with increased dynamism among commercial and investment banks, should have left upstarts better prepared fiscally to mount challenges to dominant firms than would have been the case in the 1950s, 1960s, and 1970s. Pressure on public company executives should have ratcheted up in turn.

The Public Company Executive in Transition

In an analysis of changes affecting chief executives between 1890 and 2015 sociologists Mark Mizruchi and Limroy Marshall have said of the 1980s "(t)he environment within which corporate chief executives operated was, in a relatively brief period, turned upside down."[536] It indeed was in various ways a dizzying decade for those running US public companies. Entrepreneurial acumen substantially discounted during the heyday of managerial capitalism was suddenly in vogue. A market for corporate control operating at an unprecedented level of intensity meant that executives who might have preferred to balance shareholder interests with those of other corporate constituencies were under an onus to treat stockholder returns as a top managerial priority. Market power that had provided executives of dominant firms

[528] Beltz, *supra* note 526, at 19–20; Buzz Wooley, *Realism Tempers Venture Capital*, LA TIMES, Jan. 7, 1986, SD, C2A; William Dawkins, *A Steep and Painful Learning Curve*, FIN. TIMES, May 30, 1986, 22.

[529] Beltz, *supra* note 526, at 14.

[530] *Id.* at 22; Andrew Pollack, *Venture Capital Loses Its Vigor*, NY TIMES, Oct. 8, 1989, F1.

[531] Beltz, *supra* note 526, at 21.

[532] ZOLTAN J. ACS & DAVID B. AUDRETSCH, INNOVATION AND SMALL FIRMS 71 (1990).

[533] *Id.*; Richard Florida, *Keep Government Out of Venture Capital*, *in* FINANCING, *supra* note 526, at 51, 53.

[534] William A. Sahlman, *The Structure and Governance of Venture-Capital Organizations* 27 J. FIN. ECON. 473, 475 (1990).

[535] Andrea Gabor, *Here Come the Venture Capitalists—Again*, US NEWS & WORLD REPORT, May 18, 1987, 52.

[536] Mark S. Mizruchi & Limroy J. Marshall, *Corporate CEOs, 1890–2015: Titans, Bureaucrats, and Saviors*, 42 ANN. REV. SOCIOLOGY 143, 150 (2016).

with a buffer during the managerial capitalism era ebbed away as competitors, both domestic and foreign, pushed incumbents hard.

There were, however, compensations for 1980s executives. Depending on the industry involved, those seeking to press advantages their firms had would have had additional room to maneuver due to deregulation and organized labor's waning influence. There also was greater access to capital needed to scale up to challenge rivals and to carry out acquisitions. In addition, as we will see now, those executives who navigated the 1980s successfully could anticipate being paid considerably more than their managerial capitalism counterparts. They could also achieve public notoriety unfamiliar to mid-twentieth century executives. Indeed, the 1980s did much to pave the way for the "imperial" chief executive who would take center stage by the end of the 1990s.[537]

There was awareness in the 1980s that it was a tumultuous period for public company executives. *Business Week* suggested in 1983 "management is beset by a variety of almost unbearable pressures" and said that "(t)o cope, managers perceive a need to scrap old ways of doing things."[538] Four years later, an article in the same magazine on the changing role of chief executives said that "(r)ight now many CEOs are simply longing for the bygone days."[539] Stephen Harper, a management professor, indicated in 1989 that while "'(c)hange used to be sporadic,' (m)anagers are now confronted with the most broad-based, comprehensive change ever," with "(t)he corporate game ... now being played with all new rules, new opponents and on new playing fields."[540] Rosabeth Moss Kanter told *Harvard Business Review* readers the same year "(m)anagerial work is undergoing such enormous and rapid change that many managers are reinventing their profession as they go."[541]

For senior executives during the 1980s, the type of change most likely to cause them concern personally would have been an increased possibility of a forced exit, whether in the wake of a takeover or due to action by the board. Michael Jensen and coauthor Kevin Murphy said in a 1990 article on executive pay "the CEO position is not a very risky job" and indicated job security for CEOs was greater than that for a baseball manager.[542] Executives perceived things differently. The *New York Times* quoted an executive recruiter in 1984 as saying "(y)ou'd be amazed at the insecurity at high levels—it's not even a stigma to be fired any more" and observed the "threat of hostile takeovers appears to be especially troubling."[543]

Available data indicated that feelings of insecurity in the executive suite were at least to some extent justified. The proportion of large public firms recruiting a new CEO between 1983 and 1988 was nearly 13 percent, as compared with nearly 11 percent between 1971 and 1976 and 10 percent between 1977 and 1982.[544] Concomitantly CEO tenure declined, with

---

[537] Chapter 5, notes 464–65 and related discussion.

[538] *Turnover at the Top*, BUS. WK., Dec. 19, 1983, 104.

[539] *Changing Role, supra* note 320.

[540] Stephen C. Harper, *The Manager as Change Agent: "Hell No" to the Status Quo*, INDUST. MGMT., May–June 1989, 8, 8.

[541] Rosabeth Moss Kanter, *The New Managerial Work*, HARV. BUS. REV., Nov./Dec. 1989, 85, 85.

[542] Michael C. Jensen & Kevin J. Murphy, *CEO Incentives—It's Not How Much You Pay, But How*, HARV. BUS. REV., May/June 1990, 138, 142.

[543] Ann Crittenden, *The Age of "Me-First" Management*, NY TIMES, Aug. 19, 1984, F1.

[544] Mark R. Huson, Robert Parrino & Laura T. Starks, *Internal Monitoring Mechanisms and CEO Turnover: A Long-Term Perspective*, 56 J. FIN. 2265, 2275 (2001) (based on a sample of just over 1,800 CEOs).

the mean number of years *Fortune* 500 chief executives were serving falling from 9.7 in 1982 to 8.7 in 1990.[545] Most departures were voluntary, but in numerous instances the voluntariness would have been open to debate. Thomas Whisler, a management professor at the University of Chicago, said of the typical CEO in 1987 when commenting on data indicating that turnover was on the increase, "I don't think that is because he is appointed at a later age or is retiring earlier."[546]

While public company executives experienced considerable change during the 1980s, various critics of public companies suggested bureaucratic rigidity remained excessive. Eli Ginzberg, a Columbia business school academic, and George Vojta, a bank executive, argued in a 1985 book on corporations that "(t)he large enterprise, hobbled by a rigid organizational structure and a slow-responding decision-making mechanism, finds it difficult to adjust to a volatile market."[547] Richard Darman, undersecretary of the Treasury, assailed in 1986 America's "corpocracy," drawing attention is so doing to "large-scale corporate America's tendency to be like the government bureaucracy that corporate executives love to malign: bloated, risk-averse, inefficient and unimaginative."[548] Entrepreneurs, in a decade where there was growing admiration of entrepreneurial flair,[549] generally felt large US companies were "lumbering bureaucracies that have lost the creative, competitive drive that accounted for their growth in the first place."[550] For instance, Ross Perot, in the midst of his brief mid-1980s stint as an entrepreneurial catalyst for General Motors,[551] offered an evocative description of the challenge he had faced:

> I come from an environment where if you see a snake you kill it. At GM, if you see a snake, the first thing you do is go hire a consultant on snakes. Then you get a committee on snakes, and then you discuss it for a couple of years. The most likely course of action is—nothing. You figure, the snake hasn't bitten anybody yet, so you just let him crawl around on the factory floor. We need to build an environment where the first guy who sees the snake kills it.[552]

Another charge leveled against members of the "executive elite" of the 1980s was that they were "obsessed primarily with their own self-preservation."[553] Some bias in this direction was fully understandable. While investors owning shares in public companies could readily

---

[545] MIZRUCHI, *supra* note 159, 215–16.

[546] Richard B. Stolley & Marta F. Dorion, *How to Fire the CEO*, FORTUNE, Aug. 31, 1987, 38.

[547] ELI GINZBERG & GEORGE VOJTA, BEYOND HUMAN SCALE: THE LARGE CORPORATION AT RISK 218 (1985).

[548] George Melloan, *New Debate over Corporate Governance*, WALL ST. J., Nov. 11, 1986, 36.

[549] *Supra* notes 16–18, 21–30 and accompanying text.

[550] Joel Kotkin & Don Gevirtz, *Why Entrepreneurs Trust No Politician*, WASH. POST, Jan. 16, 1983, B1.

[551] *Supra* notes 45–46 and accompanying text

[552] GRAMM, *supra* note 45, 96–97, quoting from Thomas Moore, *The GM System Is Like a Blanket of Fog*, FORTUNE. Feb. 15, 1988.

[553] CHRISTOPHER MEEK, WARNER WOODWORTH & W. GIBB DYER, MANAGING BY THE NUMBERS: ABSENTEE OWNERSHIP AND THE DECLINE OF AMERICAN INDUSTRY 21 (1988).

diversify, executives were economically wedded to the firms they ran, and, "stuck with their eggs in one basket," they had strong incentives to "treat that basket cautiously."[554]

Though a bias in favor of self-preservation was to be expected, the hostile takeovers of the Deal Decade indicated starkly how shareholders could be disadvantaged. Fending off a takeover bid could save management's jobs but the stockholders would lose the opportunity to be bought out at a substantial premium.[555] A *Wall Street Journal* columnist said in 1984 that there was "no denying" in this context "that managers have been putting their own interests above those of their investors. Time and again, rather than accede to takeovers that would clearly benefit shareholders managers have ... taken steps that damaged the business but left themselves in charge."[556] Alfred Conard, a corporate law academic, argued similarly in 1988 "that as takeover bids proliferated, managers found ways to frustrate them with defensive tactics," meaning "managers not only deprived their shareholders of millions of dollars of potential gains but also insulated themselves from the discipline of future tender offers."[557]

Other observers were more optimistic about where matters stood with 1980s senior executives, particularly in the revised market context confronting public companies. The *New York Times* indicated in a 1987 article on remaking the CEO "a new set of management precepts is emerging, with profound impact on individual companies and the country as a whole. The early returns seem heartening."[558] *Business Week* concurred in its "Changing Role" article from the same year, saying "(t)he good old days are gone, and with them the old-style executive. A new hardier breed is evolving, and not a moment too soon for tomorrow's tougher corporate world."[559] It added in an article on rising corporate earnings "(s)hareholders are starting to reap the benefit of owning shares in leaner, more sharply managed companies."[560]

A bonus was that fraud and illicit self-dealing were not a major concern in the public company context. A media commentator told *Business Week* in 1987 "(t)here's a hell of a lot of dishonest behaviour going on in business these days."[561] This was an exaggeration. There was no 1980s repeat, for instance, of the widespread illicit payment revelations that cast doubt on corporate credibility in the 1970s.[562] A 1992 20th Century Fund study of corporate corruption seeking to underscore the magnitude of the problem for the reader only offered a modest list from the 1980s, comprised of improprieties related to Michael Milken's investment bank Drexel Burnham Lambert, a $115 million fine imposed on Illinois-based aerospace manufacturer Sundstrand Corp. for defense procurement fraud, a $6.85 million fine paid by Hertz Rent a Car for consumer fraud (the largest ever such fine), and a tax-dodging scheme

---

[554] George W. Dent, *Toward Unifying Ownership and Control in the Public Corporation*, [1989] WISC. L. REV. 881, 889; see also Coffee, *supra* note 49, at 13, 17–20.

[555] Alfred F. Conard, *Beyond Managerialism: Investor Capitalism?*, 22 J.L. REFORM 117, 135 (1988) ("most conspicuous divergences").

[556] John C. Boland, *Missing the Bottom Line on "Greenmail,"* WALL ST. J., July 25, 1984, 26.

[557] Conard, *supra* note 555, at 123 (footnote omitted).

[558] Steven Prokesch, *Remaking the American CEO*, NY TIMES, Jan. 25, 1987, F1.

[559] *Changing Role, supra* note 320.

[560] *What's Propelling the Market? Big, Fat Earnings*, BUS. WK., July 6, 1987, 59.

[561] *Bad Guys Wear Pinstripes*, BUS. WK., Oct. 21, 1988, 61.

[562] Chapter 3, notes 144, 152–53, 165–70, 180 and related discussion.

centered in New York City's garment district.[563] Hence, as a critique of *Den of Thieves*, a 1991 book on Wall Street skulduggery, said of the 1980s "crime did not give the decade life."[564]

While criminality was a rarity in 1980s public companies, those in charge were hardly pure-hearted altruists. Self-preservation aside, more money—a lot more money—was headed their way. The *Wall Street Journal* noted in 1988 that the pay of chief executives was "rising faster than that of their white-collar spear carriers and blue-collar workers, faster than inflation, faster than profits," meaning for CEOs, "(t)hough not quite rock star rich, they're the richest hired hands in history."[565] According to *Business Week*, total average pay for chief executives rose from $624,000 in 1980 to $1.86 million in 1989, despite having declined 9 percent from 1988.[566]

Perceptions that managerial turnover was increasing likely encouraged 1980s top executives to bargain hard. Paul Hirsch, a business professor at the University of Chicago, said in 1988, "(m)anagers are now thinking like free agents.... Like their counterparts in professional baseball they are beginning to look out for themselves."[567] Executives indeed may have been citing the case of baseball stars in making their case for higher pay. *Forbes*, in a 1986 survey of executive pay, said of CEOs "(i)f you compare their earnings with the sums paid jocks, entertainers and TV personalities and some negligence lawyers ... most chief executives would score in the middle ranks at best."[568] Executives would have been well aware of this. *US News & World Report* said in 1989, "(m)oney was the mania and the manna of the '80s. It didn't just talk, it was talked about—obsessively. How much you made. Who made more. Who made the most."[569] CEOs, in this milieu, likely argued, and plausibly so, that if athletes and entertainers "can reap fabulous rewards, why not those of proven wealth-producing talents?"[570]

The tougher competitive environment in which public companies were operating during the 1980s also likely contributed to the growth in executive compensation. Increasingly the view took hold in boardrooms that it might be necessary to hire a "corporate messiah" to cope with intensifying market pressures, and to pay what was needed to recruit and retain such top-flight talent.[571] For instance, in a 1985 article where *US News & World Report* hailed "the age of the corporate star" it explained "phone number" executive pay by quoting an

---

[563] Irwin Ross, Shady Business: Confronting Corporate Corruption 1–4 (1992) (citing also Salomon Brothers breaking rules relating to US bond auctions that came to light in the early 1990s).

[564] William Taylor, *Crime? Greed? Big Ideas? What Were the 1980s All About?*, Harv. Bus. Rev., Jan./Feb. 1992, 32, 37; James B. Stewart, Den of Thieves (1991).

[565] Amanda Bennett, *Top Dollar*, Wall St. J., Mar. 28, 1988, 1.

[566] *Pay Stubs of the Rich and Corporate*, Bus. Wk., May 7, 1990, 56; *For Whom Were the Golden Eighties Most Golden?*, Bus. Wk., May 7, 1990, 60.

[567] Jim Schachter, *An Era of No Job Guarantees*, LA Times, Sept. 18, 1988, E3. See also William G. Flanagan, *How Much the Bosses Earned in 1985*, Forbes, June 2, 1986, 150 ("Whatever chief executives make, they seldom make it for very long.... They are a lot like baseball players—with no guarantee of how long they will be at the top of their game.")

[568] Flanagan, *supra* note 567.

[569] Jack Egan, *Business: The Decade of the Deal*, US News & World Report, Dec. 25, 1989/Jan. 1, 1990, 98.

[570] Michael Novak, *The Executive Joneses*, Forbes, May 29, 1989, 94 (questioning the veracity of the logic).

[571] Patricia O'Toole, Corporate Messiah: The Hiring and Firing of Million-Dollar Managers 16–21, 27 (1984) (suggesting, though, that for many companies the idea of salvation by a new CEO was an illusion). On the argument generally, see Steven A. Bank, Brian R. Cheffins & Harwell Wells, *Executive Pay: What Worked?*, 42 J. Corp. L. 59, 96–99 (2016).

executive recruiter who said "(m)ore companies are undergoing dramatic shifts in strategy, which require different leadership."[572]

Disney's Michael Eisner provided an instructive case study of the upside for executives with the new hired gun mentality. He negotiated an incentive-laden and potentially highly lucrative managerial services contract when Disney poached him from Paramount in 1984 to turn around the troubled entertainment company, and received compensation valued at $40.1 million in 1988 following a dramatic increase in Disney's share price.[573] Raymond Watson, a Disney director, said "I know that no one is complaining. Not even Scrooge McDuck," a miserly Disney cartoon character.[574]

Top executives, in addition to being better paid, became better known. It has been suggested that "the celebrity CEO was born" in the 1980s before flourishing in the 1990s.[575] In fact, most chief executives continued to follow the managerial capitalism pattern and operated largely under the radar. A coauthored study of leading US businessmen led by Ralph Nader rhetorically asked readers in 1986 how many Americans could identify the CEOs of prominent American companies, implying the answer was very few.[576] Peter Drucker did the same in 1987.[577] *Forbes* said in a report the same year on the 800 most powerful people in corporate America few "receive as much attention as the mayor, say, of Seattle."[578] Anonymity, moreover, was ostensibly preferred. *Business Week* said in its 1987 "Changing Role" article that "being a visible spokesman of the corporation. . . . (C)an be a terrifying experience for today's corporate chiefs, most of whom have risen through the bureaucratic ranks by blending in rather than sticking out."[579] Jack Welch, appointed chief executive of General Electric in 1981 after having started his career there, declined to participate in Nader's 1986 study, saying he was "just a grungy, lousy manager. . . . I don't want a high profile. . . . I'm just a grunt."[580]

Executive reticence toward publicity, however, was eroding. A turnaround by automaker Chrysler in the early 1980s following Lee Iacocca's high-profile appointment as chief executive in 1979 "set off a chain of events that gave rise to the celebrity CEO" of the 1990s and early 2000s.[581] Iacocca, who appeared regularly in Chrysler television advertisements and published a smash hit autobiography in 1984, not only became the first businessperson to

---

572 Clemens P. Work & Robert J. Morse, *The New Star System*, US NEWS & WORLD REPORT, Apr. 29, 1985, 60.

573 *Is the Boss Getting Paid Too Much?*, BUS. WK., May 1, 1989, 46; Graef S. Crystal, *CEO Compensation: The Case of Michael Eisner, in* EXECUTIVE COMPENSATION: A STRATEGIC GUIDE FOR THE 1990S 353, 353–55 (Fred K. Foulkes ed., 1991).

574 *Is the Boss, supra* note 573.

575 Betsy Morris, *The New Rules*, FORTUNE, July 24, 2006, 70.

576 NADER & TAYLOR, *supra* note 380, at xi.

577 Peter F. Drucker, *The Mystery of the Business Leader*, WALL ST. J., Sept. 29, 1987, 38.

578 *The 797 Most Powerful Men and 3 Most Powerful Women in Corporate America*, FORBES, June 15, 1987, 145.

579 *Changing Role, supra* note 320. See also NADER & TAYLOR, *supra* note 380, at xi.

580 NADER & TAYLOR, *supra* note 380, at xv. See also Chapter 1, notes 246–47, 260 and related discussion; Thomas J. Lueck, *Why Jack Welch Is Changing G.E.*, NY TIMES, May 5, 1985, F1.

581 Nicholas Varchaver, *Glamour! Fame! Org Charts!*, FORTUNE, Nov. 11, 2004, 136 (quoting Rakesh Khurana). See also Chapter 3, note 23 and accompanying text; CHRISTOPHER BYRON, TESTOSTERONE INC.: TALES OF CEOS GONE WILD 159 (2004) (Iacocca was "the trailblazer in a form of leadership that Americans had never before encountered: the CEO celebrity").

top Gallup's list of most admired men since 1958 but was chosen twice.[582] Iacocca's peers started to take notice. A 1988 study of changes affecting American business that identified him as "the epitome of the charismatic, celebrity CEO" suggested that being a celebrity was "a status to which many business leaders aspire."[583]

According to Howard Rubenstein, a public relations expert, in the 1980s "publicity affected certain CEOs like a drug" and "corporate titans moved from being content to have their own publicist to hiring extra ones for their trophy wives so that they could snag mentions in magazines such as *Town & Country* and *People*."[584] Nader, in his coauthored 1986 study, acknowledged Roger Smith, chairman of General Motors, had "become a master of the colorful photo opportunity, the big event.... [and] a consummate corporate media handler."[585] Even Welch's "relative anonymity" began to dissipate in the mid-1980s when General Electric acquired investment bank Kidder Peabody and RCA, including its national broadcast network NBC.[586] When a leadership expert at Wharton Business School was asked in 1988 about who in the corporate world had charisma, he mentioned Iacocca and Welch, saying of the latter that he "is a terrific presence. No question about it, he's got charisma—and leadership ability, too."[587] As managerial capitalism receded into history during what was a tumultuous decade for many top managers, the stage was set for chief executives to achieve unprecedented prominence and prosperity in the 1990s, with Welch at the forefront as the quintessential corporate executive icon.

---

[582] Chapter 3, note 22 and related discussion; McGill, *supra* note 38, 86.

[583] McGill, *supra* note 38, at 86.

[584] Varchaver, *supra* note 581.

[585] Nader & Taylor, *supra* note 380, at 109.

[586] Chapter 1, note 274 and related discussion.

[587] *The Charisma Factor*, Forbes, Dec. 12, 1988, 272 (quoting Thomas North Gilmore).

5 The 1990s

GLOOM TO EUPHORIA . . . AND BACK

THE 1990S WAS a roller-coaster ride for the public company. Momentum built rapidly after a gloomy start, propelling much of the corporate sector to giddy heights by the end of the decade, which in turn presaged a steep drop as the 2000s began. Events surrounding a blockbuster merger between Time Warner and America Online (AOL) that was announced in January 2000 provide an instructive case study of the momentum swings that would do much to shape the environment in which 1990s public companies and their executives operated.

Time Inc. and Warner Communications Inc. agreed in mid-1989 to a merger that resulted in the formation of Time Warner Inc., the world's largest communications company.[1] The Time Warner merger marked the end of 1980s—the Deal Decade—not only chronologically but also symbolically. Hostile takeovers that yielded generous windfalls for target company shareholders were a hallmark of the 1980s. Nevertheless, when Paramount Communications stepped forward with a lucrative unsolicited offer to Time's shareholders to secure control of Time, Time's board pressed forward with the merger with Warner Communications. A ruling by the Delaware Supreme Court vindicating Time's board helped to marginalize the hostile takeover offer as a governance mechanism as the 1990s began.[2]

The Time Warner merger was finalized January 10, 1990.[3] Exactly a decade later negotiations between Steve Case, chairman of America Online, and his counterpart Gerald Levin of Time Warner that had begun in the fall of 1999 culminated in an announcement that the

---

[1] Mark Landler & Judith H. Dobrzynski. *Time Warner*, BUS. WK., July 22, 1991, 70.

[2] Chapter 4, notes 220–26 and related discussion.

[3] *Time Finishes Warner Buyout*, NY TIMES, Jan. 11, 1990, D19.

The Public Company Transformed. Brian R. Cheffins.

firms would merge.[4] What would ensue, according to a 2009 study of media moguls, would be "an epic drama that ultimately resulted in a historically unprecedented destruction of value" that was "chock full of vivid characters and life lessons related to every aspect of corporate governance and decision making."[5]

Media reports on the exact price tag varied, but there was no doubt the AOL/Time Warner deal was—and continues to be—the largest corporate combination in US history.[6] The merger was, however, not thought of as "just another awesome megadeal."[7] A *Washington Post* columnist's instant verdict was that "it's hard to overhype the significance of yesterday's announcement."[8] The *Economist* characterized the merger as "an 'inflection point'—one of those events that have the potential to change the competitive landscape so fundamentally that nothing can be the same again."[9]

It was the America Online side of the merger that gave the deal its seemingly transformative quality. AOL raised a relatively modest $66 million when it went public in 1992 as a provider of online services such as email, chat rooms, and electronic bulletin boards via telephone lines.[10] The internet, underpinned by the early 1990s launch of the World Wide Web, posed a major threat to AOL's proprietary online offerings.[11] AOL, however, managed to capitalize by offering subscribers full internet access in 1995.[12] By the end of the decade, AOL was the leading internet service provider in the United States with 22 million subscribers.[13] AOL's stock had climbed nearly 80,000 percent since its 1992 initial public offering (IPO), making the company the top performer during a "golden decade" for the stock market.[14]

By the end of 1999, AOL's market capitalization of over $160 billion was nearly double that of Time Warner.[15] Case therefore was on strong ground when he argued that AOL should have a majority stake in the new merged company. The exchange ratio ended up being 55/45 in AOL's favor, implying the pricing in of a huge 71 percent premium for Time Warner's shares.[16] Assurances were offered that a merger of equals was occurring but it was generally assumed that "the torch has passed" with "new economy" AOL subsuming "old economy"

---

[4] NINA MUNK, FOOLS RUSH IN: STEVE CASE, JERRY LEVIN, AND THE UNMAKING OF AOL TIME WARNER 138–39, 179 (2004).

[5] JONATHAN A. KNEE, BRUCE C. GREENWALD & AVA SEAVE, THE CURSE OF THE MOGUL: WHAT'S WRONG WITH THE WORLD'S LEADING MEDIA COMPANIES 218 (2009).

[6] Patrick McGeehan, *By Any Measure, A Big Deal,* NY TIMES, Jan. 12, 2000, C6; Laura Brodbeck Benzinga, *The 15 Biggest Mergers of All Time,* FINANCE.YAHOO.COM, Oct. 19, 2015, https://finance.yahoo.com/news/15-biggest-mergers-time-175152979.html (accessed Dec. 19, 2017) (listing Vodafone's 2000 acquisition of Mannesmann as the largest deal ever).

[7] *Welcome to the 21st Century,* BUS. WK., Jan. 24, 2000, 37.

[8] David Ignatius, *AOL Grows Up,* WASH. POST, Jan. 11, 2000, A17.

[9] *The Big Leap,* ECONOMIST, Jan. 15, 2000, 17.

[10] ALEC KLEIN, STEALING TIME: STEVE CASE, JERRY LEVIN, AND THE COLLAPSE OF AOL TIME WARNER 47 (2003).

[11] David Streitfeld, *AOL Rode a Wave, Time Missed the Boat,* WASH. POST, Jan. 16, 2000, A1.

[12] JOHN CASSIDY, DOT.CON: THE GREATEST STORY EVER TOLD 77–78 (2002).

[13] *The Net Gets Real,* ECONOMIST, Jan. 15, 2000, 23.

[14] E.S. Browining, *Goodbye, Golden Decade. Now What Will the 'oos Bring?,* WALL ST. J., Dec. 13, 1999, C1.

[15] Streitfeld, *supra* note 11; *Net Gets, supra* note 13.

[16] MUNK, *supra* note 4, at 153, 181; KLEIN, *supra* note 10, at 95.

Time Warner.[17] As the *Washington Post* said, "(t)he legendary Henry Luce, Time's founder, labeled the last 10 decades 'the American Century'; his company made it only 10 days into what AOL's founder, Steve Case, is calling 'the Internet Century.' "[18]

Time Warner's share price increased dramatically when the merger with AOL was announced but fell back soon thereafter and AOL investors reacted coolly.[19] Otherwise, news of the AOL/Time Warner merger elicited an enthusiastic response.[20] An investment banker working with AOL at the time of the deal said a decade later:

> If you go back and read what was written in The [*Wall Street*] *Journal* and what was written in The [*New York*] *Times* about this transaction, you would have thought that it was the second coming of the Messiah. I'm sure that if one were to read those today one would find it amusing, maybe dated, but it was, for financial reporting, it was as soaring and this is the great epiphany-of-life kind of journalism and you read it and it brought tears to your eyes.[21]

The enthusiasm would soon dissipate. When AOL Time Warner's chief operating officer resigned in July 2002, the *Economist* acknowledged that it had been excited when AOL and Time Warner had announced they were merging but confessed "(h)ow wrong we were—as, it must be said, was almost everybody else."[22] That year AOL Time Warner went nearly $100 billion in the red, the biggest annual loss in American corporate history.[23] In October 2003 the company dropped "AOL" from its name and its stock began trading under the ticker symbol TWX rather than AOL.[24] Two years later, with Time Warner's market capitalization having fallen to $81 billion, the company set aside $3 billion to settle lawsuits alleging that with the AOL/Time Warner merger there had been misleading disclosures regarding AOL's financial condition and the merged company's prospects.[25] In 2009 Time Warner spun off AOL into a separate company.[26] The AOL/Time Warner merger is widely regarded as the worst corporate transaction ever.[27]

The AOL/Time Warner merger was very much a product of trends in the 1990s. It would have been impossible to contemplate the tie-up occurring as the decade got underway. America Online was still known as Quantum Computer Services and the telephone based online service it offered had just been christened AOL.[28] The World Wide Web, a

---

17 *Welcome to the 21st*, *supra* note 7. Levin apparently believed a merger of equals was occurring—MUNK, *supra* note 4, at 153.

18 Streitfeld, *supra* note 11.

19 MUNK, *supra* note 4, at 181; KLEIN, *supra* note 10, at 186; Andrew Hill & Richard Waters, *Time for the Megamerger to Smooth Out the Creases*, FIN. TIMES, Jan. 17, 2000, 24.

20 MUNK, *supra* note 4, at 180; *Dotcom Downsizing*, ECONOMIST, July 27, 2002, 63.

21 Tim Arango, *How It Went So Wrong*, NY TIMES, Jan. 11, 2010, B1.

22 *Dotcom Downsizing*, *supra* note 20.

23 KLEIN, *supra* note 10, at 300.

24 David Carr, *No Use Crying Over Spilled Billions*, NY TIMES, June 20, 2004, Business, 1.

25 Richard Siklos, *Time Warner Offers $3 Billion to End AOL Hangover*, NY TIMES, August 4, 2005, C1.

26 Kenneth Li, *The Big Turnaround*, FIN. TIMES, May 29, 2010, FT Magazine, 24.

27 *Id.*; *A Deal Too Far*, ECONOMIST, Oct. 7, 2017, 68.

28 KLEIN, *supra* note 10, at 45–46.

combination of a formatting language (HTML, or HyperText Markup Language), universal address identifiers such as URIs (Uniform Resource Identifiers) or URLs (Uniform Resource Locators), and a retrieval system for linked internet resources (HTTP, or Hypertext Transfer Protocol) that made it feasible to navigate the internet by way of a browser, was only developed as the 1990s commenced.[29] Even as of the mid-1990s the AOL/Time Warner deal, as it was ultimately constructed, was beyond contemplation. The *Washington Post* said as the transaction was announced "the mere fact that it is happening is remarkable. Five years ago, the suggestion that AOL would be a dominant partner in such a deal would have been ridiculous. Three years ago, it would have been amusing. Last week, everyone said it was inevitable."[30]

The AOL/Time Warner hangover in the 2000s also was integrally related to historical context. In the second half of the 1990s key stock market indices rose sharply amidst general corporate prosperity, with the surge in the stock prices of companies associated with the internet being particularly robust. The trend reversed dramatically as the 2000s began. Share prices fell substantially, with internet-related stocks being hit particularly hard. A number of major public companies would soon be implicated in serious corporate scandals. Numerous 1990s corporate heroes were quickly reduced to early 2000s zeroes. The scandal angle aside, the AOL/Time Warner merger hangover exemplified the pattern.

The dramatic swings of opinion concerning the AOL/Time Warner merger reflected a general pattern, namely that timing dramatically affected perceptions of 1990s public companies and their executives. With corporations there was considerable pessimism as the decade began, growing confidence during the middle of the decade, and borderline euphoria by the time the decade was drawing to a close, exemplified by AOL's dizzying share price increase. The standing of chief executive officers (CEOs) paralleled the fortunes of public companies, meaning executives chastised for being overpaid in the early 1990s were riding high by the end of the decade in a manner that was unmatched throughout the post–World War II era. Indeed, as the concluding section of this chapter describes, CEOs were verging on iconic status immediately before a dramatic fall from grace in the early 2000s.

Changing economic and market conditions similarly affected how internal and external constraints impacting public company management were perceived of and functioned. The sharp reversal of fortunes at the beginning of the 2000s meant, for instance, that positive corporate governance verdicts offered in the mid- and late-1990s seemed in retrospect to be unjustifiably optimistic. Given the influence economic and market trends had on assessments of public companies, their executives, and the constraints applicable to those executives, an overview of these trends is in order before we consider those constraints and the status of public company management during the 1990s.

---

[29] Johnny Ryan, A History of the Internet and the Digital Future 106–07 (2010); *History of the Web*, available at http://webfoundation.org/about/vision/history-of-the-web/ (accessed Dec. 10, 2017).

[30] Streitfeld, *supra* note 11.

From Stagnation to Overdrive to Hangover

Newsweek observed in October 1992 "the stagnation of the 1990s has created a roaring bull market in doom and gloom" and noted that presidential candidate "Bill Clinton expressed the fashionable sentiment in last week's first presidential debate, '(w)e're weak in the world.' "[31] Clinton, having won the election, held in December a two-day conference on the economy in Little Rock that was described as "a vindication of sorts" for those who had been saying "America's economic competitiveness . . . is eroding slowly but steadily."[32] Just five years later, to the mild irritation of his audience at a multinational economic summit, Clinton "extolled, again and again, America's magic formula for growth."[33] In 1999, *Business Week* observed "(a)s the American Century draws to a close, times have rarely been better. Eight years into an expansion that just won't quit, the robust US economy is the envy of the world."[34] However, in 2002, on the heels of a recession, revelations of corporate scandals, and falling share prices, noted economist Joseph Stiglitz said "(t)he history of the 1990s needs to be rewritten. How are we to assess that decade in light of what we are seeing today?"[35]

Reinterpretations of governance arrangements and managerial effectiveness in public companies would occur with some frequency in the 1990s and the early 2000s, with the economic mood and market conditions being highly influential. To put into context changes affecting the public company during the concluding decade of the twentieth century, we will consider now the key economic trends that shaped perceptions. Awareness of the basic trajectory cannot be taken for granted, even only a quarter century or so later. In 2017 a *Wall Street Journal* columnist accused Democratic Party leaders who characterized Bill Clinton's years in office as an economic disappointment of "self-defeating historical amnesia."[36]

AMERICA FALLING BEHIND?

As the 1990s began, the United States was in the midst of an economic expansion extending from 1983 to 2000, the longest during the post–World War era.[37] There was a recession in late 1990 and early 1991 but it was the mildest of the twentieth century.[38] The stock market fell sharply in the autumn of 1990 but the lost ground was made up by the following spring.[39] A dramatic share price increase was in prospect for the remainder of the decade (Figure 5.1).

While the economic downturn at the beginning of the 1990s would prove to be relatively mild, the country was in a pessimistic mood. The *Washington Post* declared in 1990 "America is depressed."[40] The pessimism extended to the corporate sector. The general consensus was

---

31 Marc Levinson, *The Hand Wringers*, NEWSWEEK, Oct. 26, 1992, 44.

32 Ronald E. Yates, *The Comeback Country*, CHI. TRIB., Dec. 27, 1992, C1.

33 Joan Warner, *A New Breed of Blue Chips*, BUS. WK., July 7, 1997, 52.

34 Jennifer Reingold, *Executive Pay*, BUS. WK., Apr. 19, 1999, 72.

35 Joseph Stiglitz, *The Roaring Nineties*, ATLANTIC MONTHLY, Oct. 2002, 75.

36 William A. Galston, *The Clinton Economy, The Left's Ingratitude*, WALL ST. J., May 3, 2017, A13.

37 GEORGE KOZMETSKY & PIYU YUE, THE ECONOMIC TRANSFORMATION OF THE UNITED STATES, 1950–2000, at 1, 15–16 (2005).

38 JOHN STEELE GORDON, AN EMPIRE OF WEALTH: THE EPIC HISTORY OF AMERICAN POWER 416 (2004).

39 KOZMETSKY & YUE, *supra* note 37, at 435.

40 Henry Allen, *Red, White & Truly Blue*, WASH. POST, Nov. 26, 1990, B1.

FIGURE 5.1 S&P 500 Index, 1990–2002 (Opening Prices, monthly).
Source: S&P 500—Historical Data, Yahoo! Finance, available at https://uk.finance.yahoo.com/quote/%5EGSPC/history?p=%5EGSPC (accessed May 26, 2018).

that US corporations were losing ground to German and Japanese rivals,[41] implying time had passed corporate America by. The fact that the number of US companies qualifying as one of the top 500 firms in the world, ranked by sales, fell from 298 in 1962 to 160 in 1993 seemed to confirm this downbeat assessment.[42]

Expert stock analysts assumed gloomily—and incorrectly—that the stock market decline occurring in the fall of 1990 would continue as 1991 got underway.[43] Abby Joseph Cohen, a Goldman Sachs stock market strategist who would achieve notoriety later in the decade for her unwavering faith in the stock market, said in late 1990 "(w)e believe that the basic trend in equity prices remains downward."[44] Rank-and-file workers were on edge, with iconic corporations such as General Electric (GE), IBM, and Sears cutting their workforces by 31 percent, 30 percent, and 22 percent respectively between 1987 and 1993.[45] A downbeat *Chicago Tribune* told readers in 1993 of "a bleak wasteland of disenfranchised American workers forsaken by corporations that are eliminating benefits and shrinking themselves in an unprecedented orgy of downsizing."[46]

The economic gloom was matched by "declinism" in intellectual circles, with prominent advocates of a pessimistic view of America's prospects including Harvard historian Paul Kennedy and MIT economist Lester Thurow.[47] Mediocrity was in prospect, the thinking

---

41 Ira M. Millstein, *The Evolution of the Certifying Board*, 48 Bus. Law. 1485, 1487 (1993).

42 Alfred D. Chandler & Takashi Hikino, *The Large Industrial Enterprise and the Dynamics of Modern Economic Growth*, *in* Big Business and the Wealth of Nations 24, 53 (Alfred D. Chandler, Franco Amatori & Takashi Hikino eds., 1997).

43 Randall Smith, *Stock Market Swing Shows How Wrong Professionals Can Be*, Wall St. J., Feb. 26, 1991, A1.

44 *Id.*; *infra* note 114 and related discussion.

45 Terence Deal & Allan Kennedy, The New Corporate Cultures: Revitalizing the Workplace after Downsizing, Mergers and Reengineering 69 (1999).

46 Ronald E. Yates, *Downsizing's Bitter Pill*, Chi. Trib., Nov. 21, 1993, Sunday Magazine, 14.

47 Paul M. Kennedy, The Rise and Fall of the Great Powers: Economic Change and Military Conflict from 1500 to 2000 (1987); Michael Prowse, *Is America in Decline?*, Harv. Bus. Rev., July–Aug.

went, not a second "American century" to follow the first Henry Luce identified.[48] Americans seemed inclined to agree. Those polled who thought the United States was "in decline" increased from 31 percent in October 1990 to 53 percent in October 1991 and 66 percent in February 1992.[49] Dissatisfaction with economic trends likely cost George H.W. Bush the 1992 presidential election.[50] Bill Clinton, with a sign reading "the economy, stupid" in his Little Rock campaign headquarters that provided a reminder to the campaign to stay on message,[51] duly capitalized.

RALLYING

While negativity regarding the economy hurt George Bush badly in the 1992 presidential election, the US economy in fact had begun in March 1991 what would become its longest period of uninterrupted growth to that point.[52] The stock market had already started to rally by the end of 1990, and unemployment, which hit nearly 8 percent in the summer of 1992, fell steadily thereafter and stood at 4 percent at the end of the decade.[53] The *Wall Street Journal* said in 1995 "American companies are enjoying a huge comeback."[54] In 1996, the World Economic Forum, famous for organizing its annual meetings each year in Davos, Switzerland, ranked the United States as the most competitive economy in the world for the second year in a row.[55] As part of Bill Clinton's successful 1996 re-election campaign Democrats could point proudly to an economic triple crown of solid economic growth, falling unemployment, and low inflation.[56]

There was by no means unvarnished optimism during the mid-1990s. Polls indicated that while Americans were somewhat more upbeat in 1996 than 1992, well under half thought their country was on the right track.[57] Bill Clinton, in his 1995 State of the Union address,

---

1992, 34, 34–35; LESTER THUROW, HEAD TO HEAD: THE COMING ECONOMIC BATTLE BETWEEN JAPAN, EUROPE AND AMERICA (1992).

[48] *Supra* note 18 and related discussion; Paul Krugman, *Can America Stay on Top?*, 14 J. ECON. PERSP. 169, 169 (2000); *Lessons of Prosperity*, BUS. WK., Feb. 14, 2000, 156.

[49] EVERETT CARLL LADD & KARLYN H. BOWMAN, WHAT'S WRONG: A SURVEY OF AMERICAN SATISFACTION AND COMPLAINT 19 (1998).

[50] *The Economy, Stupid*, WALL ST. J., Nov. 6, 1992, A14; WYATT WELLS, AMERICAN CAPITALISM, 1945–2000: CONTINUITY AND CHANGE FROM MASS PRODUCTION TO THE INFORMATION SOCIETY 162–63 (2003).

[51] David E. Rosenbaum, *Skipping Ahead: On the Economy, Bush Tries to Keep Focus on the Future*, NY TIMES, Sept. 13, 1992, E1. Those distilling the wisdom underpinning the message would subsequently add "it's" in front of the core phrase. See, for example, A.M. Rosenthal, *It's the Economy, Stupid*, NY TIMES, Oct. 30, 1992, A31.

[52] Robert J. Hershey, *Down and Out on Wall Street*, NY TIMES, Dec. 26, 1999, Business, 1; MICHAEL J. MANDEL, THE COMING INTERNET DEPRESSION 4 (2001).

[53] *Supra* note 39 and accompanying text; Federal Reserve Bank of St. Louis, *FRED Economic Data—Civilian Unemployment Rate*, Apr. 6, 2018, available at https://fred.stlouisfed.org/series/UNRATE (accessed Apr. 4, 2018).

[54] Ralph T. King, *No, Thanks*, WALL ST. J., June 19, 1995, R16.

[55] Mortimer B. Zuckerman, *Creators of the 21st Century*, US NEWS & WORLD REPORT, July 1, 1996, 64.

[56] MARINA V.N. WHITMAN, NEW WORLD, NEW RULES: THE CHANGING ROLE OF THE AMERICAN CORPORATION 3 (1998).

[57] LADD & BOWMAN, *supra* note 49, at 48.

said too many Americans "are still working harder and harder for less and less," and "still can't be sure of having a job next year or even next month."[58] Continuing apprehension about the adverse effects of downsizing for working people was the most obvious explanation for wariness.[59] US corporations were announcing nearly half-a-million job cuts per year during the mid-1990s, only modestly off levels in 1993, the peak downsizing year in the early 1990s.[60] In early 1996, nearly one-third of Americans said downsizing had had an impact on them personally.[61] This coincided with the publication of a series of hefty articles on the phenomenon in both the *New York Times* and *USA Today*.[62]

OVERDRIVE

Charles Geisst, in a 1997 history of Wall Street, noted that while "the largest bull market in Wall Street history" had been occurring, "only the stock and bond markets seemed to boom, not the economy itself."[63] That qualification would very soon be unnecessary. The *Financial Times* said the same year "(t)he US economy is flying high" and may well have returned to a 1950s-style "golden era of steady growth, low inflation and low unemployment."[64] *Business Week* told its readers in 1999 "(a)s the American Century draws to a close, times have rarely been better.[65] In a 2000 book offering advice on how to profit from "the new era of wealth" economic forecaster Brian Wesbury cited America's "fabulous economic performance" in the late 1990s and maintained that economic trends were "overwhelmingly positive."[66]

As a 2003 study of downsizing noted, that practice "retreated to the backburner during the boom years of the late 1990s."[67] Those companies that were cutting jobs were often simultaneously hiring, meaning that net job losses were minimal or nonexistent.[68] Moreover, with unemployment falling, finding new work was easier for those laid off. While in early 1992 nearly half of Americans surveyed believed jobs were "hard to get," this figure had fallen to 14 percent by 1998.[69] Law professor Bernard Black observed in 2000 "labor complaints about layoffs are muted, and hard to take seriously when made, when we have a 4 percent unemployment rate" and suggested somewhat caustically that "(m)ost people understand

---

[58] *Whistling While They Work*, Economist, Jan. 28, 1995, 47.

[59] *Id.*

[60] William J. Baumol, Alan S. Blinder & Edward N. Wolff, Downsizing in America: Reality, Causes, and Consequences 33 (2003).

[61] Susan Page, *Workers on the Edge—Job Fears Push Button*, USA Today, Feb. 20, 1996, B1.

[62] *Id.*; Bill Montague, *Feeling the Squeeze of Downsizing*, USA Today, Feb. 19, 1996, A1; Bill Montague, *Workers on the Edge—Building Solutions*, USA Today, Feb. 21, 1996, B1. The seven *New York Times* articles, published in March 1996, were listed in *The Downsizing of America*, NY Times, Mar. 9, 1996, 12 and repackaged as The New York Times, The Downsizing of America (1996).

[63] Charles R. Geisst, Wall Street: A History 366 (1997).

[64] *The New US Economy*, Fin. Times, July 19, 1997, 8.

[65] Reingold, *supra* note 34.

[66] Brian S. Wesbury, The New Era of Wealth: How Investors Can Profit from the 5 Economic Trends Shaping the Future 76 (2000).

[67] Baumol, Blinder & Wolff, *supra* note 60, at 2.

[68] *Id.* at 25, 40, 44; *The Revolving Door*, Economist, Oct. 26, 1996, 111.

[69] Robert J. Samuelson, *Why We're All Married to the Market*, Newsweek, Apr. 27, 1998, 47.

that anyone who is willing to show up for work, on time and sober, can get a job, even if it is not always a great job."[70]

An economy seemingly moving smoothly into overdrive reversed early 1990s pessimism concerning America's economic stature. In 1997 the *New York Times* published an essay saying "(t)he United States as No. 1 and soaring that was not supposed to happen. . . . One has to go back to the Roman Empire for a similar instance of cultural hegemony."[71] That same year, 36 percent of Americans surveyed said the United States was the world's number one economic power, up from 17 percent in 1992.[72] Media proprietor Mort Zuckerman proclaimed in *Foreign Affairs* in 1998 "American business should widen its lead over the rest of the world. France had the seventeenth century, Britain the nineteenth, and America the twentieth. It will also have the twenty-first."[73] Marina von Neumann Whitman, a business school professor and former General Motors executive, said the following year of "(w)orldwide convergence around the American model of entrepreneurial capitalism" that "nations on every continent . . . have paid us the ultimate compliment of imitation."[74] In early 2000 *Business Week* proclaimed "the declinists turned out [to] be very wrong. Americans have prospered beyond what anyone would have imagined 10 years ago."[75]

As buoyant as the economy was in the second half of the 1990s, its performance was second-best as compared to the stock market.[76] Share prices on an upward trajectory since 1990 became turbocharged in the mid-1990s (Figure 5.1). *Fortune* said of the stock market in 1996

> It's epic. Running rampant, and carrying our dreams, our wallets, and the future of millions of working-class stiffs with it. Behold the bull, the great stock market advance that has stolen more financial headlines in the past year than anything else. Its stamina is awe inspiring; the belief that stocks must go up, a new religion.[77]

The same year the stock market passed a milestone that symbolized its growing importance relative to the economy. For the first time since records were kept in the mid-1920s, the aggregate market capitalization of publicly traded stocks exceeded US gross domestic product. An analyst at Arbor Trading, a research and brokerage firm, said of the milestone "(i)t used to be that the economy was the biggest thing around. Now it's the stock market."[78]

The growing prominence of the stock market was partly due to a substantial increase in the number of publicly traded companies. The trend ran counter to gloomy forecasting by

---

[70] Bernard S. Black, *The First International Merger Wave (and the Fifth and Last US Wave)*. 54 U. MIA. L. REV. 799, 807 (2000).

[71] Josel Joffe, *America the Inescapable*, NY TIMES, June 8, 1997, Sunday Magazine, 38.

[72] LADD & BOWMAN, *supra* note 49, at 18.

[73] Mortimer B. Zuckerman, *A Second American Century*, FOREIGN AFFAIRS, May–June 1998, 18, 31.

[74] WHITMAN, *supra* note 56, at 203.

[75] *Lessons of Prosperity*, *supra* note 48.

[76] JEFF MADRICK, AGE OF GREED: THE TRIUMPH OF FINANCE AND DECLINE OF AMERICA, 1970 TO THE PRESENT 322 (2011).

[77] Susan E. Kuhn, *How Crazy Is This Market?*, FORTUNE, Apr. 15, 1996, 78.

[78] *Untested Waters*, BARRON'S, Nov. 25, 1996, 17.

business school professor Michael Jensen, who claimed in 1989 leveraged buyouts (LBOs) of public companies would result in the public company's eclipse.[79] Instead, LBO activity fell off markedly.[80] In contrast, joining the stock market proved to be a popular proposition. More than 3800 companies carried out IPOs in the 1990s.[81]

Due to the robust IPO market, the number of public companies grew steadily from 1990 to 1996 (Figure 5.2). A powerful counter-trend was coming into operation, namely substantial merger activity that resulted in numerous acquired firms leaving the stock market.[82] Mergers became sufficiently prevalent in the late 1990s to result in a net decline in the public company population. Nevertheless, the number of publicly traded companies was considerably higher as the 1990s concluded than it was when the decade began.

By 1999, the stock market capitalization/GDP ratio that attracted notoriety in 1996 at 1:1 had risen to 1.46:1.[83] With the number of public companies declining modestly as the decade came to an end, this late 1990s surge was attributable fully to existing public companies trading at higher share prices. Higher share prices in their turn were the object of considerable fascination. In March 1999, the *Wall Street Journal* said in a front page article of an iconic stock market benchmark, "(t)he Dow Jones Industrial Average closed above 10000 for the first time yesterday, capturing in a single number both the astonishing success and giddy

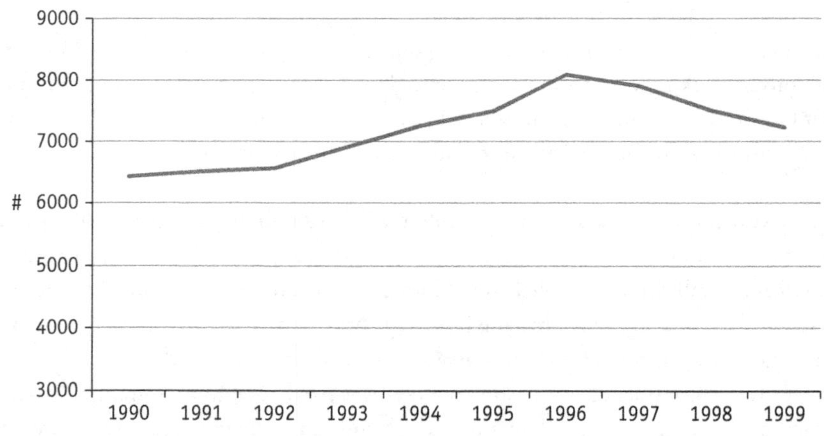

FIGURE 5.2 Number of Listed Companies, 1990–1999.
Source: World Bank, *Listed Domestic Companies, Total*, available at https://data.worldbank.org/indicator/CM.MKT.LDOM.NO?locations=US (accessed Feb. 9, 2018).

[79] Michael C. Jensen, *Eclipse of the Public Corporation*, HARV. BUS. REV., Sept.–Oct., 1989, 61.

[80] Chapter 4, note 148 and related discussion.

[81] Jay R. Ritter & Ivo Welch, *A Review of IPO Activity, Pricing, and Allocations*, 57 J. FIN. 1795, 1797 (2002).

[82] Craig Doidge, G. Andrew Karolyi & René M. Stulz, *The US Listing Gap*, 123 J. FIN. ECON. 464, 464, 475–77, 481 (2017). On merger activity in the 1990s, see *infra* note 146 and accompanying text.

[83] Federal Reserve Bank of St. Louis, *FRED Economic Data: Stock Market Capitalization to GDP for United States*, available at https://fred.stlouisfed.org/series/DDDM01USA156NWDB (accessed Apr. 15, 2018).

exuberance of the US economy this decade."[84] The *Journal* conceded that the smashing "of every standard benchmark for valuing stocks" inspired anxiety as well as awe.[85] *Newsweek*, perhaps deducing that caveats were unnecessary with the Dow having increased to nearly 11,500 at the end of 1999,[86] observed

> Maybe it's too early for this perpetually rising stock market to join death and taxes among The Only Certain Things in Life. But at this rate, the day is likely to come soon, and when it does, the next logical step will seem obvious: the stock market will take over just about every aspect of society. Granted, it can often seem as if that day has arrived already.[87]

Newsweek even speculated that America could be evolving into Wallstreetville, "(a) country of publicly traded families," with every household being a publicly traded stock.[88] Though this prognostication was somewhat tongue-in-cheek, speculation about the future of the public company had clearly moved far, far away from its demise.

Various stock market observers skeptical of the borderline investor euphoria of the late 1990s pointed out that the market was worryingly unbalanced, in the sense that a small number of outperforming stocks were driving stock market indices upward.[89] Large firms able to generate sustained profit growth indeed were disproportionately popular with investors as the 1990s drew to a close.[90] There also was a strong high-tech bias. As Alan Greenspan, chairman of the Federal Reserve from 1987 to 2006, observed in his 2007 memoirs, "hi-tech excitement brought extra sizzle to what was already a hot market for stocks."[91] Even though as of 1997 technology and communications stocks made up only about one-fifth of the market value of the S&P 500, the tech sector accounted for nearly one-half of the S&P 500's gains between mid-1995 and mid-2000.[92] In the late 1990s the technology-laden NASDAQ stock market index dramatically outpaced the S&P 500 despite the latter's robust growth (Figure 5.3).

Belying *Newsweek*'s suggestion in 1999 that rising share prices were pretty close to certain, concerns were quite often expressed that the stock market had become unhealthily detached from economic fundamentals. A *Barron's* columnist observed in 1997 following a week in which the Dow Jones Industrial Average increased nearly 5 percent that "(t)his is the kind of market that has old-timers reaching for superlatives and despondent bears talking about tulip bulbs, South Sea bubbles and other manias of the past."[93] Even a year

[84] Greg Ip, *Dow Industrials Top 10000*, Wall St. J., Mar. 30, 1999, A1.

[85] *Id.*

[86] Cassidy, *supra* note 12, at 258.

[87] Adam Bryant, *Markets Rule*, Newsweek, Jan. 1, 2000, 42.

[88] *Id.*

[89] Ip, *supra* note 84; Laszlo Birinyi, *Whoosh!*, Forbes, Feb. 22, 1999, 150.

[90] Joel Kotkin & David Friedman, *Up? Down? Who Cares? The Dow Doesn't Mean Much*, Wash. Post, Nov. 8, 1998, C1; Geoffrey Smith, *Why Small-Caps Will Keep Getting Trampled*, Bus. Wk., Apr. 12, 1999, 38.

[91] Alan Greenspan, The Age of Turbulence: Adventures in a New World 164 (2007).

[92] Mandel, *supra* note 52, at 76–77.

[93] Andrew Bary, *"Relentless" Dow Ends the Week Setting a Sixth Straight Record; It's Like a Force of Nature*, Barron's, June 16, 1997, Market Week, 3.

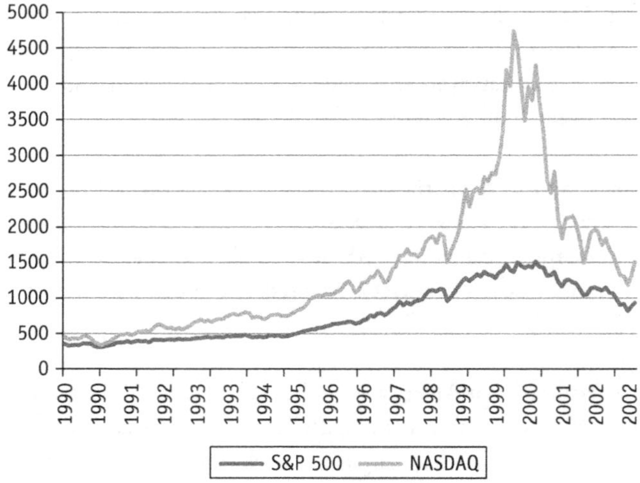

FIGURE 5.3 S&P 500 Index/NASDAQ, 1990–2002 (Opening Prices, monthly).
Source: S&P 500—Historical Data, Yahoo! Finance, available at https://uk.finance.yahoo.com/quote/%5EGSPC/history?p=%5EGSPC (accessed May 26, 2018).

before, debate was underway on Wall Street about whether there was a nascent speculative stock market bubble.[94] Greenspan seemed to suggest there might be in a December 1996 speech where he referred to "irrational exuberance" while acknowledging that "unduly escalated asset values" could affect how the Federal Reserve dealt with monetary policy.[95] Stock markets around the world fell briefly in response to the speech but recovered quickly as investors deduced that the Fed would not raise interest rates to put downward pressure on share prices.[96]

Companies associated with the internet, frequently referred to as dot.coms due to the labeling protocol for commercially oriented websites,[97] constituted the most obvious target for those making the case that stock prices were taking on a bubble-like quality. The 1995 IPO of Netscape Communications Corporation, which had created the first widely used browser software that enabled computer users to "surf" the web, marked the start of intense investor enthusiasm for internet stocks.[98] Netscape shares initially priced at $28 rocketed upward to $75 on the first day of trading before retreating to $58.25, a price still high enough to imply the company was worth more than $2 billion even though it was only 15 months old and had yet to make a profit.[99] Investor enthusiasm for internet-themed stocks intensified as the 1990s concluded. The 50 company Inter@ctive Week Internet Index, developed by the

---

[94] CASSIDY, *supra* note 12, at 118.

[95] MAGGIE MAHAR, BULL: A HISTORY OF THE BOOM, 1982–1999, at 248 (2003).

[96] CASSIDY, *supra* note 12, at 133–34.

[97] Network Working Group, *Request for Comments: 920*, Oct. 1984, available at http://www.rfc-editor.org/pdfrfc/rfc920.txt.pdf (accessed May 26, 2018).

[98] CASSIDY, *supra* note 12, at 6; MAHAR, *supra* note 95, at 150.

[99] MAHAR, *supra* note 95, at 152.

American Stock Exchange to measure a cross-section of firms with a strong internet dimension, rose nearly 600 percent between October 1998 and March 2000.[100]

There were numerous warnings that the pricing of internet stocks had lost touch with reality. As early as 1995 *Newsweek*'s Allan Sloan was characterizing share prices as "insanely high" and labeling Netscape as "the prime example of Internet Insanity."[101] He warned readers in 1997 that "it's frenzy time again in cybergreed land."[102] *US News & World Report* argued in 1999 that internet-related market speculation was destined a "place in future economics textbooks under Great Financial Manias" and speculated on what "could finally pop the bubble."[103] Barton Biggs, senior analyst for investment bank Morgan Stanley, said the same year of internet stocks "I promise you that, like all bubbles, this bubble will come to a very, very bad end. The only trouble is that none of us knows when."'[104] Though Biggs had a reputation for being bearish,[105] on this point he had company. When *Barron's* surveyed 200 major professional money managers, also in 1999, the general consensus was that internet stocks were "out of control."[106]

Though internet stocks were the most obvious contenders for bubble status, the same point was made with some regularity about the stock market more generally in the late 1990s. With the 200 money managers *Barron's* surveyed in 1999, while a sizeable proportion remained generally bullish, 72 percent nevertheless said there were signs of a speculative bubble in the market.[107] Various publications, such as London's *Economist* and *Financial Times*, offered strong warnings that the American stock market was dangerously overpriced.[108] Nobel Prize winning economists Milton Friedman and Paul Samuelson both said stocks were in bubble territory, though Samuelson did suggest any forthcoming correction would be modest.[109]

With stock market indices surging upward, warnings about the veracity of share prices seemingly did little to halt the upward momentum of stocks. Perhaps American investors tuned out because they only wanted to hear good news.[110] There also was what Joe Nocera, writing for *Fortune* in 1999, characterized as "a kind of intellectual capitulation," namely forsaking, if perhaps grudgingly, traditional valuation measures that were failing to explain the buoyant stock market.[111] For investment professionals, a desire to remain relevant and avoid

---

[100] Kozmetsky & Yue, *supra* note 37, at 448–50; NASDAQ, *The Inter@ctive Week Internet Index*[AM]*—IIX*, available at http://www.nasdaq.com/options/indexes/iix.aspx (accessed Feb. 14, 2018).

[101] Allan Sloan, *High Wired*, Newsweek, Dec. 25, 1995, 39.

[102] Allan Sloan, *Trains You Can Miss*, Newsweek, June 2, 1997, 48.

[103] James Pethokoukis, *Forget the Cyclone. The Net Ride Is Scarier*, US News & World Report, Feb. 22, 1999, 55.

[104] Peter de Jonge, *Riding the Wild, Perilous Waters of Amazon.com*, NY Times, Mar. 14, 1999, Sunday Magazine, 36.

[105] Alex Berenson, The Number: How the Drive for Quarterly Earnings Corrupted Wall Street and Corporate America 158 (2003).

[106] Lauren R. Rublin, *Party On!*, Barron's, May 3, 1999, 31.

[107] *Id.*

[108] Cassidy, *supra* note 12, at 171–72; Alan Reynolds, *Let's Burst the Bubble Theory*, Wall St. J., May 14, 1998, A22.

[109] John Cassidy, *Pricking the Bubble*, New Yorker, Aug. 17, 1998, 37; Jonathan R. Laing, *The New Dr. Doom*, Barron's, May 22, 2000, 37.

[110] Cassidy, *supra* note 12, at 172.

[111] Joseph Nocera, *Do You Believe?*, Fortune, June 7, 1999, 76.

embarrassment fostered the process. As the *New York Times* said in 1999, "(i)t is not easy being a bear. As the days have passed, some have suffered from tarnished reputations and the loss of clients—even jobs. And they've had to endure the withering scorn of market evangelists."[112] For instance, in 1996 Jeffrey Vinik was criticized in the press and pushed out as the manager of Fidelity Investments' high-profile Magellan fund because the fund underperformed due to his decision to sell what he thought were overpriced tech stocks and buy bonds.[113]

What reasoning underpinned the upward momentum of the stock market in the face of admonitions from skeptics? Abby Joseph Cohen, the Goldman Sachs analyst who was pessimistic in 1990, changed tack in 1991 and would become "the prophet of Wall Street" due to her unwavering faith in the market as share prices rose,[114] told *Business Week* for a 1998 article profiling her "(i)t's said that the five scariest words about the market are 'This time it is different' . . . but sometimes it really is different."[115] The key distinguishing feature was thought to be an economy, bolstered by technological innovations destined to improve productivity, which was well-positioned to grow smartly over the long haul without fostering inflation.[116] Alan Greenspan, having previously warned of irrational exuberance, concurred with this optimistic assessment, saying "the revolution in information technology has altered the structure of the way the American economy works."[117] President Clinton agreed, citing in 1997 massive investment in labor-saving technology to explain why "it's possible to have more sustained and higher growth without inflation than we previously thought."[118]

The rapid development of the internet was a potent part of the heady late 1990s optimism mix. Various observers predicted the Web's economic contribution would equal that of the electric dynamo, the printing press, and the wheel.[119] As early as 1995 Bill Clinton was telling his senior economic advisers "with the internet, with technology, I can feel the change. I can see growth everywhere."[120]

The phrase "New Economy" would become shorthand for an American business regime characterized by internet underpinned high growth and low inflation. *Business Week* led the way, even claiming in 1997 that Greenspan was "the avant-garde advocate of the New Economy."[121] Greenspan in fact was ambivalent about the nomenclature, the usage of which

---

[112] Hershey, *supra* note 52. See also JUSTIN FOX, THE MYTH OF THE RATIONAL MARKET: A HISTORY OF RISK, REWARD, AND DELUSION ON WALL STREET 361, n.260 (2011).

[113] MAHAR, *supra* note 95, at 227–28; BERENSON, *supra* note 105, at 162–63.

[114] *Supra* note 44 and related discussion; MAHAR, *supra* note 95, at 86–87; ROGER LOWENSTEIN, ORIGINS OF THE CRASH: THE GREAT BUBBLE AND ITS UNDOING 23–24 (2004).

[115] Anthony Bianco, *The Prophet of Wall Street*, BUS. WK., June 1, 1998, 125.

[116] Joan Warner, *The Atlantic Century*, BUS. WK, Feb. 8, 1999; Gerard Baker, *Recession or Soft-Landing: How Will the Boom End?*, FIN. TIMES, Dec. 20, 1999, 8.

[117] MICHAEL LEWIS, THE NEW NEW THING: A SILICON VALLEY STORY 383 (1999). On the evolution of Greenspan's thinking, see CASSIDY, *supra* note 12, at 130–31, 158–59.

[118] Dean Foust, *Alan Greenspan's Brave New World*, BUS. WK., July 14, 1997, 44.

[119] CASSIDY, *supra* note 12, at 1.

[120] GREENSPAN, *supra* note 91, at 171.

[121] CASSIDY, *supra* note 12, at 155; Foust, *supra* note 118. The term was in fact first used in *Business Week* in 1981: William Wolman, *He's Not Just a Bear—He's a Grizzly*, BUS. WK., Apr. 3, 2000, 20.

initially was by no means widespread.[122] The term "New Economy" would soon be commonplace, however, with the President's Council of Economic Advisers using the phrase 127 times in a January 2001 report to Congress describing economic changes occurring during the Clinton presidency.[123] Energy company Enron was thus slightly ahead of the curve when it said in its 1999 annual report to shareholders "(w)e are participating in a New Economy, and the rules have changed dramatically."[124] Within a year the company was trading "everything from gas to copper to financial instruments" on the Web.[125] Enron's president said the internet "puts the afterburner" on the company.[126] Enron would soon be flaming out as part of a tumultuous start to the 2000s that seemed to vindicate those skeptical of the buoyant stock market and the "new" economy with which it was associated.

HANGOVER

In mid-April 2000, with NASDAQ having dropped 34 percent over the previous three weeks and with the Dow Jones Industrial Average having gone down 12 percent, the *Wall Street Journal* observed "(i)n a market once priced for perfection, investors are trying to cope with a suddenly imperfect world."[127] Stock prices steadied over the next few months.[128] By the end of 2000, however, the S&P 500 had suffered its worst year since 1977 with a 10 percent decline and the NASDAQ had fallen 39 percent, the worst year for a major stock index since 1931.[129] Many prominent analysts predicted there would be a modest rally in 2001.[130] Share prices continued to fall, however (Figure 5.1), amidst anemic economic growth, the shock of terrorist attacks occurring September 11, 2001, and corporate scandals afflicting Enron and various other prominent companies.[131]

The stock price reversal powerfully reinforced the case stock market and New Economy skeptics had been making. A 2002 essay in the *New York Times* said "(a) newly sober Wall Street shudders when recalling the stock market bubble, as a groggy partygoer regrets the excesses of the night before."[132] *Barron's* told readers the same year "no prior market mania saw anything resembling the magnitude and excesses of the most recent stock-market bubble."[133]

---

[122] Robert Shiller, Irrational Exuberance xxiv (2001); Alan Greenspan, *Question: Is There a New Economy?*, Federal Reserve Board, Sept. 4, 1998, available at https://www.federalreserve.gov/boarddocs/speeches/1998/19980904.htm (accessed May 15, 2018).

[123] Economic Report of the President/Annual Report of the Council of Economic Advisers (2001). See also Shiller, *supra* note 122, at xxiv.

[124] David Skeel, Icarus in the Boardroom: The Fundamental Flaws in Corporate America and Where They Came From 147 (2005).

[125] Wendy Zellner, *Enron Electrified*, Bus. Wk, July 24, 2000, E.Biz, 54.

[126] *Id.*

[127] Greg Ip & E.S. Browning, *What Are Tech Stocks Worth, Now That We Know It Isn't Infinity?*, Wall St. J., Apr. 17, 2000, 19.

[128] Berenson, *supra* note 105, at 181–82.

[129] Adam Shell, *Investing Lesson Proves Costly*, USA Today, Jan. 2, 2001, B1.

[130] Lauren R. Rublin, *Partied Out?*, Barron's, Jan. 1, 2001, 23.

[131] Berenson, *supra* note 105, at 195, 205, 212–13.

[132] Harris Collingwood, *The Earnings Cult*, NY Times, June 9, 2002, Sunday Magazine, 68.

[133] Jonathan R. Laing, *After the Bubble*, Barron's, July 1, 2002, 19.

Gary Hamel, an influential management thinker, argued that "in the end—and the end came damn fast—the new economy turned out to have been a ruse to sell dumb as dirt business models to naïve investors and loads of IT gear to panicked CEOs."[134] Roger Lowenstein, in a 2004 book on the stock market gyrations occurring in the late 1990s and early 2000s, argued "the new economy was among the gaudiest conceits of American business."[135]

Such wholesale condemnations of the late 1990s stock market and the New Economy with which it became affiliated appear in retrospect to be somewhat overdone. Two decades later the five largest public companies in the world would be American tech companies relying heavily on the internet as part of their business models (Apple, Microsoft, Alphabet/Google, Facebook, and Amazon).[136] Even if only two of those companies were launched in the 1990s—Amazon was founded in 1994 and went public in 1997, and Google was incorporated in 1998—subsequent events vindicated the basic intuition of late 1990s investors that the internet was a major business phenomenon.[137] Be that as it may, the foregoing illustrates clearly how changing economic trends altered thinking regarding public companies and their executives. With respect to constraints on managerial autonomy there were analogous market-driven swings of confidence in their potency. The pattern perhaps was most pronounced with boards and shareholders, the primary "internal" checks on public company executives. We turn to these now.

Internal Constraints

During the 1980s, the market for corporate control overshadowed boards and shareholders as a constraint on the discretion of public company executives. As the 1990s began hostile takeovers fell into abeyance, creating a corporate governance vacuum boards and shareholders seemed to be filling to a significant degree. In the mid- and late-1990s, corporate governance, though by no means theoretically ideal, was apparently operating effectively, as evidenced by the outstanding returns public companies were delivering for investors. The share price reversals and corporate scandals occurring as the 2000s got underway indicated that oversight of public company executives by boards and shareholders in fact left much to be desired in the 1990s. Bearing this basic narrative arc—seemingly activated boards and shareholders at least partially discredited—in mind clarifies considerably potentially conflicting evidence regarding the extent to which directors and shareholders actually impinged upon managerial discretion during the 1990s.

A GOVERNANCE VACUUM

Peter Bernstein, a prolific author on financial markets and former fund manager, observed in 1992 "voluble critics ... demonstrate remarkable zest in painting corporate America as

---

[134] GARY HAMEL, LEADING THE REVOLUTION: HOW TO THRIVE IN TURBULENT TIMES BY MAKING INNOVATION A WAY OF LIFE 4 (2002).

[135] LOWENSTEIN, *supra* note 114, at 103.

[136] Chapter 7, note 389 and related discussion.

[137] *A Look Back at Modern Finance: Accomplishments and Limitations*, J. APP. CORP. FIN., Fall 2015, at 10, 12–13 (interview with Eugene Fama).

lethargic and arthritic."[138] For instance, the *Washington Post*, in a 1991 article entitled "The Numskull Factor," noted that "(i)n many US industries, leading companies are faltering: autos (General Motors), banking (Citicorp), photography (Kodak) and retailing (Sears)," argued "the dreary performance of so many huge companies in so many industries is an indictment of something about American management practices and style" and suggested "(w)hat produces a lot of bad corporate decisions is executives' insularity."[139] A *Business Week* columnist claimed the following year that "as overseas rivals have grown more agile, many American corporations have seemed to be lumbering and misdirected."[140] In 1993's *Reengineering the Corporation*, "the business blockbuster of the early nineties,"[141] Michael Hammer and James Champy asked readers rhetorically "why are so many American companies bloated, clumsy, rigid, sluggish, noncompetitive, uncreative, inefficient, disdainful of customer needs, and losing money?" [142]

During the Deal Decade the obvious corrective for "lumbering" and "sluggish" performance would have been the hostile takeover bid, with poorly run, underachieving firms attracting offers from acquirers seeking to create value by obtaining control and appointing a new management team. The theory remained familiar in the 1990s. Law professor Jonathan Macey wrote in 1998 "the market for corporate control serves as a mechanism for replacing weak managers with superior managers, and for giving managers greater incentives to perform better."[143] Takeover activity, however, declined markedly as soon as the 1980s ended.[144] Former Securities and Exchange Commission (SEC) commissioner Joseph Grundfest said in 1993, "(t)he takeover wars are over. Management won. Although hostile tender offers remain technically possible, the legal and financial barriers in their path are far higher today than they were a few short years ago."[145]

In the mid- and late-1990s merger activity would soar to unprecedented levels. In 1995 the record for annual aggregate value of deals set in 1988 fell, and fell again each year thereafter in the 1990s (Figure 5.4).[146] The disciplinary aspect of the market for corporate control nevertheless was very much a sideshow. Strategically motivated acquisitions carried out with the cooperation of the companies being bought underpinned the 1990s merger wave rather than "raiders" seeking out targets underperforming due to poor management.[147] Hostile takeovers

---

138 Peter L. Bernstein, *Are Financial Markets the Problem or the Solution? A Reply to Michael Porter*, J. App. Corp. Fin., Spring 1992, at 17, 17.

139 Robert J. Samuleson, *The Numskull Factor*, Wash. Post, June 26, 1991, A19.

140 Judith H. Dobrzynski, *A Wake-Up Call for Corporate Boards*, Bus. Wk., Apr. 20, 1992, 35.

141 Stuart Crainer, *The Gurus and the Ghosts*, Globe & Mail, Nov. 30, 1998, B15.

142 Michael Hammer & James Champy, Reengineering the Corporation: A Manifesto for Business Revolution 7 (1993).

143 Jonathan R. Macey, *The Legality of the Shareholder Rights By-Law in Delaware: Preserving the Market for Corporate Control*, J. App. Corp. Fin., Winter 1998, at 63, 65. See also Michael C. Jensen, *The Modern Industrial Revolution, Exit, and the Failure of Internal Control Systems*, 48 J. Fin. 831, 852 (1993).

144 Chapter 4, notes 152–53 and related discussion.

145 Joseph A. Grundfest, *Just Vote No: A Minimalist Strategy for Dealing with Barbarians inside the Gates*, 45 Stan. L. Rev. 857, 858 (1993).

146 Marcel Kahan & Edward B. Rock, *How I Learned to Stop Worrying and Love the Pill: Adaptive Responses to Takeover Law*, 69 U. Chi. L. Rev. 871, 879 (2002).

147 Brian R. Cheffins, *Delaware and the Transformation of Corporate Governance*, 40 Del. J. Corp. L. 1, 11 (2015).

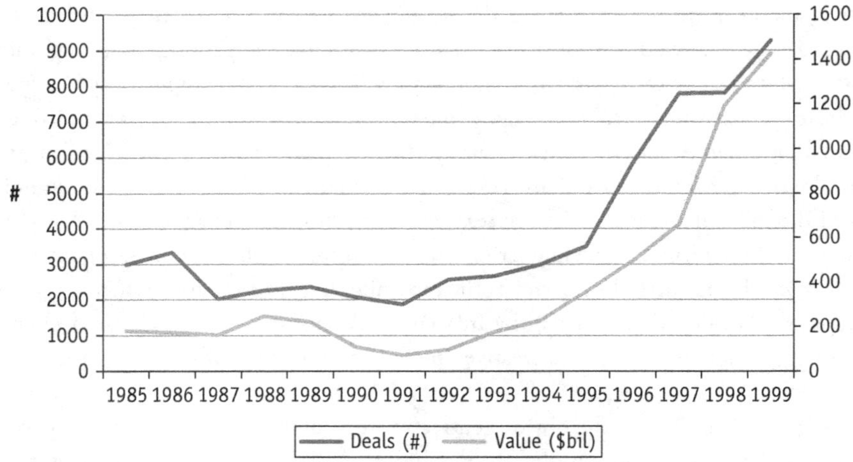

FIGURE 5.4 M&A Activity (Number and Value of Deals), 1985–1999.
Source: Marcel Kahan & Edward B. Rock, *How I Learned to Stop Worrying and Love the Pill: Adaptive Responses to Takeover Law*, 69 U. CHI. L. REV. 871, 879-80 (2002).

did occur in the 1990s, with the success rate for bids actually launched being similar to that prevailing in the 1980s.[148] The likelihood of a takeover offer being hostile was, however, considerably lower.[149] The controversy, aggression, and outrage that had permeated the market for corporate control in the 1980s duly ebbed away.[150]

As the 1990s began, there was widespread awareness that because the market for corporate control could operate as a potent check on public company executives a marked retreat in contested takeover activity might substantially reduce managerial accountability.[151] For instance, in 1992 academics John Byrd and Kent Hickman said of hostile takeovers "(a)s this once powerful disciplinary device wanes, other corporate governance mechanisms must play a larger role."[152] Numerous observers, including Byrd and Hickman, argued that boards, and more particularly outside directors, should fill the governance vacuum.[153] Others said shareholders, and more particularly institutional shareholders, could and should step forward.[154] During the early 1990s there was considerable optimism about what boards and institutional

---

[148] *Id.*

[149] *Id.* at 12; Matthew D. Cain, Stephen B. McKeon & Steven Davidoff Solomon, *Do Takeover Laws Matter? Evidence from Five Decades of Hostile Takeovers*, 124 J. FIN. ECON. 464, 468 (2017).

[150] ROBERT TEITELMAN, BLOODSPORT: WHEN RUTHLESS DEALMAKERS, SHREWD IDEOLOGUES, AND BRAWLING LAWYERS TOPPLED THE CORPORATE ESTABLISHMENT 335 (2016).

[151] Cheffins, *supra* note 147, at 56–57.

[152] John Byrd & Kent Hickman, *The Case for Independent Outside Directors*, J. APP. CORP. FIN., Fall 1992, at 78, 78.

[153] *Id.* at 78–79; Sarah Bartlett, *Life in the Executive Suite after Drexel*, NY TIMES, Feb. 18, 1990, F1; Myron Magnet, *Directors, Wake Up!*, FORTUNE, June 15, 1992, 85.

[154] Victor F. Zonana, *Activist Shareholders Spur Growth of a New Kind of Advice Industry*, LA TIMES, July 21, 1991, D3 (quoting David Eisner, senior vice president of Providence); John H. Matheson & Brent A. Olson, *Corporate Law and the Longterm Shareholder Model of Corporate Governance*, 76 MINN. L. REV. 1313, 1317–18 (1992).

shareholders could and would achieve. Disappointment, in contrast, was the order of the day a decade later.

BOARDS

Harvard Business School professor Jay Lorsch argued in *Pawns and Potentates*, a coauthored 1989 study of boards, that norms of polite boardroom behavior compromised substantially the effectiveness of boards as a constraint on potentially wayward executives.[155] *Fortune* offered a similar verdict in 1990, acknowledging that the board could be seen "as the missing link in the chain of managerial accountability" but suggesting "(t)oo often, the directors are in management's hip pocket."[156] The reputation of the board would soon improve markedly, albeit temporarily.

In the 1970s and 1980s, outside director representation on boards increased significantly and key board committees staffed primarily by non-executives became considerably more prevalent.[157] Citing such trends, consulting firm Korn Ferry argued in 1991 that "(d)irectors have become stronger and more independent partners in corporate leadership" and that "(t)he CEO no longer reigns as an absolute monarch, expecting corporate policy to be rubberstamped."[158] *Fortune* told readers the same year "directors have begun flexing atrophied muscles and forcing out chief executives at laggard companies."[159] CEOs of a number of prominent companies indeed were fired in 1991 or resigned under strong pressure from the board. The firms affected included computer maker Compaq, Goodyear Tire & Rubber, the conglomerate Tenneco, and Allied Signal, an aerospace, auto parts, and engineering firm.[160]

The boardroom intrigue of 1991 was merely a warm-up act for 1992 and 1993. *Forbes* said in 1994 of the forced CEO departures in these years, "(n)ever have so many heads fallen, in such quick succession, at so many big companies; never have so many been so rudely thrust from power. It was a reversal of historic proportions."[161] In October 1992, General Motors' board dismissed CEO and chairman of the board Robert Stempel, prompting *USA Today* to proclaim "a new era of accountability for chief executives" and the *Los Angeles Times* to argue "the bloodletting" was "heavily symbolic of a changing of the guard for the nation's industries as they try to remake themselves to survive in the global marketplace."[162] Over a period of a week at the end of January 1993, the bosses of IBM, Westinghouse, a diversified industrial firm, and financial services giant American Express lost their jobs.[163] In August of that year,

---

[155] Jay W. Lorsch & Elizabeth MacIver, Pawns and Potentates: The Reality of America's Corporate Boards 96 (1990); Chapter 4, notes 276, 280–81 and related discussion.

[156] Brett Fromson et al., *The Big Owners Roar*, Fortune, July 30, 1990.

[157] Chapter 3, notes 276–81 and related discussion; Chapter 4, notes 252-56 and accompanying text.

[158] Timothy D. Schellhardt, *More Directors Are Recruited from Outside*, Wall St. J., Mar. 20, 1991, B1.

[159] Rob Norton & Suneel Ratan, *Who Owns This Company Anyhow?*, Fortune, July 29, 1991, 131.

[160] Brian Bremner, *Tough Times, Tough Bosses*, Bus. Wk., Nov. 25, 1991, 174.

[161] Dana Wechsler Linden & Nancy Rotenier, *Good-Bye to Berle & Means*, Forbes, Jan. 3, 1994, 100.

[162] James Kim, *Ineffective CEOs Walk Plank*, USA Today, Oct. 28, 1992, B1; Amy Harmon & Donald Woutat, *New Leadership Named at GM; Dividend Slashed*, LA Times, Nov. 3, 1992, A1.

[163] *Getting Rid of the Boss*, Economist, Feb. 6, 1993, 11; Bill Saporito, *A Week of Woe for the CEO*, Fortune, Feb. 22, 1993, 10.

Kodak's Kay Whitmore joined the parade "of CEO departures that shattered the corporate equivalent of Mount Rushmore."[164]

Not everyone was convinced that the various high-profile CEO dismissals truly signaled a "new era." A common complaint was that the boards that pressured their chief executives to leave should have moved faster, with action having been taken only after huge losses in stock market value.[165] It was also argued that there remained numerous companies with underperforming executives where boards were failing to take any corrective action.[166]

Despite the misgivings expressed, the prevailing view was that the CEO dismissals of the early 1990s represented an important change in public company dynamics. *USA Today* argued "(a)ll this pushing and prodding by board members reflects basic changes in the way US companies are governed. Power is shifting away from chief executives."[167] Ira Millstein, chief legal counsel to General Motors' outside directors as the board moved toward dismissing Stempel,[168] suggested in 1993 "the era of total managerial dominance of the governance process is over" due partly to "empowered and legitimized boards of directors."[169] Even Lorsch, who was critical of the boards that dismissed their chief executives for failing to move more promptly, conceded directors were "becoming stronger and taking their responsibilities more seriously. That's good news for all of us."[170]

The sense of optimism about the contribution that boards were making to managerial accountability was generally sustained throughout the remainder of the 1990s, even if doubters remained. *Business Week*, when it launched in 1996 "the first-ever corporate-governance ranking system" justified the initiative partly on the basis that "cronyism still prevails on scores of boards. The movement to transform the boardroom from a cozy club of the CEO's buddies into an independent, active body representing owners is taking way too long."[171] Academics Sanjai Bhagat and Bernard Black, seeking to account in 1999 for empirical findings indicating that having a board where independent directors dominated numerically failed to improve corporate performance, cited anecdotal evidence indicating "(i)ndependent directors often turn out to be lapdogs rather than watchdogs."[172] The general tenor of opinion was, however, considerably more hopeful.

---

[164] *Change's Pace Costs Kodak CEO*, CHI. TRIB., Aug. 7, 1993, 1; Robert A.G. Monks, *To Change the Company, Change the Board*, WALL ST. J., Apr. 27, 1993, A20.

[165] Judith Dobrzynski, *A GM Postmortem: Lessons for Corporate America*, BUS. WK., Nov. 9, 1992, 87; *Focus at Kodak*, FIN. TIMES, Aug. 20, 1993; C.K. Prahalad, *Corporate Governance or Corporate Value Added? Rethinking the Primacy of Shareholder Value*, J. APP. CORP. FIN., Winter 1994, at 40, 42.

[166] *Management Incentive Compensation and Shareholder Value*, J. APP. CORP. FIN., Spring 1992, 110, 118 (quoting Bernard Black).

[167] James Kim, *Power Shuffle*, USA TODAY, Jan. 28, 1993, B1.

[168] Joseph B. White & Paul Ingrassia, *Behind Revolt at GM, Lawyer Ira Millstein Helped Call the Shots*, WALL ST. J., Apr. 13, 1992, A1.

[169] Millstein, *supra* note 41, at 1486.

[170] Kim, *supra* note 162.

[171] *A Tough World Needs Tough Boards*, BUS. WK., Nov. 25, 1996, 190.

[172] Sanjai Bhagat & Bernard Black, *The Uncertain Relationship between Board Composition and Firm Performance*, 54 BUS. LAW. 921, 922 (1999).

The evolving views of erstwhile board skeptic Lorsch illustrated the growing sense of optimism about boards in the 1990s. He wrote in the *Harvard Business Review* in 1995 "(c)hief executives who resist empowered boards must change their attitude. If they do not, they and their companies will be the losers because the empowered board is here to stay."[173] In a 2001 interview, having acknowledged that 1980s directors "were more like the pawns," he said "(t)oday they are more like the potentates."[174] *Business Week* had also become more optimistic, telling readers in January 2000 as it unveiled the results of its most recent assessment of America's best and worst boards, "(t)he governance revolution that swept through Corporate America's boardrooms in the 1990s has led to far more active oversight. Composed largely of independent directors, they are more accountable than ever."[175] Ira Millstein concurred, saying in 1997 "(i)n the past decade, the historically passive US board of directors has been transforming itself into an independent, active monitor, capable of real—rather than merely nominal—management and business performance oversight."[176] The upshot, according to the president of the National Association of Corporate Directors, was that "(t)he CEO isn't going to be God anymore."[177]

The corporate scandals of the early 2000s, which will be considered in detail in Chapter 6, scotched substantially the 1990s optimism concerning boards. In January 2002, with "the corporate disaster count" still going up, *Fortune* observed "(t)hese are all man-made disasters, and when you search for the people to blame, you end up quickly at the board of directors."[178] A 2003 study of why boards failed maintained that "(a) striking symptom of all the recent corporate scandals is how unquestioned and powerful the bosses' leadership was."[179] John Bogle, founder of the Vanguard mutual fund group, said in 2005 of "the Great Bull Market of 1997–2000," "(c)orporate America went largely astray because the power of managers went virtually unchecked by our gatekeepers for too long. Our corporate directors were primarily to blame."[180]

Was the improvement of boards hailed in the mid- and late-1990s merely a mirage? The *New York Times* suggested this might well have been the case. A 2003 article published to coincide with the 10-year anniversary of the 1993 dismissal of IBM's CEO entitled "The Revolution That Wasn't" said "10 years later, it looks very much as if the corporate governance revolution of 1993 is back at Square 1."[181] A more charitable verdict was that boards might have improved in general terms in the 1990s but that they let their guard down as share prices rose inexorably. Bogle, for instance, argued that "during an era of remarkable prosperity" it was likely "directors relaxed their vigilance."[182] *Fortune* speculated similarly that while directors of the iconic companies that dismissed their CEOs in the early 1990s

---

[173] Jay W. Lorsch, *Empowering the Board*, HARV. BUS. REV., Jan./Feb. 1995, 107, 107.

[174] *The Professor: Jay Lorsch*, DIRECTORS & BOARDS, Fall 2001, at 18, 18.

[175] John A. Byrne, *The Best & Worst Boards*, BUS. WK., Jan. 24, 2000, 143.

[176] Ira M. Millstein, *The Responsible Board*, 52 BUS. LAW. 407, 410 (1997).

[177] Joann S. Lublin, *CEOs Give Up More Clout to Boards*, WALL ST. J., July 26, 1996, A9.

[178] Geoffrey Colvin, *The Boardroom Follies*, FORTUNE, Jan. 7, 2002, 32.

[179] RALPH D. WARD, SAVING THE CORPORATE BOARD: WHY BOARDS FAIL AND HOW TO FIX THEM 17 (2003).

[180] JOHN C. BOGLE, THE BATTLE FOR THE SOUL OF CAPITALISM 33, 45 (2005).

[181] Claudia H. Deutsch, *The Revolution That Wasn't*, NY TIMES. Jan. 26, 2003, Business, 1.

[182] BOGLE, *supra* note 180, at 40.

acted out of fear of embarrassment of possible corporate failure, generally "(d)uring the '90s economic expansion and bull market madness, fear went into hiding."[183] Vigilance moreover, was not relaxed entirely. In 1999, 23 of the companies in the *Fortune* 500 replaced their chief executives.[184] The CEO turnover rate was sufficient to prompt a *Business Week* columnist to observe "(t)he last year of the century has been a tough one for the struggling chief executive."[185]

Evidence regarding board structure confirms that even if assessments of boards offered in the mid- and late-1990s were overly optimistic, changes were occurring. The proportion of inside directors on boards of larger companies, which declined in both the 1970s and 1980s, continued to shrink.[186] Key board committees were increasingly staffed exclusively by independent directors.[187] Lorsch, in a 2013 essay providing a retrospective analysis of his 1989 *Pawns and Potentates* book, said that the adoption of these and related best practices in the 1990s collectively amounted to "a remarkable change" that "enhanced the power of boards in relation to management and other top executives."[188] In sum, though the corporate scandals of the early 2000s revealed directors did not qualify as potentates or even fully vigilant gatekeepers, boards likely were a more meaningful constraint for public company executives at the end of the 1990s than at the beginning.

SHAREHOLDERS

Shareholder value, having emerged as a leading priority for public company executives in the 1980s,[189] took on a talismanic quality in the 1990s. A logical assumption is that direct shareholder pressure dictated this outcome. Shareholder activism did indeed intensify during the early 1990s. However, stockholder interventions played only a subsidiary role as public company executives increasingly fixated on shareholder returns. A desire by public company CEOs to hit earnings targets investors focused on closely was of greater importance.

Shareholder Value Tops the Priority List

In 1990, a columnist for the *Globe & Mail*, a Toronto-based newspaper, inferred from a dramatic increase in usage of the term "stakeholder" in his newspaper "the concept of

---

[183] Geoffrey Colvin, *CEO Knockdown*, FORTUNE, Apr. 4, 2005, 19.

[184] Joann S. Lublin & Matt Murray, *CEOs Depart Faster than Ever as Boards, Investors Lose Patience*, WALL ST. J., Oct. 27, 2000, B1.

[185] John A. Byrne, *Boards Share the Blame When the Boss Fails*, BUS. WK., Dec. 27, 1999, 58.

[186] Chapter 3, notes 276-77 and related discussion; Chapter 4, note 254 and accompanying text; Jeffrey N. Gordon, *The Rise of Independent Directors in the United States, 1950–2005: Of Shareholder Value and Stock Market Prices*, 59 STANFORD L. REV. 1465, 1473–74, 1530 (2007).

[187] AMERICAN SOCIETY OF CORPORATE SECRETARIES, CURRENT BOARD PRACTICES: THIRD STUDY 3–4, 34–41 (2000) (survey of more than 600 public companies, identifying practices changing between 1997 and 1999).

[188] Jay W. Lorsch, *America's Changing Corporate Boardrooms: The Last Twenty-Five Years*, 3 HARV. BUS. L. REV. 119, 123, 124 (2013).

[189] Chapter 4, notes 293–305 and related discussion.

stakeholders could become the corporate flummox of the 1990s, a populist substitute for 'maximizing shareholder value,' the presumably harsh dominant corporate ethic of the 1980s."[190] Stakeholders would indeed remain on the corporate radar screen in the 1990s, with a 1999 study of corporate governance suggesting there was "no clear consensus on whose interests corporate governance serves."[191] Matters in fact were rather more cut and dried than this for American executives. During the 1990s most remaining doubts about relative priorities dissipated—shareholder value trumped other concerns. As management professor Gerald Davis subsequently observed, "(b)y the late 1990s the question of the purpose of the corporation evidently had been resolved.... Corporations existed to create shareholder value."[192]

Consistent with Davis's conjecture, usage of the term "shareholder value" surged in the press and in annual reports of US public companies in the mid- and late-1990s.[193] Rhetoric deployed by public company executives also illustrated the priority being attached to shareholder returns. David Coulter, who became chief executive of Bank of America in 1996, recounted the following year "(t)he first thing we decided was that the governing objective of B of A would be to maximize shareholder value." When he received pushback within the bank he responded, "(w)ell, if we don't say that, what do we say? I don't see any alternative."[194] Bernie Ebbers, chief executive of WorldCom, was even more forthright, saying "(o)ur goal is not to capture market share or be global. Our goal is to be the No. 1 stock on Wall Street."[195]

A change in the stance of the Business Roundtable, the trade association of chief executives of leading US corporations, was an additional "telling piece of anecdotal evidence" on shareholder value's rise to preeminence.[196] The Business Roundtable declared in 1981 that managers were "expected to serve the public interest as well as private profit."[197] It adopted a similar neutral tone in 1990 when it said in a statement on corporate governance that it was "the directors' responsibility to carefully weigh the interests of all stakeholders as part of their responsibility to the corporation or to the long-term interests of its shareholders."[198] Neutrality was shelved in 1997. The Business Roundtable declared "the paramount duty of management and of boards of directors is to the corporation's stockholders" and indicated

---

[190] Terence Corcoran, *Disclosing the Great Stakeholder Hoax*, GLOBE & MAIL, Dec. 15, 1990, B4.

[191] DAN A. BAWLEY, CORPORATE GOVERNANCE AND ACCOUNTABILITY: WHAT ROLE FOR THE REGULATOR, DIRECTOR, AND AUDITOR? 116 (1999).

[192] GERALD F. DAVIS, MANAGED BY THE MARKETS: HOW FINANCE RESHAPED AMERICA 96 (2009).

[193] Johan Heilbron, Joachim Verheul & Sander Quak, *The Origins and Early Diffusion of "Shareholder Value" in the United States*, 43 THEO. SOC. 1, 8 (2014); Blake Edward Taylor, *Reconsidering the Rise of "Shareholder Value" in the United States*, London School of Economics Economic History Working Paper No. 214/2015, 12–13.

[194] David Coulter, *Managing for Shareholder Value at Bank of America*, J. APP. CORP. FIN., Summer 1997, at 68, 68.

[195] Collingwood, *supra* note 132.

[196] Bengt Holmstrom & Steven N. Kaplan, *Corporate Governance and Merger Activity in the United States: Making Sense of the 1980s and 1990s*, 15 J. ECON. PERSP. 121, 136 (2001). See also Lynne L. Dallas, *Is There Hope for Change? The Evolution of Conceptions of Good Corporate Governance*, 54 SAN DIEGO L. REV. 491, 530 (2017).

[197] Chapter 4, note 288 and related discussion.

[198] Business Roundtable, *Corporate Governance and American Competitiveness March, 1990*, 46 BUS. LAW. 241, 244 (1990).

"the interests of other stakeholders" were merely "relevant as a derivative of the duty to stockholders."[199]

Shareholder Activism

In the 1980s shareholder value emerged as a pivotal measuring stick of executive achievement primarily because top management feared anemic shareholder returns would prompt an unwelcome takeover bid.[200] Paradoxically from a 1980s perspective in the 1990s shareholder value moved to the top of the priority list as hostile takeovers went into retreat.[201] What then explains the ascendancy of shareholder interests? More robust activism is a plausible candidate. There was considerable speculation in the early 1990s that growing shareholder participation in public company affairs was destined to erode considerably managerial discretion. For instance, management expert Peter Drucker said in 1992 the rise of institutional ownership was creating "one of the most startling power shifts in American history."[202] Some were even proclaiming the dawn of an era of "investor capitalism."[203] In fact, stockholder involvement was not the primary factor motivating public company executives to treat the promotion of shareholder value as the top corporate priority.

From the 1950s through to the 1980s, the proportion of shares owned by institutional investors grew steadily.[204] The trend stalled in the 1990s (Figure 5.5). Nevertheless, the importance of institutional shareholders from a corporate governance perspective was hailed with some regularity. The *Wall Street Journal* said in 1990 that the "growing concentration of stock ownership in a few hands has the potential to shift the balance of power between shareholders and corporate managements."[205] Management professor Michael Useem suggested in 1996 "(i)nstitutional investors are the new high priests, the new repositories of wealth and power."[206] Richard Koppes, recently departed general counsel and number two executive at the California Public Employees Retirement System (CalPERS), argued in 1997 that "(n)othing has defined the revolution of corporate governance over the last 20 years as the rise of institutional investors."[207]

Despite the growth in institutional share ownership between the 1950s and 1980s, during this period institutional investors largely refrained from intervening in the affairs of public companies in which they held shares.[208] As the 1990s began, it was widely believed that the

---

[199] Business Roundtable, Statement on Corporate Governance 3 (1997).

[200] Chapter 4, notes 365–72 and accompanying text.

[201] Gordon, *supra* note 186, at 1530.

[202] Ellen Neuborne & Michelle Osborn, *Shareholders Revolt at Sears*, USA Today, May 15, 1992, B1.

[203] Michael Useem, Investor Capitalism: How Money Managers Are Changing the Face of Corporate America (1996).

[204] Chapter 2, notes 320–23 and related discussion; Chapter 3, Figure 3.1, note 205 and accompanying text; Chapter 4, notes 327–28 and related discussion.

[205] James A. White, *Giant Pension Funds' Explosive Growth Concentrates Economic Assets and Power*, Wall St. J., June 28, 1990, C1.

[206] Useem, *supra* note 203, at 38.

[207] Richard H. Koppes, *Corporate Governance*, Nat'l. L.J., Apr. 14, 1997, B5.

[208] Chapter 2, notes 327–30 and related discussion; Chapter 3, notes 190–92, 207 and accompanying text; Chapter 4, notes 343–47, 354, 357–61 and related discussion.

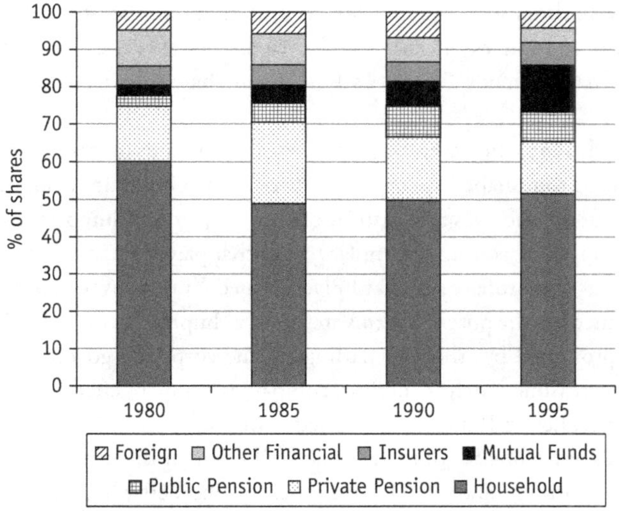

FIGURE 5.5 US Corporate Stock Held by Households and Institutions, 1980–1995.
Source: OECD, OECD ECONOMIC SURVEYS—UNITED STATES 124 (1996).

situation was changing, with institutional shareholders being on the verge of becoming active monitors of public company executives.[209] Advocates for this point of view argued that, with institutional ownership having grown substantially the sums at risk were too substantial for institutional investors to stand by if management went off the rails.[210] Institutional shareholders also would be motivated to intervene, the thinking went, because the stakes they held were too large to unwind without putting substantial downward pressure on the share price.[211] The *New York Times* said, for instance, in 1990 "as the investment funds hold ever-larger portions of major American companies, they feel they face no alternative but to get more involved. They cannot sell their holdings without taking big losses because the act of selling would drive down the value of the shares."[212]

The dismantling of some legal deterrents to intervention in the early 1990s was an additional reason increased institutional shareholder activism was anticipated. In 1992 the SEC cut back on securities law requirements applicable to parties seeking support from neutral stockholders, most notably those necessitating the submission of documentation to the SEC for review because proxies were being solicited.[213] For instance,

---

[209] John C. Coffee, *Liquidity versus Control: The Institutional Investor as Corporate Monitor*, 91 COLUM. L. REV. 1277, 1281 (1991).

[210] John Pound, *Beyond Takeovers: Politics Comes to Corporate Control*, HARV. BUS. REV., Mar./Apr. 1992, 83, 87; Bernard S. Black, *Institutional Investors and Corporate Governance: The Case for Institutional Voice*, J. APP. CORP. FIN., Fall 1992, at 19, 24.

[211] Kathleen Day & Robert McCartney, *Who's Minding the Managers?*, WASH. POST, Aug. 19, 1990, H1; *Not Awakening the Dead*, ECONOMIST, Aug. 10, 1996, 57.

[212] Sarah Bartlett, *Big Funds Pressing for Voice in Management of Companies*, NY TIMES, Feb. 23, 1990, A1.

[213] Brian R. Cheffins & John Armour, *The Past, Present, and Future of Shareholder Activism by Hedge Funds*, 37 J. CORP. L. 51, 90 (2011).

SEC filing safe harbors were created for all oral communications, for any discussions between fewer than 10 investors and for advertisements, speeches, and statements in the media.[214] The changes made it less costly to form shareholder coalitions to lobby for desired changes.[215]

During the early 1990s there were numerous vocal champions for the institutional activism seemingly destined to reshape US corporate governance. One claim made, as the *Financial Times* pointed out in 1990, was that institutions "could prove an important spur to business efficiency in the 1990s, performing a similar role to that played by the threat of a takeover in the last decade."[216] Law professor Bernard Black argued "(m)ore oversight doesn't guarantee better performance but the potential gains are large."[217] Improved corporate decision-making and efficiency prompted by "the new darlings of the corporate governance movement"[218] also could, some reasoned, help American companies compete effectively against overseas rivals. For instance, Lester Thurow, who argued in the early 1990s that the American version of capitalism was in decline,[219] contended that "(t)he nub of the matter is having long-term owners in the boardroom" and cited institutional shareholders when saying "(t)he only way for capitalism to work is for owners to take responsibility."[220]

Amongst advocates of institutional shareholder activism, there was good reason for optimism in the early 1990s. The *Wall Street Journal* remarked in 1992 on how the mood of institutions that had thought of themselves merely as investors had been changing.[221] In so doing it quoted the chairman of a firm offering advice to companies on securing shareholder support through the solicitation of proxy documentation as saying institutional investors were having "a tremendous impact on corporate culture."[222] *Newsweek* indicated in 1993 "(p)owerful shareholders are holding boards and CEOs more accountable."[223] The same year the president of the board overseeing CalPERS declared "(w)e are in corporate America's face and intend to stay there."[224]

Institutional shareholder involvement with high-profile CEO dismissals boards carried out in the early 1990s was an eye-catching manifestation of institutional investors getting "in corporate America's face." When boards at General Motors, IBM, American Express, and Kodak pushed out their chief executives, the directors' feet had been held to the fire by

---

214 Joseph Evan Calio & Rafael Xavier Zahralddin, *The Securities and Exchange Commission's 1992 Proxy Amendments: Questions of Accountability*, 14 PACE L. REV. 459, 494–500 (1994).

215 Stuart L. Gillan & Laura T. Starks, *Corporate Governance Proposals and Shareholder Activism: The Role of Institutional Investors*, 57 J. FIN. ECON. 275, 279 (2000).

216 Martin Dickson, *Investors Wake Up to Their Power*, FIN. TIMES, Dec. 3, 1990, 18.

217 Bernard S. Black, *Next Steps in Corporate Governance Reform: 13(D) Rules and Control Person Liability*, J. APP. CORP. FIN., Winter 1993, at 49. 49.

218 Jill E. Fisch, *Relationship Investing: Will It Happen? Will It Work?*, 55 OHIO STATE L.J. 1047 (1994).

219 *Supra* note 47 and related discussion.

220 *How to Make Capitalism Work*, NY TIMES, Apr. 12, 1992, F5.

221 Kevin G. Salwen & Joann S. Lublin, *Giant Investors Flex Their Muscles More at US Corporations*, WALL ST. J., Apr. 27, 1992, A1.

222 *Id.*.

223 Jolie Solomon, *Dialing for More Deals*, NEWSWEEK, Dec. 27, 1993, 34.

224 David A. Vise, *Calif. Pension Fund Plans an Investment in Power*, WASH. POST, Nov. 7, 1993, H1.

institutional investors.[225] Such institutionally prompted boardroom coups meant shareholders had "emphatically gotten corporate America's attention."[226]

Even though institutional shareholder involvement in some high-profile CEO dismissals elicited attention, changes to executive pay constituted the most tangible byproduct of institutional shareholder activism that occurred in the early 1990s.[227] With managerial compensation having risen substantially in the 1980s,[228] executive pay was a lightning rod for discontent amidst early 1990s pessimism. Generous managerial compensation elicited harsh criticism with the economy slumping, with layoffs mounting and with US public companies not simply losing ground to foreign rivals but to foreign rivals with considerably lower executive pay.[229] Institutional shareholders were among the critics. James Heard, president of Institutional Shareholder Services, a firm specializing in advising shareholders how to vote on resolutions put before them, said in 1992 "executive pay is the real hot-button issue for institutional investors" because "(i)t's typical of what's wrong with American management and why the US is not more competitive economically."[230]

Institutional investors were much more concerned about the configuration of executive pay than the amounts involved, believing a much stronger relationship between pay and performance would result in better management.[231] Jon Lukomink, overseer of five pension funds with assets of about $55 billion as New York City's deputy controller for pensions, said in 1995 "(w)e don't care how much someone gets paid as long as we get paid; it's our dirty little secret."[232] Institutions successfully pushed a pay-for-performance agenda in the 1990s.[233] In large public companies, the proportion of CEO compensation that was equity based, primarily in the form of stock options, rose from under 20 percent in 1990 to 60 percent by 1999.[234] The fact that the proportion of a public company's shares owned by institutional investors was a strong predictor of the extent to which 1990s executives were paid using stock options indicates institutional shareholder preferences contributed to the shift.[235]

While there were tangible manifestations of institutional shareholder influence, the traditional bias in favor of passivity remained largely intact in the early- and mid-1990s. In 1993

---

225 Thomas A. Stewart et al., *The King Is Dead*, FORTUNE, Jan. 11, 1993, 34; Steve Lohr, *Big Business in Turmoil*, NY TIMES, Jan. 28, 1993, A1; Martin Dickson, *Big Blue Soothes Its Big Investors*, FIN. TIMES, Sept. 24, 1993, 14.

226 Myron Magnet & John Labate, *What Activist Investors Want*, FORTUNE, Mar. 8, 1993, 59.

227 Frank Dobbin & Dirk Zorn, *Corporate Malfeasance and the Myth of Shareholder Value*, 17 POLITICAL POWER & SOCIAL THEORY 179, 189 (2005).

228 Chapter 4, note 566 and accompanying text.

229 Steve Lohr, *Recession Puts a Harsh Spotlight on Hefty Pay of Top Executives*, NY TIMES, Jan. 20, 1992, A1.

230 *Id.*

231 James E. Heard, *Executive Compensation: Perspective of the Institutional Investor*, 63 U. CIN. L. REV. 749, 749, 751 (1995).

232 Lisa Bransten, *Matching Executive Compensation with Corporate Performance*, FIN. TIMES, Aug. 18, 1995, 19.

233 Randall Thomas, *Explaining the International CEO Pay Gap: Board Capture or Market Driven*, 57 VAND. L. REV. 1171, 1247 (2004).

234 Brian J. Hall, *Six Challenges in Designing Equity-Based Pay*, J. APP. CORP. FIN., Spring 2003, at 21, 23.

235 Parthiban David, Rahul Kochhar & Edward Levitas, *The Effect of Institutional Investors on the Level and Mix of CEO Compensation*, 41 ACAD. MGMT. J. 200, 205 (1998) (finding the pattern only applied with institutional shareholders lacking any additional relationship with the companies in which they owned shares); Jay C. Hartzell & Laura T. Starks, *Institutional Investors and Executive Compensation*, 58 J. FIN. 2351, 2352–53, 2372 (2003).

the *Wall Street Journal*, having acknowledged that "(t)o hear some people tell it, corporate chieftains are on the run," indicated "the reality, however, is quite different," with most CEOs being "unscathed."[236] Law professor Louis Lowenstein noted the same year that while "there has been an increasing concentration of ownership by institutional investors.... (T)hese institutions have shown surprisingly little interest in the ongoing oversight of the businesses in which they invest."[237] The *Financial Times* concurred, saying in 1995 "(u)ntil now, shareholder activism in the US has been a tepid affair."[238]

Even the institutional investor activism that did occur in the early- and mid-1990s was very much a minority pursuit, oriented around a subset of public pension funds. Mutual funds, for instance, had little appetite for an active role in corporate governance matters.[239] Lobbying by Fidelity Investments, operator of a large family of mutual funds, did help to prompt the 1993 dismissal of Kodak's CEO.[240] Still, even with Fidelity controlling at the time around 2 percent of shares of US public companies, Robert Pozen, Fidelity's general counsel, emphasized Fidelity would not make a habit of intervening and would instead continue to sell when it saw problems at particular companies.[241]

Private pension funds—those established by companies on behalf of employees—"rarely (were) visible in the new institutional investor activism of the 1990s,"[242] perhaps due in part to a reluctance to antagonize executives of other companies.[243] Public pension funds were less reticent, but only those from a handful of states and municipalities were inclined to step forward.[244] Among those, CalPERS was the prime moving force.[245] It was christened in 1993 by the *Chicago Tribune* as "the leader of the growing shareholder activist movement that is changing American corporate culture."[246] Even CalPERS dialed back its activism, however, as the 1990s progressed.

In the early 1990s CalPERS' combative chief executive Dale Hanson did much to drive an ambitious governance agenda.[247] In 1994, however, he stepped down in favor of a more circumspect successor.[248] Koppes, described in the shareholder activism realm as "one of the

---

[236] Stuart Mieher, *Shareholder Activism, Despite Hoopla, Leaves Most CEOs Unscathed*, WALL ST. J., May 24, 1993, A1.

[237] Louis Lowenstein, *Dear Mr. Clinton*, BARRON'S, Feb. 8, 1993, 20.

[238] Richard Waters, *Hostile Offers on Increase*, FIN. TIMES, May 4, 1995, International Corporate Finance, III.

[239] Jayne W. Barnard, *Institutional Investors and the New Corporate Governance*, 69 N.C. L. REV. 1142–43 (1991).

[240] *Reluctant Owners*, ECONOMIST, Jan. 29, 1994, Survey of Corporate Governance, 16.

[241] *Id.*

[242] MARK J. ROE, STRONG MANAGERS, WEAK OWNERS: THE POLITICAL ROOTS OF AMERICAN CORPORATE FINANCE 135 (1994).

[243] Nell Minow, *Do Your Duty, Retirement Managers*, NY TIMES, Jan. 30, 1994, F11.

[244] Steve Lohr, *Pulling Down the Corporate Clubhouse*, NY TIMES, Apr. 12, 1992, 1.

[245] JONATHAN CHARKHAM, KEEPING GOOD COMPANY: A STUDY OF CORPORATE GOVERNANCE IN FIVE COUNTRIES 211 (1994).

[246] George de Lama, *Corporations Feeling Shove from Shareholders*, CHI. TRIB., Feb. 14, 1993, D1.

[247] James A. White, *Calpers' Chief Wields Big Stick for Institutional Shareholders*, WALL ST. J., Apr. 3, 1990, C1; Claire E. Crutchley, Carl D. Hudson & Marlin R.H. Jensen, *Shareholder Wealth Effects of CalPERS' Activism*, 7 FIN. SERV. REV. 1–2 (1998).

[248] Crutchley, Hudson & Jensen, *supra* note 247, 1–2; Eric Schine, *Calpers' New Chief: Same Fire, Less Flash*, BUS. WK., Oct. 3, 1994, 114.

great leaders in this field," resigned as general counsel in 1996.[249] CalPERS' public profile duly dropped. Hanson said in 1997 "(y)ou don't hear about CalPERS. If you don't keep that constructive tension, that's unfortunate."[250] None of the handful of other public pension funds with an activism track record was prepared to step into the breach.[251] The chief executive of the California State Teachers' Retirement System, then the third largest public pension fund, said in 1997 "(o)ur corporate governance program has been dormant for five years. Our board just isn't convinced that it's worth it."[252]

Passivity remained the byword generally for mainstream institutional shareholders in the late 1990s. Economists Franklin Edwards and Glenn Hubbard observed in a 2000 article entitled "The Growth of Institutional Stock Ownership: A Promise Unfulfilled," "institutional investors on the whole have not taken an active role in corporate governance."[253] In mitigation, the late 1990s was an unlikely time for institutional shareholders to step up their activism efforts, given that the strong returns public companies were delivering left stockholders little room for complaint. As the *New York Times* suggested in 1998, "(m)ost investors are feeling fat and happy and are much less interested in picking fights. And many managers look like geniuses because their stock has been swept along with the rising tide."[254] Harvard Business School professor Quinn Mills said more caustically of the late 1990s in the wake of the corporate scandals and stock market swoon of the early 2000s "(a)s long as stock prices were rising, investors didn't seem to care whether there were shenanigans going on."[255] The *Economist* offered a similar retrospective verdict, saying "of the extremes of the 1990s . . . (m)uch . . . occurred because owners allowed it to," in large part because with "the general market rise . . . shareholders could afford to be indifferent."[256] Whatever the underlying cause, direct participation in corporate affairs played at most a supporting role in prompting shareholder value's move to the top of the managerial priority list during the 1990s. Share trading patterns, as we will see next, were much more influential.

The Quarterly Earnings Obsession

Public company executives, when asked in the early 2000s to identify the key price-setters for their stocks, put institutional investors top of the list.[257] This was a reasonable supposition. Not only did institutions own a large proportion of public company shares but their trading

249 Judith H. Dobrzynski, *A Shareholder-Rights Leader Is Leaving Calpers*, NY TIMES, May 22, 1996, D1 (quoting Nell Minow).

250 Barry Rehfeld, *Low-cal CalPERS*, INSTITUTIONAL INVESTOR, Mar. 1997, 41.

251 *The Loneliness of the Shareholder Activist*, INSTITUTIONAL INVESTOR, Mar. 1997, 46.

252 *Id.*

253 Franklin R. Edwards & R. Glenn Hubbard, *The Growth of Institutional Stock Ownership: A Promise Unfulfilled*, J. APP. CORP. FIN., Fall 2000, 92, 93.

254 Reed Abelson, *Proxy Peace*, NY TIMES, May 28, 1998, D1.

255 D. QUINN MILLS, WHEEL, DEAL, AND STEAL: DECEPTIVE ACCOUNTING, DECEITFUL CEOS, AND INEFFECTIVE REFORMS 23 (2003).

256 *Beyond Shareholder Value*, ECONOMIST, June 28, 2003, Radical Thoughts on Our 160th Birthday—A Survey of Capitalism and Democracy, 9.

257 John R. Graham, Campbell R. Harvey & Shiva Rajgopal, *The Economic Implications of Corporate Financial Reporting*, 40 J. ACCTING. & ECON. 3, 50, 52 (2005).

was much more frequent than used to be the case. The portfolios of fund managers acting on behalf of institutional investors turned over at a rate exceeding 100 percent annually in 1999 as compared to just 20 percent in 1950.[258] In the 1990s, decisions these fund managers made about which shares to buy and sell were increasingly oriented around a single metric: quarterly earnings. It was this pattern more than any other that fostered a shareholder-first mentality in public companies.

The *New York Times*, in a 2002 analysis of what it termed "the earnings cult," observed "(a)s the long bull market recouped the losses of the early-90's downturn, a single, stark equation took firm hold in the minds of the mass of investors: more earnings equals more shareholder value."[259] Executives listened. John Bogle, in diagnosing in 2005 what had "gone wrong in corporate America" in the 1990s, noted that "(e)xecutives don't need to be told what to do: achieve strong, steady earnings growth and tell Wall Street about it."[260] Ram Charan, a management consultant, said more pointedly in 1999 that for boards and management "meeting quarterly earnings numbers is virtually mandatory."[261]

Under federal securities law, public companies are required to submit to the SEC each year a Form 10-K that includes a company's audited annual financial statements, a discussion of the company's business results and disclosures concerning various other facets of the business.[262] Since 1970 such firms have also been obliged to file in other quarters a Form-10Q.[263] These 10-Qs contain unaudited financial statements and updated information about a company's business, set out financial results for the previous three months and for the year to date, and compare the company's performance in the current quarter and year to date with the same periods in the previous year.[264]

The fascination with quarterly earnings that was so marked in the 1990s was a relatively recent phenomenon, having first emerged in the 1980s.[265] The chairman of Champion International, a forest products company, groused in 1986 "(e)verything is pegged nowadays to immediate earnings."[266] Executives began to fret about quarterly earnings in the 1980s because of concerns about a hostile takeover offer.[267] Harold Williams, a former chairman of

---

[258] Robert McGough & Pui-Wing Tam, *Bogle Urges Role in Corporate Governance*, WALL ST. J., Oct. 21, 1999, C23. See also FOX, *supra* note 112, at 280; Joseph L. Bower & Lynn S. Paine, *The Error at the Heart of Corporate Leadership*, HARV. BUS. REV., May/June 2017, 50, 54 (indicating the average holding period for public company shares fell from just over five years in 1976 to a year by the end of the 1990s).

[259] Collingwood, *supra* note 132.

[260] BOGLE, *supra* note 180, at 15.

[261] Ram Charan, *Five Lessons for Active Boards*, FORTUNE, June 7, 1999, 220.

[262] Forms, Securities and Exchange Act of 1934, 17 C.F.R. § 249.310 (2018).

[263] Patricia M. Dechow, Richard G. Sloan & Jenny Zha, *Stock Prices and Earnings: A History of Research*, 6 ANN. REV. FIN. ECON. 343, 345 (2014).

[264] Forms, Securities and Exchange Act of 1934, 17 C.F.R. § 249.308a (2018); BERENSON, *supra* note 105, at xvi.

[265] Nancy Ryan, *Some Say Profit Play-by-Plays Are Spoiling the Game*, CHI. TRIB., Feb. 1, 1993, B1; GEOFFREY MOORE, LIVING ON THE FAULT LINE: MANAGING FOR SHAREHOLDER VALUE IN THE AGE OF THE INTERNET 79 (2000); Frank Dobbin & Jiwook Jung, *The Misapplication of Mr. Michael Jensen: How Agency Theory Brought Down the Economy and Why It Might Again*, 30B RESEARCH SOCIOLOGY ORG. 29, 39 (2010).

[266] Steven Greenhouse, *The Folly of Inflating Quarterly Profits*, NY TIMES, Mar. 2, 1986, F1.

[267] *Id.*; Lester Thurow, *Where Management Fails*, FORTUNE, Dec., 7, 1981, 78; Mark S. Mizruchi, The Power Elite *in Historical Context: A Reevaluation of Mills's Thesis, Then and Now*, 46 THEORY & SOC. 95, 109–10 (2017).

the SEC, explained why in 1985: "(c)orporations become vulnerable if their stock prices flag, and managers believe that stock prices flag if quarterly earnings dip or just stay flat. Managers therefore struggle to keep earnings on an uptrend lest they be remembered as the ones who 'lost' General Widget."[268]

By the early 1990s "earnings season"—the months when the majority of public companies release their quarterly figures—was often "a frenzy" with investors and stock market analysts hungry for business information using the data to deduce how companies were performing.[269] Quarterly financial results would qualify as an "obsession" as the decade drew to a close.[270] Among the quarterly data companies divulged earnings per share garnered the most attention. As *Business Week* noted in 1998, "(f)or many on Wall Street, the only number that counts is the quarterly growth of earnings per share."[271] Earnings per share indeed was known on Wall Street simply as "the number."[272]

The value of a company's shares is a function of the anticipated aggregate future stream of income that a company will pay out to shareholders during its lifetime.[273] "The number" and associated earnings related data, in contrast, are backward looking, indicating what a company has done in the most recent quarter. Nevertheless in the 1990s quarterly earnings were doing more to shape expectations of future returns than anything else.[274] Fund managers and security analysts offering recommendations on shares to buy and sell were attracted to data perceived to be objective, comparable, and verifiable in a way a management team's forecasts of business prospects were not.[275]

Faith in the veracity of corporate accounting underpinned the heavy reliance on quarterly financials.[276] Goldman Sachs' influential analyst Abby Joseph Cohen told the *New York Times* in 1997 that company balance sheets "are the cleanest that they have been in most investors' professional lives" and that "(i)nvestors, in general, are increasingly comfortable that what is being reported by a company is close to the truth."[277] Such faith in accounting data would soon seem almost touchingly naïve, given that accounting improprieties were an integral element of the corporate scandals of the early 2000s.[278]

Not all earnings were created equal during the 1990s, in the sense that sizeable profits did not automatically translate into high share prices. There was, for instance, a predictability premium, with the stock market rewarding companies that featured regular, consistent

[268] Harold M. Williams, *It's Time for a Takeover Moratorium*, FORTUNE, July 22, 1985, 133.

[269] Ryan, *supra* note 265.

[270] D.N. Ghosh, *Wall Street Capitalism and the World of Professional Managers*, ECON. POLITICAL WEEKLY, Sept. 14, 2002, 3803, 3809.

[271] Nanette Byrnes, Richard A. Melcher & Debra Sparks, *Earnings Hocus-Pocus*, BUS. WK., Oct. 5, 1998, 134.

[272] BERENSON, *supra* note 105, at xvi.

[273] See Merritt B. Fox, Randall Morck, Bernard Yeung & Artyom Durnev, *Law, Share Price Accuracy, and Economic Performance: The New Evidence*, 102 MICH. L. REV. 331, 345 (2003).

[274] Ryan, *supra* note 265.

[275] Louis Lowenstein, *Financial Transparency and Corporate Governance: You Manage What You Measure*, 96 COLUM. L. REV. 1335, 1343 (1996).

[276] *Id.* at 1346, 1361; Jon E. Hilsenrath, *On the Books, More Fact and Less Fiction*, NY TIMES, Feb. 16, 1997, F1.

[277] Hilsenrath, *supra* note 276.

[278] Chapter 6, Table 6.1, notes 31, 65 and related discussion.

earnings growth.[279] Meeting expectations was also crucial. Some context is required here. In the 1970s, a handful of securities analysts and other stock market followers began using 3-by-5-inch index cards to collect for investor analysis estimates of forthcoming quarterly earnings data for particular companies.[280] By the 1990s, the arrangement had been formalized to the extent that First Call/Thomson Financial and IBES International Inc. were compiling the earnings predictions of analysts following a given stock, computing the consensus estimate on earnings, and circulating the information to investors and companies.[281] Hitting or beating this consensus number became the single most watched measure of corporate success.[282] Companies worked hard in their turn to ensure announced results would at least match the consensus figures. They sought, for instance, to influence earnings estimates by providing informal guidance to securities analysts and by issuing earnings preannouncements, and used discretion available under accounting guidelines to adjust quarterly earnings toward the consensus number.[283] The proportion of firms that met or beat their earnings target increased from about half in the 1980s to nearly two-thirds by the end of the 1990s.[284]

With the norm being to meet or exceed quarterly earnings expectations, if a company failed to do so, this could "kill a stock."[285] The CEO of Cypress Semiconductor Corp. told *Business Week* in 1998 "(t)he penalties for missing your earnings are intense. . . . If you miss one or two quarters, you can see your . . . market cap cut in half."[286] The sharp reaction occurred because of a tendency on the part of investors to infer that a failure to hit the consensus number was a signal of deeper problems. A chief financial officer interviewed for a 2005 study of financial reporting explained "if you see one cockroach, you immediately assume that there are hundreds behind the walls, even though you may have no proof that this is the case."[287]

The negative stock price hit for a company that missed a consensus earnings target was usually the same regardless of whether the company missed by a penny or by a much wider margin.[288] Given the effort companies would put in to align expectations and announced

---

[279] Graham, Harvey & Rajgopal, *supra* note 257, at 5; Mary E. Barth, John A. Elliott & Mark W. Finn, *Market Rewards Associated with Patterns of Increasing Earnings*, 37 J. Accting. Res. 387 (1999); David Millon, *Why Is Corporate Management Obsessed with Quarterly Earnings and What Should Be Done about It?*, 70 Geo. Wash. L. Rev. 890, 897 (2002).

[280] Robert D. Hershey, *A Flourishing Industry, Predicting What Is and Isn't Flourishing*, NY Times, May 17, 1998, Business, 7.

[281] Collingwood, *supra* note 132; Hershey, *supra* note 280.

[282] Justin Fox, *Can We Trust Them Now?*, Fortune, Mar. 3, 2003, 97.

[283] Greg Ip, *Rise in Profit Guidance Dilutes Positive Surprises*, Wall St. J., June 23, 1997, C1; Ira M. Millstein, *Introduction to the* Report and Recommendations of the Blue Ribbon Committee on Improving the Effectiveness of Corporate Audit Committees, 54 Bus. Law. 1057, 1059 (1999); Dirk Zorn et al., *Managing Investors: How Financial Markets Reshaped the American Firm, in* The Sociology of Financial Markets 269, 281–82 (Karin Knorr-Cetina & Alex Preda eds., 2005).

[284] Zorn et al., *supra* note 283, at 281.

[285] Gretchen Morgenson, *Forecasts Made Rosy for Investors, But Results Are Sometimes Paler*, NY Times, Dec. 21, 1999, A1.

[286] Byrnes, Melcher & Sparks, *supra* note 271.

[287] Graham, Harvey & Rajgopal, *supra* note 257, at 29.

[288] Morgenson, *supra* note 285; Kevin J. Murphy, *Executive Compensation: Where We Are, and How We Got There, in* 2 Handbook of the Economics of Finance 211, 246–47 (George Constantinites et al. eds., 2013).

results, investors inferred with a close miss that much worse news could well be around the corner.[289] As *Fortune* observed in 1999, "(c)ustom says those expectations must not be disappointed by even a penny, since a management's inability to come up with a measly cent, when so many opportunities to manipulate earnings exist, will often be interpreted as a stark sign of failure and a reason to bomb the stock."[290]

Executives complained in the 1990s about the stock market's fixation with quarterly earnings, grumbling that evaluations of their companies were carried out without sufficient appreciation of competitive positions and strategies.[291] Referring to young equity analysts who helped to shape Wall Street's reactions to disclosures companies made, one exasperated chief financial officer remarked, "I don't see why we have to place these disclosures in the hands of children that do not understand the information."[292] With hostile takeovers in retreat in the 1990s it might have been thought executives ostensibly "forced into slavish obeisance to Wall Street's incessant demands for a penny or two more in earnings per share"[293] would have felt they had an opportunity to break free of a system with which they had serious misgivings. Indeed, not all 1990s executives opted to play the earnings game.[294] Nevertheless, for most public company executives meeting or beating analysts' forecasts was the yardstick against which they were prepared to be measured.[295]

Job security was one incentive for 1990s public company executives to respond to the investment community's singular focus on quarterly earnings. The various high-profile CEO dismissals early in the decade remained fresh in the memory throughout the decade.[296] Boards of companies that missed earnings targets correspondingly found themselves not merely under an onus to investigate but to consider putting dismissal of the chief executive on the agenda.[297]

Executive pay also motivated senior management to hit "the number." Awards under annual bonus schemes were under board control, and directors of a public company were considerably more likely to exercise their discretion in favor of management when the company was meeting earnings targets.[298] The growing popularity of stock options in the 1990s[299] provided executives with an additional compensation-related reason to ensure there were no nasty earnings surprises. Stock options only have value to an executive to the extent that the executive's company's share price exceeds the specified "strike" price. Executives to whom

---

289 BOGLE, *supra* note 180, at 26.

290 Carole J. Loomis, *Lies, Damned Lies, and Managed Earnings*, FORTUNE, Aug. 2, 1999, 74. See also Harris Collingwood, *The Earnings Game: Everyone Plays, Nobody Wins*, HARV. BUS. REV., June 2001, 65, 68 (discussing Cisco).

291 Amar Bhide, *Deficient Governance*, HARV. BUS. REV., Nov./Dec. 1994, 128, 134.

292 Graham, Harvey & Rajgopal, *supra* note 257, at 52.

293 Nanette Byrnes, *Internet Anxieties*, BUS. WK., June 28, 1999, 79.

294 Robert McGough, *Executive Critical of "Managed" Earnings Doesn't Mind if the Street Criticizes Him*, WALL ST. J., Apr. 16, 1999, C1.

295 Millon, *supra* note 279, at 892.

296 *Supra* notes 160–64 and related discussion.

297 Charan, *supra* note 261.

298 Steve R. Matsunaga & Chul W. Park, *The Effect of Missing a Quarterly Earnings Benchmark on the CEO's Annual Bonus*, 76 ACCTING. REV. 313 (2001).

299 *Supra* note 234 and related discussion.

potentially lucrative stock options had been awarded correspondingly had a strong financial incentive to play the earnings game to keep the stock price up, particularly when they held a substantial number of options eligible to be exercised.[300] As *Business Week* said in 1998 of share prices falling due to a failure to hit "the number," "the resulting pain is intensely personal, since more than half of CEO pay comes from stock options."[301]

The quarterly earnings obsession, in sum, was a meaningful constraint on public company executives. A "well-regarded" *Fortune* 500 CEO told that magazine in 1999 that he probably spent "35% of his time talking to analysts and big shareholders, and otherwise worrying about the concerns of the Street."[302] The unnamed CEO conceded that his company's bottom line might have ultimately been better off if he devoted more time to the business, but said that he had to think of today's stock price, particularly given the structure of his managerial compensation. This was, as *Fortune* pointed out, not the only opportunity cost associated with "the cult of consistent earnings."[303] *Fortune* postulated that at the time of writing there likely was someone "high up" in a *Fortune* 500 company perpetrating an accounting fraud that could result in jail time, with the "fundamental reason" being that "the company . . . was 'managing earnings'—trying to meet Wall Street expectations or those of the boss, trying also to pretend that the course of business is smooth and predictable when in reality it is not."[304]

Fortune was hardly engaging in idle speculation. The desire to meet Wall Street expectations had been identified as the major driver of accounting chicanery that came to light in the late 1990s at Waste Management, a waste services firm, and Cendant, a travel and real estate company.[305] With the stock market having performed well since the early 1980s, however, the prevailing tendency with companies delivering better results on paper than circumstances seemed to dictate was to believe in financial miracles rather than to ask questions about aggressive accounting.[306] The default setting would soon change dramatically, a pattern we will consider in detail in Chapter 6.

External Constraints

We know now that "internal" constraints on public company executives, namely boards and shareholders, grew in potency in the 1990s, though perceptions about their veracity would change radically as the 2000s got underway amidst falling share prices and corporate scandals. With "external" constraints, we have also seen that the market for corporate control receded considerably as compared with the 1980s.[307] With other external constraints, unions and regulation each declined in importance in the 1990s, consistent with trends in place in the 1980s. There also was continuity in the opposite direction. As was the case in the 1980s,

---

[300] Zorn et al., *supra* note 283, at 277.

[301] Byrnes, Melcher & Sparks, *supra* note 271.

[302] Loomis, *supra* note 290.

[303] *Id.*

[304] *Id.*

[305] Byrnes, Melcher & Sparks, *Earnings, supra* note 271.

[306] Bernard Condon, *Pick a Number, Any Number*, FORBES, Mar. 23, 1998, 124.

[307] *Supra* notes 144–45, 148–50 and related discussion.

in a wide range of industries pressure from competitors was intensifying. Complacency thus seemed to be ill-advised even for executives running companies accustomed to benefitting from substantial market power.

UNIONS

Unions faded as a source of countervailing power for public company executives during the 1970s and 1980s.[308] There was a possibility this trend would abate in the 1990s. Highly publicized downsizing exercises in which larger companies were engaging[309] plausibly might have convinced employees otherwise ambivalent about unions to think of organized labor as a beneficial counterweight. For instance, a 1993 *New York Times* article entitled "Labor Takes a Happy Breath" speculated "America—the part that's at the mercy of downsizing, restructuring and revamping—may be catching up with the union movement."[310]

Bill Clinton's move into the White House also implied the political winds were blowing in the unions' favor. The *New York Times*, in its 1993 "Happy Breath" article, suggested "(n)ow Citizen Clinton is in the White House and, labor would say, finally a few things are right with the world."[311] Robert Reich, secretary of labor from 1993 to 1997, was tagged by *Forbes* as "an aggressive proponent" of trade unionism.[312] The Clinton administration's appointees to the National Labor Relations Board were more favorably disposed toward unions than Ronald Reagan's or George H.W. Bush's.[313]

Despite some counter-trends, the 1990s would not be a banner decade for organized labor. A Senate filibuster blocked passage of a 1993 bill that would have banned employers from hiring replacement workers during a strike.[314] *Fortune* labeled American unions as "hopeless losers" in 1994 and the formerly optimistic *New York Times* said in 1996 that "labor faces an uphill fight" and was "on the defensive almost everywhere."[315]

Union density in the workforce, which had been falling since the 1950s,[316] continued to drop as the proportion of workers who were unionized declined from 16 percent in 1990 to 13 percent in 1999.[317] The equivalent figures for private sector employers were 12 percent and 9 percent respectively.[318] Strike activity declined as well, with the number of large strikes

---

[308] Chapter 3, notes 385–87 and related discussion; Chapter 4 notes 405–6 and accompanying text.

[309] *Supra* notes 45, 60–62 and related discussion.

[310] Barbara Presley Noble, *Labor Takes a Happy Breath*, NY TIMES, Feb. 14, 1993, F23.

[311] *Id.*

[312] Janet Novack, *An Agency Out of Step with the Times*, FORBES, Jan. 16, 1995, 37.

[313] WELLS, *supra* note 50, at 172.

[314] DOUGLAS M. EICHAR, THE RISE AND FALL OF CORPORATE SOCIAL RESPONSIBILITY 292–93 (2015).

[315] Daniel Seligman, *Why Labor Keeps Losing*, FORTUNE, July 11, 1994, 178; Peter T. Kilborn, *Organized Labor's Hope for a Comeback*, NY TIMES, Mar. 8, 1996, A22.

[316] Chapter 2, note 463 and related discussion; Chapter 3 note 401 and accompanying text; Chapter 4, notes 415-16 and related discussion.

[317] GERALD MAYER, UNION MEMBERSHIP TRENDS IN THE UNITED STATES 22 (2004) (calculated using non-agricultural workers as the denominator).

[318] Unionstats.com, *Union Membership and Coverage Database from the CPS*, available at http://unionstats.gsu.edu/ (accessed Apr. 6, 2018).

averaging 35 a year in the 1990s as compared with 83 in the 1980s and 289 in the 1970s.[319] The director of corporate affairs of the AFL-CIO federation of unions even acknowledged in 1999 that "(i)t takes an incredibly courageous group of workers to go out on strike."[320] Unionized workers feared that if they hit the picket lines strike replacement workers might well displace them permanently.[321] Even a successful shutdown could be counterproductive because employers might shift work to nonunion plants or even go out of business at the hands of competitors with harmonious labor relations.[322] The fact that the strike was very much a weapon of last resort in the 1990s helped to tilt the balance of power at the bargaining table in management's favor.[323]

Organized labor was not marginalized completely. For some companies unions remained a constraining factor on particular issues.[324] Moreover, facets of employment law, such as rules precluding discrimination and sexual harassment, were increasingly impinging upon employer flexibility.[325] Harvard Business School professor Linda Hill even said of weaker unions in 1997 "I don't know if that means workers have less power, what with lawsuits and regulations."[326] Nevertheless, while during the managerial capitalism era unions were a meaningful source of countervailing power for public company executives,[327] by the time the twentieth century concluded it was doubtful whether this was the case.

REGULATION

Deregulation began in earnest in the late 1970s and gained momentum in the 1980s, meaning that as the 1980s ended governmental oversight was a less potent constraint on public company executives than it had been in living memory.[328] With Democrat Bill Clinton becoming president in 1993, a reversal seemed possible. Deregulation, however, remained a significant trend, with it being analogized to a "tidal force" in the late 1990s.[329] Some regard the 1990s as "the decade of deregulation."[330]

---

[319] Bureau of Labor Statistics, *Work Stoppages Involving 1,000 or More Workers, 1947–2017*, available at https://www.bls.gov/news.release/wkstp.t01.htm (accessed Apr. 6, 2018).

[320] Jeffrey Ball, Glenn Burkins & Gregory L. White, *Why Labor Unions Have Grown Reluctant to Use the "S" Word*, Wall St. J., Dec. 16, 1999, A1.

[321] Frank Swoboda, *Labor Loses the Strike as a Weapon*, Wash. Post, July 5, 1992, H1.

[322] Ball, Burkins & White, *supra* note 320; *Brothers in Alms*, Economist, Sept. 21, 1996, 91.

[323] Swoboda, *supra* note 321.

[324] Ralph Estes, Tyranny of the Bottom Line: Why Corporations Make Good People Do Bad Things 63 (1996).

[325] Robert J. Samuelson, *The Limits of the Law*, Newsweek, June 30, 1997, 58 (discussing Walter Olson, The Excuse Factory: How Employment Law Is Paralyzing the American Workplace (1997)).

[326] Thomas A. Stewart & Rajiv M. Rao, *Get With the New Power Game*, Fortune, Jan. 13, 1997, 58.

[327] Chapter 2, notes 444-51 and related discussion; Chapter 3, notes 382-84 and accompanying text.

[328] Chapter 3, notes 372–75 and related discussion; Chapter 4, notes 386–390, 392–94, 400–03 and accompanying text.

[329] Charles Derber, Corporation Nation: How Corporations Are Taking Over Our Lives and What We Can Do about It 149 (1998).

[330] Charles R. Geisst, Undue Influence: How the Wall Street Elite Puts the Financial System at Risk 241 (2005); Alexander Styhre, The Making of Shareholder Welfare Society: A Study in Corporate Governance 146, 150 (2018).

The fact that Bill Clinton treated the economy as a top priority in his 1992 election campaign and argued that America was being left behind implied that an activist federal government might soon be intervening to try to correct deregulation mistakes from the 1980s but matters would work out much differently.[331] Clinton retained faith in government as a matter of principle throughout his presidency.[332] He shifted rightward, however, in response to a Republican sweep in the 1994 congressional elections backed by a "Contract With America" that translated the voting into a referendum where the electorate signaled unease with Clinton's first two years in office and with big government more generally.[333] Joseph Stiglitz, who served in the Clinton administration from 1993 to 1997, said ruefully in 2003 "in too many instances ... we succumbed to the deregulation mantra."[334] Clinton even proclaimed in his 1996 State of the Union address "the era of big government is over."[335]

Clinton's pivot matched the mood of the times. There was considerable faith in markets, a sentiment that the flourishing economy of the mid- and late-1990s powerfully reinforced.[336] Confidence in government was also at a low ebb. Senator Phil Gramm said in 1995 "America clearly wants less regulation."[337] Public opinion polls suggested he was right. When asked in 1995 whether the federal government created more problems than it solved, 72 percent of Americans surveyed agreed.[338]

Throughout much of the 1990s, deregulatory legislation was passed at an energetic pace matching that set in the late 1970s when the late twentieth century deregulation movement commenced.[339] The Energy Policy Act of 1992 dismantled restrictions on sales of power between utility companies so as to foster competition in a sector local monopolies traditionally dominated.[340] The Riegle-Neal Interstate Banking and Branching Efficiency Act of 1994 eliminated most regulatory obstacles to interstate bank acquisitions and put in place a national framework for banks to operate across state lines, culminating a trend in favor of facilitating multistate banking various states had begun in the late 1970s.[341]

---

331 *Supra* notes 31–32, 50–51 and accompanying text; DANIEL YERGIN & JOSEPH STANISLAW, THE COMMANDING HEIGHTS: THE BATTLE BETWEEN GOVERNMENT AND THE MARKETPLACE THAT IS REMAKING THE MODERN WORLD 362 (1998).

332 Garry Wills, *The Clinton Principle*, NY TIMES, Jan. 19, 1997, Sunday Magazine, 28.

333 James Fallows, *Washington and The Contract With America*, ATLANTIC.COM, 1994, available at https://www.theatlantic.com/past/docs/unbound/jfnpr/jfreview.htm (accessed May 15, 2018).

334 JOSEPH E. STIGLITZ, THE ROARING NINETIES: A NEW HISTORY OF THE WORLD'S MOST PROSPEROUS DECADE 112 (2003).

335 Alison Mitchell, *Clinton Offers Challenge to the Nation, Declaring "Era of Big Government Is Over,"* NY TIMES, Jan. 24, 1996, A1.

336 STIGLITZ, *supra* note 334, at 81–82.

337 Diana B. Henriques, *Efforts to Harness SEC Worry Agency Critics Too,* NY TIMES, Oct. 23, 1995, A1.

338 LADD & BOWMAN, *supra* note 49, at 101.

339 Joseph D. Kearney & Thomas W. Merrill, *The Great Transformation of Regulated Industries Law*, 98 COLUM. L. REV. 1323, 1381–82 (1998).

340 Pub. L. No. 102-486, 106 Stat. 2776; CHARLES R. GEISST, DEALS OF THE CENTURY: WALL STREET, MERGERS, AND THE MAKING OF MODERN AMERICA 243 (2001).

341 Pub. L. No. 103-328, 108 Stat. 2338 (1994); James R. Barth, Tong Li & Wenling Lu, *Bank Regulation in the United States*, 56 CESFIO ECON. STUD. 112, 126–27 (2010).

In 1995, the Interstate Commerce Commission, which had regulated interstate surface transportation since 1887, was shut down but President Clinton still chided Congress for failing to back bolder steps to deregulate transportation industries.[342] The Telecommunications Act of 1996 permitted long distance and local telephone companies, such as the "Baby Bells" created when AT&T was broken up in 1982, to compete against each other.[343] The legislation also relaxed restrictions on ownership of television and radio stations and allowed cable communication companies and telephone companies to enter each other's markets.[344] Finally, the 1999 Gramm-Leach-Bliley Act formalized the dismantling of already crumbling barriers between commercial and investment banking encompassed in the Glass Steagall Act of 1933 and explicitly authorized the creation of full-service financial holding companies.[345] These various measures proved to be a powerful stimulant for dealmaking activity in the 1990s, with media/telecommunications, financial services, and utilities being among the most active M&A sectors in a merger-intensive decade.[346]

Many contemporaries praised the deregulation occurring during the 1990s. A 1999 *Wall Street Journal* essay seeking to explain the robust stock market that put the 10,000 mark for the Dow Jones Industrial Average within reach emphasized the retreat of government, saying "(t)he dominant event of the late 20th century is the bull-market prosperity of the 1980s and 1990s. This was caused largely by a shift back to free-market economics, a reduction in the role of the state and an expansion of personal liberty."[347] Treasury Secretary Larry Summers said of recent deregulation initiatives the same year that that they would "make the economy more efficient and consumers will benefit from that," reasoning "archaic restrictions reduce choice and raise prices."[348] Business historian Louis Galambos, in a 2000 analysis of the twentieth century corporate economy, suggested that deregulation had "an important positive impact on America's large corporations" by bringing "market discipline to a growing number of firms" that forced them "to improve the general efficiency of their operations."[349]

With share prices falling and corporate scandals hitting the headlines in the early 2000s the verdict on 1990s deregulation was considerably less favorable. Joseph Stiglitz wrote in 2003 "we were too trapped into the mantra of deregulation, mindlessly stripping back on

---

[342] ICC Termination Act of 1995, Pub. L. 104–88, 109 Stat.803; William J. Clinton, *Statement on Signing the ICC Termination Act of 1995* (Dec. 29, 1995), available at http://www.presidency.ucsb.edu/ws/?pid=52436 (accessed Feb. 14, 2018).

[343] Pub. L. No. 104-104, 110 Stat. 56; Chapter 1, notes 117, 119–20 and accompanying text.

[344] Hanglong Fu, Yi Mou & David Atkin, *The Impact of the Telecommunications Act of 1996 in the Broadband Age*, 8 ADVANCES COMMUNICATIONS & MEDIA RES. 117, 122–23 (2011).

[345] Pub. L. 106–102, 113 Stat. 1338; Arthur E. Wilmarth, *The Transformation of the US Financial Services Industry, 1975–2000: Competition, Consolidation, and Increased Risks* [2002] U. ILL. L. REV. 217, 319–20.

[346] *Supra* note 146 and related discussion; David R. Francis, *Big Business Gets Bigger, Record Pace*, CHRISTIAN SCI. MONITOR, June 4, 1997, 8; BRUCE WASSERSTEIN, BIG DEAL: 2000 AND BEYOND 12 (2000).

[347] Lawrence Kudlow, *The Road to Dow 10000*, WALL ST. J., Mar. 16, 1999, A26.

[348] Stephen Labaton, *Despite a Tough Stance or Two, White House Is Still Consolidation Friendly*, NY TIMES, Nov. 8, 1999, A22.

[349] Louis Galambos, *The US Corporate Economy in the Twentieth Century*, THE CAMBRIDGE ECONOMIC HISTORY OF THE UNITED STATES, VOLUME III: THE TWENTIETH CENTURY 927, 959–60 (Stanley L. Engerman & Robert E. Gallman eds., 2000).

regulation" and argued "(i)t was no coincidence that many of the problems of the Roaring Nineties can be traced back to the newly deregulated sectors—electricity, telecommunications and finance."[350] John Bogle argued similarly in 2005 that an important contributor to the "fatal breakdown" of corporate accountability resulting in scandals in the early 2000s was that "(g)overnment regulations were relaxed. Our elected public officials not only didn't care but actually stood by, aiding and abetting the malfeasance."[351]

The verdicts offered on deregulation, whether pro or con, could give the impression that the state was in full-scale retreat in the 1990s. This was not the case. Regulation remained a significant constraint for public company executives throughout the decade. For instance, sociologist Charles Derber, in a 1998 critique of the corporate order, suggested that "(g)overnment remains the most important potential countervailing threat to corporate power."[352] Despite deregulation, throughout the course of the 1990s the federal government's regulatory expenditures increased 51.5 percent on an inflation-adjusted basis.[353] Also, while Reagan appointments to federal agencies typically shared his bias against governmental burdens, Clinton chose personnel intellectually committed to the underlying regulatory mission of the agencies they served and the legislation they were administering.[354]

Antitrust law was also a factor 1990s public company executives needed to bear in mind, at least with high-profile mergers. A number of major deals failed to proceed due to pressure from antitrust regulators.[355] In 1995, for example, Microsoft abandoned plans to acquire Intuit, a leading producer of personal-finance software, after the Justice Department filed a suit challenging the deal on antitrust grounds.[356] In 1997, the Federal Trade Commission blocked a proposed $4 billion merger between Office Depot, Inc. and Staples, Inc., the nation's two largest office supply retailers.[357] The following year Lockheed Martin Corp. abandoned a planned acquisition of fellow aerospace and defense firm Northrop Grumman Corp. after the Department of Justice opposed the transaction on antitrust grounds.[358]

While antitrust scrutiny sidetracked some major acquisitions in the 1990s, corporate dealmakers were offered a free hand for the most part.[359] Only a small proportion of merger transactions were formally investigated, let alone challenged explicitly.[360] *US News & World*

---

[350] STIGLITZ, *supra* note 334, at 11.

[351] BOGLE, *supra* note 180, at 33.

[352] DERBER, *supra* note 329, at 65.

[353] Susan Dudley & Melinda Warren, *Regulators' Budget Reflects President Trump's Priorities: An Analysis of the U.S. Budget for Fiscal Years 1960 to 2018*, Weidenbaum Center on the Economy, Government, and Public Policy/The George Washington University Regulatory Studies Center, July 18, 2017, 8.

[354] Chapter 4, note 402 and related discussion; EICHAR, *supra* note 314, at 292.

[355] GEISST, *supra* note 340, at 234.

[356] G. Christian Hill, Don Clark & Viveca Novak, *Microsoft Drops Bid for Intuit—A Victory for Antitrust Agency*, WALL ST. J., May 22, 1995, A1.

[357] John R. Wilke & Joseph Pereira, *Office Depot, Staples Deal Is Blocked*, WALL ST. J., July 1, 1997, A3.

[358] Leslie Wayne, *Lockheed Cancels Northrop Merger, Citing US Stand*, NY TIMES, July 17, 1998, A1.

[359] GEISST, *supra* note 340, at 235.

[360] David R. Francis, *Mega-Merger Madness*, CHRISTIAN SCI. MONITOR, June 29, 1998, B8; Joseph H. Flom, *Mergers & Acquisitions: The Decade in Review*, 54 U. MIA. L. REV. 753, 770 (2000).

Report correspondingly observed in 1995 that "the government is far more lenient about consolidation than it was in the distant past."[361] The *New York Times* even told readers in 1999 "Mr. Clinton and his administration will go down in history as encouraging the largest number of business mergers—and in some industries the greatest concentration of economic power—in many years."[362] As with regulation more generally, then, 1990s public company executives would have borne antitrust law in mind when exercising managerial discretion but in material respects had greater room to move than their managerial capitalism era peers.

COMPETITORS

While during the 1980s regulation and organized labor receded in importance as constraints on public company executives, the pressure brought to bear by competitors intensified markedly.[363] Challenges by rivals continued to mount as a source of concern for management in the 1990s. As with Chapter 4's discussion of competitive pressure in the 1980s, we will consider initially here the evidence indicating that market forces were intensifying. We will then turn to explanations why this was happening.

"Speed Is of the Essence"

Views expressed by management expert Gary Hamel captured evocatively fears competitors were eliciting in the corporate ranks during the 1990s. He and coauthor C.K. Prahalad wrote in their 1994 book *Competing for the Future* "(t)he future is now," "speed is of the essence," and "(t)here should be no mushy-headed wishfulness involved."[364] Hamel intensified the rhetoric in 1999, saying "(f)ace it: Out there in some garage, an entrepreneur is forging a bullet with your company's name on it. Once that bullet leaves the barrel, you won't be able to dodge it."[365]

Many contemporaries, while not necessarily adopting Hamel's hyperbolic tone, agreed that for large US corporations pressure from rivals was robust, particularly by historical standards. In a 1996 study of corporate governance in the United States the Organisation for Economic Co-operation and Development invoked the concept of "creative destruction," a term coined by economist Joseph Schumpeter to describe how markets can displace preexisting economic structures, saying it was "alive and thriving in the United States."[366] In 1998 Joel Klein, head of the Justice Department's Antitrust Division, declared "our economy is more competitive today than it has been in a long, long time."[367] Treasury Secretary Lawrence Summers concurred, indicating in 1999 "in the majority of industries, the degree

---

[361] Don L. Boroughs & David Fischer, *Big!*, US NEWS & WORLD REPORT, Sept. 11, 1995, 46.

[362] Labaton, *supra* note 348. See also Leslie Wayne, *Wave of Mergers Is Recasting Face of Business in US*, NY TIMES, Jan. 19, 1998, A1 (saying the Clinton administration's approach to mergers was governed by "flexible economic analysis that allows more big companies to unite").

[363] Chapter 4, notes 423–26, 428–33 and related discussion.

[364] GARY HAMEL & C.K. PRAHALAD, COMPETING FOR THE FUTURE 24, 28, 36 (1994).

[365] Gary Hamel, *Bringing Silicon Valley Inside*, HARV. BUS. REV., Sept./Oct. 1999, 70, 72.

[366] Chapter 2, note 483 and related discussion; OECD, OECD ECONOMIC SURVEYS—UNITED STATES 158 (1996).

[367] *Too Much of a Good Thing*, ECONOMIST, Mar. 26, 2016, 23.

of competition has increased."[368] The same year Lester Thurow, a critic of American competitiveness in the early 1990s,[369] said that "(f)or new firms the economic opportunities have never been better," and that "(f)or those with skills and a fondness for risks . . . who are willing to cannibalize their old activities . . . the times have never been more favorable."[370]

The tribulations of various well-known corporations provided anecdotal evidence confirming conjectures about increased competitive pressure. "All around us we hear the thuds of dinosaur organizations hitting the decks" management professor Thomas Vollmann declared in 1996.[371] "The most visible hulks in Dinosaurland" in the early 1990s were companies that engaged in newsworthy CEO turnover, such as GM, IBM, Sears and Kodak.[372] Though Apple's rise in the late 1970s and early 1980s "became a sort of American business fable" it was a victim as well.[373] In the mid-1990s three of its CEOs departed under pressure during a four-year span with losses mounting as Apple lost out to competitors responding effectively to consumer demand even if they lacked Apple's overall vision.[374]

Even software giant Microsoft was supposedly under the gun. There was speculation in the mid-1990s that Microsoft would, IBM-style, "be washed away by a new wave of competitors in the computer business."[375] Microsoft, which achieved dominance with its Windows operating system and related software, was thought to be vulnerable because it had failed to develop a strategy to counter the possibility that the internet would provide a platform for rivals to challenge Windows' hegemony.[376] Marc Andreessen, cofounder of Netscape, reputedly boasted his company would reduce Windows to a "mundane collection of not entirely debugged device drivers."[377]

Available data confirmed competition intensified during the 1990s. Thurow, to buttress his claim that about the dynamic environment in which companies were operating, cited the fact that of the 25 biggest American firms in 1960 only 6 were still on the list in 1997.[378] Economist Paul Krugman struck a similar note in 1999, saying "(t)he turnover rate among firms is increasing markedly," noting that a quarter of the top 100 US companies by market capitalization did not exist a generation previously.[379] Data on aggregate concentration, measured by the percentage of corporate profits generated by the 500 largest private sector companies as a proportion of all corporate profits, also indicated incumbents were losing out to rivals. This measure of market power declined steadily from the early 1980s through to 1998, and an increase in 1999 only brought aggregate concentration levels back to where they had been in the late 1980s.[380]

---

368 Labaton, *supra* note 348.

369 *Supra* note 47 and accompanying text.

370 Lester C. Thurow, *Building Wealth*, ATLANTIC MONTHLY, June 1999, 57, 69.

371 THOMAS E. VOLLMANN, ACHIEVING MARKET DOMINANCE THROUGH RADICAL CHANGE 11 (1996).

372 *Supra* notes 161–64 and related discussion; Carol J. Loomis & Joshua Mendes, *Dinosaurs*, FORTUNE, May 3, 1993, 36.

373 Chapter 3, notes 481, 495–96 and accompanying text; Chapter 4, notes 26–28, 446 and accompanying text; Walter S. Mossberg, *Apple of America's Eye Falls Victim to Pride*, WALL ST. J., Jan. 24, 1996, B1.

374 Mossberg, *supra* note 373; John Simons, *Bobbing for CEOs at Apple*, US NEWS & WORLD REPORT, July 21, 1997, 55.

375 Kathy Rebello, *Inside Microsoft*, BUS. WK., July 15, 1996, 56.

376 *Id.*

377 Adam Lashinsky, Oliver Ryan & Patricia Neering, *The Birth of the Web*, FORTUNE, July 25, 2005, 144.

378 Thurow, *supra* note 370, at 58.

379 Gerard Baker, *Winning Ways: Ready Bucks and a Flair for Risk*, FIN. TIMES, Dec. 14, 1999, 16.

380 Lawrence J. White, *Aggregate Concentration in the United States*, 16 J. ECON. PERSP. 137, 156 (2002).

Awareness of the seeming prevalence of "creative destruction" affected the managerial mindset. In 1998 Marina von Neumann Whitman argued that for present-day executives "(i)ntense competitive pressures" were diluting "the concentration of managerial power" and had "reduced managerial complacency."[381] Vollman made the point more starkly, saying "(t)oday the sentiment dominate or die is as common in the boardroom as computer games in the teenage bedrooms."[382]

Executives had no shortage of advice on how to respond to the challenges intensifying competition posed. Management consultants David and Mark Nadler, in their 1998 book *Champions of Change*, said "(t)he past few years have brought about a staggering outpouring of books, articles, lectures, and seminars touting an avalanche of ideas about managing change."[383] A different book, Clayton Christensen's *The Innovator's Dilemma*, would be the one that would dominate discussion during the late 1990s.[384] Christensen, a Harvard Business School academic, explained in his 1997 book how even well-run companies dominating an industrial sector were vulnerable to "disruption" from newcomers deploying innovative strategies to capture market share by appealing to customers the incumbents were overlooking because of success with their premium-priced products. With disruptive scenarios apparently occurring in a wide variety of contexts, such as film versus digital cameras and human versus online stockbroking, Christensen's analysis of "disrupters" resulted in "sudden celebrity on the corporate circuit."[385]

There were various high-profile examples of public company executives moving beyond theory and deploying robust strategies to meet competitive challenges they were facing. Sears implemented in the mid-1990s a wide range of changes to update its look and feel, resulting in *Fortune* naming the company the most innovative general merchandise retailer in 1997 after calling it a "dinosaur" four years before.[386] At Apple, in 1997 its board asked Steve Jobs to return after a 12-year hiatus to run the company, initially as iCEO (interim chief executive officer).[387] He oversaw the 1998 launch of the iMac, a stylish PC that became a best-seller and catapulted Apple's share price from $13 at the beginning of 1998 to over $100 per share at the end of 1999.[388] Apple's successes multiplied in the 2000s,[389] leading some to suggest that the board's rehiring of Jobs was one of "the greatest business decisions of all time."[390]

---

381 WHITMAN, *supra* note 56, at 30, 43, 199.

382 VOLLMANN, *supra* note 371, at 9.

383 DAVID A. NADLER & MARK B. NADLER, CHAMPIONS OF CHANGE: HOW CEOS AND THEIR COMPANIES ARE MASTERING THE SKILLS OF RADICAL CHANGE 3 (1998).

384 CLAYTON M. CHRISTENSEN, THE INNOVATOR'S DILEMMA: WHEN NEW TECHNOLOGIES CAUSE GREAT FIRMS TO FAIL (1997).

385 WESBURY, *supra* note 66, at 140–41; Jerry Useem, *Internet Defense Strategy: Cannibalize Yourself*, FORTUNE, Sept. 6, 1999, 141.

386 Loomis & Mendes, *supra* note 372; Patricia Sellers, *Sears: The Turnaround Is Ending: The Revolution Has Begun*, FORTUNE, Apr. 28, 1997, 106; ROBERT A.G. MONKS & NELL MINOW, CORPORATE GOVERNANCE 371–72 (2d ed. 2001).

387 Leander Kahney, *The Wilderness Years*, NEWSWEEK, Oct. 10, 2011, 20.

388 THOMAS KUCZMARKSI, ARTHUR MIDDLEBROOKS & JEFFREY SWADDLING, INNOVATING THE CORPORATION: CREATING VALUE FOR CUSTOMERS AND SHAREHOLDERS 8, 220 (2001).

389 Chapter 6, note 397 and related discussion.

390 RAM CHARAN, DENNIS CAREY & MICHAEL USEEM, BOARDS THAT LEAD: WHEN TO TAKE CHARGE, WHEN TO PARTNER, AND WHEN TO STAY OUT OF THE WAY 14 (2013).

Microsoft's response to the challenge the internet posed to its business model was similarly forthright. *Business Week* said in 1996

> Microsoft, already the ultimate hardcore company, is entering a new dimension. It's called Internet time: a pace so frenetic it's like living dog years—each jammed with the events of seven normal ones. Microsoft employees are pulling allnighters to make up for the precious time the company has lost to Internet go-getters such as Netscape.[391]

Later that year Microsoft launched Internet Explorer, a free web browser as capable as Netscape's Navigator, and bundled it with every new Windows operating system Microsoft sold.[392] The tactic crippled Netscape and was subsequently ruled by a federal court to be illegally monopolistic under antitrust law in a case that was ultimately settled with Microsoft acceding to various restrictions on its methods of doing business.[393]

Why the Pressure Intensified

Microsoft's robust response in the mid-1990s to the threat the internet reputedly posed to its business model illustrated that the rise of the World Wide Web was a significant reason that public company executives felt the pressure from rivals was intensifying as the twentieth century drew to a close. *Business Week* picked up on the theme in a 1999 cover story entitled "Internet Anxiety":

> Simply put, there's a revolution under way, and mastering the Net has moved front and center on Corporate America's agenda.... Throughout Corporate America, executives are suddenly waking to the realization that those who don't move fast to get in on the game risk having their lunch eaten by tiny rivals who may have barely existed just a few years ago.[394]

GE CEO Jack Welch bought into the logic. He said of his company "(w)here does the Internet rank in priority? It's No. 1, 2, 3, and 4."[395]

Those in charge of corporations dominant within a market sector were apprehensive of the internet because the Web opened up for fledgling firms the possibility of catching up quickly while operating with "freedom from the hierarchical management structure of most of Corporate America."[396] Suddenly it was much easier for buyers and sellers to find each other and for customers to engage in comparison shopping for the best deal.[397] As bestselling

---

391 Rebello, *supra* note 375.

392 William H. Page & John E. Lopatka, The Microsoft Case: Antitrust, High Technology and Consumer Welfare 26–27 (2007).

393 *Id.* at 35, 203, 220–21; Lewis, *supra* note 117, 288–93; United States v. Microsoft Corp., 87 F. Supp. 2d 30, 44 (D.D.C. 2000).

394 Byrnes, *supra* note 293.

395 *Id.*

396 *Id.*

397 Gordon, *supra* note 38, at 412; Robert Kuttner, *Bill Gates, Robber Baron*, Bus. Wk., Jan. 19, 1998, 20.

author Michael Lewis observed in a 1999 book about Netscape's cofounder Jim Clark "(t)he Internet created many opportunities for people like Clark—outsiders, troublemakers—to think thoughts that would turn entire industries on their heads."[398] Prime examples were Jeff Bezos of Amazon, which used the internet to revolutionize book retailing, and the founders of eBay, which had upended the auction business.[399]

Apprehension about competition in the 1990s was by no means purely a product of the internet. Hamel and Prahalad were, after all, telling readers "the future is now" in 1994, when the internet had yet to go mainstream. Similarly, Michael Hammer and James Champy said in a 1993 bestselling book on corporate re-engineering, "(t)oday, companies must move fast, or they won't be moving at all."[400]

Hammer and Champy, in making their case that companies were operating in a more challenging environment, cited a factor frequently mentioned in the 1980s as a source of competitive pressure for US companies, namely the foreign dimension.[401] They said "(w)ith globalization of the economy, companies face a greater number of competitors, each one of which may introduce product and service innovations to the market."[402] Andrall Pearson, a Harvard Business School professor and former president of PepsiCo, argued similarly in 1992 "(t)oday global US companies in nearly every major industry find themselves tormented in a competitive purgatory largely of their own making, where their old successes look increasingly like gross excesses."[403] According to a 1993 survey of representatives of 132 American manufacturing firms, most of which were large and active in foreign markets, three-quarters agreed strongly that their firm faced much stiffer competition than had been the case a decade earlier.[404]

Overseas rivals receded somewhat as a source of concern during the mid- and late-1990s as a buoyant US economy laid to rest fears of American economic decline.[405] The *Financial Times* observed in 1994 "if business is war, the Americans now seem to be winning it."[406] The typical large American corporation reputedly was evolving into a "nimble global competitor."[407] A 1994 *Newsweek* column on the reinvention of corporate America noted "(p)opular rhetoric dwells upon foreign threats: Toyota menacing General Motors. In truth, the more common threats are homegrown. Microsoft and Compaq menace IBM. Southwest Air menaces American. MCI and Sprint menace AT&T."[408]

---

398 LEWIS, *supra* note 117, at 383.

399 *Id.*

400 HAMMER & CHAMPY, *supra* note 142, at 23.

401 Chapter 4, notes 437–38 and related discussion.

402 HAMMER & CHAMPY, *supra* note 142, at 23.

403 Andrall E. Pearson, *Corporate Redemption and the Seven Deadly Sins*, HARV. BUS. REV., May/June 1992, 65, 65.

404 WHITMAN, *supra* note 56, at 20.

405 *Supra* notes 71–75 and related discussion.

406 *Once More Unto the Breach*, FIN. TIMES, Feb. 7, 1994.

407 WHITMAN, *supra* note 56, at 1.

408 Robert J. Samuelson, *Reinventing Corporate America*, NEWSWEEK, July 4, 1994, 53. See also Lohr, *supra* note 225.

Deregulation was as an additional factor fostering competitive pressures in the 1990s.[409] The *Wall Street Journal* noted, for instance, in 1999 that with "even long-protected industries . . . being pried open to market competition . . . the most hidebound *Fortune* 500 companies feel forced to act like scrappy entrepreneurs."[410] At least in those industries directly affected, deregulation would have been a two-edged sword for executives. On the one hand, assuming deregulation reduced barriers to entry the executives running formerly insulated incumbents would, as the *Wall Street Journal* was indicating, have been forced to navigate a novel and challenging competitive environment. On the other hand, the dismantling of industry-specific restrictions opened up fresh opportunities for management teams suitably positioned to capitalize on the enhanced discretion available to them.

A final factor amplifying competitive pressure in the 1990s had similar potentially conflicting ramifications for public company executives, this being improved access to finance. If capital is being allocated conservatively, ambitious executives who need cash to execute plans they have can end up with little room to maneuver. The effects will be mixed for managers of large public companies. Absent robust retained earnings, grand plans they have may well not come to fruition. On the other hand, challengers seeking to seize market share might well lack the financial wherewithal to proceed, thereby insulating the incumbents from unwelcome competition.[411]

During the 1980s, the venture capital (VC) industry expanded, commercial banks adopted a more liberal approach when lending to businesses, and investment banks became more creative in raising capital for their corporate clientele, most tangibly with the explosion of the market for junk bonds.[412] Access to capital correspondingly improved for incumbents and challengers alike. The trends were similar in the 1990s, at least when the economy picked up after the mild recession at the beginning of the decade. Mort Zuckerman, when he argued in 1998 that a second American century was beginning, praised "the unique and remarkable world of finance capital" on the basis that it had "proven its capacity to provide the multiple sources of entrepreneurial capital needed by entrepreneurial management, thereby demonstrating its ability to meet the needs of a modern, rapidly changing, globalized economy."[413] This would have been worrying for those managing well-established market leaders already nervous due to the internet, foreign competition, and deregulation. In contrast, for ambitious executives awareness that securing financing to execute bold initiatives was a realistic possibility was potentially invigorating.

While corporate borrowing grew in popularity in the 1980s,[414] during the mild recession at the beginning of the 1990s "American credit markets went through a period of convalescence."[415] Debt, according to one investment banker, became "a four-letter word."[416] US

---

409 Whitman, *supra* note 56, at 21; Paul Osterman, Securing Prosperity—The American Labor Market: How It Has Change and What to Do about It 32 (1999).

410 Alan Murray, *The Economy Is New; Human Nature Isn't*, Wall St. J., May 24, 1999, A1.

411 Chapter 2, notes 388–89 and accompanying text.

412 Chapter 4, notes 473–78, 487–91, 500–01, 511–13, 516, 519–20 and related discussion.

413 Zuckerman, *supra* note 73, at 23.

414 Chapter 4, notes 468–70 and accompanying text.

415 Henry Kaufman, On Money and Markets: A Wall Street Memoir 280 (2000).

416 Leslie Wayne, *Balance Sheets in 90s: Less Debt*, NY Times, July 23, 1990, D1.

companies, having borrowed heavily, reversed course and deleveraged as the 1990s began, taking advantage of rising share prices to raise equity to shore up their balance sheets.[417] In the second half of the 1990s, however, companies were again borrowing at a healthy clip. By the first quarter of 2000, corporate debt equaled 46 percent of GDP, up from 38 percent in 1995.[418] Ira Kay, an executive pay consultant, said in 2000 that rising debt was "the dirty little secret of corporate America."[419]

Bank policy contributed both to the conservative debt climate of the early 1990s and to the liberalization in the years that followed. As the 1980s concluded, the financial sector was roiled by a crisis affecting savings and loans (S&L) associations, also known as thrifts, which specialized in residential mortgage lending but diversified in the 1980s with often disastrous consequences.[420] With the S&L crisis prompting worries about the soundness of the wider banking system federal regulators clamped down on what they classified as highly leveraged transactions and banks looked askance at potentially risky corporate borrowers.[421] As *US News & World Report* said in 1990, "credit standards have changed dramatically and banks have become much tougher in their negotiations with corporate borrowers. Many financial institutions won't lend to companies where credit quality is even a distant worry."[422]

In the risk-averse environment of the early 1990s, "only the safest loans got made."[423] The mindset was still prevalent during 1993.[424] Change was imminent, however. *Business Week* said in 1997 "(t)oday is heaven for corporations looking to raise money."[425] A revised approach to lending banks adopted was an important reason. By the late 1990s, bank loans to commercial and industrial companies were growing substantially faster than GDP.[426] The money was not merely available but also available on advantageous terms. Banks were accommodating because they knew that larger corporations had the option to issue commercial paper to raise debt and smaller firms could turn to flourishing nonbank lenders such as GE Capital and Green Tree Financial.[427]

Junk bonds, which rose to prominence in the 1980s,[428] provided another reason that by the late 1990s it was "heaven for corporations looking to raise money." As the 1990s commenced the junk bond market was "comatose."[429] The *New York Times* suggested in 1990 "it

---

[417] Kenneth P. Gilpin, *Balance Sheets Are Healthier*, NY TIMES, Nov. 15, 1993, D1; Terence P. Pare & Eileen P. Gunn, *Today's Hot Concept, Tomorrow's Forest Fire*, FORTUNE, May 15, 1995, 197.

[418] Floyd Norris, *As Profits Soar, Corporate America Takes on More Debt*, NY TIMES, July 7, 2000, C1.

[419] David Leonhardt, *Will Today's Huge Rewards Devour Tomorrow's Earnings?*, NY TIMES, Apr. 2, 2000, Business, 1.

[420] WELLS, *supra* note 50, at 158.

[421] Wayne, *supra* note 416.

[422] Jack Egan, Robert F. Black & Gary Cohen, *Now, It's Crunch Time*, US NEWS & WORLD REPORT, Nov. 19, 1990, 56.

[423] Suzanne Wooley, *The Floodgates Inch Open*, BUS. WK., Nov. 2, 1993, Enterprise, 96.

[424] *Id.*

[425] Peter Coy, *Money, Money Everywhere*, BUS. WK., Mar. 10, 1997, 96.

[426] *A Hazardous Journey*, ECONOMIST, Jan. 27, 2001, The Party's Over: A Survey of Corporate Finance, 17.

[427] ROBERT E. LITAN, AMERICAN FINANCE FOR THE 21ST CENTURY 2, 75 (1998); *The Party's Over*, ECONOMIST, Jan. 27, 2001, The Party's Over: A Survey of Corporate Finance, 5.

[428] Chapter 4, notes 472–78 and related discussion.

[429] Chapter 4, note 160 and accompanying text.

is unlikely that there will soon be a sizable market for new issues even of relatively high-quality junk."[430] By the middle of the decade, however, it was clear that junk bonds were "here to stay."[431] As of 1998 the high-yield bond market was "sizzling."[432] Default was a rarity in the benign economic environment of the mid- and late-1990s, which made junk bonds popular with debt investors looking for yields higher than those offered by government bonds.[433] Junk bond issuers used most of the funds raised to pay for capital expenditures, to make other general investments in their operations or to refinance existing debt.[434]

Venture capital was an additional form of finance potentially available to those seeking to challenge incumbents that was in the doldrums as the 1990s began but grew in prominence as the decade progressed. Fresh investment in venture capital firms, which peaked for the 1980s in 1987 at $4.2 billion, was only $1.8 billion in 1990 and $1.4 billion in 1991.[435] In 1991 a *Los Angeles Times* business columnist warned that "(v)enture capital has become Wimp Capital" due to shifting away from start-ups to late-round financing and argued that "(t)he change isn't just cyclic; it's structural," meaning "(f)or Americans concerned about competitiveness" there was "excellent reason to worry."[436] This implied that for entrepreneurs "the odds against raising big money (were) daunting."[437]

It soon was evident the *Los Angeles Times* had been too pessimistic. New venture capital commitments in 1995 equaled the previous 1987 peak.[438] This presaged a "golden age of venture capital investing."[439] In the mid-1990s, returns for venture capital funds were stellar (44 percent in 1995 and 34 percent in 1996 according to one estimate).[440] Venture capital funds run by Kleiner Perkins profited wildly, for instance, with Netscape's 1995 initial public offering, and the same happened for its rival Sequoia when Yahoo!, the operator of a popular internet search engine, joined the stock market in 1996.[441] Such successes were a magnet for new investment, which hit a record $6.5 billion in 1996.[442] Expansion of the venture capital industry then went into overdrive, with the number of venture capital firms in operation increasing by two-thirds between 1996 and 1999 and with funds under management growing from $52 billion to $164 billion over the same period.[443]

---

430 Floyd Norris, *As Defaults Keep Rising, A Market Dies*, NY TIMES, Sept. 9, 1990, F1.

431 Franklin R. Edwards & Frederic S. Mishkin, *The Decline of Traditional Banking: Implications for Financial Stability and Regulatory Policy*, FRBNY ECON. POL'Y. REV., July 1995, 27, 32.

432 Toddi Gutner, *Junk Bonds Have Grown Up*, BUS. WK., May 18, 1998, 202.

433 Jeffrey M. Laderman, *In Bonds, the Junkier the Better*, BUS. WK., July 7, 1997, 116; Edward I. Altman, *Revisiting the High Yield Bond Market: Mature but Never Dull*, J. APP. CORP. FIN., Spring 2000, at 64, 65, 68.

434 Altman, *supra* note 433, at 70–71.

435 Cynthia A. Beltz, *Introduction, in* FINANCING ENTREPRENEURS 1, 14 (Cynthia A. Beltz ed., 1994); Bernard S. Black & Ronald J. Gilson, *Venture Capital and the Structure of Capital Markets: Banks versus Stock Markets*, 47 J. FIN. ECON. 243, 247 (1998).

436 Michael Schrage, *Venture Capital Loses Its Spirit of Adventure*, LA TIMES, Sept. 5, 1991, 49.

437 Amar Bhide, *Bootstrap Finance: The Art of Start-Ups*, HARV. BUS. REV., Nov./Dec. 1995, 109, 110.

438 Black & Gilson, *supra* note 435, at 247.

439 Tom Foremski, *Living in the Golden Age*, FIN. TIMES, May 5, 1999, FT-IT Review, 7.

440 Shawn Tully & Ani Hadjian, *How to Make $400,000,000 in Just One Minute*, FORTUNE, May 27, 1996, 84; *Money to Burn*, ECONOMIST, May 27, 2000, 103.

441 Tully & Hadjian, *supra* note 440.

442 Black & Gilson, *supra* note 435, at 246.

443 CASSIDY, *supra* note 12, at 236.

Venture capital firms, with their bulging coffers, liberalized considerably the deployment of funds. As *Forbes* said in 2000, "(t)he once-staid venture capital community has morphed into a free-for-all brawl, and the obvious culprit is money, oodles and oodles of it."[444] Venture capitalists "were accustomed to dictating to entrepreneurs, not vice versa."[445] Their default position was to be patient before relying on an initial public offering as an exit option, with a venture capital partner explaining, "(w)e'd rather get $100m five years out than $20m after two years."[446] During the late 1990s, however, "money was chasing deals" and the balance of power shifted in favor of entrepreneurs with promising prospects and an eye on public markets.[447] Amidst intense enthusiasm for stocks, especially for enterprises with an internet dimension, venture capital firms frequently succumbed to the temptation to go for a quick blockbuster IPO payoff.[448] For VC-funded companies the typical time lag between the venture capital stage and the IPO stage fell from about six-and-a-half years in 1995 to about two-and-a-half years in 1999.[449]

For those seeking to challenge incumbents the dramatic growth of the venture capital industry in the late 1990s was potentially welcome news. "It is now much easier for entrepreneurs to raise money" noted a *New York Times* guest columnist in 1999.[450] The same year Harvard Business School's William Sahlman cited venture capital as a key reason money was flowing to entrepreneurs "with enormous ease."[451] An executive from consumer goods giant Procter & Gamble who quit to launch an internet start-up concurred in a 1999 interview with the *Financial Times*, saying "(t)he availability of venture capital is what compels us to leave the large corporations and put our own stake in the ground. A lot of smart money is looking for really good ideas out there."[452]

Though the venture capital industry grew dramatically in the 1990s, a number of factors muted its impact as a catalyst for creative destruction. First, the phenomenon was a fleeting one. Venture capitalists quickly forced companies in which they had invested to rein in costs and shelve plans to go public when investor enthusiasm for IPOs, particularly of the internet variety, cooled in 2000.[453] By the end of 2000 a venture capital partner was even referring to the 1990s as "the good ol' days."[454]

---

444 Eric W. Pfeiffer, *Why Oh Why?*, FORBES, May 29, 2000, ASAP, 115.

445 CASSIDY, *supra* note 12, at 61.

446 *A Really Big Adventure*, ECONOMIST, Jan. 25, 1997, 20.

447 Ulrich Hege & Sébastien Michenaud, *The Internet Boom in a Corporate Finance Retrospective, in* INTERNET AND DIGITAL ECONOMICS: PRINCIPLES, METHODS AND APPLICATIONS 142, 146 (Eric Brousseau & Nicolas Curien eds., 2007).

448 Bijan Khezri, *Lost in the Valley*, FIN. TIMES, June 5, 2001, 21.

449 Fred Barbash, *Valuing Dot-Coms: Counting Eyeballs Isn't Enough*, WASH. POST, Nov. 14, 1999, H1.

450 Charles Ferguson, *Is There Too Much Venture Capital?*, NY TIMES, Dec. 11, 1999, A19.

451 William Sahlman, *The New Economy Is Stronger than You Think*, HARV. BUS. REV., Nov./Dec. 1999, 99, 105.

452 Baker, *supra* note 379.

453 Luisa Krull, *When the Music Stops*, FORBES, May 15, 2000, 182; Margaret E. Popper, *Public Access Denied*, BUS. WK., May 22, 2000, Frontier, 12.

454 *Day of E-tonement*, FORBES, Dec. 25, 2000, 262.

Second, even at its peak, the venture capital industry was small relative to the economy, with VC investments amounting to only 0.59 percent of GDP as of 1999.[455] Despite the relaxation of standards in the late 1990s, venture capitalists only provided backing for a tiny proportion of the thousands of business plans they reviewed.[456] Third, repeating a pattern evident in the 1980s,[457] there was a strong sectoral bias with venture capital disbursements. In 1999, about 60 percent went to companies in the information technology realm, around 10 percent was invested in life sciences and medical companies, and the rest was spread amongst other types of company.[458]

Despite the qualifications, the 1990s venture capital industry did leave a significant imprint on corporate America. VC-financed Netscape came out second-best to Microsoft in the browser war between them before it was acquired by AOL in 1998, but VC-backed Yahoo! operated what was the top search engine in the late 1990s and the early 2000s.[459] Google.com, started by youthful doctoral students Larry Page and Sergey Brin, received $25 million in VC funding to launch in the late 1990s the search engine that would usurp Yahoo!.[460] Internet-oriented consumer services revolutionaries Amazon and eBay were also backed by VC firms.[461] When Larry Summers claimed in 1999 that it was the first economy where "entrepreneurs may raise their first $100 million before buying their first suits" venture capital was a significant contributor to the situation.[462] Not bad for "Wimp Capital."

The CEO as Corporate Icon

The 1980s was a dizzying decade for senior executives of public companies with managerial turnover increasing, pay rising substantially, and public notoriety becoming increasingly common.[463] These trends were present, and more robust, in the 1990s. By the end of the decade, CEOs were prominent in a way they had never been before. In an era of corporate prosperity, the best-known achieved something approaching iconic status, setting the stage for chief executives to be labeled "imperial CEOs."[464] A 1997 *Wall Street Journal* article

---

455 Roy C. Smith, The Wealth Creators: The Rise of Today's Rich and Super-Rich 79 (2001); Mary O'Sullivan, *Finance and Innovation, in* The Oxford Handbook of Innovation 240, 253 (Jan Fagerberg, David C. Mowery & Richard R. Nelson eds., 2005).

456 Leslie Walker, *Venture Capital: Doorway to Internet Dreams*, Wash. Post, June 27, 1999, H1: R.D. Norton, Creating the New Economy: The Entrepreneur and the US Resurgence 246 (2001).

457 Chapter 4, notes 534–35 and accompanying text.

458 Paul Gompers & Josh Lerner, *The Venture Capital Revolution*, 15 J. Econ. Persp. 145, 148 (2001).

459 Hege & Michenaud, *supra* note 447, at 150; *War of the Worlds*, Economist, Nov. 28, 1998, 16; Mike Tekula, *Your Approach to Organic Search Is Obsolete: How to Evolve in 2014*, Distilled, Jan. 21, 2014, available at https://www.distilled.net/blog/your-seo-approach-is-obsolete-evolve-in-2014/ (accessed Feb. 14, 2018).

460 Lewis, *supra* note 117, at 390; Chapter 6, note 398 and accompanying text.

461 Cassidy, *supra* note 12, at 140–41, 194.

462 Mandel, *supra* note 52, at 5.

463 Chapter 4, notes 538–46, 565–66, 575, 581–87 and related discussion.

464 The term "imperial CEO" was first deployed with considerable frequency in 2002, by which time the dethroning had begun. See Chapter 6, notes 407, 418 and related discussion; David Leonhardt, *The Imperial Chief Executive Is Suddenly in the Cross Hairs*, NY Times, June 24, 2002, A1; *Downsizing the Imperial CEO*, NY Times, Aug. 9, 2002, A14.

saying "(t)he celebrity CEO is the current ideal if not the standard" quoted a media consultant who advised 300 chief executives on image making as saying that "(a)ll of a sudden, ordinary people can name CEOs."[465] This left America's newly minted iconic chief executives a considerable distance to fall when the tide went out on public companies in the early 2000s.

The increased prominence of chief executives was not mere happenstance. Instead, the scope senior management had to influence outcomes likely was greater in the 1990s than it had been at any previous point. Regulation and unions had declined in importance as constraints and there was ample access to capital to finance bold corporate initiatives. Competitive pressure had intensified, but with enhanced discretion available in various ways, executives had greater room to respond. Subsequent empirical research indeed suggested that during the second half of the 20th century "the CEO effect" peaked as the 1990s came to an end.[466]

There was during the 1990s a dearth of empirical evidence on the impact chief executives had, through their efforts or reputation, on corporate performance.[467] Conjectures about the impact CEOs had on their companies nevertheless abounded. A *Wall Street Journal* columnist argued in 1990 that the CEO effect was modest, saying "(e)xecutive ability is far, far more common than the talent needed to spear a ground ball hit to the hole [in baseball]. Anyone who has a fair amount of common sense, energy and humanity can do a creditable or even exemplary job of running a business. Parenthood is a lot harder."[468] As the decade progressed, however, it became increasingly widely accepted that executives were a key determinant of corporate success.

Columbia Business School professor Leonard Sayles claimed in 1993 that "the subject of leadership has been rediscovered by business as a critical factor in organizational performance," due partly to "a gnawing sense among American business managers that they have been doing something wrong."[469] Management consultant Mike Davidson told readers in 1996 "(w)e are now in yet another kind of economic time" and said that to identify "the Dynasties of the next wave.... (T)he answer is to look at their leaders."[470] The *Economist* claimed in 1999 that while "a chief executive might once have got by with good managers, cost control, and a beady eye on the accounts," "a chief executive now ... needs to be an innovator and an entrepreneur," with the result being "(a)n able chief executive has extraordinary power to make or break a company."[471] Psychoanalyst Michael Maccoby, who said in the late 1970s that "the corporate gamesman" had replaced "the other-directed organization man" as

---

[465] G. Pascal Zachary, *CEOs Are Stars Now, But Why? And Would Alfred Sloan Approve?*, Wall St. J., Sept. 3, 1997, A1.

[466] Chapter 1, note 18 and related discussion.

[467] Derek Bok, The Cost of Talent: How Executives and Professionals Are Paid and How It Affects America 256 (1993); Leslie Gaines-Ross, CEO Capital: A Guide to Building CEO Reputation and Company Success 6 (2003).

[468] William E. Blundell, *A Modest Proposal*, Wall St. J., Apr. 18, 1990, R31.

[469] Leonard R. Sayles, The Working Leader: The Triumph of High Performance over Conventional Management Principles 2 (1993).

[470] Mike Davidson, The Transformation of Management 83 (1996).

[471] *Firing the Boss*, Economist, Oct. 30, 1999, 17.

the prototypical executive,[472] wrote in *Harvard Business Review*'s first issue of 2000 "there's something new and daring about the CEOs who are transforming today's industries" with "the business world . . . experiencing enormous changes that call for visionary and charismatic leadership."[473]

The investment community concurred that executives mattered. When AT&T indicated in 1997 that Michael Armstrong, poached from Hughes Electronics, would replace lackluster Bob Allen as CEO, "Wall Street voted its approval by investors sending the stock up more than 5 percent, adding more than $3 billion to AT&T's worth."[474] This healthy market reaction nevertheless paled in comparison to that following the 1996 announcement by troubled appliance maker Sunbeam Corp. that it had hired as CEO Al Dunlap, nicknamed "Chainsaw" because of his reputation of ruthless cost-cutting.[475] Sunbeam's stock price soared 52 percent on the news, boosting Sunbeam's roughly $1 billion market capitalization by $521 million.[476]

With both Dunlap and Armstrong investors were far too optimistic. Dunlap "was the first of the Great Bull Market's most celebrated CEOs Gone Wild to go from hero to zero in barely the blink of an eye," leaving Sunbeam in 1998 amidst revelations of accounting chicanery.[477] The company declared bankruptcy in 2001.[478] Armstrong would resign as AT&T CEO under a cloud in 2002 after an acquisition spree he orchestrated delivered disappointing results.[479] Nevertheless, the stock market reaction to the hiring of Dunlap and Armstrong indicates how important CEOs were thought to be during the second half of the 1990s.[480] Survey evidence confirmed the point. Financial analysts and institutional investor representatives polled by consulting firm Burson-Marsteller in 1999 indicated that 47 percent of a company's reputation was attributable to the reputation of its chief executive officer.[481] Ninety-five percent of analysts said the attributes of a corporation's CEO influenced their decision whether to recommend that a stock was worth buying.[482]

Boards apparently concurred. A series of widely publicized dismissals of CEOs at leading companies in the early 1990s implied directors thought having the right person at the helm was a top priority.[483] In 1993 the *Wall Street Journal*, having cited the high-profile firings, said "(a) CEO's tenure is growing shorter than ever, subject to abrupt cancellation when things go wrong."[484] The trend in favor of boards orchestrating managerial change

---

[472] MICHAEL MACCOBY, THE GAMESMAN: THE NEW CORPORATE LEADERS 35–36 (1977); Chapter 3, note 16 and related discussion.

[473] Michael Maccoby, *Narcissistic Leaders*, HARV. BUS. REV., Jan./Feb. 2000, 69, 69–70.

[474] Seth Schiesel, *AT&T Introduces Executive Who'll Take Over Company*, NY TIMES, Oct. 21, 1997, D4.

[475] Glenn Collins, *For a Struggling Sunbeam, Shock Therapy*, NY TIMES, Aug. 11, 1996, F1; CHRISTOPHER BYRON, TESTOSTERONE INC.: TALES OF CEOS GONE WILD 203–04, 255–56 (2004).

[476] Collins, *supra* note 475; BYRON, *supra* note 475, at 256–57.

[477] BYRON, *supra* note 475, at 295–96.

[478] *Id*. at 300.

[479] Chapter 1, notes 168, 178, 182 and accompanying text.

[480] Janice Revell, *Should You Bet on the CEO?*, FORTUNE, Nov. 18, 2002, 189.

[481] GAINES-ROSS, *supra* note 467, 19; *CEOs Make Up Half of Corporate Reputations*, INVESTOR RELATIONS BUS., June 12, 2000, 21.

[482] *CEOs Make Up*, *supra* note 481.

[483] *Supra* notes 160–64 and related discussion.

[484] Gilbert Fuchsberg, *Chief Executives See Their Power Shrink*, WALL ST. J., Mar. 15, 1993, B1.

was not restricted to the most prominent firms. Amongst the several hundred companies included in *Forbes*' annual surveys of executive pay, between 1989 and 1994 23.4 percent of CEO departures involved forced turnover as compared with 13.9 percent between 1971 and 1988.[485]

CEO turnover became even more robust throughout the remainder of the 1990s. With *Fortune* 500 companies, 12.6 percent of companies had a new CEO in post annually between 1992 and 1996, implying an average CEO tenure of 7.9 years, as compared with 19.2 percent turnover between 1997 to 2002, implying an average tenure of 5.2 years.[486] The *New York Times* pointed out in 1997 that for CEOs "the leash is short and getting shorter," with the dismissal pace of the early 1990s being "almost leisurely by current standards."[487] This, according to the paper, was because "(c)orporate boards are under greater pressure than ever to acknowledge management problems and act quickly."[488]

An increased willingness on the part of boards to depart from a norm of elevating a current executive to the CEO post in favor of appointing an outsider was an additional indication that directors felt it was pivotal to find the right chief executive, regardless of lineage. With CEO appointments occurring in the 800 largest corporations in the United States, the proportion of outside hires rose from 15 percent in the 1970s and 17 percent in the 1980s to 26 percent in the 1990s.[489] Among the largest 500 public firms that experienced CEO turnover in 1997 and 1998, outsiders were brought in 36 percent of the time.[490]

While growing faith in executive talent as a determinant of corporate success was reducing job security it was also making CEOs rich. The *New York Times* observed in 1997 "(e)xecutive pay seems to rise inexorably."[491] Among S&P 500 industrial companies, the median CEO earned nearly $6 million in 1999 as compared with $1.25 million in 1990.[492] With boards and investors being increasingly convinced that talented senior management was a crucial ingredient of corporate success, a desire to hire the right person helped to drive pay upward. For instance, IBM's board was praised for its efforts to improve shareholder returns when in 1993 it offered prospective CEO Louis Gerstner options to buy 500,000 shares, a huge quantity at the time, to lure him away from RJR Nabisco.[493]

Concerns about retention also served to push managerial compensation upward in the 1990s. The *Economist*, in a 1999 survey of executive pay, quoted an American compensation consultant as saying "(i)f a company has a CEO it likes, the last thing it wants is to have to

---

[485] Mark R. Huson, Robert Parrino & Laura T. Starks, *Internal Monitoring Mechanisms and CEO Turnover: A Long-Term Perspective*, 56 J. FIN. 2265, 2279 (2001). With *Forbes*, there were, for example, 800 companies included in its 1992 executive pay survey—*What 800 Companies Paid*, FORBES, May 25, 1992, 182.

[486] Steven N. Kaplan & Bernadette A. Minton, *How Has CEO Turnover Changed?*, 12 INT'L. REV. FIN. 57, 61 (2012).

[487] Steve Lohr, *Leashes Get Shorter for Executives*, NY TIMES, July 18, 1997, D1.

[488] *Id.*

[489] Kevin J. Murphy & Ján Zábojník, *CEO Pay and Appointments: A Market-Based Explanation for Recent Trends*, 94 AMER. ECON. REV. (PAPERS & PROCEEDINGS) 192, 193 (2004).

[490] Margarethe Wiersema, *Holes at the Top: Why CEO Firings Backfire*, HARV. BUS. REV., Dec. 2000, 70, 72.

[491] Judith H. Dobrzynski, *New Road to Riches Is Paved with Options*, NY TIMES, Mar. 30, 1997, F1.

[492] Hall, *supra* note 234, at 23 (measured in 2001 dollars; the figure for 1990 is derived from a sample of *Forbes* 500 companies).

[493] LOWENSTEIN, *supra* note 114, at 21.

go out and search for a new one," and reasoned "(s)o companies err on the side of generosity."[494] For instance, Kodak, having poached George Fisher from Motorola in 1993, gave him a two-year contract extension and stock options to buy 2 million shares in 1997 when rumors surfaced that AT&T was considering hiring him as its CEO.[495]

Use of equity-based executive compensation, particularly stock options, grew substantially in the 1990s.[496] The growing conviction that top management's efforts were a key determinant of corporate success contributed to the trend. Linking pay with performance implicitly presupposes that the recipients can influence outcomes and, as we have just seen, it was widely believed during the 1990s that this was the case with CEOs.[497] The shift toward performance-oriented pay in the 1990s in turn helps to explain why executives were paid more.

As the 1990s began, executives were telling Ira Kay, a leading executive pay consultant, that they were "reluctant to be paid primarily or heavily or even a little bit on stock price performance."[498] Executives indicated they didn't "want to be subject to the 'vagaries' of the stock market."[499] There also would have been diversification related apprehension about tying pay to the performance of the company in which the executives had already tied up virtually all of their human capital.[500] For companies wanting to link pay with performance but also assuage these managerial doubts, the obvious solution was to structure executive compensation to provide for a highly lucrative outcome if all went well.[501] Kay said, for instance, that a corporation seeking to fortify the link between pay and performance "must build large upside potential into its programs to offset the introduction of downside risk."[502] Public companies did exactly that.

There are various additional plausible explanations why executive pay increased dramatically in the 1990s. Pliant directors stand out as one contender. Boards ostensibly were a more robust check on executives in the 1990s than they had been previously.[503] Nevertheless, perhaps among directors responsible for setting executive pay "no one want(ed) to be the resident spoil-sport."[504] Boards, and the compensation consultants advising them, also may have been caught off guard by just how quickly shares rose in value as the 1990s went on. There was, for instance, a strong bias in favor of awarding senior management the same number of stock options each year, apparently with little regard for how dramatically their value would increase as stock prices rose.[505] As *Time* observed in 1997, "it is that bull market that has

---

494 *Who Wants to Be a Billionaire?*, ECONOMIST, May 8, 1999, The Best . . . and the Rest: A Survey of Pay, 14.

495 Daniel Kadlec & Bernard Baumohl, *How CEO Pay Got Away*, TIME, Apr. 28, 1997, 59.

496 *Supra* note 234 and related discussion; K. J. Martijn Cremers, Saura Masconale & Simone M. Sepe, *CEO Pay Redux*, 96 TEX. L. REV. 205, 240 (2017).

497 *Supra* notes 469–76 and accompanying text.

498 IRA T. KAY, VALUE AT THE TOP: SOLUTIONS TO THE EXECUTIVE COMPENSATION CRISIS 195 (1992).

499 *Id.*

500 Steven A. Bank, Brian R. Cheffins & Harwell Wells, *Executive Pay: What Worked?*, 42 J. CORP. L. 59, 68 (2016).

501 *Id.*

502 KAY, *supra* note 498, at 195.

503 *Supra* notes 167–70, 174–77, 186–88 and related discussion.

504 Lucian Bebchuk, Jesse Fried & David Walker, *Managerial Power and Rent Extraction in the Design of Executive Compensation*, 69 U. CHI. L. REV. 751, 754, 764–71 (2002).

505 Kelly Shue & Richard R. Townsend, *Growth through Rigidity: An Explanation for the Rise in CEO Pay*, 123 J. FIN. ECON. 1 (2017).

turned millions upon millions of stock options into pure CEO gold, in cartloads unforeseen by anyone."[506]

Ironically, regulation introduced in the early 1990s to constrain executive pay likely was an additional cause of the substantial increases that occurred throughout the remainder of the decade. As 1992 got underway, *Newsweek* told readers "America is headed off on a witch hunt—and this year's features the overpaid corporate executive as witch."[507] With the US in recession and with downsizing being a highly publicized phenomenon, critics zeroed in on top executives because CEOs had enjoyed substantial pay increases in the 1980s and their pay was still "galloping forward."[508] For perhaps the first time ever, a corporate governance issue became a true media sensation, moving from the financial pages to the editorial and front pages.[509] The anger reached its apex in early 1992 when President Bush went to Japan accompanied by a retinue of top executives to seek trade concessions and the public became aware that the annual pay of those executives averaged $3.4 million, six times as much as their Japanese counterparts.[510]

The controversy took on a strong political dimension, with Congress threatening to hold hearings and pass legislation.[511] Executive pay also became a campaign issue in the 1992 presidential race.[512] For instance, while competing for the Democratic nomination Bill Clinton railed that "executives continue to raise their pay and their perks while the workers get the shaft."[513]

The early 1990s executive pay furor also elicited regulatory changes. In October 1992 the SEC substantially revamped and bolstered rules governing disclosure of managerial compensation, shifting from a narrative-based regime to a tabular system to try to provide investors with an easily understood overview of executive pay in a single location.[514] Tax law was also deployed. To be deductible by a corporation managerial compensation has to be "reasonable" in relation to the services rendered.[515] In 1993 amounts paid in excess of $1 million to a public corporation's chief executive and to any of its other four highest-paid executives were deemed nondeductible unless the pay was based on performance goals, was set by a

[506] Kadlec & Baumohl, *supra* note 495. See also Tamar Hausman, *Predicting Pay*, WALL ST. J., Apr. 8, 1999, R9 (citing the views of a consultant on corporate governance associated with TIAA-CREF).

[507] Marc Levinson, *Lay Off the Pricey CEOs*, NEWSWEEK, Feb. 10, 1992, 44.

[508] *Supra* notes 38, 46, 62, 309 and accompanying text; Geoffrey Colvin, *How to Pay the CEO Right*, FORTUNE, Apr. 6, 1992, 60; Kevin Maney & Michelle Osborn, *Outcry over CEO Pay*, USA TODAY, Mar. 27, 1992, B1.

[509] MONKS & MINOW, *supra* note 386, at 139, 221.

[510] Alison Leigh Cowan, *The Gadfly CEO's Want to Swat*, NY TIMES, Feb. 2, 1992, F1. See also Charles C. Pak, *Toward Reasonable Executive Compensation: Outcry for Reform and Regulatory Response*, [1994] ANN. SURVEY AMER. LAW 633, 634–35 (making the same point with somewhat different figures).

[511] Maney & Osborn, *supra* note 508.

[512] Martin Dickson, *A Check on the Bosses' Cheque*, FIN. TIMES, Mar. 31, 1992, 20; Kevin J. Murphy, *The Politics of Pay: A Legislative History of Executive Compensation, in* RESEARCH HANDBOOK ON EXECUTIVE PAY 11, 23 (Randall Thomas & Jennifer Hill eds., 2012).

[513] *Pressure to Perform*, US NEWS & WORLD REPORT, Apr. 6, 1992, 49.

[514] Executive Compensation Disclosure (1992) 57 Fed. Reg. 48,126; Bank, Cheffins & Wells, *supra* note 500, at 70; *Shadow SEC Roundtable on the New Disclosures of Executive Pay*, J. APP. CORP. FIN., Winter 1993, at 62, 63.

[515] I.R.C. § 162(a)(1) (2018).

compensation committee comprised of independent directors, and was approved by a vote of shareholders.[516]

These early 1990s regulatory changes likely had the opposite effect to what reformers intended. On the disclosure front, *Fortune* in 2001 sought to explain to readers why executive compensation had "become highway robbery," and said of the 1992 reforms requiring companies to report CEO pay in greater detail that "(a)mbitious CEOs now knew better than ever what their peers were getting—and could push for packages that were superior in every particular."[517] With the prevailing wisdom in the 1990s being that executive talent was a key determinant of corporate success, those CEOs would have been well-positioned to drive a hard bargain.

As for the $1 million deductibility cap, the fact that there was an exemption for performance related compensation likely provided a tax-related catalyst for the generous granting of stock options that fueled the dramatic rise of executive pay during the 1990s.[518] The cap also may have been treated as an implicit endorsement of CEO pay of at least $1 million annually, thereby prompting companies paying less to play catch up.[519] On this point *Fortune*'s take in 2001 was that "(m)any salaries that were below $1 million now rose to that level, since it was virtually government-endorsed."[520]

The timing of *Fortune's* critique of executive pay was not coincidental. As of 2001 "the backdrop (was) a dragging economy and a market collapse that hurt millions of people,"[521] which prompted considerable disquiet about executive pay that had risen so dramatically through the 1990s. Michael Jensen, who, when pressing the case in 1990 for companies to link pay more closely with performance argued that chief executives were underpaid,[522] was quoted by *Fortune* as saying "now even I'm troubled."[523] Criticism of this sort was much less prevalent during the mid- and late-1990s, with the economic context being a crucial variable. As *Fortune* said in 2001 of the executive pay debates of the early 1990s "(p)ay kept right on rocketing after that, but when the economy got back on track and the stock markets caught fire, who cared?"[524]

---

[516] I.R.C. § 162(m) (2018); Bank, Cheffins & Wells, *supra* note 500, at 70.

[517] Geoffrey Colvin, Ann Harringion & Paola Hejlt, *The Great CEO Pay Heist*, FORTUNE, June 25, 2001, 64. See also Mark J. Loewenstein, *The Conundrum of Executive Compensation*, 35 WAKE FOREST L. REV. 1, 23–24, (2000); Jerry Useem et al., *Have They No Shame?*, FORTUNE, Apr. 28, 2003, 56.

[518] Cremers, Masconale & Sepe, *supra* note 496, 242–43.

[519] Gregg D. Polsky, *Controlling Executive Compensation through the Tax Code*, 64 WASH. & LEE L. REV. 877, 917–20 (2007).

[520] Colvin, Harringion & Hejlt, *supra* note 517. Empirical research indicates, however, that any such effect may well have been modest. See, for example, Nancy L. Rose & Catherine D. Wolfram, *Regulating Executive Pay: Using the Tax Code to Influence Chief Executive Officer Compensation*, 20 J. LABOR ECON. S138, S166 (2002).

[521] Colvin, Harringion & Hejlt, *supra* note 517. On falling share prices and the "dragging economy," see *supra* notes 127, 131 and accompanying text.

[522] Michael C. Jensen & Kevin J. Murphy, *CEO Incentives—It's Not How Much You Pay, But How*, HARV. BUS. REV., May/June 1990, 138, 145, 148–49.

[523] Colvin, Harringion & Hejlt, *supra* note 517.

[524] *Id.*

Nearly three-quarters of Americans polled in 1997 indicated executives were paid too much.[525] Managerial compensation, however, was not a cause célèbre as the 1990s drew to a close in the way it was as the beginning of the decade. Lists of the highest paid executives compiled and distributed by the business press caused little protest.[526] Unlike in 1992, presidential candidates eight years later ignored the issue.[527] The *New York Times* said in a report on executive pay in 2000 "(t)o a large extent, the debate is over, and the executives have won.... And eight years after Bill Clinton made exorbitant executive pay an issue in his first presidential campaign, the topic has disappeared from the political scene."[528]

The strong performance of public companies in the mid- and late-1990s did much to defuse concerns about executive pay. *Business Week*, seeking to explain in 1995 why "few complaints are being heard" about rapid increases in managerial compensation, quoted an executive pay consultant as saying of executives "(t)heir greed isn't hurting anybody.... It's benefiting people. It's making the shareholders richer."[529] Robert Reich, having returned to academic life after serving in the Clinton administration, said in early 2000, "(a)s long as the economy stays good and most people are very hopeful about their personal economic future, no one's terribly concerned about excessive CEO pay."[530]

As the 1990s came to an end, perceptions of top executives also likely muted concerns about their lucrative pay. CEOs were increasingly being thought of as iconic symbols of corporate America's success, and such individuals logically would have been thought of as appropriate recipients of generous compensation. In a 1997 front page article analyzing the growing prominence of chief executives the *Wall Street Journal* noted that "(w)ith US companies booming and trumping foreign competitors, CEOs have emerged as a kind of royalty."[531] According to a 1998 poll, 7 of the 10 most admired Americans were chief executives.[532] Management professors C.K. Prahalad and Yves Doz wrote in 2000 "during the past decade, many CEOs of large companies have become highly visible public figures.... (L)aunching a new style of corporate leadership—one that includes a public persona for the CEO."[533] Executives thus were perceived much differently than in the heyday of managerial capitalism, when William Whyte characterized the typical corporate manager as "organization man."[534] A 2000 *Financial Times* book review elaborated on the point, observing that "(w)hile businesses are less hierarchical, today's chief executives tend to dominate even more than their predecessors did. In Whyte's companies, the organisation itself set the tone; now it is charismatic corporate leaders who give it meaning."[535]

---

525 Jennifer Reingold, *Even Executives Are Wincing at Executive Pay*, BUS. WK., May 12, 1997, 40.

526 David Leonhardt, *Executive Pay Drops Off the Political Radar*, NY TIMES, Apr. 16, 2000, Weekend, 5.

527 *Id.*

528 Leonhardt, *supra* note 419.

529 John A. Byrne, *CEO Pay: Ready for Takeoff*, BUS. WK., Apr. 24, 1995, 88.

530 Leonhardt, *supra* note 526.

531 Zachary, *supra* note 465.

532 GIDEON HAIGH, FAT CATS: THE STRANGE CULT OF THE CEO 97 (2004).

533 C.K. Prahalad & Yves Doz, *The CEO: A Visible Hand in Wealth Creation?*, J. APP. CORP. FIN., Fall 2000, 20, 20.

534 Chapter 2, note 203 and related discussion; WILLIAM WHYTE, THE ORGANIZATION MAN (1956).

535 Holly Yeager, *The Rise of Consumption Man*, FIN. TIMES, Apr. 26, 2000, 19.

The media contributed substantially to bolstering the profile of executives of large firms in the mid- and late-1990s. Coverage of chief executives in major national publications increased by half between 1995 and 2000, based on the number of stories on point.[536] CNBC, a business oriented cable news channel launched in 1989 that grew substantially in the 1990s, welcomed chief executives for interviews and was reliably upbeat in orientation.[537] CNBC was in no way an outlier in this regard. *Business Week* said of coverage of chief executives in 1999 "(t)he media celebrate CEOs as larger than- life individuals who single-handedly communicate a vision and lead the way, earning millions for themselves in the process."[538]

Given the media's general tilt when reporting on public company executives as the 1990s drew to a close, it is far from surprising that when Steve Case and Gerard Levin announced the AOL/Time Warner merger in January 2000 the general tone of the initial coverage was "soaring."[539] Enthusiasm for the deal would soon dissipate,[540] as it would generally for public companies and the executives running them. The marked shift in sentiment would set the scene for changes in market practice and regulatory reforms that would recalibrate substantially the constraints relevant to public company executives. The "new style of corporate leadership" that Prahalad and Doz referred to would necessarily be of a substantially different character than what they envisaged when writing in 2000. We turn to these developments in Chapter 6.

---

[536] *CEOs Make Up, supra* note 481.

[537] John Cassidy, *Striking It Rich*, NEW YORKER, Jan. 14, 2002, 63, 67–68.

[538] John A. Byrne, *The Global Corporation Becomes the Leaderless Corporation*, BUS. WK., Aug. 30, 1999, 88.

[539] Arango, *supra* note 21.

[540] *Supra* note 22 and related discussion.

6 The 2000s

THE DECADE FROM HELL

WHILE THE 1990S was a prosperous and successful decade for the public company, the 2000s was a much different proposition. The opening sections of this chapter provide an overview of the dramatically altered circumstances and summarize challenges the public company faced as conditions changed. Next, we will, as in other chapters, consider the internal and external constraints applicable to public company executives, with a key theme being that the challenges the public company was facing had a significant impact on the nature of a number of these constraints. The chapter then canvasses an early 2000s retreat by chief executive officers (CEOs) from quasi-iconic status secured as the 1990s drew to a close. It concludes with an analysis of a corporate governance "free pass" those running banks enjoyed in the mid-2000s that ended abruptly with the 2008 financial crisis.

Changing Circumstances for the Public Company

"Soaring" media coverage that accompanied the January 2000 merger of AOL and Time Warner provided a suitable exclamation point for the 1990s, which developed into a highly successful decade for the US public company, its senior executives, and the American economy more generally.[1] Share prices rose sharply from the early 1990s through to the end of the decade, IPO activity was robust, and chief executives of public companies thought to be fulfilling a perceived need for visionary and charismatic leadership were becoming celebrities. After a mild recession at the beginning of the decade, the US economy featured robust

[1] Chapter 5, Figure 5.1, notes 7–9, 21, 63–66, 81, 84–86, 492, 506, 531–33, 536–39 and related discussion.

The Public Company Transformed. Brian R. Cheffins.

growth, falling unemployment, and low inflation. Economic consultant Allen Sinai suggested immediately after the 1990s ended that "(t)he nineties have been the best decade for the US economy going back to the 1950s."[2] A *New York Times* columnist, seeking to evoke nostalgia for the period, claimed more broadly in 2015 that "the final 10 years of the 20th century . . . was simply the happiest decade of our American lifetimes."[3]

The 2000s would be a much different proposition for the United States, its economy, its public companies, and its CEOs. *Time* said of the decade in December 2009 "just give thanks that it is nearly over."[4] Citing the infamous terrorist attacks that occurred on September 11, 2001 and the economic fallout from the financial crisis that roiled Wall Street seven years later, the magazine's verdict was that "the first 10 years of this century will very likely go down as the most dispiriting and disillusioning decade Americans have lived through in the post-World War II era."[5] It was, in short, "the decade from hell."[6]

With the economy at large, during the 2000s annual GDP growth averaged 2.0 percent compared with 3.4 percent from 1980 to 2000.[7] The unemployment rate, which was just below 4 percent as the 2000s got underway, hit 10 percent in October 2009.[8] Pessimism understandably took hold. According to a 2009 NBC/*Wall Street Journal* poll, only 27 percent of Americans were confident their children's standard of living would be better than their own.[9]

The 2000s amounted to a hellish decade in various ways for public companies as well. The noughties were the worst decade for the stock market since the Depression plagued 1930s, with the S&P 500 falling by 24 percent despite a rally beginning in the spring of 2009 (Figure 6.1).[10] The number of publicly traded companies, which had begun to decline in the late 1990s, fell further throughout the 2000s (Figure 6.2).

The discouraging public company statistics were accompanied by diminished public faith in large corporations. Polling data indicated that confidence in big business, having

---

[2] Quoted in DOUG HENWOOD, AFTER THE NEW ECONOMY 4 (2003).

[3] Kurt Andersen, *The Best Decade Ever? The 1990s, Obviously*, NY TIMES, Feb. 8, 2015, Sunday Review, 6.

[4] Andy Serwer & Beth Kerwitt, *The Decade from Hell . . . and How the Next One Can Be Better*, TIME, Dec, 7, 2009, 30.

[5] *Id.*

[6] *Id.* See also Noah Smith, *The 2000s Sure Were a Horrible Decade for the US*, NEWSDAY, Jan. 29, 2015, available at https://www.newsday.com/opinion/oped/the-2000s-sure-were-a-horrible-decade-for-the-u-s-noah-smith-1.9876065 (accessed Feb. 10, 2018).

[7] Jeffrey D. Sachs, *The GDP Doesn't Tell the Whole Story about Economic Growth*, BOS. GLOBE, Feb. 4, 2016, available at https://www.bostonglobe.com/opinion/2016/02/04/the-gdp-doesn-tell-whole-story-about-economic-growth/aC4sXAnQ6H5wX1SxrgldGP/story.html (accessed Feb. 10, 2018); Chegg Study, Average Annual Growth Rate 2000–2009, available at http://www.chegg.com/homework-help/questions-and-answers/refer-table-average-annual-growth-rate-2000-2009-gdp-population-per-capita-gdp-high-income-q12871007 (accessed Feb. 10, 2018).

[8] Federal Reserve Bank of St. Louis, *FRED Economic Data—Civilian Unemployment Rate*, Apr. 16, 2018, available at https://fred.stlouisfed.org/series/UNRATE (accessed Apr. 4, 2018).

[9] Daniel Gross, *The Comeback Country*, NEWSWEEK, Apr. 19, 2010, 28.

[10] The S&P 500 stood at 1469 at the beginning of January 2000 and at 1117 at the beginning of January 2010. See *S&P 500/Historical Data*, available at https://finance.yahoo.com/quote/%5EGSPC/history/ (accessed May 26, 2018). On the 1930s versus the 2000s, see John Authers, *The Noughties and the 1930s Look Very Alike*, FIN. TIMES, Dec, 29, 2009, 7.

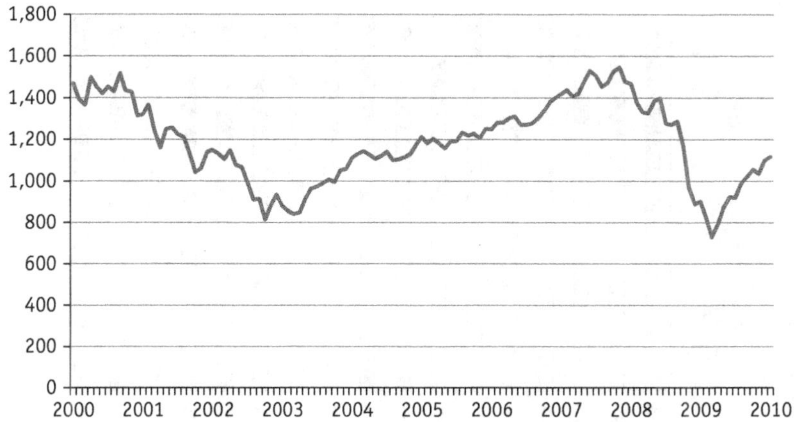

FIGURE 6.1 S&P 500, 2000–2009 (Opening Prices, monthly).
Source: S&P 500—Historical Data, Yahoo! Finance, available at https://uk.finance.yahoo.com/quote/%5EGSPC/history?p=%5EGSPC (accessed May 26, 2018).

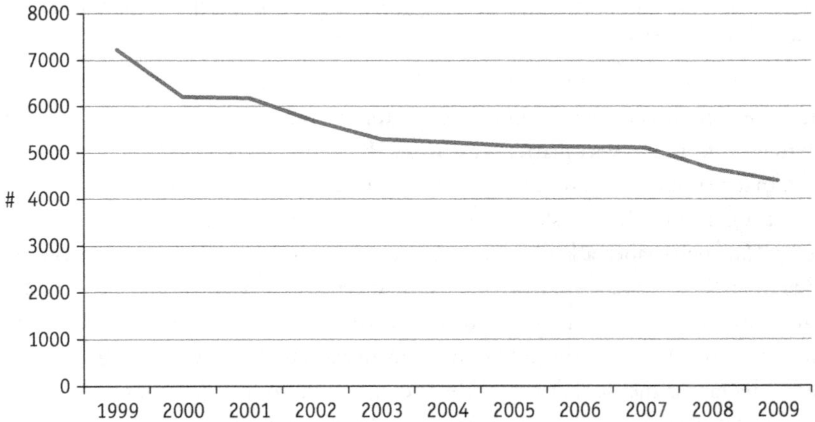

FIGURE 6.2 Number of Listed Companies, 1999–2009.
Source: World Bank, *Listed Domestic Companies, Total*, available at https://data.worldbank.org/indicator/CM.MKT.LDOM.NO?locations=US (accessed Feb. 9, 2018).

increased amidst the prosperity of the mid- and late-1990s, fell substantially in the 2000s (Figure 6.3). William Donaldson, chairman of the Securities and Exchange Commission (SEC), told business leaders in 2003 that the public's view of American business "is as low as it has ever been."[11] As the noughties came to an end Indra Nooyi, CEO of beverage giant PepsiCo, warned that corporate America was in the midst of "a crisis in trust" that was bad for companies and the economy more generally.[12]

[11] *Tough at the Top*, ECONOMIST, Oct. 25, 2003, Tough at the Top: A Survey of Corporate Leadership, 3.

[12] Indra Nooyi, *We Have a Job to Do: Rebuild Trust*, FORTUNE, May 4, 2009, 67.

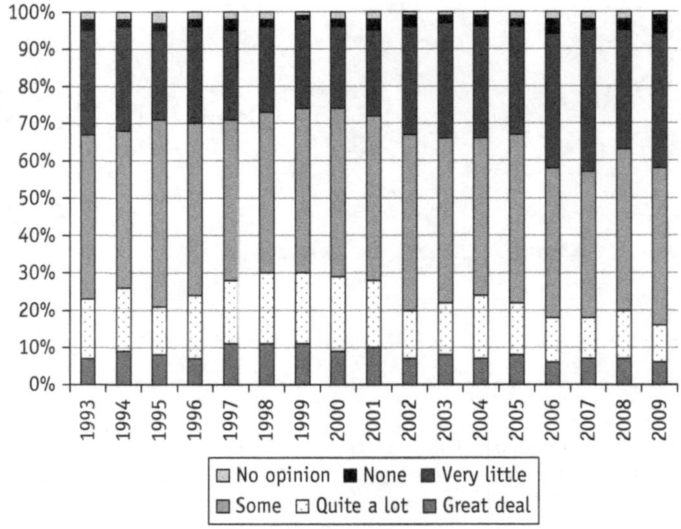

FIGURE 6.3 Confidence in Big Business, 1993–2009.
Source: Gallup, *Confidence in Institutions*, available at http://www.gallup.com/poll/1597/confidence-institutions.aspx (accessed Mar. 16, 2018).

Circumstances became challenging enough for the public company in the 2000s for its future to become the subject matter for debate. The *Wall Street Journal* referred in 2007 to a "fear . . . that the public corporation, which was the great wealth-generating machine of the 20th century, may be dying a slow death in the 21st."[13] A 2007 essay in the Toronto-based *Globe & Mail* newspaper asked readers rhetorically "how does one . . . commemorate the death of the publicly traded company?"[14] Those speculating on the future of the public company not surprisingly tended to invoke financial economist Michael Jensen in so doing.[15] His predictions of the demise of the public company in the late 1970s and again in the late 1980s proved to be far off the mark,[16] prompting ridicule from some.[17] Jensen, some suggested in the 2000s, could yet be vindicated, at least partially, before long.[18]

Chief executives, who had been emerging as celebrities in the 1990s,[19] took a sizeable reputational hit alongside their companies in the 2000s. *Grant's Interest Rate Observer* made light

---

[13] Alan Murray, *After the Revolt, Creating a New CEO*, WALL ST. J., May 5, 2007, A1.

[14] Sinclair Stewart, *Liquid Enough for You?*, GLOBE & MAIL, Apr. 27, 2007, Report on Business, 58.

[15] *Id.*; Stephen F. Diamond, *Private Equity and Public Good*, DISSENT, Winter 2008, at 55, 59–60; Ronald J. Gilson & Charles K. Whitehead, *Deconstructing Equity: Public Ownership, Agency Costs, and Complete Capital Markets*, 108 COLUM. L. REV. 231, 233–34 (2008).

[16] Michael C. Jensen & William H. Meckling, *Can the Corporation Survive?*, FIN. ANALYSTS J., Jan./Feb. 1978, 31; Michael C. Jensen, *Eclipse of the Public Corporation*, HARV. BUS. REV., Sept.–Oct., 1989, 61; Chapter 3, notes 49–52 and related discussion; Chapter 4, notes 146–48 and accompanying text; Chapter 5, notes 79–80 and related discussion.

[17] For discussion of examples see Stewart, *supra* note 14; Francesco Guerrera & Carola Hoyos, *Hidden Value: How Unlisted Companies Are Eclipsing the Public Equity Market*, FIN. TIMES, Dec. 15, 2006, 13.

[18] Stewart, *supra* note 14; Diamond, *supra* note 15, at 60; Guerrera & Hoyos, *supra* note 17.

[19] Chapter 5, notes 464–65 and related discussion.

of chief executives having been discredited due to a series of corporate scandals in the early 2000s with a cartoon showing a mother separating two quarreling boys where one explained "he called me a CEO first."[20] Arthur Levitt, former chairman of the SEC, proclaimed in 2005 "(t)he imperial CEO is no more."[21] A 2011 study of management theory noted that "(t)he first decade of the twenty-first century has seen a striking backlash against the cult of the superman CEO," to the point where one had to go back to the era of "the organization man" of the 1950s "to find such a cult of facelessness."[22]

The diminished status of public companies and the executives who ran them was a product in large measure of various challenges the 2000s posed for the public company. We will consider next the nature of these challenges. The treatment of these topics is not intended to be definitive; the literature on each is extensive. The objective instead is to provide essential background for the topics canvassed in the remainder of the chapter.

The Public Company's Challenges

Chapter 5 has already considered one of the major challenges that the public company faced in the 2000s, this being a dramatic decline in stock market prices at the beginning of the decade.[23] Four others merit consideration. The first was a set of corporate scandals that afflicted a series of major public companies during 2001 and 2002. The second was the regulatory response to the scandals, which increased the costs associated with being a publicly traded corporation. The third was a surge in buyouts of public companies conducted by private equity firms that peaked in the mid-2000s. Fourth and finally, there was the economic turmoil associated with the financial crisis of 2008.

CORPORATE SCANDALS

Public companies in the United States were afflicted by a series of scandals in the early 2000s. The malfeasance involved was the most egregious from the managerial capitalism era through to the present day. Economist Joseph Stiglitz said in 2003 of "the worst corporate scandals in more than 70 years," "(t)he offenses . . . put most acts of political crookedness to shame."[24] Jeff Madrick, in a 2011 history of financial excess that addressed the 2008 financial crisis as well as the early 2000s scandals maintained, "(t)he 1990s through 2002 was the most corrupt 'decade' since the 1920s and one of the most corrupt in American business history."[25]

---

[20] Alan Elsner, *The Era of CEO as Superhero Ends amid Corporate Scandals*, GLOBE & MAIL, July 10, 2002, C1.

[21] Arthur Levitt, *The Imperial CEO Is No More*, WALL ST. J., Mar. 17, 2005, A16. See also *infra* notes 405–8, 418–19.

[22] ADRIAN WOOLDRIDGE, MASTERS OF MANAGEMENT 309, 310 (2011).

[23] Chapter 5, notes 127–31 and related discussion.

[24] JOSEPH E. STIGLITZ, THE ROARING NINETIES: A NEW HISTORY OF THE WORLD'S MOST PROSPEROUS DECADE 7, 167 (2003).

[25] JEFF MADRICK, AGE OF GREED: THE TRIUMPH OF FINANCE AND DECLINE OF AMERICA, 1970 TO THE PRESENT 320 (2011).

The macroeconomic consequences of the 2008 financial crisis no doubt were more profound than the fallout from the early 2000s scandals. During the first half of 2002, when the scandal revelations peaked, industrial output was picking up, housing starts were accelerating, and consumer confidence was improving.[26] In contrast, the recession of 2008–2009 may have been the most severe since the late 1930s.[27] Nevertheless, misbehavior by public company executives was more blatant in the early 2000s.

How many instances of corporate impropriety coming to light in the early 2000s merit the appellation "scandal"? Answers vary. A June 2002 *Wall Street Journal* article that acknowledged "(m)easuring the volume of corporate skullduggery precisely is difficult," listed 18 firms in a table of "big companies fac(ing) serious questions about their business."[28] In a scathing 2003 critique of America's corporate and political culture, prominent media commentator Arianna Huffington identified 11 scandalized corporations as meriting inclusion in "Satan's stock portfolio."[29] Among 30 companies accountancy professor Zabihollah Rezaee listed in a 2007 volume on corporate governance as being involved in high-profile financial scandals between 1977 and 2004, with 17 their stock price bottomed out in 2001 or 2002.[30]

Enron, Tyco, an industrial conglomerate, Global Crossing, a telecommunications firm, Adelphia Communications Corp., a cable company, and WorldCom, another telecommunications firm, were each listed by the *Wall Street Journal*, Huffington and Rezaee.[31] Hallmarks of these "super scandals" included massive destruction of shareholder value, usually resulting in bankruptcy, dubious related party transactions, and egregious accounting chicanery (Table 6.1).

The Tyco saga, revolving around Dennis Kozlowski, provided the most colorful details among the "super scandals." Kozlowski, Tyco's CEO from 1992 until his dismissal in 2002, was riding high as the 2000s began. *Business Week* characterized him as "supremely self-assured" in a 2001 article hailing Tyco as the best performing US company over the previous year and cited his "relentless dealmaking and lean operating style" in naming him in early 2002 as one of the top 25 managers from 2001.[32] Robert Monks, a former Tyco director and a shareholder activist who cultivated a substantial media profile as a corporate scold, said of Kozlowski "I don't think there's a better CEO in America."[33]

---

[26] James Surowiecki, *Did This Man Ruin American Business?*, GUARDIAN, July 23, 2002, A2; James C. Cooper & Kathleen Madigan, *Don't Blame the Economy for the Bear Market*, BUS. WK., July 29, 2002, 29.

[27] ALAN S. BLINDER, AFTER THE MUSIC STOPPED: THE FINANCIAL CRISIS, THE RESPONSE AND THE WORK AHEAD 14, 22–23 (2013); DAVID M. KOTZ, THE RISE AND FALL OF NEOLIBERAL CAPITALISM 151–52 (2015).

[28] David Wessel, *Venal Sins: Why the Bad Guys of the Boardroom Emerged en Masse*, WALL ST. J., June 20, 2002, A1.

[29] ARIANNA HUFFINGTON, PIGS AT THE TROUGH: HOW CORPORATE GREED AND POLITICAL CORRUPTION ARE UNDERMINING AMERICA 41 (2003).

[30] ZABIHOLLAH REZAEE, CORPORATE GOVERNANCE POST-SARBANES-OXLEY: REGULATIONS, REQUIREMENTS AND INTEGRATED PROCESSES 28–29 (2007).

[31] One other company was cited by all three, namely Qwest. The accounting practices of this telecommunications company became the subject of a criminal investigation.

[32] Joseph Webber, *Best Performers*, BUS. WK., Apr. 3, 2001, 10; *The Top 25 Managers of the Year*, BUS. WK., Jan. 14, 2002, 52.

[33] William Symonds, *The Most Aggressive CEO,* BUS. WK, May 28, 2001, 68. On Monks, see, for example, Alison Maitland, *A Life's Investment in the Investor*, FIN. TIMES, July 21, 2005, 11.

TABLE 6.1

Corporate "Super Scandals," early 2000s

Company/ Stock price bottom/date	Market value lost/Bankrupt?	Self-Dealing Allegations	Accounting Improprieties
Enron/$0/ Dec. 12, 2001	$66.5 billion/ Yes	Enron's chief financial officer and other senior Enron officials served as general partner with a number of special purpose entities (SPEs) Enron established that kept ventures the corporation was undertaking off of its balance sheet. The executives could benefit by charging management fees and by sharing in the profits the ventures might generate.[1] Enron directors and officers also sold in the two years preceding the bankruptcy $1.2 billion worth of Enron shares they owned.[2]	Enron's accounting ploys were overlapping and complex.[3] Enron, for instance, overstated revenues by relying on "mark to market" accounting to book profits immediately for transactions where the ultimate outcome was unresolved. Enron also exploited rules for SPEs to conceal debts and losses associated with poorly performing ventures.[4]
Global Crossing/$0/ Jan. 28, 2002	$25.4 billion/ Yes	Gary Winnick, who founded Global Crossing in 1997, sold $735 million worth of shares before the corporation went bankrupt and other directors and executives sold $582 million worth. This was characterized as "one of the most extravagant stings in the history of public securities."[5] Nevertheless, the Justice Department and the SEC refrained from bringing proceedings against Winnick.[6]	In 2000 Global Crossing concocted fake revenue by swapping parts of its fiber-optic network capacity with other carriers and reporting revenue immediately while amortizing costs gradually. No criminal charges were brought.[7]

(*Continued*)

TABLE 6.1

(Continued)

Company/ Stock price bottom/date	Market value lost/Bankrupt?	Self-Dealing Allegations	Accounting Improprieties
Adelphia/$0/ June 25, 2002	$7.7 billion/Yes	The Rigas family, which had voting control of Adelphia, borrowed $2.3 billion pursuant to a co-borrowing arrangement under which Adelphia as well as the family was liable to repay. "(O)ne of the most extensive financial frauds ever to take place at a public company" resulted in criminal convictions for founder John Rigas and one of his sons.[8]	The SEC filed accounting-related civil charges against the Rigas family, citing improper exclusion of liabilities via off-balance sheet affiliates, falsified operational statistics (e.g. inflating the number of cable subscribers) and a failure to disclose the co-borrowings by Adelphia and the family.[9]
WorldCom/$0/ July 21, 2002	$119.9 billion/ Yes	WorldCom lent CEO Bernie Ebbers $408 million on terms that were advantageous to Ebbers and risky for WorldCom.[10]	WorldCom treated fees paid to other service providers for use of their transmission networks ("line costs") as capital expenses, meaning the expenses could be depreciated slowly rather being recorded on the books immediately.[11] Expenses erroneously capitalized amounted to a total of $11 billion. Five WorldCom executives, including CEO Ebbers, were subsequently found guilty of securities fraud.[12]

Tyco/$8.25/ July 25, 2002 (peak, $62.80, Jan. 30 2001)	$93.3 billion/No	CEO Dennis Kozlowski, fired in June 2002, was subsequently convicted of over 20 felony counts and sentenced to at least eight years in prison. Most of the charges centered on executive compensation bonuses awarded between 1995 and 2002 that had not been properly authorized.[13]	Tyco, after a lengthy investigation, acknowledged at the end of 2002 the use of aggressive accounting techniques but maintained generally accepted accounting practice had not been violated. The company wrote off $382 million in profits it had previously claimed.[14]

Source: ZABIHOLLAH REZAEE, CORPORATE GOVERNANCE POST-SARBANES-OXLEY: REGULATIONS, REQUIREMENTS AND INTEGRATED PROCESSES 28-29 (2007) (for stock price/market capitalization data)

[1] KENNETH R. GRAY, LARRY A. FRIEDER & GEORGE W. CLARK, CORPORATE SCANDALS: THE GREAT HEIST, FINANCIAL BUBBLES, AND THE ABSENCE OF VIRTUE 52 (2005); JERRY W. MARKHAM, A FINANCIAL HISTORY OF MODERN US CORPORATE SCANDALS 71 (2006).

[2] ROGER LOWENSTEIN, ORIGINS OF THE CRASH: THE GREAT BUBBLE AND ITS UNDOING 171 (2004).

[3] Floyd Norris, *Lies My CFO Told Me, Act XIII*, NY TIMES, June 30, 2002, C5.

[4] Marianne M. Jennings, *Restoring Ethical Gumption in the Corporation: A Federalist Paper on Corporate Governance—Restoration of Active Virtue in the Corporate Structure to Curb the "Yeehaw Culture" in Organizations*, 3 WYO. L. REV. 387, 395–96 (2003).

[5] LOWENSTEIN, *supra* note 2.

[6] Timothy O'Brien, *A New Legal Chapter for a 90's Flameout*, NY TIMES, Aug. 15, 2004, Business, 1; Deborah Solomon, *SEC Won't Charge, Fine Global Crossing Chairman*, WALL ST. J., Dec, 13, 2004, A1.

[7] LOWENSTEIN, *supra* note 2, 160–61; O'Brien, *supra* note 6; Andy Kessler, *Winnick's Voyage to the Bottom of the Sea*, WALL ST. J., Mar. 21, 2002, 22; Jeremy Kahn, *How Telecom's Bad Boy Did It*, FORTUNE, Mar. 4, 2002, 36.

[8] MARKHAM, *supra* note 1, at 325–26; Roger Lowenstein, *The Company They Kept*, NY TIMES, Feb. 1, 2004, Sunday Magazine, 27.

[9] MARKHAM, *supra* note 1, at 326–27; Gary Giroux, *What Went Wrong? Accounting Fraud and Lessons from the Recent Scandals*, 75 SOCIAL RESEARCH 1205, 1230 (2008).

[10] MARKHAM, *supra* note 1, at 336; Jennings, *supra* note 4, 438–39.

[11] JOHN C. COFFEE, GATEKEEPERS: THE PROFESSIONS AND CORPORATE GOVERNANCE 37–38 (2006).

[12] GARY GIROUX, BUSINESS SCANDALS, CORRUPTION AND REFORM: AN ENCYCLOPEDIA 649–51 (2013).

[13] CATHERINE S. NEAL, TAKING DOWN THE LION: THE TRIUMPHANT RISE AND TRAGIC FALL OF TYCO'S DENNIS KOZLOWSKI 142–43, 191–93 (2014).

[14] Andrew Ross Sorkin & Alex Berenson, *Tyco Admits Using Accounting Tricks to Inflate Earnings*, NY TIMES, Dec. 31, 2002, A1.

By the end of 2002, everything had changed. There were revelations of an $18 million Manhattan apartment Tyco purchased in 2001 with Kozlowski named as the owner that was redecorated at a cost of $11 million, including a $6,000 shower curtain.[34] Details also became available of a $2 million Roman-themed 40th birthday party in Sardinia for Kozlowski's new wife for which Tyco partly footed the bill that featured an ice sculpture of Michelangelo's *David* that urinated vodka.[35] *Business Week* was saying of Kozlowski as 2002 concluded "(t)he history of American business contains few figures who were unhinged by greed as theatrically."[36]

Despite the salacious Tyco revelations, the Enron and WorldCom debacles achieved the greatest prominence among the scandals afflicting US public companies in the early 2000s. Economist Paul Krugman, in a January 2002 *New York Times* column, controversially predicted "that in the years ahead Enron, not Sept. 11, will come to be seen as the greater turning point in US society."[37] The claim was off the mark, given the massive political ramifications of the 9/11 terrorist attacks for the United States, both domestically and abroad.[38] Nevertheless, in the weeks following Enron's late 2001 collapse there was "wall-to-wall cable coverage and endless opining about what it all means."[39] Three-fourths of Americans polled said in January 2002 that they were paying attention to the Enron debacle.[40]

Within 18 months of Enron's demise the firm was being called "the most notorious company ever" and books on the scandal became "their own cottage industry," with dozens being published.[41] A *New York Times* columnist said in 2006 as two key Enron executives went on trial "for their roles in the highest-profile scandal in more than 70 years. . . . (O)ur fascination with—our hunger to know what really happened; our thirst to punish those responsible for its demise—hasn't really diminished."[42] The passage of time ultimately would loosen Enron's grip on the public's imagination, particularly with the occurrence of the 2008 financial crisis.

---

34 Mark Maremont & Laurie P. Cohen, *Interior Design on a Budget—The Tyco Way*, WALL ST. J., Sept. 18, 2002, B1; CATHERINE S. NEAL, TAKING DOWN THE LION: THE TRIUMPHANT RISE AND TRAGIC FALL OF TYCO'S DENNIS KOZLOWSKI 15–20 (2014).

35 NEAL, *supra* note 34, at 67–71; Mark Maremont & Laurie P. Cohen, *How Tyco's CEO Enriched Himself*, WALL ST. J., Aug. 7, 2002, A1.

36 Anthony Bianco, William Symonds & Nanette Byrnes, *The Rise and Fall of Dennis Kozlowski*, BUS. WK., Dec. 23, 2002, 64.

37 Paul Krugman, *The Great Divide*, NY TIMES, Jan. 29, 2002, A21. On the controversy, see James Heskett, *Will the Societal Effects of Enron Exceed Those of 9/11?*, HARVARD BUSINESS SCHOOL, WORKING KNOWLEDGE: BUSINESS RESEARCH FOR BUSINESS LEADERS, Feb. 2, 2002, available at http://hbswk.hbs.edu/item/will-the-societal-effects-of-enron-exceed-those-of-september-11 (accessed Mar. 14, 2018).

38 Andrew Hill, *Besieged, Conflicted and Under Pressure: Why We Should Feel Sorry for Leaders*, FIN. TIMES, Nov. 20, 2017, 12 ("the greatest geopolitical inflection point the western world has seen in the last 25 years").

39 Daniel McGinn, *The Ripple Effect*, NEWSWEEK, Feb. 18, 2002, 29.

40 Richard L. Berke & Janet Elder, *Poll Finds Enron's Taint Clings More to G.O.P. than Democrats*, NY TIMES, Jan. 27, 2002, A1.

41 Jeffrey D. Van Niel & Nancy B. Rapoport, *Dr. Jekyll & Mr. Skilling: How Enron's Public Image Morphed from the Most Innovative Company in the* Fortune *500 to the Most Notorious Company Ever, in* ENRON: CORPORATE FIASCOS AND THEIR IMPLICATIONS 79, 87 (Nancy B. Rapoport & Bala G. Dharan eds., 2004) (listing titles in fn. 36).

42 Joe Nocera, *A Revenge, Except It's Reality*, NY TIMES, Jan. 28, 2006, C1.

Nevertheless, a 2013 encyclopedia of business scandals characterized Enron as "one of the premier scandals in American history."[43]

There were in the late 1990s revelations of public company accounting chicanery at Cendant, a consumer services conglomerate, Sunbeam, and Waste Management, but these failed to set off major alarm bells.[44] One reason Enron was different was the scale and suddenness of the collapse. In 2000 Enron was ranked seventh in the *Fortune* 500, was the world's largest trader of electricity and natural gas, and also operated in the telecommunications and financial services sectors.[45] Its shares were trading at nearly $40 in early October 2001, well off an August 2000 peak of $90 but reasonably respectable given falling share prices (Figure 6.1) and the abrupt resignation in August of CEO Jeffrey Skilling six months after he had taken up the job.[46] A quick downfall ensued. When Enron disclosed in mid-October that it was reducing shareholder equity on its books to account for special purpose entities under the control of Andrew Fastow, Enron's chief financial officer (CFO), this set off a hasty death spiral featuring Fastow's resignation, further damaging accounting revelations, and a failed merger with energy rival Dynergy.[47] At the beginning of December, Enron declared bankruptcy, with the $63.4 billion filing being almost as large as the two next biggest previous failures combined, Texaco Inc. and Financial Corp. of America in the late 1980s.[48]

The Enron scandal grabbed attention additionally because it prompted serious concerns among investors about the veracity of robust financial results that had been associated with stock prices that rose rapidly in the mid- and late-1990s. *Business Week* said in the immediate aftermath of Enron's bankruptcy filing in December 2001

> Enron's tale is a clarifying event. It reveals key weaknesses in the financial system that must be corrected as the US moves forward in the 21st century. If America is to have an equity culture in which individuals invest in stocks and provide the capital for fast economic growth, the market must be able to correctly value companies. This requires making financial data readily available and easily comprehensible.[49]

As 2002 got underway there was tangible evidence of the Enron effect on the stock market, with the share prices of companies known for their opaque or complex financial reporting falling substantially.[50] A portfolio manager explained to the *New York Times* that it was "cockroach theory," in the sense there were likely to be additional as yet unidentified companies (cockroaches) deploying dubious accounting practices.[51] Skepticism regarding financial

---

[43] Gary Giroux, Business Scandals, Corruption and Reform: An Encyclopedia xxxvi (2013).

[44] Allan Sloan & Michael Isikoff, *The Enron Effect*, Newsweek, Jan. 28, 2002, 34. See also Chapter 5, notes 305–6, 477 and related discussion.

[45] Allen R. Myerson, *With Enron's Fall, Many Dominoes Tremble*, NY Times, Dec. 2, 2000, Business, 1.

[46] Rezaee, *supra* note 30, 28 (peak share price); Kurt Eichenwald, *Audacious Climb to Success Ended in a Dizzying Plunge*, NY Times, Jan. 13, 2002, 1.

[47] Eichenwald, *supra* note 46.

[48] Steve Liesman, *Enron Fallout May Cut Stock Prices in General*, Wall St. J., Jan. 21, 2002, A1.

[49] *Enron: Let Us Count the Culprits*, Bus. Wk., Dec, 17, 2001, 154.

[50] Gretchen Morgenson, *Worries of More Enrons to Come Give Stock Prices a Pounding*, NY Times, Jan. 30, 2002, C1.

[51] *Id.* For another example of the cockroach theory, see Chapter 5, note 287 and related discussion.

reporting extended even to various prominent "blue chip" companies accused of nothing illegal.[52]

The Enron scandal also resonated in ways the Cendant, Sunbeam, and Waste Management revelations did not because it fueled doubts about the overall direction in which the corporate economy was headed after the euphoric 1990s. The dramatic decline in share prices associated with the end of the dot.com stock market boom was a blow to the corporate sector but blame could be cordoned off to flaky internet start-ups and a subset of excitable investors getting ahead of themselves. Enron, in contrast, had firm roots in the real corporate economy as well as operating on the cutting edge. As of 2000, Enron had been selected as *Fortune's* most innovative company for six straight years and ranked 25th overall on the magazine's list of most admired companies.[53] Enron, according to *Newsweek*, "was supposed to be the next new thing, a New Economy company with substance to it," having "real businesses, real assets, real revenues and what seemed to be real profits."[54] Enron's ignominious collapse thus could quite plausibly be thought of as "not merely the death of a company but the end of an era."[55]

The *Wall Street Journal* indicated in February 2002 "it's inevitable that new laws and regulations will be waved in the direction of accounting and management."[56] By March more than 10 congressional committees were pursuing Enron-related inquiries and a total of 32 bills had been introduced to Congress to address ills associated with the company's collapse.[57] Revelations involving Global Crossing, Tyco, Adelphia Communications, and some other companies kept corporate scandals in the news.[58] Nevertheless, as June began the initial shock Enron's collapse had induced was fading and the prospects of Congress passing meaningful legislation were receding.[59]

WorldCom's announcement in late June 2002 of accounting improprieties involving billions of dollars changed the reform equation. The scandal gave "a powerful boost of energy to the drive in Congress to clean up business practices."[60] By the end of June, 77 percent of respondents were telling pollster Gallup they felt business scandals were either a crisis or a major problem.[61] At the beginning of July *Barron's* said of WorldCom's accounting revelations that this "was more than just a body blow to another troubled company. It means that what the pundits are calling a 'crisis of confidence' in corporate America got wider and deeper."[62]

---

[52] Daniel Kadlec, Bernard Baumohl & Unmesh Kher, *Under the Microscope*, TIME, Feb. 4, 2002, 28.

[53] Vince Kaminski & John Martin, *Transforming Enron: The Value of Active Management*, J. APP. CORP. FIN., Winter 2001, at 39, 41.

[54] Allan Sloan, *Who Killed Enron?*, NEWSWEEK, Jan. 21, 2002, 18.

[55] BETHANY MCLEAN & PETER ELKIND, THE SMARTEST GUYS IN THE ROOM: THE AMAZING RISE AND SCANDALOUS FALL OF ENRON xxiv (2003).

[56] Daniel Henninger, *Enron's Decline Tracks the Fall of Good Advice*, WALL ST. J., Feb. 8, 2002, A18.

[57] *Enron Triggers a Slew of Proposed Fixes, But What Will Stick?*, WALL ST. J., Mar. 7, 2002, A1.

[58] Anthony Bianco, *The Angry Market*, BUS. WK., July 29, 2002, 32.

[59] Deborah McGregor & Peter Spiegel, *King of Corporate Reform*, FIN. TIMES, July 27, 2002, 11; ALEX BERENSON, THE NUMBER: HOW THE DRIVE FOR QUARTERLY EARNINGS CORRUPTED WALL STREET AND CORPORATE AMERICA 214 (2003).

[60] Tom Hamburger, Greg Hitt & Michael Schroeder, *Sorry Wrong Number*, WALL ST. J., June 27, 2002, A8.

[61] Lee Walczak, Richard S. Dunham & Paula Dwyer, *Let the Reforms Begin*, BUS. WK., July 22, 2002, 26.

[62] Howard R. Gold, *The Graft Next Door*, BARRON'S, July 1, 2002, Technology Week, 8.

WorldCom's collapse re-energized the reform bandwagon partly because the accounting fraud involved was on a larger scale than Enron's and was more brazen.[63] Also important was that WorldCom had the highest pre-collapse profile of the super-scandal companies. WorldCom, both in terms of assets and market capitalization, was nearly twice as big as Enron at their respective peaks.[64] Though Enron received favorable coverage in the business media before its collapse,[65] it was unfamiliar to most consumers until its scandal hit the headlines.[66] In contrast, WorldCom was, with its well-known brand MCI, America's No. 2 long-distance phone company, serving 20 million customers.[67] Basketball superstar Michael Jordan was even the corporate pitchman.[68]

Representative Michael Oxley, who had sponsored a modest reform bill the House of Representatives passed in April,[69] remarked on the changed mood in the Senate in mid-July, saying of scandalized public company executives "(s)ummary executions would get about 85 votes in the Senate right now."[70] By the end of July the House had swung around, and, together with the Senate, overwhelmingly endorsed a tougher measure than Oxley's modeled primarily on a bill Senator Paul Sarbanes had proposed.[71] President George W. Bush, who had been advocating caution with respect to reform,[72] was won over as well and said when signing the legislation Congress put before him that the new law included "the most far-reaching reforms of American business practices since the time of Franklin D. Roosevelt."[73] What became known as the Sarbanes-Oxley Act (SOX)[74] was enacted barely six weeks after WorldCom formally acknowledged its massive accounting irregularities and only 10 days after WorldCom filed for bankruptcy.[75]

SOX

The sharp decline in share prices occurring between 2000 and 2002 and corporate scandals such as Enron and WorldCom constituted obvious reputational hits for the American public company. Surveys of US corporate governance by economists Bengt Holmstrom and Steven Kaplan published in 2001 and 2003 illustrate the point. In their 2001 article,

---

[63] Kurt Eichenwald, *The Latest Corporate Scandal Is Sudden, Vast and Simple*, NY Times, June 27 2002, A1.

[64] See Table 6.1 (market capitalization); Kevin Maney & Andrew Backove, *WorldCom's Bomb*, USA Today, July 22, 2002, B1 (assets).

[65] *Supra* notes 53–54 and related discussion; James Ledbetter, *The Boys in the Bubble*, NY Times, Jan. 2, 2003, A17 ("Do a search, for example, of the word 'Enron' in the databases of those publications prior to 2000 and you'll find little but praise for its market innovations.")

[66] Gold, *supra* note 62; Maney & Backove, *supra* note 64.

[67] Maney & Backove, *supra* note 64.

[68] Gold, *supra* note 62.

[69] Michael Schroder, *Corporate Reform: The First Year*, Wall St. J., July 22, 2003, C1.

[70] Richard A. Oppel, *GOP in Congress Moving Past Bush on Business Fraud*, NY Times, July 12, 2002, C4.

[71] Allan Sloan, *Reform? Don't Celebrate Yet*, Newsweek, Aug. 4, 2003, 45; *A Cleaner Bill of Health for US Companies*, Fin. Times, Sept. 5, 2003, Survey on Corporate Governance, 4.

[72] McGregor & Spiegel, *supra* note 59; Gerard Baker & Alan Beattie, *Unstoppable Reform*, Fin. Times, July 25, 2002, 16.

[73] Elisabeth Bulmiller, *Bush Signs Bill Aimed at Fraud in Corporations*, NY Times, July 31, 2002, A1.

[74] Pub. L. 107-204, 116 Stat. 745.

[75] Maney & Backove, *supra* note 64; Joseph Nocera, *For All Its Cost, Sarbanes Law Is Working*, NY Times, Dec, 3, 2005, C1.

mindful of prosperity enjoyed by US corporations in the 1990s and ideological and market-driven momentum that had built up for companies elsewhere to converge toward a US-style shareholder-oriented corporate governance model,[76] they observed optimistically "since the mid-1980s, the US style of corporate governance has reinvented itself, and the rest of the world seems to be following the same path."[77] They conceded two years later "(t)o a casual observer, the United States corporate governance system must seem to be in terrible shape."[78]

Holmstrom and Kaplan maintained in their later article that US corporate governance was in fact not "really that bad."[79] Nevertheless, falling share prices and the scandals of the early 2000s had seriously discredited the US model of corporate governance internationally, making it much more difficult to sell abroad.[80] Domestically, the scandals "rattled a lot of investors."[81] The percentage of Americans who thought that investing in the stock market was a bad idea indeed increased markedly in mid-2002 following a sizeable blow to investor confidence in 2000 prompted by falling share prices (Figure 6.4).

While it is obvious that the bear market and the corporate scandals of the early 2000s constituted challenges for the public company, it is less obvious why this should also be the case with reforms introduced in response to the scandals, with the Sarbanes Oxley Act of 2002 as the centerpiece. Jeffrey Immelt, General Electric's CEO, said reform was "simply the right thing to do" and indicated he believed the new law would "help restore investor

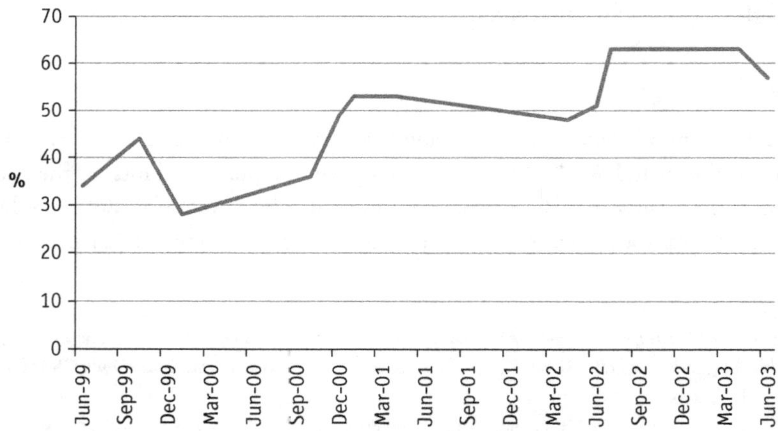

FIGURE 6.4 Americans Thinking That Investing in the Stock Market Was a Bad Idea, 1999–2003, percent.

Source: Gallup, *Stock Market*, http://www.gallup.com/poll/1711/stock-market.aspx (accessed Mar. 14, 2018).

[76] See, for example, Henry Hansmann & Reinier Kraakman, *The End of History for Corporate Law*, 89 GEO. L.J. 439 (2001).

[77] Bengt Holmstrom & Steven N. Kaplan, *Corporate Governance and Merger Activity in the US: Making Sense of the 1980s and 1990s*, 15 J. ECON. PERSP. 121, 133 (2001).

[78] Bengt Holmstrom & Steven N. Kaplan, *The State of US Corporate Governance: What's Right and What's Wrong*, J. APP. CORP. FIN., Spring 2003, at 8, 8.

[79] *Id.*

[80] Evelyn Iritani, *US Business Model a Tough Sell Overseas*, L.A. TIMES, July 7, 2002, A1.

[81] Rob Norton, *Don't Blame It All on WorldCom*, FORTUNE, July 22, 2002, 42.

confidence."[82] Such a restoration was the core goal of SOX and related reforms. Harvey Pitt, SEC chairman as debates about legislative change proceeded, indicated that bringing back investor "confidence is the No. 1 goal on our agenda."[83] Paul Sarbanes affirmed this indeed was the chief objective with SOX in an interview a few years after its enactment.[84]

How could legislation designed to restore investor confidence the corporate scandals of the early 2000s had shattered contribute to the "decade from hell" afflicting public companies? Surely revived confidence would benefit rather than challenge the public corporation. The particular measures introduced, however, created substantial unease among public company executives who believed SOX's costs substantially outweighed the benefits.

Reform topics SOX addressed included accounting and auditing, executive conduct, and boards. With accounting and auditing, the Act created a new oversight panel, the Public Company Accounting Oversight Board, to regulate accountants and to discipline auditors.[85] Auditing firms were also prohibited from offering a broad range of consulting services to companies they audited.[86] With executive conduct, SOX prohibited public corporations from granting loans to top management.[87] SOX also required the chief executive and CFO of a publicly traded corporation to attest together with the corporation's auditor as to the existence of a robust internal financial control system and to certify personally the accuracy and completeness of quarterly and annual financial reports filed with the SEC.[88] Knowingly false certifications were made punishable by criminal penalties.[89] Executives could also be required to reimburse any bonuses received after the filing of inaccurate financial reports that failed to comply with securities law requirements.[90] As for boards, SOX mandated changes to the listing rules of the New York Stock Exchange (NYSE) and its rival NASDAQ (National Association of Securities Dealers Automated Quotations) that spelled out the formal duties of audit committees, required a listed company to have an audit committee composed entirely of independent directors, and obliged such firms to offer an explanation if their audit committees lacked a member who was a financial expert.[91]

The NYSE reinforced the campaign to fortify investor confidence via board reform. It amended its listing rules with provisions binding as of 2004 that required corporations traded on the NYSE to have boards with a majority of directors who were independent, to have boards convene at least annually an "executive session" a "presiding" director would

---

[82] Andrew Hill & Adrian Michaels, *Hostile Terrain*, Fin. Times, Aug. 13, 2002, 16.

[83] Stephen M. Bainbridge, The Complete Guide to Sarbanes-Oxley: Understanding How Sarbanes-Oxley Affects Your Business 19 (2007).

[84] Thomas Olson, *Sarbanes-Oxley Law Eased Blow, Former Congressman Says at Duquesne*, Pittsburgh Trib. Rev., Apr. 22, 2009, available at https://www.highbeam.com/publications/tribune-reviewpittsburgh-tribune-review-p61204/apr-22-2009 (accessed Feb. 14, 2018).

[85] Sarbanes-Oxley Act of 2002, § 101.

[86] *Id.* § 201.

[87] *Id.* § 402.

[88] *Id.* §§ 302, 404.

[89] *Id.* § 304.

[90] *Id.* §§ 906.

[91] *Id.* §§ 301, 407. Companies listed on the NYSE were required to have independent audit committees beginning in the late 1970s—Chapter 3, note 313 and related discussion.

oversee where management would not be present, to have nomination and compensation committees staffed exclusively by independent directors, and to give shareholders the opportunity to approve all equity-based compensation plans.[92] NASDAQ adopted similar requirements.[93]

Business leaders refrained from criticizing SOX at the time of enactment, at least in public.[94] For at least a year, executives maintained official silence.[95] Nevertheless, those running public companies were increasingly viewing SOX as a challenge to be navigated rather than as a salutary mechanism for restoring investor confidence. Even between October 2002 and June 2003 the proportion of executives surveyed favorably disposed toward SOX fell from 42 percent to 30 percent.[96]

Antipathy toward SOX was greatest among smaller public companies. In a 2004 survey of 115 such firms two-thirds said the new regime was too strict.[97] Janet Dolan, CEO of Tennant Co., a Minneapolis-based maker of industrial cleaning products, elaborated in an interview the same year with the *Wall Street Journal*. She said of SOX "(t)his has been pretty much a one- size-fits-all-approach," falling "much more heavily on small-cap companies in terms of the expense" because "(w)e're all having to do about the same thing, but it's less of a burden for General Electric than for us."[98]

The requirement to attest to the existence and veracity of internal financial control systems, imposed by section 404 of SOX, proved particularly vexing. The provision quickly became thought of as "the corporate equivalent of root canal."[99] Conceptions of adequate financial controls supposedly were "interpreted to be almost anything that paranoid auditors could dream up."[100] A survey of more than 100 public companies carried out in 2004 by Foley & Lardner, a law firm, found that for a public company with revenue under $1 billion the average cost of being publicly traded had increased 130 percent due to SOX, with section 404 having the most significant financial impact.[101] A 2010 study of smaller public companies just above and just below a $75 million market capitalization threshold under which firms were at least temporarily exempted from complying with section 404 revealed that up

[92] Andrew Hill, *NYSE Approves Shake-Up in Standards*, Fin. Times, Aug. 2, 2002, 15; John Nofsinger & Kenneth Kim, Infectious Greed: Restoring Confidence in America's Companies 220–22 (2003); Raymond Gilmartin, *The Argument for a Lead Director, in* The Future of Boards: Meeting the Governance Challenges of the Twenty-First Century 155, 159–60 (Jay W. Lorsch ed., 2012). The rules regarding nomination and compensation committees were not applicable to companies with controlling shareholders.

[93] Gilmartin, *supra* note 92, at 160.

[94] Hill & Michaels, *supra* note 82.

[95] Neil Weinberg, *Criminalizing Capitalism*, Forbes, May 12, 2003, 75; Louis Lavelle, *Governance: Backlash in the Executive Suite*, Bus. Wk., June 14, 2004, 36.

[96] Nanette Byrnes, *Reform: Who's Making the Grade*, Bus. Wk., Sept. 22, 2003, 80.

[97] Lavelle, *supra* note 95.

[98] Judith Burns, *Is Sarbanes-Oxley Working?*, Wall St. J., June 21, 2004, R8.

[99] Amy Borrus, *Learning to Love Sarbanes-Oxley*, Bus. Wk., Nov. 21, 2005, 126.

[100] Thomas G. Donlan, *Sarbanes-Oxley Messes Up*, Barron's, July 24, 2006, 39.

[101] Scott Green, Sarbanes-Oxley and the Board of Directors: Techniques and Best Practices for Corporate Governance 272 (2005).

to 2007 the attestation requirement increased annual audit fees by an average of 86 percent, or $528,000, a meaningful amount for companies on the exemption borderline.[102]

Out-of-pocket compliance costs were not the only source of concern in the business community with SOX. Another, shared by bigger and smaller public companies alike, was a counterproductive diversion of managerial talent.[103] The chief accounting officer of General Motors complained to the *Wall Street Journal* in 2004, "(t)he real cost isn't the incremental dollars, it is having people that should be focused on the business focused instead on complying with the details of the rules."[104] There also were fears SOX could change executives "from entrepreneurs to hall monitors."[105] For instance, William Donaldson, who took over as chairman of the SEC from Harvey Pitt in February 2003, told the *Financial Times* later that year "I worry about the loss of risk-taking zeal."[106] Donaldson said "Sarbanes-Oxley unleashed batteries of lawyers across the country," resulting in "a huge preoccupation with the dangers and risks of making the slightest mistake, as opposed to a reasonable approach to legitimate business risk."[107]

The fact that during the 2000s the number of public companies fell markedly (Figure 6.2) lends credence to the notion that SOX posed a challenge for public companies rather than being a regulatory boon. Concerns that SOX could discourage companies from being traded publicly arose quickly. In 2003 *Forbes*, having described SOX as "the sweeping assault that Congress hurriedly passed" observed "(t)he regulatory onslaught already is wreaking unintended consequences on the US economy. Dozens of public firms are going private."[108] The 2004 survey of public companies by Foley & Lardner found that about 20 percent of firms polled were considering leaving the stock market as a result of the increased regulatory burden.[109] Dolan, the Minneapolis-based CEO, elaborated in her *Wall Street Journal* interview on why SOX could prompt a stock market exit: "(w)e all support good governance. The question is, at what price? If you keep adding expense, at some point it tips the scale," adding that for many smaller firms, "the cost of being public anymore is really starting to be questionable."[110]

Speculation about the impact SOX was having on the viability of the public company continued thereafter. The *New York Times*, in a 2010 article on the falling number of public companies it characterized as "a remarkable turnabout" that was "to some, deeply unsettling,"

---

[102] Peter Iliev, *The Effect of SOX Section 404: Costs, Earnings Quality and Stock Prices*, 45 J. FIN. 1163, 1177–78 (2010). Audit fees would peak in 2008 and then either levelled off or fell modestly, depending on the size of the company. See Paul Rose & Steven Davidoff Solomon, *Where Have All the IPOs Gone? The Hard Life of the Small IPO*, 6 HARV. BUS. L. REV. 83, 89–90 (2016).

[103] HENRY N. BUTLER & LARRY E. RIBSTEIN, THE SARBANES-OXLEY DEBACLE 50–51 (2006); Ivy Xiying Zhang, *Economic Consequences of the Sarbanes-Oxley Act of 2002*, 44 J. ACCTING. & ECON. 74, 80 (2007).

[104] Deborah Solomon & Cassell Bryan-Low, *Companies Complain about the Cost of Corporate Governance Rules*, WALL ST. J., Feb. 10, 2004, A1.

[105] BUTLER & RIBSTEIN, *supra* note 103, at 51.

[106] Adrian Michaels, *American Boardrooms Must Stop Being Frightened and Get Back to Business*, FIN. TIMES, July 24, 2003, 15.

[107] *Id.*

[108] Weinberg, *supra* note 95.

[109] Adrian Michaels, *The Downside to Staying Public*, FIN. TIMES, June 4, 2004, 10.

[110] Burns, *supra* note 98.

speculated that "the incredible shrinking stock market is one of the unexpected results of regulations like the Sarbanes-Oxley Act of 2002."[111] The *New York Times* was not focusing on companies leaving the stock market but rather was exploring reasons that initial public offerings (IPOs) had been scarce, meaning that potentially viable candidates for public markets were staying away.

Despite speculation about SOX discouraging companies from going public, basic chronology suggests SOX did not have a substantial impact. IPO activity did fall off considerably in the 2000s, with the number occurring annually averaging 130 as compared to 307 for the 1980s and 1990s.[112] However, the average number of IPOs per year was greater between 2003 and 2009 (118.8)—after SOX was enacted—than in 2001 and 2002 (64).[113] The pattern was replicated with small firms (Figure 6.5), despite SOX supposedly having a disproportionately adverse impact on smaller public companies. Empirical studies making allowances for a range of potential explanatory variables confirm that SOX was not a dominant cause of the decline in IPO activity in the 2000s as compared with earlier decades.[114]

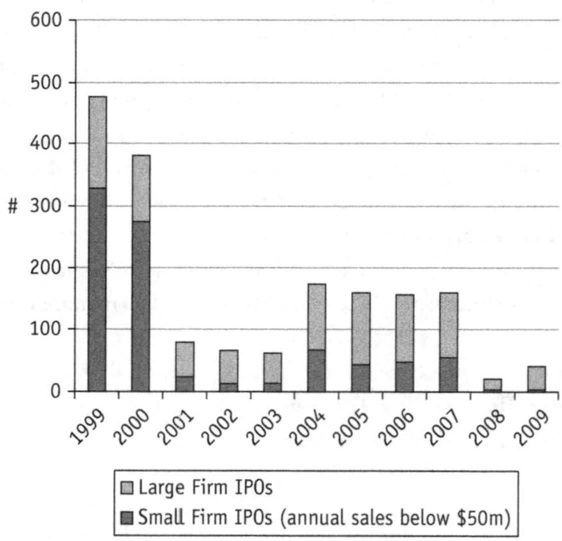

FIGURE 6.5 Number of IPOs, Large Firm/Small Firm, 1999–2009.
Source: Xiaohui Gao, Jay R. Ritter & Zhongyan Zhu, *Where Have All the IPOs Gone?*, 48 J. FIN. QUANT. ANALYSIS 1663, 1668 (2013).

[111] Graham Bowley, *Wall Street, the Home of the Vanishing IPO*, NY TIMES, Nov. 18, 2010, B1.

[112] Xiaohui Gao, Jay R. Ritter & Zhongyan Zhu, *Where Have All the IPOs Gone?*, 48 J. FIN. QUANT. ANALYSIS 1663, 1668 (2013) (table with annual data on IPOs indicating 6,139 occurred between 1980 and 1999 and 1,301 took place during the 2000s).

[113] *Id.*

[114] *Id.* at 1665, 1675–77, 1690; Jay R. Ritter, *Reenergizing the IPO Market*, 1 J. APP. FIN. 37, 38 (2014); Craig Doidge, G. Andrew Karolyi & René M. Stulz, *The US Left Behind? Financial Globalization and the Rise of IPOs outside the US*, 110 J. FIN. ECON. 546, 549, 566–68 (2013).

What about SOX driving companies that were already public away from the stock market? Public-to-private buyouts, such as the record-setting 1989 RJR Nabisco deal,[115] are one method by which companies can depart the stock market. This transactional form, having faded into relative obscurity in the 1990s,[116] roared back in the mid-2000s with a new label, "private equity" buyouts, arising from the moniker used to describe the firms conducting the buyout transactions. As the next subsection discusses, private equity buyouts posed a challenge to the public company, regulatory variables aside. The point that merits scrutiny now is speculation by many commentators and policy analysts that SOX reduced the number of public companies by helping to foster the surge in public-to-private buyouts.[117] For instance, David Bonderman, founding partner of private equity giant Texas Pacific Group, quipped in a 2004 interview that Messrs. Sarbanes and Oxley were among his firm's "best friends."[118]

In fact, SOX likely did little to foster public-to-private buyouts. While public-to-private buyout activity increased after SOX was enacted, benchmarking against international buyout trends unaffected by SOX indicates that SOX's enactment had little independent impact.[119] Moreover, contrary to what would be expected if escaping SOX was prompting public-to-private buyouts, the proportion of large companies bought out by private equity firms between 2003 to 2006 that remained subject to federal securities law—including SOX—due to having publicly traded debt was nearly one-half as compared with one-third prior to SOX's enactment.[120]

While SOX did little to affect the number of public companies by discouraging IPOs and encouraging public-to-private transactions, it may have contributed to the downward trend by prompting companies to "go dark." A company goes dark when it deregisters from the SEC on the basis that it has fewer than 300 holders of record, a threshold governing the applicability of the federal securities laws of which SOX is a part.[121] With a total of 305 companies going dark in 2003 and 2004 compared with an average of only 35 per year between 1998 and 2002, it would seem that SOX prompted deregistrations.[122] On the other hand, companies going dark were usually small enough—those doing so between 1998 and 2004 had a median market value of just $4 million[123]—to mean they would have had little reason to try to escape SOX because their small size would have exempted them from complying with many of its strictures. The upshot is that while SOX imposed meaningful and

---

[115] Chapter 4, notes 136–37, 140–41 and accompanying text.

[116] Chapter 4, note 148 and related discussion; Chapter 5, note 80 and accompanying text.

[117] Robert P. Bartlett, *Going Private but Staying Public: Reexamining the Effect of Sarbanes-Oxley on Firms' Going-Private Decisions*, 76 U. Chi. L. Rev. 7, 8 (2009).

[118] Deborah Orr, *The New Titans*, Forbes, Apr. 19, 2004, 68.

[119] Ehud Kamar, Pinar Karaca-Mandic & Eric Talley, *Going-Private Decisions and the Sarbanes-Oxley Act of 2002: A Cross-Country Analysis*, 25 J.L. Econ. & Org. 107, 117–18, 129 (2009).

[120] Bartlett, *supra* note 117, at 30, 36–37.

[121] Butler & Ribstein, *supra* note 103, at 54; Christian Leuz, Alexander Triantis & Tracy Yue Wang, *Why Do Firms Go Dark? Causes and Economic Consequences of Voluntary SEC Deregistrations*, 45 J. Accting. & Econ. 181, 182, 206–07 (2008); Jesse M. Fried, *Firms Gone Dark*, 76 U. Chi. L. Rev. 135, 135–36 (2009).

[122] Leuz, Triantis & Wang, *supra* note 121, at 189.

[123] *Id.* at 191.

presumably unwelcome costs on public companies, its impact on the number of such firms was modest at best.

PRIVATE EQUITY

While private equity buyouts would become a plausible threat to the viability of the public company in the mid-2000s, this seemed unlikely as the decade got underway. The public-to-private buyout was very much a sideshow amidst the hectic merger and acquisition (M&A) activity of the mid- and late-1990s.[124] The tide had not turned at the start of the 2000s. Private equity firms, perhaps still known better as "buyout shops," could raise funds readily enough from investors attempting to beat a now poorly performing stock market.[125] Nevertheless, a paucity of deals where publicly traded companies were taken private led a senior investment banker to claim that "(f)or the most part, the day of the large buyout shop is over."[126] Private equity firms were focusing instead on acquiring business units companies were divesting, taking small, non-controlling stakes in publicly traded corporations, and making early stage investments akin to those in which venture capital firms specialized.[127]

With debt being a prominent feature of leveraged buyouts (LBOs), market conditions were a major stumbling block to public-to-private transactions as the 2000s commenced. The swooning stock market meant there were numerous potential targets attractively priced.[128] Investors, however, were reluctant to buy risky corporate debt, initially due to recessionary conditions and then as a result of uncertainties created by the 9/11 terrorist attacks.[129] Correspondingly, as a Goldman Sachs research analyst said of the buyout shops," (t)hey're ready to go, but with the markets the way they are, they are stuck on the runway."[130]

It also seemed possible as the 2000s began that the governance logic underpinning public-to-private buyouts had been undercut. An oft-cited rationale for going-private transactions is that they provide opportunities to restructure out of the limelight companies that have lost their way while being publicly traded.[131] Economists Bengt Holmstrom and Steven Kaplan, in the 2001 article where they praised corporate governance arrangements in the United States, suggested that due to improvements with public companies there was little scope to generate value

[124] Chapter 5, note 146 and related discussion; *supra* note 116 and accompanying text.

[125] Deborah Sparks, *Return of the LBO*, BUS. WK., Oct. 16, 2000, 130 (deploying both terms).

[126] *Id.*

[127] *Id.*; Robert Clow & Peter Smith, *Scandals Help to Break the Deal Drought*, FIN. TIMES, Dec, 12, 2002, Private Equity—The Buy-Out Market, 1; Felix Barber & Michael Gould, *The Strategic Secret of Private Equity*, HARV. BUS. REV., Sept. 2007, 53, 54, 56.

[128] David Franecki, *Here's the Deal*, BARRON'S, Feb. 12, 2001, 20; Riva D. Atlas, *What's an Aging Barbarian to Do?*, NY TIMES, Aug. 26, 2001, Business, 1.

[129] Andrew Ross Sorkin, *It's Buying Time Again*, NY TIMES, Jan. 11, 2001, C1; DAVID CAREY & JOHN E. MORRIS, KING OF CAPITAL: THE REMARKABLE RISE, FALL, AND RISE AGAIN OF STEVE SCHWARZMAN AND BLACKSTONE 165–67 (2010).

[130] Sorkin, *supra* note 129.

[131] Chapter 4, note 125 and related discussion; *Is the Boom in Buyouts Good for Business?*, WALL ST. J., June 3, 2006, A7; Brian Cheffins & John Armour, *The Eclipse of Private Equity*, 33 DEL. J. CORP. L. 1, 59 (2008).

in this way.[132] Public company executives, Holmstrom and Kaplan reasoned, were already focusing intently on maximizing shareholder value, spurred on by governance changes resulting in the increased use of incentive-based executive compensation and closer monitoring by shareholders and directors.[133]

While the public-to-private buyout got off to a slow start in the 2000s, the situation would soon change markedly. In early 2004 *Business Week* told readers "(l)everaged-buyout firms are on a tear," citing a $2.6 billion purchase of Warner Music Group by a private equity consortium.[134] This LBO was just a warm-up act. Warner Music was a unit of Time Warner, meaning the transaction was the sort of divestment transaction that was prevalent as the 2000s began. A major shift to buyouts involving the removal of companies from the stock market was imminent, however.

During 2004 the aggregate value of full-scale public-to-private LBOs equaled that for the acquisition of divisions from public companies.[135] For three years after that public-to-private buyout activity largely eclipsed the buying of units from public companies.[136] The past was similarly overshadowed. Between 2004 and 2007, public-to-private buyouts worth $535 billion were completed as compared with $50 billion between 1996 and 2003 (in 2007 dollars) and $227 billion between 1986 and 1989 (again in 2007 dollars).[137] In 2006 and 2007, 9 of the 10 largest public-to-private buyouts ever would be announced, with the only outlier being the 1989 RJR Nabisco acquisition.[138] Topping the list was the $44.4 billion acquisition of TXU Corp., a Texas energy company. There was talk of $100 billion and $150 billion deals.[139] Even software giant Microsoft was mooted as a possible target.[140]

Very "loose" credit markets, featuring cheap and plentiful debt, fueled the dramatic mid-2000s growth of public-to-private buyouts.[141] Large banks took the lead in financing private equity activity, and while they paid close attention to credit quality as late as 2004, they then "started letting their guard down."[142] The banks, confident that fixed income investors eager for yields higher than those offered by government debt would buy up buyout loans repackaged by way of securitization, hustled to lend to private equity firms.[143] Private equity firms, in their turn, could negotiate when borrowing highly favorable interest rates as well as relaxed terms, such as "covenant lite" loans issued without standard loan conditions relating

---

[132] Holmstrom & Kaplan, *Corporate*, *supra* note 77, at 132–33, 136.

[133] *Id.* at 130–33.

[134] Emily Thornton, *Those Bulging Buyouts*, BUS. WK., Feb. 9, 2004, 74.

[135] Barber & Gould, *supra* note 127, at 56.

[136] *Id.*

[137] Anil Shivdasani & Yihui Wang, *Did Structured Credit Fuel the LBO Boom?*, 66 J. FIN. 1291, 1291 (2011).

[138] STEVEN M. DAVIDOFF, GODS AT WAR: SHOTGUN TAKEOVERS, GOVERNMENT BY DEAL, AND THE PRIVATE EQUITY IMPLOSION 35 (2009).

[139] David Reilly, *Game of Buyout Bingo May Be Ending*, WALL ST. J., June 28, 2007, C1.

[140] John Plender, *Private Equity Folk Could Do Wonders with Microsoft*, FIN. TIMES, Aug. 18, 2006, 13.

[141] Cheffins & Armour, *supra* note 131, at 23–24.

[142] JOSH KOSMAN, THE BUYOUT OF AMERICA: HOW PRIVATE EQUITY IS DESTROYING JOBS AND KILLING THE AMERICAN ECONOMY 36 (2009).

[143] *Id.* at 36–37; Andy Kessler, *Blackstone's World of Cash*, WALL ST. J., June 21, 2007, A17.

to the financial performance of the leveraged companies being acquired.[144] For private equity firms "it was like having a credit card without a limit."[145]

Corporate governance was also invoked to explain the popularity of private equity buyouts. The falling share prices and corporate scandals that characterized the early 2000s tarnished the public company governance model Holmstrom and Kaplan had cited approvingly in 2001 to explain the dearth of public-to-private buyouts.[146] The governance arrangements private equity firms put in place for companies taken private were also singled out for praise. Michael Jensen, the primary academic booster of LBOs in the 1980s,[147] said of private equity in 2007 "(i)t's not a transaction business—it's a governance business."[148]

As was the case with LBOs in the 1980s, the incentive package in place for executives running companies taken private that combined sizeable stock ownership stakes as the carrot and the servicing of sizeable corporate debt as the stick was cited as a crucial private equity governance plus compared with public companies.[149] Another plus cited in the 1980s, namely the freedom executives had to run the business without justifying choices made to investment analysts and the media,[150] not only remained relevant but was of greater salience. The quarterly earnings "cult" that flourished in the 1990s remained a feature of being public in the 2000s.[151] The opportunity to run a firm free from "the tyranny of quarterly earnings expectations" was correspondingly viewed as a key benefit of being private.[152]

Boards were an additional feature of what the managing partner at Clayton, Dubilier & Rice, a leading private equity firm, referred to in 2006 as private equity's "great corporate governance advantage."[153] The fact independent directors serving on a part-time basis dominated public company boards theoretically fostered objectivity but also implied potentially counterproductive detachment.[154] With a company taken private, in contrast, the outside directors would typically be representatives of the private equity firm that orchestrated the buyout who, as such, would be eager to get the corporation in shape to sell at an advantageous price.[155] The result, according to advocates of the private equity model, was stronger strategic leadership at the board level than public companies experienced, allied with more effective performance oversight.[156]

---

[144] Cheffins & Armour, *supra* note 131, at 24.

[145] Carey & Morris, *supra* note 129, at 229.

[146] See Chapter 5, notes 127–31 and accompanying text; *supra* notes 31, 80, 131–32 and related discussion.

[147] See Chapter 4, note 128 and related discussion.

[148] Stewart, *supra* note 14.

[149] See Chapter 4, note 126 and accompanying text; Cheffins & Armour, *supra* note 131, at 13; Geoffrey Colvin & Ram Charan, *Private Lives*, Fortune, Nov. 27, 2006, 190; Ronald W. Masulis & Randall S. Thomas, *Does Private Equity Create Wealth? The Effects of Private Equity and Derivatives on Corporate Governance*, 76 U. Chi. L. Rev. 219, 227–28 (2009).

[150] See Chapter 4, note 125 and accompanying text.

[151] *Infra* notes 275–279 and related discussion.

[152] Emily Thornton, *Going Private*, Bus. Wk., Feb. 27, 2006, 53; Erin White & Gregory Zuckerman, *The Private Equity CEO*, Wall St. J., Nov. 6, 2006, B1.

[153] Francesco Guerrera & James Politi, *Life on the Other Side—Why Private Equity Is Luring Top Talent*, Fin. Times, Dec. 22, 2006, 13.

[154] Chapter 5, note 172 and related discussion; *infra* notes 240–41 and accompanying text.

[155] Cheffins & Armour, *supra* note 131, at 13–14; Masulis & Thomas, *supra* note 149, at 228.

[156] Jonathan Drance & Edward Waitzer, *Make Directors Work*, Nat'l Post, July 16, 2009, Financial Post, 11.

The dramatic increase in public-to-private buyout activity in the mid-2000s and praise for the governance advantages of private equity combined to prompt speculation that Jensen's 1989 buyout-driven prediction of the eclipse of the public corporation would be vindicated belatedly.[157] Indeed, David Rubenstein, cofounder of Carlyle Group, a major private equity firm, told *Fortune* at the start of 2007 "[We are] the face of 21st-century American capitalism," a claim the magazine labeled "mildly self-serving" but not "outlandish."[158] Jensen, for his part, had doubts about private equity's imminent preeminence, in large part because of what he characterized as a private equity non sequitur in the form of a mooted move by leading private equity firms away from the previously universal pattern of private ownership.[159] Blackstone, a private equity giant, in fact carried out a public offering in mid-2007, accompanied by speculation key competitors would follow soon.[160] Developments in credit markets would, however, very soon render moot for the moment debate about private equity eclipsing the public company.

The cheap debt that fostered the private equity boom became available partly due to low interest rates prompted by an expansionary monetary policy the Federal Reserve had been pursuing.[161] The Fed, having slashed interest rates in 2001, refrained from raising them for months thereafter due to discouraging economic data, weak share prices, and the 9/11 terrorist attacks.[162] The Fed's stance helped to push mortgage rates down to 40-year lows, which kicked the housing market into high gear.[163] House prices increased by nearly 10 percent annually between mid-2001 and mid-2005 and rose even faster in hot markets such as California and Florida.[164] Lending standards associated with residential mortgages eroded, with "subprime" mortgages (mortgages to borrowers lacking sound credit histories) proliferating.[165] Losses in the event of default were thought to be unlikely given that the value of the underlying assets—residential real estate—was increasing steadily.[166] Lenders were also passing on much of whatever risk there was through the financial system via securitization of mortgage debt, ostensibly with the risk being reduced along the way through pooling and diversification.[167] In 2006, the

---

[157] *Supra* note 18 and related discussion.

[158] Nicholas Varchaver et al., *Private Equity Forecast*, FORTUNE, Jan. 22, 2007, 21.

[159] Gretchen Morgenson, *It's Just a Matter of Equity*, NY TIMES, Sept. 16, 2007, B1.

[160] Cheffins & Armour, *supra* note 131, at 60–61.

[161] *Id.* at 23.

[162] DAVID FABER, AND THEN THE ROOF CAVED IN: HOW WALL STREET'S GREED AND STUPIDITY BROUGHT CAPITALISM TO ITS KNEES 15–17 (2009); FINANCIAL CRISIS INQUIRY COMMISSION, THE FINANCIAL CRISIS INQUIRY REPORT 84 (2012).

[163] FINANCIAL CRISIS INQUIRY COMMISSION, *supra* note 162, at 85.

[164] *Id.* ROBERT J. BARBERA, THE COST OF CAPITALISM: UNDERSTANDING MARKET MAYHEM AND STABILIZING OUR ECONOMIC FUTURE 133 (2009).

[165] FINANCIAL CRISIS INQUIRY COMMISSION, *supra* note 162, at 67; SIMON JOHNSON & JAMES KWAK, 13 BANKERS: THE WALL STREET TAKEOVER AND THE NEXT FINANCIAL MELTDOWN 126–27 (2010).

[166] Markus K Brunnermeier, *Deciphering the Liquidity and Credit Crunch 2007–2008*, 23 J. ECON. PERSP. 77, 82 (2009).

[167] FINANCIAL CRISIS INQUIRY COMMISSION, *supra* note 162, at 128–29; JOHNSON & KWAK, *supra* note 165, at 127–29.

housing market peaked and prices began to fall, loss-making foreclosures proliferated, and "mortgage-backed securities began to blow up like time bombs."[168]

In May 2007, Ben Bernanke, who succeeded Alan Greenspan as chairman of the Federal Reserve in 2006, said "we believe the effect of the troubles in the subprime sector on the broader housing market will likely be limited, and we do not expect significant spillovers from the subprime market to the rest of the economy or to the financial system."[169] The collapse the following month of two heavily leveraged Bear Stearns hedge funds that invested almost exclusively in mortgage-backed securities and mortgage-related derivatives provided an early indication that such confidence was misplaced.[170] In July 2007 Standard & Poor's cut its credit ratings on billions of dollars' worth of mortgage-backed securities.[171] The downgrade in turn prompted investors to worry about the riskiness of high-yield debt more generally and even the creditworthiness of substantial holders of investments related to that debt.[172] The *Financial Times* said in late July "(t)here is widespread recognition that something has changed: after five years in which credit has been freely available, the tide has turned."[173] In early August, Bear Stearns' CFO, instead of reassuring investors as his firm's share price fell due to its problems with its mortgage-oriented hedge funds, cautioned with the fixed income debt market "(i)t's about as bad as I've seen it."[174] A few days later BNP Paribas, a large French bank, halted withdrawals on three of its funds heavily invested in subprime mortgages due to difficulties valuing the assets fairly. What had been thought of as "a niggle in an arcane corner of the US mortgage market" was developing into a full blown "credit crunch."[175]

In the case of private equity, symptoms of a debt market chill were apparent a few weeks before the credit crunch had developed fully. In late June 2007, investors spurned $3.6 billion worth of bonds and loans issued to finance a proposed buyout of US Foodservice Inc., a major food distributor.[176] The news prompted Carl Icahn, a prominent 1980s corporate raider and a leading shareholder activist in the 2000s, to say of private equity "it's peaked."[177]

---

[168] Rick Newman, *A New Direction on Wall Street*, US News & World Report, Sept. 29, 2008, 22. See also Steven Gjersted & Vernon Smith, *From Bubble to Depression?*, Wall St. J., Apr. 6, 2009, A15; Dean Baker, Plunder and Blunder: The Rise and Fall of the Bubble Economy 104–06 (2009).

[169] William W. Lang & Julapa A. Jagtiani, *The Mortgage and Financial Crises: The Role of Credit*, 38 J. Atl. Econ. 295, 296 (2010).

[170] Financial Crisis Inquiry Commission, *supra* note 162, at 135–36; Roger Lowenstein, The End of Wall Street 90 (2010).

[171] Faber, *supra* note 162, at 163.

[172] Serena Ng & Tom Lauricella, *Loan Slump May Crimp Buyout Deals*, Wall St. J., July 13, 2007, C1; Norm Alster, *Signs of Weakness in a Sector Known for Its Strength*, NY Times, Aug. 12, 2007, B4; John Cassidy, How Markets Fail: The Logic of Economic Calamities 301 (2009).

[173] Peter Thal Larsen, *Debt Bubble Denial Bears Resemblance to Dotcoms*, Fin. Times, July 25, 2007, Survey of Corporate Finance, 6.

[174] John Gapper, *The Cost of a Wrong Turn*, Fin. Times, Aug. 5, 2008, 9.

[175] Richard Beales, *US Niggle Became Global Problem*, Fin. Times, Aug. 11, 2007, 2; see also Faber, *supra* note 162, at 162–63.

[176] Serena Ng, Tom Lauricella & Michael Aneiro, *Market's Jitters Stir Some Fears for Buyout Boom*, Wall St. J., June 28, 2007, 1.

[177] Thomas Heath, *Private Equity Deals Slow Down*, Wash. Post, June 29, 2007, D1. On Ichan's 1980s raiding, see Chapter 4, notes 66, 71, 81 and related discussion.

Not everyone agreed a debt market-driven reversal of fortune had occurred for the private equity industry. When in early July 2007 the *Financial Times* asked Chuck Prince, CEO of Citigroup, whether his bank, a leading financier of private equity deals, was contemplating stepping back from the private equity market, he indicated that was not the case. Prince said instead "(w)hen the music stops, in terms of liquidity, things will be complicated. But as long as the music is playing, you've got to get up and dance. We're still dancing."[178]

Prince's reply to the *Financial Times*' query about private equity would become the most famous—or infamous—quote associated with the 2008 financial crisis.[179] His remarks seemed to exemplify the counterproductively cavalier way Wall Street viewed financial risk as the financial crisis loomed.[180] In fact, with the particular market segment Prince was referring to everyone would be sitting down very soon. The *Financial Times* observed in mid-August 2007:

> Just days after Chuck Prince, Citigroup's chief executive, had confidently proclaimed that he was "still dancing" to the tune of the buy-out boom, the music stopped and the self- proclaimed "golden age" of private equity came to an end. Indeed, since the end of July, discussions about large private equity takeovers have virtually ground to a halt, say Wall Street bankers."[181]

The *New York Times* similarly proclaimed "the buyout boom has officially gone bust and the credit markets are in meltdown."[182] LBO volume indeed fell by 94 percent in the fourth quarter of 2007 from a year previously.[183]

Through to the middle of August 2008, the total value of private equity buyout deals for the year was one-sixth the outlay in the corresponding 2007 period.[184] The eclipse of private equity seemed a more likely outcome than the eclipse of the public company.[185] Somewhat astonishingly, in mid-2008 private equity executives' mood reportedly remained "one of almost hypnotic confidence."[186] Such confidence would, however, very soon be undercut by an economic reversal that would also be the final major challenge the public company faced during the 2000s, namely the financial crisis of 2008.

---

178 Michioyo Nakamoto & David Wighton, *Bullish CitigroupIs "Still Dancing" to the Beat of the Buy-Out Boom*, FIN. TIMES, July 10, 2007, 1.

179 BLINDER, *supra* note 27, at xv.

180 DONALD C. LANGEVOORT, SELLING HOPE, SELLING RISK: CORPORATIONS, WALL STREET, AND THE DILEMMAS OF INVESTOR PROTECTION 145 (2016).

181 Francesco Guerrera & James Politi, *Not Dancing Anymore*, FIN. TIMES, Aug. 14, 2007, 9.

182 Andrew Ross Sorkin, *Sorting through the Buyout Freezeout*, NY TIMES, Aug. 12, 2007, B6.

183 Shivdasani & Wang, *supra* note 137.

184 Andrew Bary, *Look Out Below!*, BARRON'S, Sept. 1, 2008, 25 ($67 billion vs. $400 billion).

185 Cheffins & Armour, *supra* note 131.

186 *Private Investigations*, ECONOMIST, July 5, 2008, 94.

THE FINANCIAL CRISIS

Private equity executives were not alone in feeling confident in mid-2008 despite challenging circumstances. In March of that year Bear Stearns was encountering a destructive negative feedback loop. It was on the brink of failure because creditors it counted on to provide short-term debt financing, financial institutions that were counterparties in derivatives trades with the investment bank and ultimately its prime brokerage clients, all were considering how to disassociate themselves from Bear Stearns because they were losing faith in its financial wherewithal.[187] Though Bear Stearns, as an investment bank, was overseen by the SEC and did not fall directly within the Federal Reserve's bank regulation remit, the Fed orchestrated a "rescue merger" at a knockdown price with the large commercial bank J.P. Morgan Chase as buyer.[188] This was backstopped by the Fed using its lending powers creatively to protect J.P. Morgan Chase against losses the bank might incur due to $30 billion of problematic mortgage-related assets Bear Stearns held.[189]

The Bear Stearns rescue buoyed spirits. In April 2008 J.P. Morgan Chase's CEO Jamie Dimon said the credit crunch that had started the previous summer was "maybe 75% to 80%" over.[190] Richard Fuld and John Mack, CEOs of leading investment banks Lehman Brothers and Morgan Stanley, told their shareholders respectively "the worst is behind us" and that the US subprime mortgage crisis was in "the eighth or ninth inning."[191] Investors seemed to agree. During the summer of 2008 stock prices approached record levels set in the fall of 2007 and markets generally were, in hindsight, "surprisingly stable and almost seemed to be neutral."[192]

Belying the post-Bear Stearns rescue calm, the financial crisis hit with dizzying strength in September 2008. At the beginning of the month the federal government placed the Federal Home Loan Mortgage Co. (a.k.a. "Freddie Mac") and the Federal National Mortgage Association (a.k.a. "Fannie Mae"), troubled government sponsored but also publicly traded enterprises, into conservatorship.[193] A few days later Lehman Brothers announced very poor quarterly financial results and, afflicted by the same negative feedback loop as Bear Stearns in March, it was teetering.[194] Merrill Lynch, another investment bank experiencing financial difficulties, grasped, at the Federal Reserve's urging, a rescue merger opportunity and agreed

---

[187] *The $2 Bail-Out*, ECONOMIST, Mar. 22, 2008, 94; Steven M. Davidoff & David Zaring, *Regulation by Deal: The Government's Response to the Financial Crisis*, 61 ADMIN. L. REV. 463, 476–77 (2009); Charles K. Whitehead, *Reframing Financial Regulation*, 90 B.U. L. REV. 1, 22–23 (2010).

[188] On the "rescue merger" characterization, see Brian R. Cheffins, *Did Corporate Governance "Fail" during the 2008 Stock Market Meltdown? The Case of the S&P 500*, 65 BUS. LAW. 1, 3, 25, 29 (2009); *Panel 2: Banking Reform*, 7 N.Y.U. J.L. & BUS. 479, 490 (2011) (comments of Thomas C. Baxter, an in-house lawyer with the Federal Reserve Bank of New York).

[189] BLINDER, *supra* note 27, at 105–08; Davidoff & Zaring, *supra* note 187, at 477–83.

[190] Joseph Schuman, *Parsing a US Economy As Bleak, Weak and Soft. . . .*, WALL ST. J., Apr. 17, 2008 (online edition), available via ProQuest/ABI Inform Collection.

[191] *Id.*; Susanne Craig et al., *The Weekend That Wall Street Died*, WALL ST. J., Dec, 29, 2008, A1.

[192] FINANCIAL CRISIS INQUIRY COMMISSION, *supra* note 162, at 292 (quoting Morgan Stanley's treasurer). See also BLINDER, *supra* note 27, at 114.

[193] BLINDER, *supra* note 27, at 115–18; FINANCIAL CRISIS INQUIRY COMMISSION, *supra* note 162, at 309, 319–21.

[194] Davidoff & Zaring, *supra* note 187, at 491, 493.

to sell out to Bank of America for $50 billion.[195] There was no Fed-led rescue in store, however, for Lehman Brothers and, when the investment bank filed for bankruptcy, panic set in. The stock market fell sharply and the Reserve Primary Fund, an ostensibly ultra-safe money market fund with sizeable holdings in now worthless Lehman commercial paper, shocked investors when it announced it was going to "break the buck" and lower its net asset value below $1 per share.[196]

American International Group (AIG), an insurance giant imperiled due to prolific writing of credit default swaps protecting mortgage lenders, was next on the radar of federal government officials.[197] Unlike with Lehman, a rescue was arranged, with the Federal Reserve ultimately agreeing to lend up to $85 billion to the insurer in return for a 79.9 percent equity stake.[198] The Treasury and the Fed then turned to money market funds, seeking to shore up the $3.4 trillion industry by putting in place guarantees that afforded protection against "breaking the buck."[199] In addition, the Bush administration proposed a Troubled Assets Relief Program (TARP) that would give the federal government scope to purchase up to $700 billion worth of illiquid mortgage-backed securities from financial institutions.[200]

Despite federal intervention, the market convulsions continued throughout the remainder of September for major financial firms. With the encouragement of the Federal Reserve, Goldman Sachs and Morgan Stanley, the only large publicly traded investment banks regulated by the SEC that were still operating, converted themselves to bank holding companies under the Fed's jurisdiction. This provided ready access to the Fed's bank rescue mechanisms should trouble accelerate, introduced a backstop of stricter regulation, and implied a stable source of financing in the form of customer deposits.[201] Next was the largest bank failure in US history, with federal regulators taking control of publicly traded Washington Mutual and transferring to J.P. Morgan Chase for $1.9 billion the banking operations and loan portfolio of what had been a $307 billion thrift.[202] Wachovia, recently the fourth largest bank in the United States by market value, then agreed under a deal federal regulators brokered to transfer most of its operations and debt obligations to Citigroup for $2 billion.[203]

---

[195] Greg Farrell & Henny Sender, *The Shaming of John Thain*, FIN. TIMES, Mar. 14, 2009, FT Magazine, 21; GREG FARRELL, CRASH OF THE TITANS: GREED, HUBRIS, THE FALL OF MERRILL LYNCH, AND THE NEAR-COLLAPSE OF BANK OF AMERICA 262–63, 279–305 (2010).

[196] FINANCIAL CRISIS INQUIRY COMMISSION, *supra* note 162, 356–57; Joe Nocera, *Lehman Had to Die, It Seems, So Global Finance Could Live*, NY TIMES, Sept. 12, 2009, A1.

[197] Karl S. Okamoto, *After the Bailout: Regulating Systemic Moral Hazard*, 57 U.C.L.A. L. REV. 183, 200–02 (2009).

[198] Davidoff & Zaring, *supra* note 187, at 494–97.

[199] Diana B. Henriques, *Rescue Plan for Funds Will Come With a Price*, WALL ST. J., Sept. 20, 2008, C1;

[200] FINANCIAL CRISIS INQUIRY COMMISSION, *supra* note 162, at 371; Peter Baker, *Administration Is Seeking $700 Billion for Wall St.; Bailout Could Set Record*, NY TIMES, Sept. 21, 2008, 1.

[201] LOWENSTEIN, *supra* note 170, at 230, 234; Davidoff & Zaring, *supra* note 187, at 494; Jon Hilsenrath, Damian Paletta & Aaron Luchetti, *Goldman, Morgan Scrap Wall Street Model*, WALL ST. J., Sept. 22, 2008, A1.

[202] Robin Sidel, David Enrich & Dan Fitzpatrick, *WaMu Is Seized, Sold Off to J.P. Morgan, In Largest Failure in US Banking History*, WALL ST. J., Sept. 26, 2008, A1; Bill Virgin, Andrea James & Dan Richman, *WaMu Seized, Sold*, SEATTLE POST-INTELLIGENCER, Sept. 26, 2008, A1.

[203] Dan Fitzpatrick & Diva Gullapalli, *Storm of Fear Enveloped Wachovia*, WALL ST. J., Sept. 30, 2008, A7; Richard Craver, *Shareholders Weigh Options at Wachovia*, WINSTON-SALEM J., Oct. 3, 2008, 1.

As September ended, the House of Representatives rejected the White House's TARP proposal, which contributed to the biggest numerical point drop in the history of the Dow Jones Industrial Average stock market index to that point (777.68, or 7 percent in percentage terms).[204] Congress, spooked by the adverse market reaction, passed the TARP legislative package in early October.[205] The dizzying restructuring of the banking industry abated but times remained tumultuous. Citigroup, which had its September offer to buy Wachovia trumped by a higher bid from Wells Fargo,[206] had to be rescued by federal regulators in November with Citigroup issuing more than $20 billion in preferred stock to the government.[207] In December, the Bush administration authorized the use of TARP funds to underwrite $17 billion worth of loans to financially distressed automakers General Motors and Chrysler, issued in return for nonvoting stock warrants.[208] Stock price declines following the onset of the financial crisis meant that 2008 was the worst year for the S&P 500 since 1937 and the worst for the Dow Jones since 1931.[209] Across all US stock markets, an estimated $6.9 trillion in market value was wiped out.[210]

There was speculation as 2009 got underway that a 1930s-style depression could be in the offing.[211] While the unemployment rate would not peak until October,[212] the worst in fact was now over. A strong stock market rally began in the spring of 2009 (Figure 6.1) and GDP increased 1.3 percent and 3.9 percent in the third and fourth quarters of the year respectively.[213] The May release of results of "stress tests" of 19 major banks federal regulators conducted under the federal Supervisory Capital Assessment Program indicating the banks could withstand a severe economic downturn lent valuable credence to assurances leading government figures were offering that the banking system was secure.[214] As disruptive as the financial crisis was, as economist Alan Blinder put it, "(o)nly the homebuilding sector . . . experienced anything close to Great Depression 2.0."[215]

A decade after the financial crisis, important open questions remain. What caused the crisis?[216] Did efforts by federal regulators to rescue the financial sector beneficially forestall a

---

[204] Sarah Lueck, Damian Paletta & Greg Hitt, *Bailout Plan Rejected, Markets Plunge*, WALL ST. J., Sept. 30, 2008, A1.

[205] Emergency Economic Stabilization Act of 2008, Pub. L. No. 110-343; Greg Hitt & Deborah Solomon, *Historic Bailout Passes As Economy Slips Further*, WALL ST. J., Oct. 4, 2008, A1.

[206] David Enrich & Dan Fitzpatrick, *Wachovia Chooses Wells Fargo*, WALL ST. J., Oct. 4, 2008, A1.

[207] FINANCIAL CRISIS INQUIRY COMMISSION, *supra* note 162, at 381–82; LOWENSTEIN, *supra* note 170, at 278.

[208] John D. McKinnon & John D. Stoll, *US Throws Lifeline to Detroit*, WALL ST. J., Dec, 20, 2008, A1.

[209] Matt Krantz, *Markets' Fall Was Worst in Seven Decades*, USA TODAY, Jan. 2, 2009, B1.

[210] *Id.*

[211] RICHARD A. POSNER, A FAILURE OF CAPITALISM: THE CRISIS OF '08 AND THE DESCENT INTO DEPRESSION ix (2009).

[212] *Supra* note 8 and related discussion.

[213] Federal Reserve Bank of St. Louis, *Economic Data*, Table 1.1.1. Percent Change from Preceding Period in Real Gross Domestic Product—Quarterly, available at https://fred.stlouisfed.org/release/tables?rid=53&eid=38375 (accessed Feb. 14, 2018).

[214] JOHNSON & KWAK, *supra* note 165, at 170–71.

[215] BLINDER, *supra* note 27, at 6.

[216] For brief discussion of this point, see *infra* notes 507–10, 519, 538–542 and accompanying text.

cataclysmic financial meltdown or amount to a costly, ad hoc, and largely superfluous intervention?[217] One point, however, that is clear is that the financial crisis was a major reputational setback for public companies.

There was some criticism of non-financial firms. Executives of General Motors and Chrysler left themselves open to ridicule when they flew by private jet in late 2008 to Washington, DC to lobby Congress for financial aid. Gary Ackerman, a New York congressman, chided them for the optics, asking, "(c)ouldn't you all have downgraded to first class or jet-pooled, or something, to get here? It would have at least sent a message that you do get it."[218] Financial firms, however, were singled out particularly for criticism.

Americans were upset with financial firms partly because it looked as if Wall Street was being bailed out while there was scant relief for Americans suffering the consequences of banker irresponsibility. Washington, DC, seemingly cared "more about people who wear Guccis than people who wear Levi's."[219] It also seemed illogical to "reward the greed that created the mess to begin with."[220] As Robert Reich, an academic who served in the Clinton administration, observed, the primary beneficiaries of the rescue efforts appeared to be "the Wall Streeters who've made out like bandits in the past few years."[221] It was hardly surprising, then, that among those asked by Gallup about their level of confidence in big business, in 2009 an all-time low of 16 percent replied a great deal or quite a lot.[222] There was for public company executives, however, one consolation—the "decade from hell" was over. We will consider now how events during that decade reconfigured the constraints under which they operated.

Internal Constraints

With public companies riding high in the 1990s, those in charge of the firms were riding high as well. Executive pay rose dramatically as CEOs of America's leading corporations began to acquire iconic status.[223] Given that the 2000s were hellish in various ways for public companies, not surprisingly the decade would be a difficult one for public company executives. Indeed in a 2010 law review article Marcel Kahan and Ed Rock described US CEOs as "embattled," likening the chief executive to Jonathan Swift's Gulliver being tied

---

[217] Contrast, for example, Jonathan R. Macey, *Failure Is an Option: An Ersatz-Antitrust Approach to Financial Regulation*, 120 YALE L.J. 1368, 1376 (2011); Allan Sloan & Doris Burke, *The Five Myths of the Great Financial Meltdown*, FORTUNE, July 2, 2012, 37 (pro rescue) with POSNER, *supra* note 211, at 269, 277–78; JOHN A. ALLISON, THE FINANCIAL CRISIS: WHY PURE CAPITALISM IS THE WORLD ECONOMY'S ONLY HOPE 164–73 (2013) (con).

[218] John Schwartz, *Contrite Over Misstep, Auto Chiefs Take to Road*, NY TIMES, Dec, 3, 2008, B1.

[219] David M. Herszenhorn, *About Those Charges of Bailout Bias*, NY TIMES, Dec, 7, 2008, Weekend, 3 (quoting a Michigan congressman).

[220] Rana Foroohar, *A New Age of Global Capitalism Starts Now*, NEWSWEEK (Int'l. ed.), Oct. 13, 2008, available at http://www.newsweek.com/new-age-global-capitalism-starts-now-91697 (accessed Mar. 14, 2018).

[221] *Id.*

[222] Gallup, *Confidence in Institutions*, available at http://www.gallup.com/poll/1597/confidence-institutions.aspx (accessed Mar. 16, 2018) (providing data for most years between 1973 and 2017).

[223] Chapter 5, notes 464–65, 491–92, 531–35 and accompanying text.

down by Lilliputians.[224] According to Kahan and Rock, the key Lilliputians were outside directors and shareholders, with chief executives losing power to both.[225] The result was potentially

> the emergence of a new era of corporate governance for the early part of the twenty-first century, where power over the US corporate enterprise is more evenly distributed between various participants-inside managers, outside directors, and shareholders-rather than concentrated in the hands of the CEO.[226]

In other words, events occurring during the 2000s implied that power within public companies could soon be arranged in a manner that was unprecedented since managerial capitalism came to the fore in the middle of the twentieth century.

Given that Kahan and Rock were writing in 2010, given that public company CEOs were riding high as the 1990s concluded, and given the identity of their Lilliputians, internal constraints on management seemingly must have tightened considerably in the 2000s. There are also potentially confounding facts to bear in mind, though. One might have expected the embattled CEOs of the noughties to have had to endure a substantial reduction in pay, particularly given that executive compensation had recently rocketed upward. In fact, even though executive pay fell in tandem with the stock market meltdown associated with the financial crisis, CEOs pay levels were much the same in 2009 as they were as the decade began.[227] Moreover, if chief executives were tied down in the manner Gulliver was, who was let loose in the run-up to the financial crisis to drive major financial firms to the edge of the cliff, and sometimes over?

Directors and shareholders were indeed both more robust sources of managerial discipline at the end of the 2000s than at the beginning. The story during the decade, however, was mixed. There was some evidence that boards were upping their game and, largely due to the rise of activist hedge funds, shareholders grew in prominence as a check on public company management. However, boards were criticized heavily in relation to the corporate scandals of the early 2000s and neither boards nor shareholders substantially compromised the discretion available to executives running major financial firms in the mid-2000s. We will look at the special case of banks after considering in a general way the intensity with which both internal and external constraints affected executives of public companies in the 2000s.

---

[224] Marcel Kahan & Edward Rock, *Embattled CEOs*, 88 TEX. L. REV. 987, 989–90 (2010), citing JONATHAN SWIFT, GULLIVER'S TRAVELS (1726).

[225] Kahan & Rock, *supra* note 224, at 989, 1022.

[226] *Id.* at 989.

[227] Steven A. Bank, Brian R. Cheffins & Harwell Wells, *Executive Pay: What Worked?*, 42 J. CORP. L. 59, 67–68 (2016) ($7.2 million on average in 2001 and $7.4 million in 2009); Kelly Shue & Richard R. Townsend, *Growth through Rigidity: An Explanation for the Rise in CEO Pay*, 123 J. FIN. ECON. 1, 4 (2017) ($6.8 million in 2000 and $6.7 million in 2009); Alex Edmans, Xavier Gabaix & Dirk Jenter, *Executive Compensation: A Survey of Theory and Evidence*, *in* 1 THE HANDBOOK OF THE ECONOMICS OF CORPORATE GOVERNANCE 383, 388–89 (Benjamin E. Hermalin & Michael S. Weisbach eds., 2017) (indicating that the pay of S&P 500 CEOs was slightly lower in 2009 than in 2000).

BOARDS

By the end of the 1990s, amidst substantial corporate prosperity, there was a general feeling that boards were making meaningful progress as a check on managerial excess.[228] The upbeat tone continued as the 2000s began. A *Barron's* columnist said in 2001 "(i)t seems that America's corporate boards are finally getting it."[229] Corporate governance experts typically concurred, offering in so doing optimistic assessments of boards as monitors of public company executives.[230]

Matters would change in short order. A different *Barron's* columnist told readers in mid-2002 "(b)oards of directors rubber-stamp chief executives' decisions" and quoted a representative of an advisory service to institutional shareholders as saying "(y)our average board today is still under the thumb of the CEO."[231] A *New York Times* columnist concurred, saying "(i)t has become all too clear in recent months that corporate directors are more often lap dogs for executives than tough-minded protectors of shareholders' interests."[232]

The corporate scandals of the early 2000s prompted the change of heart. *Forbes* said in 2003 of the major scandal afflicted companies "(a)ll had boards of directors that looked the other way while their chief executives ran roughshod over the auditing committees and often fattened their personal bank accounts while the businesses fell apart."[233] John Reed, whose 35-year career in banking culminated as co-CEO of Citigroup, said similarly in 2005 of "the seemingly broad-based breakdown of values and responsibilities" that "(o)ne of the most striking features of this history is the failure of boards."[234]

Enron provided a stark illustration of a seemingly well-positioned board failing to keep wayward executives in check. Outside directors, apparently highly qualified, substantially outnumbered executives on the board, which was widely hailed an exemplar of good corporate governance.[235] *Chief Executive* ranked Enron's board in 2000 as third-best among public companies, saying it "works hard to keep up with things."[236] Nevertheless, a 2002 Senate report on the board's role in the Enron scandal condemned the directors for missing a dozen obvious "red flags" that should have put them on alert.[237]

Various commentators on board behavior suggested little changed through the remainder of the 2000s, with senior management in most public companies continuing in practice to dominate the outside directors serving on boards.[238] Michael Jensen maintained in 2007 that in most publicly traded corporations "the CEO has no boss," with outside directors viewing

---

[228] Chapter 5, notes 167–70, 173–77 and related discussion.

[229] Ralph D. Ward, *Twilight of the Gods*, BARRON'S, Apr. 9, 2001, 57.

[230] Marcel Kahan & Edward B. Rock, *How I Learned to Stop Worrying and Love the Pill: Adaptive Responses to Takeover Law*, 69 U. CHI. L. REV. 871, 882–83 (2002) (summarizing and agreeing with views expressed).

[231] Gold, *supra* note 62.

[232] Gretchen Morgenson, *Pick Up the Proxy and Exert Some Control*, NY TIMES, Aug. 25, 2002, B1.

[233] Michael K. Ozanian & Scott Decarlo, *Does the Board Have a Backbone?*, FORBES, May 12, 2003, 106.

[234] John S. Reed, *Values and Corporate Responsibility: A Personal Perspective, in* RESTORING TRUST IN AMERICAN BUSINESS 35, 35, 39 (Jay W. Lorsch, Leslie Berlowitz & Andy Zelleke eds., 2005).

[235] JONATHAN R. MACEY, CORPORATE GOVERNANCE: PROMISES KEPT, PROMISES BROKEN 80–81 (2008).

[236] Robert W. Lear & Boris Yavitz, *Boards on Trial*, CHIEF EXEC., Oct. 2000, 40, 48.

[237] NOFSINGER & KIM, *supra* note 92, at 104–05.

[238] Masulis & Thomas, *supra* note 149, at 229 (summarizing points made).

themselves "as employees of the CEO" absent a crisis.[239] A *New Yorker* columnist argued in 2009 that collegiality prevailed counterproductively at board meetings and said that with independent directors being part-time "moonlighters" they were susceptible to "being pushed around by CEOs, who are professionals."[240] John Bogle, founder of the giant mutual fund group Vanguard, characterized directors in 2012 as "tail-wagging puppy dogs."[241]

Others were more optimistic. Alan Murray, in his 2007 book *Revolt in the Boardroom,* said "CEOs had to take their boards much more seriously" and directors, "no longer hand-picked" by the chief executive, were "acting with new energy" as part of a "shift in power from the chief executive's office to the corporate boardroom."[242] Law professor Steve Bainbridge wrote in 2008 there was "a substantial body of evidence that boards of directors are becoming far more effective than their predecessors."[243] The *Economist*, citing in 2009 a working paper version of Kahan and Rock's "Embattled CEOs" article, maintained "boards are not bosses' poodles."[244]

A continuation of a trend in favor of independent director representation extending back to the managerial capitalism era lent credence to the view that boards became more effective monitors of management in the 2000s.[245] The proportion of publicly traded companies with boards where independent directors were in the majority jumped from 76 percent in 2000 to 94 percent in 2005.[246] Representation of independent directors on audit committees increased from 81 percent to 95 percent between 1998 and 2005, with equivalent jumps of 85 percent to 94 percent and 72 percent to 92 percent occurring for compensation and nominating committees respectively.[247]

Other changes to boards also indicated they became better positioned to monitor executives in the 2000s. The proportion of S&P 500 companies with a "lead director" specifically charged with liaising between the CEO (and usually also chairman of the board) and the cohort of independent directors increased from 36 percent in mid-2003 to 85 percent in mid-2004 and to 94 percent as of 2007.[248] Amongst companies with CEOs who were members of the Business Roundtable in 2005, 71 percent organized in conjunction with board meetings executive sessions with only independent directors present, as compared with 55 percent in 2003.[249] This, according to board expert Jay Lorsch, was "absolutely the most important thing that's happened" because

---

[239] Quoted in John Gillespie & David Zweig, Money for Nothing: How CEOs and Boards Are Bankrupting America 97 (2010).

[240] James Surowiecki, *Board Stiff*, New Yorker, June 1, 2009, 34.

[241] John C. Bogle, The Clash of Cultures: Investment vs. Speculation 61 (2012) (quoting Warren Buffett).

[242] Alan Murray, Revolt in the Boardroom: The New Rules of Power in Corporate America xvii, 265 (2007).

[243] Stephen M. Bainbridge, The New Corporate Governance in Theory and Practice 199 (2008).

[244] *Attacking the Corporate Gravy Train*, Economist, May 20, 2009, 78.

[245] Chapter 2, notes 279, 281 and accompanying text; Chapter 3, notes 276–81 and related discussion.

[246] Ran Duchin, John G. Matsusaka & Oguzhan Ozbas, *When Are Outside Directors Effective?*, 96 J. Fin. Econ. 195, 198 (2010).

[247] *Id.*

[248] Bart Friedman, *An Independent Voice on the Board*, N.Y.L.J., Nov. 17, 2008, 9; see also Gilmartin, *supra* note 92, at 161.

[249] Alan Murray, *Emboldened Boards Tackle Imperial CEOs*, Wall St. J., Mar. 16, 2005, A2.

meeting without the CEO present afforded independent directors a realistic opportunity to discuss frankly delicate topics such as the chief executive's performance and CEO succession.[250]

The changes bolstering the board's capabilities as a monitor occurred in a context where corporate governance attracted attention like never before. *Business Week* told readers in a 2002 analysis of the best and worst boards that "(a)cross Corporate America, a governance revolution is under way."[251] *Business Week*'s story was part of a broader trend, with the number of articles in the media about corporate governance jumping sharply in the early 2000s to historically high levels and remaining above historical norms throughout the remainder of the decade.[252] Corporations also talked more about governance, as reflected in disclosures in proxy documentation sent to stockholders prior to annual shareholder meetings to solicit voting support. The proportion of companies using the term "corporate governance" rose from 51 percent in 2002 to 91 percent in 2003 and then to 99 percent in 2004.[253] The frequency with which the term was used continued to increase thereafter.[254]

The Sarbanes Oxley Act of 2002 also contributed to change in the boardroom.[255] SOX and associated scandal-induced amendments to stock exchange listing rules fortified independence standards and introduced regulatory treatment of the "presiding" (akin to "lead") director and executive sessions for boards.[256] The *Wall Street Journal*, in a 2006 article declaring "the boardroom walls are coming down," noted that "(t)o some extent, boards have little choice in becoming more aggressive. New rules and regulations guiding director duties are forcing major changes."[257] A 2008 empirical study of the impact SOX had on the market for directorial talent reported similarly that "(o)ur results are consistent with the conjecture that firms are making substantial adjustments directly in response to SOX and contemporary changes to the exchange listing rules."[258]

SOX's implications for managerial accountability went beyond boards. Anecdotal evidence indicated that requiring CEOs and CFOs to attest, subject to criminal penalties, to the accuracy of financial disclosures and the veracity of internal financial control systems prompted improvements to management information systems and fostered increased attention to financial detail by executives.[259] The founder of an accounting research service told

---

250 *Where's All the Fun Gone?*, ECONOMIST, Mar. 20, 2004, 93.

251 Louis Lavelle, *The Best & Worst Boards*, BUS. WK., Oct. 7, 2002, 104.

252 Lucian A. Bebchuk, Alma Cohen & Charles C.Y. Yang, *Learning and the Disappearing Association between Governance and Returns*, 108 J. FIN. ECON. 323, 324, 330 (2013).

253 Alon Bebchuk & Robert J. Jackson, *The Rise of Corporate Governance*, Columbia Law School Data Lab Working Paper 3 (2016).

254 *Id.* at 4–6.

255 Jason Q. Zhang, Hong Zhu & Hung-bin Ding, *Board Composition and Corporate Social Responsibility: An Empirical Investigation in the Post-Sarbanes-Oxley Era*, 114 J. BUS. ETHICS 381, 382 (2013).

256 *Supra* note 92 and related discussion.

257 Kaja Whitehouse, *Move Over CEO*, WALL ST. J., Oct. 9, 2006, R1.

258 James S. Linck, Jeffry M. Netter & Tina Yang, *The Effects and Unintended Consequences of the Sarbanes-Oxley Act on the Supply and Demand for Directors*, 22 REV. FIN. STUD. 3287, 3290 (2008).

259 Nocera, *supra* note 75; Louis Osmont, *Time to Bite the Bullet*, FIN. TIMES, Jan. 8, 2004, 44; Robert C. Clark, *Corporate Governance Changes in the Wake of the Sarbanes-Oxley Act: A Morality Tale for Policymakers Too*, 22 GA. ST. UNIV. L. REV. 251, 266 (2005).

the *New York Times* in 2017 "(t)hose accounting scandals were a crisis we should be thankful for; we got through it, a law was passed, and it works."[260] Empirical research on SOX's impact was more ambiguous, though, indicating that the legislation may have done little to foster the detection and disclosure of internal control weaknesses.[261] Also, while criminal sanctions associated with false financial report certifications may have resulted in CEOs and CFOs being less cavalier about financial disclosure, the fact that prosecutions turned out to be a rarity may well have muted the deterrent effect over time.[262]

An additional caveat with the impact SOX and stock exchange listing rule amendments had on boards and managerial accountability more generally is that an upgrade in board capabilities may have occurred without regulatory reform. Voluntary restructuring indeed was the predominant pattern with boards during the closing decades of the twentieth century.[263] Given all of the attention the corporate scandals generated, boardroom vigilance and director scrutiny of executives likely would have intensified regardless of whether SOX was passed or not.[264] For instance, despite being unrelated to SOX settlements in 2005 of class actions arising from allegations of breaches of securities law involving Enron and WorldCom reputedly prompted "new defiance among directors."[265] While outside directors of public companies almost never pay damages out of their own pocket as a result of litigation, outside directors of these two scandal-ridden companies strikingly did so to the tune of $37.5 million.[266] Regardless, however, of the precise ways in which the corporate scandals of the early 2000s affected directors of public companies, boards likely were a more meaningful constraint on executives after the scandals than they were beforehand.

SHAREHOLDERS

Kahan and Rock, while acknowledging that "embattled" CEOs had been losing power to boards in the 2000s, suggested "perhaps more so, they are losing power to shareholders."[267] The extent to which chief executives were emasculated through the noughties is open to debate.[268] Nevertheless, Kahan and Rock likely were correct that with whatever diminution of influence occurred growth in the power of shareholders had a greater role to play than did changes affecting boards. This was primarily due to a novel source of shareholder influence.

---

260 Gretchen Morgenson, *The Reflections of a Truth Seeker*, NY TIMES, Nov. 12, 2017, B1.

261 Sarah C. Rice, David P. Weber & Biyu Wu, *Does SOX 404 Have Teeth? Consequences of the Failure to Report Existing Internal Control Weaknesses*, 90 ACCTING. REV. 1169, 1196 (2015).

262 Michael Rapoport, *Law's Big Weapon Sits Idle*, WALL ST. J., July 30, 2012, C3.

263 Chapter 3, notes 276–81, 303 and related discussion; Chapter 4, notes 252–53 and accompanying text; Chapter 5, notes 186–87 and related discussion.

264 ROGER LOWENSTEIN, ORIGINS OF THE CRASH: THE GREAT BUBBLE AND ITS UNDOING 207 (2004).

265 David Henry, Mike France & Louis Lavelle, *The Boss on the Sidelines*, BUS. WK., Apr. 25, 2005, 86; see also Geoffrey Colvin, *CEO Knockdown*, FORTUNE, Apr. 4, 2005, 19.

266 On the settlements and the rarity of out-of-pocket liability generally, see Bernard Black, Brian Cheffins & Michael Klausner, *Outside Director Liability*, 58 STAN. L. REV. 1055 (2006).

267 Kahan & Rock, *supra* note 224, at 989.

268 *Supra* note 227 and related discussion.

As the twentieth century drew a close, institutional shareholders were frequently hailed as "the new darlings of the corporate governance movement."[269] The level of activism in which they engaged failed to live up to the hype, but during the 1990s shareholder value was a top priority for public company executives focusing intently on corporate earnings.[270] In the 2000s, the fixation with earnings continued and "mainstream" institutional shareholders increased to some degree their involvement in corporate governance. The emergence of hedge funds as a corporate governance force was, however, the primary reason that shareholder pressure became a more potent check on public company executives.

The Earnings Fixation Continues

During the 1990s if a company failed to meet the investment community's earnings expectations its share price could fall dramatically in a way that would render potentially lucrative executive stock options worthless and put the CEO's job at risk.[271] Apprehension about hitting quarterly earnings targets played a role in the corporate scandals of the early 2000s. It was said of the Enron and WorldCom debacles a shared pattern was that "(w)hen these companies don't generate the anticipated (and needed) earnings, they pull out the books and start relabelling stuff."[272] SOX in turn zeroed in on accounting lapses with reforms intended to restore the integrity of financial reporting.[273]

After SOX's enactment, companies became less inclined to use accounting-related earnings management techniques to "make the numbers."[274] Nevertheless, as the *New York Times* presciently observed in 2002, "(o)bsessions die hard," predicting accurately that "the earnings fixation ... will withstand whatever reform measures eventually emerge from Washington."[275] A 2006 study intending to explain why executives might go "rogue" observed "(e)xecutives are both tempted and pressured to devote too much of their efforts to managing accounting and fretting over the next quarter's report."[276] A representative of a firm specializing in financial analytics was quoted in 2008 in the *New York Times* as saying "(t)he market abundantly rewards companies that put together long strings of good news, but severely penalizes those companies when they begin to disappoint," a point borne out by research his firm had done indicating that traders dumped unceremoniously stocks where companies that had beaten expectations for a number of quarters suddenly failed to do so.[277] This was a pattern the typical public company executive was not prepared to ignore.

---

[269] Jill E. Fisch, *Relationship Investing: Will It Happen? Will It Work?*, 55 Ohio State L.J. 1009, 1047 (1994).

[270] Chapter 4, notes 343–47 and accompanying text; Chapter 5, 192–99, 236–39, 242, 253, 255–56, 258-61 and related discussion.

[271] Chapter 5, notes 295–301 and accompanying text.

[272] Leo Hindery, It Takes a CEO: It's Time to Lead with Integrity 93 (2005).

[273] *Supra* notes 85–86, 88–89 and related discussion; Lowenstein, *supra* note 264, at 205; John C. Coffee, Gatekeepers: The Professions and Corporate Governance 16 (2006).

[274] June Y. Aono & Liming Guan, *The Impact of Sarbanes-Oxley Act on Cosmetic Earnings Management*, 20 Research Accting. Reg. 205, 206–07, 210–11 (2008).

[275] Harris Collingwood, *The Earnings Cult*, NY Times, June 9, 2002, Sunday Magazine, 68.

[276] Leonard R. Sayles & Cynthia J. Smith, The Rise of the Rogue Executive: How Good Companies Go Bad and How to Stop the Destruction 46 (2006).

[277] Norm Alster, *At the End of a Winning Streak, A Painful Reckoning*, NY Times, Apr. 20, 2008, Business, 9.

Clay Christensen, well known for his work on "disruption" by upstart firms,[278] remarked in 2008 together with two Harvard Business School colleagues on the "almost singular focus on earnings per share and EPS growth as *the* metric for corporate performance," and said for executives "others' perception of their success is tied up in those numbers, leading to a self-reinforcing cycle of obsession."[279]

Mainstream Institutional Shareholders

Did direct pressure from "mainstream" institutional shareholders in the 2000s add meaningfully to the earnings-driven constraints public company executives were operating under? With pension funds and mutual funds their theoretical importance was in little doubt. The proportion of shares owned by institutional shareholders, having increased rapidly from the 1950s through the 1980s before the trend stalled in the 1990s,[280] rose again in the 2000s, albeit modestly.[281] However, institutional holdings of stocks in the 1,000 largest public companies increased from 61 percent in 2000 to 73 percent in 2009.[282] Vanguard's John Bogle may have been dismissive of directors as a check on executives but he saw hope with institutional investors, citing in 2005 their potentially "awesome power" and referring to the largest institutional holders as "the King Kong of investment America."[283] Executive pay expert Ira Kay concurred in 2007, saying "(i)t is difficult to overestimate the power of US institutional investors."[284]

The potential for institutional investor activism was cited frequently during the closing decades of the twentieth century but institutional shareholders biased in favor of passivity flattered to deceive.[285] There were suggestions in the 2000s that the pattern had changed, at least to some degree. A 2004 study of boards indicated "the days of the passive . . . stockholder appear to be over."[286] Steve Bainbridge and Alan Murray observed respectively in 2007 that institutional investors were "feeling their oats" and "flexing their muscles."[287] Awareness that institutional shareholders disliked the theoretical possibility of board nominees running unopposed being elected without majority support ("plurality voting")

---

[278] Chapter 5, notes 384–85 and accompanying text.

[279] Clayton M. Christensen, Stephen P. Kaufman & Willy C. Shih, *Innovation Killers: How Financial Tools Destroy Your Capacity to Do New Things*, HARV. BUS. REV., Jan. 2008, 98, 104.

[280] Chapter 5, Figure 5.5, note 204 and related discussion.

[281] Kahan & Rock, *supra* note 224, at 996 (indicating, based on Federal Reserve data, that stock ownership of institutional investors rose from 44 percent to 50 percent between 2000 and 2002 and then changed little for the remainder of the decade); CONFERENCE BOARD, THE 2010 INSTITUTIONAL INVESTMENT REPORT—TRENDS IN ASSET ALLOCATION AND PORTFOLIO COMPOSITION 22 (2010) (reporting, again based on Federal Reserve data, that institutions owned 49 percent of public company shares in 1999 and 51 percent in 2009).

[282] CONFERENCE BOARD, *supra* note 281, at 27.

[283] *Supra* note 241 and related discussion; JOHN C. BOGLE, THE BATTLE FOR THE SOUL OF CAPITALISM xxi, 76 (2005).

[284] IRA T. KAY & STEVEN VAN PUTTEN, MYTHS AND REALITIES OF EXECUTIVE PAY 59 (2007).

[285] Chapter 5, notes 208, 221–24, 236–39, 242, 253, 255–56 and related discussion.

[286] PAUL B. BROUNTAS, BOARDROOM EXCELLENCE: A COMMONSENSE PERSPECTIVE ON CORPORATE GOVERNANCE 16 (2004).

[287] BAINBRIDGE, *supra* note 83, at 160; MURRAY, *supra* note 242, at xviii.

prompted numerous public companies to change their director election rules to require that an unopposed nominee obtain a majority of votes cast to be elected ("majority voting").[288] Union pension funds emerged as prolific filers of resolutions to be voted on by shareholders of public companies, with 506 being submitted between 2003 and 2005.[289] Mutual funds, which traditionally would only cast their votes in favor of management and would sell out if they lost faith in a company, became willing to contemplate seriously voting in a manner contrary to what management recommended while retaining a stake.[290] A 2003 SEC rule change requiring registered mutual funds to disclose publicly how they voted shares in the companies in which they held shares was credited with prompting the change of heart.[291]

While there was something of a departure from past trends in the 2000s, activism by mainstream institutional investors did not emerge as a substantial check on managerial discretion. Affirmative challenges to management rarely extended beyond the union pension funds filing their resolutions, joined on some occasions by state employee pension funds.[292] With the proposals that were filed, they rarely attracted majority support unless the dismantling of takeover defenses was involved.[293] Otherwise, activism with pension funds was restricted to low-visibility efforts such as participation in corporate governance organizations and periodically refraining from backing management-sponsored board nominees.[294] As for mutual funds, even though they became prepared to contemplate voting against management, they still rarely did so in practice.[295] Disclosure obligations regarding voting practices were often addressed by paying for recommendations from a shareholder advisory service such as Institutional Shareholder Services, voting accordingly, and then describing voting decisions by reference to what was recommended.[296]

---

[288] George W. Dent, *Corporate Governance: Still Broke, No Fix in Sight*, 31 J. CORP. L. 36, 73 (2005); Lori Verstegen Ryan, Ann K. Buchholtz & Robert W. Kolb, *New Directions in Corporate Governance and Finance: Implications for Business Ethics Research*, 20 BUS. ETHICS Q. 673, 675 (2010).

[289] Luc Renneboog & Peter G. Szilagyi, *The Role of Shareholder Proposals in Corporate Governance*, 17 J. CORP. FIN. 167, 170 (2011).

[290] James Cotter, Alan Palmiter & Randall Thomas, *ISS Recommendations and Mutual Fund Voting on Proxy Proposals*, 55 VILL. L. REV. 1, 21–22, 52, 55–56 (2010).

[291] *Disclosure of Proxy Voting Policies and Proxy Voting Records by Registered Management Investment Companies*, Securities Act Release No. 8188, Exchange Act Release No. 47,304, Investment Company Act Release No. 25,922 (Jan. 31, 2003); Geoffrey Colvin, *Undercutting CEO Power*, FORTUNE, Mar. 5, 2007, 42; *Hail, Shareholder*, ECONOMIST, June 2, 2007, 73.

[292] BAINBRIDGE, *supra* note 83, at 161; Ronald J. Gilson & Jeffrey N. Gordon, *The Agency Costs of Agency Capitalism: Activist Investors and the Revaluation of Governance Rights*, 113 COLUM. L. REV. 863, 887 (2013) (reporting that only 0.9 percent of shareholder proposals formally made between 2007 and 2009 were by mutual funds raising governance or performance issues).

[293] Renneboog & Szilagyi, *supra* note 289, at 172.

[294] Stephen J. Choi & Jill E. Fisch, *On Beyond CalPERS: Survey Evidence on the Developing Role of Public Pension Funds in Corporate Governance*, 61 VAND. L. REV. 315, 318 (2008).

[295] Joann S. Lublin & Phred Dvorak, *How Five New Players Aid Movement to Limit CEO Pay*, WALL ST. J., Mar. 13, 2007, A1.

[296] Mark Hodak, *The Growing Executive Compensation Advantage of Private Versus Public Companies*, J. APP. CORP. FIN., Winter 2014, at 20, 24. When recommendations by management and ISS conflicted, mutual funds typically gave greater weight to what ISS said. Other institutional shareholders usually did the opposite. See Cotter, Palmiter & Thomas, *supra* note 290, at 50–52.

The bias in favor of passivity prevailed even in circumstances where substantial destruction of shareholder value was occurring. With the corporate scandals of the early 2000s, institutional shareholders were criticized for being "sleeping giants" that were "shockingly indifferent to bad management" and for standing by when it should have been evident that boards were not up to scratch.[297] The California Public Employees Retirement System, widely known as the most activist of all institutional shareholders, even invested $250 million in an Enron special purpose entity, a mechanism Enron used with some regularity to conceal its true financial position.[298] As the financial crisis of 2008 mounted mainstream institutional shareholders generally prized stability and correspondingly refrained from rocking the boat even in companies poised to suffer major financial setbacks.[299]

Hedge Fund Activism

In 2005, a *New York Times* columnist noted that "(f)our years after Enron's bankruptcy shocked investors ... reforms have changed many things in corporate America" but said "one change that seemed likely—an increase in shareholder power—has not been realized."[300] This assessment was largely on the mark with mainstream institutional shareholders. However, corporate America was beginning to experience a novel and meaningful form of stockholder pressure in the form of activism by hedge funds.[301] In the 2000s activist hedge funds targeted with considerable regularity companies believed to be underperforming, "offensively" building up a sufficiently sizeable minority stake to capture management's attention and pressing hard for changes intended to increase shareholder value if management proved unresponsive.

In 2005, the *Wall Street Journal* proclaimed "Hedge Funds Are New Sheriffs of the Boardroom" and *Business Week* referred to an "onslaught from hedge funds."[302] The *New York Times* indicated in 2007 "a wide-ranging, merry band of hedge fund managers have risen to power by holding their poison pens to the throats of corporate executives and directors" with the results being "staggering: activists have put dozens of companies, large and small, into play and helped prop up the stock price of dozens of others."[303] Law professor Jonathan Macey said in a 2008 book on corporate governance that hedge funds were "the newest big thing in corporate governance" and a "great shining beacon of hope on an otherwise bleak landscape."[304] Prominent public companies targeted by the "merry band" in the 2000s included media conglomerate Time Warner, food and beverage producers H.J. Heinz

---

[297] Nofsinger & Kim, *supra* note 92, at 197; *Is Greed Good?*, Economist, May 18, 2002, Survey of International Finance, 23; *A Helluva Problem*, Economist, Sept. 21, 2002, 81.

[298] See Table 6.1; Kurt Eichenwald, Conspiracy of Fools: A True Story 145 (2005).

[299] Cheffins, *supra* note 188, at 47–49. See also *infra* note 321 and accompanying text.

[300] Floyd Norris, *Do Companies Need a Little Democracy?*, NY Times, Dec, 9, 2005, C1.

[301] The account of hedge fund activism offered here is derived primarily from Brian R. Cheffins & John Armour, *The Past, Present, and Future of Shareholder Activism by Hedge Funds*, 37 J. Corp. L. 51 (2011). That article provides citations for various propositions advanced here unsupported by footnote references.

[302] Alan Murray, *Hedge Funds Are New Sheriffs of the Boardroom*, Wall St. J., Dec, 14, 2005, A2; *Take Your Best Shot, Punk*, BusinessWeek, Nov. 7, 2005, 118.

[303] Andrew Ross Sorkin, *Will the Credit Crisis End the Activists' Run?*, NY Times, Aug. 26, 2007, B7.

[304] Macey, *supra* note 235, at 241, 272.

Company and Kraft, restaurant groups McDonald's and Wendy's, and retailers Circuit City, Home Depot, and Target.[305]

With mainstream institutional investors during the 2000s, as in earlier decades, a key obstacle to activism was that they emphasized diversification as an investment philosophy. Diversification is a prudent risk mitigation strategy. However, with respect to activism, since improved returns in a particular company are only likely to have a marginal impact on a highly diversified investment portfolio, and since challenging management is time-consuming, costly, and not always successful, the sums simply do not add up. The business model of activist hedge funds that gained prominence in the 2000s was considerably different, oriented around owning shares in a small cohort of carefully screened public companies with the stakes being sufficiently large to result in meaningful gains in the event of strong returns.

There is a substantial overlap in investment philosophies between activist hedge funds and "value investors" who seek through diligent analysis of corporate fundamentals to purchase shares trading at a bargain price, the proverbial dollar for 50 cents.[306] The subset of hedge funds that engage in "offensive" shareholder activism typically relies on this "value approach" to identify suitably priced companies as potential targets. As and when an activist hedge fund's analysis is borne out by a market correction rather than due to any prompting by the hedge fund this will be relatively "easy money" for the hedge fund. The situation will be much the same if the board of a targeted company, aware of an activist hedge fund on its share register, makes changes purely on its own initiative that serve to increase shareholder returns.

Activist hedge funds that buy sizeable stakes in target companies where shareholder returns improve without any form of intervention are essentially engaging in the successful "stock picking" to which value investors aspire. The readiness to take a hands-on role to shake things up is the crucial additional dimension of offensive shareholder activism executed by hedge funds. Instead of simply waiting for the market to self-correct in the manner a typical value investor would, activist hedge funds are prepared to take the initiative and accelerate matters by pressing for changes to boost shareholder returns. Activist hedge funds periodically engage in costly, aggressive tactics such as launching a proxy contest to secure board representation or proposing to make a tender offer to buy a controlling stake. Ratcheting up the pressure on occasion using such strategies signals to potential future targets a willingness to invest heavily in pursuing an activist campaign should this be required to achieve desired results.

Hedge funds were by no means the first "offensive" shareholder activists. As far back as the opening decades of the twentieth century there were instances that generated press coverage where insurgent investors bought a sizeable stake and sought board seats and sometimes board control to improve management.[307] Nevertheless, it was only in the 1980s that investment funds,

---

[305] Kahan & Rock, *supra* note 224, at 998–99.

[306] Bruce C.N. Greenwald, Judd Kahn, Paul D. Sonkin & Michael van Biema, Value Investing: From Graham to Buffett and Beyond xv (2004).

[307] John H. Armour & Brian R. Cheffins, *Origins of "Offensive" Shareholder Activism in the United States*, *in* Origins of Shareholder Advocacy 253, 255–58 (Jonathan G.S. Koppell ed., 2011).

as opposed to individuals or corporations, began to adopt the tactics activist hedge funds would subsequently popularize. Even hedge funds themselves were slow starters. When a few began to take an activist stance in the banking sector in the 1990s, *US Banker* labeled them as "little-known investment operations."[308]

The tide turned in the early 2000s. In 2001, the *Wall Street Journal* drew attention to the fact "dissatisfied shareholders are aggressively pushing companies to find new ways to unlock shareholder value" and said that "(a)mong the growing ranks of activists are . . . even hedge-fund managers, who historically have been relatively passive."[309] *Business Week* featured hedge funds Highfields Capital Management and Chapman Capital LLC in a 2002 article on "value investors" minded to challenge existing management for the sake of value creation, saying "(t)heir style of investing is taking off like a Fourth of July bottle rocket."[310] *Institutional Investor* observed similarly in 2003 "(n)o-nonsense, seize-the-board, put-the-company-in-play, do-whatever-it-takes-to-increase-the-stock-price corporate activism is coming back into style—and hedge funds are at the cutting-and-slashing edge."[311]

The stock market swoon at the beginning of the 2000s set the scene nicely for activist hedge funds because shares in potential targets were cheap. Bargain pricing was, however, insufficient in isolation for hedge fund activism to thrive. Since hedge fund activists only acquire minority stakes in companies they target, they know management can ignore them unless other shareholders are sympathetic. As the 2000s began, activist hedge funds sought to rally support from major institutional shareholders. Fund managers acting on behalf of these institutional investors proved in turn to be receptive to the dissident campaigns in a way they had not been previously. *Institutional Investor* said in 2003 of the change of heart "(a) gruelling, two-year bear market is probably the biggest factor: What companies could get away with when most stocks were rising is no longer acceptable when they are plunging."[312]

Crucially, when share prices swung upward in the mid-2000s (Figure 6.1) mainstream institutional investors remained responsive to the entreaties of hedge fund activists rather than reverting to old manager-deferent habits. The *New York Times* spelled out the implications in 2006, saying "the greatest shift in the influence that activist shareholders have gained is the role once-conservative institutional investors—big money managers like the mutual fund giant Fidelity—have begun to take."[313] This did not mean leading money managers were themselves taking the activism initiative. They still preferred to retain the option to cut their losses by selling out promptly and wanted to avoid the adverse publicity that confronting public company executives could generate. Still, to a greater extent than had been the case previously, key institutional investors were prepared to back activists prepared to do the dirty work, thus lending valuable credibility to campaigns to challenge managers of target companies.

A mid-2000s combination of corporate prosperity and financial conservatism also helped to foster hedge fund activism. Corporate profits rose with the economy rebounding but executives, still shell-shocked by memories of the bear market and scandals of the early

---

308 Andrew E. Serwer, *Mr. Price Is on the Line*, FORTUNE, Dec, 9, 1996, 70.

309 Robin Sidel, *More Investors Turn Activist in Tough Times*, WALL ST. J., Apr. 13, 2001, C1.

310 *The Ultimate Value Investors*, BUS. WK., June 10, 2002, 124.

311 *Proxy Warriors*, INSTIT. INVESTOR, Jan. 2003, 52.

312 *Id.* See also James Surowiecki, *Gadfly Inc.*, NEW YORKER, Sept. 10, 2001, 42.

313 Andrew Ross Sorkin, *To Battle, Armed with Shares*, NY TIMES, Jan. 4, 2006, C1.

2000s, kept capital expenditures and wage increases very much in check. As a result, by 2006 the corporations comprising the S&P 500 had accumulated between them \$2.7 trillion in cash, up from \$1.6 trillion in 2001 and \$0.88 trillion in 1996.[314] With the cash earning paltry returns in the corporate treasury, activist hedge funds pressed public company executives to put the funds to work in a shareholder-friendly manner.

A favorable market for corporate borrowing also strengthened the hand of hedge funds. Hedge fund activists commonly agitated for a target company to unlock shareholder value by making a big cash payout, by disposing of underperforming divisions, or by putting itself up for sale. Debt was plentiful and cheap during the mid-2000s.[315] It correspondingly was relatively painless for companies pressured by hedge funds to borrow to distribute cash to shareholders or to find buyers for subsidiary operations. Even putting an entire company up for sale could be fairly straightforward, particularly with private equity firms carrying out buyouts at a frantic pace.[316]

The influence of hedge fund activism on managerial thinking extended beyond companies explicitly targeted. As Macey said in his 2008 book, "the key role being played by hedge funds ... in corporate governance affects *all* companies in a very profound way. Even companies that want to *avoid* being the target of an activist fund can only do this by improving corporate governance extensively so that there are no longer any arbitrage possibilities that allow fund managers to take a position in the target company and then start agitating for reform."[317] Share buy-backs by public companies illustrate the impact hedge funds were having. Share repurchases increased dramatically in the mid-2000s (Figure 6.6). Part of the reason for the surge likely was that public company executives

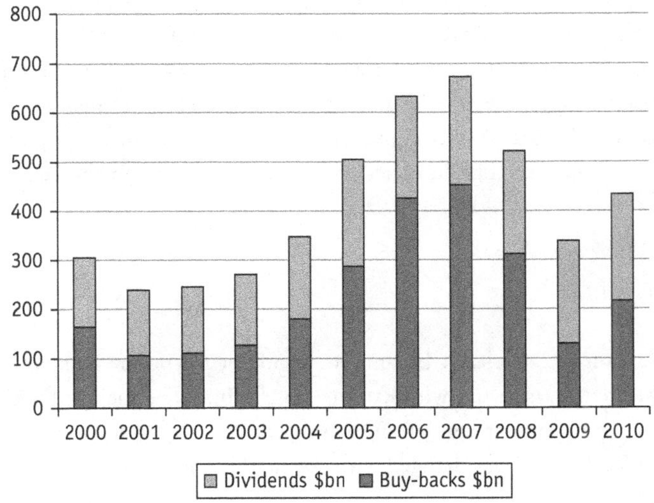

FIGURE 6.6 Cash Distributions by Public Companies, 2000–2010 (constant 2012 dollars).
Source: Eric Floyd, Nan Li & Douglas J. Skinner, *Payout Policy through the Financial Crisis: The Growth of Repurchases and the Resilience of Dividends*, 118 J. FIN. ECON. 299, 305 (2015).

[314] Robert C. Pozen, *If Private Equity Sized Up Your Business*, HARV. BUS. REV., Nov. 2007, 78, 80.

[315] *Supra* note 141 and related discussion.

[316] *Supra* notes 136 to 140 and accompanying text.

[317] MACEY, *supra* note 235, at 250 (emphasis in original).

were returning cash to shareholders to forestall preemptively an unwelcome hedge fund intervention.[318]

As was the case with private equity, the financial crisis was a major challenge for activist hedge funds. The savage bear market meant buying up shares was cheaper. On the other hand, as a *Financial Times* columnist observed during the 2007 "credit crunch," "(a)ctivist investors may find they have a greater choice of legitimate targets, but fewer tools to work with."[319] With the tightening of debt markets it suddenly became "harder to persuade boards to gear up balance sheets with debt or push companies into the arms of prospective bidders."[320]

In the midst of the 2008 financial crisis hedge fund activists also could not take for granted shareholder backing for the challenges they launched. Mainstream institutional investors who otherwise may have been receptive to activist overtures tended, with markets gripped by uncertainty, to back management due to fears disrupting the status quo would make matters worse. As an investor familiar with an unsuccessful 2009 proxy battle launched by hedge fund Pershing Square against discount retailer Target said, "(c)onservatism is a big problem. Big long-only investors [i.e., major mutual funds and pension funds] don't want to know about unlocking value right now. They're still just concentrated on preserving it."[321]

The rapidly declining stock prices associated with the financial crisis created problems in another way for hedge fund activists. With the shares of companies which activist hedge funds already owned falling in value, nervous investors sought redemptions with some regularity. Funds available for activism campaigns could in turn decline markedly. For instance, Cerberus Capital received financial crisis-induced redemption requests for $5.5 billion with its $7.7 billion activist hedge fund portfolio. The founder of activist firm Bulldog Investments said in 2009, "(i)t's like being in the store where everything is 80% off but you have just $2 in your pocket."[322]

While the financial crisis clearly dealt a blow to hedge fund activism the market turmoil induced a reasonably orderly retreat rather than an outright rout. The number of hedge fund interventions did drop markedly in 2009 but hedge funds continued to target publicly traded companies with reasonable regularity.[323] Hence, for executives in public companies who thought of reduced hedge fund activism as a silver lining in the larger cloud of the financial crisis, the respite was merely partial.

External Constraints

While internal constraints clearly became more potent for public company executives in the 2000s, the trend was mixed with external constraints. The market for corporate control, unions, and government regulation each receded in importance as constraints in the 1990s. During the 2000s little changed with the market for corporate control and unions.

[318] John Authers, *Investors Show Their Faith Lies with Dividend Returns*, FIN. TIMES, Dec, 10, 2005, 33; William W. Bratton & Michael W. Wachter, *The Case against Shareholder Empowerment*, 158 U. PA. L. REV. 653, 686 (2010).

[319] Peter Thai Larsen, *Life after the Golden Age*, FIN. TIMES, Sept. 10, 2007, FT fm, 9.

[320] Kate Burgess, *Activists Flex Muscles as Markets Falter*, FIN. TIMES, Jan. 8, 2008, 19.

[321] Sam Jones, *Activist Funds Find Going Tough*, FIN. TIMES, Aug. 31, 2009, 19.

[322] Jay Akasie, *Missing in Action*, AR (ABSOLUTE RETURN + ALPHA), May 15, 2009.

[323] Cheffins & Armour, *supra* note 301, at 95–96.

Government regulation, however, became a more potent limitation for public company executives. Pressure from competitors also grew in importance as a check on management. There was evidence emerging, though, that suggested at least some firms were accumulating market power sufficient to act as a partial buffer against challenges by rivals.

THE MARKET FOR CORPORATE CONTROL

While the possibility of being displaced by way of a hostile takeover was a robust external constraint on management in the 1980s there was something of "a governance vacuum" when the market for corporate control receded considerably in importance in the 1990s.[324] During the 2000s, the hostile takeover remained on the corporate governance radar. Nevertheless, as was the case in the 1990s, the market for corporate control was a constraint of secondary importance for public company executives.

Hectic M&A activity that characterized much of the 1990s came to "a screeching halt" in 2001 due to falling share prices and economic uncertainty.[325] The situation changed little through 2003.[326] The tide then turned, with the dealmaking environment being "pretty ripe" by 2005.[327] At the beginning of 2007 the *New York Times* was asking rhetorically "(f)or deal makers, does it get any better than this?"[328] Then with the 2007 credit crunch and the 2008 financial crisis "mergers plunged along with the markets as executives grappled with trying to understand how best to survive."[329]

The explosion of private-equity buyouts helped to fuel the mid-2000s M&A boom, with financial buyers accounting for roughly one-third of total acquisition volume as merger activity peaked.[330] If private equity firms had regularly followed the approach taken by Kohlberg, Kravis & Roberts with the iconic 1989 RJR Nabisco leveraged buyout and launched bids for control against the wishes of management,[331] the hostile takeover perhaps would have returned to 1980s-style prominence in the 2000s. This did not happen. A 2002 *Business Week* article proclaiming "(t)he buyout kings are back" noted "(t)his time around, LBO shops are invited guests" and quoted a cofounder of the Carlyle Group as saying "(h)ostile takeovers are a thing of the past."[332] Private equity firms retained their antipathy toward hostile bids even as buyout activity became increasingly frenzied before the 2007 credit crunch short-circuited public-to-private transactions.[333]

---

[324] Chapter 5, notes 149–54 and related discussion.

[325] Lina Saigol, *A Giddy Ride on the M&A Carousel*, FIN. TIMES, Dec, 28, 2009, 18. See also Chapter 5, note 146 and accompanying text; Adrian Michaels & Peter Thal Larsen, *Making M&A Child's Play*, FIN. TIMES, Jan. 18, 2001, 14.

[326] Saigol, *supra* note 325.

[327] Roben Farzad, *Sweet Times for Dealmakers*, BUS. WK., Dec, 26, 2005, 114.

[328] Heather Timmons, *The Year That Made Deal Makers Giddy*, NY TIMES, Jan. 5, 2007, C6.

[329] Andrew Ross Sorkin, *In Flurry of Big Merger Deals, Signs of Restored Confidence*, NY TIMES, Sept. 29, 2009, A1.

[330] Dana Cimilluca, *Private Equity Fuels Record Merger Run*, WALL ST. J., July 2, 2007, C8; HARRY CENDROWSKI, LOUIS W. PETRO, JAMES P. MARTIN & ADAM A. WADECKI, PRIVATE EQUITY: HISTORY, GOVERNANCE, AND OPERATIONS 65 (2nd ed., 2012).

[331] Chapter 4, note 138 and related discussion.

[332] Emily Thornton, *Embracing Barbarians at the Gate*, BUS. WK., Nov. 18, 2002, 120.

[333] Cheffins & Armour, *supra* note 131, 12; Miriam Gottfried & Dawn Lim, *Private-Equity Firm Breaks from the Pack*, WALL ST. J., Dec, 16, 2017, B1 (reporting there had only been nine hostile public-to-private buyouts since 1995, all involving targets valued at less than $2 billion).

Even with private equity buyers refraining from going hostile, public company executives could not dismiss outright the possibility of an unwelcome takeover bid. Many public companies ended up the 2000s theoretically less well protected against a hostile offer than they had been in the late 1980s and 1990s.[334] During the 2000s, companies dismantled at a rapid clip both poison pills and "staggered" boards, which postponed for a bidder the possibility of securing full board control because only a prescribed proportion of directors (typically one-third) would be standing for election annually. As of 2000, 60 percent of S&P 500 companies had a poison pill in place and the same proportion had a staggered board.[335] These figures fell to 17 percent and 32 percent respectively by 2009.[336]

There also was some high profile hostile takeover activity in the 2000s. In 2004, software powerhouse Oracle acquired rival PeopleSoft for $10.3 billion after a bitter takeover fight that PeopleSoft's chief executive likened to buying a beloved pet dog and then shooting the dog.[337] The same year Disney rejected a $54 billion hostile takeover bid from cable giant Comcast, and in 2008 Yahoo! spurned a $47.5 billion takeover offer from Microsoft.[338] Still, while a hostile takeover offer remained a theoretical possibility during the 2000s, the number of hostile bids launched with public companies as targets rarely broke double figures annually.[339] Some contended hostile tender offers "almost disappeared" and were "virtually obsolete."[340] This may well overstate matters, but certainly among constraints executives of public companies needed to bear in mind the market for corporate control would not have been at the top of the list in the 2000s in the way it would have been in the 1980s.

UNIONS

With the 2000s being a decade from hell for public companies, adverse consequences for employees of large firms inexorably followed. When the economy slowed down in 2001 and 2002, corporations responded with job cuts greater than any year during the 1990s, a decade when downsizing was highly publicized.[341] In some companies there was "almost a layoff panic."[342] Press coverage of early 2000s downsizing was modest in comparison with the 1990s,

---

[334] Davidoff, *supra* note 138, at 188.

[335] Ram Charan, Denis Carey & Michael Useem, Boards That Lead: When to Take Charge, When to Partner, and When to Stay Out of the Way 245 (2013).

[336] *Id.*

[337] Randall Stross, *The New Silicon Valley: A Dog-Eat-Dog World*, NY Times, Sept. 26, 2004, Business, 5; Steve Lohr & Laurie J. Flynn, *Oracle to Acquire PeopleSoft for $10.3 Billion, Ending Bitter Fight*, NY Times, Dec. 14, 2004, C1.

[338] Davidoff, *supra* note 138, at 190–96; James B. Stewart, Disney War: The Battle for the Magic Kingdom 489–91 (2006).

[339] William W. Bratton, *Private Equity's Three Lessons for Agency Theory*, 3 Brook. J. Corp. Fin. & Com. L. 1, 10 (2008) (chart, total number of hostile takeover offers relative to total public company acquisitions, 1974–2007); Vyacheslav Fos, *The Disciplinary Effects of Proxy Contests*, 63 Mgmt. Sci. 655, 658 (2017) (chart, with average annual number of hostile tender offers for 1991–2001 and 2002–2012).

[340] Macey, *supra* note 235, at 10; Bratton, *supra* note 339, 9.

[341] Chapter 5, notes 59–61 and accompanying text; William J. Baumol, Alan S. Blinder & Edward N. Wolff, Downsizing in America: Reality, Causes, and Consequences 32–33 (2003).

[342] Daniel McGinn & Keith Naughton, *How Safe Is Your Job?*, Newsweek, Feb. 5, 2001, 36.

however.[343] One explanation may have been that companies were managing downsizing better, at least in part to preserve the morale of the workers left behind.[344]

The financial crisis brought fresh employee pain. Twenty-five corporate "layoff kings" announced between them job cuts of 700,000 staff between late 2007 and mid-2010.[345] *Newsweek* reported in 2009 "many offices feel like an episode of 'The Apprentice,' [a reality television show hosted by future president Donald Trump] as employees jockey for position, form alliances, backstab and constantly recalculate the odds they'll survive the next round of cuts."[346] Even those continuing to work faced headwinds, as the share of US national income going to workers as wages fell from 65 percent at the start of the 2000s to 60 percent by the end.[347]

Given the challenges employees were facing in the 2000s, it might have seemed the timing was propitious for unions to reverse the decline they suffered as the twentieth century drew to a close.[348] The president of the AFL-CIO union federation indeed told the *New York Times* in 2002 that he was seeing "a pendulum swing in favor of collective protections," citing an employee who told him "(w)e trusted our employer, and liked our job, but when they threw us on the street, we lost all trust," and arguing that many workers were "saying to themselves, 'The same thing can happen to me.' "[349] This optimistic conjecture was not entirely fanciful. A 2005 poll indicated 53 percent of nonunion workers would vote for a union if they got the chance, up from 30 percent in 1984 and 39 percent in 1994.[350]

In practice, unions continued to lose ground. Union density, which had already fallen markedly in the second half of the twentieth century, declined slightly from 13 percent to 12 percent during the 2000s, with the equivalent figures for private sector workers being 9 percent and 7 percent.[351] A 2006 text on the corporation indicated that even when a workforce was unionized, "(t)oday unions are not a threat to corporations provided management treats workers with fairness and respect."[352] A work stoppage, for instance, was highly unlikely, with the number of large strikes averaging merely 20 a year in the 2000s compared with nearly 290 annually in the 1970s.[353] Hence, only in exceptional situations were unions a meaningful constraint for public company executives in the 2000s.

---

343 BAUMOL, BLINDER & WOLFF, *supra* note 341, at 36.

344 *The Jobs Challenge*, ECONOMIST, July 14, 2001, 70.

345 Douglas McIntyre, *The Layoff Kings: The 25 Companies Responsible for 700,000 Lost Jobs*, AOL.COM, Aug. 18, 2010, available at https://www.aol.com/2010/08/18/the-layoff-kings-the-25-companies-responsible-for-700-000-lost/ (accessed Mar. 4, 2018).

346 Daniel McGinn, *Managing Along the Cutting Edge*, NEWSWEEK, Feb. 9, 2009, 46.

347 Robin Harding, *$740bn Pay Gap Threat to US Recovery*, FIN. TIMES, Dec, 15, 2011, 1, 12.

348 On the decline, see Chapter 5, notes 308, 315–23 and accompanying text.

349 Steven Greenhouse, *Update on Capitalism: What Do You Mean "Us", Boss?*, NY TIMES, Sept. 1, 2002, C3.

350 DOUGLAS M. EICHAR, THE RISE AND FALL OF CORPORATE SOCIAL RESPONSIBILITY 332 (2015).

351 GERALD MAYER, UNION MEMBERSHIP TRENDS IN THE UNITED STATES 22 (2004) (calculated using non-agricultural workers as the denominator); Unionstats.com, *Union Membership and Coverage Database from the CPS*, available at http://unionstats.gsu.edu/ (accessed Apr. 6, 2018).

352 WESLEY B. TRUITT, THE CORPORATION 236 (2006).

353 Chapter 5, note 319 and related discussion; Bureau of Labor Statistics, *Work Stoppages Involving 1,000 or More Workers, 1947-2017*, available at https://www.bls.gov/news.release/wkstp.t01.htm (accessed Apr. 6, 2018).

REGULATION

Deregulation commenced in the late 1970s, gained momentum in the 1980s and remained a meaningful trend in the 1990s when the election of Democrat Bill Clinton as president might have been expected to lead to a reversal.[354] As a result, as the twentieth century drew to a close government regulation tended to be a less potent constraint for public company executives than it had been during the managerial capitalism era. As the 2000s got underway, it appeared the trend would continue. George W. Bush, in his successful 2000 presidential election campaign, sought to woo business community support by promising to scale back federal interference.[355] In fact, the deregulatory tide would ebb in the 2000s, leading the *New York Times* in 2005 to harken back to a 1996 proclamation by Bill Clinton on the perilous state of big government and declare "(t)he era of big government being over is over."[356] The era of regulation declining as a constraint on public company executives correspondingly ended in the 2000s.

Events partially dictated the step back from deregulation. The 9/11 terrorist attacks prompted Congress to create the Transportation Security Administration, the first big new federal bureaucracy set up in more than a quarter century.[357] Enron, WorldCom, and other significant corporate scandals provided the catalyst for the new regulations SOX introduced.[358] The financial crisis prompted before the 2000s concluded federal bailouts and rescues of various major corporations.[359]

The retreat from deregulation was not entirely event-driven, however. Homeland security activities launched after 9/11 explain to a significant extent why federal regulatory expenditures and staffing levels were significantly higher in 2009 than in 2000.[360] However, even with economic regulatory agencies expenditures grew 45 percent in real terms in the 2000s and staffing levels increased by 12 percent.[361] This growth in governmental activity chimed with public attitudes. According to a 2008 poll Americans wanted government to "do more to solve problems" by a 53-to-42 percent margin whereas a dozen years previously respondents opposed additional government intervention by a 2-to-1 margin.[362]

Under the Bush administration antitrust was at least a partial departure from the step back from deregulation. Price-fixing and similar cartelization activity was subject to close scrutiny but with mergers the perception was that antitrust authorities took a more relaxed stance than they had in the 1990s.[363] The reputation for laxity may not have been deserved. Available data suggest

---

[354] Chapter 5, notes 328–35 and related discussion.

[355] Jeanne Cummings, Jacob M. Schlesinger & Michael Schroeder, *Bush Crackdown on Business Fraud Signals New Era*, WALL ST. J., July 10, 2002, A1.

[356] Chapter 5, note 335 and accompanying text; Sheryl Gay Stolberg, *The Revolution That Wasn't*, NY TIMES, Feb. 12, 2005, D1.

[357] MURRAY, *supra* note 242, 31.

[358] *Supra* notes 56–60 and accompanying text.

[359] *Supra* notes 198–200, 207–08 and related discussion.

[360] VERONIQUE DE RUGY & MELINDA WARREN, REGULATORY AGENCY SPENDING REACHES NEW HEIGHT: AN ANALYSIS OF THE US BUDGET FOR FISCAL YEARS 2008 AND 2009 3, 18 (2008).

[361] *Id.* at 6, 9.

[362] Bob Davis, Damian Paletta & Rebecca Smith, *Unraveling Reagan*, WALL ST. J., July 25, 2008, A1.

[363] Steve Labaton, *New View of Antitrust Law: See No Evil, Hear No Evil*, NY TIMES, May 5, 2006, C5; *The Beat Goes On*, ECONOMIST, May 12, 2007, 81.

that merger enforcement activity under the Clinton and Bush administrations did not differ markedly.[364] Nevertheless, with M&A, contrary to the general trend with regulation, public company executives may well have perceived that state intervention was a less potent constraint in the 2000s than it had been in the 1990s.

COMPETITORS

While there was awareness throughout the second half of the twentieth century that rivals vying for customers and clients could be a potent check on management, it was during the 1990s that competitive pressure flourished particularly as a constraint on public company executives.[365] There was ample anecdotal evidence suggesting competitors remained a headache for public company management in the 2000s. Robert Reich even suggested that "supercapitalism" had taken hold in the United States, characterized by "ever more intensifying competition among businessmen."[366] There were also some indications, however, that the tide could be turning in favor of accumulation of market power.

Various trends suggested that in the 2000s US public companies were operating in a dynamic competitive environment that put management under considerable pressure. The first was the foreign angle. As the 1990s proceeded, apprehension about the economic standing of the United States in the world receded as American companies thrived.[367] The pattern was the opposite in the 2000s, with concerns growing that the competitiveness problems many Americans found vexing in the late 1970s and the 1980s were in fact not "as obsolete as leg warmers and Jazzercise."[368] In particular, China's strength was drawing attention in a manner akin to the Japanese challenge in the 1980s.[369] For instance, a 2006 study of public company executives warned "the current global economy has little patience for companies that can't 'hack it'" and that "(t)he Asian tigers are back, fiercer than before, now that China is among them."[370]

Second, there were information technology advances, such as the continued growth of the internet, which bolstered challengers. *Forbes* observed in 2006 "(w)e are going through a transition that will interest historians centuries from now," citing "the digital revolution and the information-based economy it spawns" and saying of this trend "(b)y freeing companies from physical assets, it has made them both more flexible and more vulnerable to competitors."[371] A 2011 study of the evolution of management theory echoed the same sentiment,

---

[364] Ronan P. Harty, Howard A. Shelanski & Jesse Solomon, *Merger Enforcement across Political Administrations in the United States*, CONCURRENCES, issue #2, 1, 8 (2012), available at https://www.davispolk.com/publications/merger-enforcement-across-political-administrations-united-states/ (accessed May 7, 2018); Ning Gao, Ni Peng & Norman Strong, *What Determines Horizontal Merger Antitrust Case Selection*, 46 J. CORP. FIN. 51, 57 (2017) (table providing annual data indicating that of 164 major mergers in the 1990s there were challenges on 14 occasions whereas 17 of 171 such mergers in the 2000s were challenged).

[365] Chapter 2, notes 351–53 and accompanying text; Chapter 5, notes 364–82 and accompanying text.

[366] ROBERT REICH, SUPERCAPITALISM: THE BATTLE FOR DEMOCRACY IN AN AGE OF BIG BUSINESS x (2007).

[367] Chapter 5, notes 405–08 and related discussion.

[368] Gary P. Pisano & Wily C. Shih, *Restoring American Competitiveness*, HARV. BUS. REV., July–Aug. 2009, 114, 116.

[369] Keith Bradsher, *Like Japan in the 1980s, China Poses Big Economic Challenge*, NY TIMES, Mar. 2, 2004, A1.

[370] SAYLES & SMITH, *supra* note 276, 27, 46.

[371] Geoffrey Colvin, *Managing in Chaos*, FORTUNE, Oct. 2, 2006, 72.

indicating "(t)he internet has made it easier for Davids to take on Goliaths." [372] This, in turn, had "forced established Goliaths to improve their game."[373]

Third, there was improved access to finance. Challengers seeking to make inroads will usually need capital to make their move, and availability was generally good in the 2000s. Venture capital was an exception due to a hangover after the exuberant dot.com era. According to *Fortune*, "(w)hen the bubble burst in 2000, the industry practically collapsed."[374] There was residual psychic shock, with concerns about future bubbles haunting many venture capital practitioners and investors for a number of years after.[375] Funding of start-ups suffered accordingly, particularly in the technology sector.[376] Nevertheless, venture capital backing did help to launch YouTube, a video-sharing website that would achieve great popularity after Google bought the company in 2006 for $1.6 billion, and Facebook, the social networking platform that would soon dominate that market.[377]

While venture capital was not as promising a source of finance as was the case in the frantic late 1990s, for much of the 2000s borrowing was never easier. Soon after the noughties began a sluggish economy and the 9/11 terrorist attacks knocked the wind out of debt markets.[378] For much of remainder of the decade, however, "hypercompetition in the capital markets" meant there was easy credit available generally to companies seeking to borrow.[379] The amount of commercial paper companies issued nearly doubled between 2000 and 2007.[380] With junk bonds, "(t)he high-yield bond market" was "all but begging borrowers to take on low-cost debt" due to historically low spreads between interest rates for risky debt and ultra-safe Treasury bills.[381] A formerly obscure market in leveraged loans—speculative-grade loans secured by company assets offering floating interest rates rather than the fixed interest rates associated with junk bonds—flourished.[382] A *Wall Street Journal* columnist summed up the situation in June 2007, saying "(n)o exaggeration is required to pronounce unequivocally that money is available today in quantities, at prices and on terms never before seen in the 100-plus years since US financial markets reached full flower."[383]

As the 2000s came to an end, a debt market chill set in.[384] Conditions were particularly harrowing as the financial crisis peaked in the fall of 2008. In mid-September the market for commercial paper collapsed as banks hoarded cash and the issuance of corporate bonds,

---

[372] Adrian Wooldridge, Masters of Management 148 (2011).

[373] *Id.*

[374] Adam Lashinsky, Elias Rodriquez & Patricia Neering, *Google's Banker*, Fortune, May 3, 2005, 105.

[375] Gary Rivlin, *In Silicon Valley, the Crash Seems Like Just Yesterday*, NY Times, June 3, 2007, C5.

[376] *Id.*

[377] *Id.*; Miguel Helft, *A Kink in Venture Capital's Gold Chain*, NY Times, Oct. 7, 2006, C1; *infra* note 396 and related discussion.

[378] Carey & Morris, *supra* note 129, 167; *A Hazardous Journey*, Economist, Jan. 27, 2001, Corporate Finance Survey, 17; Anna Bernask, *Will the Economy Get Well Soon?*, Fortune, Dec, 24, 2001, 89.

[379] William C. Taylor & Polly LaBerre, Mavericks at Work: Why the Most Original Minds in Business Win 143 (2007).

[380] Financial Crisis Inquiry Commission, *supra* note 162, at 251 (Fig. 13.1).

[381] Michael Santoli, *LBOs Are Back*, Barron's, Mar. 14, 2005, 21.

[382] David Henry, *Why Junk Bonds Are Getting Junked*, Bus. Wk., Feb. 13, 2006, 72.

[383] Steven Rattner, *The Coming Credit Meltdown*, Wall St. J., June 18, 2007, A17.

[384] Kirk Shinkle, *A New Era for Stocks*, US News & World Report, July 1, 2009, 66.

even of investment grade, virtually ceased.[385] Many companies could not borrow at any price and even corporate icon General Electric was crimped for cash.[386] The sharp reversal in debt markets would have impinged considerably on corporate insurgents seeking to displace market leaders. Nevertheless, for most of the 2000s there was a congenial financial setting for challenging incumbents.

With conditions generally being propitious for rivals to vie with market leaders during the 2000s, there was a general consensus that for companies and their executives the pace of change had never been greater.[387] *Fortune* told readers in 2006 that the business world was "truly rocking."[388] There reputedly were "few protected markets, few natural or unnatural monopolies."[389] The fact that markets could "rise and fall with breathtaking speed" meant "strengths today . . . often provide nothing but false comfort."[390] Executives, in turn, were under pressure to exercise the leadership skills needed to respond effectively "to an extraordinary lack of certainty."[391]

There was data that substantiated the received wisdom that pressure from rivals was robust. While in 1985 Standard & Poor's categorized 35 percent of companies in its iconic S&P 500 index as "high risk" based on the ability to achieve long-term stable earnings growth and 41 percent as "low risk," by 2006 the ratio was 71 percent to 13 percent.[392] Other empirical evidence suggested, however, that already dominant firms might be more than holding their own. In a substantial majority of industries the revenue share enjoyed by the 50 largest firms increased between 1997 and 2012.[393] Over the same period, in two-thirds of 900 economic sub-sectors the market share of the largest four firms grew, with the average weighted by total revenues increasing from 26 percent to 32 percent.[394] The turnover of S&P 500 companies also decreased in the 2000s as compared with the 1980s and 1990s.[395] Perhaps despite the rhetoric regarding the pace of change dominant incumbents were enjoying a somewhat quieter life than their late twentieth century peers.

---

[385] *The Doctor's Bill*, ECONOMIST, Sept. 27, 2008, 92.

[386] Chapter 1, note 320 and accompanying text; LOWENSTEIN, *supra* note 170, at 223, 256.

[387] Rune Todnem By, *Organisational Change Management: A Critical Review*, 5 J. CHANGE MGMT. 369, 378 (2005).

[388] Colvin, *supra* note 371. For other similar proclamations, see TIMOTHY R. CLARK, EPIC CHANGE: HOW TO LEAD CHANGE IN THE GLOBAL AGE 17–18 (2008).

[389] SAYLES & SMITH, *supra* note 276, 27.

[390] CLARK, *supra* note 388, 12.

[391] *Id.* at 19.

[392] Colvin, *supra* note 371.

[393] *Benefits of Competition and Indicators of Market Power*, COUNCIL OF ECONOMIC ADVISERS ISSUE BRIEF, Spring 2016, at 4. See, though, Carl Shapiro, *Antitrust in a Time of Populism*, unpublished working paper, 8–9, 15 (2017) (casting doubts on whether this data support the proposition that market power of leading firms actually increased).

[394] *Too Much of a Good Thing*, ECONOMIST, Mar. 26, 2016, 23. As with the Council of Economic Advisers statistics, it is open to question whether the data indicate that the market power of leading firms increased—Shapiro, *supra* note 393, at 410, 10–15.

[395] Dane Stangler & Sam Arbesman, *What Does Fortune 500 Turnover Mean?*, Ewing Marion Kauffman Foundation Working Paper 6 (2012).

Another indication that market forces may not have been as robust as was often suggested was that various companies that would be widely recognized as having considerable market power in the 2010s made substantial progress in the 2000s. By the beginning of 2010, Facebook was dominating social networking, with 52 percent of visits, well ahead of its closest rival, YouTube, at 16 percent.[396] Courtesy of the runaway success of the iPod, Apple's share of the digital music player market went from 0 percent in 2001 to 24 percent in 2002 and 74 percent in 2009.[397] Google's search engine became more popular than Yahoo!'s in 2002 and achieved over 50 percent market share in 2003 on the way to capturing 80 percent of the market by 2007.[398] In 2007 Amazon launched Kindle, an e-book reader, catching rivals flat-footed on its way to revolutionizing the book business, with Amazon ultimately capturing a 93 percent market share of e-commerce for books by 2016.[399] Still, while the steady erosion of market power that featured as the twentieth century drew to a close was not a given in the 2000s, due to the dominant perception that market leaders were continuing to become more vulnerable to competitors under "supercapitalism" public company executives likely would have conducted themselves as if the threat of incursion by rivals was a substantial constraint on their discretion.

The Retreat of the Iconic Chief Executive

By the time the 1990s ended, amidst a buoyant economy and rising share prices, CEOs of public companies appeared to be verging on iconic status.[400] By the end of the 2000s chief executives reputedly were "embattled."[401] CEOs likely were not humbled to the extent this rhetoric might imply. Nevertheless, there was a marked retreat by chief executives of non-financial companies following the bear market and the corporate scandals that characterized the early 2000s. In contrast, CEOs in the banking sector continued to fly high in the mid-2000s. The financial crisis ended that. We will consider general trends before focusing on the special case of Wall Street.

As the 2000s began CEOs pretty much carried on where they left off during the euphoric late 1990s. The fact George W. Bush felt he would appeal to voters in his 2000

---

[396] Roy Morejon, *Top 10 Social Networking Websites: March 2010 Statistics*, SOCIAL MEDIA TODAY, Apr. 12, 2010, available at http://www.socialmediatoday.com/content/top-10-social-networking-websites-march-2010-statistics (accessed Feb. 7, 2018).

[397] Peter Burrows, *Show Time!*, BUS. WK., Feb. 2, 2004, 56; James Delahunty, *iPod Market Share at 73.8%*, AFTERDAWN, Sept. 9, 2009, available at http://www.afterdawn.com/news/article.cfm/2009/09/09/ipod_market_share_at_73_8_percent_225_million_ipods_sold_more_games_for_touch_than_psp_nds_apple (accessed Feb. 7, 2018).

[398] Mike Tekula, *Your Approach to Organic Search Is Obsolete: How to Evolve in 2014*, DISTILLED, Jan. 21, 2014, available at https://www.distilled.net/blog/your-seo-approach-is-obsolete-evolve-in-2014/ (accessed Feb. 14, 2018).

[399] BRAD STONE, THE EVERYTHING STORE: JEFF BEZOS AND THE AGE OF AMAZON 314, 349–50 (2013); Tonya Garcia, *20 Years after IPO: How Amazon Came to Dominate Books, Electronics and the Cloud*, MarketWatch, May 21, 2017, available at http://www.marketwatch.com/story/how-amazon-came-to-dominate-books-electronics-and-the-cloud-2017-05-12 (accessed Feb. 7, 2018).

[400] Chapter 5, notes 64–66, 76–77, 464–65, 531–35 and related discussion.

[401] *Supra* note 224 and related discussion.

election campaign by pledging to be the "CEO president" illustrated that "the cult of the omnipotent corporate chief" was continuing.[402] A research officer at the consulting firm Burson-Marsteller who led analysis of executive reputation observed the same year "CEOs have done a masterful job of imprinting their companies with their own personality, leadership style and image. In the mind's eye, these CEOs are the company."[403] Harvard Business School academic Jay Lorsch said the following year "(w)e in America have the image of the CEO as John Wayne on his white horse—all-powerful, all-knowing."[404]

A sharp decline in share prices that began in late 2000 (Figure 6.1) put chief executives on the back foot in a way they had not been for quite some time. The *New Yorker* said in 2001 "(i)n the bull market almost every executive was a genius. . . . But in a bear market the goodwill evaporates. Shareholders grow restless and reach for the pitchforks. These days, CEOs have more explaining to do."[405] Enron and the other high-profile corporate scandals then "punctured the inflated cult of the CEO."[406] In June 2002, citing both the scandals and falling share prices, the *New York Times* said "the imperial chief executive, hailed not long ago as the savior of entire companies and the driving force behind the turnaround of the American economy, is suddenly under siege."[407] *USA Today* observed later in the year that "the image of CEO as crook changes everything. It changes the way millions of investors view Corporate America. It changes the way the nation's best and brightest leaders of the future view the executive seat. It changes the way honest, hardworking CEOs view themselves and their peers."[408]

Executive pay grew sharply in the 1990s as the reputation of CEOs soared.[409] The situation changed markedly in the new environment. The *Wall Street Journal* suggested in 2003 that "all across America, being the top boss looks less like a get-rich-quick scheme these days," noting that "(s)tunned by a tsunami of accounting scandals, bankruptcies and investor outrage over option abuses, many boards are taking a fresh look at almost every aspect of their leader's pay package."[410] CEO pay indeed fell in large companies in 2002 and 2003 even though stock prices began to rally (Figure 6.1).[411]

There also was a change in managerial style. "The model of CEO as showman" that was taking hold in the late 1990s fell out of favor in the early 2000s as companies presented

---

402 Justin Schack, *Hail to the Chiefs*, INSTIT. INVESTOR, Jan. 2003, 27.

403 Sathnam Sanghera, *Suitable Style in an Age of Uncertainty*, FIN. TIMES, July 21, 2000, 15.

404 Michael Skapinker, *Under Pressure*, FIN. TIMES, May 31, 2001, 20.

405 Surowiecki, *supra* note 312.

406 JOHN W. CIOFFI, PUBLIC LAW AND PRIVATE POWER: CORPORATE GOVERNANCE REFORM IN THE AGE OF FINANCE CAPITALISM 109 (2010).

407 David Leonhardt, *The Imperial Chief Executive Is Suddenly in the Cross Hairs*, NY TIMES, June 24, 2002, A1.

408 Bruce Horovitz, *Scandals Grow Out of CEOs' Warped Mind-Set*, USA TODAY, Oct. 11, 2002, B1.

409 Chapter 5, notes 491–92, 536–38 and related discussion.

410 Joann S. Lublin, *Why the Get-Rich-Quick Days May Be Over*, WALL ST. J., Apr. 14, 2003, R1.

411 Shue & Townsend, *supra* note 227, at 4; Edmans, Gabaix & Jenter, *supra* note 227, at 390 (both providing data for S&P 500 companies illustrating the trend); Louis Lavelle, *Living Large in the Corner Office*, BUS. WK., Feb. 23, 2004, 47 ("(f)or the past two years, CEOs have watched as their pay cratered"). *Cf.* Steven N. Kaplan, *Are US CEOs Overpaid?*, ACAD. MGMT. PERSP., May 2008, 5, 9 (indicating that after falling substantially in 2001 and 2002, CEO pay recovered modestly in 2003).

themselves more as business institutions than as extensions of the chief executive.[412] Integrity and character moved up the list of desirable CEO traits at the expense of brand-name status and visibility.[413] The shift appeared to fit the mood of the time, with *Newsweek* saying "(f)or a public tired of self-promotional corporate bosses, there's something refreshing about this quieter breed of leader."[414]

Many, including CEOs, anticipated that the changes would be temporary. Investors, the media, and the public at large, it was thought, would quickly forget the sins of the early 2000s once the most notorious corporate wrongdoers had been punished and stock prices recovered.[415] There were some signs matters might work out this way. Executive pay began to increase again in the mid-2000s with stock prices continuing to rally.[416] The business press also continued to run numerous stories on CEOs with a personal dimension that merged their success with that of their companies.[417]

While there was a rally from the nadir of the early 2000s, there would not be for the remainder of the 2000s a return to the heady CEO-as-icon era. Former SEC chairman Arthur Levitt, writing in 2005, said "(g)one are the days of the autocratic, muscular CEO whose picture appeared on the covers of business magazines.... The imperial CEO is no more."[418] A *Washington Post* columnist said of CEOs the same year "(t)hey've gone from heroes to bums. Hardly a day passes when the press or prosecutors don't thrash some corporate CEO for alleged managerial blunders or accounting illegalities."[419] As if on cue, in late 2005 and through 2006 there were revelations that at dozens of companies the pay of executives had been artificially and perhaps illegally boosted through fictionalized dating of stock options.[420] Even though the "options backdating" had almost all occurred prior to mid-2002 when SOX tightened relevant disclosure rules, the controversy fostered the perception that corporate America and its executives had not learned their lessons from the corporate scandal heyday.[421]

During the mid-2000s, reports of rapid CEO turnover appeared to prove "that CEOs at major, publicly traded companies are on a shorter leash than ever before."[422] For instance, the *Wall Street Journal* in a 2006 editorial said "(i)t wasn't long ago that the scolds among our

---

[412] David Olive, *How Celebrity CEOs Failed to Deliver*, TORONTO STAR, Aug. 24, 2002, A1; *Humbled*, ECONOMIST, Dec, 20, 2003, 109.

[413] *Churning Heads*, ECONOMIST, June 22, 2002, 80; Karen Lowry Miller, *The Quiet CEOs*, NEWSWEEK, Dec, 20, 2004, 38.

[414] Daniel McGinn, *The CEO's Challenge*, NEWSWEEK, Apr. 28, 2003, 50.

[415] MURRAY, *supra* note 242, xvi, 33; Jennifer Pellet, *Restoring Confidence in Chief Executives*, CHIEF EXEC., Nov. 2004, 56, 61.

[416] Shue & Townsend, *supra* note 227, at 4; Edmans, Gabaix & Jenter, *supra* note 227, at 390.

[417] Terence Corcoran, *Overkill in the Hunt for Imperial CEOs*, NATIONAL POST, Apr. 5, 2005, Financial Post, 23.

[418] Levitt, *supra* note 21.

[419] Robert J. Samuelson, *The New Economic Warriors*, WASH. POST, Apr. 13, 2005, A17.

[420] Mark Maremont, *Authorities Probe Improper Backdating of Options*, WALL ST. J., Nov. 11, 2005, A1; Eric Dash, *Study Charts Broad Manipulation of Options*, NY TIMES, Nov. 17, 2006, C2; Christy L. Abbott, *The Shareholder Derivative Suit as a Response to Stock Option Backdating*, 53 ST. LOUIS U. L.J. 593, 597–99 (2009).

[421] Maremont, *supra* note 420; Jeremy Grant, *Academic Who Shook Up Wall Street*, FIN. TIMES, Sept. 11, 2006, 24; Kevin Allison & Francesco Guerrera Open Season, FIN. TIMES, Apr. 2, 2007, 13.

[422] Peter Hadekel, *Days of "Imperial CEO" Are Fading Fast*, MONTREAL GAZETTE, June 17, 2005, B6.

self-appointed corporate watchdogs were saying that CEOs were too imperial, 'owning' their boards of directors and dictating their own 'excessive' salaries without oversight or accountability for underperformance. These days, if anything, the opposite seems to be true. Perform or die."[423] The opening months of 2005 proved to be particularly challenging for incumbent CEOs in leading companies. It seemed "high-profile chiefs were dropping like bowling pins," which prompted *Fortune* to say "(t)here hasn't been this much sacking since the Goths dropped in on Rome."[424] Michael Eisner, for instance, was eased out at Disney a year earlier than he had planned regardless of considerable past success.[425] Hewlett-Packard's board dismissed Carly Fiorina despite her having been an "omega" celebrity CEO earlier in her tenure.[426] Hank Greenberg, fired as boss of AIG, reportedly right until the end "clung to the model of the imperial chief executive, steadfast in his belief that the market would lose faith in the company without him."[427]

CEO dismissal trends from the mid-2000s do not provide in isolation authoritative evidence of a post-scandal demise of the imperial CEO.[428] CEO turnover was also substantial in 2000 and 2001, prior to the corporate scandals.[429] Other facets of public company behavior, however, do indicate post-bear-market/post-scandal CEOs conducted themselves in a more restrained manner. "Risky" investments, defined as research and development outlays, acquisitions, and net capital expenditures, fell as a proportion of total assets.[430] Financial reporting became more conservative and earnings management was less aggressive.[431] Earnings restatements, which grew in number and severity as companies corrected for the wayward accounting of the early 2000s,[432] ultimately became more modest affairs with dollar amounts being lower and with errors less likely to have been intentional.[433] A 2007 *Forbes* editorial entitled "Timid CEOs" identified SOX as a contributor to a conservative approach large US companies had recently been taking, saying because of the legislation "corporate chieftains have to focus more on crossing t's and dotting i's than on aggressively expanding their businesses."[434] A benefit was that corporate scandals became markedly less common, particularly

---

[423] *The Un-Imperial CEO*, WALL ST. J., Sept. 16, 2006, A8.

[424] Geoffrey Colvin, *CEO Knockdown*, FORTUNE, Apr. 4, 2005, 19.

[425] STEWART, *supra* note 338, at 523–26, 537–38.

[426] MURRAY, *supra* note 242, 59-62; Allan Sloan, *Now Playing!!! The Celebrity CEO*, NEWSWEEK, Sept. 17, 2001, 55.

[427] Kurt Eichenwald & Jenny Anderson, *How a Titan of Insurance Ran Afoul of the Government*, NY TIMES, Apr. 4, 2005, C1;

[428] See Hongxia Wang, Wallace N. Davidson & Xiaoxin Wang, *The Sarbanes-Oxley Act and CEO Tenure, Turnover, and Risk Aversion*, 50 Q. REV. ECON. & FIN. 367, 375 (2010) (indicating that CEO dismissal trends were not markedly different at the beginning of the 2000s and after the enactment of SOX).

[429] Ward, *supra* note 229; Anthony Bianco & Louis Lavelle, *The CEO Trap*, BUS. WK., Dec, 11, 2000, 86;

[430] Wang, Davidson & Wang, *supra* note 428, at 370–71.

[431] *Supra* note 274 and related discussion; Robert A. Prentice & David B. Spence, *Sarbanes-Oxley as Quack Corporate Governance: How Wise Is the Received Wisdom?*, 95 GEO. L.J. 1843, 1906–07 (2007) (summarizing and explaining empirical studies); Jian Zhou, *Financial Reporting after the Sarbanes-Oxley Act: Conservative or Less Earnings Management?*, 20 RES. ACCTING. REG. 187, 191 (2008).

[432] Jonathan D. Glater, *Restatements Are at a High, and Lawsuits Are Rising*, NY TIMES, Jan. 20, 2005, C2.

[433] John C. Coates & Suraj Srinivasan, *SOX after Ten Years: A Multidisciplinary Review*, 28 ACCTING. HORIZONS 627, 648 (2014); *Custodians of Capitalism*, ECONOMIST, Dec. 16, 2017, 59.

[434] *Timid CEOs*, FORBES, June 4, 2007, 33.

once allowance is made for the fact that with options backdating the problematic conduct predated SOX.[435]

Modest use of debt financing provides further evidence of the post-bear-market/post-scandal conservatism of larger public companies and their executives. Measured by decade, debt/capital ratios for non-financial public firms were at their lowest level in the 2000s since the 1950s.[436] In 2002 "net borrowing fell off the cliff," with those running public companies acquiring substantial respect for cash with debt markets being tight.[437] Conservative cash management was sustained thereafter, despite low interest rates and relaxed lending terms arising from "hypercompetition in the capital markets" that paved the way for unprecedented public-to-private buyout activity.[438]

With caution being the order of the day and with corporate profits rising in the mid-2000s as the economy recovered, larger public companies rapidly accumulated cash in amounts substantial enough to prompt activist hedge funds to press for the unlocking of shareholder value.[439] With private equity firms using leverage aggressively and apparently successfully, public company executives were criticized for having gone too far with deleveraging and for failing to "realize that too much cash can be too much of a good thing."[440] Criticism on grounds of excessive caution abated, though, when the corporate sector had to weather the turmoil brought on by the financial crisis. *Newsweek* praised big business in late 2008 for behaving "quite responsibly over the past five years," particularly because it "hoarded cash to prepare for rainy days."[441] The *Economist* said of American non-financial public companies in 2009 "whisper it quietly, but most were just sensible."[442]

Fortune speculated in mid-2007 that "(t)he 5 1/2-year humiliation of American business ... has run its course" with the result "businesspeople at long last sense it's okay to become public figures again."[443] The credit crunch and the financial crisis, however, halted any immediate return to the swashbuckling executive style of the 1990s. During 2009, public companies were reputedly asking headhunting firms to find them "humble" bosses and business journalists were resorting "to producing glowing profiles of self-effacing and self-denying bosses."[444] The downgrade from iconic status would not be fleeting.

---

[435] Gary Giroux, *What Went Wrong? Accounting Fraud and Lessons from the Recent Scandals*, 75 SOCIAL RESEARCH 1205, 1231, 1235 (2008).

[436] John R. Graham, Mark T. Leary & Michael R. Roberts, *A Century of Capital Structure: The Leveraging of Corporate America*, 118 J. FIN. ECON. 658, 661 (2015).

[437] *Getting Rid of Corporate Debt*, BUS. WK., July 1, 2002, 30; Barrett Sheridan, *Big Business Is Not to Blame*, NEWSWEEK, Dec, 15, 2008 (Atlantic ed.), 48.

[438] *Supra* notes 141–43, 379–83 and related discussion; Megan Barnett & Richard J. Newman, *Merger Madness*, US NEWS & WORLD REPORT, Dec, 27, 2004, 20; *Betting the Balance-Sheet*, ECONOMIST, June 26, 2010, Special Report on Debt, 8.

[439] *Supra* note 314 and related discussion.

[440] Andrew Bary, *Who's Afraid of Leverage? Not the Buyout Kings*, BARRON'S, Nov. 27, 2006, 21.

[441] Sheridan, *supra* note 437.

[442] *The Sensible Giants*, ECONOMIST, May 2, 2009, 65.

[443] Geoffrey Colvin, *Business Is Back*, FORTUNE, May 14, 2007, 40.

[444] *The Cult of the Faceless Boss*, ECONOMIST, Nov. 14, 2009, 86.

Banks, Their "Free Pass," and the Financial Crisis

The foregoing analysis of CEOs ostensibly under siege begs an important question. If corporate scandals and SOX had tamed public company executives, why were swashbuckling banks at the epicenter of the economic meltdown the United States experienced as the 2000s drew to a close? The banks and their executives, it transpired, secured a corporate governance "free pass" that provided ample scope for them to contribute to the onset of the 2008 financial crisis.

Between the mid-twentieth century and the 2000s commercial and investment banks moved some distance from being the models of conservatism and propriety they were during the heyday of managerial capitalism.[445] The bias in favor of caution began to ebb away in the 1970s, and the process continued in the 1980s.[446] The momentum stalled in the early 1990s, with commercial and investment banks retrenching as the economy slowed.[447]

As for the remainder of the 1990s, a reasonable assumption would be that investment banks would have thrived, with share prices increasing dramatically and with IPO and M&A activity being robust.[448] In fact, the industry bifurcated. Numerous firms struggling with the burden of managing rapid growth opted to merge with a stronger partner.[449] Merrill Lynch, Goldman Sachs, and Morgan Stanley flourished, emerging in so doing as the very top tier of American investment banks, and Bear Stearns and Lehman Brothers prospered as well, the latter after being spun off from American Express in 1994.[450]

Consolidation also featured prominently with commercial banks. Mergers occurred at a torrid pace in the 1990s, resulting in a marked decline in the number of banks as well as substantial growth of the biggest banks.[451] The share of bank assets held by the 10 largest banks grew from 26 percent to 45 percent between 1990 and 1999.[452] By the late 1990s, Bank of America could even make a legitimate claim to being the first genuinely national bank,[453]

---

[445] Chapter 2, notes 391–93, 409–13 and related discussion.

[446] Chapter 3, notes 425, 435–48, 452–56 and accompanying text; Chapter 4, notes 483–88, 500–02, 507–8, 511–12 and accompanying text.

[447] Matthew Schifrin, *Financial Services*, FORBES, July 7, 1991, 156; BRUCE WASSERSTEIN, BIG DEAL: 2000 AND BEYOND 300 (2000).

[448] Chapter 5, Figures 5.1, 5.3 and 5.4, notes 81, 146 and related discussion; ROY C. SMITH, THE WEALTH CREATORS: THE RISE OF TODAY'S RICH AND SUPER-RICH 188 (2001).

[449] SMITH, *supra* note 448, at 188–89; Roy C. Smith, *Strategic Directions in Investment Banking—A Retrospective Analysis*, J. APP. CORP. FIN., Spring 2001, at 111, 112.

[450] SMITH, *supra* note 448, 189–91; Smith, *supra* note 449, 119; Tracy Corrigan, *Wall Street's Big Bang*, FIN. TIMES, Sept. 25, 1997, 23.

[451] Allen E. Berger, Rebecca S. Demsetz & Philip E. Strahan, *The Consolidation of the Financial Services Industry: Causes, Consequences, and Implications for the Future*, 23 J. BANKING & FIN. 135, 136, 138–40 (1999); Robert DeYoung, *Mergers and the Changing Landscape of Commercial Banking (Part I)*, CHI. FED LETTER, No. 145, Sept. 1999, available at https://www.chicagofed.org/publications/chicago-fed-letter/1999/september-145 (accessed May 25, 2018).

[452] JOHNSON & KWAK, *supra* note 165, at 85–86.

[453] John Authers, *Banking on Moving Targets*, FIN. TIMES, Apr. 14, 1998, 21.

facilitated by regulatory reforms culminating in the mid-1990s with a federally sanctioned framework for the establishment of interstate banking.[454]

Commercial banks did not merely get bigger in the 1990s. They also expanded the scope of their operations, primarily by moving into investment banking. Barriers between commercial and investment banking encompassed in the Glass Steagall Act of 1933 were formally dismantled only by the 1999 Gramm-Leach-Bliley Act.[455] Commercial banks, however, capitalized on the Federal Reserve relaxing in 1996 restrictions on their activities to build up substantial investment banking operations by acquiring small and mid-size securities firms.[456] The Federal Reserve also cleared the way in 1998 for Citibank and insurer/investment bank Travelers Group to join to form Citigroup by authorizing a five-year waiver of a Glass Steagall prohibition against banks underwriting insurance.[457] At that point in time, the merger was the largest in corporate history.[458]

As the 2000s began the investment and commercial banks that had come to dominate their respective market sectors were conducting themselves quite differently from their cautious managerial capitalism era forebears. Investment banks are prone to a tension between an intention to build up over the long-term a reputation for prudence and probity and a temptation to cut corners to maximize short-term fee revenues from underwriting and brokerage activities.[459] While accumulating and sustaining reputational capital was the top priority in the decades following World War II, in the frothy stock market conditions of the late 1990s and the opening half of 2000 reputedly "many leading US financial firms threw out their business standards and started grabbing the loot."[460]

With the investment banking community "grabbing the loot," the reputation of Wall Street securities analysts were sullied the most. They were tagged, for instance, as "public enemy number one" of the stock market crash of 2000–2001.[461] Analysts were criticized for offering doggedly optimistic assessments of companies they followed, an unsurprising predilection given they were operating in a system that rewarded them as much for helping their employers to attract and retain corporate investment banking clients as for accurate forecasts.[462] Perceived conflicts of interest put analysts at the center of a high-profile criminal investigation of investment banking New York state attorney general Elliot Spitzer launched.[463] The

---

[454] Chapter 5, note 341 and accompanying text.

[455] Chapter 5, note 345 and related discussion.

[456] Anthony Saunders, *Consolidation and Universal Banking*, 23 J. BANKING & FIN. 693, 694 (1999); Arthur E. Wilmarth, *The Transformation of the US Financial Services Industry, 1975–2000: Competition, Consolidation, and Increased Risks* [2002] UNIV. ILL. L. REV. 217, 319.

[457] WASSERSTEIN, *supra* note 447, at 10–11, 332–33; Jim McTague, *Empty Glass-Steagall?*, BARRON'S, Apr. 13, 1998, 20.

[458] WASSERSTEIN, *supra* note 447, 333.

[459] ALAN D. MORRISON & WILLIAM J. WILHELM, INVESTMENT BANKING: INSTITUTIONS, POLITICS & LAW 15, 75–76, 301 (2007).

[460] Peter Elmstrom, *The Great Internet Money Game*, BUS. WK., Apr. 16, 2001, EB, 16. See also Shawn Tully, *Betrayal on Wall Street*, FORTUNE, May 14, 2001, 84; JONATHAN A. KNEE, THE ACCIDENTIAL INVESTMENT BANKER xxi, 127–28, 147–49 (2007).

[461] *Is Greed Good?*, ECONOMIST, May 18, 2002, Survey of International Finance, 23.

[462] *Id.*; John Byrne, *How to Fix Corporate Governance*, BUS. WK., May 6, 2002, 68.

[463] DAVID SKEEL, ICARUS IN THE BOARDROOM: THE FUNDAMENTAL FLAWS IN CORPORATE AMERICA AND WHERE THEY CAME FROM 180–81 (2005).

end result was a 2003 "global settlement" involving Spitzer, the SEC, the New York Stock Exchange, and 10 of the largest investment banks (including subsidiaries of commercial banks) under which the firms agreed to pay as penalties a total of nearly $1.4 billion and to implement structural reforms designed to insulate securities analysts from investment banking pressure.[464]

As for major commercial banks, a number conducted themselves sufficiently adventurously to become supporting actors in the corporate scandals of the early 2000s. Citigroup and its leading commercial banking competitor, J.P. Morgan Chase, were lenders to many of the companies implicated and thus seemed "to be in the hot seat every time a financial scandal . . . pops up."[465] Citigroup was also lead financial advisor and underwriter for WorldCom, prompting Citigroup's general counsel (and later CEO) Chuck Prince to remark when deposed in a WorldCom related lawsuit against the bank "I wish we had never heard of (WorldCom CEO) Bernie Ebbers."[466] With the Enron scandal, among various commercial banks and investment banks characterized as "enablers," Citigroup and J.P. Morgan Chase topped the list.[467] The two banks agreed subsequently to pay $2 billion and $2.2 billion respectively to settle a massive class action alleging securities fraud in relation to stocks and bonds Enron issued in which defendants collectively paid out a total of $7.3 billion.[468] The two also paid a combined $4.6 billion of $6 billion banks handed over to settle similar litigation involving WorldCom.[469]

While commercial and investment banks were carrying on business in a sufficiently adventurous manner to mean they did not escape the public company travails of the early 2000s unscathed, the blow was merely a glancing one for the banking sector. By the time banks were settling the Enron and WorldCom securities fraud class actions, the news failed to attract front page treatment despite the sizeable amounts involved.[470] As for the Spitzer-orchestrated global settlement, the *Wall Street Journal* observed in an editorial "Mr. Spitzer hasn't so much fixed Wall Street's business model as bailed it out."[471] Investors were pleased, as the shares of major banks rose substantially when a preliminary version of the global settlement was announced at the end of 2002.[472] The penalty of $100 million

---

[464] Kenneth R. Gray, Larry A. Frieder & George W. Clark, Corporate Scandals: The Great Heist, Financial Bubbles, and the Absence of Virtue 109–14 (2005).

[465] Julie Creswell, *Banks on the Hot Seat*, Fortune, Sept. 2, 2002, 79.

[466] Monica Langley, Tearing Down the Walls 392–93 (2003); Gretchen Morgenson, *The Big Winner, Again, Is "Scandalot,"* NY Times, Jan. 1, 2006, B1.

[467] McLean & Elkind, *supra* note 55, at 162, 408.

[468] Jeff Bailey, *CIBC Pays to Settle Enron Case: An Agreement for $2.4 Billion*, NY Times, Aug. 3, 2005, C1; Julie Creswell, *Court Rejects Suit against Enron Banks*, NY Times, Mar. 20, 2007, C1.

[469] Robin Sidel, *J.P. Morgan to Pay $2 Billion as Street's Bill for Bubble Soars*, Wall St. J., Mar. 17, 2005, C1.

[470] See Bailey, *supra* note 468; Sidel, *supra* note 469. The out-of-pocket payments by WorldCom and Enron directors arising from the same litigation (see *supra* note 266 and accompanying text) were, on the other hand, front page news. See, for example, Gretchen Morgenson, *10 Ex-Directors from WorldCom to Pay Millions*, NY Times, Jan. 6, 2005, A1.

[471] *The Spitzer-Weill Stock Trade*, Wall St. J., Dec, 23, 2002, A14.

[472] Langley, *supra* note 466, at 423; Silvia Ascarelli, *Americans Are Warier of Stock-Market Investing*, Wall St. J., Dec, 23, 2002, C3.

Merrill Lynch agreed to pay was, according to one critical media commentator, "less than one third of what the firm paid for office supplies and postage" annually and amounted to little more than a "business expense for deceiving the public."[473] Nevertheless, the public seemed to believe justice was done.[474] When the settlement was finalized a few months later all concerned were ready to move on, with Spitzer turning his attention to alleged mutual fund misconduct and lucrative compensation that had been awarded to the NYSE's chairman.[475]

In addition to sidestepping a major reputational hit with the corporate scandals of the early 2000s, banks were thriving relative to their non-financial counterparts. Financial company profits increased at an average of 13.8 percent annually between 1996 and 2006, compared with 8.5 percent for non-financial companies.[476] While the S&P 500 dropped nearly 50 percent between March 2000 and September 2002 as the "dot.com" bull market went into reverse and corporate scandals hit,[477] share prices of banks in the S&P 500 actually increased (Figure 6.7). The *New York Times* remarked in 2003 "bank shares have been among the most resilient investments of the last three years."[478] Bank shares then continued to perform well through to 2007 while the stock market overall was struggling to recover ground lost during the 2000–2002 bear market (Figure 6.7).

Within a strongly performing financial sector, Lehman Brothers shone through. Its share price rose sixteenfold between 1994, when Lehman was relaunched as an independent going concern, and 2005.[479] *Barron's* ranked the firm as number one in its 2006 survey of the financial performance of the largest 500 US and Canadian corporations, just ahead of rival Goldman Sachs.[480] *Barron's* explained

> Lehman Brothers has transformed itself from a bond shop into a diversified financial-services powerhouse with sterling investment-banking and asset-management franchises. The makeover culminated in record profits last year, a near-doubling of its stock price and the No. 1 ranking in this year's *Barron's* 500 survey.[481]

While in the early 2000s the bear market afflicting stocks and corporate scandals fostered conservatism among public companies and knocked CEOs off their 1990s pedestal, the same momentum was absent in a banking sector that was performing well and had not

---

[473] MAGGIE MAHAR, BULL: A HISTORY OF THE BOOM, 1982–1999, at 352 (2003), citing Bill Moyers, a journalist at PBS. Merrill Lynch also agreed to pay $100 million to fund independent research and investor education—GRAY, FRIEDER & CLARK, *supra* note 464, at 111.

[474] ROY C. SMITH & INGO WALTER, GOVERNING THE MODERN CORPORATION: CAPITAL MARKETS, CORPORATE CONTROL, AND ECONOMIC PERFORMANCE 209 (2006).

[475] *Id.* at 209–10.

[476] Arthur E. Wilmarth, *The Dark Side of Universal Banking: Financial Conglomerates and the Origins of the Subprime Financial Crisis*, 41 CONN. L. REV. 963, 1003 (2009).

[477] Cheffins, *supra* note 188, at 10.

[478] Conrad De Aenlle, *As Interest Rates Climb, Must Bank Stocks Fall?: Time to Sell?*, NY TIMES, Sept. 21, 2003, Business 6.

[479] LOWENSTEIN, *supra* note 170, 49.

[480] Christopher C. Williams, *Barron's 500*, BARRON'S, May 15, 2006, 27.

[481] *Id.*

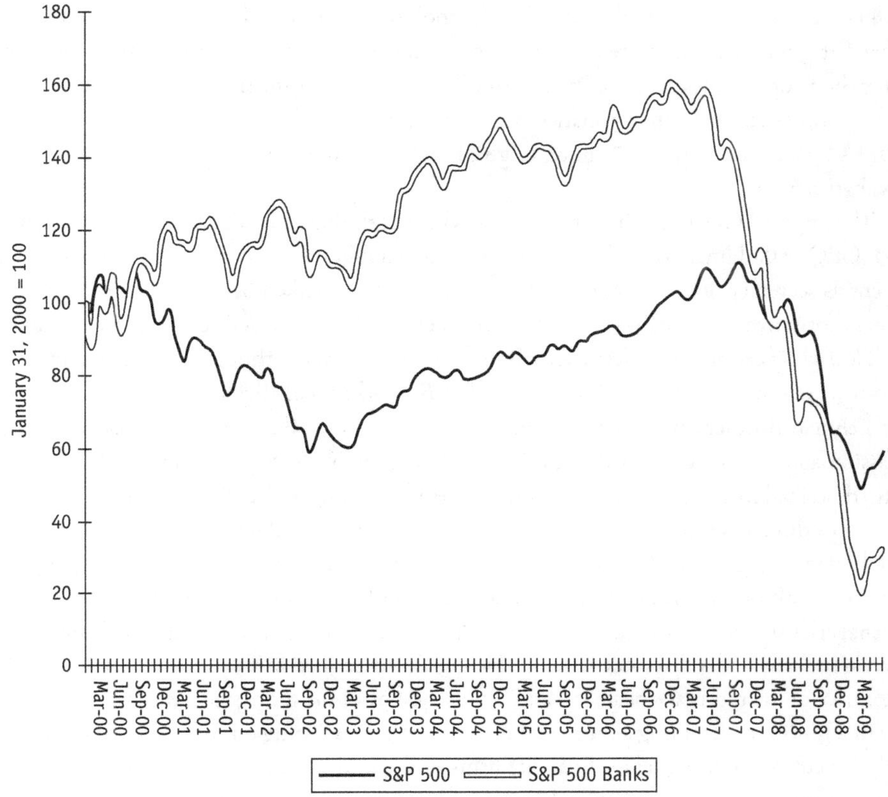

FIGURE 6.7 S&P 500/S&P 500 Banks, 2000–2009.
Source: William W. Bratton & Michael W. Wachter, *The Case against Shareholder Empowerment*, 158 U. PA. L. REV. 653, 718 (2010).

been tarnished markedly by scandal. According to a July 2008 *American Banker* article, "the passage of that reform legislation [SOX] coincided with an extended run of profitability in the banking industry, and discussions about the consequences of weak corporate governance were mostly theoretical."[482] The banks, in other words, received a mid-2000s governance "free pass" unavailable to their non-financial counterparts, and their management teams correspondingly had a license to freewheel in a manner that would have been entirely foreign to their cautious managerial capitalism era peers.

Citigroup's chairman and CEO Sandy Weill, described by *Fortune* in 2001 as a "big-ego boss . . . sitting imperially center stage," did in the midst of the various controversies swirling around the bank in the early 2000s give up the CEO post in 2003 to general counsel Chuck Prince.[483] Prince, for his part, was not used to operating in the limelight, and prioritized

[482] Kevin Dobbs, *Crisis Casts Bank Boards as Activists*, AM. BANKER, July 14, 2008, 1. Part of the explanation for SOX being thought of as "mostly theoretical" with banks was that auditing regulation for which SOX provided was introduced for banks by reforms in the early 1990s—ALLISON, *supra* note 217, at 134.

[483] LANGLEY, *supra* note 466, at 403–35; Carol J. Loomis, *Sandy Weill's Monster*, FORTUNE, April 16, 2001, 106.

adherence to rules and regulations when he took over.[484] Prince, however, quickly deduced that Citigroup needed "more than competence and accountability in the corner office" and launched "operation charisma."[485] He emerged as "king within the walls of Citigroup."[486] Citigroup's share price performance was mediocre in the mid-2000s.[487] Nevertheless, the bank's board reputedly was "willing to give more and more rope" to Prince, who took over as chairman in 2006.[488]

The imperial CEO was alive and well elsewhere in the banking sector. Hank Paulson, who was CEO of Goldman Sachs from when it became a public company in 1999 until his appointment as secretary of the Treasury in 2006, was "a guy who liked being in charge ... seemed so authoritative ... (and) was very decisive when a decision needed to be made."[489] Stanley O'Neal, chief executive of Merrill Lynch from 2003 to 2007, was thought of as "brutally ambitious ... remote, difficult and intimidating."[490] *Barron's* said of Richard Fuld, chief executive of Lehman Brothers, when naming him one of the best 30 CEOs of 2007 that he "brings passion and competitiveness that are powerful even by (Wall) Street standards."[491] Fuld was also described in a 2009 book on the firm's collapse as "King Richard" who "turned Lehman's board of directors into a kind of irrelevant lower chamber."[492] Angelo Mozilo, cofounder of leading mortgage lender Countrywide Financial and chief executive when the company was sold to Bank of America at a financial crisis-related knockdown price in early 2008, had a managerial style that provided scope for a "friends of Angelo" list that afforded politicians access to loans under favorable terms.[493] He was also described in a 2000 *Forbes* article as "the Rommel of the mortgage business" and "(t)he bad boy of the mortgage industry."[494]

In addition to retaining an imperial demeanor that was going out of fashion more generally, executives running major financial firms in the mid-2000s did not adopt the conservative managerial outlook that had become prevalent among public companies generally. Aware that debt was cheap and plentiful and that securitization provided a convenient means of offloading downside risk, commercial banks took a very relaxed stance with lending to prospective home buyers, private equity firms, and other borrowers.[495] Commercial banks also relied increasingly heavily on trading financial assets to boost their profits.[496] It was said of J.P. Morgan Chase "its multi-trillion exposures look like typographical errors."[497]

---

[484] Mara Der Hovanesian, *Rewiring Chuck Prince*, Bus. Wk., Feb. 20, 2006, 75.

[485] *Id.*

[486] *The A Listers*, American Banker, Mar. 2005, 43.

[487] Eric Dash, *Citi's Stormy First Decade*, NY Times, Apr. 3, 2008, C1.

[488] David Enrich, *For Rubin Pressure's On*, Wall St. J., Nov. 5, 2007, C1.

[489] William D. Cohan, Money & Power: How Goldman Sachs Came to Rule the World 414–15, 431, 453–55 (2011).

[490] Lowenstein, *supra* note 170, at 71.

[491] Andrew Bary, *The World's Best CEOs*, Barron's, Mar. 26, 2007.

[492] Larry MacDonald, A Colossal Failure of Common Sense: The Incredible Inside Story of the Collapse of Lehman Brothers 97, 224 (2009).

[493] *A Case of Note*, Economist, Sept. 28, 2013, 79.

[494] Bernard Condon, *Last Man Standing*, Forbes, Nov. 27, 2000, 108.

[495] Davidoff, *supra* note 138, at 101.

[496] Benjamin M. Friedman, *Is Our Financial System Serving US Well?*, Daedalus, Fall 2010, 9, 11.

[497] John Plender, *Corporate Quicksilver*, Fin. Times, Feb. 6, 2002, 12.

While commercial banks were adventurous by historical standards in the mid-2000s, they "were seen as slow-footed and dull" compared to leading investment banks.[498] The capital structure of elite investment banks was, for example, considerably more aggressive. For commercial banks their maximum permissible leverage ratio under applicable banking regulations was 20:1 (equity capital valued at 5 percent of total assets).[499] On the eve of the financial crisis, among major commercial banks only Citigroup, with a 19:1 ratio, was close to the prescribed limit, and the ratio of US commercial banks collectively was slightly lower than 10:1.[500] In contrast, the leverage ratios of Goldman Sachs, Merrill Lynch, Morgan Stanley, Bear Stearns, and Lehman Brothers ranged between 28:1 and 33:1 in early 2008, up from an already high 21:1 to 29:1 spectrum in mid-2006.[501] This was partly due to a policy change by the SEC that permitted those firms to opt out of a net capital rule the SEC had in place in favor of a regime oriented around SEC monitoring of capital adequacy.[502]

As well as being highly leveraged, leading investment banks were shifting away from generating revenue by charging underwriting fees and brokerage commissions, once the industry's bread and butter, in favor of the potentially volatile business of trading on their own accounts.[503] For instance, Goldman Sachs' revenue generated from trading and principal investments rose from two-fifths of total net revenue in the late 1990s to two-thirds in 2007.[504] The leading investment banks, with their aggressive capital structure, had to rely increasingly on short-term borrowing to finance the principal trading in which they were engaging, and began to look like "hedge funds in disguise."[505] Lehman Brothers, Bear Stearns, and Merrill Lynch also added to the mix sizeable operations packaging and selling mortgage-backed securities, the financial product that would spark the 2007 credit crunch that set the scene for the financial crisis.[506]

Aside from involvement in the mortgage market that acted as a catalyst for the financial crisis, were banks, with their mid-2000s free pass, to blame for the 2008 meltdown? A plausible conjecture is that banks and their executives, extended substantial discretion due to healthy financial performance, squandered the latitude provided to them and engaged in reckless banking that brought on economic ruin. Indeed, after the financial crisis hit, a consensus quickly developed that deficient corporate governance at US financial firms was largely responsible.[507]

---

[498] LOWENSTEIN, *supra* note 170, at 220.

[499] JEFFREY FRIEDMAN & WLADIMIR KRAUS, ENGINEERING THE FINANCIAL CRISIS: SYSTEMIC RISK AND THE FAILURE OF REGULATION 40 (2011).

[500] *Id.* at 40–41.

[501] Securities and Exchange Commission, Office of Inspector General, *SEC's Oversight of Bear Stearns and Related Entities: The Consolidated Supervised Entity Program 120* (Report No. 446-A, Sept. 25, 2008), available at https://www.sec.gov/files/446-a.pdf (accessed Feb. 7, 2018).

[502] John C. Coffee, Jr. & Hillary A. Sale, *Redesigning the SEC: Does the Treasury Have a Better Idea?*, 95 VA. L. REV. 707, 735–37 (2009).

[503] Chapter 2, notes 411–12 and related discussion; *Capital Spenders*, ECONOMIST, May 19, 2007, Special Report on International Banking, 12.

[504] MORRISON & WILHELM, *supra* note 459, at 302.

[505] CASSIDY, *supra* note 172, at 313.

[506] *Supra* notes 168, 170–72, 175 and related discussion; BLINDER, *supra* note 27, at 151; GIROUX, *supra* note 43, at 61, 341.

[507] Paul Rose, *Regulating Risk by "Strengthening Corporate Governance,"* 17 CONN. INSUR. L.J. 1, 2 (2010); STEPHEN M. BAINBRIDGE, CORPORATE GOVERNANCE AFTER THE CRISIS 9 (2012).

Carl Icahn, the shareholder activist, was one among many who blamed the financial crisis on reckless bankers. He wrote in 2009 "(l)ax and ineffective boards, self-serving managements, and failed short-term strategies all contributed to the entirely preventable financial meltdown."[508] A 2009 report commissioned by the Organisation for Economic Co-operation and Development steering group on corporate governance concluded the financial crisis could be "attributed to failures and weaknesses in corporate governance arrangements" in financial firms.[509] In a 2011 report to the president and Congress the National Commission on the Causes of the Financial and Economic Crisis in the United States indicated "dramatic failures of corporate governance and risk management at many systemically important financial institutions were a key cause of this crisis."[510]

Top executives at major banks may indeed have been afforded in the early and mid-2000s excessive discretion, reinforced by ill-advised incentives. *American Banker* magazine suggested in a 2008 cover story "(a)t far too many banks . . . the attitude was to let the good times roll when executives should have been nibbling their fingernails down to the quick."[511] For instance, Robert Rubin, who joined Citigroup as a director and part-time executive after serving in the Clinton administration, admitted that he was unaware of $43 billion worth of shaky derivatives on Citigroup's books until losses on them were written down publicly in 2007.[512] The corporate governance culture at Bear Stearns was said to be "straight out of the 1920s," with Bear's board of directors meeting only every other month and leaving primary oversight of management to an all-insider executive committee of directors.[513] Fuld indicated four days before Lehman went bankrupt that its board had been "wonderfully supportive," hardly an ideal stance when financial ruin was imminent.[514]

Banks and their boards were also criticized for missing the plot when setting executive pay. The charge was that compensation arrangements in place encouraged excessive risk-taking that fostered ill-advised gambles.[515] Particularly problematic were potentially lucrative bonus schemes and equity compensation plans where bank executives could cash in quickly and in effect hedge personally against the possibility of things going awry due to risky bets by their banks going sour.[516] For instance, the top five executives of Bear Stearns and Lehman Brothers pocketed collectively $1.4 billion and $1 billion respectively from equity sales and bonuses between 2000 and 2007.[517] Economist Alan Blinder described the dangers this

---

[508] Carl C. Icahn, *The Economy Needs Corporate Governance Reform*, WALL ST. J., Jan. 23, 2009, A13.

[509] Grant Kirkpatrick, *The Corporate Governance Lessons from the Financial Crisis*, FIN. MKT. TRENDS, July 2009, 1, 2.

[510] FINANCIAL CRISIS INQUIRY COMMISSION, *supra* note 162, at xviii.

[511] Glen Fest, *Risk without Reward*, AMERICAN BANKER, Feb. 2008, 26.

[512] MADRICK, *supra* note 25, at 314, 371, 396.

[513] Jill E. Fisch, *The Overstated Promise of Corporate Governance*, 77 U. CHI. L. REV. 923, 923 (2010).

[514] GILLESPIE & ZWEIG, *supra* note 239, at 17.

[515] Lucian A. Bebchuk & Holger Spamann, *Regulating Bankers' Pay*, 98 GEO. L.J. 247, 249 (2010).

[516] John C. Coffee, *The Political Economy of Dodd-Frank: Why Financial Reform Tends to Be Frustrated and Systemic Risk Perpetuated*, 97 CORNELL L. REV. 1047, 1051 (2012).

[517] Lucian A. Bebchuk, *How to Fix Bankers' Pay*, DAEDALUS, Fall 2010, at 52, 53.

compensation format created in a 2009 *Wall Street Journal* column, saying of CEOs and other top executives:

> it's often: Heads, you become richer than Croesus ever imagined; tails, you receive a golden parachute that still leaves you richer than Croesus. So they want to flip those big coins, too. From the point of view of the companies' shareholders ... this is madness. To them, the gamble looks like: Heads, we get a share of the winnings; tails, we absorb almost all of the losses. The conclusion is clear: ... managers ... want to flip more coins—and at higher stakes—than shareholders would if they had any control, which they don't.[518]

While those running various major financial companies did receive a post-corporate-scandal free pass unavailable to public company executives generally in the mid-2000s, it is open to question whether reckless bankers ostensibly untrammeled by lax bank governance were the primary cause of the financial crisis. To the extent that abuse of excessive managerial discretion was a catalyst for the meltdown, financial firms with sound corporate governance would have been expected to outperform less prudent rivals as trouble grew. In fact, large banks with theoretically better corporate governance arrangements, such as a high proportion of independent directors, substantial financial expertise on the board, and executives owning large equity stakes, performed no better than rivals that seemingly should have been at greater risk.[519]

Also noteworthy is that governance mechanisms in place were by no means inert as the financial crisis loomed. Instead, whatever free pass bank executives had been issued was largely revoked before the havoc of September 2008. The June 2008 *American Banker* article that indicated that corporate governance concerns had been largely theoretical in the banking sector after the enactment of SOX observed "(n)o longer."[520] Fears that a bad situation might be made worse may well have discouraged some disgruntled shareholders from publicly challenging bank executives in the midst of the financial crisis.[521] On the other hand, there was strong shareholder-led criticism of generous executive pay arrangements of various financial companies as the crisis mounted.[522] In addition, between 1994 and 2010 2008 was the year when bank shareholders made the highest number of filings with the SEC indicating an intention to engage in activism.[523]

Boards also stepped up as the financial crisis loomed. Amidst growing criticism of board practice in the banking sector and various recommendations by shareholder advisory firms to

---

[518] Alan S. Blinder, *Crazy Compensation and the Crisis*, WALL ST. J., May 28, 2009, A15. See also BLINDER, *supra* note 27, at 82.

[519] René M. Stulz, *Risk-Taking and Risk Management by Banks*, J. APP. CORP. FIN., Winter 2015, at 8, 12 (summarizing relevant empirical studies).

[520] Dobbs, *supra* note 482.

[521] Cheffins, *supra* note 188, at 47.

[522] *Id.* at 41–44.

[523] Raluca A. Roman, *Shareholder Activism in Banking*, Federal Reserve Bank of Kansas City Research Working Papers, RWP 15-09 46 (2015), tbl. 2 (103 instances in 2008; the total did not exceed a hundred in any other year).

clients to vote against nominations to board seats that banks proposed, boards began orchestrating managerial turnover at a rapid clip.[524] Chuck Prince was a prominent casualty. At the urging of the Citigroup board he resigned in November 2007 as Citigroup's CEO and chairman, and Citigroup's directors resolved to split the CEO and chairman roles so the chairman could monitor the new CEO's performance.[525] Merrill Lynch's CEO Stanley O'Neal also resigned under board pressure in late 2007.[526] More generally, of the 15 financial companies included in the S&P 500 that were sufficiently adversely affected by the onset of the financial crisis to be removed from the index during 2008 (Merrill Lynch was one of these but Citigroup was not), seven fired their CEOs in the months before removal, and lower ranking top officials were replaced at three other such firms.[527]

The fact that corrective measures were taken does not absolve bank governance from blame for the financial crisis. Arguably the reaction at large financial firms was belatedly futile. Lax oversight may have created scope for irresponsible behavior and imprudent risk-taking the consequences of which could not be reversed once sufficient momentum had been achieved.[528] As ex-General Electric CEO Jack Welch said in 2009, "(w)ithout a doubt and with perfect hindsight, some boards could have acted more boldly in trying to avert the current meltdown."[529]

The "perfect hindsight" qualification Welch offered merits closer scrutiny. Those critical of corporate governance at leading banks in the early- and mid-2000s implicitly assume boards or shareholders should have stepped forward to rein in bank executives. But was it realistic to expect this given the banks were doing well and given that very few observers were predicting with accuracy the forthcoming calamity? This seems doubtful. As a 2013 study of post-crisis banking said of boards, "(i)t takes courage to challenge what everyone else regards as a record of success."[530] Moreover, as *Time* magazine asked rhetorically at the financial crisis nadir in late September 2008, "who could have seen this coming in the fall of 2006, when things were booming and the world was awash in cheap money?"[531]

To be sure, there were "notable voices of doom, who got important bits of the puzzle correct even if the timing or other details eluded them."[532] Prescient observers were, however, a tiny minority. Alan Greenspan, admittedly seeking to justify why he did not spot the housing bubble that presaged the late 2000s financial calamity, observed "(e)verybody missed it—academia, the Federal Reserve, all regulators."[533] Warren Buffett, known as "the Sage of Omaha" because of a long-standing reputation for investing wisdom as operator of Berkshire

---

[524] Cheffins, *supra* note 188, at 34–35; *Tightrope Artists*, ECONOMIST, May 17, 2008, Paradise Lost: A Special Report on International Banking, 19.

[525] Dobbs, *supra* note 482.

[526] FARRELL, *supra* note 195, at 79–81.

[527] Cheffins, *supra* note 188, at 21, 37–39.

[528] Michael E. Murphy, *Assuring Responsible Risk Management in Banking: The Corporate Governance Dimension*, 36 DEL. J. CORP. L. 121, 143–44 (2011).

[529] Jack & Suzy Welch, *Of Boards and Blame*, BUS. WK., Jan. 26, 2009, 102.

[530] ANAT ADMATI & MARTIN HELLWIG, THE BANKERS' NEW CLOTHES: WHAT'S WRONG WITH BANKING AND WHAT TO DO ABOUT IT 126 (2013).

[531] Andy Serwer & Allan Sloan, *The Price of Greed*, TIME, Sept. 29, 2008, 32.

[532] Chris Giles, *The Vision Thing*, FIN. TIMES, Nov. 26, 2008, 13.

[533] Frank Rich, *No One Is to Blame for Anything*, NY TIMES, Apr. 11, 2010, Weekend, 10.

Hathaway, said of the housing market "very, very few people could appreciate the bubble . . . a mass delusion" shared by "300 million Americans."[534]

Top banking executives were apparently caught out as much as anyone else. If they had been aware a financial calamity was a serious risk, with respect to shares they owned in the banks for which they worked they logically would have sought to sell before September 2008 as many as possible. Instead, more than three-quarters of bank CEOs did not report any insider sales in 2007 and 2008 even though the value of the shares they continued to own fell sharply.[535] More generally, while the rescues federal officials arranged and bailouts the federal government provided cushioned at least partially the blow for ill-advised risk-taking in which bankers engaged, there is little tangible evidence indicating awareness that large banks would be saved because they were "too big to fail" provided the strategic departure point for the freewheeling banking that occurred.[536] As a *Wall Street Journal* columnist pointed out a few years after the crisis, "(n)obody has found an email from a CEO saying, 'Go ahead, roll the dice. If the worst happens, we've always got the Fed.' "[537]

A final reason to doubt the extent to which the financial crisis can be blamed on reckless bank executives operating unconstrained is that with the meltdown financial firms were hardly the only culprits. A *Newsweek* columnist observed in late 2008 "Wall Street serves as an ideal scapegoat for the deepening global recession, but the emerging consensus is that there's plenty of blame to go around."[538] The Federal Reserve, for instance, has a case to answer. The Fed, by cutting interest rates in the early 2000s and then keeping them low, did much to foster the housing "bubble" as well as a "reach for yield" that fueled the demand for risky fixed-income securities that underpinned the loose debt market of the mid-2000s.[539] Ordinary Americans also must be assigned some blame for borrowing excessively and buying unwisely on the strength of misplaced faith in the strength of the housing market.[540] As *Business Week* observed a few months before the 2008 crisis hit with full force "this whole exercise invariably circles back to the public: our rapacity, our naïveté, our willing suspension of disbelief toward all things credit. But who wants to ponder that?"[541]

Identifying exactly what caused the financial crisis is not a simple task, and debate over the issue continues today and will likely continue for years to come.[542] It suffices to say for present purposes that the corporate governance "free pass" banks received as compared to nonfinancial companies is a contender as a culprit but that there was much more to the story. One point that is clear is that the free pass was not restored once revoked, with managerial

---

[534] Financial Crisis Inquiry Commission, *supra* note 162, at 3.

[535] Rüdiger Fahlenbrach & René M. Stulz, *Bank CEO Incentives and the Credit Crisis*, 99 J. Fin. Econ. 11, 23 (2011).

[536] Greg Ip, *Critics of "Too Big to Fail" Go Too Far on Banks*, Wall St. J., Mar. 3, 2016, A2.

[537] Holman Jenkins, *Bank Bashing, the Modern Nero's Fiddle*, Wall St. J., May 23, 2015, A11.

[538] Sheridan, *supra* note 437.

[539] *Supra* notes 162–63 and related discussion; Allison, *supra* note 217, at 6, 26–33.

[540] Allison, *supra* note 217, at 9; Allan Sloan, *What's Still Wrong with Wall Street*, Time, Nov. 9, 2009, 24.

[541] Robin Farzad, *In Search of a Subprime Villain*, Bus. Wk., Feb. 4, 2008, 77.

[542] Timothy Spangler, One Step Ahead: Private Equity and Hedge Funds after the Global Financial Crisis 164 (2013); Justin Baer & Ryan Tracy, *Lasting Legacy of the Bear Stearns Bailout*, Wall St. J., Mar. 14, 2018, A1.

discretion in banks receiving heightened attention in the wake of the financial crisis.[543] The bank sector version of the imperial CEO who featured in the mid-2000s was a noteworthy casualty. In February 2009 a columnist for the *Globe & Mail* observed that historians would be able to "carbon-date that extinct species known as the celebrity CEO" to hearings of the House Financial Services Committee where members of the Committee were grilling chief executives of the eight largest financial firms in the United States.[544] There would subsequently be a formal regulatory response imposing restrictions on banks but it would not arrive until after the decade from hell had ended. We will consider the nature of the constraints the Dodd-Frank Act of 2010[545] imposed on financial firms and other public companies in the concluding chapter.

---

[543] Hugh Grove, Lorenzo Patelli, Lisa M. Victoravich & Pisun Xu, *Corporate Governance and Performance in the Wake of the Financial Crisis: Evidence from US Commercial Banks*, 19 Corp. Gov: Int'l. Rev. 418, 418 (2011); Group of Thirty, Toward Effective Governance of Financial Institutions 12 (2012).

[544] Sinclair Stewart, *Let Us Prey*, Globe & Mail, Mar. 27, 2009, 42. On the identity of those testifying, see Stacy Kaper, *Spotlight on 8 CEOs, and Pandit Grabs It*, Am. Banker, Feb. 12, 2009, 1.

[545] Dodd–Frank Wall Street Reform and Consumer Protection Act of 2010, Pub. L. 111-203.

7 The Future of the Public Company

BETWEEN THE MID-TWENTIETH century heyday of managerial capitalism and the end of the opening decade of the twenty-first century, the American public company was transformed along various dimensions. The previous six chapters have identified the key trends. This concluding chapter draws upon the historical analysis that has been provided thus far to offer conjectures about the direction of travel for the public company. It cannot be taken for granted that looking at past trends will provide insights regarding the future. For instance, with share prices of public companies the strategy is likely to be fruitless because the current price of shares likely reflects all past trading behavior.[1] Generally, however, history can provide helpful insights regarding future patterns.[2] As Theodore Roosevelt said in 1910, "(f)ull knowledge of the past helps us in dealing with the future."[3]

The prediction exercise engaged in here will not be a matter of pure historical deduction. Instead, salient developments from the 2010s will be taken into account, with particular emphasis on those that suggest a path different from that implied by changes occurring from

[1] In economics nomenclature, this will be the case if share prices conform to what is known as the weak form of the efficient capital markets hypothesis. See John Armour & Brian Cheffins, *Stock Market Prices and the Market for Corporate Control* [2016] U. ILL. L. REV. 761, 766, 769.

[2] *Does the Past Predict the Future?*, ECONOMIST.COM, Sept. 23, 2009, available at https://www.economist.com/blogs/freeexchange/2009/09/does_the_past_predict_the_futu (accessed May 9, 2018) ("Historical data maybe imperfect, but it remains the only unbiased way to measure risk and make assumptions about the future").

[3] Theodore Roosevelt, *The Progressives, Past and Present*, THE OUTLOOK, Sept. 3, 1910, available at http://www.theodore-roosevelt.com/images/research/treditorials/0160.pdf (accessed May 9, 2018).

The Public Company Transformed. Brian R. Cheffins.

the mid-twentieth century through to the opening decade of the twenty-first century. The methodology should appeal to those who believe that deploying a Bayesian approach to prediction (named for eighteenth century English mathematician Thomas Bayes) involving the adjustment of base probabilities in light of new evidence leads to more accurate (but hardly flawless) forecasting.[4]

Prediction is undertaken here with full awareness of the challenges involved. Successful prognostication is a difficult trick to execute. Distinguished physicist Niels Bohr and baseball legends Yogi Berra and Casey Stengel have each been credited with offering the warning that one should "never make predictions, especially about the future."[5] The 1982 sci-fi classic film *Blade Runner*, set in 2019 Los Angeles, illustrates how corporate-related forecasting can go awry. Numerous thriving early 1980s brands featured in the movie became defunct within a few years, prompting speculation that a cinematic curse jinxed the corporations affected.[6]

Despite the challenges involved, offering predictions is an appropriate exercise for this concluding chapter. Pragmatism plays a role. Forecasting future trends by reference to past developments is a convenient method by which to draw together key themes this book has explored.

Prediction is also needed to frame the book appropriately. From the managerial capitalism era through to the present day, the publicly traded company has been a dominant force in the American economy. Throughout the same period the typical large public company has had widely dispersed share ownership that has underpinned substantial discretion potentially available to public company executives. There has recently been considerable speculation that the public company's days are numbered. It has also been argued that, due to changes in share ownership patterns, it is no longer appropriate to assume that shareholder passivity is the appropriate governance departure point. If these conjectures are borne out, the history of the public company provided here could take the form of an epitaph. In fact, neither the public company nor a basic shareholder bias in favor of passivity is going anywhere soon. Correspondingly, the transformation of the public company described here is part of a larger story still being written.

As is the case with the book generally, the internal and external constraints that shape the discretion of public company executives will be considered in some detail. This chapter argues radical departures from present-day arrangements are unlikely any time soon. With internal constraints, board reform, a consistent theme since the 1970s, may well be reaching its limits. Hedge fund activism, which emerged in the 2000s as a meaningful form of shareholder pressure on public company executives, may likewise have peaked. Regardless, the promotion of shareholder value will likely continue to be the top priority of public company executives, to the disappointment of those hoping for the sort of balancing of interests frequently associated with managerial capitalism.

---

[4] On the contribution Bayesian analysis can make, see NATE SILVER, THE SIGNAL AND THE NOISE: THE ART AND SCIENCE OF PREDICTION 240–49, 258–61 (2012). On possible limits, see PHILIP E. TETLOCK & DAN GARDNER, SUPERFORECASTING: THE ART AND SCIENCE OF PREDICTION 171–73 (2012).

[5] Peter Patau, *According to Yogi Berra, or Niels Bohr, or Albert Einstein, or Mark Twain, or Somebody*, Dec. 2, 2006, available at http://www.peterpatau.com/2006/12/bohr-leads-berra-but-yogi-closing-gap.html (accessed Feb. 8, 2018); Adi Ignatius, *Preparing for the New World*, HARV. BUS. REV., Oct. 2015, 14.

[6] Don Steinberg, *Science Affliction: Will Brands Flop after* Blade Runner *Cameos?*, WALL ST. J., Sept. 26, 2017, A1.

As for external constraints, neither unions nor the market for corporate control are likely to impinge substantially on managerial discretion in the foreseeable future. State intervention will remain a potent constraint for public company executives, despite recent nods toward deregulation. Competitors will continue to be a source of concern as well, even though leading tech companies have been accumulating market power under controversial circumstances. A byproduct of all of this continuity is that the imperial CEO who held court during the late 1990s will not be returning anytime soon, nor will an updated version of managerial capitalism.

Drawing matters together, for those anticipating bold predictions, this chapter does not offer them. Change no doubt will occur. As *Forbes* noted in 1986, "in business as in life, nothing stays the same."[7] At this point, however, neither historical trends nor current developments provide clear guidance regarding changes affecting the public company.

Extinction of the Public Company?

With speculation regarding the future of the public company, a threshold issue is whether there is a meaningful future at all. Numerous observers have surmised recently there is not. A *Financial Times* columnist suggested in 2014 that in the United States and elsewhere publicly traded companies "are dying off, if not like flies then perhaps more like other things no longer suited to their environment—dinosaurs, say."[8] The *New York Times* indicated in 2016 that "(p)ublicly listed companies in the United States have become something of a dying breed."[9] A core claim in management professor Gerald Davis's 2016 book *The Vanishing American Corporation* is that "the public corporation will no longer be the default way of doing business."[10] Britain's *Telegraph* newspaper ran a story in 2018 under the headline "Demise of the Listed Company Is Holding the US Back."[11] In fact, nothing akin to extinction is on the agenda for the foreseeable future for the American public company.

WHAT'S NEW?

Claims that the public company's economic predominance is at risk are hardly novel. Financial economists Michael Jensen and William Meckling predicted in the late 1970s that excessive regulation would spell the end of the public company.[12] In fact, deregulation became a byword for the 1980s as share prices soared. Unbowed, in 1989 Jensen proclaimed the "eclipse" of the public company, citing the governance advantages of leveraged public-to-private buy-outs that had grown quickly in popularity.[13] Wrong again. During the 1990s

[7] M.S. Forbes, *Milken Helps Swing the Pendulum*, FORBES, Aug. 25, 1986, 23.

[8] Simon Caulkin, *On Management*, FIN. TIMES, Oct. 20, 2014, FT Business Education, 12.

[9] Andrew Ross Sorkin, *Chiefs Meet in Secret to Examine Governance*, NY TIMES, July 21, 2016, B6.

[10] GERALD F. DAVIS, THE VANISHING AMERICAN CORPORATION: NAVIGATING THE HAZARDS OF A NEW ECONOMY 93 (2016).

[11] Supriya Menon, *Demise of the Listed Company Is Holding the US Back*, TELEGRAPH, Mar. 28, 2018, Business, 2.

[12] Chapter 3, notes 40–41 and related discussion.

[13] Chapter 4, note 128 and accompanying text; Michael C. Jensen, *Eclipse of the Public Corporation*, HARV. BUS. REV., Sept.–Oct., 1989, 61.

leveraged buyouts became an afterthought and initial public offering activity soared.[14] In the mid-2000s fevered leveraged buyout activity executed by what had become known as private equity firms prompted fresh speculation that the public company was on the ropes. This time a "credit crunch" in 2007 and the financial crisis of 2008 brought the public-to-private buyout frenzy to a shuddering halt.[15]

Given the track record with prior predictions regarding the demise of the public company, it might be tempting to dismiss current speculation cursorily as yet another false alarm. The trend with the number of publicly traded companies does suggest, however, a potentially adverse long-term trend. There was a substantial drop from the late 1990s through to the late 2000s, and no significant rally has been forthcoming (Figure 7.1).[16] The Wilshire 5000 Total Market Index, established in the 1970s to capture the 5,000 or so stocks which had readily available price data at that time, was comprised of only 3,492 stocks as 2017 drew to a close.[17]

Ascertaining whether the public company is destined for oblivion merits investigation before we proceed further because its prospects contextualize in an important way the conjectures this concluding chapter offers. If the public company is on the verge of extinction the relevance of the exercise is substantially diminished, and perhaps could be entirely superfluous. In fact, despite speculation to the contrary, the public company should remain a crucial element of the American economy for the foreseeable future. As we will see now,

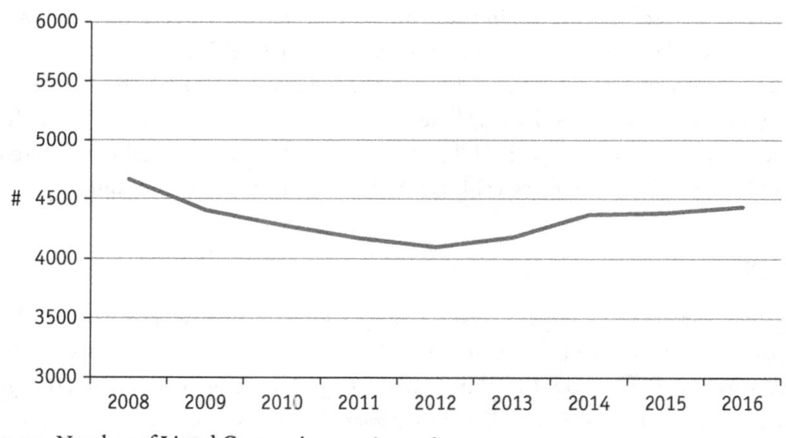

FIGURE 7.1 Number of Listed Companies, 2008–2016.
Source: World Bank, *Listed Domestic Companies, Total*, available at https://data.worldbank.org/indicator/CM.MKT.LDOM.NO?locations=US (accessed Feb. 9, 2018).

---

[14] Chapter 5, notes 80–81 and accompanying text.

[15] Chapter 6, notes 176–77, 181–85 and accompanying text.

[16] Chapter 5, Figure 5.2; Chapter 6, Figure 6.2; *Proof of Life*, ECONOMIST, Mar. 17, 2018, 69.

[17] Michael J. Mauboussin, Dan Callahan & Darius Majid, *The Incredible Shrinking Universe of Stocks: The Causes and Consequences of Fewer US Equities*, CREDIT SUISSE: GLOBAL FINANCIAL STRATEGIES, Mar. 22, 2017, 2, available at http://www.cmgwealth.com/wp-content/uploads/2017/03/document_1072753661.pdf (accessed Feb. 10, 2018); Wilshire, *Wilshire 5000 Total Market Index: Index Fact Sheet* (Dec. 31, 2017), available at https://wilshire.com/Portals/0/analytics/indexes/fact-sheets/wilshire-5000-fact-sheet.pdf (accessed Feb. 9, 2018).

neither public-to-private buyouts nor a growing reluctance of fledgling companies experiencing rapid growth to go public compromises fundamentally the public company's future prospects.

PRIVATE EQUITY

Unlike in the late 1980s and mid-2000s, public-to-private buyout activity has been something of a sideshow with the most recent speculation regarding the possible demise of the public company. The *Wall Street Journal* even suggested in 2015 "(p)rivate equity is done. Stick a fork in it."[18] This is an overwrought assessment, though it is true that the public-to-private buyout is a considerably lower profile transaction than it was in the late 1980s or mid-2000s.

Private equity firms have by no means been idle since the financial turmoil of the late 2000s knocked their public-to-private buyout business sideways. Confirming speculation engaged in when leading private equity firm Blackstone carried out a public offering in 2007,[19] a small handful of major rivals, including Kohlberg, Kravis & Roberts (KKR), Apollo Global Management, and the Carlyle Group, became publicly listed partnerships as the 2010s got underway.[20] These publicly traded private equity firms have in turn transformed their business model by diversifying away from buyout transactions. Sometimes styled now as "alternative asset managers," the firms have been developing significant international operations, providing mergers and acquisition advice, underwriting securities issues, running hedge funds, and managing funds dedicated to business lending, infrastructure projects, and property investments.[21] The *Economist*, analogizing leading private equity firms to formerly youthful rebels entering middle age, suggested in 2014 "the leveraged buy-out, the mainstay of private equity, is turning into a marginal activity."[22] By that time, only a third of the investor assets Apollo managed were tied to corporate buyouts and at Blackstone the share was below 25 percent, down from 75 percent a decade previously.[23] By 2016, less than half of Carlyle and KKR's assets were so allocated.[24]

Private equity firms, despite diversifying, continue to engage in buyout activity. They generally refrain, however, from taking private large public companies in the mid-2000s manner. Secondary buyout transactions, where a private equity firm buys a company already owned by another private equity firm, are now rivalling conventional first time-buyouts in popularity.[25] Private equity firms have also been active in acquiring divisions of companies. For instance, when in 2015 General Electric sold off most of GE Capital, its once sprawling

---

[18] Andy Kessler, *The Glory Days of Private Equity Are Over*, WALL ST. J., Mar. 30, 2015, A13.

[19] Chapter 6, note 160 and related discussion.

[20] Robert Teitelman, *Private Equity's Giants Take an Alternative Route*, INSTIT. INVESTOR, Apr. 2013, 18; Sujeet Indap, *Private Equity Chiefs Feel Misunderstood—and Undervalued*, FIN. TIMES, Mar. 22, 2016, 16.

[21] Andrew F. Tuch, *The Remaking of Wall Street*, 7 HARV. BUS. L. REV. 315, 340–47 (2017).

[22] *Barbarians at Middle Age*, ECONOMIST, Apr. 19, 2014, 65.

[23] Ryan Dezember & Nicholas Barivo, *Private-Equity Firms Build Instead of Buy*, WALL ST. J., May 15, 2013, A1.

[24] *The Barbarian Establishment*, ECONOMIST, Oct. 22, 2016, 15.

[25] Ryan Dezember, *Buyout Shops Look to Rivals*, WALL ST. J., July 31, 2014, C1; Liz Hoffman, *A MultiPlan Bonanza for Private Equity*, WALL ST. J., May 9, 2016, C1.

finance arm, private-equity firms were involved in a quarter of the more than 100 transactions involved.[26] Public-to-private buyouts also continue to occur. The number of public company delistings occurring as a result of a public-to-private buyout has been higher in the 2010s than in any decade other than the 2000s.[27]

The various types of buyout activity private equity firms oversee mean that the top private equity houses are major employers, albeit indirectly because it is the limited partnership funds they oversee that actually own the controlling stakes in the businesses in question. The portfolio companies of Carlyle and KKR each employ collectively over 700,000 workers, with the equivalent figures for Blackstone being approximately 600,000 and Apollo 300,000.[28] Each is among the 10 largest employers in the United States.[29]

While public-to-private buyouts continue to occur, this has been happening largely under the radar. The deals being carried out are smaller and less flashy than those executed in the mid-2000s.[30] During the 2010s, there have only been a handful of public-to-private transactions valued at more than $5 billion, and deals exceeding $10 billion in value have been virtually unknown.[31] In 2013 Michael Dell, founder of Dell Inc., did work together with the private equity firm Silver Lake to take the computer manufacturer private for $25 billion.[32] This was by far the largest public-to-private buyout since the financial crisis but it was not the start of a trend.[33] The Dell transaction was exceptional because of the participation of a wealthy founder able and willing to buy the bulk of the equity component of the company being taken private.[34] Restricted access to debt has helped to deter similarly scaled deals, with banks adhering to guidance regulators provided in 2013 to refrain from corporate related lending where this would mean borrowing would exceed earnings by six times or more.[35]

When asked in 2015, 84 percent of *Fortune* 500 chief executives said they would find it easier to manage their company if it was private.[36] Nevertheless, with mid-2000s mega-public-to-private buyouts having largely disappeared, it is rare for major US corporations to operate under the umbrella of private equity. At first glance 2013 data compiled by Bain, a management consultancy, suggests differently. According to Bain private-equity-backed companies accounted for 11 percent of America's "large" companies as well as 23 percent of medium-sized companies.[37] The definition of "large"—an enterprise value exceeding $500 million

---

[26] Chapter 1, note 324 and related discussion; *Barbarian Establishment, supra* note 24.

[27] Mauboussin, Callahan & Majid, *supra* note 17, at 7, exhibit #5.

[28] *Barbarian Establishment, supra* note 24; Gillian Tett, *Private Equity and Trump's Quest for Jobs*, FIN. TIMES, May 5, 2017, 11.

[29] Tett, *supra* note 28.

[30] Ryan Dezember & Sharon Terlep, *Buyouts Boom, But Not Like '07*, WALL ST. J., Aug. 23, 2012, C1.

[31] Paul J. Davies, *Cash Is Piling Up at Buyout Funds*, WALL ST. J., Aug. 28, 2017, B11; Miriam Gottfried, *Private Equity Hoards $1 Trillion in Cash*, WALL ST. J., Mar. 23, 2018, B6.

[32] Andrew Bary, *A Wind-Fall for Michael Dell*, BARRON'S, Sept. 16, 2013, 16.

[33] Ryan Dezember, *Wave of Large Buyouts Unlikely to Follow Dell*, WALL ST. J., Feb. 7, 2013, C1.

[34] *Id.*; Bary, *supra* note 32.

[35] Kessler, *supra* note 18; Gillian Tan, *Buyout Firms Feel the Pinch*, WALL ST. J., Mar. 26, 2015, C1; Gillian Tett, *The US Has Picked the Wrong Time to Ease Up on Banks*, FIN. TIMES, April 27, 2018, 11 (indicating that bank regulators were contemplating abandoning the "six times" rule).

[36] Alan Murray, *Myth-Busting the* Fortune *500*, FORTUNE, June 15, 2015, 14.

[37] *Barbarian Establishment, supra* note 24.

qualified—was very generous given the size of bigger public companies. J.C. Penney, the smallest company on the S&P 500 in 2013, had a market capitalization of nearly $2.5 billion.[38]

A 2017 ranking of America's largest private companies by *Forbes*, measured by revenue, indicates private equity's sideshow status among the very biggest firms.[39] The top 20 companies on the list had revenue exceeding the 200th-ranked company in the 2017 *Fortune* 500, which only included those private companies that filed financial documentation with government regulators.[40] Of those 20, only Albertsons, a grocery retailer that also placed 49th in the 2017 *Fortune* 500, was under private equity control.[41] Dell, ranked 4th among private companies in 2016 and 41st in the 2017 *Fortune* 500, was dropped from the 2017 largest private company list after acquiring EMC Corporation, another technology company.[42] The acquisition provided Dell with indirect exposure to public markets through VMware, a publicly traded EMC subsidiary, and in 2018 Dell announced a plan to return to the stock market.[43]

UNICORNS AND IPOS

While public-to-private buyouts were the primary focal point for gloomy predictions regarding the public company in 1989 and in the mid-2000s, recently public company pessimists have focused primarily on "unicorns." Since it was unknown before the financial crisis for a tech start-up to achieve a valuation greater than $1 billion without carrying out an initial public offering (IPO), "unicorn" became the Silicon Valley term of art used to describe still private tech companies exceeding that threshold.[44] Unicorns have since proliferated, and the phenomenon has thrown into sharp relief the possibility that the public company's status is being undermined. Exits from the stock market occur due to bankruptcies, mergers, public-to-private transactions, moves to other jurisdictions, and the process of "going dark" after a decline in shareholder numbers.[45] If companies worth more than $1 billion are

---

[38] Dan Caplinger, *Will JC Penney, JDS Uniphase, and US Steel Leave the S&P 500?*, The Motley Fool, Nov. 2, 2013, available at https://www.fool.com/investing/general/2013/11/02/will-jc-penney-jds-uniphase-and-us-steel-leave-the.aspx (accessed May 11, 2018).

[39] Andrea Murphy, *America's Largest Private Companies 2017*, FORBES.COM, Aug. 9, 2017, available at https://www.forbes.com/sites/andreamurphy/2017/08/09/americas-largest-private-companies-2/#2255a3f5247c (accessed May 21, 2018).

[40] *Fortune 500*, link to methodology and credits, FORTUNE.COM, available at http://fortune.com/fortune500/ (accessed March 21, 2018).

[41] *Largest US Corporations*, FORTUNE, June 15, 2017, F1. Albertsons was taken private in 2006. See http://www.albertsons.com/wp-content/uploads/2015/07/Albertsons-75-Anniversary-Timeline.pdf (accessed May 21, 2018).

[42] Murphy, *supra* note 39.

[43] *Dell: The Revenant*, FIN. TIMES, Jan. 27/28, 2018, 22; Jay Greene, *Dell and CEO Return to Public Spotlight*, WALL ST. J., July 3, 2018, B3.

[44] Gideon Lewis-Krauss, *Bubble Indemnity*, NY TIMES, May 10, 2016, Sunday Magazine, 20; Corrie Driebusch & Maureen Farrell, *IPO Misfires Shake Silicon Valley Startups*, WALL ST. J., Aug. 2, 2017, B1.

[45] On going dark, see Chapter 6, note 121 and related discussion.

refraining from joining the stock market, how will the pool of public companies ever be replenished?[46]

The unicorn phenomenon has developed in a wider context where it is assumed the IPO market has not been fulfilling its potential with regard to launching public companies. The chair of the Securities and Exchange Commission (SEC) acknowledged in 2011 IPO activity "was not as robust . . . as we would like it to be."[47] The *Economist* said in 2016 the US IPO market had "shrunk into insignificance."[48] In 2017, the *Wall Street Journal* drew attention to "concern that the public markets are being used as a last resort."[49] The number of IPOs indeed has been modest in the 2010s compared with the 1990s, having failed to rebound meaningfully after an abrupt decline following the end of the dot.com frenzy at the beginning of the noughties (Figure 7.2).

Lukewarm investor interest has helped to suppress IPO activity.[50] During the dot.com boom there was a voracious appetite for tech-related IPOs, sustained by enthusiasm so robust numerous individuals quit their jobs to invest in stocks.[51] No more. Kathleen Smith, cofounder of a firm specializing in IPO research, said in 2016 of retail investors "(t)hey are not in there flipping IPOs. The individual investor participation, which tends to be the easy money, is not there, and it's very unlikely to come back."[52]

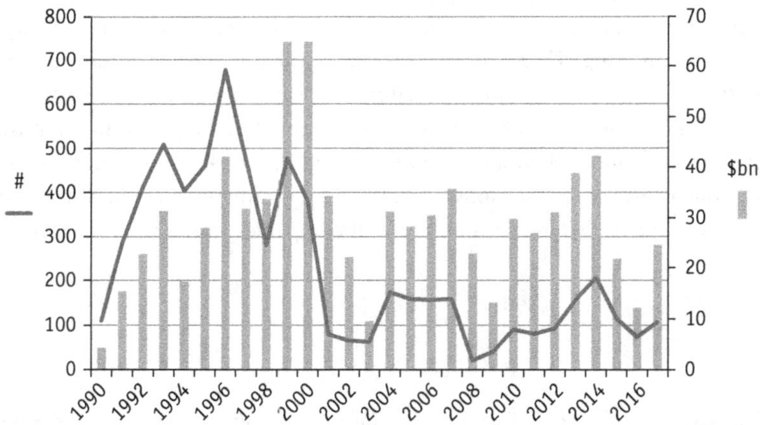

FIGURE 7.2 Number of IPOs and Aggregate Proceeds, 1990–2017.

Source: Jay R. Ritter, *Initial Public Offerings: Updated Statistics*, Jan. 17, 2018, 3, available at https://site.warrington.ufl.edu/ritter/files/2018/01/IPOs2017Statistics_January17_2018.pdf (accessed Feb. 9, 2018).

[46] Kopin Tan, *Now, It's the Wilshire 3,666*, BARRON'S, Feb. 24, 2014, 9; *Life in the Public Eye*, ECONOMIST, Apr. 22, 2017, 62; Alexander Ljungqvist, Lars Persson & Joacim Tåg, *Private Equity's Unintended Dark Side: On the Economic Consequences of Excessive Delistings*, NBER Working Paper 21909, 7 (2016).

[47] Aaron Lucchetti, *US Falls Behind in Stock Listings*, WALL ST. J., May 26, 2011, A1.

[48] *The New Methuselahs*, ECONOMIST, Sept. 17, 2016, Survey—Rise of the Superstars, 7.

[49] Corrie Driebusch & Maureen Farrell, *Market Fuels an IPO Push but Biggest Names Hold Off*, WALL ST. J., May 8, 2017, A1.

[50] Alexander Eule, *The Disappearing IPO Market*, BARRON'S, June 6, 2016, 23.

[51] *To Fly, to Fall, to Fly Again*, ECONOMIST, July 25, 2015, 17.

[52] Eule, *supra* note 50. See also Akane Otani & Chris Dieterich, *Many Investors Bailed Out Early*, WALL ST. J., Jan. 5, 2018, A1.

Reluctant sellers have dampened IPO activity as much, if not more than, discerning buyers. The *New York Times* said in 2015 about IPO wariness among tech sector proprietors

> The initial public offering of stock has become déclassé. For start-up entrepreneurs and their employees across Silicon Valley, an initial public offering is no longer a main goal. Instead, many founders talk about going public as a necessary evil to be postponed as long as possible because it comes with more problems than benefits.[53]

Regulatory concerns are often identified as a primary reason for IPO skepticism.[54] *Barron's*, for instance, indicated in 2014 that "(i)ncreased regulation and the climbing costs of a public listing have weakened the resolve of managers who once dreamt of ringing the opening bell at the New York Stock Exchange."[55] Continuing with a trend from the 2000s, additional compliance costs the Sarbanes-Oxley Act of 2002 (SOX) imposed on publicly traded companies are frequently singled out as the primary regulatory deterrent to going public.[56] SOX's impact in fact probably has been marginal, as evidenced by the fact that IPO activity started to decline before it was enacted.[57] Nevertheless, fears of overregulation deterring IPOs yielded policymaking dividends in 2012.

In 2011 the IPO Task Force, struck as a result of deliberations launched by the US Treasury, made proposals for statutory change designed to solve what the Task Force characterized as an "IPO crisis."[58] A key recommendation was the creation of an "IPO on-ramp" that would give "emerging growth companies" going public while generating less than $1 billion of revenue in their most recently completed fiscal year up to five years to scale up to full compliance with disclosure obligations federal securities law imposed.[59] The Task Force said that emerging growth companies should also be able to "test the waters" prior to committing fully to an IPO by filing draft registration statements confidentially with the SEC and by conferring informally with qualified institutional investors.[60] The Jumpstart Our Business Startups (JOBS) Act, enacted by Congress in 2012,[61] implemented these and various other recommendations the IPO Task Force made.[62]

---

[53] Farhad Manjoo, *The Next Big Tech IPO Could Be a Private One*, NY Times, July 2, 2015, B1.

[54] Elisabeth de Fontenay, *The Deregulation of Private Capital and the Decline of the Public Company*, 68 Hastings L.J. 445, 447 (2017).

[55] Tan, *supra* note 46.

[56] Sarbanes-Oxley Act of 2002, Pub. L. 107–204, 116 Stat. 745; Chapter 6, note 111 and related discussion; Eule, *supra* note 50; Xiaohui Gao, Jay R. Ritter & Zhongyan Zhu, *Where Have All the IPOs Gone?*, 48 J. Fin. Quant. Analysis 1663, 1663–64 (2013); Scott S. Powell, *A Pox on SOX, It's Bad for Stocks*, Wall St. J., Feb. 14, 2018, A19.

[57] See Figure 7.2; Chapter 6, note 113 and accompanying text; de Fontenay, *supra* note 54, at 464–65; Craig Doidge, G. Andrew Karolyi & René M. Stulz, *The US Listing Gap*, 123 J. Fin. Econ. 464, 486 (2017).

[58] IPO Task Force, Rebuilding the IPO On-Ramp: Putting Emerging Companies and the Job Market Back on the Road to Growth 1–3 (2011).

[59] *Id.* at 2, 19–20.

[60] *Id.* at 28–29.

[61] Pub. L. No. 112-106, 126 Stat. 306.

[62] For an overview of the "on ramp" and "test the waters" provisions, see Carlos Berdejo, *Going Public after the JOBS Act*, 76 Ohio St. L.J. 1, 22–27 (2015). For a summary of these and other key measures in the legislation, see Thaya Brook Knight, *A Walk through the JOBS Act of 2012: Deregulation in the Wake of Financial Crisis*, CATO Institute Policy Analysis, No. 790, May 3, 2016.

There is academic research suggesting the JOBS Act helped to foster IPO activity.[63] Nevertheless, the fact that the number of IPOs remained well below pre-2001 levels post-JOBS (Figure 7.2) indicates factors other than regulation have contributed to the aversion to public offerings on the part of reluctant sellers.[64] For proprietors of a growing company, there indeed are various "frustrations of publicness" aside from regulation that mean going public is not all it has been cracked up to be.[65] *Fortune* offered a pithy summary in 2017:

> To startup founders, going public meant jumping through hoops to get a bunch of bean-counting Wall Streeters to see their world-changing vision, diluting their ownership, and paying massive banker fees for the privilege. And if it was successful, their reward would be earnings reports, every quarter, for the rest of time, while a bunch of high-frequency trading bots threaten to tank the stock anytime the company misses its overly lofty revenue projections or an employee tweets something dumb.[66]

Fortune framed matters in the past tense because it was asserting that an "IPO fever" not seen since the dot.com era was underway.[67] The primary example of the new trend was said to be Snap, the operator of the messaging app Snapchat, where investor demand for shares available in a $3.4 billion IPO was sufficiently robust to drive the share price up 44 percent on the first day of trading.[68] Snap, however, would soon find out about the rigors of public markets. The company's share price fell 21 percent after Snap announced a $2.2 billion loss in its first earnings report as a public company.[69] The ensuing conference call involving analysts following Snap and Snap executives, including 26-year old cofounder and CEO Evan Spiegel, illustrated the harsh scrutiny a public company that disappoints investors can face. According to the *New York Times*

> During the event, many analysts' questions about the company were dismissed by Mr. Spiegel. None of the executives made a particularly impassioned case for why the business would be a success over the long term. On Thursday, Jim Cramer, the investor and CNBC host, said Mr. Spiegel needed to be "hazed" and put through a "gauntlet" by investors because "he is so arrogant."[70]

---

[63] Michael Dambra, Laura Casares Field & Matthew T. Gustafson, *The JOBS Act and IPO Volume: Evidence That Disclosure Costs Affect the IPO Decision*, 116 J. Fin. Econ. 121 (2015); Marlin R. H. Jensen, Beverly B. Marshall & John S. Jahera, *JOBS Act: Has It Brought Back the IPO?*, J. Corp. Accounting & Fin., Jan./Feb. 2015, 9, 15–17.

[64] Steven Davidoff Solomon, *Deregulation Isn't a Quick Fix for Decline in IPOs*, NY Times, Mar. 29, 2017, B6; Gerald F. Davis, Post-Corporate: The Disappearing Corporation in the New Economy 18 (2017) (available at http://www.thirdway.org/report/post-corporate-the-disappearing-corporation-in-the-new-economy) (accessed Jan. 10, 2018).

[65] Donald C. Langevoort, Selling Hope, Selling Risk: Corporations, Wall Street, and the Dilemmas of Investor Protection 112 (2016); see also John Authers, *Vote of No-Confidence in Shareholder Capitalism*, Fin. Times, Oct. 24, 2015, 24.

[66] Erin Griffith, *Goodbye, Unicorns. Hello, IPOs!*, Fortune, May 1, 2017, 7.

[67] *Id.*

[68] Michael J. de la Merced, *Will Snap's Value Disappear? Investors Focus on the Positive*, NY Times, Mar. 3, 2017, A1.

[69] Katie Benner, *In Snap's Tumble, StartUps See the Hazards of Public Offerings*, NY Times, May 12, 2017, B1.

[70] *Id.*

Snap's rough initiation to public markets was characterized as "a powerful lesson to other start-ups" and likely helped to quell the IPO "fever" *Fortune* had diagnosed.[71] IPO activity in 2017 was up modestly as compared with 2016 but was less robust than it was between 2013 and 2015.[72]

Even taking into account the hassle associated with being publicly traded, a desire to provide a convenient exit option for current owners of shares can furnish the impetus for an IPO. While shares in a private company will usually be illiquid investments, with a stock market listing stockholders seeking to diversify or cash out fully can typically count on being able to sell shares they own promptly at or near the market price.[73] Exit options, however, have become more promising recently with firms that have not moved to the stock market. Sales of sizeable holdings in still private companies, known as secondary sales, have become easier recently with private equity funds, sovereign wealth funds, and even some public companies stepping forward as buyers.[74] For smaller stakes, NASDAQ may well be able to provide the answer. It established in 2013 the Nasdaq Private Market as an online marketplace to match buyers and sellers of shares in private companies and in 2015 acquired leading rival SecondMarket, which had been in the business since 2009.[75]

For a privately held company with promising prospects that is currently producing relatively little cash flow the possibility of raising capital by issuing shares is an additional potentially compelling reason to go public. It is now possible, however, for a promising venture to scale up more cheaply than used to be the case. With the economy having become increasingly technology-intensive there is a reduced need to spend on costly fixed assets such as plants and equipment.[76] Moreover, innovations such as e-mail, social media, outsourced "cloud" infrastructure and open-source software mean start-up ventures can access readily and economically computing and communication capabilities formerly restricted to large corporations.[77]

Private companies with promising growth prospects not only need less capital but they can now get what they need more easily without a public offering. In various ways "(f)unding dedicated to private startups is robust."[78] Web-based financing interfaces have made it

---

[71] *Id.*; Jack Nicas, *IPO Wave Is Coming, And Investors Spy a Payday*, NY TIMES, April 16, 2018, B1 (acknowledging that Snap's problems afflicted IPOs in 2017 but predicting fresh IPO momentum was building in 2018).

[72] See Figure 7.2; Jay R. Ritter, *Initial Public Offerings: Updated Statistics*, Jan. 17, 2018, 3, available at https://site.warrington.ufl.edu/ritter/files/2018/01/IPOs2017Statistics_January17_2018.pdf (accessed Feb. 9, 2018).

[73] BRIAN R. CHEFFINS, CORPORATE OWNERSHIP AND CONTROL: BRITISH BUSINESS TRANSFORMED 65 (2008). Major shareholders may have to wait to sell due to a "lock up" arrangement.

[74] Eliot Brown & Greg Bensinger, *Firms Buy Stakes of Startups Privately*, WALL ST. J., Nov. 20, 2017, B1.

[75] Tess Stynes & Bradley Hope, *Nasdaq Buys SecondMarket*, WALL ST. J., Oct. 23, 2015, C3; *SharesPost Sells Interest in NASDAQ*, COMPUTER WEEKLY NEWS, Oct. 29, 2015.

[76] Mauboussin Callahan & Majid, *supra* note 17, at 12; *Life in the Public Eye*, ECONOMIST, Apr. 22, 2017, 62; Craig Doidge et al., *Eclipse of the Public Corporation or Eclipse of the Public Markets?*, ECGI Working Paper in Finance, No 547/2018, 13 (2018).

[77] Nathan Heller, *Bay Watched*, NEW YORKER, Oct. 14, 2013, available at https://www.newyorker.com/magazine/2013/10/14/bay-watched (accessed May 20, 2018); Keith C. Brown & Kenneth W. Wiles, *In Search of Unicorns: Private IPOs and the Changing Markets for Private Equity Investments and Corporate Control*, J. APP. CORP. FIN., Summer 2015, at 34, 45; Hal Varian, *There Is No Hope of a Quiet Life in the Age of Disruption*, FIN. TIMES, Oct. 4, 2016, 13.

[78] Driebusch & Farrell, *supra* note 44. See also Mauboussin, Callahan & Majid, *supra* note 17, at 12; Doidge et al. *supra* note 76, at 12; Jason M. Thomas, *Where Have All the Public Companies Gone?*, WALL ST. J., Nov. 17, 2017, A15; Jean Eaglesham & Coulter Jones, *Powering US Business: Private Capital*, WALL ST. J., Apr. 3, 2018, A1.

easier for those running fledgling ventures to link up with affluent "angels" looking to back promising start-ups with seed capital.[79] Large asset managers, hedge funds, and sovereign wealth funds have joined venture capitalists in participating in later stage financing of up-and-coming private enterprises, meaning "hot startups are living in a brave new world of big capital."[80] Sovereign wealth funds have also been major backers of Visionfund, a $100 billion investment vehicle that Japanese conglomerate Softbank has set up which has, with substantial capital outlays in tech startups, reinforced the "tendency for highly valued private companies to shun the public markets for longer."[81] The venture capital industry itself has been growing, with $359 billion being invested through it in 2017, double the amount in 2005.[82] Drawing on such sources, unicorn Uber, an app-oriented ride-hailing service founded in 2009, had by 2017 raised $14 billion and has been valued as highly as $70 billion.[83]

With the financial and shareholder liquidity hitches associated with private company status having been at least partly alleviated, unicorns have proliferated. As of 2018, 105 still private US start-ups were valued at $1 billion or more, with the number having more than tripled in four years.[84] The term "decacorns," attributed to private companies such as Uber with a valuation of $10 billion or more, has even entered the financial lexicon.[85]

Despite a growing reticence among those operating rapidly growing private companies to go public and the associated rise of unicorns, the economic significance of the public company has not been compromised fundamentally. One reason is that a common fate for companies that formerly might have carried out an IPO is now to "exit" by selling themselves to a large, established, and probably public company. In 2015, a year when 157 companies went public in the United States, there were nearly 20 additional firms that were pursuing an IPO but stopped due to being acquired.[86] With most large companies being publicly traded,[87] when promising start-ups sidestep IPOs by selling to major established businesses the assets most often end up in the public company realm, albeit by a different route. Apple, Alphabet (the parent company of Google), Amazon, Facebook, and Microsoft, each a publicly traded tech giant, bought up nearly 330 small firms between them between 2013 and 2018.[88]

---

[79] *Reinventing the Deal*, ECONOMIST, Oct. 24, 2015, 23; Stephen Foley, *Flurry of Innovation Prompts Easier Access to Funding*, FIN. TIMES, Feb. 9, 2016, Raising Capital, 2.

[80] Dan Primak, *Dear Tech CEOs: Go Public, for the Good of the Country*, FORTUNE, Aug. 11, 2014, 44. See also Gillian Tett, *The Legend of the Silicon Valley Unicorns*, FIN. TIMES, Feb. 27, 2015, 9; Renee Jones, *The Unicorn Governance Trap*, 166 U. PA. L. REV. ONLINE 165, 173 (2017); Nicole Bullock & Robin Wigglesworth, *US Seeks Depth in the Listings Pool*, FIN. TIMES, Jan. 9, 2018, 9.

[81] *The Son Kingdom*, ECONOMIST, May 10, 2018, 21.

[82] NATIONAL VENTURE CAPITAL ASSOCIATION, 2018 YEARBOOK 10 (2018).

[83] Chad Bray & Matthew Goldstein, *US Gives All Firms Secrecy in IPOs*, NY TIMES, July 1, 2017, B1.

[84] Eaglesham & Jones, *supra* note 78.

[85] Jones, *supra* note 80, at 178.

[86] Telis Demos & Corrie Driebusch, *Forget IPOs, Firms Want to Get Bought*, WALL ST. J., Nov. 30, 2015, C1.

[87] Chapter 1, note 1 and accompanying text.

[88] *Infra* notes 389, 413 and accompanying text; *Chicago Bears*, ECONOMIST, April 28, 2018, 62.

If a sale to an established company is not forthcoming and if success is sustained, factors that motivate IPOs will ultimately likely tip the balance in favor of a public offering despite misgivings proprietors might have. As the *Financial Times* observed in 2016, "(e)ven the flushest unicorn, however, lacks billions of dollars for big purchases. It could attempt to use its own private stock but battle-scarred investors say that is difficult."[89] Facebook's experience is instructive. Mark Zuckerberg, the firm's cofounder and CEO, made clear his antipathy toward a move to the stock market in a 2010 interview on the TV news show *60 Minutes*, saying "(a) lot of people who I think build start-ups or companies think that selling the company or going public is this endpoint. . . . And that's just not how I see it."[90] Nevertheless, in 2012, Facebook carried out what *Barron's* heralded as "the mostly eagerly awaited initial public offering ever."[91]

With IPOs having "become déclassé"[92] but not defunct those companies that join the stock market now do so later than used to be the case. The median age of companies going public between 2001 and 2016 was 50 percent higher than it was between 1976 and 2000.[93] Companies joining the stock market are also bigger than they used to be,[94] a trend evidenced by the fact that a decline in annual aggregate IPO proceeds since 2000 has been much less precipitous than the decline in the number of IPOs (Figure 7.2). With companies joining the stock market later, public investors have less scope to capture the upside with fledgling companies experiencing rapid initial growth and may well struggle to gain exposure to fast-growing industry segments.[95] With respect to the future of the public company, however, the key point is that "(p)eople have been staying private for longer, not forever."[96] Until "forever" becomes the choice, trends relating to IPOs and unicorns will not foretell the demise of the public company.

THE PUBLIC COMPANY RETAINS CENTER STAGE

One might deduce from the foregoing account of IPOs and unicorns that the decline of the public company is less precipitous than is widely perceived but is occurring nevertheless. A revised assessment of this nature is closer to the mark but still implies an ultimately dismal outlook for the public company. In fact, the "winners" in the public company sector have been thriving and likely are as influential as they ever have been.[97]

---

[89] Tom Braithwaite, *Private Pressures*, FIN. TIMES, Oct. 24, 2016, 9. See also Andy Kessler, *Unicorns Need IPOs*, WALL ST. J., Jan. 8, 2018, A15.

[90] *Friending Private Capital*, WALL ST. J., Jan. 5, 2010, A14.

[91] Andrew Bary, *Mad about Facebook*, BARRON'S, May 14, 2012, 15.

[92] *Supra* note 53 and accompanying text.

[93] Mauboussin, Callahan & Majid, *supra* note 17, at 11. See also Michael Wursthorn & Gregory Zuckerman, *Number of Listed Companies Is Falling*, WALL ST. J., Jan. 5, 2018, A8 (the average age of companies carrying out IPOs was 18 years in 2017 versus 12 in 1996).

[94] Rana Foroohar, *Public Offerings That Serve a Wealthy Few*, FIN. TIMES, July 24, 2017, 11.

[95] Powell, *supra* note 56; Merryn Somerset Webb, *Money Manager Capitalism Harms Us All*, FIN. TIMES, Jan. 30, 2016, FT Money, 24; *The Lessons of Amazon*, WALL ST. J., May 19, 2017, A16.

[96] Bullock & Wigglesworth, *supra* note 80 (quoting the head of capital markets at KKR).

[97] Conrad S. Ciccotello, *The State of the Public Corporation: Not So Much an Eclipse as an Evolution*, J. APP. CORP. FIN., Fall 2014, at 8, 10.

The American economy rallied from the 2008 financial crisis that concluded a "decade from hell" for public companies, but only hesitantly. Measured in terms of GDP growth, the recovery was the weakest rebound from a recession in the post–World War II era.[98] In contrast, after-tax corporate profits were healthy.[99] Stock prices also rallied sharply. Investors who bought the S&P 500 as it hit its pre-financial-crisis high in October 2007 and held on for a decade would, including dividends, have more than doubled their money despite the financial crisis meltdown.[100] The annualized return of 5.6 percent above inflation for that decade was only marginally below historical norms over the past two centuries.[101]

Due in part to the post-financial-crisis stock market rally publicly traded companies are, when measured in terms of the ratio between aggregate market capitalization and US GDP, as important an element of the US economy as they ever have been (Figure 7.3).[102] With the number of public companies having declined, a corollary is that those companies that are listed have become bigger. Indeed, in 2017 the average market capitalization of listed companies was almost $7 billion, more than 10 times as large on an inflation-adjusted basis as the average mid-1970s public company.[103]

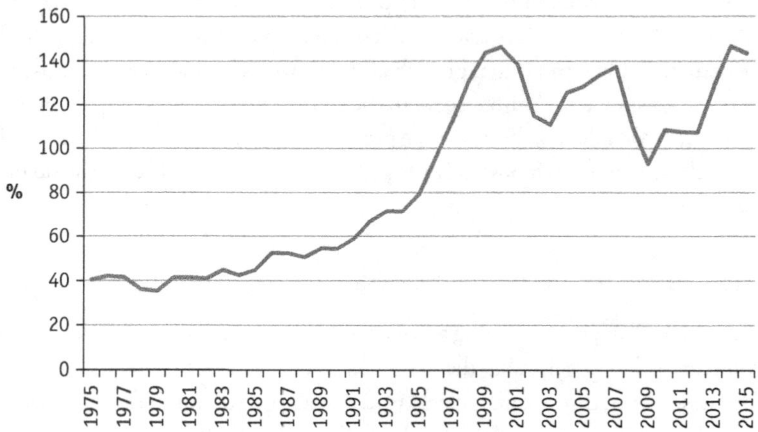

FIGURE 7.3 Stock Market Capitalization/GDP, Percent, 1975–2015.
Source: Federal Reserve Bank of St. Louis, *FRED Economic Data—Stock Market Capitalization to GDP for United States, Percent, Annual,* Aug. 30, 2017, available at https://fred.stlouisfed.org/series/DDDM01USA156NWDB (accessed Feb. 15, 2018).

98 Rich Karlgaard, *Why Economic Growth Stinks*, FORBES, Sept. 13, 2016, 44.

99 Ted Kavadas, *Corporate Profits as a Percentage of GDP*, EconomicGreenfield, May 26, 2017, https://www.economicgreenfield.com/2017/05/26/corporate-profits-as-a-percentage-of-gdp-19/ (accessed Feb. 15, 2018).

100 James Mackintosh, *The False Prophet of "Long-Term Investing,"* WALL ST. J., Oct. 10, 2017, B1.

101 *Id.* See also James Mackintosh, *US Stock Returns Belie A Postcrisis Landscape*, WALL ST. J., June 5, 2018, B1 (annualized inflation adjusted stock market returns between June 2008 and June 2018 exceeded post-1900 norm).

102 *Cf.* Kathleen M. Kahle & René M. Stulz, *Is the US Public Corporation in Trouble?*, 31 J. ECON. PERSP. 67, 71 (2017) (acknowledging the basic trend but emphasizing the volatility of the aggregate market capitalization/GDP ratio as a measure of financial development and maintaining that this ratio remained somewhat lower in 2015 than it was in 1999).

103 Mauboussin, Callahan & Majid, *supra* note 17, at 8; Doidge et al. *supra* note 76, at 4–5.

There is other evidence that those American corporations that are publicly traded have been thriving and have remained influential even as the number of companies listed on the stock market has fallen. While public companies comprise only a tiny and recently declining fraction of America's 28 million businesses, they continue to account for half of capital spending by business.[104] Total sales generated by the *Fortune* 500 increased from 59 percent of US gross domestic product in 1995 to 65 percent in 2017, which, given that 470 of the 2017 *Fortune* 500 companies were publicly traded, is a statistic driven primarily by public corporations.[105] Among the 100 largest public corporations in the world ranked by market capitalization as of 2017, 55 were American as compared with 35 in 2008.[106]

The continued vibrancy of the public company has not translated into public admiration. According to polling data, confidence in big business, having fallen in the 2000s,[107] has not rallied substantially since the financial crisis (Figure 7.4). Despite this, and despite a decline in the number of public companies since the 1990s, the public company remains a crucial element of the US economy. Absent the economic or regulatory equivalent of the asteroid

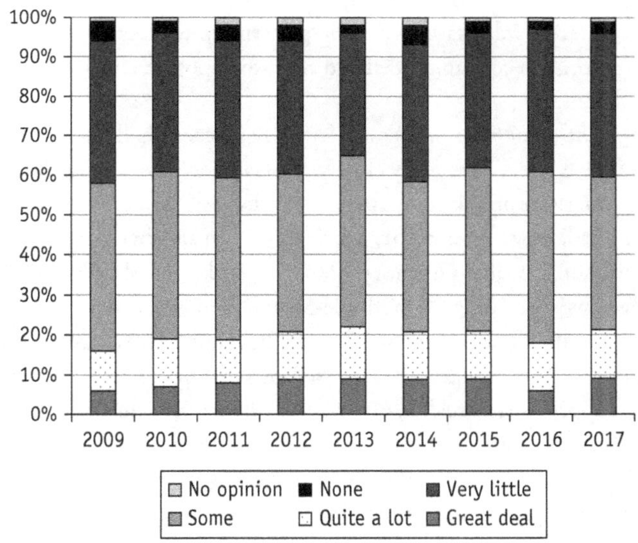

FIGURE 7.4 Confidence in Big Business, 2009–2017.
Source: Gallup, *Confidence in Institutions*, available at http://www.gallup.com/poll/1597/confidence-institutions.aspx (accessed Mar. 16, 2018).

[104] Jamie Dimon & Warren E. Buffett, *Short-Termism is Harming the Economy*, WALL ST. J., June 7, 2018, A17.

[105] Laura Entis, *America: A Growth Industry*, FORTUNE, June 15, 2017, 149 (*Fortune* 500/GDP data). With the 2017 *Fortune* 500 list, there were 30 companies that had no market value listed and thus would not have been publicly traded. Most were mutually owned companies such as State Farm Insurance, with various others being employee owned (e.g., Publix Super Markets) or co-operatives (e.g., Minnesota's CHS). See *Largest US Corporations*, FORTUNE, June 15, 2017, F1.

[106] PWC, *Global Top 100 Companies by Market Capitalisation: 31 March 2017 Update*, available at https://www.pwc.com/gx/en/audit-services/assets/pdf/global-top-100-companies-2017-final.pdf (accessed Feb. 16, 2018).

[107] Chapter 6, note 222 and related discussion.

that left behind the Chicxulub crater off Mexico and was "ground zero of the Cretaceous extinction event,"[108] the public company is hardly a dinosaur destined for oblivion or even obscurity.

The End of the Berle-Means Corporation?

Even if the American public company is destined to continue to play a predominant economic role, an integral feature could be in jeopardy. What Adolf Berle and Gardiner Means characterized in 1932 as a separation of share ownership from managerial control has been a hallmark of corporate life in the United States since the heyday of managerial capitalism.[109] The fact that dominant shareholders have been the exception to the rule has expanded considerably the scope for executives to pursue their own agenda, potentially in a manner that is detrimental for shareholders as well as others affected by corporate activity.[110] The separation of ownership and control has in turn constituted the "core fissure" in US corporate governance.[111] There has been speculation recently that the diffuse pattern of stock ownership associated with the US public company since the managerial capitalism era has been substantially displaced. In fact, while share ownership patterns have undergone change, a separation of ownership and control continues to afford executives potentially wide discretion in most large public companies.

The separation of ownership and control that has been a hallmark of corporate life in the United States has been sufficiently closely associated with Berle and Means for the prototypical large American public company to be styled as "the Berle-Means corporation."[112] Gerald Davis argued, however, in a 2011 article that "(i)n another generation, the Berle and Means corporation may be just a memory."[113] Corporate law scholars Ronald Gilson and Jeff Gordon claimed two years later "(t)he Berle-Means premise of dispersed share ownership is now wrong."[114] Fellow legal academics Lucian Bebchuk, Alma Cohen, and Scott Hirst asserted in 2017 that "the scenario of dispersed ownership described by Berle and Means (1932) no longer approximates reality, not even for the largest publicly traded corporations" and suggested "current share ownership is significantly more concentrated than the level described by Berle and Means (1932)."[115] Despite the protestations to the contrary, a separation of ownership and control in fact remains a hallmark of large public corporations in the United States, albeit with a significant institutional shareholder twist.

[108] Nicholas St. Fleur, *Cosmic Collision: Dinosaur-Killing Asteroid's Deep Impact*, NY TIMES, Nov. 22, 2016, D2.

[109] Chapter 1, note 47 and related discussion; ADOLF A. BERLE & GARDINER C. MEANS, THE MODERN CORPORATION & PRIVATE PROPERTY (1932).

[110] Chapter 2, notes 169, 171 and accompanying text.

[111] Chapter 2, note 172 and related discussion.

[112] Chapter 2, note 73 and accompanying text.

[113] Gerald F. Davis, *The Twilight of the Berle and Means Corporation*, 34 SEATTLE UNIV. L. REV. 1121, 1122 (2011).

[114] Ronald J. Gilson & Jeffrey N. Gordon, *The Agency Costs of Agency Capitalism: Activist Investors and the Revaluation of Governance Rights*, 113 COLUM. L. REV. 863, 865 (2013).

[115] Lucian A. Bebchuk, Alma Cohen & Scott Hirst, *The Agency Problems of Institutional Investors*, 31 J. ECON. PERSP. 89, 92 (2017).

The Berle-Means corporation came to dominate the American corporate economy when shareholders with sufficiently large ownership stakes to dictate outcomes when stockholders voted became the exception to the rule in large companies.[116] One might logically expect that the supposedly imminent demise of the Berle-Means corporation is due to a revival of shareholders of this sort. There has been no such trend, as a 2016 study of ownership patterns in the S&P 1500 stock market index carried out on behalf of the Investor Responsibility Research Center Institute (IRRCI) and Institutional Shareholder Services (ISS) makes clear.[117]

The IRRCI/ISS study focused on "controlled" companies, with corporations qualifying in one of two circumstances. The first was where a significant shareholder, or shareholder group, owned 30 percent or more of the voting shares. The second was where there was a multi-class capital structure in place that allocated de facto control through share classes providing disproportionately large voting rights or enhanced board election rights.[118] The IRRCI/ISS study found "(c)ontrary to common belief the number of controlled companies has declined recently," with only 105, or 7 percent, of firms in the S&P 1500 qualifying.[119] As per the Berle-Means corporation characterization, then, stockholders with sufficient voting clout to dictate reliably the fate of the companies in which they own shares are very much the exception to the rule.

The small number of controlled companies needs to be borne in mind when considering Bebchuk, Cohen, and Hirst's claim that ownership and control is currently more concentrated than it was in 1932. When they drew upon Berle and Means's data to compare 1932 with the present day they excluded from their calculations corporations that had a shareholder or tight coalition of shareholders with substantial voting power.[120] While such companies are a rarity among larger public companies today, they made up a majority of the 200 companies Berle and Means considered.[121] Comparing all large companies rather than just those lacking a major shareholder would no doubt reveal ownership is considerably more widely dispersed today than it was in 1932.

Among the 105 companies in the IRRCI/ISS study with controlling shareholders, there were 27 firms with a shareholder group owning 30 percent or more of the shares and 78 with multi-class capital structures. The growing popularity of multi-class shares among tech-oriented companies going public has been widely reported, with prominent examples including Mark Zuckerberg with Facebook in 2012 and Fitbit Inc. and Box Inc. in 2015.[122] Typically, though, only a small minority of VC-backed companies that go public have such arrangements in place and among those firms it is exceptional for there to be a CEO/founder

---

116 Chapter 2, notes 81–88 and accompanying text.

117 Edward Kamanjoh, Controlled Companies in the Standard & Poor's 1500: A Follow Up Review of Performance and Risk (2016).

118 *Id.* at 4, 15.

119 *Id.* at 15. See also María Gutiérrez & Maribel Sáez Lacave, *Strong Shareholders, Weak Outside Investors*, 18 J. Corp. L. Stud. 1, 4 (2018) (indicating that among the largest 100 American public corporations as of 2016, 85 percent lacked a shareholder owning 25 percent or more of the shares).

120 Bebchuk, Cohen, & Hirst, *supra* note 115, at 91.

121 Chapter 2, notes 74–75 and related discussion; Berle & Means, *supra* note 109, at 106, 109.

122 John Plender, *Governance Lessons Lost on Facebook*, Fin. Times, Feb. 28, 2012, FT fm, 27; Kristin Lin, *The Big Number*, Wall St. J., Aug. 18, 2015, B6.

who retains voting control.[123] Indeed, the IRRCI/ISS study indicated the number of S&P 1500 companies where control existed due to a multi-class capital structure actually declined slightly from 79 in 2012.[124] The IRRCI/ISS study did not take into account an increase in 2017 and 2018 of the number of venture-capital backed tech IPOs that provided for founder friendly voting arrangements, exemplified by Snap becoming the first major company since at least 2000 to go public while offering shares with no voting rights attached.[125] Nevertheless, multi-class capital structures likely remain too rare and too controversial—S&P Dow Jones announced in 2017 that it would no longer add companies with multi-class shares to its iconic S&P 500 index[126]—to disrupt the dominance of the Berle-Means corporation in the foreseeable future.

If the Berle-Means corporation's days are not numbered because of shareholders with substantial voting clout, whether due to large ownership blocs or multi-class capital structures, what threat is there? Stakes held collectively by institutional intermediaries are said to be responsible. As Bebchuk, Cohen, and Hirst say, "the trend toward dispersion has been reversed in subsequent decades by the rise of institutional investors."[127] The prominence of institutional shareholders, however, is hardly news. As far back as the 1990s, the sizeable ownership stakes of institutional investors were being cited as evidence that a new era of management/shareholder relations was underway, with shareholders having the upper hand.[128] Mainstream institutional investors (primarily pension funds and mutual funds) remained largely passive, however, in the 1990s and the 2000s, implicitly vesting executives of public companies with substantial discretion.[129]

Those who have recently been hailing the demise of the Berle-Means corporation suggest the size of the collective stake of the largest institutional shareholders has now sealed its fate. For instance, when Bebchuk, Cohen, and Hirst claim "the prospects for stewardship by shareholders are substantially better today than in Berle–Means corporations" they cite data for 2016 for the 20 largest US corporations lacking a controlling shareholder indicating that, on average, the largest five institutional shareholders owned 21 percent of the shares, the largest 20 owned 33 percent, and the largest 50 owned 44 percent.[130] Gilson and Gordon concluded on the basis of similar data they collected for 2009 for the 10 largest US corporations that "representatives of institutions that collectively represent effective control of many large US corporations could fit around a boardroom table."[131]

---

[123] Brian Broughman & Jesse M. Fried, *Do Founders Control Start-up Firms That Go Public?*, ECGI Working Paper, European Corporate Governance Institute Law Working Paper No. 405/2018 12 (2018).

[124] KAMANJOH, *supra* note 117, at 15.

[125] Maureen Farrell, *Tech Founders Want IPO Cash—and Control*, WALL ST. J., Apr. 4, 2017, A1; Rolfe Winkler & Maureen Farrell, *Tech Founders Gain Power*, WALL ST. J., May 29, 2018, A1.

[126] Chris Dieterich, Maureen Farrell & Sarah Krouse, *S&P 500 Blocks Multiple Classes*, WALL ST. J., Aug. 2, 2017, B1.

[127] Bebchuk, Cohen & Hirst, *supra* note 115, at 91.

[128] Chapter 5, notes 154, 205–07, 216, 221–24 and related discussion.

[129] Chapter 5, notes 236–38 and related discussion; Chapter 6, notes 292–99 and accompanying text.

[130] Bebchuk, Cohen & Hirst, *supra* note 115, at 92, 93.

[131] Gilson & Gordon, *supra* note 114, at 875.

Undertakers for the Berle-Means corporation appear to be assuming that collective institutional stakes of the sort prevailing in the largest US public companies today will translate into meaningful shareholder oversight of corporate executives. This can by no means be taken for granted. In the mid-1990s, US corporate law academics Bernard Black and Jack Coffee examined levels of institutional shareholder activism in the United Kingdom to gauge the prospects for activism in the United States, citing the fact that there were fewer barriers to intervention in Britain.[132] One such consideration was that sizeable institutional stakes were more prevalent than in the United States. According to Black and Coffee, it was typical for the 25 largest institutional shareholders to hold a majority of the stock of UK public companies,[133] a higher ownership concentration than Bebchuk, Cohen, and Hirst cite for large US public companies today. Nevertheless, a separation of ownership and control remained a hallmark of corporate Britain. Black and Coffee acknowledged "the complete passivity announced by Berle and Means" was absent in the UK but remarked upon "the reluctance of even large shareholders to intervene."[134]

The bias in favor of passivity that prevailed among powerful institutional shareholders in early 1990s corporate Britain is paralleled today in the United States. Gilson and Gordon acknowledge that while theoretically the substantial collective stakes held by major institutional shareholders in US public companies "should mitigate the managerial agency cost problems of the Berle-Means corporationt.... Reality has fallen short."[135] Gilson and Gordon say of the possibility of US institutional investors acting as "real" owners or "stewards," "institutions have continually failed to play this role; despite the urging of academics and regulators, they remain stubbornly responsive but not proactive."[136] Other observers concur. John Bogle, founder of the giant mutual fund group Vanguard, conceded in 2012 that while he had been optimistic earlier in his career that asset managers acting on behalf of mutual funds and pension funds would exercise greater influence as the percentage of shares owned grew, "the strong voice I expected to hear is barely a whisper."[137] Eminent investment bankers Joseph Perella and Peter Weinberg wrote in the *New York Times* in 2014 "the big shareholders, the institutional shareholders who invest for pension funds and the like, need to stop being silent and speak out."[138] The *Economist* said in 2015 of major American asset managers "their business is running diversified portfolios and they would rather sell their shares in a struggling firm than face the hassle of fixing it."[139]

If institutional shareholders are failing to address the challenges of managerial accountability diffuse share ownership poses, why might it be that, as Gilson and Gordon and Bebchuk, Cohen, and Hirst posit, that the Berle-Means corporation is passé? According to Gilson and Gordon, what has emerged is a regime of "agency capitalism" where

---

[132] Bernard S. Black & John C. Coffee, *Hail Britannia? Institutional Investor Behavior Under Limited Regulation*, 92 MICH. L. REV. 1997, 2001–02 (1994).

[133] *Id.* at 2002.

[134] *Id.* at 2086.

[135] Gilson & Gordon, *supra* note 114, at 889.

[136] *Id.* at 888.

[137] JOHN C. BOGLE, THE CLASH OF CULTURES: INVESTMENT VS. SPECULATION 66–67 (2012).

[138] Joseph Perella & Peter Weinberg, *Powerful, Disruptive Shareholders*, NY TIMES, Apr. 9, 2014, A23.

[139] *An Investor Calls*, ECONOMIST, Feb. 7, 2015, 19.

institutional shareholders, as agents for end investors, are "not 'rationally apathetic' . . . but instead are 'rationally reticent.' "[140] With respect to the discretion available to executives running public companies, this could well be a distinction without a difference. Unless institutional shareholders begin conducting themselves in the manner that would be expected of "real" owners, the managerial accountability challenges that characterize the Berle-Means corporation will remain largely intact despite substantial collective institutional ownership. Correspondingly, absent concrete evidence of shareholders taking meaningful steps to keep management in check, the term "Berle-Means corporation" remains appropriate shorthand for the paradigmatic American public company. As we turn now to internal constraints relevant to public company executives, we will see that the prospects for shareholder engagement with management have not improved in a way that means a change in terminology is due.

Internal Constraints

In the 1950s and 1960s internal constraints, in the form of boards and shareholders, were rarely strongly binding upon the executives who ran larger public companies.[141] In the 1970s, the monitoring role of boards began to take shape in earnest as corporate governance was emerging as a topic for debate and analysis.[142] In subsequent decades, despite board restructuring due to a combination of market and regulatory initiatives, high expectations of improved corporate governance were rarely more than partially fulfilled. The pattern was similar with stockholders. The growing importance of institutional investors created the potential for meaningful stockholder oversight that was unrealistic during the managerial capitalism era. Nevertheless, hopes they would keep executives in check were never more than partly realized. Hence, the Berle-Means corporation nomenclature remained apt.

With the board of directors, though it has not emerged as an ideal monitoring body, there likely is little scope to push boards substantially further in that direction. Board reform remains a topic for debate, but the emphasis has begun to shift to objectives other than improved monitoring, such as fostering the ability of directors to work together with executives in the formulation of corporate strategy. As for shareholders, hedge fund activists, who emerged as significant corporate governance players in the 2000s, appear destined to remain a meaningful but ultimately episodic source of pressure on executives. Otherwise, the growing popularity of investment in funds that track well-known stock market indices could, due to a bias in favor of passivity on the part of these index trackers, simultaneously foster more highly concentrated share ownership and guarantee executives continued sustained autonomy.

[140] Gilson & Gordon, *supra* note 114, at 867.

[141] Chapter 2, notes 270–71, 283–86, 312–15, 327–30 and related discussion.

[142] Chapter 3, notes 57, 244, 265, 282–84 and accompanying text.

BOARDS

The Dodd-Frank Act of 2010 was the primary federal legislative response to the financial crisis that concluded the 2000s.[143] It was one of the most complex pieces of legislation ever, with the electronic version clocking in at 849 pages and with more than 22,200 pages of supporting rules having been adopted as of 2016.[144] The Dodd-Frank Act focused primarily on overhauling financial regulation, particularly with respect to banking. Corporate governance was one topic addressed, which is not surprising given that deficiencies banks suffered from on this count were identified by many as a main cause of the financial crisis.[145] Most of Dodd-Frank's corporate governance reforms, however, did not specifically target financial services firms and instead were made applicable to all issuers falling under the SEC's jurisdiction.[146] This was quixotic, since corporate governance generally functioned well in non-financial companies given the challenges the 2007 credit crunch and the 2008 financial crisis posed.[147] However, no doubt mindful of the invocation of President Barack Obama's first chief of staff that "you never want a serious crisis to go to waste" a cohort of state, local government, and union pension funds and various activists in the institutional investor community lobbied successfully to ensure Dodd-Frank reformed corporate governance generally rather than focusing solely on banks.[148]

With the board of directors, Dodd-Frank's impact has generally been modest. The proportion of *Fortune* 500 companies with a separate CEO and chair of the board increased from 35 percent in 2007 to 43 percent in 2012 and to 51 percent in 2017.[149] A Dodd-Frank provision requiring companies to disclose and explain their stance on this issue plausibly consolidated the trend in favor of a split.[150] On the other hand, a Dodd-Frank measure mandating that stock exchange listing rules require that publicly traded companies have an independent compensation committee was largely superfluous.[151] Since 1993 companies seeking to deduct executive compensation from their taxes have been obliged to have a compensation committee comprised of independent directors and since 2004 NYSE and NASDAQ

---

143 Dodd–Frank Wall Street Reform and Consumer Protection Act of 2010 [hereinafter Dodd-Frank Act], Pub. L. 111–203, 124 Stat. 1376.

144 The electronic version is available at https://www.gpo.gov/fdsys/pkg/PLAW-111publ203/pdf/PLAW-111publ203.pdf (accessed Feb. 18, 2018). On supporting rules, see Kirsten Grind & Emily Glazer, *Inside Enforcers Shake Up Bank Culture*, Wall St. J., May 31, 2016, A1.

145 Chapter 6, notes 507–10 and related discussion.

146 Title IX, Sub-title E., encompassing §§ 951-57; Title IX, Sub-title G., encompassing §§ 971-72. Section 956, which requires disclosure of executive pay arrangements to regulators, was an exception as it only applies to "covered financial institutions."

147 Brian R. Cheffins, *Did Corporate Governance "Fail" during the 2008 Stock Market Meltdown? The Case of the S&P500*, 65 Bus. Law. 1, 50–51, 60–61 (2009); Stephen M. Bainbridge, Corporate Governance after the Crisis 10–11 (2012).

148 Gerald F. Seib, *In Crisis, Opportunity for Obama*, Wall St. J., Nov. 21, 2008, A2; Stephen M. Bainbridge, *Dodd-Frank: Quack Federal Corporate Governance Round II*, 95 Minn. L. Rev. 1779, 1816, 1818 (2011).

149 SpencerStuart, 2017 Spencer Stuart U.S. Board Index 8, 24 (2017).

150 Dodd-Frank Act, § 972.

151 Dodd-Frank Act, § 952.

listing rules have provided for such committees.[152] In addition, a 2011 judicial ruling against the SEC rendered at least temporarily moot a Dodd-Frank provision affirming that the SEC could promulgate a "proxy access" rule giving dissident stockholders seeking board representation the opportunity to use the proxy documentation their corporations circulate to communicate to their fellow shareholders.[153]

Despite Dodd-Frank's modest impact on boards, "(t)o a significant extent, the dreams of yesterday's corporate governance advocates have come true."[154] A monitoring model of the board that achieved notoriety in the 1970s implied that outside directors should substantially outnumber executives on the board and that boards would establish audit, compensation, and nomination committees staffed by such directors.[155] This is what we currently see. As of 2017, 85 percent of directors of S&P 500 companies qualified as "independent," up from 80 percent in 2007.[156] Audit, compensation, and nomination committees staffed by independent directors are now essentially universal in large public companies,[157] with reforms introduced in the early 2000s by SOX and by key stock exchanges having, in effect, made such committees mandatory.[158]

Recent voluntary changes by large public companies to director election procedures that have theoretically "handed investors the keys to their boardrooms" may have enhanced the monitoring capabilities of boards further.[159] There was in the 2000s a substantial move away from "staggered" boards that can delay the assumption of control by an insurgent shareholder with sufficient voting clout to a win a contest for board seats.[160] The trend has continued, with the proportion of S&P 500 companies with staggered boards falling from 24 percent in 2011 to 8 percent in 2017.[161] The proportion of S&P 500 companies with "majority" rather than "plurality" voting, meaning a nominee has to obtain a majority of votes cast to be elected even when running unopposed, stood at 89 percent in 2018 as compared with 16 percent in 2006.[162] While the 2011 judicial ruling on proxy access was a setback for the SEC, as of

---

[152] Chapter 5, note 516 and related discussion; Chapter 6, notes 92–93 and accompanying text; Kevin J. Murphy, *Executive Compensation: Where We Are, and How We Got There, in* 2A HANDBOOK OF THE ECONOMICS OF FINANCE 211, 312 (George M. Constantinites et al. eds., 2013).

[153] Dodd-Frank Act, § 971; John C. Coffee, Jr. & Darius Palia, *The Wolf at the Door: The Impact of Hedge Fund Activism on Corporate Governance*, 41 J. CORP. L. 545, 570–71 (2016).

[154] Mariana Pargendler, *The Corporate Governance Obsession*, 42 J. CORP. L. 359, 401 (2016).

[155] Chapter 3, notes 265, 272–75 and related discussion.

[156] SPENCERSTUART, *supra* note 149, at 8.

[157] SPENCERSTUART, *supra* note 149, 29 (indicating that 100 percent of S&P 500 companies had an audit and compensation committee staffed entirely by independent directors, as did 99.6 percent in the case of nomination committees).

[158] Chapter 6, notes 91–93 and accompanying text; SPENCERSTUART, *supra* note 149, at 29 (noting that stock exchange listing requirements are not applicable to companies with controlling shareholders).

[159] Joann S. Lublin, *Investors Gain More Clout over Boards*, WALL ST. J., Jan. 11, 2016, B1.

[160] Chapter 6, notes 335–36 and related discussion.

[161] SPENCERSTUART, *supra* note 149, at 16; Liz Hoffman, *Bidders Pounce on Firms' Weakened Defenses*, WALL ST. J., Aug. 26, 2014, C1.

[162] Claudia H. Allen, *Study of Majority Voting in Board Elections*, Neal, Gerber & Eisenberg, Nov. 12, 2007, 1, available at http://www.nge.com/files/uploads/documents/majoritystudy111207.pdf (accessed May 19, 2018) (indicating additionally that the figure had increased to 66 percent at the time of writing); EY Center for Board Matters, *Corporate Governance by the Numbers*, Feb. 28, 2018, available at http://www.ey.com/us/en/issues/governance-and-reporting/ey-corporate-governance-by-the-numbers (accessed Apr. 16, 2018).

2017 more than three out of five S&P 500 companies had changed their by-laws to introduce the procedure for significant shareholders, up from about 21 percent in early 2016 and just 1 percent in 2014.[163]

Anecdotally, structural changes affecting boards have been matched by changes in practice that mean boards operate quite effectively as monitors of executives. Corporate law academic Omari Scott Simmons said in 2013 "(o)ver the past thirty years, corporate governance, despite occasional bumps, has undoubtedly improved. Today's corporate boards are much more informed, organized, skilled, and accountable than their historical predecessors."[164] Ram Charan, Dennis Carey, and Michael Useem, in a study of boards published the same year, maintained that regulatory changes had "significantly sharpened the board's role as monitors of management" and helped to move boards "a long way from the ceremonial status in the earlier era of managerial dominance."[165] Journalist Alan Murray wrote in the *Wall Street Journal* in 2014 "post-Worldcom, post-Enron, post-Sarbanes-Oxley, post-Dodd-Frank, boards have become the big guys on the block."[166] Rav Gupta, a former CEO of a *Fortune* 500 chemical concern and an outside director of additional *Fortune* 500 companies, maintained in 2016 "we have moved the needle a lot in the last 15 years," exemplified by " 'radical change' in the boardroom" since the financial crisis.[167] The *New York Times* suggested in 2017 boards "have changed, evolving from country club like collections of the same familiar faces into a much more diverse and demanding constituency."[168]

History shows that boards can fail to match expectations such optimistic rhetoric logically engenders. In the 1970s, 1980s, 1990s, and 2000s assurances were offered about the increased vigilance of boards and yet criticism continued, reaching a crescendo with corporate governance scandals during the early 2000s and the financial crisis of 2008.[169] Today's boards certainly continue to have their critics. Concerns have been expressed that "(m)any boards lack the time necessary to fulfill their monitoring obligations and oversee management."[170] Independent directors are also said to have insufficient access to information needed to fulfill their potential as monitors of public company executives.[171] Ira Millstein, a venerable authority on corporate governance, maintained in 2016 that a counterproductive

---

163 EY Center for Board Matters, *supra* note 162; Joann S. Lublin, *Big Firms Resist Boardroom Entry*, WALL ST. J., Apr. 18, 2017, B2.

164 Omari Scott Simmons, *The Corporate Immune System: Governance from the Inside Out* [2013] U. ILL. L. REV. 1131, 1135.

165 RAM CHARAN, DENNIS CAREY & MICHAEL USEEM, BOARDS THAT LEAD: WHEN TO TAKE CHARGE, WHEN TO PARTNER, AND WHEN TO STAY OUT OF THE WAY 17–18 (2013).

166 Alan Murray, *The Big Guys on the Block*, WALL ST. J., Jan. 16, 2014, A13.

167 *The Role of Corporate Boards: A Roundtable Discussion of Where We're Going and Where We've Been*, J. APP. CORP. FIN., Winter 2017, at 22, 25–26.

168 Nelson D. Schwartz, *Decline of the Baronial CEO*, NY TIMES, June 18, 2017, Business, 1.

169 Chapter 3, notes 282–88 and accompanying text; Chapter 4, notes 258–64, 269–81 and related discussion; Chapter 5, notes 158–59, 169–83 and accompanying text; Chapter 6, notes 228–34, 238–44, 508–10 and related discussion.

170 Nicola Faith Sharpe, *The Cosmetic Independence of Corporate Boards*, 34 SEATTLE U. L. REV. 1435, 1436, 1453 (2011).

171 Kobi Kastiel & Yaron Nili, *Captured Boards: The Rise of Super Directors and the Case for a Board Suite* [2017] WIS. L. REV. 19, 27–30.

"unspoken norm ... to get along" was being sustained in boardrooms because nomination committees and CEOs are not "interested in bringing in squeaky wheels, or people with new ideas about how to do things."[172] Former media executive Steven Clifford concurred in a 2017 book criticizing executive pay arrangements in public companies, characterizing boards as detrimentally "collegial and consensual."[173]

To the extent that boards in fact are counterproductively collegial it is unlikely that recent changes to director election procedure supposedly handing the keys to investors will change the equation any time soon. By-laws offering proxy access are almost never relied upon.[174] With votes opposing directorial candidates put forward by incumbent boards having recently averaged less than 5 percent of the all votes cast,[175] only in highly exceptional situations will staggering, or lack thereof, affect board composition materially. Similar overwhelming shareholder backing for nominees companies put forward should also ensure that requiring majority support for unopposed board candidates is no more than a footnote in the director selection process. Of more than 24,000 S&P 1500 director nominees that went up for election under a majority voting regime between 2007 and 2013 only 8 came up short.[176]

Calls for additional boardroom reform will no doubt continue as they have since the managerial capitalism era was drawing to a close. New corporate governance controversies crop up regularly, with debates being sustained by a corporate governance reform "industry" operating out of the shareholder community, academia, and professional advisory firms with a vested interest in keeping change permanently on the agenda.[177] With women holding not even one out of four S&P 500 directorships, fostering increased diversity in the boardroom stands out as a likely priority.[178] There have also been calls for boards to move beyond monitoring and take on a leadership role by actively partnering with management in the formulation of corporate strategy.[179]

While board reform is destined to remain on the agenda, there appears to be little additional scope for boards to be restructured to constrain management through monitoring. With independent directors dominating boards, with the board committees assumed to be crucial from a governance perspective being all but universal, and with shareholders having

---

[172] *The Case for Activist Directors: A Conversation with Ira M. Millstein*, J. App. Corp. Fin., Winter 2017, at 10, 11.

[173] Steven Clifford, The CEO Pay Machine: How It Trashes America and How to Stop It 108 (2017).

[174] Lublin, *supra* note 159 (citing a corporate law partner who said that proxy access had not been relied on to that point and speculating that this might happen once or twice over the next two to three years); Skadden, *Proxy Access: Highlights of the 2017 Proxy Season* (June 20, 2017), available at https://www.skadden.com/insights/publications/2017/06/insights-articles-june-2017/proxy-access-highlights-2017-proxy-season (accessed Feb. 19, 2018).

[175] EY Center for Board Matters, *supra* note 162 (data for 2017).

[176] Stephen J. Choi et al., *Does Majority Voting Improve Board Accountability?*, 83 U. Chi. L. Rev. 1119, 1122 (2016). See also Emily Glazer & Joann S. Lublin, *Key Vote Tests Wells Fargo's Directors*, Wall St. J., Apr. 17, 2017, B1 (indicating that in the previous five years only nine directors had left boards of companies in the S&P 500 after failing to receive majority support).

[177] Marcel Kahan & Edward Rock, *Symbolic Corporate Governance Politics*, 94 Bos. U. L. Rev. 1997, 1998 (2014).

[178] SpencerStuart, *supra* note 149, at 21; Pargendler, *supra* note 154, at 392; Vanessa Fuhrmans, *Pressure Tactics Diversify Boards*, Wall St. J., April 26, 2018, B6.

[179] Charan, Carey & Useem, *supra* note 165; Ira M. Millstein, The Activist Director: Lessons from the Boardroom and the Future of the Corporation vii, 179–82 (2017).

ample theoretical scope to use their voting power to turf out underperforming directors, there are few obvious moves left to upgrade the board's monitoring capabilities. The fact that outside directors are part-timers imposes inevitable limitations on their ability to act as corporate watchdogs, but reputedly boards work noticeably harder than they used to.[180] Hence, absent changes barely on the radar screen at present, such as compelling corporations to appoint workers or taxpayers as directors,[181] it is unlikely that boards will operate as a markedly more robust check on corporate executives in the future than they do currently.

SHAREHOLDERS

Just as the extent to which boards constrain managerial discretion is unlikely to change markedly soon, continuity should be the order of the day on the shareholder front for the foreseeable future. Enhancing shareholder value should remain the top managerial priority. Hedge funds are not going anywhere soon but their influence is unlikely to continue to increase in the manner prevailing since the early 2000s. Passivity will remain the byword for mainstream institutional shareholders despite (or perhaps more accurately because of) the growing influence of index tracking funds.

Managerial Priorities

During the managerial capitalism era public company executives who were balancing the interests of various corporate constituencies rather than seeking to maximize shareholder returns fit the mood of the times.[182] By the late 1990s, promoting shareholder value was widely recognized as the primary goal of public companies.[183] Matters were the same as the 2000s got underway. *Business Week* indicated in 2000 "the fundamental task of today's CEO is simplicity itself: Get the stock price up. Period."[184]

Management professor Gerald Davis said in 2009 "(i)n the American system, share price is like a global positioning system for those managing corporations."[185] Yet doubts grew about corporate prioritization of shareholder value during the 2000s. The corporate scandals of the early 2000s posed a challenge to the prevailing orthodoxy, with the pressure to conjure market-pleasing numbers for investors being identified as a primary cause of executive wrongdoing.[186] The financial crisis reinforced skepticism of shareholder primacy.[187] The *Financial Times* said in 2009 "(l)ong-held tenets of corporate faith," including "the pursuit of shareholder valuet . . . are being blamed for the turmoil and look likely to be overhauled"

---

[180] Geoff Colvin, *Inside the Boardroom: The Party Is Over!*, FORTUNE, May 20, 2013, 219; Jay W. Lorsch, *America's Changing Corporate Boardrooms: The Last Twenty-Five Years*, 3 HARV. BUS. L. REV. 119, 130 (2013).

[181] For an example of an advocate of board reform of this sort, see William Lazonick, *Profits without Prosperity*, HARV. BUS. REV., Sept. 2014, 46, 54.

[182] Chapter 2, notes 239–50; Chapter 3, notes 239–42 and accompanying text.

[183] Chapter 5, notes 192–96, 199 and related discussion.

[184] Anthony Bianco & Louis Lavelle, *The CEO Trap*, BUS. WK., Dec. 11, 2000, 86.

[185] GERALD F. DAVIS, MANAGED BY THE MARKETS: HOW FINANCE RESHAPED AMERICA 96 (2009).

[186] Harris Collingwood, *The Earnings Cult*, NY TIMES, June 9, 2002, Sunday Magazine, 68; John A. Byrne, *After Enron: The Ideal Corporation*, BUS. WK., Aug. 26, 2002, 68.

[187] Pargendler, *supra* note 154, at 397.

and suggested there could be "(a) palace revolution . . . toppling the dictatorship of shareholder value maximisation."[188] Even former General Electric CEO Jack Welch, sometimes heralded as a pioneer of the shareholder value movement, suggested that making shareholder value the core of corporate strategy was "the dumbest idea in the world."[189]

Law professor Lynn Stout predicted in 2013 "shareholder primacy seems poised to fall, perhaps even more quickly than it ascended."[190] The *New York Times* observed in 2018 that, as part of corporate statesmanship initiatives with a 1970s flavor, "more chief executives have begun speaking out on issues that at first glance have little to do with the bottom line, including immigration policy, climate change and gay rights."[191] It nevertheless seems unlikely that shareholder primacy will be displaced in any sort of thoroughgoing fashion in the near future.

Chief executives continue "to watch their stocks like hawks."[192] Reportedly "it's rare to find a CEO of a publicly traded company who doesn't publicly buy into the idea of shareholder value."[193] A *Wall Street Journal* columnist has said most executives "have been taught that maximizing shareholder value is their sole responsibility—and if this means ignoring the needs of workers and the well-being of local communities, so be it."[194] Numerous chief executives may privately resent pressure to deliver for shareholders.[195] However, according to Margaret Blair, another legal academic, "(t)he notion that corporations are supposed to focus exclusively on maximizing share value has become so deeply instilled in the culture of corporate boardrooms that challenging this notion is like swimming upstream against a strong current."[196]

When shareholder value became a corporate buzzword in the 1980s and achieved preeminence in the 1990s, direct pressure from shareholders was a minor factor. It was widely recognized that while a substantial increase in the percentage of shares owned by institutional investors had bolstered the potential for meaningful shareholder interventions, this potential was going largely unfulfilled.[197] Instead, other transmission mechanisms from market to boardroom were pivotal.[198] In the 1980s, corporate executives prioritized shareholder value

---

188 Francesco Guerrera, *A Need to Reconnect*, FIN. TIMES, Mar. 13, 2009, 11; *Shareholder Value Re-evaluated*, FIN. TIMES, Mar. 16, 2009, 12.

189 Chapter 1, note 249 and accompanying text; Francesco Guerrera, *Welch Slams the Obsession with Shareholder Value as a "Dumb Idea,"* FIN. TIMES, Mar. 13, 2009, 1.

190 Lynn A. Stout, *On the Rise of Shareholder Primacy, Signs of Its Fall, and the Return of Managerialism (in the Closet)*, 36 SEATTLE U. L. REV. 1169, 1180 (2013).

191 David Gelles, *Businesses Step In to Fill a Public Void*, NY TIMES, Feb. 4, 2018, Business, 1. See also Rana Foroohar, *The Backlash against Shareholder Value*, FIN. TIMES, Mar. 5, 2018, 11.

192 Dana Mattioli & Dana Cimilluca, *Fear of Losing Out Drives Deal Boom*, WALL ST. J., June 27, 2015, A1.

193 RANA FOROOHAR, MAKERS AND TAKERS: THE RISE OF FINANCE AND THE FALL OF AMERICAN BUSINESS 107 (2016).

194 William A. Galston, *A Ford Exec Who Took the Long View*, WALL ST. J., Nov. 15, 2017, A17.

195 Steven Pearlstein, *When Shareholder Capitalism Came to Town*, AMERICAN PROSPECT, Mar./Apr. 2014, 40, 45–46.

196 Margaret M. Blair, *What Must Corporate Directors Do? Maximizing Shareholder Value versus Creating Value through Team Production*, Center for Effective Public Management at Brookings, June 2015, 2.

197 Chapter 4, notes 326–30, 343–47 and related discussion; Chapter 5, notes 204–12, 236–38, 253 and accompanying text.

198 On the nature of transmission mechanisms in this context, see Mark J. Roe, *Corporate Short-Termism—In the Boardroom and in the Courtroom*, 68 BUS. LAW. 977, 985 (2013).

to reduce the possibility that a bidder targeting companies with underperforming shares would try to secure control by way of a hostile tender offer.[199] The hostile takeover was marginalized in the 1990s, partly due to case law and statutory measures providing incumbent management with ample scope to take defensive action.[200] The primary impetus for executives to prioritize shareholder value became stock market pressure arising from a single metric, namely quarterly earnings data.[201]

The market for corporate control remains a marginalized shareholder value transmission mechanism. Hostile bids do occur, with examples periodically generating media coverage.[202] Widespread dismantling of staggered boards occurring since 2000 theoretically makes it easier for hostile offers to succeed because potentially antagonistic directors can be replaced more rapidly.[203] Nevertheless, hostile takeovers remain rare, and arguably are "on life support."[204]

The quarterly earnings "cult" that flourished in the 1990s remained a feature of public companies in the 2000s.[205] It continues to operate. Concerns are frequently expressed that executives who treat hitting quarterly financial targets as a priority create for themselves counterproductive incentives to meet analysts' estimates by cutting costs in a shortsighted manner or by meddling with the accounts.[206] There is support for the idea of forsaking the provision of quarterly earnings guidance.[207] A substantial majority of public companies nevertheless attend closely to quarterly earnings forecasts.[208] Moreover, investors remain ready to penalize companies that miss predicted numbers, with stock prices often being hammered.[209] Roughly three-fifths of the annual pay of a typical CEO of a large public corporation is currently equity-based, which provides chief executives with a potent incentive to watch the stock

---

199 Chapter 4, notes 365–72 and related discussion.

200 Chapter 4, notes 194–214, 219–23, 226 and accompanying text; Chapter 5, note 2 and related discussion.

201 Chapter 5, notes 259–61, 295–301 and accompanying text.

202 Steven Davidoff Solomon, *Hostile Takeovers Abound, but Success Is No Guarantee*, INT'L. NY TIMES, May 31, 2016, 17.

203 *Supra* notes 160–61 and related discussion; Ron Barusch, *Attention Shareholders: Beware of the Board*, WALL ST. J., Sept. 15, 2015, C2.

204 Steven M. Davidoff, *With Fewer Barbarians at the Gate, A New Threat Emerges*, NY TIMES, July 31, 2013, B4. See also Steven Davidoff Solomon, *Poison Pill's Relevance in the Age of Shareholder Activism*, NY TIMES, Apr. 18, 2014, available at https://dealbook.nytimes.com/2014/04/18/poison-pills-relevance-in-the-age-of-shareholder-activism/ (accessed May 21, 2018); Matthew D. Cain, Stephen B. McKeon & Steven Davidoff Solomon, *Do Takeover Laws Matter? Evidence from Five Decades of Hostile Takeovers*, 124 J. FIN. ECON. 464, 468 (2017) (empirical data).

205 Chapter 6, notes 151, 275–79 and related discussion.

206 Mackintosh, *supra* note 100; LYNN STOUT, THE SHAREHOLDER VALUE MYTH: HOW PUTTING SHAREHOLDERS FIRST HARMS INVESTORS, CORPORATIONS, AND THE PUBLIC 49 (2012); Steven Pearlstein, *Social Capital, Corporate Purpose and the Revival of American Capitalism*, Center for Effective Public Management at Brookings, Jan. 2014, 21.

207 Russ Banham, *Letting Go of Guidance*, CFO, Nov. 2012, 44; David Benoit, *A Daring Idea: End Quarterly Reports*, WALL ST. J., Aug. 20, 2015, C1. Business Roundtable, *Business Roundtable Supports Move Away from Short-Term Guidance*, June 7, 2018, https://www.businessroundtable.org/media/news-releases/business-roundtable-supports-move-away-short-term-guidance (accessed July 10, 2018).

208 Banham, *supra* note 207; Theresa Hamacher & Robert Pozen, *Fight against Short-Termism Is Misdirected*, FIN. TIMES, June 30, 2014, 8 (saying three-quarters of public companies do so).

209 Pearlstein, *supra* note 206, at 9; *Managing Investors*, HARV. BUS. REV., June 2014, 81, 82.

price closely.[210] It is hardly surprising, then, that stock market reactions to quarterly earnings reports continue to constitute a meaningful shareholder value transmission mechanism in public companies.

While direct shareholder pressure was merely a secondary consideration when generating shareholder value became a top priority for public company executives as the twentieth century drew to a close, shareholder activism has evolved considerably in the meantime. Hedge fund interventions became "the newest big thing in corporate governance" in the 2000s,[211] and the pattern has grown in prominence in the years since. As for mainstream institutional shareholders, through to the end of the 2000s they flattered to deceive on the activism front. A reconfiguration, however, of institutional ownership in favor of investment funds with passive investment strategies oriented around mimicking well-known stock market indices such as the S&P 500 could be changing the equation. We will now consider the extent to which interventions by hedge funds activists and mainstream institutional shareholders currently dictate the priorities of public company executives. We will also assess possibilities for change in the future.

Hedge Fund Activism

The turmoil associated with the 2008 financial crisis posed challenges for hedge fund activists but activism continued, albeit without quite the same intensity as during the mid-2000s.[212] Hedge fund activism then rallied strongly as the 2010s got underway, with law professors Jack Coffee and Darius Palia saying in 2016 it had "recently spiked, almost hyperbolically."[213] The number of "high intensity" activist interventions, namely those where a shareholder activist sought to obtain board representation, dismiss top executives, or otherwise campaigned strongly to bolster shareholder value, increased from 221 in 2010 to 377 in 2015.[214]

In the 2000s, hedge fund activists focused heavily on "small cap" companies. With very large targets too many eggs would have to have been put in one investment basket to buy up the sort of sizeable minority stake normally required to improve the odds of success and yield meaningful profits.[215] An increase in assets under management by activist hedge funds from

---

[210] Theo Francis & Joann S. Lublin, *Should Bar Be Lifted on CEO Bonuses?*, Wall St. J., June 2, 2017, B3; Alex Edmans, Xavier Gabaix & Dirk Jenter, *Executive Compensation: A Survey of Theory and Evidence*, *in* 1 The Handbook of the Economics of Corporate Governance 383, 401 (Benjamin E. Hermalin & Michael S. Weisbach eds., 2017); K.J. Martijn Cremers, Saura Masconale & Simone M. Sepe, *CEO Pay Redux*, 96 Tex. L. Rev. 205, 242, 269 (2017) (emphasizing a recent switch in equity-based compensation from options to the awarding of stock and recognizing that performance-related executive pay can foster "earnings hysteria").

[211] Chapter 6, note 304 and related discussion.

[212] Chapter 6, note 323 and related discussion.

[213] Coffee & Palia, *supra* note 153, at 548.

[214] FactSet, *2016 Shareholder Activism Review*, Feb. 1, 2017, 7, available at https://insight.factset.com/hubfs/Resources/Research%20Desk/Market%20Insight/FactSet%27s%202016%20Year-End%20Activism%20Review_2.1.17.pdf (accessed Jan. 23, 2018).

[215] Brian R. Cheffins & John Armour, *The Past, Present, and Future of Shareholder Activism by Hedge Funds*, 37 J. Corp. L. 51, 63 (2011).

$36 billion in 2009 to $115.5 billion at the end of 2014 bolstered considerably, however, the firepower available to target bigger firms.[216]

Among hedge fund activists the bias in favor of smaller public company targets remains pronounced.[217] Nevertheless, hedge funds began in the 2010s to zone in on large firms more often. The proportion of target companies with a market capitalization under $1 billion fell from 91 percent in 2009 to 68 percent in 2013 while the proportion with a market capitalization exceeding $10 billion increased from 3 percent to 7 percent.[218] The *New York Post* warned in 2013 that "no company is safe as corporate cage rattlers take aim at some of the biggest names in business."[219] The *Economist* provided readers with examples in 2015, saying "Americans encounter firms that activists have targeted when they brush their teeth (Procter & Gamble), answer their phone (Apple), log in to their computer (Microsoft, Yahoo and eBay), dine out (Burger King and PepsiCo) and watch television (Netflix)."[220] Forays involving iconic public companies DuPont and General Electric would follow.[221]

Hedge fund activists almost never seek to acquire voting control in targets.[222] Instead, their preferred tactic is to obtain sizeable but not dominant minority stakes. Under such circumstances, "they get their way when the board believes that a majority of shareholders supports the thrust of an activist's criticism."[223] Considerable success on this front has put many targeted companies on the back foot.

During the 2000s mainstream institutional investors proved receptive to hedge fund entreaties, thereby increasing substantially the clout of hedge fund activists.[224] The bonds involved solidified following the financial crisis, meaning companies pushing back hard against hedge fund provocateurs have risked alienating their broader shareholder base.[225] Executives, bristling as a result of being second-guessed, can be tempted when facing an activist campaign to fight back in any way they can.[226] Wary, however, that opposing change fruitlessly can alienate otherwise neutral shareholders and tarnish managerial reputations,

---

216 Jacob Bunge & David Benoit, *At DuPont, Gains Didn't Ward Off Trian*, WALL ST. J., Jan. 10, 2015, B1.

217 FactSet, *supra* note 214, at 8.

218 *Id.*

219 Kaja Whitehouse, *Street Fightin' Men*, NY POST, Mar. 9, 2013, 24. See also Adam Shell, *Rich Activist Investors Go Gunning for Big Game*, USA TODAY, Aug. 15, 2013, B1 (quoting Claudia Allen, a senior lawyer specializing in corporate governance).

220 *Capitalism's Unlikely Heroes*, ECONOMIST, Feb. 7, 2015, 11.

221 Chapter 1, notes 325–26; *infra* note 461 and related discussion; Coffee & Palia, *supra* note 153, at 579–80; Steve Lohr, *G.E., Pressured by Its Investors, Changes Leader*, NY TIMES, June 12, 2017, A1.

222 Ajay Khorana, Anil Shivdasani & Gustav Sigurdsson, *The Evolving Shareholder Activist Landscape (How Companies Can Prepare for It)*, J. APP. CORP. FIN., Summer 2017, at 8, 16 (indicating that an activist offered to purchase a target outright in less than 4 percent of hedge fund activist campaigns targeting S&P 1500 companies since 2006).

223 Stephen Foley, *All-Singing, All-Dancing Activist Hedge Funds*, FIN. TIMES, Jan. 4, 2016, 10.

224 Chapter 6, notes 312–13 and accompanying text.

225 David Benoit, *Companies, Activists Declare Truce in Boardroom Battles*, WALL ST. J., Dec. 10, 2013, A1; William D. Cohan, *The Investors CEOs Most Fear*, FORTUNE, Dec. 22, 2014, 120.

226 Andrew Hill, *Carl Icahn and Daniel Loeb Can't Be Shut Out*, FIN. TIMES, Oct. 15, 2013, 16; Brooke Masters, *Poison Pills Are a Toxic Temptation for Hidebound Chiefs*, FIN. TIMES, Apr. 26, 2014, 14.

public company executives have found themselves under an onus to take seriously credible hedge fund proposals to enhance shareholder value.[227] For example, various major public companies, including Apple, DuPont, General Motors, and telecommunications equipment company Qualcomm, have launched substantial share buy-back schemes in response to activist lobbying.[228] There have been instances where lobbying by hedge fund activists has prompted large firms to announce they would spin off key assets to release value for shareholders, with examples including Kraft Foods Inc. in 2011 and internet auctioneer eBay in 2014.[229] Where hedge fund activists have demanded representation on the board, it has become increasingly common for companies to accede to the request rather than engage in a costly, publicized proxy battle.[230] High-profile instances involved Microsoft in 2013 and General Electric in 2017.[231]

The influence that hedge funds wield plays an important part in Ronald Gilson and Jeff Gordon's claim that the Berle-Means corporation has been relegated to a historical curiosity. Having noted that institutional shareholders fail to act like "real owners" despite substantial collective ownership, Gilson and Gordon hail hedge fund activists as "governance intermediaries" who identify underperforming firms and put forward concrete proposals for changes intended to improve shareholder returns.[232] Gilson and Gordon point out that mainstream institutional investors are often receptive, meaning hedge fund activists frequently have sufficient voting power at their disposal to swing around otherwise recalcitrant executives of targeted companies.[233] This "happy complementarity" generates, according to Gilson and Gordon, effective shareholder-related governance unknown to the Berle-Means corporation.[234]

Gilson and Gordon likely overestimate the clout of activist hedge funds, which is significant but has been compromised from a governance perspective by the continued bias in favor of targeting smaller companies as well as by the episodic nature of hedge fund interventions. Caveats aside, hedge fund activism has been a meaningful shareholder value catalyst and likely will remain so for the foreseeable future.[235] As a corrective mechanism, hedge fund activism is

---

227 Barry Rosenstein, *Skipping the Pointless Battle against Activists*, FIN. TIMES, Jan. 20, 2014, 12; *Active Measures*, ECONOMIST, May 13, 2017, 67.

228 Emily Chasan & Maxwell Murphy, *Activist Investors Go Big*, WALL ST. J., Oct. 1, 2013, B6; *Anything You Can Do, Icahn Do Better*, ECONOMIST, Feb. 15, 2014, 55; Karen Brettell, David Gaffen & David Rohde, *Surging US Buybacks Dwarf Innovation Spending*, REUTERS NEWS, Nov. 16, 2015.

229 Gina Chon, Anupreeta Das & Paul Ziobro, *Activists Pressed for Kraft Spin-Off*, WALL ST. J., Aug. 5, 2011, B1; Shira Ovide & Don Clark, *Silicon Valley Grits Teeth over Activist Investors*, WALL ST. J., May 27, 2015, B1.

230 FactSet, *supra* note 214, at 12; Jeffrey A. Sonnenfeld, *The CEOs Who Didn't Deserve the Boot*, WALL ST. J., July 13, 2017, A15.

231 David Benoit & Kirsten Grind, *Activists' Secret Ally: Big Mutual Funds*, WALL ST. J., Aug. 10, 2015, A1; Thomas Gryta, David Benoit & Joann S. Lublin, *GE Adds Activist to Board as Stock Slumps*, WALL ST. J., Oct. 10, 2017, A1.

232 Gilson & Gordon, *supra* note 114, at 866, 896. See also *Anything You Can, supra* note 228 (endorsing Gilson and Gordon's analysis).

233 Gilson & Gordon, *supra* note 114, at 896–97.

234 *Id.* at 898–900, 916–17.

235 Khorana, Shivdasani & Sigurdsson, *supra* note 222, at 17; James D. Cox & Randall S. Thomas, *Corporate Darwinism: Disciplining Managers in a World with Weak Shareholder Litigation*, 95 N.C. L. REV. 19, 65 (2016);

less disruptive and expensive than the hostile takeover, and the strategy is potentially appealing for neutral shareholders because they do not have to worry the intervention will end up being primarily a windfall for a canny bidder.[236] Nevertheless, with hedge fund activism an inflection point may have been reached marking the end of the upward trajectory that began in the early 2000s.[237]

Public company executives, realizing they can end up on the back foot once a hedge fund activist arrives, are increasingly taking advance precautions. Reputedly, " 'think like an activist' has become a boardroom mantra as companies strive to anticipate potential hedge fund demands and address perceived weaknesses."[238] Numerous companies have, for instance, been engaging in activist "fire drills," identifying areas of vulnerability and making changes so as to try to forestall a hedge fund foray.[239] With public companies reading the playbook of hedge fund activists and taking anticipatory measures, hedge funds seem to be pulling back as they realize there are fewer instances where activism will add value.[240] The number of activist interventions indeed declined substantially in 2016 and 2017 as compared to 2014 and 2015, including among large public companies.[241]

In addition to dialing back interventions, activist hedge funds have been delivering poor returns lately.[242] Perhaps with public company executives endeavoring to think like activists there are now few instances where underperformance is sufficiently egregious for intervention to yield bumper returns. Whatever the explanation, investors, disappointed with results activist hedge funds have been delivering, have begun taking their money out of the sector, a trend that inevitably would throw the brakes on activist hedge fund growth if it continues in earnest.[243] Hedge fund activism thus appears to be stalling, even if there is no full-scale retreat on the horizon. If in fact a ceiling is coming into view for hedge fund activism, the extent to which direct pressure by shareholders will operate as a constraint on public company executives going forward will depend primarily on the stance mainstream institutional investors take. We turn to this next.

John C. Coffee, *Preserving the Corporate Superego in a Time of Stress: An Essay on Ethics and Economics*, 33 Oxford Rev. Econ. Pol. 221, 235 (2017).

236 *Activist Investors and Their Implications for Corporate Managers*, J. App. Corp. Fin., Summer 2015, at 8, 29.

237 Stephen Foley, *The So-Called Death of Event-Driven Investing*, Fin. Times, Mar. 7, 2016, FT fm, 10.

238 Khorana, Shivdasani & Sigurdsson, *supra* note 222, at 10.

239 David Gelles, *Boardrooms Rethink Tactics to Defang Activist Investors*, NY Times, Nov. 12, 2013, F10.

240 David Benoit, *Activists Start Thinking Smaller*, Wall St. J., Nov. 15, 2016, A1; Stephen Foley, *The Hard Task of Working Out Where Activists Will Pounce*, Fin. Times, Jan. 24, 2017, 28.

241 FactSet, *supra* note 214, at 7–8 (the proportion of campaigns involving companies with market capitalizations exceeding $10 billion fell from 8 percent in 2015 to 5 percent to 2016); Khorana, Shivdasani & Sigurdsson, *supra* note 222, at 8; Mike Coranto, *2017 Proxy Fights: High Cost, Low Volume*, FactSet Insight, Nov. 6, 2017, available at https://insight.factset.com/2017-proxy-fights-high-cost-low-volume ("high impact" campaigns fell from 382 in 2015 to 328 in 2016 and 273 in 2017) (accessed Mar. 28, 2018).

242 Sonnenfeld, *supra* note 230; Leslie Picker, *Hedge Fund Industry's Stars Are Stumbling as Stock Picks and Proxy Fights Fizzle*, CNBC.com, Jan. 23, 2018, available at https://www.cnbc.com/2018/01/23/wall-streets-star-activists-stumbled-in-2017.html (accessed Mar. 28, 2018); David Benoit, *Investors Flee Star Activist Ackman*, Wall St. J., Apr. 6, 2018, A1.

243 Foley, *supra* note 240; Benoit, *supra* note 242.

Mainstream Institutional Shareholders

Extending back at least to the 1970s, institutional investors have disappointed those anticipating that substantial ownership of shares in public companies would translate into meaningful oversight of corporate executives.[244] Today's mainstream institutional shareholders may be going somewhat further than their predecessors in fulfilling their activism potential. Mutual funds and pension funds pretty much always vote their shares, due in large part to a strong steer to do so from the SEC and Department of Labor rules.[245] The default setting for mainstream institutional investors also is not as management-friendly as it used to be.[246] They reputedly voice concerns directly to management more often than used to be the case, though with engagements of this type being private it is difficult to know how widespread the practice has become.[247] Also, with the viability of hedge fund activism hinging on support from mainstream institutional investors and with hedge fund activism having proliferated since the early 2000s, hedge fund provocateurs have clearly had some success forcing "America's lazy money" off the sidelines.[248] Sometimes the ideas hedge fund activists promote arise from suggestions by institutional shareholders that have significant knowledge of shortcomings with particular companies but lack the mandate, aptitude, or appetite to lead an activism campaign.[249]

Though mainstream institutional shareholders may have come off the sidelines to some degree it is yet not time to send the Berle-Means corporation to the retirement home based on a changed stance with such investors.[250] Passivity remains the departure point. The continued bias against activism is betrayed by the fact that even the largest asset managers acting on behalf of mutual funds and pension funds have only a small department dedicated to shareholder voting and other governance-related stewardship activities for the hundreds of corporations in which they invest.[251] Modest staffing reflects, as the *Financial Times* said of the situation in the United States in 2015, "the Cinderella status of governance within fund

---

[244] Chapter 3, notes 190–92, 195 and accompanying text; Chapter 6, notes 285, 292–99 and related discussion.

[245] Chapter 6, note 291 and related discussion; Coffee, *supra* note 235, at 230; James K. Glassman, *Regulators Are a Proxy Adviser's Best Friend*, Wall St. J., Dec. 18, 2014, 19; Dorothy Shapiro Lund, *The Case against Passive Shareholder Voting*, 43 J. Corp. L. 493, 526 (2018) (indicating that, contrary to common perception, SEC rules introduced in 2003 do not directly compel voting).

[246] Benoit & Grind, *supra* note 231.

[247] Lund, *supra* note 245, at 501; Michael J. de la Merced, *Taking Recipes from the Activist Cookbook*, NY Times, Dec. 11, 2014, B10. McCahery, Sautner and Starks report on the basis of responses to questionnaires sent in 2012 and 2013 to representatives of institutional shareholders "widespread use of behind-the-scenes engagement"—Joseph A. McCahery, Zacharias Sautner & Laura T. Starks, *Behind the Scenes: The Corporate Governance Preferences of Institutional Investors*, 71 J. Fin. 2905, 2908 (2016). Given that the survey response rate was only 4.3 percent and that only 24 percent of the institutional shareholders were based in the United States (see at 2908, 2910) the extent to which this conclusion can appropriately be generalized in the American context is impossible to gauge.

[248] *Capitalism's Unlikely*, *supra* note 220.

[249] Gregory V. Milano & John R. Cryan, *Be Your Own Activist*, J. App. Corp. Fin., Summer 2015, at 61, 61; Lindsay Fortado, *Asset Manager Adopts Legal Strategy*, Fin. Times, Feb. 19, 2018, 18.

[250] The argument presented here is canvassed in greater detail in Brian R. Cheffins, *The Rise and Fall (?) of the Berle-Means Corporation*, forthcoming Seattle Univ. L. Rev.

[251] Bebchuk, Cohen & Hirst, *supra* note 115, at 101.

management businesses. While trumpeted as important, it is not an area on which institutions have historically lavished pay and investment."[252] With a small governance contingent in place it is feasible for major asset managers to make reasoned decisions whether to back firm-specific proposals hedge fund activists periodically make and to adopt a voting stance opposing generic management-friendly governance mechanisms such as staggered boards, poison pills, and plurality voting.[253] However, shareholders almost never exercise rights they might have to veto transactions executives propose and taking a sufficiently close interest in a particular company to lead a public activism campaign will be off the agenda.[254]

To manage the costs associated with the potentially daunting number of resolutions on which public companies ask their shareholders to vote—250,000 per year by one count—asset managers rely heavily on advice they pay to receive from proxy advisors such as Institutional Shareholder Services and Glass Lewis.[255] In 2015 Jamie Dimon, J.P. Morgan Chase's CEO, charged investment managers with being "lazy capitalists" due to the farming out of voting decisions to these advisory services.[256] The extent to which recommendations are adopted differs depending on the circumstances but deference typically is substantial.[257] Justin Fox, a financial journalist, and Jay Lorsch, a Harvard Business School expert on corporate governance, have said of the result "(i)t's better than nothing, which is what most individual investors do, but it's a standardized and usually superficial sort of oversight."[258]

While today's mainstream institutional shareholders seem unlikely to break with tradition and fulfill hopes they will be "real owners," there is a recent twist in the plot of which account must be taken. Dramatic growth in the popularity of "passive" index tracking funds has resulted in fears of "a concentration of ownership not seen since the days of the Rockefeller Trust" oriented around Standard Oil at the turn of the twentieth century.[259] Perhaps this "re-concentration of corporate ownership" is "a fundamental reorganization of the system of corporate governance"[260] that could yet spell doom for the Berle-Means corporation.

From an investor perspective, the logic with index tracking funds is seemingly compelling. Big tracker funds drive down fees through economies of scale and the deployment of a plain vanilla investment approach—mimic as closely as possible the performance of a prominent stock market index. For instance, the expense ratio for the main S&P tracker fund which the Vanguard Group operates is 0.04 percent of the fund's assets, as compared with 0.8 percent for the average actively managed American mutual fund.[261] If actively managed funds

---

[252] Jonathan Ford, *Dimon's Criticisms over Proxy Advisers Deserve Consideration*, FIN. TIMES, June 1, 2015, 18.

[253] Coffee, *supra* note 235, at 230.

[254] *Id.*; Sujeet Indap, *Board Directors are Enjoying a More Permissive Climate*, FIN. TIMES, June 5, 2018, 14.

[255] SUNEELA JAIN ET AL., THE CONFERENCE BOARD CORPORATE GOVERNANCE CENTER WHITE PAPER: WHAT IS THE OPTIMAL BALANCE IN THE RELATIVE ROLES OF MANAGEMENT, DIRECTORS AND INVESTORS IN THE GOVERNANCE OF PUBLIC CORPORATIONS? 23 (2014).

[256] *Reinventing the Deal*, *supra* note 79.

[257] Coffee & Palia, *supra* note 153, at 558.

[258] Justin Fox & Jay W. Lorsch, *What Good Are Shareholders?*, HARV. BUS. REV., July/Aug. 2012, 48, 55–56.

[259] Burton G. Malkiel, *Index Funds Still Beat "Active" Portfolio Management*, WALL ST. J., June 6, 2017, A17.

[260] Jan Fichtner, Eelke M. Heemskerk & Javier Garcia-Bernardo, *Hidden Power of the Big Three? Passive Index Funds, Re-concentration of Corporate Ownership, and New Financial Risk*, 19 BUS. & POLITICS 298, 302 (2017).

[261] *The Big Squeeze*, ECONOMIST, May 13, 2017, 74.

outperformed the market, the higher fees would be good value. Few do so consistently, however. Between 1985 and 2015 the annual return of the S&P 500 was 11.2 percent as compared with 9.6 percent for the average mutual fund focusing on large market cap companies.[262]

Investors have increasingly been swung around by the logic of index tracking funds. In 2016, of the more than $400 billion of new retail investments coming through financial advisers 82 percent was placed in index funds and their close relative, exchange trading funds.[263] With the money pouring in, the proportion of the S&P 500 owned by US-based index trackers increased from 4.6 percent in 2005 to 13.9 percent in 2017.[264]

The three largest US-based asset management firms, BlackRock, Vanguard, and State Street, dominate the rapidly growing index tracking industry.[265] A substantial majority of the assets under management by "the Big Three" is invested in passive index funds.[266] The dramatic growth of index tracking funds has correspondingly meant the stakes of each in public companies have increased substantially recently. Vanguard's passive funds alone held a stake of 5 percent or more in 468 S&P 500 companies as of 2016, up from just three in 2005.[267] The proportion of S&P 500 companies where BlackRock, Vanguard, and State Street combined would constitute the largest shareholder increased from 25 percent in 2000 to 88 percent in 2015.[268]

The large collective stake the Big Three hold in US public companies has been referred to as "(a)n economic blockbuster" that "has recently been exposed."[269] In particular, the anti-competitive effects of "common ownership," which exists where a single investor owns shares of competing firms, have set off alarm bells.[270] An investor in this position will potentially prefer that the co-owned corporations refrain from competing intensely so as to create scope for charging higher prices that will bolster profits and shareholder returns.[271] With the Big Three having emerged as "the dominant capital market players of our time"[272] concerns exist that their collective common ownership is substantial enough to impact upon the behavior

---

262 John C. Bogle, *The Index Mutual Fund: 40 Years of Growth, Change, and Challenge*, FIN. ANALYSTS J., Jan./Feb. 2016, 9, 11.

263 Jason Zweig, *Mindless Robots, Overblown Worries*, WALL ST. J., Feb. 25, 2017, B1.

264 Dieterich, Farrell & Krouse, *supra* note 126.

265 Lund, *supra* note 245, 509; Fichtner, Heemskerk & Garcia-Bernardo, *supra* note 260, at 299, 304.

266 Fichtner, Heemskerk & Garcia-Bernardo, *supra* note 260, at 299, 304. Hortense Bioy et al., *Passive Fund Providers Take an Active Approach to Investment Stewardship*, MORNINGSTAR, Nov. 2017, 4.

267 Sarah Krouse & David Benoit, *Passive Funds Embrace Their New Power*, WALL ST. J., Oct. 25, 2016, A1.

268 Lund, *supra* note 245, 496, 509; Fiona Scott Morton & Herbert Hovenkamp, *Horizontal Shareholding and Antitrust Policy*, 127 YALE L.J. 2026, 2029 (2018).

269 Einer Elhauge, *Horizontal Shareholding*, 129 HARV. L. REV. 1267, 1267 (2016). Elhuage treats Fidelity, a major asset manager that does not specialize in passive investing, as part of the "economic blockbuster" phenomenon.

270 Jacob Gramlich & Serafin Grundl, *Testing for Competitive Effects of Common Ownership*, Board of Governors of the Federal Reserve System Finance and Economics Discussion Series 2017-029 2 (2017); *Europe Targets U.S. Asset Managers*, WALL ST. J., Mar. 28, 2018, A16 (discussing an investigation European Union competition law officials were launching).

271 Fichtner, Heemskerk & Garcia-Bernardo, *supra* note 260, at 322.

272 Eric A. Posner, Fiona Scott Morton & E. Glen Weyl, *A Proposal to Limit the Anti-competitive Power of Institutional Investors*, 81 ANTITRUST L.J. 669, 669 (2017).

of market leaders in key industries and create substantial anticompetitive effects throughout the US economy.[273]

Regardless of who the shareholders might be, executives running firms that dominate an industry with oligopolistic features have incentives to throw the competitive brakes on so as to avoid difficult decisions and enjoy a "quiet life."[274] The manner in which the Big Three operate indicates that they are unlikely to do much, if anything, to reinforce whatever tendencies already exist with dominant firms to ease off competitively. Any highly diversified investment fund will have a bias in favor of passivity. There is, after all, no guarantee that intervening will yield a beneficial outcome, the benefits arising from successful interventions have to be shared amongst all shareholders, and incurring costs to step forward could result in losing out in terms of relative performance to less energetic, free-riding rivals.[275] Index tracker funds have particularly weak incentives to act as engaged shareholders.[276] Operators of index funds do not compete over the performance of the index they are set up to mimic, which is taken as a given, and instead focus on keeping costs as low as possible and eliminating tracking errors.[277] Correspondingly, if those running an index fund expend resources to identify and correct underperformance in particular companies, any gains will be shared with the market at large, fees will increase, and market share could well be lost rapidly to cheaper, fully passive rivals in an industry where price competition has a significant effect on investor inflows.[278]

Operators of index tracking funds insist they are not mere "professional snoozers."[279] Larry Fink, BlackRock's CEO, maintains "(t)he time has come for a new model of shareholder engagement—one that strengthens and deepens communication between shareholders and the companies that they own."[280] Similarly Vanguard Principal and Fund Controller Glenn Booraem has said its funds seek to be "passive investors but active owners."[281] Booraem reasons Vanguard and other investment firms operating index tracking funds must exercise their voices because with the level of investment in companies being predetermined by the market "(w)e're riding in a car we can't get out of" and "(g)overnance is the seat belt and air bag."[282] Fear of criticism provides an additional incentive to speak up. A State Street official said in

---

[273] See, for example, Elhauge, *supra* note 269; Posner, Morton & Weyl, *supra* note 272; José Azar, Martin C. Schmalz & Isabel Tecu, *Anti-competitive Effects of Common Ownership*, unpublished working paper (2017).

[274] Marianne Bertrand & Sendhil Mullainathan, *Enjoying the Quiet Life? Corporate Governance and Managerial Preferences*, 111 J. POL. ECON. 1043, 1047 (2003).

[275] Chapter 6, text following note 305; Gilson & Gordon, *supra* note 114, at 889–93; BAINBRIDGE, *supra* note 147, at 243–46.

[276] Bebchuk, Cohen & Hirst, *supra* note 115, at 90.

[277] Edward B. Rock & Daniel L. Rubinfeld, *Defusing the Antitrust Threat to Institutional Investor Involvement in Corporate Governance*, New York University School of Law Law and Economics Research Series Working Paper No. 17-05, 7, 27 (2017).

[278] Bebchuk, Cohen & Hirst, *supra* note 115, at 98; *Passive, Aggressive*, ECONOMIST, Nov. 18, 2017, 69; Chris Flood, *Price War Becomes "Winner Take All,"* FIN. TIMES, May 7, 2018, FT fm, 1.

[279] On the characterization, see *Snaptrap*, ECONOMIST, Feb. 11, 2017, 58.

[280] Sarah Krouse, *BlackRock's Fink Pledges to Intensify Shareholder Activism*, WALL ST. J., Jan. 17, 2018, B12.

[281] *Reinventing the Company*, ECONOMIST, Oct. 24, 2015, 11.

[282] Amy Deen Westbrook & David A. Westbrook, *Unicorns, Guardians, and the Concentration of the US Equity Markets*, 96 NEB. L. REV. 688, 736 (2018).

2018 "(w)e are stewards of a large part of the US economy, and it's important that we do that properly. If we didn't do that, we'd open ourselves up to opprobrium from our investors."[283]

The Big Three have added staff recently to deal with governance and stewardship.[284] Nevertheless, each is poorly situated to impinge substantially on the discretion of public company executives, whether to encourage those executives to throw the competitive brakes on or otherwise. BlackRock's governance team is comprised of around 35 employees tasked with overseeing the 14,000 companies in which BlackRock owns shares.[285] Vanguard has just over 20 people for its 13,000 companies and State Street has approximately a dozen for its 9,000.[286] The governance teams of the Big Three carry out dozens of engagements each year with management of companies in which their index tracking funds own shares.[287] Nevertheless, with most portfolio companies it is not feasible to arrange a meeting even annually.[288] The head of corporate governance for State Street's asset management funds has told her team that because of time constraints they should not agree to every meeting company executives might request.[289] Public company executives notice. A CEO told the *Financial Times* in 2017 "(w)e'd love to talk to the passive guys, they control 20 percent of our shares, but they don't want to see us."[290]

Given the modest amount of direct contact between the Big Three indexers and public companies in which they own shares, anything approaching the sort of firm-specific meddling in which activist hedge funds engage is unrealistic. BlackRock's head of corporate governance has acknowledged "(i)t's not the shareholders' role to second guess what management is doing in every single issue."[291] The largest passive investors do throw their weight around sometimes.[292] For instance, votes against board nominees companies put forward occur with some regularity.[293] Critics nevertheless charge index trackers with failing to devote any more attention to the voting process than is required to satisfy regulators "or perhaps to satisfy their own conscience and . . . boost their firm's image."[294]

Whatever the attentiveness level of leading passive investors, they most often back management.[295] In 2017, BlackRock supported management proposals in US public companies 91 percent of the time, State Street did so with 86 percent of resolutions, and Vanguard's

---

283 Attracta Mooney & Robin Wigglesworth, *Biggest Fund Managers Face Showdown in US Gun Debate*, FIN. TIMES, Mar. 5, 2018, FTfm, 6.

284 John Authers, *Passive Phenomenon Sparks Stewardship and Governance Fears*, FIN. TIMES, Dec. 14, 2017, 28; Jill Fisch, Assaf Hamdani & Steven Davidoff Solomon, *Passive Investors*, University of Pennsylvania Institute for Law and Economics Working Paper 18-12 26 (2018).

285 Bioy et al., *supra* note 266, at 19; Krouse & Benoit, *supra* note 267.

286 Lund, *supra* note 245, at 516; Bioy et al., *supra* note 266, at 19; Jason Zweig, *This Index Argument Doesn't Hold Water*, WALL ST. J., April 21, 2018, B1.

287 Bioy et al., *supra* note 266, at 16 (listing 1480, 817, and 611 for BlackRock, Vanguard, and State Street respectively for 2016).

288 Lund, *supra* note 245, at 516, 519.

289 Krouse & Benoit, *supra* note 267.

290 John Authers, *How Passive Investors Morphed Into the Bad Guys*, FIN. TIMES, Oct. 14, 2017, 24.

291 Krouse & Benoit, *supra* note 267.

292 Reshma Kapadia, *Passive Investors Are Turning Active*, BARRON'S, July 10, 2017, L10.

293 Fichtner, Heemskerk & Garcia-Bernardo, *supra* note 260, at 318 (indicating that on nearly half of the occasions where the "Big Three" voted against management recommendations a board nomination was involved).

294 Dick Weil, *Passive Investors, Don't Vote*, WALL ST. J., Mar. 9, 2018, A9.

295 Authers, *supra* note 284; Lindsay Fortado & Anna Nicolaou, *Peltz's P&G Loss Unlikely to Stop Activist Tide*, FIN. TIMES, Oct. 12, 2017, 15.

support level was 94 percent.[296] The *Financial Times* has said of this pattern that it signals "a degree of inattention at odds with dynamic stewardship claims."[297]

Voting patterns on executive pay confirm the tendency among the largest passive investors to support management. Under the Dodd-Frank Act of 2010, a "say on pay" scheme was introduced giving shareholders of publicly traded companies the right to vote on executive pay policy on an advisory basis at least once every three years.[298] Shareholders rarely vote against what companies put forward. With S&P 500 companies shareholder votes cast in favor were 91 percent in 2016 and 92 percent in 2017.[299] BlackRock and Vanguard have been particularly strong supporters. During 2016 each voted 98 percent in favor of pay practices at S&P 500 companies.[300] A *New York Times* columnist has said of BlackRock's voting power on executive pay that its "big stick is more like a wet noodle."[301]

Developments with say on pay voting are instructive not only in relation to index trackers but also with respect to limits generally on the potency of institutional shareholders as a constraint on public company executives. Essentially the story is a consistent one—shareholder input has increased but management retains wide discretion. Supporters of the introduction of say on pay believed shareholder votes on executive pay policy would foster transparency, encourage the alignment of pay and performance, and preclude CEO compensation from spiraling upward.[302] Vanguard's Jack Bogle characterized the reform as "a nice step forward."[303]

The manner in which matters have worked out in practice has tempered considerably optimism about say on pay. With shareholders voting heavily in favor of executive pay policies put before them, the embarrassment of a majority "no" vote has proved to be a rarity. In the seven proxy seasons from 2011 through 2017, only 1.9 percent of the votes at corporations in the Russell 3000 stock market index went against the company.[304] Executive pay has also increased noticeably since say on pay was introduced. The median pay of S&P 500 CEOs was $11.6 million in 2017 as compared with just under $9 million in 2010.[305] Such evidence has prompted harsh verdicts on the say on pay experiment such as "tinkering at the edges at best,"[306] "a bust,"[307] and "ineffective."[308]

---

[296] Bioy et al., *supra* note 266, at 13.

[297] Lex, *Index Funds—Cut Price Consciences*, FIN. TIMES, Dec. 29, 2017, 12.

[298] Dodd Frank § 951(c).

[299] EY Center for Board Matters, *supra* note 162.

[300] Gretchen Morgenson, *Your Fund Has Your Say, Like It or Not*, NY TIMES, Sept. 25, 2016, Business, 1. See also Zweig, *supra* note 286 (citing a study indicating that with "leading S&P index funds" the approval rate with executive pay proposals was 97 percent in 2016).

[301] Gretchen Morgenson, *Wet Noodle Where a Stick Ought to Be*, NY TIMES, Apr. 17, 2016, Business, 1.

[302] Randall S. Thomas, Alan R. Palmiter & James F. Cotter, *Dodd-Frank's Say on Pay: Will It Lead to a Greater Role for Shareholders in Corporate Governance?*, 97 CORNELL L. REV. 1213, 1235 (2012).

[303] BOGLE, *supra* note 137, at 95.

[304] *See* SEMLER BROSSY, 2017 SAY ON PAY RESULTS, Aug. 30, 2017, available at http://www.semlerbrossy.com/wp-content/uploads/SBCG-2017-SOP-Report-08-30-2017.pdf (accessed Jan. 27, 2018) (calculated using annual data for 2011 through to 2017).

[305] Theo Francis & Joann S. Lublin, *CEO Pay Reached New High in 2017*, WALL ST. J., Mar. 22, 2018, B1.

[306] Steven M. Davidoff, *Furor over Executive Pay Is Not the Revolt It Appears to Be*, NY TIMES, May 2, 2012, B5.

[307] Jesse Eisenger, *In Shareholder Say-on-Pay Votes, Whispers, Not Shouts*, NY TIMES, June 27, 2013, B5.

[308] James Surowiecki, *Why CEO Reform Failed*, NEW YORKER, Apr. 20, 2015, available at https://www.newyorker.com/magazine/2015/04/20/why-c-e-o-pay-reform-failed (accessed Dec. 20, 2017).

While say on pay has not unleashed substantial opposition to executive pay or prompted material reductions in managerial compensation, the mechanism has not been a corporate governance irrelevance.[309] As the *Wall Street Journal* noted in 2014, even though outcomes are nonbinding "most corporate boards consider a negative vote a black eye and work hard to respond to shareholder concerns."[310] The say on pay process has correspondingly prompted many companies to increase board outreach to shareholders, accompanied by the opening of new lines of communication.[311] Boards in their turn have been prepared to make modifications to head off dissent, which likely has bolstered the high approval rates that have been obtained.[312] The fact that executive pay is a key topic for discussion with nearly half of the engagements BlackRock has with public companies despite BlackRock rarely actually voting against management on executive pay lends credence to this conjecture.[313]

The say on pay regime, where public companies listen to their shareholders but retain considerable scope to proceed in the manner they see fit, reflects broader trends concerning institutional investors. Rav Gupta, the former *Fortune* 500 CEO, likely was correct when he suggested in 2016 that due primarily to large institutional investors "shareholders are exerting a more effective and powerful influence on corporate management than in the past."[314] On the other hand, there remains a continued bias against activism by mainstream institutional investors that means public company executives have wide discretion to run their firms without provoking active pushback. Correspondingly, despite institutional shareholders owning a large proportion of shares in public companies and despite the collective stake of the biggest institutions being substantial, there remains a separation of ownership and control in public firms not very far removed from the Berle and Means's 1930s version.

The growing popularity of index tracking funds likely will reinforce the institutional bias against activism. Only time will tell exactly what corporate governance role BlackRock, Vanguard, and State Street will assume in the likely event their collective stake in US public companies continues to increase.[315] Given the business model underpinning index tracking funds, however, it is unlikely that the voting power available to passive indexers will substantially compromise existing managerial prerogatives in the foreseeable future. Concrete, sustained evidence of institutional shareholders taking meaningful, proactive steps to keep management in check would mean that it would no longer be appropriate to refer to the

---

309 Cox & Thomas, *supra* note 235, at 50.

310 Emily Chasan, *Companies Say "No Way" to "Say on Pay,"* WALL ST. J., Aug. 26, 2014, B1.

311 Vipal Monga, *Boards Cozy Up to Investors*, WALL ST. J., Jan. 8, 2013, B7; Paul H. Edelman, Randall S. Thomas & Robert B. Thompson, *Shareholder Voting in an Age of Intermediary Capitalism*, 87 S. CAL. L. REV. 1359, 1432 (2014).

312 MICHAEL B. DORFF, INDISPENSABLE AND OTHER MYTHS: WHY THE CEO EXPERIMENT FAILED AND HOW TO FIX IT 245 (2014).

313 Caleb Melby, *A Millionaire Is Telling BlackRock to Say No to Big CEO Pay*, BLOOMBERG, May 20, 2016, available at https://www.bloomberg.com/news/articles/2016-05-20/a-millionaire-is-telling-blackrock-to-say-no-to-big-ceo-pay (accessed Mar. 15, 2018).

314 *Role of Corporate Boards, supra* note 167, at 25.

315 MILLSTEIN, *supra* note 179, at 20.

paradigmatic American public company as the Berle-Means corporation. That evidence is currently lacking and probably will be for some time yet.

External Constraints

Earlier chapters have shown that both boards and shareholders have become more potent as constraints on public company executives since the managerial capitalism era, albeit often in a fitful fashion. These trends, as we have just seen, have continued recently. It is doubtful, however, whether the boards or shareholders of tomorrow will impose markedly greater checks on managerial conduct than their present-day counterparts. Correspondingly, for the foreseeable future "external" constraints are destined to remain an important determinant of the scope of managerial discretion. We have already seen that one historically important external constraint, the market for corporate control, might now be on life support.[316] We will consider now the current state of play and likely prospects for other potentially significant external constraints.

UNIONS

For many public company executives during the managerial capitalism era, dealing with organized labor impinged quite substantially on choices they made.[317] In the decades that followed unions receded steadily in importance as a variable with which management had to be concerned.[318] Organized labor's decline has not been reversed lately. Union density slumped to 10.7 percent of the workforce in 2016, an all-time low, and remained unchanged in 2017.[319] With private sector employers, only 6.5 percent of workers were unionized in 2017, a proportion just fractionally above the all-time low of 6.4 percent in 2016.[320] Strike activity has continued to decline as well. Between 2010 and 2017 there was an average of 14 major work stoppages annually, a decline from the already historically low rate of 20 per year in the 2000s.[321]

There is some good news for unions, namely public support. In 2017, 61 percent of Americans polled indicated they approved of unions, the highest level of support since 2003.[322] Nostalgia for the stability of family-based factory life during the prosperous union-friendly 1950s and 1960s has perhaps bolstered support for organized labor.[323]

---

[316] *Supra* note 204 and accompanying text.

[317] Chapter 2, notes 444–51; Chapter 3, notes 381–84 and related discussion.

[318] Chapter 6, note 348, 351–52 and accompanying text; Louis Uchitelle, *How Labor's Decline Hurt American Manufacturing*, NY TIMES, Apr. 22, 2018, Business, 4.

[319] Bureau of Labor Statistics, *Union Membership Rate 10.7 Percent in 2016*, February 9, 2017, available at https://www.bls.gov/opub/ted/2017/union-membership-rate-10-point-7-percent-in-2016.htm (accessed Apr. 6, 2018); Bureau of Labor Statistics, *Economic News Release: Union Members Summary*, Jan. 19, 2018, available at https://www.bls.gov/news.release/union2.nr0.htm (accessed Apr. 6, 2018).

[320] Unionstats.com, *Union Membership and Coverage Database from the CPS*, available at http://unionstats.gsu.edu/ (accessed Apr. 6, 2018).

[321] Chapter 6, note 353 and related discussion; Bureau of Labor Statistics, *Work Stoppages Involving 1,000 or More Workers, 1947–2017*, available at https://www.bls.gov/news.release/wkstp.t01.htm (accessed Apr. 6, 2018).

[322] Art Swift, *Labor Union Approval Best since 2003, at 61%*, GALLUP WORKPLACE, Aug. 31, 2017, available at http://news.gallup.com/poll/217331/labor-union-approval-best-2003.aspx?g_source=position4&g_medium=related&g_campaign=tiles (accessed Jan. 28, 2018).

[323] Noam Cohen, *How Trump Disrupted Silicon Valley*, NY TIMES, Nov. 18, 2016, A31.

Americans may view unions favorably but they harbor serious doubts about the future of organized labor, with less than a quarter believing unions will become stronger in the future.[324] This pessimism appears to be justified. In the private sector context an ideal setting to put collective bargaining in place is one where workplaces are large and staffed by sizeable contingents of full-time employees.[325] This arrangement, however, has become very much the exception to the rule with employers depending heavily on automation to economize on labor costs and outsourcing work to independent contractors whenever possible.[326] Continued antipathy toward unions in the southern United States and in sectors such as high-tech and restaurants has also hamstrung organized labor.[327] The upshot is that it is unlikely that unions will rally substantially in the private sector for the foreseeable future, meaning in turn that organized labor is unlikely to return soon as a highly relevant constraint for public company executives.

REGULATION

A late twentieth century trend in favor of deregulation that had bolstered the discretion available to public company executives ended in the 2000s.[328] From the beginning of the current decade through to the end of Barack Obama's presidency, regulatory pressure on business intensified. The banking sector was the poster child for the trend. A double back in favor of deregulation appears to be underway with Donald Trump. Astute political clairvoyance would be needed to predict accurately the legacy of this latest change of course.

While George W. Bush promised to curtail regulation as president, government intervention was scaled up while he was in office.[329] The trend continued, and accelerated, when Barack Obama became president in 2009. A total of 486 regulations expected to have an economic impact of $100 million or more were promulgated during the eight years Obama was president, as compared with 358 under Bush.[330] Moreover, Obama's "regulations were, on the whole, bigger and bolder than what had come before."[331] The *New York Times*, in a 2016 retrospective series on the Obama presidency, even labeled him "the Regulator in Chief."[332]

---

324 Swift, *supra* note 322.

325 William E. Forbath & Brishen Rogers, *New Workers, New Labor Laws*, NY TIMES, Sept. 4, 2017, A21.

326 *Labour Pains*, ECONOMIST, Nov. 2, 2013, 73; Lauren Webb, *The End of Employees*, WALL ST. J., Feb. 2, 2017, A1.

327 Gregory Ferenstein, *Why Labor Unions and Silicon Valley Aren't Friends, In 2 Charts*, TECHCRUNCH, July 29, 2013, available at https://techcrunch.com/2013/07/29/why-labor-unions-and-silicon-valley-arent-friends-in-2-charts/ (accessed Jan. 28, 2018); Richard Berman, *Honey, I Shrunk the Union*, WALL ST. J., Apr. 12, 2017, A13 (restaurant sector); *The United Auto Workers Lose Again*, WALL ST. J., Aug. 7, 2017, A16 (the South).

328 Chapter 6 notes 354, 357–59 and related discussion.

329 Chapter 6, notes 355, 360–61 and accompanying text.

330 Derived from data available at George Washington Regulatory Studies Center, *Reg Stats—Economically Significant Regulations Issued Each Year*, available at https://regulatorystudies.columbian.gwu.edu/reg-stats (accessed May 20, 2018).

331 *Grudges and Kludges*, ECONOMIST, Mar. 4, 2017, 30.

332 In the series, the label was used to tag an online version of a print story that did not include the phrase. See https://www.nytimes.com/2016/08/14/us/politics/obama-era-legacy-regulation.html (accessed Jan. 29, 2018).

The scaling up of regulation during the Obama administration impinged upon managerial discretion in public companies. According to an analysis of disclosures by publicly traded companies regulatory risk jumped nearly 80 percent across industries between 2010 and 2015.[333] Corporate executives were well aware increased regulation was circumscribing options. *Fortune* indicated in a 2016 article on "red tape" that "right now the hue and cry from the business community is louder than at just about any time in recent memory."[334] The Business Roundtable, the association of chief executives of leading public companies, joined those complaining. The introduction to a set of corporate governance principles the Business Roundtable issued in 2016 noted "(t)he increased regulatory burdens imposed on public companies in recent years have added to the costs and complexity of overseeing and managing a corporation's business and bring new challenges from operational, regulatory and compliance perspectives."[335]

New regulations the Obama administration generated addressed a wide range of issues, including healthcare, the environment, and workplace safety.[336] Due, however, to the Dodd-Frank Act of 2010 and regulatory initiatives associated with that statute, banking was the industry where managerial discretion was most substantially compromised. Even prior to Dodd-Frank banking was one of the most heavily regulated industries in America.[337] Nevertheless, a freewheeling culture characterized banking in the 2000s, led by a coterie of highly leveraged investment banks increasingly trading on their own accounts to bolster profits.[338] There was a radical change post-financial crisis.

The financial crisis flattened the swashbuckling investment bank, meaning "glamour is out and stability is in."[339] Investment banking now occurs under the umbrella of major commercial banks or is conducted in small boutiques that refrain from large-scale high-risk proprietary trading.[340] With the high-flying investment banks of the mid-2000s Lehman Brothers went bankrupt, Bear Stearns and Merrill Lynch were bought in distress sales by commercial banks, and Goldman Sachs and Morgan Stanley each converted into a bank holding company, the corporate vehicle of choice for major commercial banks.[341] Following its conversion Morgan Stanley "changed from a run-and-gun investment bank," curtailed "(g)o-go trading businesses once hailed as its future," and prioritized retail brokerage business and the managing of investment assets for affluent individual clients, companies, and institutions.[342] As for Goldman Sachs, while it was "the undisputed king of the investment-banking industry" when

---

333 Clark S. Judge, *The Rust Belt Is Right to Blame Obama*, WALL ST. J., Dec. 19, 2016, A21 (discussing research by VogelHood Group).

334 Brian O'Keefe, *The Red Tape Conundrum*, FORTUNE, Nov. 1, 2016, 76.

335 BUSINESS ROUNDTABLE, PRINCIPLES OF CORPORATE GOVERNANCE 1 (2016).

336 *How the President Came to Embrace Executive Power*, NY TIMES, Aug. 14, 2016, A1.

337 John D. "Jay" Cornet, *Bank Governance: An Independent Director's Perspective*, 7 N.C. BANKING INST. 1, 2 (2003).

338 Chapter 6, notes 495–506 and related discussion.

339 *Sorpasso on the Street*, ECONOMIST, Jan. 27, 2018, 9.

340 William M. Isaac & Richard M. Kovacevich, *The Shattered Arguments for a New Glass-Steagall*, WALL ST. J., Apr. 26, 2017, A17.

341 Chapter 6, notes 188, 195–96, 201 and accompanying text.

342 Aaron Lucchetti & Julie Steinberg, *Life on Wall Street Grows Less Risky*, WALL ST. J., Sept. 10, 2013, A1; Avi Salzman, *The Makeover*, BARRON'S, June 9, 2014, 23; *Tediously Does It*, ECONOMIST, Jan. 27, 2018, 63.

"investment banking seemed to rule the world," recently it has been forsaking a predilection for trading assets on its own account to push into lending and has been "producing returns more commonly associated with a utility."[343] Correspondingly, "(r)ival banks view it with indifference, not awe."[344]

Restraint has also been the order of the day with other major financial firms, with regulation helping to make "finance a more mundane place."[345] In the years following the financial crisis large commercial banks shrank operations, cut staff, jettisoned risky businesses, and capped banker bonuses.[346] Analogies have regularly been drawn between post-financial crisis banks and cautiously run public utilities so as to underscore the level of risk aversion.[347] The banking sector imperial CEO, a casualty of the financial crisis, has yet to return, even if the CEOs of leading banks are well paid.[348] With J.P. Morgan Chase having navigated the financial crisis relatively adeptly its chief executive Jamie Dimon stayed in control but he was "the last of the old-style loudmouths."[349] Otherwise, according to the *Wall Street Journal*, "(l)arge banks, burned by years of scandal, often with swashbuckling CEOs at the helm" have been "turning to new bosses who sport well-polished veneers of boringness. The goal is to avoid further controversy."[350]

The cautious approach to banking prevailing since the financial crisis has been due in large measure to increased regulation. The core rationale underlying the Dodd-Frank Act of 2010 was that nothing like the financial crisis of 2008 should happen again.[351] This was to be achieved by reforming the financial system to reduce risk before the fact and by limiting the damage in the event of a fresh crisis by introducing a new insolvency framework designed to ensure the orderly resolution of the affairs of troubled large financial institutions.[352]

One way in which the Dodd-Frank Act sought to limit risk-taking by banks was by introducing what became known as "the Volcker rule," arising from a 2009 recommendation by former Federal Reserve chairman Paul Volcker that large commercial banks should be precluded from trading and investing for their own profit and loss.[353] Dodd-Frank also directed

---

[343] Gillian Tett, *How the Vampire Squid Became a Fattened Slug*, FIN. TIMES, Apr. 22, 2016, 11; Ben McLannahan, *Selling to America*, FIN. TIMES, Apr. 20, 2018, 9.

[344] *Goldman Sags*, ECONOMIST, Oct. 7, 2017, 66.

[345] Liz Hoffmann, *Once Near Death, Morgan Stanley Gets Its Mojo Back*, WALL ST. J., May 4, 2018, A1.

[346] Alexandra Frean, *Big Banks Are Learning at Last That It Pays to Address the Bonus Culture*, TIMES, Apr. 26, 2016, 41.

[347] Grind & Glazer, *supra* note 144; Patrick Jenkins, *Too Dull to Fail?*, FIN. TIMES, Sept. 7, 2016, 9; DAVID M. SMICK, THE GREAT EQUALIZER: HOW MAIN STREET CAPITALISM CAN CREATE AN ECONOMY FOR EVERYONE 87 (2017).

[348] Chapter 6, note 544 and related discussion; Liz Hoffman, Christina Rexrode & Aaron Lucchetti. *Big Bank CEOs Reap Rich Pay Packages*, WALL ST. J., Feb. 17, 2018, B1.

[349] Patrick Jenkins, *RBS Headhunter Starts Search for Anti-hero*, FIN. TIMES, June 15, 2013, 17.

[350] Max Colchester, *Today's Bank Chiefs Can Spin a Yawn*, WALL ST. J., Aug. 12, 2013, C1.

[351] ALAN S. BLINDER, AFTER THE MUSIC STOPPED: THE FINANCIAL CRISIS, THE RESPONSE AND THE WORK AHEAD 7 (2013).

[352] DAVID SKEEL, THE NEW FINANCIAL DEAL: UNDERSTANDING THE DODD-FRANK ACT AND ITS (UNINTENDED) CONSEQUENCES 6 (2011); Tom Braithwaite & Nasiripour Shahien, *Out to Break the Banks*, FIN. TIMES, May 1, 2013, 11.

[353] Dodd-Frank Act, § 619; Steven L. Schwarcz, *Misalignment: Corporate Risk-Taking and Public Duty*, 92 NOTRE DAME L. REV. 1, 12 (2016).

the Federal Reserve to conduct annual "stress tests" for large banks so as to identify and address significant downside risks that might otherwise preclude survival should a financial crisis be looming.[354] Otherwise, the Act generally steered clear of enacting specific risk reduction measures for banks thought to be "too big to fail" and instead in various ways authorized bank regulators to set relevant ground rules.[355]

Regulators, fortified by their Dodd-Frank mandate, stepped up considerably their scrutiny of banks, a process characterized by the *Wall Street Journal* in 2017 as "politicians and bureaucrats join(ing) in a remorseless and determined effort to tighten regulation."[356] Bankers were well aware of the pattern. Morgan Stanley's CEO agreed when his predecessor suggested in 2013 "(y)our No. 1 client is the government."[357]

Mindful of heightened scrutiny post-Dodd-Frank, the six largest banks increased their collective compliance expenditures from $34.7 billion in 2007 to $70.2 billion in 2013.[358] Large financial firms also adjusted key policies; "(s)ince the crisis, banks have not needed an excuse to be bureaucratic or timid."[359] Sizeable acquisitions were off the agenda for large financial firms because regulators had indicated such dealmaking was unwelcome.[360] Major banks sought Federal Reserve clearance for dividend policies, being aware that the Fed was taking into account cash distributions to shareholders when deciding the outcome of the annual stress tests it was conducting.[361] It was well understood that equity capital was a crucial element of the stress tests, and banks facing such scrutiny correspondingly rebuilt their equity base from 5.5 percent of risk-weighted assets in 2009 to 12.5 percent in 2017.[362] Decisions about which businesses to move into or leave were tailored accordingly, with bankers being cognizant that carrying out riskier activities could quickly erode a capital cushion that was potentially costly and time-consuming to replenish.[363]

For many apprehensive about dangers the financial sector pose to the wider economy, bankers dialing back risk in response to regulation might be welcome but does not suffice. The fear is that the intensity of regulatory supervision will weaken as the 2008 crisis fades from memory, opening the door for banks to return to their destructive freewheeling ways.[364]

---

[354] Dodd-Frank Act, § 165(i); Mehrsa Baradaran, *Regulation by Hypothetical*, 67 VAND. L. REV. 1247, 1286–88 (2014).

[355] John C. Coffee, *The Political Economy of Dodd-Frank: Why Financial Reform Tends to Be Frustrated and Systemic Risk Perpetuated*, 97 CORNELL L. REV. 1019, 1059 (2012).

[356] Tim Congdon & Steve H. Henke, *More Bank Capital Could Kill the Economy*, WALL ST. J., Mar. 14, 2017, A17.

[357] Lucchetti & Steinberg, *supra* note 342.

[358] Grind & Glazer, *supra* note 144.

[359] *If the Cap Fits*, ECONOMIST, Feb. 10, 2018, 69.

[360] Lawrence G. Baxter, *Betting Big: Value, Caution and Accountability in an Era of Large Banks and Complex Finance*, 31 REV. BANKING & FIN. L. 765, 871 (2011–2012); Patrick Jenkins, *Banks Adapt to Being Kept in Check*, FIN. TIMES, Sept. 9, 2013, 21; *Banking in the Age of Dodd-Frank*, WALL ST. J., June 15, 2017, B14 (chart indicating that the total value of bank acquisitions had yet to exceed $30 billion in any one year during the 2010s while doing so every year but one in the 2000s).

[361] Ryan Tracey & Andy Ackerman, *Where Financial Regulation Goes from Here*, WALL ST. J., Apr. 25, 2017, R1.

[362] Ben McLannahan, *Big Banks Prepare for "Payout Party Time,"* FIN. TIMES, June 30, 2017, A14; *Spring in Their Step*, ECONOMIST, Apr. 21, 2018, 66.

[363] Nathaniel Popper, *Has Wall Street Been Tamed?*, NY TIMES, Aug. 7, 2016, Sunday Magazine, 14.

[364] John C. Coffee, *Systemic Risk after Dodd-Frank: Contingent Capital and the Need for Regulatory Strategies beyond Oversight*, 111 COLUM. L. REV. 795, 821 (2011).

In addition, while the preamble to the Dodd-Frank Act indicated that the legislation would end bank bailouts for good,[365] this may well be a vain hope.[366] Bank regulators are optimistic that if a leading financial institution got into dire straits an orderly failure would ensue.[367] The largest banks, however, are bigger now than they were before the financial crisis, with the top six having total assets of $10.2 trillion in 2017 as compared with just over $8 trillion a decade earlier.[368] With the top banks operating on such a massive scale, if any one of them was at risk of collapse and delays with deploying the Dodd-Frank resolution mechanisms created the risk of 2008-style economic havoc, a bailout seemingly would be politically inevitable.[369]

Given the unappetizing prospect of future bailouts of supersized banks, Simon Johnson and James Kwak said in a 2010 book on banking and the financial crisis "(t)he right solution is obvious: do not allow financial institutions to be too big to fail; break up the ones that are."[370] The idea of breaking up mega-banks has resonated politically. In 2013 Senators Elizabeth Warren and John McCain co-sponsored a bill they styled "the 21st Century Glass-Steagall Act," a reference to the 1933 legislation that split commercial and investment banking activities before its 1999 repeal.[371] Warren, who launched a Twitter campaign to rally support for the bill with the motto "Banking Should Be Boring,"[372] teamed up with McCain to reintroduce the bill in 2015.[373] Neither bill made headway but the 2016 Republican and Democratic Party platforms both called for reinstatement of the Glass-Steagall Act.[374] Political discussion of bank breakups continued after the election. Donald Trump said in a 2017 interview "(t)here's some people that want to go back to the old system, right? So we're going to look at that."[375]

Since antipathy toward Wall Street remains robust a decade after the financial crisis, some type of restoration of Glass-Steagall theoretically could happen.[376] The tougher regulation of banks that would be involved would, however, be out of character for a Trump administration with a distinct deregulatory orientation. Trump said on the campaign trail "I would say 70 percent of regulations can go. It's just stopping businesses from growing."[377] A year into

[365] Dodd-Frank Act, preamble.

[366] Roberta S. Karmel, *Is the Public Utility Holding Company Act a Model for Breaking Up the Banks That Are Too-Big-to-Fail?*, 62 HASTINGS L.J. 821, 827 (2010).

[367] Justin Baer & Ryan Tracy, *Lasting Legacy of the Bear Stearns Bailout*, WALL ST. J., Mar. 14, 2018, A1.

[368] Jesse Eisinger, *Despite Changes, an Overhaul of Wall Street Falls Short*, NY TIMES, Mar. 5, 2015, B5; Christina Rexrode & Ryan Tracy, *Bank Size Threshold Comes under Scrutiny*, WALL ST. J., May 31, 2017, B3.

[369] Coffee, *supra* note 364, at 799–800; Jonathan R. Macey & James P. Holdcroft, *Failure Is an Option: An Ersatz-Antitrust Approach to Financial Regulation*, 120 YALE L.J. 1368, 1382, 1389–90 (2011); Charles W. Calomiris, *Four Principles for Replacing Dodd-Frank*, WALL ST. J., June 16, 2017, A17.

[370] SIMON JOHNSON & JAMES KWAK, 13 BANKERS: THE WALL STREET TAKEOVER AND THE NEXT FINANCIAL MELTDOWN 208 (2010).

[371] Chapter 2, note 64 and related discussion; Chapter 5, note 345 and accompanying text; Peter Eavis, *Senators Introduce Bill to Separate Trading Activities from Big Banks*, NY TIMES, July 12, 2013, B3.

[372] Michael R. Crittenden, *New Glass-Steagall Is Urged*, WALL ST. J., July 12, 2013, C3.

[373] WILLIAM D. COHAN, WHY WALL STREET MATTERS 69 (2017).

[374] Edward Robinson, *The Taming of Wall Street*, BUS. WK., Aug. 1, 2016, 33.

[375] Andrew Ross Sorkin, *Wall Street Shudders as Trump Muses*, NY TIMES, May 2, 2017, B1.

[376] John Authers, *Call for Glass-Steagall Shows Need to Create a New Banking Model*, FIN. TIMES, Apr. 15, 2017, 18.

[377] O'Keefe, *supra* note 334.

his presidency, Trump claimed "(w)e have undertaken the most extensive regulatory reduction ever conceived."[378] In fact, cases where active regulations have been stripped clean off the books have been rare.[379] Nevertheless, rule-making has tailed off dramatically from the Obama era, numerous executive orders and executive branch agency directives have scaled back regulations in place, and the regulatory style has become more congenial for the regulated as Trump appointees have been installed.[380]

Somewhat quixotically given Trump's bank breakup ruminations, the supervisory style of banking regulators has become less abrasive and the Treasury Department has spelled out plans for adopting a lighter touch in the many areas where Dodd-Frank offers discretion.[381] Then again, Trump did call Dodd-Frank a "disaster," vowed after taking office to "do a big number" on it, and indicated overregulation had left the financial industry "devastated and unable to properly serve the public."[382] Nevertheless, legislation enacted in 2018 to scale back Dodd-Frank left "most of the sprawling Obama-era statute in place."[383]

It is unclear at present whether the deregulatory stance the Trump administration has taken will constitute a mere hiatus in a larger pro-regulatory trend or is the beginning of a deregulation pattern akin to that in operation as the twentieth century came to a close.[384] Future election results will do much to dictate in which direction things go. Absent an unlikely wholesale regulatory bonfire, however, governmental rule-making should remain a meaningful constraint on public company behavior for the foreseeable future.

COMPETITORS

As the twentieth century drew to a close, executives of companies dominating the market sectors in which their firms operated had to be mindful of competitors to a greater extent than their counterparts in the managerial capitalism era.[385] As the twenty-first century got underway, it appeared to some that intensifying competition had evolved into a form of "supercapitalism."[386] At the same time, that there were signs that some large firms were accumulating market power that could permit them a somewhat quieter life than their late twentieth century peers.[387]

---

[378] Barney Jopson, *Trump's Bonfire of Red Tape Proves a Slow Burn*, FIN. TIMES, Jan. 30, 2018, 6.

[379] *Id.*; *Trump v the Rule Book*, ECONOMIST, Oct. 14, 2017, 61.

[380] *Trump v the Rule*, *supra* note 379; Gerald F. Seib, *Trump's Deregulatory Juggernaut Is Rolling*, WALL ST. J., Oct. 31, 2017, A2; Binyamin Appelbaum & Jim Tankersley, *Red Tape Losing Its Grip, Firms Ante Up*, NY TIMES, Jan. 2, 2018, A1; *A Boom Like No Other*, ECONOMIST, May 24, 2018, 24.

[381] *Turn of the Wheel*, ECONOMIST, June 17, 2017, 73; Matthew Goldstein & Stacey Cowley, *Casting Wall Street as Victim, Trump Leads Charge on Deregulation*, NY TIMES, Nov. 28, 2017, B1; Ben McLannahan & Barney Jopson, *US Banks Applaud Trump's Shift in Tone on Regulation*, FIN. TIMES, Feb. 22, 2018, 6.

[382] Goldstein & Cowley, *supra* note 381; *Shearing and Shaving*, ECONOMIST, Feb. 11, 2017, 59.

[383] Ryan Tracy & Andrew Ackerman, *Regulators' To-Do List Grows With Banking Bill*, WALL ST. J., May 25, 2018, B10.

[384] *Trump v the Rule*, *supra* note 379.

[385] Chapter 2, notes 354–58 and related discussion; Chapter 5, notes 364–80 and accompanying text.

[386] Chapter 6, note 366 and related discussion.

[387] Chapter 6, notes 393–99 and accompanying text.

Conflicting signals on the extent to which market pressure from rivals impinges upon public company executives continue today. The competitive pressure businesses face is still widely hyped. On the other hand, the growing sway of incumbents, particularly in the tech sector, is capturing attention to an extent unknown since the managerial capitalism era ended.

A popular theory is that "business is more competitive than ever," which translates into "a hyper-competitive world in which established giants are constantly being felled by the forces of disruption."[388] Turnover at the corporate pinnacle seems to confirm such conjectures. Between 2007 and 2017 the world's five largest companies, ranked by market capitalization, all changed, with the exception of Microsoft. Apple, Alphabet/Google, Amazon, and Facebook replaced Exxon Mobil, General Electric, Citigroup, and Shell Oil.[389]

Big Bang Disruption: Strategy in the Age of Devastating Innovation, a 2014 book by Larry Downes and Paul Nunes described by a *Forbes* columnist as "(o)ne of the most important business books to come along in a while," exemplifies the thinking that business is operating in an unprecedentedly hypercompetitive world.[390] Clay Christensen achieved considerable notoriety in the late 1990s by using the concept of "disruption" to characterize competitive threats industry incumbents could face.[391] Downes and Nunes justify adding the intensifier "big bang" on the basis that a new stage of innovation is underway which is "devastating" because "(t)he new disrupters attack existing markets not just from the top, bottom and sides, but from all three at once."[392]

Downes and Nunes have had plenty of company in hailing an age of competition-driven unrelenting change. Gerald Davis, in making his case that the days of the public company as the dominant business form are numbered, has suggested "being disruptive is an essential virtue for any new business plan," and that "lightweight entrants" are well situated to challenge public company incumbents because "(t)he economies of scale that gave birth to the modern corporation have disappeared in many sectors."[393] A team of analysts from the influential management consultancy McKinsey wrote in 2016 "(i)ncumbents that have long focused on perfecting their industry value chains are often stunned to find new entrants introducing completely different ways to make money," meaning "many business leaders live in a heightened state of alert."[394] Or as a *New York Times* columnist observed in 2016 when describing how Dollar Shave Club, a start-up selling razors, had challenged market leader Procter & Gamble and its key brand Gillette, "all companies should be fearful."[395]

---

[388] *Out With the Old*, ECONOMIST, Dec. 17, 2016, 64.

[389] Jonathan Taplin, *Is It Time to Break Up Google?*, NY TIMES, Apr. 23, 2017, Sunday Review, 4.

[390] LARRY DOWNES & PAUL NUNES, BIG BANG DISRUPTION: STRATEGY IN THE AGE OF DEVASTATING INNOVATION (2014); Steven Denning, *The Business Disease with No Cure: Big Bang Disruption*, FORBES.COM, Feb. 22, 2014, available at https://www.forbes.com/sites/stevedenning/2014/02/22/the-business-disease-without-a-cure-big-bang-disruption/#5b40c70f69ff (accessed Jan. 28, 2018).

[391] Chapter 5, notes 384–85 and related discussion.

[392] DOWNES & NUNES, *supra* note 390, at 7.

[393] DAVIS, *supra* note 10, x, 81.

[394] Angus Dawson, Martin Hart & Jay Scanlan, *The Economic Essentials of Digital Strategy*, MCKINSEY Q. (2016), issue #2, 32, 33, 41.

[395] Steven Davidoff Solomon, *In Comfort of a Close Shave, a Distressing Disruption*, NY TIMES, July 27, 2016, B3.

Explanations for the ostensible competitive free-for-all that has prompted a heightened state of alert are typically oriented around technological advances and a congenial financial environment for potential disrupters. With the popularity of the iPhone and its smartphone rivals expanding the reach of the internet and with apps making it easier to reach consumers directly,[396] in the words of Google economist Hal Varian "(c)ompetition is a click away, so competitive advantage can erode quickly."[397] Due to a healthy venture capital industry, increased investing by wealthy business "angels" and by sovereign wealth funds, and the possibility of soliciting funding online ("crowdfunding"), entrepreneurs eager to challenge incumbents reputedly "have a broader range of funding sources to choose from than ever before, for almost every stage of their company's growth."[398] Stewart Butterfield, the founder of Slack, a popular messaging service that achieved "unicorn" status the fastest of any company after launch,[399] declared in 2015 "(i)t might be the best time for any kind of business in any industry to raise money for all of history, like since the time of the ancient Egyptians."[400]

The financing outlook for start-ups is not as universally rosy as Butterfield's rhetoric implies. Access to risk capital in the United States features a strong geographic bias, with more than three-quarters of venture capital assets under management being run by funds based in California, Massachusetts, and New York and being invested in those states.[401] Traditionally, entrepreneurs starting a business have turned to banks to borrow when personal resources are proving to be inadequate but the post-financial crisis banking sector has been criticized for being unenthusiastic about making commercial loans.[402] Donald Trump argued as much in 2017, blaming overregulation. He said "(f)rankly, I have so many people, friends of mine, that have nice businesses and they can't borrow money. They just can't get any money because the banks just won't let them borrow because of the rules and regulations in Dodd-Frank."[403] In fact, commercial lending has been increasing since 2011, but the rate of growth has been considerably slower than it was before the financial crisis.[404] There correspondingly may well be a sizeable number of entrepreneurs theoretically well positioned to challenge incumbents who cannot finance their plans readily.

---

[396] Betsy Morris, *What the iPhone Wrought*, WALL ST. J., June 24, 2017, B3.

[397] Varian, *supra* note 77.

[398] Foley, *supra* note 79; see also *supra* notes 78–83 and related discussion; Ahmed Murad et al., *"Disrupters" Bring Destruction but Opportunity*, FIN. TIMES, Dec. 29, 2014, 15.

[399] Bhavik Sarkhedi, *From WB21 to Slack, These Are the 10 Fastest Unicorns to Reach a $1 Billion Valuation*, ENTREPRENEUR.COM, Dec. 15, 2016, available at https://www.entrepreneur.com/article/286558 (accessed May 25, 2018).

[400] Foley, *supra* note 79.

[401] NATIONAL VENTURE CAPITAL ASSOCIATION, *supra* note 82, 14 ($272.2 billion out of $333.5 billion assets under management); *Gazelles in the Heartland*, ECONOMIST, Sept. 30, 2017, 62; Steve Lohr, *Seeking Midwest Start-Up Gold*, NY TIMES, Nov. 20, 2017, Business, 1 (acknowledging the situation but saying it might be improving).

[402] Knight, *supra* note 62, at 2; *A Boom Like*, *supra* note 380 ("(t)he mid-sized banks to which small firms tend to turn for money . . . show no signs of limbering up for a big burst of borrowing"); Clayton M. Christensen & Derek van Bever, *The Capitalist's Dilemma*, HARV. BUS. REV., June 2014, 60, 66.

[403] Gretchen Morgenson, *Yes, Mr. President, Banks Are Lending*, NY TIMES, Feb. 19, 2017, Business, 1.

[404] *Banking in the Age*, *supra* note 360 (chart, indicating weekly changes in lending, 2005–2017).

"Disrupt or be disrupted is the cliché of the moment and no one dares question it" a *Financial Times* columnist proclaimed in 2015.[405] In fact, a potent counter-narrative has emerged challenging the notion that upstarts are engaging in the regular felling of corporate giants.[406] As Senator Elizabeth Warren said in 2016, there are fears "today, in America, competition is dying."[407] The President's Council of Economic Advisers indicated in a 2016 report "(w)hile there are many benefits of competition for consumers and workers, competition appears to be declining in at least part of the economy."[408] *The Atlantic* flagged up the same year "America's Monopoly Problem," claiming that "the economy has come to resemble something . . . like a stagnant pool" and that "America has become the land of the big and the home of the consolidated."[409] The *Economist* concurred in 2018, saying "(t)he past two decades of profitable torpor have been an incumbent's paradise."[410]

Ironically, given that the internet is seen as a primary catalyst for "big bang disruption," the technology industry has become the major source of fears about the anticompetitive accumulation of market power. History can account for the apparent contradiction—competitive dynamics in the tech sector have been changing dramatically. As the *Economist* said in 2016 "(i)n the 1990s Silicon Valley was a playground for startups. It is now the fief of a handful of behemoths."[411] Stock market investors have been sold on the idea that Apple, Alphabet/Google, Amazon, Facebook, and Microsoft "are the dominant oligopolies of the 21st century and will extract a vast, rising, flow of profits."[412] Their collective market value of $2.8 trillion as of early 2018 was greater than that of any five firms in history.[413]

What distinguishes Apple, Alphabet/Google, Amazon, Facebook, and Microsoft as purveyors of market power in the tech world is that they have each built up and now control platforms that users are highly dependent upon, akin to customers of railroads in the late nineteenth and early twentieth centuries.[414] These dominant firms benefit from and exploit powerful "network effects" associated with their platforms—for a customer switching to a lightly used competing platform is a self-defeating strategy—that operate as powerful barriers to entry to potential rivals.[415] The dominant tech firms are also vigilant in responding

---

[405] Lucy Kellaway, *My New Rule of Competition Begins with a War on Talent*, FIN. TIMES, Oct. 19, 2015, 14.

[406] *Out With the Old, supra* note 388; Carl Shapiro, *Antitrust in a Time of Populism*, unpublished working paper, 2–4 (2017).

[407] Brent Kendall, *Elizabeth Warren Says Competition "Dying," More Merger Scrutiny Needed*, WSJ.COM BLOGS—WASHINGTON WIRE, June 29, 2016, available at https://blogs.wsj.com/washwire/2016/06/29/elizabeth-warren-says-competition-dying-more-merger-scrutiny-needed/ (accessed Feb. 15, 2018).

[408] *Benefits of Competition and Indicators of Market Power*, COUNCIL OF ECONOMIC ADVISERS ISSUE BRIEF, Spring 2016, at 4.

[409] Derek Thompson, *America's Monopoly Problem*, THE ATLANTIC, October 2016, available at https://www.theatlantic.com/magazine/archive/2016/10/americas-monopoly-problem/497549/ (accessed May 30, 2018).

[410] *A Boom Like, supra* note 380. See also *Too Much of a Good Thing*, ECONOMIST, Mar. 26, 2016, 23.

[411] *Out With the Old, supra* note 388.

[412] *Money Mountains*, ECONOMIST, June 3, 2017, 70.

[413] *Id.*; Scott Galloway, *Silicon Valley's Tax-Avoiding, Job-Killing, Tax-Avoiding Machine*, ESQUIRE, Mar. 2018, available at http://www.esquire.com/news-politics/a15895746/bust-big-tech-silicon-valley/ (accessed Feb. 8, 2018).

[414] Don Clark & Robert McMillan, *Giants Tighten Grip on Internet Economy*, WALL ST. J., Nov. 6, 2015, B1.

[415] Jason Furman, *Beyond Antitrust: The Role of Competition Policy in Promoting Inclusive Growth*, Searle Center Conference on Antitrust Economics and Competition Policy, Sept. 16, 2016, 17, available at

to potential threats, being apprehensive about losing first-mover advantages in the way that Netscape, as a browser, or Yahoo, as a search engine, did in the late 1990s and early 2000s.[416] Today's tech giants reputedly "love start-ups, but in the same way that orcas love baby seals," buying up fledgling rivals or replicating key innovations to eliminate perceived competitive advantages with sufficient alacrity to prompt talk of a tech "kill-zone".[417]

The concerns about market power could translate into regulatory reform that would impact materially upon managerial decision-making in large public companies. For instance, in 2017 Democrats in Congress issued a policy agenda document pitched as a preview of what would occur when their party wins back control of the House and Senate that promised "cracking down on corporate monopolies," including the creation of "a 21st-century 'Trust Buster' to stop abusive corporate conduct and the exploitation of market power."[418] There have also been calls to treat the tech giants as natural monopolies and dismantle them or regulate them like public utilities.[419] There are too many variables in play to offer confident predictions about the regulatory fate of the tech giants, other than to say that regulatory risk poses a meaningful threat to sky-high valuations that have been ascribed to these firms.[420] We will consider instead at this point the extent to which over the next while public company executives are likely to think of competition from rivals as a significant constraint on their discretion.

If dominant firms are becoming sufficiently insulated by market power for their executives to feel they can ease off, there could be a return to circumstances prevalent during the managerial capitalism era. Mid-twentieth century public company executives did not ignore competitors.[421] Nevertheless, the impact rivals had on managerial discretion often was muted because the dominant firms in an industry benefitted from what legendary investor Warren Buffett referred to in 2007 as "a moat around it with a very valuable castle in the middle."[422] Perhaps the same could be happening again. Tyler Cowen, an economics professor, claimed in a 2017 book where he said American society had become counterproductively complacent "(w)e're coming uncomfortably close to that static, conformist caricature of the 1950s oligopolistic business life where the relative status of the major companies just doesn't

https://obamawhitehouse.archives.gov/sites/default/files/page/files/20160916_searle_conference_competition_furman_cea.pdf (accessed Feb. 15, 2018); Grep Ip, *The Antitrust Case against America's Technology Behemoths*, WALL ST. J., Jan. 17, 2018, A1; *Taming the Titans*, ECONOMIST. Jan. 20, 2018, 11.

416 Chapter 5, notes 392–93, 459 and related discussion; Chapter 6, note 398 and accompanying text; Steven Davidoff Solomon, *Tech Giants Gobble Start-Ups in a Regulatory Blind Spot*, NY TIMES, Aug. 17, 2016, B3.

417 Farhad Manjoo, *A Frightful Stranglehold on Tech Start-Ups*, NY TIMES, Oct. 19, 2017, B1; *Into the Danger Zone*, ECONOMIST, June 2, 2018, 61.

418 Clare Foran, *Democrats Bet on a Populist Message to Win Back Congress*, ATLANTIC.COM, July 24, 2017, available at https://www.theatlantic.com/politics/archive/2017/07/democrats-message-populist-monopolies-congress-trump/534603/ (accessed Feb. 15, 2018).

419 Taplin, *supra* note 389; Galloway, *supra* note 413; Lina M. Khan, *Amazon's Antitrust Paradox*, 126 YALE L.J. 710, 797–802 (2017); *Silicon Valley, We Have a Problem*, ECONOMIST, Jan. 20, 2018, 21.

420 *Chicago Bears, supra* note 88; Dan Gallagher, *The Biggest Risk Big Tech Faces*, WALL ST. J., Sept. 28, 2017, B12; James Mackintosh, *The Market Awakens to Risks Facing Tech*, WALL ST. J., Mar. 29, 2018, B1.

421 Chapter 2, notes 351–53, 359–60, 362–63 and accompanying text.

422 Chapter 2, notes 354–58 and related discussion; Robert Harding, *How Buffett Broke American Capitalism*, FIN. TIMES, Sept. 13, 2017, 9.

change that much over time."[423] The *Economist* has argued similarly that in the United States "(s)luggishness is everywhere" and that "(m)any big firms wallow in lucrative stagnation."[424]

The market power available to leading public companies may well have increased somewhat lately. Nevertheless, it is unlikely that the executives in charge feel sufficiently confident in whatever moat they might have to protect to ease off and enjoy the quiet life. Again, the tech giants, being cognizant of eclipsed predecessors, are well aware that "(i)n the technology industry, the sharks have never long been safe from the minnows"[425] and thus have sought to avoid coasting. The *New York Times* has said of Apple, Alphabet/Google, Amazon, Facebook, and Microsoft that none has

> slowed down investing intended to further expand its area of control—for instance, Google keeps investing in search, Facebook is still spending heavily to create new social-networking features, and Amazon remains relentless in creating new ways to let people shop. At the same time, they are all locked in intense battles for new markets and technologies.[426]

Moreover, future complacency seems unlikely in the tech sector. The *Economist*, despite its warnings about cosseted incumbents, has said that with China's tech industry being on course for parity with America's in 10 to 15 years "(f)or Silicon Valley, it is time to get paranoid."[427]

A possibility is that tech giants which retain their economic vigor will become the main source of competition in an otherwise laconic American corporate economy.[428] In fact, for large public companies outside the tech sector coasting is an unlikely prospect. Buffett told Berkshire Hathaway shareholders in 2018 "(t)here are some pretty good moats around" but acknowledged "(t)here have been more moats that have become susceptible to invasion than seemed to be the case earlier."[429] Consider, as well, the *New York Times* explanation in 2013 of a series of then recently executed and proposed mega-mergers, based on analysis by Carl Shapiro, formerly chief economist at the Antitrust Division:

> Together, Penguin and Random House may be able to better stave off Amazon; American Airlines and US Airways can contend with Delta. Similarly, Office Depot and OfficeMax, once merged, may finally be large enough to really scare Staples. Fear, Shapiro says, is the key. Markets work best, he says, when "everyone has to watch their back."[430]

---

[423] Tyler Cowen, The Complacent Class: The Self-Defeating Quest for the American Dream 75 (2017).

[424] *The Age of the Torporation*, Economist, Oct. 24, 2015, 59; *Myopium*. Economist, Feb. 18, 2017, 64.

[425] Farhad Manjoo, *Frightful but Not Invincible*, NY Times, Jan. 5, 2017, B1.

[426] Farhad Manjoo, *The Upside of Bowing to Big Tech*, NY Times, Nov. 2, 2017, B1.

[427] *Chinese Tech v American Tech*, Economist, Feb. 17, 2018, 69.

[428] *A Boom Like*, *supra* note 380.

[429] Andrew Ross Sorkin, *Mogul on a Contrarian Mission To Fill In Buffett's Sacred Moat*, NY Times, May 8, 2018, B1.

[430] Adam Davidson, *Buzzkilled?*, NY Times, Mar. 3, 2013, Sunday Magazine, 16.

Also instructive are recent e-commerce initiatives of retail giant Wal-Mart, christened "the most powerful, most influential company in the world" in 2006.[431] A 2010 book aiming to convince readers the US economy was afflicted by monopoly capitalism argued that Wal-Mart's leverage was so substantial that it determined "who shall buy what and how much they shall pay."[432] By 2016, with Amazon's online sales growing rapidly, Wal-Mart was very much on the back foot, with its market share of US retail sales having declined from 11.6 percent in 2009 to 10.6 percent.[433] In response, Wal-Mart invested nearly $15 billion in information technology, including paying $3.3 billion in 2016 to buy shopping website Jet.com, a "unicorn" that had been selling products for barely a year.[434] The corporation even changed its legal name in 2017 from Wal-Mart Stores Inc. to Walmart Inc. to reflect its shift of emphasis away from physical stores in favor of online shopping.[435]

Available data tend to confirm that even if the competitive pressure under which businesses operate has eased off since the late 1990s, today's public company executives have good reason to be more apprehensive than their managerial capitalism era counterparts. With *Fortune* 500 companies, 57 percent of those on the 1995 list were gone by 2015 as compared with only 45 percent of 1955 companies having exited by 1975.[436] Concentration levels calculated taking into account both the number of the companies operating in an industrial sector and the market share of the biggest companies reveal the same pattern. Measures of concentration increased 45 percent across industries between 1995 and 2015 but were 18 percent lower in 2015 than 1975.[437] It follows that even if executives of public corporations need not be quite as fearful of competitors as they were as the twentieth century drew to a close, it will be quite some time before there is market power insulating executives of dominant firms to the same extent as in the mid-twentieth century.

What Does the Future Hold for Public Company Executives?

Having considered the internal and external constraints that impact upon the discretion of those running public companies, we are now in a position to consider directly the prospects for corporate management. In the managerial capitalism era, the standard characterization of a major corporate executive was the reserved, bureaucratically oriented "organization man." As the 1990s came to an end, charisma was much in demand in the executive suite and CEOs of America's largest companies were approaching iconic status. A sharp reversal of fortunes then ensued during a "decade from hell" for the public company, leaving the

[431] CHARLES FISHMAN, THE WAL-MART EFFECT: HOW THE WORLD'S MOST POWERFUL COMPANY REALLY WORKS--AND HOW IT'S TRANSFORMING THE AMERICAN ECONOMY 5 (2006).

[432] BARRY C. LYNN, CORNERED: THE NEW MONOPOLY CAPITALISM AND THE ECONOMICS OF DESTRUCTION 29 (2010).

[433] *Thinking outside the Box*, ECONOMIST, June 4, 2016, 61.

[434] *Id.* ($10.5 billion invested before the purchase of Jet.com); Leslie Picker & Rachel Abrams, *Teaming Up against Amazon*, NY TIMES, Aug. 9, 2016, Business, 1; *Boxed-in Unicorn*, ECONOMIST, Aug. 13, 2016, 47.

[435] Sarah Nassauer, *A Storied Retail Name Bows to Internet Age*, WALL ST. J., Dec. 7, 2017, B1.

[436] Murray, *supra* note 36.

[437] Kahle & Stulz, *supra* note 102, at 72.

formerly "imperial" CEO "embattled" by 2010.[438] Where next on the roller coaster for public company executives? In answering this question, it is prudent to start by considering but then setting aside a much publicized though small subset of chief executive, namely those who launched the companies they are running.

CEO/FOUNDERS

Barron's spoke for many who follow business affairs when saying in 2011 "(w)e've got a weakness for founder CEOs like (Apple's Steve) Jobs."[439] A *Wall Street Journal* columnist explained in 2015 the appeal of CEO/founders:

> Many Americans, regardless of their feelings about CEOs, cheer when the founder of a company earns billions for turning an idea into something that saves us money and enriches our lives. Perhaps that reflects their understanding that visionaries might easily have failed, and they should be rewarded for taking risks.[440]

Jobs passed away in 2011. However, Jeff Bezos (Amazon), Larry Page (Alphabet/Google), Reed Hastings (Netflix), Mark Zuckerberg (Facebook), and Elon Musk (Tesla) currently are high-profile CEOs who founded or cofounded their companies.

While CEO/founders have undoubted appeal, they have drawbacks too. A compensation consultant said in 2013 of Larry Ellison, founder of software powerhouse Oracle, shortly before Ellison stepped down as CEO (Ellison remained chairman of the board), "(h)e doesn't care what shareholders think. . . . He's one of the richest guys in the world, and he has the company pay for his bodyguards. I don't think he's going to change."[441] Ellison was by no means unique. Due to the odds being stacked against start-ups in the tech industry and due to the fact those few companies that move to the forefront in the market sector in which they operate often succeed emphatically, reputedly "CEOs in Silicon Valley now have God complexes."[442]

Despite the risks CEO/founders can pose, governance checks on them tend to be modest, particularly in the tech sector. Steven Davidoff Solomon, a corporate law academic, suggested in a 2012 *New York Times* column that shareholders and boards could be leaving "the wunderkinder of the Internet free to run their companies without interference."[443] This is a realistic concern. Some tech company founders rely on ownership of a class of shares with special voting rights to lock in outsize influence amongst the stockholders.[444] Others dominate through the sheer force of personality more than naked voting power, such as Jeff Bezos

---

[438] Chapter 6, notes 6, 224, 400–01 and accompanying text.

[439] Andrew Bary, *30 Best CEOs*, BARRON'S, Mar. 28, 2011, 31.

[440] John Tamny, *Misguided Political Attacks on CEO Pay*, WALL ST. J., July 20, 2015, A13.

[441] Nelson D. Schwartz, *The Infinity Pool of Executive Pay*, NY TIMES, Apr. 7, 2013, Business, 1. On Ellison stepping down as CEO, see Dan Gallagher, *Oracle's Shuffle Doesn't Change Its Hand*, WALL ST. J., Sept. 19, 2014, C8.

[442] Farrell, *supra* note 125 (quoting Vivek Wadhwa, a well-known engineer).

[443] Steven M. Davidoff, *In Silicon Valley, Chieftains Hold Sway with Few Checks and Balances*, NY TIMES, July 25, 2012, B4. Soon after writing this column, Davidoff added Solomon to his surname.

[444] *Supra* notes 122, 125 and related discussion.

(a 16 percent shareholder in Amazon as of 2017), Elon Musk (owner of a 20 percent stake in Tesla), and Reed Hastings (a 3 percent stockholder in Netflix).[445] Silicon Valley boards also tend to be rather "clubby" by public company standards, with insider representation being somewhat higher than the norm and with high-profile independent directors often being thoroughly networked in a cliquey industry.[446]

Davidoff Solomon, as well as suggesting boards and shareholders tend to give tech company CEO/founders a free pass, wondered whether the relaxed corporate governance stance in cutting edge technology firms could be "a trend that will spread to the rest of corporate America."[447] That is highly unlikely. With companies that go public, CEO/founders are the exception to the rule and many of the founders who are serving as chief executive at the time of the IPO exit within a few years.[448]

Then there is the high-tech angle. It is a sector apart in the American economy. Management theorist Tom Peters observed in 2014 when cautioning about drawing inferences from "5 percent of leading edge companies.... (T)here's Silicon Valley and then there's ROP, Rest of Planet."[449] Or as a book reviewer for the *Wall Street Journal* said in 2015 of "the Silicon Valley high technology crowd... these people are different. Not just superficially different, but profoundly so."[450] Charles Munger, long-time right-hand man of Warren Buffett at conglomerate Berkshire Hathaway, has even said of Amazon's CEO/founder "Jeff Bezos is a different species."[451] CEO/founders of super-successful tech companies such as Bezos and Zuckerberg, and Jobs and Bill Gates before them, have been objects of fascination since the 1980s, and this will no doubt continue. Extrapolating, however, from what such tech sector megastars say and do to ascertain general trends regarding public company executives must be done with considerable care.

RETURN OF THE IMPERIAL CEO?

Turning from CEO/founders to general trends affecting public company executives, one possible future trajectory would be for the imperial CEO of the 1990s to return. As the twentieth century concluded a buoyant stock market and a flourishing economy provided a congenial setting for successful public company CEOs to acquire iconic status.[452] If we turn to the present day, we see that stock prices have rallied strongly following the "decade from hell" for the public company.[453] Might history repeat itself, leading to a reprise of the imperial chief executive?

---

445 *Control Freaks*, ECONOMIST, Nov. 25, 2017, 72.

446 Davidoff, *supra* note 443; FENWICK & WEST, CORPORATE GOVERNANCE PRACTICES AND TRENDS: A COMPARISON OF LARGE PUBLIC COMPANIES AND SILICON VALLEY COMPANIES 12 (2016) (reporting 20 percent inside directors for 150 Silicon Valley companies as compared with 14 percent for S&P 100 companies).

447 Davidoff, *supra* note 443.

448 Broughman & Fried, *supra* note 123, at 1, 9–11.

449 *Tom Peters on Leading the 21st-century Organization*, MCKINSEY Q. (2014), issue #3, 88, 95.

450 Philip Delves Broughton, *Go Big or Go Home*, WALL ST. J., Feb. 17, 2015, A9.

451 Andrew Ross Sorkin, *20 Years On, Bezos Proves His Naysayers Were Wrong*, NY TIMES, May 16, 2017, B1.

452 Chapter 5, *supra* notes 64–66, 76–77, 464–65, 529–33 and accompanying text.

453 *Supra* note 100 and related discussion; *Akane Otani, Stocks'Bull Run Hits 9 Years Going Strong*, WALL ST. J., Mar. 9, 2018, B12.

The possibility of an imperial CEO rerun cannot be dismissed out of hand. Venerable shareholder activist Bob Monks claimed back in 2013 that "emperor" CEOs were "commonplace. Far too much of American business is being run for the personal enrichment and glorification of its manager-kings."[454] More recently, when it was revealed in 2017 that for a number of years General Electric had a "chase plane" follow the corporate jet of chief executive Jeffrey Immelt to provide back-up in case of an emergency, a horrified analyst who had covered GE for years said the practice showed that Immelt "was the imperial CEO."[455]

Despite some speculation that the imperial CEO is alive and well, for now the past remains in the past. As the *New York Times* suggested in 2017 when indicating that the era of the "baronial" CEO was over, "for most of the *Fortune* 500, the unquestioned power and perks, the imperviousness to criticism from the likes of shareholders, and the outsize public profile that once automatically came with the corner office have gone the way of the typewriter and the Dictaphone."[456] Unlike in the halcyon days of the iconic chief executive,[457] with the exception of attention-catching tech company founders such as Bezos and Zuckerberg, media coverage of public company CEOs currently is modest.[458] Chief executives do not appear to be interested in changing the situation, as they usually seek to keep their egos in check and cultivate a modest image.[459]

Even if public company executives start aspiring to the restoration of "baronial" status, the constraints applicable to them should preclude such an outcome. Boards are more vigilant than they used to be, shareholder pressure on underperforming companies has grown, and the regulatory strictures relevant to public companies have been intensifying, at least until recently.[460] Chief executives of public companies today correspondingly are subject to tighter constraints than their imperial brethren circa 2000. Consider Jeffrey Immelt. Contrary to what would be expected with an emperor CEO, he left office in 2017 earlier than he had been planning amidst pressure from prominent hedge fund activist Nelson Peltz and other investors disappointed with the company's lagging share price.[461] Boards, shareholders, and regulation are unlikely to recede markedly as constraints on public company executives for the foreseeable future.[462] The imperial CEO, late-1990s style, then, should not be returning any time soon.

EMBATTLED?

While a reprise of the imperial CEO is unlikely soon, what about the opposite scenario, namely a continuation of the erosion of power and influence that reputedly resulted in CEOs

---

[454] Robert A.G. Monks, Citizens Disunited: Passive Investors, Drone CEOs, and the Corporate Capture of the American Dream 1 (2013).

[455] James B. Stewart, *A Corporate Jet with No Passengers*, NY Times, Nov. 4, 2017, B1.

[456] Schwartz, *supra* note 168.

[457] Chapter 5, notes 536–38 and accompanying text.

[458] Pearlstein, *supra* note 206, at 14.

[459] *The Imperial CFO*, Economist, June 18, 2016, 71.

[460] *Supra* notes 164–68, 245–49, 329–36 and related discussion.

[461] Steve Lohr, *GE, Pressured by Its Investors, Changes Leader*, NY Times, June 13, 2017, B1.

[462] *Supra* notes 154–59, 235, 245–47, 314, 384 and accompanying text.

becoming "embattled" by the end of the 2000s? There are some indications such a trend could be in operation. The *Economist* suggested in 2012 that "shackled" CEOs had "become ever more embattled" over the previous couple of years, noting "the latest buzz phrases in the C-suite are 'humble leadership', 'servant leadership' and 'bottom-up leadership.'"[463] The *Wall Street Journal* said of the CEO post in 2017 "(a)n array of challenges—from increasing impatience on Wall Street and in boardrooms to a corporate landscape rapidly transformed by new technologies and rival upstarts—have made the top job tougher and more precarious than just a few years ago, top executives say."[464] A *Financial Times* columnist suggested the same year "chief executives are pestered and pursued as never before. They have to carry out a far broader and more complex set of tasks than their antecedents did, at a time of chaotic change, under constant pressure from short-term activists, and all while in competition with lavishly funded, privately held start-ups."[465]

While public company executives face pressures from a variety of directions, CEOs will not be harried managerial afterthoughts any time soon. Law professors Marcel Kahan and Ed Rock, who christened chief executives as embattled in 2010,[466] have acknowledged CEOs continue to matter. They said in 2014 "CEOs remain a dominant force, if less so than twenty years ago. On day-to-day matters, the CEO calls most of the shots, and is left to do so as long as she does a reasonably good job in managing the corporation."[467]

Trends relating to CEO employment indicate the position of the chief executive within the public company hierarchy may indeed be strengthening rather than weakening. CEO pay, for instance, has increased significantly during the 2010s.[468] In addition, contrary to the image that has been conveyed of a harried chief executive at risk of being chased from office by shareholder activists and eager competitors, CEO tenure has been lengthening recently. A *Newsweek* columnist said in 2013 "(t)he life of a top executive may be cushy and full of perks. But for many, it has also become Hobbesian—nasty, brutish, and short. Two years is the new 10 years."[469] The *Wall Street Journal* struck the same tone in 2017, suggesting "(t)he bosses of America's biggest and best-known companies are learning a common lesson this year: The pay is great, but job security has rarely been shakier."[470] In fact S&P 500 CEOs have been staying in office longer since Kahan and Rock suggested chief executives were embattled. According to Conference Board data on the tenure of departing S&P 500 executives from 2001 to 2016, the shortest average in any one year was 7.2 in 2009. This figure climbed steadily to 10.8 years in 2015 before falling back to 9 years in 2016, which was the average for the entire period analyzed.[471]

---

463 *The Shackled Boss*, ECONOMIST, Jan. 21, 2012, 67.

464 Vanessa Fuhrmans & Joann S. Lublin, *For CEOs, High Pay, Higher Anxiety*, WALL ST. J., July 6, 2017, B1.

465 Andrew Hill, *Besieged, Conflicted and Under Pressure: Why We Should Feel Sorry for Leaders*, FIN. TIMES, Nov. 20, 2017, 12.

466 Marcel Kahan & Edward Rock, *Embattled CEOs*, 88 TEX. L. REV. 989, 989–90 (2010).

467 Kahan & Rock, *supra* note 177, at 2042.

468 *Supra* note 305 and related discussion.

469 Daniel Gross, *Why the Speed of Business Is Dooming America's CEOs*, NEWSWEEK.COM, May 6, 2013, available at http://www.newsweek.com/why-speed-business-dooming-americas-ceos-63241 (accessed Dec. 20, 2017).

470 Fuhrmans & Lublin, *supra* note 464.

471 Matteo Tonello, *CEO Succession Practices: 2017 Edition*, HARVARD LAW SCHOOL FORUM ON CORPORATE GOVERNANCE AND FINANCIAL REGULATION, July 31, 2017, available at https://corpgov.law.harvard.edu/2017/07/31/ceo-succession-practices-2017-edition/ (accessed Dec. 20, 2017).

With the monitoring capabilities of boards perhaps reaching their logical limits and with it being unlikely that shareholder interference in public company affairs will ratchet up markedly,[472] a substantial increase in corporate governance related shackling of CEOs looks unlikely. With any sort of immediate return to the CEO glory days of the 1990s also being unlikely, a middle ground between imperial and embattled is the most obvious future position for public company executives. Optimistically, the result could be a Goldilocks "not too hot, not too cold" outcome. Jeffrey Sonnenfeld, a leading management theorist, suggested in a 2017 *Wall Street Journal* column while cautioning boards against being too trigger-happy with their CEOs that this sort of happy medium had in fact been reached. According to Sonnenfeld, "(t)oday's corporate bosses aren't the robber barons or country-club networkers of yesteryear. Modern CEOs are generally smart, diligent and committed to their jobs."[473]

MANAGERIAL CAPITALISM REDUX?

While a "Goldilocks" scenario is plausible for CEOs if they are destined to be neither imperial nor embattled, there is an additional possible middle ground outcome for top public company executives meriting investigation. Ironically that potential future outcome would bring us back close to where we started with this analysis of how the public company has been transformed over time. A core precept of this book has been that managerial capitalism prevailed in American public companies during the middle decades of the twentieth century but was displaced as the century drew to a close. The changes that the public company has undergone have been explored to a substantial extent from this departure point. A middle ground between imperial and increasingly embattled opens up the possibility that matters might come full circle with public company executives conducting themselves in a manner akin to their managerial capitalism forebears.

We have already considered in this chapter a key check on executive discretion where conditions could be returning to those prevailing during the managerial capitalism era. In the mid-twentieth century it was widely assumed that "the possession of a substantial degree of market power is characteristic of the modern corporation,"[474] thereby enhancing managerial autonomy. If, as some have speculated, the American economy is again becoming an "incumbents' paradise"[475] the discretion available to those running dominant firms will similarly be amplified. Extended sufficiently, conditions could be congenial for the restoration of managerial capitalism. Fredrik Erixon and Björn Weigel, in a 2016 book seeking to explain the recent stagnation of Western economies, have argued the process is already largely complete, maintaining "(m)odern corporate behaviour increasingly conforms to the spirit of managerialism."[476]

---

472 *Supra* notes 180–81, 240–43, 254, 314–15 and related discussion.

473 Sonnenfeld, *supra* note 230.

474 Chapter 2, note 358 and accompanying text.

475 *Supra* note 410 and related discussion

476 Fredrik Erixon & Björn Weigel, The Innovation Illusion: How So Little Is Created by So Many Working So Hard 68 (2016)

Erixon and Weigel attribute the economic stagnation they identify to the fact "the capitalist system that used to procure eccentricity and embrace ingenuity all too often produces mediocrity," with the malaise occurring because "the capitalist spirit of contesting markets has weakened."[477] Markets are failing to self-correct because, with barriers to entry being fortified, "(n)ew market entrants will have greater problems circumventing the big firms and their production networks."[478] Innovation is suffering because of "a custodian corporate culture" where "corporate managers shy away from uncertainty" and "turn companies into bureaucratic entities ... to make capitalism predictable."[479] Hence, managerialism, which "never faded away" has "progressively anchored itself more firmly in companies," with the result "(m)anagerialists occupy the central posts of business."[480]

While Erixon and Weigel bemoan the restoration of managerial capitalism they have identified, others have been pleased that a revival could be on the way. Law professor Lynn Stout, for example, staked out this position in the early 2010s. Aware that internal constraints on public company executives were weak during the mid-twentieth century, she acknowledged managerial capitalism was "hardly perfect."[481] Nevertheless, according to Stout, it generated "good results" overall.[482] Leading American companies were globally dominant and the stock market delivered robust returns so "managerial capitalism worked surprisingly well for dispersed and powerless shareholders."[483] Others benefitted too, Stout suggested admiringly. Managerialist boards and executives did not see themselves "as mere agents of shareholders" and instead ran their companies "in the interests of a wide range of beneficiaries. Certainly they looked out for investors' interests, but they looked out for the interests of employees, customers, and the nation as well."[484]

According to Stout, the shareholder primacy model that emerged in the 1980s and 1990s failed to deliver superior returns for stockholders, the supposed beneficiaries, which implied it was "time to move on to another theory."[485] Stout predicted—"albeit with caution"—that "American corporations are likely to respond to the disappointments of shareholder primacy by returning to what worked for more than half a century: some form of managerial capitalism."[486] Stout would acknowledge this new corporate philosophy was "unlikely to be called managerial capitalism" but said it would "bear the hallmarks of managerialism."[487]

---

477 *Id.* at 2, 190.

478 *Id.* at 124–25.

479 *Id.* at 17–18.

480 *Id.* at 17, 190.

481 Stout, *supra* note 190, at 1171.

482 *Id.*

483 *Id.*

484 *Id.*

485 *Id.* at 1181.

486 *Id.* See also Chris Gay, *Are Shareholders Their Own Worst Enemies?*, US News & World Report, Sept. 5, 2012 (interview with Stout in which she was asked whether some form of managerialism would replace shareholder value, and she replied that "(t)he lovely thing about the business world is that, given a little breathing room, it's highly adaptable.")

487 Stout, *supra* note 190, at 1182.

A revival of managerial capitalism, for better or worse, in fact is unlikely. With the facet of managerial capitalism of particular interest to Stout—ample managerial regard for constituencies other than stockholders—the strong shareholder orientation that emerged in US public companies and was sustained subsequently would need to be derailed. She indeed did predict shareholder primacy's demise in the early 2010s, and quite plausibly so at the time given the criticism of shareholder value maximization in the wake of the financial crisis.[488] In fact, it is unlikely that shareholder value will be knocked down the priority list soon in a way that will open up substantially greater discretion for public company executives to favor other corporate constituencies. Share price should continue to operate as "a global positioning system for those managing corporations,"[489] assuming a substantial proportion of executive pay remains equity-linked, failing to hit earnings targets continues to punish share prices, and hedge fund activists remain a threat with companies where management is underperforming.[490]

As for Erixon and Weigel's gloomier managerial capitalism prognosis oriented around a counterproductive bureaucrat mindset, there is some supporting evidence. Managerial hierarchies remain a prominent feature of public companies, with the rate of growth in the number of managers and supervisors in the US economy being nearly double that for other employees since the early 1980s.[491] At the apex of the corporate hierarchy, chief executives of large public companies who can no longer rely on "imperial" clout frequently have to forge a consensus among executives, directors, and shareholders to launch a major corporate initiative.[492]

Erixon and Weigel's managerial capitalism prediction nevertheless is likely to founder. They are pessimistic about the capacity of the market to self-correct due to incumbents' growing dominance of the sectors within which they operate. Even the largest American companies, however, tend to lack sufficiently imposing market advantages to foreclose challenges from innovative competitors.[493] The tech giants appear to be best positioned to put a daunting competitive moat in place but it is unlikely they will be resting on their laurels any time soon.[494] A hallmark of the managerial capitalism era was the realistic possibility of a reasonably quiet life insulated by oligopolistic market structures. Today's public company executives lack this luxury, and likely will for some time to come. For the public company and managerial capitalism, then, this should not be a case of *plus ça change, plus c'est la même chose.*

* * *

A general pattern with the predictions offered here about the future of the public company is an absence of bold claims of forthcoming radical change. The public company will remain a crucial element in the American economy. A separation of ownership and control will continue to be a public company hallmark, albeit with an ongoing institutional twist. Boards, shareholders, unions, and the market for corporate control are unlikely to impose

---

488 *Supra* notes 187–190 and related discussion.

489 *Supra* note 185 and accompanying text.

490 *Supra* notes 208–210, 235 and related discussion.

491 Gary Hamel & Michele Zanini, *Bureaucracy: Where to Liberate $3 Trillion*, LONDON BUS. SCHOOL REV., Jan. 2017, 7.

492 *General Eclectic*, ECONOMIST, May 27, 2017, 66.

493 *Supra* notes 429–37 and accompanying text.

494 *Supra* notes 414–417, 425–427 and related discussion.

substantially greater constraints on management than they do currently. It is unclear whether there will be a reoccurrence of the sort of late twentieth century deregulatory wave that materially enhanced managerial discretion, but regulation will remain a meaningful constraint for public company executives regardless. Neither managerial capitalism nor the quiet life arising from public company market power will be restored in their mid-twentieth century form in the foreseeable future.

A plausible, if somewhat cynical, reaction to the foregoing forecasting pattern would be that the predictor was playing it safe to avoid the embarrassment of being incorrect. After all, no prognosticator likes to acknowledge "I was wrong."[495] There are, however, strong counter-incentives with academic forecasting, as Philip Tetlock, a psychologist who achieved considerable notoriety for an empirical study of political pundits that revealed their predictions were little better than informed non-experts,[496] has pointed out. If one aspires to achieve the profile associated with being a public intellectual, it pays "to be pretty bold and attach non-negligible probabilities to fairly dramatic change. That's much more likely to bring you attention."[497] Moreover, academics can make at least a few bold erroneous predictions without worrying too much. They are unlikely to have a direct financial stake in the outcomes, wrong calls can be finessed on the basis that the timing was just off or that the predictions were wrong for the right reasons, and memories of mistaken predictions often fade quickly.[498] Perhaps another forecast that the public company's days are numbered would have been a good idea. . . .

Even if the rather cautious predictions offered here are sound over the short-term, some inevitably will be wrong over the medium- to long-term. History shows that the public company of today will not be preserved in aspic. In each of the decades canvassed in this book, the environment in which the public company has operated has changed substantially. Assuming this pattern continues, key features of the public company will no doubt evolve in ways even the most prescient today would be unable to predict.

More broadly, the accuracy of the forecasting in this concluding chapter is really a sideshow. Offering predictions was a logical way to draw together the key themes this book has explored. Fundamentally, though, what has been presented in this book is history, if recent history. The core objective has been to describe how the public company has evolved since the managerial capitalism era, identifying and analyzing in so doing the pivotal trends driving its transformation as we approach the third decade of the twenty-first century. The speculation in which this concluding chapter has engaged should not affect materially any assessment of the extent to which this goal has been fulfilled.

---

495 Tetlock & Gardner, *supra* note 4, at 69.

496 Philip E. Tetlock, Expert Political Judgment: How Good Is It? How Can We Know? (2005).

497 Silver, *supra* note 4, at 55.

498 Tetlock & Gardner, *supra* note 4, at 52; Louis Menand, *Everyone's an Expert*, New Yorker, Dec. 5, 2005, available at https://www.newyorker.com/magazine/2005/12/05/everybodys-an-expert (accessed May 20, 2018).

Index A General

The Public Company Transformed. Brian R. Cheffins.

Index B Authors

The Public Company Transformed. Brian R. Cheffins.

Index C Corporations and Other Business Enterprises

Index D People (Other than Authors)